MW00812123

Jewish Astrology, A Cosmic Science:
Torah, Talmud and Zohar Works on Spiritual Astrology

Yaakov Kronenberg

For information regarding special discounts for bulk purchases,
please contact BN Publishing at
info@bnpublishing.net

Table of contents

Astrology according to Jewish Law

Astrology according to Jewish Law

A commentary by Yaakov Kronenberg on a Torah Astrology book written nearly 1000 years ago by the famous Rabbi Abraham bar Chiya.
R Chiya lived in Spain (1070 - 1140) and was the great-grandson of Hezekiah Gaon, the last Gaon of the Talmudic academy of Pumbedita and a direct descendant of the David dynasty.
He was the teacher of Rabbi Abraham Ibn Ezra and author of numerous books in Hebrew (*Hegyon ha-Nefesh, Megillat ha-Megalleh ect..).*
He was also a great astronomer and published in the field, and incorporated Torah astrology in his daily Torah observance. This commentary deals with the legal parameters, definitions and applications of Torah astrology.

Astrology according to Jewish law

Commentary by Yaakov Kronenberg

Introduction

Tonight I am going to start a new series of lessons, dealing with 'how the Jewish religion views astrology'. Judaism is based on a whole series of laws, positive and negative commandments, which a Jew has to fulfil in his/her everyday life. And one of the questions is, can a religious Jew follow and believe in astrology? Does it work? Are you allowed to go to astrologers? We are going to cover these and other fascinating questions by studying a book of an ancient rabbi, who lived about 1000 years ago. He lived just before the year 1100. His major works were published around 1100, so he may have been born about thirty or forty years before, around the year 1060 or 1070. His name war Rabbi Avraham Bar Chiya, he was a great rabbi during his generation in Spain, he wrote many books of all sorts of subjects, and he lived a short time before the Iben Ezra, who quotes him in his commentary of the Torah a number of times. He wrote very important books about Jewish law, astronomy and mathematics, and he also wrote an important book about ethics. He was a very prolific author and a deep scholar.
Although the Jewish books and writings were not publicized properly, during this oppressive period of history, even many Jews are not aware of someone like Rabbi Avraham Bar Chiya, nonetheless, he is known among the well read as a great writer of many books on different subjects. He was an important rabbi, but today we hardly know anything about him. In any case, he wrote a book of Sheelot Utshuvot, Questions and Answers, as known in Jewish law. Rabbis used to write such books, in order to solve legal problems. They consisted of questions people asked the rabbi, together with the answers and the logical reasons for them, based on the Jewish Law, and these books were called Questions and Answers (Sheelot Utshuvot). They were written in different times, so if you learn them you'll get some idea about the history of their times. Through these questions, it is possible to learn the history of the last 1500 years. Every generation has its own problems, and different generations ask different questions, which are relevant for the particular generation. There is no generation that is exactly like the one which came before it. Like today there are questions that were never asked and dealt with before, such as: What about cloning? How do you observe the Sabbath when you are in a spaceship going to the moon? Also all kinds of medical and reproductive questions, which were never asked before. So it is possible to realize what problems bothered each generation, and through those books it is possible to learn a tremendous amount of history of the world. Time is always changing, and with it everything in the world changes, and moves, and nothing is constant, which is one of the important ideas in astrology. There are no two days or moments which are the same as each other, or any similar pieces of time. One of the principles of one of a great Kabbalist in the last hundred years, Rabbi Sholomo Elyashiv, as he wrote in his book, was that nothing stands still, and everything is in movement. The whole world constantly moves. So things may come up, while others seem to come down, and maybe inside all this system one may seem to stand still. But things just don't stay still.
We will discuss the subject through the question and answers discussed in Rabbi Avraham Bar Chiya's book. I will tell it to you outside the text, so when we will study

this book it will be easier to get an overview of that whole question and answer the book is about. I have translated this book of about 35 pages. So we may cover it in a fairly short period of time. But it is tremendously interesting, and not only about the Jewish laws approach to astrology. We are going to learn a lot of the basic principles to the question of how the Jews approached the whole subject of astrology: If they saw problems with astrology or not, how they viewed it, if they are different kinds of astrology, and all sorts of things; it also talks about Jewish law and astrology, and many interesting subjects and matters. I have my own views on astrology and Jewish law, but I don't consider myself a rabbi, though I have studied on and off, over 30 years in yeshivas. So I don't consider myself an authority in legal areas of rabbinic matters. Today it is a generation of specialists, where each person is a specialist in a different area, and only a few people specialize on a combination of things at one time. So I consider myself a specialist on mystical matters of Kabbala. So if a question arises on matters of rabbinic areas, I think everyone should ask their own rabbi. I can tell you what I think, but you shouldn't consider me as an authority.

In any case, let us read the book of Rabbi Avraham Bar Chiya, which I think is very revelatory, and is going to add a lot to our understanding of Judaism and astrology. What I will do is read a paragraph, try to explain it, and read it over again. And we will try to talk about it a little. You can follow it too, for I have the text up as a PDF, to make things clearer and easier to get into it. So let us give an introduction to what this letter is about. Rabbi Avraham Bar Chiya was a senior rabbi in Spain, a rabbi of his town, around the year 1100, and he had a student, a talmid (in his town), whom he was very close with. The student was going to get married on Friday morning, so Rabbi Avraham and the student picked an hour during which the wedding would take place, which would be fortunate/good according to astrology. That morning, one of the congregants died, and, according to Jewish law, when a burial and a wedding have to take place at the same time, the burial takes precedence, and therefore, the wedding has to take place later.

So I don't remember the exact hour the wedding was supposed to have taken place but let us say at ten O'clock in the morning, but then they had to bury somebody, so the wedding was postponed to eleven O'clock. So the student came to the rabbi (Rabbi Avraham Bar Chiya) and asked: 'Is eleven O'clock a good time to get married?' And the rabbi replied that he didn't think eleven O'clock was a good time, and suggested the wedding would take place at one O'clock. We will later read the letter and understand why. But the congregation heard that the wedding was delayed to one O'clock, and its members wondered why is had been delayed for so long. When they heard that this was due to astrological reasons, many of them said: 'What you are doing is forbidden, it is like black magic! There is no place for this in Judaism! You go too much according to astrology!" And the rabbi eventually had to conduct the wedding at the time he concluded was not so fortunate astrologically. In any case, the rabbi wrote a letter defending himself; so I guess he wrote the question and replied to his own question. The letter is introduced by a friend (he writes the first couple of lines): "This is the letter of the brilliant scholar, the prince Rabbi Chiya the Sephardi, may his memory be blessed. He was also called Isahab El Shorta. Concerning events that happened to him. This letter was sent to Rabbi Yehuda the son of Rabbi Barzili El Bartsaloni, may his memory be blessed". Rabbi Barzili himself was also a great rabbi of his time, I think he is the same Rabbi Barzili who wrote a

commentary on the Book of Yetzira (Book of Formation), written by Avraham Avinu (Abraham), which is the most ancient work of Judaism. So the letter starts:
"It is written (Psalms 34 verse 15) 'turn away from evil and do good', in your business dealings and in the works of your hand.'Seek peace and run after it,' in your interpersonal relationships. Another explanation: 'turn away from evil and do good', if your desires turn to that which wisdom and understanding consider undesirable, turn away from evil desire and accept the advice of good wisdom.
With respect to the phrase, 'Seek peace and run after it', if you see your friend receiving improper advice, seek peace and run after it, and warn him as if you were seeking and running after the peace of your own soul. An example of this is: If you are preparing to go on a journey, and a wise man, one of your friends, says don't start that journey at that hour because it is dangerous, whether because it is an even hour or the hour of Saturn, or the hour of Mars, or he will say to you don't start out on this day because the planets are unfavourable for a journey, be concerned with what he says and don't start out on the journey. Similarly, if there will be before you food that you desire to eat and the doctor will say to you don't eat it because it is bad for people of your age group, heed his words and don't eat. This is the meaning of 'turn away from evil and do good'. Stop the evil and take the good advice. 'Seek peace and run after it': If you see your friend starting a journey or beginning a task on an even hour which is dangerous or on a day on which the planetary forces are unfavourable for that task, warn him against starting out on the journey or from beginning the task, and you will have fulfilled 'seek the peace of your friend and run after his good'. For men of understanding it is proper to guard themselves from all danger and to be cautious and not begin work at an improper hour or on a day that is astrologically unfavourable. And just like it is proper for them to be cautious and guard themselves, so it is proper for them to caution and warn their friends".

This is the 1st paragraph of the letter; let us go back and look at it again more carefully. He quotes from the holy writings: from the Book of Psalms, Chapter 34: 'Turn away from evil and do good'. What does it mean? It means in your business dealings and in the works of your hand. In other words, you should always be a proper business dealer. 'Seek peace and run after it', which is talking about your interpersonal relationships between people. This is the first explanation, which he doesn't want to talk about too much, because he is not concerned about it so much. The other explanations are: What does it mean 'Turn away from evil and do good'? if your desires turn to that which wisdom and understanding consider undesirable, turn away from evil desire and accept the advice of good wisdom; which means, turn away from your Yetzer Hara and your evil instincts, and overcome what you know you shouldn't do and turn it into something good.
'Seek peace and run after it'. What does it mean, to seek peace and run after it? If you see your friend receiving improper advice, seek peace and run after it, and warn him as if you were seeking and running after the peace of our own soul. You should be concerned with your own friends, as well as with yourself, and as much as you worry about the peace of your own soul. If you are preparing to go on a journey, and a wise man, one of your friends, says it is not advisable to start at that hour. If you are going to start a journey, and a wise man, or one of your friends, tells you that you shouldn't start it on a particular hour you planned to, for different reasons, it might be dangerous, whether because it is an even hour or a bad planetary influence. With respect to it being an even hour, the

commentaries explain that during those hours the demons/negative energies are more powerful. Or it is the hour of Saturn, Saturn is considered a bad planet, which is malefic, or the hour of Mars, which is malefic too. These two planets are malefic in astrology: Saturn, because it is too slow and too cold by nature, and Mars, because it is too hot. The worst enemies in astrology is the "too much" and the "too little". Saturn is cold, which resembles being too slow and too hesitant. Mars resembles impatience, the nature of being too hot and too fast. So even hours are hours which have negative power of the demons, Saturn hours may be too late for things, and Mars hours may be too early. He adds another reason why a friend should warn his friend, and this is where he will say to you don't start out on this day because the planets (as they are positioned in the sky at this moment) are unfavourable for a journey. Maybe he looked up in the sky at all the configuration of the planets and stars of that day, and realized it doesn't look like a good time to start your journey. So a lot of Jewish astrological matters are dealt with in these five lines mentioned above. If you think a little about it, you come back to the question of what astrology is. Basic astrology is based on each person's Birth Chart, which is erected at the time he is born. When a person is born, there is a sign at the Eastern Horizon, and all planets are in different places in the Zodiac. And we look at the planets' positions at that time and how they related to the sign of the Eastern Horizon, and from that we construct the Chart, which tells you a lot about the person. This is standard astrology, which is Western astrology and according to many of our commentators this is also Jewish astrology. The Ari Z"L and others talk about this .

And yet there is a strong second approach, coming form earlier and more important sources in the Talmud where it discusses astrology (such as Tractate Shabbat) and there in the Talmud, the Jewish astrology system shockingly has nothing to do with the idea of where the planets are in the sky at any particular moment. Time is pre-embedded with energies set during the initial moments of creation and what happens when a person is born on a certain Day is influenced by these primal energies. For example, a person who was born in Sunday is likely to be all good or all bad, Why? because God created day and night on that day. A person who is born on Monday is likely to become a thief or a contentious person or a life filled with conflict, because Monday is the day of the moon and the day God separated the firmaments. And then the Talmud proceeds to talk about something which exists in Western astrology too, which is planetary hours: The whole week had been divided into seven days, and each day has a different ruler, and each hour of a day and night has a particular ruler too. And then it goes to the area of bloodletting: Which days are good for bloodletting and which days are not etc. So you see that the Talmud also discussed what we call today (in Western astrology) Planetary Hours. I am going to show you later on that the Kabbalists had a much deeper idea about what planetary hours are. They took the system of the Talmud and expanded on it greatly, and made a very sophisticated model of the universe, which we are going to talk about some more.

In standard astrology today, you look at where everything in the sky was when you were born, and if you want to know what is going to happen to you today, you relate them to where the planets are today, compared to where they were when you were born. And that way you can figure out if what you plan to do today will go well or not.

Now, if you pay a close attention to the writing of Rabbi Avraham Bar Chiya, you see he incorporates both systems. He says that there are two systems in Jewish astrology, and

this is a tremendous insight here. There is the astrology based on where the planets are in the sky in a particular moment. This is what he says when he writes: "he will say to you don't start out on this day because the Planets are unfavourable for a journey"; which means, the expert looked in the sky, and said that a particular hour wasn't good to start a journey. So in other words, one should look at the position and condition of the planets in the sky in a particular moment, and conclude from this, if the time is good or not.
And he also distinguishes between even and odd hours which are fixed energies embedded at the onset of creation and operate in perpetuity. And this fixed system includes the Fixed Day system and the Fixed hour system as explained in the Talmud.

There is the famous Chatam Sofer (a great and very famous rabbi of the 1800s, one of the greatest rabbis in Europe in his period, whose writings are extensively quoted today), who wrote that when God created the world, He put into time the planetary influences. All six thousand years of time had different kinds of planetary influences. And if you look at Western astrology, they use the Talmudic Model, that was born on the idea that there are days and there are hours, seven days a week and 24 hours a day, and each day has a different planet ruling it, and there is a day ruler and a night ruler, and there are hourly rulers too. And they built a whole model on this. And the Kabbala explains it greatly: Judaism holds that there are six thousand years to the world, and each thousand year period is ruled by a different planet. And there are also 50 year cycles, and the seven years cycle, called the Shemita Cycle, and the monthly cycles, daily cycles, hourly cycles, and cycles for each minute. So time has different influences embedded into it, and this looks to me as a whole second system in astrology. And we will see it in depth when we study further the letter of Rabbi Avraham Bar Chiya and other Kabbala writings.
So there are 2 different systems of astrology in Judaism.
- The first system is based on a fixed time energy set at the time of creation and which is embedded into all future time each unit with a certain set of characteristics. They can be based on the fixed hourly planet influence or the fixed Day influence as set at creation, and includes the Even/Odd fixed time unit.
- The second system is based on the actual planetary positions at the moment in question, as used broadly speaking in western astrology today.
So one should check if different cycles are good for him, if he wants to delay something, how long one wants to delay, and then, bearing all in mind, decide when to do what. I have some points of my own, regarding the question of why one sometimes uses one system and other times one uses the other, which will discuss further down.
Astrology is similar to what doctors do. Doctors tell you what is good or bad for you to eat while astrologers tell you, according to the stars and planets, what is the right time, and what is a bad time to do a thing. "If there will be before you food that you desire to eat and the doctor will say to you don't eat it because it is bad for people of your age group, heed his words and don't eat". It means that astrologers have a similar objective to doctors, and one should follow their advice. Astrology is the study of time and Doctors study our bodies. The main argument is that you are allowed to help people, and just like a doctor can help people, so can astrologers.
We should all be cautious in life and take care of ourselves, to stay out of danger and take advantage of opportunities, and take advice about what is a good time for you and what is dangerous time for you.

Chapter 1

In the first lesson we learned from Rabbi Avraham Bar Chiya using the Psalms that a wise man should always be on the lookout to protect himself from dangerous situations, and also prevent his friends from bringing themselves into dangerous situations. And then he goes on to say, that one of the ways you could put yourself into danger is by starting something in an unfavourable astrological hour. One should not start things in unfavourable astrological hours, and people should warn their friends not to do so either. And then he goes on, and tells you that he learns this from the Talmud, which is an ancient Jewish book, though many Jewish people may have not heard of it. It is one of the most important books in Jewish literature after the Bible. It is a book we refer to as the Oral Torah. It is the source of the oral tradition which tells us how to learn the Bible. Whereas the Bible tells you that certain things are forbidden and others are permitted, and all kinds of laws, it doesn't really expound on this to tell you how exactly to fulfil them. All these explanations to Biblical laws are referred to as the Oral Law. This Oral law was handed down from mouth to mouth, until, at a certain point in history, the rabbis decided to write it down, because they saw that Jews were going to be exiled from Israel, and were afraid that if they didn't write it all down, it might eventually be forgotten. So this became known to us as the Talmud. The whole basis of Western civilization can be found in it, and I recommend that people should learn it properly. The Talmud is divided into two parts: The Mishnah, which is the original basic teachings from Sinai, and the Talmud itself, which is the explanation and commentary of this ancient teaching known as the Mishnah. So one should learn the Mishnah first, because it is easier Hebrew and gives you a general overview of the whole Talmud, and then you can proceed to the Talmud itself, a great part of which is in Aramaic. So if you really want to master the Talmud and really learn it, you will have to learn Hebrew first, and then you will have to learn Aramaic too. When I started out, some forty years ago, there were no translations in English, so we had to learn Hebrew and Aramaic. Today, thank God, the Talmud has been translated into English and other languages. So whereas many books of Judaism have been lost, some rabbis in America have over the last 20 years or so, managed to make Jewish books understandable to everyone again, and especially the most important books. One of these groups is known as Artscroll, and they have translated the Talmud into an understandable format, and people should not find it difficult to learn. So Jews can now learn from their own sources.

So the Talmud talks about bloodletting in the tractate of Shabbat (which is one of the 60 tractates of the Talmud) and this reference is on page 129, on the second side. There you will find a whole piece on bloodletting and what are the days which are good for doing bloodletting (which had a certain dangerous element to it) from an astrological point of view, and which days are not. Back then, the major answer doctor's had for health problems was bloodletting that was up until the early 1800's. The lancet was the instrument used to make holes in the body of a person, to drain and let out the blood of the body, so that it would hopefully cure the person. The lancet was used extensively and still today one of the main medical journals in the UK is called the Lancet as it has its roots in the early 1800's. So one of the proofs Rabbi Avraham Bar Chiya gives to the acceptance of astrology in Judaism, how to overcome time energies, how to avoid bad time energies and their effects, comes from there in the Talmud on bloodletting since that was a serious matter and a common practice.

So there are the seven days of the week, each day has 24 hours, and each hour is ruled by one of the seven planets. Later we will see how it all fits in and how it works with bloodletting. So let us start reading from the Talmud:

"One who does something exhausting should lay down a little, before getting up to do things. As the master (one of the sages in the Talmud) said: Five things are closer to death than to life, and they are: Standing up immediately after eating, standing up immediately after drinking, standing up immediately after sleeping, standing up immediately after bloodletting and standing up immediately after having sexual intercourse". So after being treated with bloodletting, especially if one has low blood pressure, it is dangerous to suddenly jump up and switch gears so quickly. Then the Talmud continues specifically about bloodletting:

"Said Shmuel: The time of blood (letting) is every thirty days." which means, it is safe to have it once in each thirty day period. That is for a person in his prime. "But for those over 40, one should not have bloodletting so often and do it once in two months, and at an older age, the age of 60, one should have it once in three months. Then the Talmud proceeds to explain what days are good for bloodletting: "Said Shmuel:

Bloodletting should take place on Sunday, on Wednesday and on Friday, but not on Monday, Tuesday or Thursday, because the upper Court of Heaven and the Lower court (Beit Din) works on these days"...and there is therefore a lot of judgement in the world on these days, and when a person does something which is a little dangerous, such as bloodletting, one's bad deeds can be remembered at that time by the negative forces, and they could cause harm to that person.

But why not do it on Tuesday? Because Mars rules during part of that day during an even hour (and Mars is the planet which rules over blood, and violence, wars etc.); especially during even hours (as opposed to odd hours), when demons rule, the combination of that and the rule of Mars can cause damage to one who does dangerous things. We should note that the discussion in the Talmud is only about the daylight hours of each day, and not during the night, as the sages were not concerned about the night hours, since these activities (bloodletting) did not occur at night. Back then it wasn't a common thing to go out at night, because there weren't street lights. So the sages didn't forbid bloodletting on specific nights. So if you look at the chart I have made, you will see that there are the seven days of the week, with 24 hours to each day, and each hour has a different planet. You can see in the table that during the even hour Mars ruled, only during the eighth hour of Tuesday, yet they forbade bloodletting during the whole of Tuesday, so people wouldn't be confused about which hour is forbidden and which hour is not. That is the tradition, to build a fence around something not good.

Then the Talmud continues: "On Friday Mars also occurs during the day". It rules during the sixth hour on Friday, and so the question is, why is bloodletting allowed on Friday and not on Tuesday? And the Talmud answers: "Since many people disregard the prohibition of not doing it on Friday, we say, as written in Psalms: 'God watches over the simpletons', and we trust God to prevent any trouble from being caused by the bloodletting on Friday. But originally it was forbidden, but since Jews are accustomed to eat meat mainly on the Sabbath, and it is healthy to eat good food right after bloodletting, it became a custom to have bloodletting before Sabbath, and so with time we began to say that we trust in God to prevent any disaster from happening on the day before Shabbat as a result. On Wednesday it is permitted to have bloodletting, even though the planet Mars rules on the twelfth hour, and this is because it is the last hour of the day, and people did not pay much attention to that, and they consider that a night hour anyway. So that is the piece from the Talmud in Tractate Shabbat.

Sunday Night	Monday Night	Tuesday Night	Wednesday Night	Thursday Night	Friday Night	Saturday Night	Time	Hours
Jupiter	Venus	Saturn*	Sun	Moon	Mars	Mercury	6-7 pm	1st Hour of night
Mars	Mercury	Jupiter	Venus	Saturn	Sun	Moon	7-8	2
Sun	Moon	Mars	Mercury	Jupiter	Venus	Saturn	8-9	3
Venus	Saturn	Sun	Moon	Mars	Mercury	Jupiter	9-10	4
Mercury	Jupiter	Venus	Saturn	Sun	Moon	Mars	10-11	5
Moon	Mars	Mercury	Jupiter	Venus	Saturn	Sun	11-12	6
Saturn	Sun	Moon	Mars	Mercury	Jupiter	Venus	12-1 am	7
Jupiter	Venus	Saturn	Sun	Moon	Mars	Mercury	1-2	8
Mars	Mercury	Jupiter	Venus	Saturn	Sun	Moon	2-3	9
Sun	Moon	Mars	Mercury	Jupiter	Venus	Saturn	3-4	10
Venus	Saturn	Sun	Moon	Mars	Mercury	Jupiter	4-5	11
Mercury	Jupiter	Venus	Saturn	Sun	Moon	Mars	5-6	12
Moon	Mars	Mercury	Jupiter	Venus	Saturn	Sun	6-7 am	1st Hour of day
Saturn	Sun	Moon	Mars	Mercury	Jupiter	Venus	7-8	2
Jupiter	Venus	Saturn	Sun	Moon	Mars	Mercury	8-9	3
Mars	Mercury	Jupiter	Venus	Saturn	Sun	Moon	9-10	4
Sun	Moon	Mars	Mercury	Jupiter	Venus	Saturn	10-11	5
Venus	Saturn	Sun	Moon	Mars	Mercury	Jupiter	11-12	6
Mercury	Jupiter	Venus	Saturn	Sun	Moon	Mars	12-1 pm	7
Moon	Mars	Mercury	Jupiter	Venus	Saturn	Sun	1-2	8
Saturn	Sun	Moon	Mars	Mercury	Jupiter	Venus	2-3	9
Jupiter	Venus	Saturn	Sun	Moon	Mars	Mercury	3-4	10
Mars	Mercury	Jupiter	Venus	Saturn	Sun	Moon	4-5	11
Sun	Moon	Mars	Mercury	Jupiter	Venus	Saturn	5-6	12

* Beginning of Time when the Planets where created on the 4th day of creation (Tuesday night 6 pm is the beginning of day 4 when God created the Planets)

Now, let us go back to the text of Rabbi Avraham Bar Chiya:
"We learn that this is proper behaviour from our rabbis, may they be blessed, who warned us about this matter and taught us to do and act like this in all places. They said (Shabbat 129 B): "Blood should be let on Sunday, Wednesday or Friday, but not on Monday or Thursday, since the master taught:
"Only those whose ancestors had great merit should draw blood on Monday or Thursday". The reason for the danger is as we said that Mars rules an even hour on those days, and it was known to the masters of Astrology that it is not proper to begin in general a new venture on an even hour, and all the more so if a destructive planet rules that hour (such as mars). They worried about bloodletting in a Martian hour, because Mars rules over blood. And they warned especially not to draw blood on a day that Mars rules over an even hour like Monday or Thursday.
A question that should be asked is if the rabbis say that bloodletting or other things shouldn't be done on hours ruled over by Mars, why are these things allowed in hours ruled over by Saturn, since the bad influence of Saturn is considered even more destructive? Mars destroys, while the power of Saturn is destructive and also causes uprooting, which prevents anything which it destroyed from reappearing! And it is a kind of power which completely annihilates every one of its enemies. "So from here we also learn that anyone who wants to build a house, or plant a vineyard or dig a well, or any

action on which Saturn rules over in an even hour, should not start on that hour even if it is on a Sunday or Wednesday, and should be careful from beginning on Monday, Tuesday and Thursday and Friday, because in those days Saturn rules over an even hour. So with all these rules one can put together a full program of when to start and when not to start certain activities, in order to have the most favourable energy affecting the start of the activity. And remember that everything that will transpire from an activity is found in its beginning, so getting the start right is important; that is a basic principle of Kabbala, everything that will evolve is in the beginning, like the seed of a Cyprus tree.
You should remember that the system discussed here is not the system of the planets in the sky at the given moment of the activity, but rather a system based on the fixed energies as set during creation which influence all future time. As we have mentioned before, there are two systems in Torah astrology: The first system is about looking at the sky at the specific moment in question, seeing where the planets are situated, and concluding the influences at play. This is also the system of Western astrology, which is based on the Archetype chart of Adam, the first man. The second system, which can only be found in the Talmud, is based on the planetary Rulership which God imbedded in all time and is fixed. These fixed energies rule over each day and even each of the thousand years of the world's existence. Remember that in Judaism we learn that the world is supposed to exist for a period of 7000 years, with each thousand years being ruled by a different planet. So we see that this second system starts from the Bible during the creation of each day of the 7 days of the week. So this is what Rabbi Avraham means when he says: "No man can protest what I said, because it is revealed before their eyes" (ie: it's in the Bible).

Now Rabbi Avraham proceeds to explain the original reason and motive behind writing this letter:
"However, it once happened to me concerning this matter, and I need to explain what happened, and make known all the complaints, doubts and questions which arose, and answer them (one by one), until the truth becomes clear".
"I had a talented student, whom I loved and cared about greatly. He was to be married on Friday (which is a good day), and he suggested to me to be married in the third hour of that day, as it was the time the congregation leaves the synagogue and they could go straight to the wedding. His suggestion appealed to me very much, because it was an odd hour (which is a favourable time), and also the moon was ruling during that hour (according to the Fixed system from creation) and it is proper to begin a thing in the moon's hour. Further more, the planetary positions (tropical system) were good at that time. However, he was forced to delay the wedding because someone who had no relatives had passed away and needed to be buried (and this type of burial takes precedent over a marriage ceremony).
"The wedding contingent saw that the heads of the congregation and the important men of the community were going to the funeral, and the entrance of the bride was delayed until the congregation returned from burying the dead at the end of the fifth hour, the beginning of the sixth hour of the day which is ruled over by Mars, and it also didn't seem right from the planetary positions and the rising sign". Again he uses the two systems: one where the planets are embedded in time in perpetuity, and the other where the planets are situated in the sky at that moment.

"When I saw this I said to him, since you waited until the sixth hour, delay a little longer and do the wedding in the seventh hour, which is an odd hour and according the fixed system (of the Bible) the sun rules, and also the planetary influence at that hour were also good". The sun is a favourable planet, it has light and warmth, and on that day it occurs in an odd hour, an hour where no negative energies operate. So starting a wedding in such a time is likely to result in less fighting and more peace and harmony, and diminished unnatural deaths.

"I explained that it is always proper to start at this time, and further more, the planetary positions are better. He listened and was convinced by my reasoning, and he and his friends decided to wait. However, there was someone who disagreed, and said, 'this waiting is similar to asking a Chaldean (idolater), and we know that our rabbis, may they be blessed, said we don't ask Chaldeans, and so whoever does this deed (of listening to the wisdom of Astrology) transgress the words of our rabbis. He also quoted the passage from the Tractate Shabbat and said that concerning what Samuel said in the Talmud, about not letting blood on Mondays etc. is only concerning actual bloodletting because of the weakness it causes the body (and is not a general astrological principle), and we can't learn other things from that ruling and build a whole planetary system out of it. He went on again and again, until the bridegroom was forced to begin his marriage in the sixth hour".

"Since all this happened because of me, I felt as if all those who heard the story considered me a transgressor and sinner. Therefore I have to give the reasoning behind what I said and to acquit myself before God and His people, as it is says (In the Book of Numbers, chapter 32 verse 22), 'you are clean before God and Israel'. I stick to my words, and say that my accuser was being strict when there was no reason for strictness, and ruled something forbidden when there was no reason to forbid. Because whoever says that hour so and so of the day is good for something, or says it is proper to start something in the hour of Jupiter or in the hour that Aries or Taurus rising, is doing the same as a doctor who tells you that the water of this grass is good for the eyes, or this food is good for the teeth or the stomach, or this medicine causes diarrhoea or this medicine causes constipation. Just like this drug and this food and this grass each work in their own way, similarly each hour affects a person in a different way. Also, as there is no reason to forbid medicine, so there is no reason to forbid acting according to the influence of the hours".

So again, Rabbi Avraham comes back to the idea that astrology is similar to medicine. And just like a doctor can tell you which medicine is good or bad, so the astrologer can tell you which hours are good or bad.

Chapter 2

I am going to start with 2 new sources as an introduction before we move on with the letter of Rabbi Avraham: the first introduction is from the Talmud of Tractate Pesachim (Pesach): "Said Raba Bar Bar Channa who said in the name of Rabbi Shmuel Bar Marta, who said in the name of Rav, who said in the name of Rabbi Yosi the man from Hutzal: We have a tradition that we do not ask for the advice from Chaldeans. This we know from the Bible, in the Book of Deuteronomy, where it is said: "be simple in your faith with God"". So we don't ask the Chaldeans/Babylonians to tell us about the future and should rather trust in God and that everything that is going to happen is for the best and if you are worried, then pray to God, but don't go to the Chaldeans to get them to tell you what will happen in the future, as this shows a lack of trust in God. The commentator Rashi explains this passage and says that the Chaldeans are people who communicate with the dead (baalei ov). Other medieval commentators known as the Tosafot, in the name of Rashbam, says that the Chaldeans are astrologers, and that appears to be the main interpretation. So this passage from Tractate Pesachim seems to be telling us that you should pray to God instead of asking for the advice from astrologers.
So this is one source Rabbi Avraham Bar Chiya will have to address in his letter to show that a Jew is not transgressing that law (of not asking the Chaldeans) when he studies astrology.

I heard another explanation to this verse in Deuteronomy from a Kabbalist and astrologer of the last generation, Rabbi Binyamin Barazani. He was born in Afghanistan, and later came over to Jerusalem, and was a rabbi in the Beit Yisrael neighborhood in Jerusalem (near Meah Shearim). His explanations of the verse "be simple in your faith with God" was that it meant that once you learned astrology and studied your horoscope and saw who you are and what your future is, and what, approximately, you can get in life, and what profession you are a natural talent for and all the other things that come out of your chart, you should then not complain to God and ask God, why did you give me those energies and hassles and not others? Rather, you should accept your mazal and move forward with life with simple faith and trust in God and with the mazal he has given you, as it is all for the good, in as much as it is the fate you require for your mission on earth. Rabbi Binyamin Barazani did not agree with the interpretation that this verse in Deuteronomy is telling us that it is forbidden to study astrology and to not inquire as to what toolbox you were given at birth to fulfil you mission; it came to tell you what is your fate, and to accept it and work within it. For you were born with a certain mission in life, everyone has a mission in their life, and you should accept yours. So this is how he learned it. It is like being given a map of your life, you should not ask for another map or complain about the one you have. You should rather study it in detail and ensure that you are well prepared for what is coming up along the journey and maximize your potential within these parameters. Not studying the map at all and just going along the path blind as to what is coming around the next corner, is not the way of being simple in your faith with God, since you are ignoring the map he gave you, and blazing your own trail and wasting much time. You should aim to turn you Fate into your Destiny. For example, if you have a mazal to have lots of children, and you fulfil the bible commandment to procreate, then you will fulfil your mazal, while if you do not fulfil the commandment to procreate, or you partially fulfil it, you will change your potential mazal and have less children, despite the fact that you could have had more. Similarly, if your mazal is that you will have an inclination to do bad things, and yet you study the bible and its commandments and you follow them, you can change this mazal and do good.

This second source I would like to introduce is from a very ancient astrology book, called the Braita of Shmuel Hakatan (which is a tradition from our sages which was not included into the Mishnah and is therefore called a "Braita" [outside] and it comes from about 2000 years ago). He wrote a book about astrology and this book contains around 20 or 30 pages, with each page containing about ten lines of the original writing and the rest of the page is a commentary by a later rabbi. So I am going to read the last chapter of the book, which is the ninth chapter, and it says: "the explanation of the stars which rule the horoscope are…" So you have to remember that there are two bad/malific planets in astrology, which are Saturn and Mars. Saturn is too cold and Mars is too hot. And there are two good/beneficent planets, Jupiter and Venus. Jupiter represents good moral behaviour, and Venus has all the pleasure of this world. You also have the two lights, the Sun and the Moon. And there is Mercury, which is neither good nor bad, but it depends on which planets it combines with.

So the chapter begins with Saturn, the planet which is furthest from the earth and it says: "Saturn/Shabtai rules over poverty, over destitution, destruction, over illness and wounds and over sinning. Mars which is hot, rules over the blood and on destruction and evil and quarrel, over stronger disputes, wounds and injuries, over wars and hate, jealousy and animosity, competition and plagues, over Iron, fire, water. Jupiter rules over life, peace, goodness and calmness, quietness, Torah, happiness, rejoicing, wealth, honour and majesty. Venus rules over beauty and kindness, love and lust, infatuation and reproduction, the children of human beings and animals, and fruits of the ground and fruits of trees. Mercury rules over wisdom and intelligence, understanding and knowledge, scientific knowledge, and is able to open or develop all sorts of ideas and to be able to think and understand all sorts of thoughts in all systems of art and writing and languages".

"The Sun rules over light and darkness, differentiating between day and night, it rules over the counting of days and months and doing all kind of work and action using its light to see, travelling everywhere and anywhere using it".

(On a side note, we will in the future talk about the three modern planets, which were known to the world from the 1700s onwards. We have the book Sefer HaBrit which discusses Uranus, Neptune and Pluto where he mentioned the modern planets and discusses the reasons why the ancient sages didn't talk about them.)

For now we will only talk about the seven planets mentioned by the sages, which after all are the planets which rule the seven days of the week, and anyway the outer 3 planets rule different matters. So let us continue with the Baraita:

"The moon has the keys of the heaven and the earth, and is involved with the good and bad that happen on earth".

So now we get to the part in this source which is my main purpose for mentioning all this now: "And although the planets rule over the doing of both the bad and the good that happens on the earth, they do not have permission to instigate good or bad according to their own understanding". And this is a point that the Baraita makes, that the Planets, according to Judaism, are just appointed to fulfil their task and are agents of God.

[In future talks we will discuss a book by a Kabbalist called the "Leshem Shvo Veachlama", where the question is asked, why did God have to create planets and the solar system to rule and channel all the energies he sends down? His answer in brief is that because Adam (the first man) sinned, God had to distance himself as it then was not possible for Him to send all his bounty directly to humanity and had to use the solar system and all the different worlds (Assiya, Yetzira, Beriah and Atzilut) as intermediaries to serve as His delivery system to bring down His energies to us. But do not think that these intermediaries are the source of the works and then start worshiping the planets and stars as if they are doing the work and are independent powers by themselves. This cuts the planets from their source, and makes idols of the planets. The Jews who followed the tradition always knew that the planets and stars are only agents of God who carry out His will, and don't have the ability to do good or bad by themselves. So if one has a problem, the solution is to pray to God, not to the planets. And this seems to be the main point that this Baraita is making. The text continues: "And although the planets rule over the bad and good, they don't have any permission to do good or bad according to their own understanding. But everything is done by the instruction of God who 'calls out' the commandments to the planets. Everything is done by God's command; everything is done by what He, who created everything, instructs. And so it is said in Jeremiah, chapter 10 verse 5: "The gratitude and praising belongs to God, don't fear the idols (planets), for they cannot cause evil'. And how do you know that everything is done from God's calling out his instructions? For it says, 'And God called out a fast upon the earth'. And it also says in Jeremiah,"For behold, I call all families of the Northern kingdoms, that I am going to do evil". And where do we learn that God calls out good? As it says: "And He calls out in the desert; make way for God's path, make a straight road for the people, for the Lord our God will do good". So you have learned that the planets have no permission to do good or bad from their own volition, unless they are given permission by the Master of all (God)".

Let us continue with the letter of Rabbi Avraham Bar Chiya the Prince:

"Similarly, one who says about a child born when Jupiter is ruling, that he will be honest or modest, or about a girl born when Venus is strong, that she will be attractive and pleasant, he is not 'asking a Chaldean', and is not behaving like a Chaldean, and is not turning away from the way of the Torah, even by the hairsbreadth. Because all Israel acknowledges and believes that the power that was delegated to the stars was delegated on condition that it fulfils Gods will, and it is not in the planets hands to benefit or to hurt according to their will and understanding. Rather, they do what they are told and commanded. This is the way of belief of all God fearing men who delve into the wisdom of astrology, and one who is suspicious of them is suspicious of kosher people, and it is his doubts and thoughts that are not kosher thoughts. It appears to us through logical reasoning, after careful consideration that one who is careful not to start his work in even hours, or in hours which are unsuitable because of the planetary positions, has not sinned. He can rely on the words of our sage from the Talmud, the Sage Shmuel, that he has not transgressed neither a rabbinical nor Biblical injunction".

So what Rabbi Chiya's student did what not 'asking a Chaldean', as is implied by the strict opinion of the one in the congregation who opposed the Sage.

So there is no problem with astrology for a religious Jew. "And one who is suspicious of them is suspicious of kosher people".

Many Jews today do not know much about the Talmud and its rules and objectives, so it is important for me to emphasise that there are two types of transgressions in Jewish Law. One is a Biblical transgression and the other is a lesser transgression which is called Rabbinic. The punishments are more severe for transgressing Biblical injunction. If one transgressed something which is specifically written in the Bible, it is more serious than transgressing what the sages/rabbis decreed. And the sages decreed that certain things are forbidden because they saw that if those things were allowed, one might come to transgress something Biblical, which is very serious. So they made a sort of a spiritual fence, to protect you from transgressing Biblical commands. So for example, if it is a Biblical law not to extinguish a flame on the Sabbath, so the Rabbis instituted a law not to even touch a candle on Shabbat in case you put it out and transgress the biblical law. In any case, if you rely on Shemuel's opinion from the Talmud, you do not transgress either a rabbinical or a Biblical injunction.

In other words, it is kosher one hundred percent. "What he did is not 'asking a Chaldean'", for it is not at all connected to that".

So we see that Rabbi Avraham Bar Chiya holds that there is no problem in studying and implementing astrology, because astrological rules are dependent on God's will, not on the will of the planets themselves, and are only God's messengers. God is running everything; He calls out to the planets and gives them orders. So our connection is with God and not with the planets.

Chapter 3

Rabbi Avraham goes on to talk about the question of what "asking a Chaldean" really means, since this is an important definition which needs to be clarified since the Bible says it is forbidden to ask them. We saw that the Rashbam defined the Chaldeans as astrologers, and therefore you would assume that it means that one should not listen to astrologers.

Now, in the next paragraph of the letter of Rabbi Avraham Bar Chiya, he is going to talk about what it really means 'not to listen to a Chaldean'. But first, as an introduction to that, and to make it more understandable, I want to quote the Talmud in Tractate Shabbat, Page 156, on the first side: "It is written in the notebook of Rabbi Yehoshua Ben Levi: One who is born on the first day of the week (in Judaism the first day of the week is Sunday), will be a man 'with only one thing in him'. What does it mean a man 'with one thing in him'? Does it mean that he is a man with only one good thing in him? Rav Ashi said: ' But I was born on the first day of the week' (and I have many good things in me!). So maybe it means that this one thing refers to only one bad thing? But Rav Ashi said:' I and Dimi Bar Kakuza are both born on the first day of the week and I became a king (a Rosh Yeshiva who is like the king of the yeshiva) and Dimi became the head of thieves'. So therefore it means that one born on the first day of the week (Sunday) will either be successful for the best, or successful for the worst". And what is the reason for this? The reason is that on the first day, Darkness and Light were created, and those extremes of either light or darkness are embedded in that day (Sunday) in perpetuity, and anyone born on that day will reflect either of these opposite characteristics of Success and getting to the top (either for good or for bad).

So you see here that the Talmud is linking the days of the week, and the type of person who was born on any one of those days, to the energy and activity that took place during the seven days of creation. What God created on each of the original days of creation hints to you about what kind of person will be born on each of these days in the week. "And one who is born on the second day of the week (Monday) is likely to be an angry person. What is the reason for this? Because on day 2 of creation the upper and lower waters were separated, and one who was born on the 3rd day of the week (Tuesday) is likely to become rich and/or be an adulterer. And what is the reason for this? Because on day 3 of creation, the grasses were created and the grasses grow very fast, which is an indication to wealth: Just as grasses grow fast, so would the person's crops grow fast, and the person is going to make a lot of money. And since it isn't said that the grasses would grow according to their species and therefore will intermingle, it indicates that a person born on that day might have a tendency to adultery, since he goes after something which is not his, and likes things that are someone else's. "One, who is born on the fourth day of the week (Wednesday), will be wise and have a good memory. What is the reason for this, because the planets and the stars were positioned on that day. The moon gives him a good memory and the sun makes him wise. And one born on the fifth day (Thursday) of the week is likely to be generous and do good deeds for others. And what is the reason for that, because the fish and the birds were created on that day". And the Fish and birds find food easily, which indicates the energy of making it easy for himself to find things that he needs. "One who is born on the 6th day (Friday) is likely to be a person who strives a lot after things; said Rav Nachman Bar Yitzchak, 'such a person would be a seeker of good deeds, because on Friday, we do the good deeds of preparing for Saturday

(the Shabbat). "One who is born on the Shabbat (Saturday) is likely to die on the Sabbath". Because since one 'disturbed' the Sabbath laws in order to be born and save his life, so will he have to die on Shabbat. The Talmud goes on and says: "And Rabba Bar Rav Shila said: And he who is born on Shabbat will be a great and a holy person.
Said Rav Chanina: Go out and tell Rabbi Yehoshua Ben Levi (who uses the Days to determine influences), it is not the day that counts, but the hour of birth". "One who is born when the sun is ruling would be good-looking and have a dynamic disposition", because the sun is bright. And he is going to eat his own food and drink from his own resources, and his secrets will be revealed, because the sun sheds light and reveals everything". I suppose you could say he will have a big ego and can't refrain from talking about himself, "and he will not succeed if he resorts to theft", because whatever he does comes to light. "One who is born when Venus rules is likely to be rich and an adulterer. For what reason, because fire is positioned in it (in Venus). One born when Mercury rules is likely to have a good memory and be wise, for Mercury is the scribe of the sun.
One who is born when the moon rules is likely to suffer a lot of evil, build and demolish, demolish and build, because the moon always gets bigger and smaller, and it takes from what is not his and drinks what is not his, because the moon can be seen sometimes during the daytime, which is not the moon's time, whereas the sun is never seen at night, so the moon has some tendency towards theft. But his secrets are not likely to be revealed, and such a person is likely to succeed if he resorts to theft. The moon resembles the unconscious, because it has no light of its own, so it doesn't really shed light on anything.
The Talmud is not suggesting that a person born under the moon hour should become a thief. And my astrology teacher used to say that, whatever a person acquires in the wrong way he will loose it, he can't hold on to it. But in any case, some people have a greater chance to succeed in doing wrong things. "One who is born when Saturn rules is likely to have his plans frustrated. Others say that it's the other way round and that those born under Saturn will be able to stop anyone who thinks against him. Saturn is the outer planet of the Solar System, it is a smart planet, which can take care of itself. And anyone who tries to rise up against Saturn is not likely to be successful. "One who is born when Jupiter rules is likely to become a righteous person. Said Rav Nachman Bar Yitzchak: And (it means) righteous in doing good deeds. One who is born when Mars rules, is likely to become a person who sheds blood. Said Rav Ashi: (such a person may become) either a bloodletter or a thug, or a butcher or a surgeon. Said Raba: but I was born in a Mars hour? Said Abayey: Master Raba you do punish and kill since you are a Judge !
Rabbi Chanina says: Your mazal which you get from the planets affects people in the area of how wise and wealthy you will be, and the people of Israel are affected from astrological/planetary influence. Rabbi Yochanan says: Israel has no astrological influence (when they keep the commandments). And Rabbi Yochanan goes according to his reasoning, for Rabbi Yochanan said, where do you see that Israel has no astrologically influence? As it is said in Jeremiah: 'So said God, don't learn from the ways of the nations, and don't fear the signs of heaven, for only the nations should fear them'. They should be frightened, not Israel. And Rav too said that Israel has no astrologically influence, for Rav Yehuda said : Where is it learned that Israel is not astrologically influenced? As it is said about Avraham (in Genesis): 'And He (God) took him (Avraham) out of planetary influence'. Said Avraham:"master of the universe, the person

of my house (the head servant Eliezer) is going to inherent me? God said to him, “no, for the one who comes out of you (your son Issac) will inherit from you'. Said he (Avraham) to Him: Master of the world, I looked in my astrology chart, and I am not likely to have a son. He said to him: get out of your astrological chart, for Israel has no astrological influence! God said, what is your reasoning? that Jupiter is in the West (and this is a sign of no children)? I will take it (Jupiter) back and put it in the east”, and you will have children.

One of the later Kabalists after the Gaon of Vilna, a Rabbi Yitzchak Chaver (a main disciple of the Gaon of Vilna), said that, it is true that it is taught in our tradition, that both Avraham and Sarah had reproductive problems and were barren, and neither of them could give birth. But God cured them and made it possible for them to produce children. And all the Jewish people came out of Abraham and Sarah, and Rabbi Chaver explains it as God re-creating them into a new creation and where they are not under the planetary influences. And the Talmud continues: "And this is what is written: 'he put Jupiter in the east, and called it (instructed it) for his sake'.

Also Shmuel too said that Israel is not under the planetary influences (when they keep the commandments). The source in the Talmud says that Shmuel and Avlat (a non-jew) were sitting and some people walked passed them towards a lake. Said Avlat to Shmuel: 'This person is going to the lake and will not come back, a snake will bite him and he will die’. Shmuel said, if he is a descendent of Israel, he will come back! And they sat down and eventually he indeed came back. Avlat went to that man and asked him for his bag and threw it the floor, and indeed, a snake was found in it, which was cut into two pieces. Shmuel asked the man: 'What did you do to be saved from this snake?' The person replied: 'Every day we the workers collect bread and eat. Today I saw there was one of us who had no bread to contribute to our group and was embarrassed by this. I said to the group that I will collect the bread, and I pretended I received some bread from him, so he should not be ashamed'. So Shmuel said to him: 'You did a good deed! And that saved you. And Shmuel declared: 'Charity saves one from death' (in other words, Charity overcomes the planetary influences).

There is a tradition in Judaism which we will discuss in later lessons which explains how we overcome our planetary influences. I have a book from the 1500s where it is explained that the Jews were given the Torah and all the commandments, and that these commandments enables them to overcome the planetary influences, which is a very deep idea, which I will discuss in latter talks. Jews were given the Torah to overcome their natural inclinations and desires which come from the planetary influences; so one who follows all the commandments may be saved from all the natural trouble as determined by his Mazal. And Rabbi Avraham is going to talk about this also.

So the important thing is that in the eyes of the non Jews, it is not so much that the Jewish astrology is better than other astrology in predicting, but that Jews were able to overcome their planetary influences, overcome those predictions. Just like what Avlat saw above, that the Jew was meant to die from the snake bite, but instead, the snake was cut into two and the man was saved.

“And from Rabbi Akiva we also see that he held that Israel is above planetary influences. For Rabbi Akiva had a daughter and a Chaldean said to him: 'On the day that your daughter has her wedding, a snake will bite her and she will die'. Rabbi Akiva was worried about it very much. On the day before her wedding she prepared a special golden crown for her head, and stored it for the next day by attaching it to the wall using 2 long pins to hold it up, and unbeknown to her these 2 pins pierced the eyes of a snake which was sitting inside the crack of the wall. On the morning of her wedding, when she took it off the wall to put it on her head and found that a dead snake was attached to it. Rabbi Akiva asked his daughter, what did you do (to kill the snake)? She replied: A poor man was there, and everyone was so busy preparing for the wedding that they did not attend to him and give him food, so I gave my portion of food to him. So Rabbi Akiva said to her, you did a good deed and he went out and declared: 'Charity saves one from death'. And not just from terrible death, but from death itself. And we also know from Rabbi Nachman Bar Yitzchak who said, Israel is not under the planetary influences (which means that even though there is an influence, one is able to overcome it), because a Chaldeans said to his mother, 'your son is going to become a thief'. So she took that seriously and made sure that he always covered his head with a kipah (and followed all the commandments) and made sure he never had his head uncovered. She said to him, 'cover your head, so you will have the fear of heaven and pray for mercy'. At the time he didn't know why she said that to him. One day he sat and studied under a palm tree and his kipah fell off and a lust to steal came upon him, and he climbed up the tree and cut a cluster of dates with his teeth (he stole it).

All these different examples show that Jews were able to change there planetary influences by doing good deeds. So we are influenced by the planets, by we can over come it only if we do the mitzvoth. A Jew is not automatically exempt from planetary influences, but has tools to overcome them, that is what is meant by Israel is above the influence of the stars.

There is also a very important Kabbalah book called Shaar Hakedusha, the Gate of Holiness, which was written by Rabbi Hayim Vital. There he mentions that the way to correct one self (and change our natural inclinations as determined by our planetary influence), one has to do the 613 commandments with the correct intention, and, by doing so, a person would correct himself and be removed from astral influence. In Jewish psychology, the best way for a person to change himself is through performing the 613 commandments with the right intention as set out in the bible. Or, for the non-Jew, he has to perform the 7 Universal laws of Noah which are required of people who are not Jewish. So the thing is to fulfil these commandments, and by doing so, you get the ability to restrain your bad character traits. Because everyone has some bad character traits and everyone has things to work on; the whole purpose of coming to the world is to fix yourself, where ever you are in what ever situation you are in. And you see in the Torah that the way to fix character traits is through action, doing the deed (which includes daily studying). If you find it difficult to give things to others (you have the trait of being a miser) you overcome it by giving charity. If you are an angry person, you should study how the rabbis describe the terrible repercussion of anger and how it causes one to sin, and so on with other character traits. So there are two things; one is to do the commandments and the other is to acquire and fashion for yourself a better character, and this you do by continuously doing the commandments that you are not used to doing, and that don't go according to your nature, and this can change the planetary influences. In other words it is the character traits that hinder or help us in fulfilling the commandments, so in a sense the major work must be on changing our natures , which we can change by doing the will of God.

Chapter 4

Rabbi Avraham is going to prove that astrology has an influence on all people's lives (Jew and Gentile), just as he explained using the example of his student who was allowed to delay his wedding by an hour, to have it in an hour which was going to be better astrologically and therefore have a better marriage potential had he done so. Remember that one of the basic principles of Kabbala and ancient Jewish astrology is that everything is in the beginning. Think of it like you have a flash of insight on something important to you, and you then think about it and further meditate about it and flesh out the idea, and as it keeps popping into your thoughts, you then get motivated and want it to happen and begin to attach all sorts of emotions to it, and you finally sign the contract (or what ever concrete starting act to manifest the idea) and start talking, drawing, sharing and spending time, effort and money to get it started. The full natural potential of this venture with all its facets is encapsulated astrologically and symbolically in the moment you signed the contract. This is broadly speaking since you still have free choice on how to manifest the expression of the nature of the venture (and by doing the mitzot you can effect the nature of the potential itself – not just the expression of the nature), but this is a topic all on its own and evolves some of the deepest ideas of Torah and Kabbala.

Now lets go back to the example I gave above on Tractate Shabbat 156b : There we see there is an discussion between Rabbi Yehoshua Ben Levi and Rabbi Chanina, about which is more important in determining fate, is it the day the person is born in, as Rabbi Yehoshua Ben Levi holds, or is it the hour the person is born in as Chanina holds ? And this is very important. I have seen in many books and texts where the writers take both opinions, combine and make a mixture out of them, where one opinion modifies the other and create synergy: There is the day of the week, which is more supreme, because it is longer than the hours and it contains them. But the hours themselves are important too, so they modify the day (remember this is the system of the fixed embedded energies set from creation in perpetuity. This is a system brought down in the Talmud and Zohar). For example, if a person in born on the day of Mars, and then his Mars hour is very strong, he is going to be a very hot person, for he has a double Mars. But if he is of a Martian day with as Saturn hour, his Saturn is going to cool his Mars off a little, and he is sometimes going to become hot and sometimes he will be cold. And his astrological makeup can somehow mess up his timing. He may delay things too much, and then rush to do it, or rush to do things and then hesitates and backs off. This may be a result of a Saturn-Mars conjunction, which is a combination of hot and cold moods. So you have to take many things into consideration when you apply this. So remember, there are seven planets in the ancient system, and each rules over three or four different hours of each day. Also there is a considerable difference between the energies imparted to a person who was born in daytime or at night. We haven't talked about this much yet, but this is part of ancient astrology too, and is of great importance, because although we made a chart of the hours of the day using the illustration of the medical procedure mention in the Talmud of bloodletting, and we divided each day into 24 hours, we were really focusing on the hours of the day, and not on the hours of the night. The question of where planets were at night didn't interest us, because people then did not let blood at night. So for bloodletting night hours are irrelevant, but for astrology there is a great difference between the times, day or night, and whether a person was born during the day or at

night. Let us give an example: Mars is considered a bad planet, because it is too hot, so its element has a nature that is too hot, which turns a person into a blood spiller or an angry person and argumentative etc. But that refers mainly to a person born in a Martian hour of the day, or on a Martian day, but if he was born at night, it would not be so bad, even if he was born on a Martian hour; because Mars is cooler at night, so it is not so hot. So a Martian person born at night is better, but this would be the opposite with Saturn, since Saturn is cold. So if a person is born during the day, he warms up his Saturn a little, but not during the night. So there are considerable differences between day and night.
Another question people ask me, is how does one determine the hours in the fixed creation system of the Talmud, because each hour, as written on the chart, is divided by sixty minutes and each planet rules over sixty minutes: From six to seven at night it is Saturn, from seven to eight at night it is Jupiter, from eight to nine is Mars, nine to ten is the sun, ten to eleven is Venus, eleven to twelve is Mercury, twelve to one is the moon, and then you start over again with Saturn: The first hour and the second starts with Saturn (then Jupiter, mars, sun, venus, mercury, moon) and it continues all week; from the furthest planet to the one closest to earth and back. And this is called using the 'regular hours'. But there are also hours called in Hebrew Shaot Zmaniyot, 'relative hours'. Like in summer the day is longer than night, so there are 18 hours of sunlight and six hours of night. So if you look at that chart and say we go according to relative hours (we divide the 18 hours of sunlight into 12 units of day time and get an hour unit of 90 minutes, which is different to the set regular 60 minute hours. Also at night each hour would be less than 60 minutes - we divide the 6 hours by 12 units and get 30 minutes hours). So the hours of the day are different to the hours of the night. So in this case, the 'relative hour' approach changes all the time with the seasons and the 'regular hour' approach which is set as shown in the chart above, would only be accurate for two days a year from the perspective of the 'relative hour' approach. So one has to take all this into consideration, and the more correct system in my opinion is the system of - regular hours. So the planetary influences are not so simple. And you see that in this system brought down in the Talmud, there are a couple of causes to human nature and planetary influences. The Kabbalists go even further by taking into consideration the week you were born in, and the month, the year etc. but in the Talmud, the rabbis discussed all this only briefly, in relation to bloodletting, so they gave the days and the hours only.
Earlier Rabbi Avraham Bar Chiya came to the conclusion that the chart of bloodletting was a practical example of a principle that comes to teach you that you have to be cautious with astrological hours when initiating something important, and not start it on a dangerous hour. And he also explained that it is not against Torah or Rabbinical laws to factor the astrological influences into your life, because the planets are not entities onto themselves, but God's agents, who fulfil His commands. And we should be in tune with God's energy flow. We also talked about the fact that one shouldn't worry that Jews who study these energies coming down from God will begin to worship the delivery system (the planets) or anything like that, and therefore go against the Torah. And if this is not a risk, then astrology as practiced by our ancient sages need not be circled and cut off from our people. Astrology is basically a study of time: Which time is good for this and which time is not good for that, that's it, and otherwise we pray to God who can change the fate that comes through these planetary influences. And we saw examples to that in the Talmud, how charity and other Mitzot change one's destiny.

Now Rabbi Avraham Bar Chiya deals with the important question of what does it mean that 'you do not ask the Chaldeans'? And especially when you take into consideration the Rashbam, one of the great rabbis of the Middle Ages, who learned that to 'not ask the Chaldeans' means one should not ask astrologers. Does it mean we don't ask astrologers about our astrology? So using the classical method of detailed Talmud analysis and definition, Rabbi Avraham Bar Chiya is going to deal with this problem, as well as with the question of what is actually the problem the Rabbis were worried about and whether there is a problem in actually asking Chaldeans, or is it that there is a problem in listening to them, and all sorts of combinations like that.

So he writes; "Now let us investigate further concerning the warning against asking the Chaldeans. Is it from the side that the science that they engage in has an element of idol worship and blasphemy in it, and we were warned from asking them because their science is forbidden? Or is it perhaps that our sages did not warn about asking except concerning the asking itself, because in their Chaldean astrological investigation they seek out that which is forbidden, and it is as if we participate in their transgression? (we should not be associated with idolatry in any form, even if they are using a correct system). To answer this question, we need to investigate what are the works of the Chaldeans and what is their wisdom, and what is there in this wisdom which has a forbidden side to it. We find in rabbinic literature (Talmud) the story of the mother of Rav Nachman, who listened to the words of the Chaldeans when they told her 'your child will be a thief'. But these words of the Chaldeans are similar words to those sages of ours who delve into the ways of the stars, and who say, 'if one is born under such and such a constellation, or if this planet rules over a person, he will be a thief or a rich person or a wise person'. We find it taught in the rabbinical literature like Talmud Tractate Shabbat, not in the name of the Chaldeans, but in the name of an important Rabbi, Rabbi Joshua Ben Levi, who said, 'one born under the sun will be like this, one born under Venus like this', and 'one born under Mars will be a blood spiller'. And then the eminant Rav Ashi who said: 'Or a thief or a blood letter or an animal slaughterer or mohel'. And the renowned Raba said: 'I am born under Mars'. And then Abaye said to him: 'You also punish and kill' ect...". That is a lot of very important Rabbi's using similar words to the words of the Chaldeans. And it must be emphasised that these words have been said by the greats of our tradition such as Rabbi Joshua Ben Levi and Raba and Abaye (and each one gave a strong reason). So how can we say there is a forbidden side to it? Rather we see from here that our rabbis engaged in the study of the planets and constellations (astrology), and they delved into it and they did not hold their hand back from it. We can say that in this respect, because what the Chaldeans said does not differ from what the rabbis said, there can be no forbidden side to astrology. Rather, the problem is not with astrology but with the way the Chaldeans used this knowledge and how they study and investigate this knowledge in a forbidden way, so our rabbis warned us about them and not about astrology. So they directed us away from asking them as people with forbidden beliefs.

Now we will explain this matter in another way and say that those sages who were investigators of the stars and their influences are similar to our farther Avraham Avinu (Abraham was the master astrologer of his generation, he wrote the oldest book on astrology, Sefer Hayetzira – The book of Formation, which is available today in English

and the best one is the commentary of Rabbi Ariye Kaplan, and in this book, at least three of the book's chapters talk about astrology. So it is almost a 4000 year old book.) Our rabbis said about him: 'Avraham said before God, Master of the universe, I looked at my horoscope, and I am not suitable to have a child. God replied: Get out from your astrology! The Jews are not under the influence of the constellations. What is your reasoning? that Jupiter is in the west? I will return it and place it in the east, as we see in Isaiah 42 (2) 'Who lights up the east with Righteousness (Tzedek, Jupiter)'.
So we see from this story that studying the movement of the planets, which speak about the fate of man and what will happen to him, is kosher. Because it is similar to what Avraham engaged in, and you can see this because Avraham our father said, 'I looked and saw that I couldn't have children', which are the words of an astrologer, words on the fate of man. And nobody can say about Avraham Avinu (who God said about him, 'since Avraham listened to my voice and guarded my commandments and Torah'), that he would engage in anything that was un-true and sinful. Rather we have to say that anything that one engages in, which is similar to what Avraham Avinu did, cannot have anything wrong with it. So we can say concerning astrology, that there is no stigma to it, and we can say about the words of the Chaldeans, if they are similar to the words of the wise astrologers, then there is no stigma attached from the fact that they are similar".

"This is the first thing we can say from the story. It also appears that astrology is a true knowledge, and it is proper to encourage and study it, because God said to Avraham Avinu, 'leave astrology, because the Jews are not under planetary influences' (once they follow the mitzvoth). And He didn't say, 'leave astrology because it is not a science and it in not true and it is not proper to study'. All of this He would have said if astrology was not a science that should be encouraged and learned. From this we can say that astrology is called a science, and its principals are true and you should search after it and study it. The third thing you can learn is that the Jews are not under the planetary influences. That is to say that the righteous ones of Israel (those who keep the commandments ect...) can nullify evil decrees by their righteous behaviour and prayers. This isn't the case of the rest of the nations of the world, of which it was said about them in the Talmud,' Rabbi Yonatan said, 'how do we know the Jews are not under the planetary influences'? Because God said, 'don't learn from the ways of the non Jews, and also from the signs of heaven do not be afraid if the non Jew is afraid'. So we learn 'the non Jew is afraid' because as opposed to the religious Jew, he is not using prayer and righteous behaviour to overcome the planetary influences. Those who do will also overcome their fate.
Now Rabbi Avraham is going to give another reason, which is much deeper, to the question of why the Jews are above the planetary influence: "Further more, it was said that the Jews are not under the planetary influences, because the whole world was created for the Jews because they accepted the Torah. If the Jews didn't accept the Torah, the whole world (the planets and constellations) would have returned to nothingness. And if the planets and constellations only exist because of the Torah and the Jews, how can they rule over the Jews (who follow the ways of the Torah)? Rather, the strength of the Jews and their merit, which allowed the world to exist, is greater than the powers of the stars". And as we have mentioned before, that the planetary influences come from the lowest of the 5 worlds, known as the world Assiya, the world of Action; but the root of the influences upon Jews is from 3 worlds higher up, a world known as the world of Atzilut,

the world of Emanation. So therefore, Jews, through the Torah, have the ability to change the planetary influences. And because of this we say that the Jews are not under the planetary influences. Because there isn't enough strength in the constellations to fulfil their decrees on Israel, since the righteous ones of Israel are able, through their merit, to nullify the power of the constellations. Like it says, 'charity saves from death'.
A great Kabbalist Rabbi Yitzchak Izik Chaver of the generation following that of the Vilna Gaon wrote a little book called “Ein Mazal Leyisrael” (The is no Mazal on Israel). Astrology is discussed a lot in that book, and in particular how the Jews are above the planetary influences. Rabbi Yitzchak also brings up the example of Avraham and how if astrology was ok for him, it is certainly ok for us. Everyone who learns Judaism knows that Avraham and Sara started it: At the age of three, Avraham came to realize that there is one creator to this world, and together with his wife, Sara, they started the Jewish religion. And it is taught that both Avraham and Sara were completely barren, and neither had any chance, even one in a million, to have children. They couldn't produce children. But God made a miracle, and they had a child, Isaac, the first Jewish child. So Rabbi Yitzchak Chaver wants to learn from this that the Jews are a special creation, who, according to natural rule, shouldn't have come into existence. So they were a Briah Chadasha, a new creation, something different from the rest of mankind, people created later than the beginnings of creation. So they have a special destiny and a special fate. And hopefully, one day we will come to the book of Yitzchak Izik Chaver, because it is a very deep book.

Chapter 5

So Rabbi Avraham Bar Chiya learns from every word in these stories; that it is not astrology which is untrue, but something in the Chaldean way of thinking which is untrue. Rabbi Avraham is going to explain that there is some difference between how Chaldeans practice astrology, and how normal astrologers do, and that there is something wrong in the way Chaldeans do it.

"Even though we said that there is no mazal to Israel, we do say that the constellations testify for Israel". Every person may learn astrology, see the planets and realize that this and that may be caused and happen in his future. Which also means all the normal things: That Venus is going to bring love, Jupiter is going to bring morality, and each planet in a person's chart is going to have meaning for him, as we saw in the notebook of Rabbi Yehoshua Ben Levi; but the righteous have the ability to be beyond the planetary influences. "Like Rabbi Chanina said, mazal makes you wealthy, mazal makes you wise, and there is mazal to Israel'". So Rabbi Chanina holds that there is mazal to Israel: Some have mazal to be very wealthy, some have mazal to be wise, some have mazal to be idiots etc. "Rabbi Chanina's words were not against Rabbi Yohanan, and Rav and Rabbi Yehuda, and Shmuel and Rabbi Akiva, he didn't really and completely argue with the five great rabbis, who all said, 'there is no mazal to Israel', they only took different approaches and different points of view. We can rather say that Rabbi Chanina comes to explain the other rabbis in that the reasoning of Rabbi Chanina is that the merit of Israel can nullify the testimony of the planets". In other words, the planets testify to things. They testify to what is going to happen in this world. If you are an astrologer, you see peoples' charts, and you may look at their charts and tell what is going to happen to them, because they testify to what is going to be. But a Jew can nullify the testimony of the planets, and cause it, by doing good deeds, not to come true. "It comes out, there is mazal to Israel and there isn't mazal to Israel". It is like a two way street: Sometimes there is mazal to Israel, but sometimes they have the ability to override the testimony of the planets by their behaviour, by doing good deeds, because the mazal doesn't testify for them and the testimony isn't established", it doesn't make a complete testimony for them, "rather it is dependent on the deeds of Israel and their merit". Rather, what happens to the Jews is more dependent on their deeds and their merit, and they can override their mazal. "If God wants to nullify the decrees of the planets from Israel, he doesn't nullify the power of the planet that testifies to that decree; rather the decree is automatically revoked from above; because the planets and signs have no rulership over Israel". This is a very deep idea, that the root of the Jews is higher than the planets, and are, therefore, not completely dependent on them. Therefore, if God wants to nullify a decree against a Jew, or even against the whole nation of Israel, He doesn't have to nullify the power of the planet that testifies to that decree. He just nullifies the decree itself higher up in the worlds above the planets. But the planet can still function, because it just gives testimony, which can be overridden. So God doesn't have to get rid of the planet or change it. "However, if God wants to nullify the planetary decrees on the nations of the world, first He removes the power of the planet which has rulership over that decree, and nullifies its rulership, and afterwards He does what He wants with that nation". So when it comes to decrees upon the nations, first the power of the planet has to be removed. But that is not what has to be done when it comes to the Jews, who are above that.

“Because we find that since it was right in God's eyes to increase the life span of King Hezekeyah and to add on to the testimony of the birth planets (add years to his life), which concerning it the prophet Isaiah prophesized, 'you will die and not live'. We do not see that He removed the planetary power, and didn't nullify the sign rulership, rather he said, ' I am adding on to your life fifteen years'. And similarly with the daughter of Rabbi Akiva, who God saved from death. Rabbi Akiva didn't say that God nullified the rulership of the constellations, rather he expounded, 'charity saves from death', and the Jews are not under the planetary influences”.

Let us go back to the story of King Hezekeyah: He was one of the righteous kings of Judea, but there was a decree on him to die. He prayed to God, asking him to nullify the decree, even though the prophet Isaiah came and told him about this prophecy that he would die. There is no way out for yourself. And yet, King Hezekeyah got a life extension of fifteen years. And Rabbi Avraham is going to talk about this a little and explain it:
“We do not see that He removed the planetary power, and didn't nullify the sign rulership”. The Bible doesn't say that the planetary power or the sign of rulership were removed, as is mentioned in the Book of Kings. “Rather He said, 'I am adding on to your life fifteen years'”, without nullifying any planet or anything. “And similarly with the daughter of Rabbi Akiva, who God saved from death. Rabbi Akiva didn't say that God nullified the rulership of the constellations, rather he expounded, 'charity saves from death', and the Jews are not under the planetary influences”. So even though the rulership and the testimony of the constellations still existed, the decree was nullified due to the act of Rabbi Akiva's daughter giving charity. So the astrological testimony was overridden, because “Charity saves from death” and the Jews are not under the planetary influences. But when a decree had been decreed upon the nations of the world, God first nullified the planetary powers:
“And it is not so with the nations of the world, rather we see with the decree that came on the generation of the flood, God said, ‘Remove one star from the constellation of Kima (Kima could be like Taurus, or maybe one star within the Constellation of Taurus) and bring on the flood’. Because the flood would not have come to the world if the influence of that constellation hadn't been nullified, and the star Kima, which is probably in the constellation of Taurus, hadn't been removed”. In other words, in order to bring the flood, God had to get rid of Kima, which probably holds the amount of rain that comes down to earth. So after that star was taken away, the flood could start. “He didn't remove the star from any other constellation, because the flood was in the month of Iyar where Taurus rises in the east or in the month of Chashvan where Taurus sets in the west. Because the rabbis argued over in which of these two months the flood took place. In these two months Taurus rises and sets, and rules over the rains and thunder, and testifies concerning all the increases and decreases in every year, according to all those versed in astrology. Because the flood was in the days of the rulership of Taurus, from there it was said, remove a star from Taurus and bring the flood. If the flood was in the month of Iyar (May), remove the star from Taurus, which is rising, and if it is in Chashvan (November), remove it when it is setting. All this is to make known that God only nullifies the planetary power which rules at that specific time, and which in the future He will

reinstate or nullify on the nations. But on Israel, God does not have to nullify the planetary powers, because the planets do not rule over them".

So let us go back again:

"He didn't remove the star from any other constellation, because the flood was in the month of Iyar", which is the second month of the Hebrew year, starting from Nissan. But actually there are two ways to count the Hebrew year: One is from Nissan, which is around April, when it is counted according to the months, and the other is from Tishrei, the time of Rosh Hashana, around October. And the second month may be Iyar, "where Taurus rises in the east", in the eastern horizon in the morning, "or Chashvan (scorpio), where Taurus sets in the west", in the evening. So there are two different opinions as to when the flood started, in what was the "Second month", Iyar or Chashvan. Is it the time of Scorpio, when Taurus sets in the west or when Taurus rises, in the Spring, Scorpio sets. Scorpio rises in the beginning of the rainy season.

So because this world has to function in a natural way of natural rules, some planetary influences had to be removed in order to enable the rain to really fall, and have a major flood. In other words, the testimony of the planets for the nations is always established, but if God wants to do something against it, He removes their power and influence of that planet or some planets.

So let us read the next paragraph, after which we will look at it again:

"God, in the story of Abraham our father, informed us of these matters. He informed us of the power of Israel", who are beyond the planetary influences and have no mazal, and He informed us of the power of the stars over the nations of the world, who do have mazal". What did He say to Abraham? "Jupiter is in the west, then I will move it to the east", so he said that because of the non-Jewish nations which came out from Avraham. "He brought those two matters, because from Avraham came forth many nations who the stars rule over, and concerning them He said, 'Jupiter is in the west, then I will move it to the east'. He nullified the power of the stars for the nations, as he said to Avraham, 'Ishmael will live before you', and for him I nullified the power of the constellations. And further, 'my covenant I will establish with Yitzhak (Isaac), whose power is greater then the hosts of heaven'. About Yitzhak He said, 'he will be called offspring', and his offspring will be established, and the stars will have no influence over them". So Rabbi Avraham wants to say that since Avraham was the father of many nations, including probably the Brahamins of the Indian society (which if you look at their name it comes from Avraham). It says in the Torah, that he sent many of his sons to the east with gifts. And the commentaries explain that these gifts were different spiritual kinds of wisdom which Avraham taught them. And Avraham is the father of the Arabs too, for Ishmael was his son, and the Arabs came from him. So there were two sides to Avraham: On the one side, for Ishmael and the other sons who were fathers of non Jewish nations, God moved Jupiter from west to east, so the planetary influence would change and Avraham would be able to have these sons. But for Yitzchak, the father of Israel, God didn't have to do that, because Israel is above the planetary influence. He made the change from above the planets in the other worlds above.

I think I should also read out a couple of verses from the Book of Genesis to you, from which Rabbi Avraham learns these points above. It is in Chapter 17, verses 17-22:

"And Avraham fell upon his face and laughed, and thought, can a hundred year old man have children? And as for Sarah, can a ninety year old woman give birth? And Avraham said to God, all that Ishmael might live before you. God said, nonetheless, your wife, Sara, will give you a son, and you should call his name Isaac, and I will fulfill my covenant with him as an everlasting covenant with his offspring after him. And as for Ishmael, I have heard you, behold, I have blessed him and he will be fruitful and produce many children, he will produce twelve princes and I will make him a great nation. But I will maintain my covenant with Isaac, who will be born to Sara, on this time next year. And when He finished speaking, God ascended from upon Avraham".

So you see that there were two sons to Avraham, and later there were two types of children to him: Isaac the Jew, who was above the planetary influences, and the non Jews who were under these influences. So you see, already from there, how there is a distinction, regarding planetary influences, between Israel and the rest of humanity. Let us further read from Rabbi Avraham's letter:

"Already we have seen from the story of Abraham that there is nothing wrong with astrology, because Avraham Avinu was engaged in it". And whatever Avraham did was always what God allowed humanity. "We see it is a true science, because God did not nullify testimony of the stars on Avraham, until He changed their placement and put Jupiter in the east". God had to move the stars around, so you see that what Avraham realized, regarding Jupiter's influence, was true, so astrology isn't nonsense. "We see that the constellations rule over the nations of the world and the testimony of the stars rule and are established over them. And if God wants to nullify it, He must remove the power of the planets and nullify their influence", in order to change what is going to happen to non-Jews. "Furthermore, we see a fifth thing, that with the knowledge of the stars, one thing can be derived from another thing, like it says, 'the son of my house inherits me'". Since Avraham saw he couldn't have children, he realized that his faithful servant of his house was going to inherit him. "He didn't see this, rather he saw that he wouldn't have a son, and he learned from it that his servant would inherit him. This is similar to the wise man, who said to a man, your children will be from illicit relationships. He answered him, where do you know this from, and where did this wisdom come from? He said, I saw that every woman that you will marry with a marriage covenant will be barren, and I also saw you will have children, and I derived from this that your children will be from an illicit relationship. This is how you derive knowledge from astrology".

Because one can see the chart of the first wife, if one looks at the house of marriage, from the seventh house, and that of the second wife from the ninth house etc. He saw the wives wouldn't have children. And he looked at the fifth house and saw the man was going to have children. So he concluded that these children were going to be from illicit relationships. So we see that we can use logic and conclude different things from signs which can be seen in astrology. So from everything we have seen up to now, we see that it is proper to study astrology and go according to it.

Chapter 6

In the letter to his student, Rabbi Avraham Bar Chiya explained his reasoning for suggesting that he should delay his wedding. He suggested that the wedding be delayed so there would be more luck in the time of the wedding. His suggestion was that it be done on an hour which was

- an odd hour, and
- a good planetary fixed hour (Talmud system), and
- a good position of the planets in the horoscope when compared with their positions at the time of the student's birth.

And managed to prove, and using all his sources, from the Talmud, the Bible and other rabbinical literature, that the Jews always considered astrology as a legitimate science. “From everything we said up to now, we see that it is proper to study astrology and to hold it. However, since it could go up in the heart of man to take the knowledge of the Chaldeans and that our rabbis warned us about doing this and consulting with them, we need to investigate the difference between the two. We must say that astrology gives us the insight as to what will be in the future in a general way, but it cannot inform us in detail or specifics or the body of the truth. If astrology informs us that this man will own fields and vineyards, it cannot tell us that he will buy this specific field or that specific vineyard at that specific location. So one only sees the power of the mazal and the testimony of the planets that testify in the sky, but we don’t see its particulars down on earth. Rather we see the categories and the general. This is a matter which is very clear, and agreed on by all who practice this science”.

Rabbi Avraham explains that you can't say that the Chaldeans learn astrology just like other people learn it. And that even though they call themselves and are called by others, astrologers, there is a difference, and they do something different from other astrologers, and because of that it is forbidden to listen to them. Because if they were normal astrologers, there would be no reason for them to be forbidden, since astrology is the science of understanding time, which is what Rabbi Avraham said in the beginning: There are times to do this, there are times to do that, and there are times to refrain from doing things. Just like doctors may say that this kind of food is good for you and the other is not, and there is a time to eat food and time not to eat, and each person eats different foods. And the same thing is in astrology as the study of time, and it is a legitimate science. So what do the Chaldeans do wrong? This is what he wants to get to know. “We must say that astrology gives us the insight to what will be in the future in a general way, but it cannot inform us in detail or specifics or the body of the matter in truth'. So astrology works only in a general way; It is the understanding of what we see in the Heaven’s part of the world of Asiya, the Heavens of the lowest world of Action. And there you don't see things in detail, you only see things in a general way. You can see that this person is going to get married this year, but it doesn't tell you who he is going to marry. So if someone comes to you and asks, 'am I going to get married this year?', you can tell him, 'yes, you are, I see it clearly in your horoscope'. But then, if he asks, 'will I marry this person?', then that you can't tell him from looking at his horoscope only, without seeing her horoscope. You can't be certain of the name of the girl he is going to marry, because it is too much. Because astrology only sees things in a general way, this is what Rabbi Avraham tries to explain. “We must say that astrology gives us the insight to what will be in the future in a general way, but it cannot inform us in detail or specifics or the body in truth.

“The Chaldeans' words are not like this, rather they testify (predict) on the specific thing and the body as it is, like it teaches”.

To illustrate the point he now quotes some famous astrology stories in the Talmud. He starts with the story of Yosef Mokir Shavi who was a Jewish man who gave great honour to the Shabbat. All week he lived a modest life, ate very little, didn't spend his money on any weekly purpose, except for things for the Sabbath, so he would have money to honour the Sabbath: To have three good meals of Shabbat, and give honour to it like you are supposed to according to the Jewish law. So he had the nickname, besides his name, Yosef: The man who honours the Seventh Day (Yosef mokir shvee). And in his neighbourhood there was a very wealthy non Jew, and one day a Chaldean came up to the wealthy man and told him his prediction, saying that all his possessions are going to get taken by the Jew Yosef, the Man who honours the Seventh Day. Your possessions would be lost to you and go to him (Yosef). When the non Jew heard this, he sold all his possessions, took all his money and bought with it a precious stone. He put it in his hat, with which he went everywhere, to make sure he didn't lose the precious stone. One day, as the wind was blowing, his hat blew off his head and went into the river. He was very unhappy but he consoled himself by thinking at least the Chaldean was wrong on one point, because Yosef did not get the precious stone. Later the stone was swallowed by a big fish that then got caught and sold in the marketplace of Friday. This was such a magnificent fish someone said ‘Let us offer this fish to Yosef Mokir Shvee, who is likely to buy this expensive fish from us to honour the Sabbath! They didn't have refrigerators back in those days, and they wanted to sell the fish as soon as possible, so it wouldn't get ruined. Of course Yosef bought the fish for the Sabbath. And the precious stone was found as he and his family opened up the fish. And Yosef became a very wealthy man”.

So you see that the Chaldean was right, but you can also see, as Rabbi Avraham learns from the story, that Chaldeans predict specific things in details. Not only that the person was going to lose all his wealth, but who exactly would inherit it. And that is a rule we have in astrology, that you can't predict the particulars. You can predict things in general, but not in details. So this is one story which proves that Chaldeans predict specifics.

And now Rabbi Avraham is going to bring another story from the Talmud (a few others in passing), where you see a Chaldean made a specific prediction:

Similarly it was said, 'a Chaldean said to the mother of Rav Nachman, 'your son will be a thief, don't let him go with his head uncovered'. This way of predicting is not the way of astrologers, because they are able to see if he is a thief, but they don't know if covering his head will help him. Because from astrology, it is impossible to know that covering his head would help him. This predicting specifics is not the same as looking at the general and surmising logically about the details. As we showed above where we discussed the story of Abraham who saw in his horoscope that he would have no children, and then logically concluded that his trusted servant was going to inherit his possessions. Abraham did not use astrology to predict WHO was going to inherit he possessions. That on the other hand is what the Chaldeans would do, predict who.

This is similar to a story in another part of the Talmud, where it says that the Chaldean said to Rabbi Akiva about his daughter, that when she enters the wedding room a snake will bite her”. Why in Rabbi Akiva’s story is the Talmud using the word ‘Chaldean’ in this case and not a generic term for astrologer ? Because he predicted to Rabbi Akiva exactly where the snake was supposed to bite her, and it would be when she enters the wedding room. “It is not in the power of the astrologers to predict where she will die”. So they called him a Chaldean. Astrologers can tell you that someone can die on a certain day or hour, and maybe even in a general area, but not in such specifics, like in which room one will die. “If they see she will die in a field, they can't say, in Mr. X's field or Mr. Y's garden. So from here we see that what astrologers do and what the Chaldeans do is not the same thing.

Another story in the Talmud is the story of Shmuel and Avlat who were sitting and they saw a man going to the lake. Avlat said to Shmuel, 'he is going but he will not return'. Now this is something that any astrologer can predict, on the road at this hour was not a good hour and something will happen to him. Because of this the Talmud called him Avlat by his name, because he was an astrologer, and didn't call him a Chaldean, like it said in the stories about Rabbi Akiva and the mother of Rav Nachman. So from the fact that the Talmud didn't use the specific name of the astrologer when he predicted specifically to Rabbi Akiva and Rav Nachman’s mother they call him a ‘Chaldean’, and yet in the story of Shmuel the astrologer Avlat is mentioned by name, because he predicted in general and therefore was a regular astrologer and not a Chaldean. So this is Rabbi Avraham’s proof from the Talmud that there is a fundamental difference between a Chaldean and a regular astrologer.

“It appears to us that astrology and the 'work of the Chaldeans' is not the same thing”. Rabbi Avraham is saying that there are two separate things: Common astrology on the one hand, and the work of the Chaldeans on the other. How are they different? “Rather the Chaldeans investigate more deeply”. They have a different way of investigating into what is going to be, much more deeply than what the astrologers do. “Because of this we say that the 'work of the Chaldeans', where they investigate what will be in the future, is not carried out in the same way as the astrologers carry out their investigations”. So the way they arrive at their conclusions is very different, and because of this the Sages forbid what the Chaldeans do. But before we talk about this, he wants to clarify something else: “If we clarify all the different sciences and works which comprise astrology”, because first we have to clarify what exactly astrology is, and all the different sciences which make up astrology, “what they are and on what side man studies the science of astrology and engages in the work of the heavenly bodies”, and what he does with the heavenly bodies, “we can see from there what the Chaldeans do, if it is one of these sciences or not”. What is the science of astrology composed versus what and where the Chaldeans get their knowledge from is it from the same sources or from some other place.

So he then talks on the subject of astrology and states that the first thing which comprises astrology is the study of astronomy. Back then, astronomy and astrology where one art, which was astronomy with part of it being astrology. Astronomy was the knowledge of how the heaven was built, where all the planets are, which one is higher then the others, how fast the planets move etc. And that is the first part of astrology. He further says that “we will say that the first of the sciences that comprise astrology is the study of the shape of the earth”. Because we want to see what the earth is like. “The shape of the earth and the heaven and their pictures”, how they look in relation to everything else, “and to give proofs and signs for them that they are circular like the picture of a ball, and the earth is planted and stands in the middle of the firmament", from our perspective the earth is in the middle of everything, which "surrounds it and travels around it from the east to the west, and to investigate the shapes of the planets and where they dwell in the firmament, and how the planets are one underneath the other". If you look at the sky, you may think that they are all at the same distance from the earth, while they are really at different distances. "To know the shape of their orbits from the east to the west (and where their northernmost point and southern most point are (Makom Hashvii BeRakia), and how the constellations move and how sometimes they are closer or farther from the earth, and to calculate all their movements in order to know where each planet is standing, in terms of the constellations", how to figure out their movements, and if they all move at the same speed, "and if it appears in the north or south of the Kav Ofen HaMazalot", the belt of the constellations, which the sun travels through, through the belt of the twelve constellations. So in each month the Sun is in a different point of the constellations, but the planets don't go through that belt, so they can be north or south of the belt, "and if they're closer or further from the earth, and if their orbit is direct or retrograde", when it appears as if they go backwards, which we call retrogression, "and many other investigations, which I don't have time to expand on. This science is the most exalted of all the sciences that comprise astrology. The wise men of Israel and those of the nations were studying and explaining it. And the wise men of Israel only disagree with the wise men of the nations on a few points".

He then tells us that the second thing which comprises astrology (the first being astronomy) is what we call today astrology, which is the study of how the planets and constellations impact on people in this world and influence their life's. "The second science which comprises astrology, and is dependent on the first", because first you have to know all about the Planets and where they are situated in the sky, before you can talk about their meanings, " and to know the rulership and the powers which were given to the planets", which Planet rules over which Sign, which is good or bad in which sign, "and the constellations in their orbits around the earth, and if this power that was given to each Planet stands when it is in every constellation", the powers of the Planets are different in each constellation, "and how this power changes as the Planet moves through the firmaments when it is in the north and in the south or when it draws closer to the earth", in which case its impact would be stronger, "and when it distances itself from the earth", when its impact would not be as strong, and "when it is travelling direct" when its impact would be more outward, and also "retrograde" which could be more internal. "Also we have the power that the planets have on the earth and everything on it; including each person on his birthday with his individual horoscope, and new events when they arise. This knowledge was handed over and expounded on by the wise men of this science; either it was handed over to them by way of the tradition (teacher), or it came to them through divine revelation, or they learned it through experience in their lifetime, or a combination". In any case this is the science of astrology.

Chapter 7

Rabbi Avraham came to the conclusion that there is nothing wrong with studying and practicing astrology and going according to its signals. So if astrology is a worthwhile science and something everybody should study, and it is a true wisdom, then what is wrong in asking a Chaldean, if it means that he is an astrologer? So now he is going to show us that what the Chaldeans did was not exactly astrology. It was different from the astrology that other people practice. He gave us the general rule, that the astrologers only see things generally: By looking on what goes on in the upper worlds, and seeing symbols of what is going to be down here, they get a general picture of the person, his life, and what will happen to him. But from that you cannot see specifics details. You can see that a person is going to get married, but it doesn't say he would marry Jane and that she lives in Street 53 in New York City. Knowing this is beyond the power of astrology. Astrology will show you that he is going to get married, but you can't see and tell him the name of the person he is going to marry. Sometimes people come to me and want to know if they are going to get married. So I might say, 'yes, you are going to get married this year, I see it clearly in your chart'. And then they ask if they are going to marry this person or that. So I tell them that this is hard to know, especially if you don't have her horoscope. So that is what Rabbi Abraham Bar Chiya wants to say, that there is a difference between the astrology that the Jews practice and the Chaldeans. The Chaldeans, for whatever reason, learned things in more details, and they went into things in a way which was more definite than they were supposed to, and because of that it wasn't considered as real astrology. Rabbi Abraham is now going to investigate to see what the Chaldeans did, whether it was proper or improper. So far he has dealt with two of these components: The one was astronomy, and in ancient times there was no distinction between astronomy and astrology, they were one science, and only later on, in the 1500s, it was split into two sciences. So the first part of astrology consists of astronomy, to understand the orbits of the planets etc. and to know when there would be eclipses, and today they talk about black holes and galaxies. The second part of astrology is going to be the constellations and their impacts over the planets and earth, together with the planets' impacts on everything which happens on earth, on all what we call in astrology the 4 levels of creation, which are the mineral world, the vegetable world, the animal world and the human world; and the planets influence everything: the weather, the environment, earthquakes, volcanoes, jungles and wild animals etc., and they also have influence on human beings.

So let us quickly go over the last paragraph we have read last time:

“And the wise men of Israel investigated this science which states that those who are born under Saturn will be like this, and under Jupiter will be like that, and their works are expanded on more for example in the Braitot of Shmuel Hakatan, who spoke in their name”. And we have talked about this Braita before. “And here also, on the rulership of the planets, there is no significant difference between the Jewish sages and the wise ones of the nations, except on their power to force an event”. The only argument is whether it is the planets themselves that can force an event, or is it that the people can alter the event. “The wicked ones of the nations, who have no fear of heaven, say that the power of the stars is a complete and full power, and these planets are able to start good or damage according to their will and understanding, and their decrees are unconditionally fulfilled. But the believers, whose strength is in the fear of God, and make themselves holy by learning His book, and who received this wisdom from the holy spirit, the mouths of the prophets, say that the power of the planets is not a complete power, and they don't have the power to start good or damage according to their understanding and will. Rather everything is in God's command, and any time God wants, He can remove their rulership and change their decree. This is the difference between the Jewish sages and the wise ones of the nations".

Don't think that Judaism is like a racist religion, and that the Jews consider themselves super superior to other people. I don't think this is the proper way to understand what is said here. The Jewish religion says that all people have the power to get to higher levels and become spiritual. What Rabbi Avraham says here is that the difference between Jews and non Jews is that the Jewish people were given a book, a Torah, in which there are details of how a person should behave in this world, and all the commandments, and this was a book given to them by God. So the uniqueness of the Jewish religion is that it holds that God appeared to all of Israel, and to a lesser degree, He appeared to all peoples in the world. Israel consisted of about 600 000 men from the age of 20 and above, and there were at least the same amount of women, which already gives you the number of one million two hundred thousand, and probably the same amount of people were those under 20, which makes 2.4 million. And then a bunch of people from other nations, who were called the large multitude (erev rav), were attached to them, and they were maybe another two million. So you already have about four million people who received the Divine Revelation: God came to them and gave them the Tablet of Laws. And you don't really see that in any other religion. Nobody, in any other religions, claims that their religion was given to millions of people by God. All other religions basically started from one person who claimed to have had some revelation and spread it from there. If you look at the Christian and Muslim religions, for instance, you see that these religions basically have the same idea: The Christians came along and said that the Jews were right and were the chosen people by God to receive his Torah, but then "God abandoned them". So even these religions who have persecuted us, stand by our experience at mount Sinai where God gave us the Torah. This is quite exceptional because if you look at the Holocaust, which happened around 70 years ago, you see that there are already books claiming that the Holocaust never happened, and it is all some people's imaginations, yet none of the ancient Gentiles disclaimed the facts about the Sinai revelation. The head of the Palestinian Authority got his PhD by "proving" that there was "no holocaust" and that the holocaust never happened. And the holocaust happened quite recently. But when we talk about the Jews being given the Torah on Mount Sinai 3500 years ago, nobody in all these ancient history argued with the authenticity of the Sinai experience and revelation. You don't see any books from the past that really argued with this, and nobody says it never happened and that it was all just a mass delusion. Then along came Christianity, which said that the Jews messed up and that our Man is supposed to start a new religion, and to take the place of the Jews and do things differently. And basically Mohammed came along too a few hundred years later and said the same thing: "The Jews were given the Torah, they messed up, Christians messed up, everyone messed up. Now I am OK, it is all given to me now, and I have to make the whole world Muslim". And that is going on till today. And so it is with the Mormons and others, all have a religion which was started by one person who claims to have had a revelation, and spreads it from there.

So really, the whole Jewish religion is very different to all these other religions, and unless you were born a Jew, or you are really interested in practicing Judaism and fulfilling its commandments, you wouldn't want to become a Jew. And indeed, we don't look for converts, and this is due to that. If you are really going to practice it, then adopt it, and you will get great reward. But if you don't follow it, after you have accepted it upon yourself, you will be punished from heaven. And so we don't actively try to convert people, because we want to do good for people and not expose them to the risk of converting to Judaism and then expose them to the downside of backing off from fulfilling its duties. But if somebody really wants to convert, we would surely be glad to accept him, after explaining to him/her all our history and suffering. We would ask him why he wants to join us and have such a hard life. But if he commits despite the potential hardships, then we would be happy to accept him. So you see it is not that we are better than other people, but rather that we were given the Holy Book of God, and this is what we are, and through this book we have the ability to go into higher spiritual levels. But it is not that we are intrinsically better than others. Anybody can come along and convert if they are really interested in doing so. They can become Jewish and follow this book too and get to the same levels. As we have said before, if you do all the commandments, you may get beyond the influences of the planets. You will be able to rise above the planetary influences if you study the Book and fulfill the different commandments. And you see that many Jews open the newspaper and read about all the troubles they have, and they have these different problems because they don't study and follow the Torah. They just go after their own logic. And this is not what the Jews were given at Mount Sinai to do in this world. And when a Jew does that and does not follow the Torah, he is not anything special. But he has the capability, because he was born with the potential to follow the book, but as long as he doesn't, he is certainly not beyond the horoscope. Non Jews also have to follow the Seven Laws of Noah, which they must follow and can in their own way get into high levels, and, to a certain degree, overcome the influences of the stars by fulfilling these seven Noachite commandments. So this is what I wanted to give you as a general introduction, to show you that Judaism is not about being racists or having a kind of a superiority complex or anything like that. No, it is just that we were born after we were given this book. And most of my listeners and clients tend to be Jewish or people who converted to Judaism. So when you think about it, the whole Jewish religion falls and stands on a divine revelation. The whole thing is that since God gave the Torah to Israel on Mount Sinai, then we are obligated to practice this religion. If God had not given it to us, or had it been a mass delusion, then we wouldn't need to. Or if you believe that the Jews were given it but messed up, and someone else took over, then inevitably you believe you may be obligated to go to them who took over. Of course, I hold that it was given and is still given to us, and we are obligated to follow it. So people, especially Jewish listeners, should really investigate this and realize what actually happened in Mount Sinai. And then one must become religious after coming to this conclusion. And it is not easy to be religious. There are a lot of responsibilities placed on you, and Judaism is not an easy religion to practice. That is why we are a small group of people in the world. An the majority of Jews now live in a little country, surrounded by 300 million people who want to destroy us, and it has been like that for the last two thousand years. So let us go back to the text:

“The wicked ones of the nations”, means the ones who don't follow God's law to any degree, not even the seven Mitzvot of the Nations (the 7 Noachite laws), “who have no fear of heaven, say that the power of the stars is a complete and full power, and are able to improve and damage according to their will and understanding, and their decrees are unconditionally fulfilled”. In other words, they say that what the planet’s decree is what has to happen, unless you supplicate them and idol worship them or something of that kind, or through mantras, like the Indian astrologers do. “But the believers, whose strength is in the fear of God, and make themselves holy by learning His book, and who received this wisdom from the holy spirit and the mouths of the prophets, they say that the power of the planets is not a complete power, and they don't have the power to start good or damage according to their understanding and will. Rather everything is in God's command, and any time God wants, He can remove their rulership and change their decree. This is the difference between the Jewish sages and the wise ones of the nations”. So in astronomy there is almost no basic difference between Jewish sages and the wise people of the nations. In astrology, the difference is based on the question of what is the power of the planets and stars: are they agents of God, or entities to themselves? Is their power absolute, or can they be modified by how the person behaves, and can God change their decrees whenever He wants? But the rules of interpretation of astrology in general and how it works are similar between Jewish and non Jewish astrologers. And as I said in the first lessons, a lot of astrology was given to Adam Harishon, and he passed it on. There is a book written by an old historian, Yosef Ben Matityahu, who says that the science of astronomy was given to one of Adam's sons, and he passed it on to the academy of Shem and Ever, which was a secret Jewish academy, after the time of Noah, where they learned the secret traditions, and Yaakov Avinu/Jacob, the grandson of Abraham, learned there for a number of years. But from there it went to the Chaldeans, via the dispersion after the tower of Babel which occurred after the great flood; and again after the Jews were exiled to Babylonia. This is basically what Yosef Ben Matityahu said. So he explains why the astrology of the West and the Jewish astrology are very similar. If you read the Ibn Ezra, for example, who was a great Jewish Rabbi, you see that he taught Western astrology. So it makes sense that there is no major difference between Western and Jewish astrology in any major way, except for differences which we have mentioned above in brief and which we will expand on later below. His book ‘The Beginning of Wisdom’, is basically a Western astrology book, even though he used a quote from the book of Mishley/Proverbs as the books title: “The beginning of wisdom is the fear of the Lord”. What he was stating emphatically through the choice of that title, is that a person who fears the Lord and follows His commandments, and doesn't run after what his eyes see and desire, or what his ears and heart decide on their own (without the mind reflecting on the Mitzvot), would be able to get beyond the planetary influences. Like my teacher used to say: ‘Life is easy if it is not important to you’. If what happens in this world is not important to you, then life is easy. If you subjugate your material life to your spiritual life, and make that your priority, then life and it challenges can come but they seem to pass in a very fast way. I am sixty years old, and I have been through a lot, and yet sometimes it seems to feel that I lived no more than one day. Because if you really believe, you are not that affected by the material world, and you don't chase after fancy dreams, and you are here basically for the next world, and even though it is not easy, you always remember that what you do here is what gets you into the next world, and then everything in this world is much easier to overcome. The main thing in Judaism is the idea of Revelation and getting beyond the planetary influences, which you do by believing that this life is really without purpose for itself, and the whole purpose is to acquire the world to come. Everything in this world is only for the world to come, and all other materiality is not really worth chasing, for in the end it the grave, and you cannot take your material accumulations with you. So what do you run after it for? If you view it this way, you would be able to overcome all the challenges in this world, just like the Jews have done up to now throughout history. This is the main difference between Jewish astrologers and the ones from other nations, what is the intention behind learning and practicing astrology. In today's times, one may go to a psychologist, to a psychiatrist or to an astrologer, and say: Help me! I am stuck. I cannot fulfill my potential or get any pleasure. Help me get my pleasure! I am here for only 60 or 70 years, and I don't have enough time. So I get people who ask me this, and sometimes I try to help them get peace of mind and relax, and I think this is the important thing which everyone actually tries to get. They chase the pleasures of this world because they think that that will bring them peace of mind, but at the end it doesn't, which is unfortunate.

Rabbi Avraham Bar Chiya continues, "Our Rabbis blessed these two sciences and studied and practiced them. And on both they obligated, 'everyone who can calculate the seasons and the constellations, that he must calculate them', to fulfill what is written, 'it is your wisdom and understanding in the eyes of the nations'. You cannot say that what they meant by 'to calculate the seasons and constellations' is talking about calculating the four seasons, because this is something easy, and it is not a difficult calculation, and not dependent on a special knowledge, and all the nations can calculate them. What it means is that the calculation of the seasons and constellations is about calculating all seven planets, where they are in the constellations. The 'seasons' is the calculation of the Sun, and the 'constellation' is said about calculating the Planets. With the calculation of the seasons, the Jewish sages know when the holidays are in the years and with the calculation of the Planets we know Wisdom. However, when the Sun orbits in the sky, so all the Planets orbit in the sky. And like the sun has four seasons in the sky that switch during its travel around the earth, so do we have these four seasons of the year for all the Planets, since they all have four points in the sky where they switch their direction, they all have these four points in the days of their orbits. So they could have just said that one needs 'to calculate the four seasons', but because they said, 'the seasons and the constellations', we know that 'the seasons' is the orbit of the planets and 'the constellations' is the calculation of their wandering, as it appears from the earth. For we call the testimony and the meanderings of the constellations 'mazalot'. We say for something good mazal tov, and for the opposite, which isn't good, mazal ra, and for this I bring a proof from the passage, 'it is your wisdom and understanding in the eyes of the nations'. Because the calculation of the planetary motions is not a singularly Jewish wisdom compared to the nations, rather the majority of the nations are more diligent in this than the Jews. Rather the wisdom of the Jews in the eyes of the nations is that their righteousness nullifies for them the decrees of the heavens, and the decrees of the nations are established and not nullified except if God removes the power of the planet and weakens it. And the power of the planet is not weakened for Israel, because it has no power over them".

There is a verse from the Book of Deuteronomy, 4:6: "it is your wisdom and understanding in the eyes of the nations". And the Talmud is going to talk about what it means. What is that wisdom and understanding, that the nations of the world considered the Jews to have a made them a wise and understanding people? The Talmud on page 75 side one:

"Said Rabbi Shmuel Bar Nachmani who said in the name of Rabbi Yochanan: Where do we see that calculating the seasons and constellations is fulfilling God's command? As it is said: 'and preserve and do so (calculate both), for it is your wisdom and understanding in the eyes of the nations'. What is the wisdom and understanding in the eyes of the nations? It means the calculation of the seasons and constellations and Israel's ability to do so". Rabbi Avraham says that "the seasons" is astronomy, and "the constellations" means what we call today astrology. Because constellation is translated in Hebrew into the word mazal, which also means fortune, and the constellations are suppose to affect the fortune of the people on the earth. "For we call the testimony and the meanderings of the planets, mazalot".

Chapter 8

"If two nativities (horoscope drawn on date, time and place of birth, known today as a 'chart') that are similar in their mazal (similar charts), one is of a non-Jew (who does not keep the 7 Noachite laws) and the second is of a Jew (who fulfils the commandments), and these charts are brought to a wise man of one of the nations, he will find that the Jew who follows the Torah was saved from all the difficult decrees in his birth chart, and the unrighteous non-Jew was tripped up by all of the difficult decrees depicted in his chart". Again, this does not mean that the Jews are better than the non-Jews. We are talking about Jews who followed the Torah, and so they are saved versus the people who don't follow the straight path and go after their instincts. And the best of peoples get lost without a guide book. So the term "unrighteous non-Jew" also includes the Jews who do not follow the path of the Torah. So let us go on: "This will be a great wonder for the wise men of the nations, and they will be startled when they see the greatness of Israel". I live in Israel, and it is a miracle that we exist at all. Once Jews used to live in Ghettos in Europe, which were situated in major cities, and there was a pogrom or massacre against them here and there, where they got kicked out or lost their money etc. And this continues today. As the world integrated there is this little country called Israel, and some want us to give away the West Bank, and thus become smaller, but we still survive here. So there are about five million Jews here, and we are surrounded by 300 million Arabs, who want to get rid of all of us. And we have another million within Israel itself who don't exactly like us, and we also have all the other nations of the world who don't exactly like us either, but we somehow keep going. And this is a kind of a miracle. Which brings you to another point: We see that sometimes people don't have eyes to see. Everyone talks about Nostradamus for instance, and how he could predict things. But nobody talks about the ancient prophets, and when you look at the books of the prophets, you realize that their prophecies came true, much more than Nostradamus' predictions. And Moses said in the Torah, that the Jews were going to be exiled and then they would come back to the land of Israel, and this was a unique prophecy which came true, and Moses lived over 3000 years ago. And still the Bible doesn't seem to be taken too seriously by some. And you see all the prophets, Isaiah, Jeremiah, Ezekiel, etc., who told Israel that they would mess up and be exiled, and then come back to the land of Israel. Predictions like these, the greatest astrologer can't predict. It is easier to predict what will be in the near future, and almost impossible for non prophets to predict what will be in the distant future. The more you move astrologers from the present, the harder it is for them to predict. My teacher told me that once someone predicted to him when the Second World War was going to start and he did this just 2 days before that war started. So even though he got it right, this was not a unique prediction. But if you are honest with yourself, especially astrologers who know how hard it is to predict, you realize that the prophecies in the Bible are something extraordinary. As there is the saying: 'If astrologers knew everything, there would be no need for prophets'. But you see that astrologers can't predict what will happen in the distant future, but the prophecies of the prophets regarding this all come true. Astrologers see things in a partial way, while prophets could see the whole thing, because they are working with a system beyond the Planets. This is a thought people should think about, and maybe then there will be more people studying astrology and maybe later prophecy. Unfortunately, in America where I grew up, the intellectuals read everything except the Bible and the prophets. It wasn't in the curricular.

"There is another difference between Israel and the nations. If there is a decree that is suitable to come on Israel and the nations, and God wants to nullify it from the nations, He removes the power of the planet and nullifies it, and when He removes the power of the planet and nullifies the decree for the Jew and non-Jew alike, because there doesn't remain to the planet damage or help". This is the standard way in which He removes the decree for the non-Jew, and so He also removes it for the Jew at the same time, if it is the same decree that was decreed on a Jew and a non-Jew. "And if God wants to nullify decrees from Israel, He doesn't weaken the power of the planet, because the planets have no rulership over Israel, but rather He does this from above the planets". So because the energies of the planets are not weakened or interfered with, they still work at full force and therefore their decree remains established over the non-Jew. "And on this the Torah passage says, 'for what great nation is there that has God so close to them, the Lord, our God, whenever we call to Him'. He says your wisdom will be for the eyes of the nations, who will see that the decrees of the planets are nullified from you in your calling out to God, and it is not nullified from them. With this you will see the wisdom of Israel, because all the astrologers saw that Hezekiah, king of Judah, was destined to rule no more then 14 years and yet because of his righteousness and prayers he ruled for double those years. The decrees of the stars were overridden, and the astrologers are cognoscente of this honor".

In other words, the astrologers said that the king of Judea had to rule for only 14 years, as was written in his chart, and in the end, despite his chart, he ruled for 28 years. And after 14 years, Prophet Isaiah came to him and said that was the end of his rule. But even so, King Hezkiyah prayed and prayed, until the decree was eventually nullified and he ruled for an extra 14 years. And this story is an example to how other nations saw that the Jews were able to overcome their planetary influences.

Now Rabbi Avraham is going to bring a second story, which is also from the Book of Kings II, at the beginning of Chapter 1:

"And Moab rebelled against Israel after the death of Achav. And Achazya (the new king) fell through the balustrade of his upper chamber in Samaria and he took ill, and he sent messengers, saying to them: Go and inquire of the Baal Zvuv, the god of Ekron, whether I will recover from this illness". He sent messengers to ask the idol if he would survive his illness. So you see that he was an idol worshiper. "And an angel of God spoke to Elijah the Tishbite (that is Eliyahu the Prophet): Rise and go up to the messengers of Samaria (the king Achazya's messengers) and say to them: Is there no God in Israel that you must go to ask Baal Zvuv the god of Ekron!? And therefore (because you did this), so said God; the bed that you came on to, you shall not come down from, for you will surely die! And Elijah went. And the messengers returned to him (Achazya), and he said to them: What did you return for? And they said to him: A man came to us and said to us: So said the Lord, is there no God in Israel that you must send to ask Baal Zvuv the god of Ekron!? Therefore, the bed you climbed onto you will not come down from, for you will surely die. He (Achazya) asked them: What is the description of the man who came up to you and said to you these things? And they said to him: A man with hair and leather belt gathered over his waist! And he said, that is Elijah the Tishbite. And he (Achazya) sent a captain and his fifty men to him, and he (the captain) came to him (Elijah) and saw him sitting on the top of a mountain, and said to him: Man of God! The king has spoken, come down! And Elijah responded by saying to the captain of the fifty: And if I am a man of God, may fire come down from heaven and consume you and your fifty! And a fire came down from heaven and consumed him and his fifty. And He (Achazya) went on and sent another captain and his fifty men, who said to him (to Elijah): Man of God! So said the king: Come down! And Elijah responded and said to them: If I am a man of God, may a fire come down from heaven and consume you and your fifty! And a fire came down from heaven and consumed him and his fifty. And he (Achazya) continued and sent a third captain of fifty to him (Elijah), and the third captain of fifty kneeled in front of Elijah and pleaded with him: Man of God, spare my soul and the souls of these fifty servants of yours. Behold, a fire came down from heaven and consumed the first two captains of fifty, but now, may my soul be spared by you. And an angel of God said to Elijah: Go down with him, don't fear him! And he (Elijah) rose and went down to the king. And he spoke to him: So said God: Since you sent messengers to ask Baal Zvuv the god of Ekron, as if there is no God in Israel that one can ask for His words, therefore the bed you climbed up onto you shall not come down from, for you will surely die! And he died, just like God's words were spoken by Elijah".

So that was the story of Achazya, the king of Israel, noted for his unrighteousness, who at a certain point went off the path and sent messengers to ask the idols for advice when he fell onto his sick bed. Now Rabbi Avraham Bar Chiya is going to show you from this that not only are Israel above their mazal, but sometimes they can ruin their own good mazal. And Achazya lost his mazal because he went after idolatry, and it was decreed that he was going to die. As Prophet Elijah said, 'because of what you did, you are never going to come down from you sick bed'. So you see that Jews can mess up their good mazal sometimes, and not just overcome bad decrees. And if the king had not sent them, it wouldn't have been decreed on him".

So you see from this story that the whole decree that he would die was because he went to ask the idol worshipers. Otherwise, there wouldn't have been a decree on him to die, and as the astrologers saw, he would have recovered. So you see that there is also the side of Mazal where a person can mess up, and therefore he would mess up with his fortune, as we see here. And we see it with Rabbi Akiva:

"And also with Rabbi Akiva, who the Chaldeans frightened (with their prediction of his daughter dying on her wedding day), when the decree was nullified, he didn't say the Chaldeans lied, rather he said, 'charity saves from death'". He didn't say that God made a mistake or lied, or that the Chaldeans lie, he only said that the merit of charity can save one from death. His daughter did a good deed on her wedding night, and this saved her from death "Similarly, with the Shmuel and Avlat (in the Talmud), when the words of Avlat the Heshoni were not fulfilled, Rav Shmuel didn't say, 'he is not telling the truth', rather he said, 'charity saves from death'. Because of this it is an obligation that everyone who knows the calculation of the seasons and the constellations to calculate them. And if he sees testimony that good things will happen, don't trust this as being guaranteed to happen, rather guard yourself and be careful, lest the sin will cause you to lose the good things. And if you see testimony that isn't good, repent, fall down and supplicate before God, maybe it will be proper in His eyes to nullify the decree".

So you see from here, that the Jews can nullify the planetary decrees on the one hand, and can mess up and cause bad decrees upon themselves and lose the good decrees on the other hand.

And this is similar to the story of Yaakov Avinu (Jacob), whom God told that he would become great and have twelve children, and everything would be alright. And the next day he worried again, because he thought that maybe he did a sin and this would be nullified. So even if God comes and gives you the prophecy, you still have to worry, because maybe you are going to mess up, do something wrong and lose your good mazal. "We find that this art is an obligation on all who know it, to strengthen it, so that his belief will be strengthened as well as his fear (of heaven), and he will increase his prayers and his righteousness at all times". At all times one has to realize, that even though according to the testimony of the planets, there may be good decrees, you still have to pray and do good deeds so as not to mess up your mazal. Sometimes you see that people have good horoscopes, but they just don't fulfill it, because they messed up somewhere along the way.

You have to learn these two things: The motion of the planets and the meanings of these motions. The wisdom of the Jews is that they can overcome the planetary influences, and this should be learned. And the calculations of the seasons (astronomy) should also be done, not only the constellations (astrology), because in order to become an astrologer, one has to know astronomy. If you don't know where the planets are, and how they are moving (and in the old days there were no computer printouts from NASA, which tell you where all the planets are), you therefore would not be able to know their meanings and decrees. "And of these two sciences that are attached to the fear of heaven, it is the wisdom of the stars that Israel is obligated to study and engage in".

So these are the first two branches of astrology which Rabbi Abraham showed are perfectly legitimate to study.

Now he is going to talk about some of the branches in astrology that are forbidden for the Jews to practice (and non-Jews):

"There are other sciences which are part of astrology, that are dependent on the planets (instead of God) which most of the nations engaged in, and the Jewish people were not permitted to engage in them. This is because they are connected to idolatry, and they degrade one's fear of heaven and our relationship with God. This is because all of the nations that believe that the planets benefit or destroy with their own knowledge and power, will eventually add to their own wickedness and brazenness until it appears to them that they are serving and making offerings to the planets themselves that help them. And it went up in the hearts of many, because of an impure spirit which came to them from the planets, who command them, and warned them and taught them the way they (the planets) must be served. These evil ones caused their generation to sin, they made idols for them and statues to be served, worshiped, and they taught them how they (the planets) should be served, and they enacted evil ceremonies to be performed before them. These false prophets, prophets of idols, are called in Arabic, 'Etziel Vathi', which means 'the founders of the ceremonies'. And their students who performed these profane religious ceremonies were called 'El Atba', meaning 'the ones who were drawn after the evil', and each of the idolatrous nations, worshipers of idols to whom they dedicated themselves and enacted forms of evil worship, were called in Arabic 'Mustonol Beel Kavi', meaning 'those that draw down the powers'".

So we see that Jews cannot be in any way connected with idolatry, which is a very severe sin, since it influences one not to believe in God, and instead to believe in materiality, and attributing Godly powers to it. It is also not permitted to the non-Jew to follow this idolatry as stipulated in the Noachite laws of the Bible. But this type of idolatry is hard to imagine today. We must remember the source in the Talmud (Tractate Sanhedrin) which brings down the events from the 2nd temple period, when the prophets enacted a special request, and prayed to God to nullify the desires Jews had for idolatry. And so God nullified the desire for idolatry. And due to that, the desire to worship idols today is not as strong as it used to be then. And it is said that if people of today had lived back at the times of idol worship, the pull was so strong, that they would run after those idols too, even though those idols degrade one's fear of heaven. If you believe in the stars, and if you think that they implement the decrees out of their own will, then eventually you would come to worship the stars. So as we said at the beginning of the letter, there is nothing wrong in astrology for the Jews, because the Jews know that the planets are just agents of God. And these planet energies don't have a free will, or any powers to decree things. The stars don't use their own rational judgment. And all the decrees and nullification of decrees are all from God. But the idol worshipers saw that the planets apparently decreed things, and went one step further, and said, 'if the planets have the power to decree things, then the next step would obviously be to please and worship the planets, to try to modify and pacify them', and so they did. And you see in India, the great Indian astrologers use mantras for the planets. So if it is a season of Saturn, and the planet "causes you trouble", you would have to say a mantra many times to appease Saturn so it would not give you such difficulty in life. But we learned that the planets themselves do not decree, it is not in their power. They are just messengers of God. So Rabbi Abraham repeats this point in a different way, in order to show you that that was the point. That one of the forbidden forms of astrology was where they dedicated idols to the planets, with different ceremonies, different theology, different times and materials, and how to worship them. The planets don't do anything besides being messengers who deliver messages. Worshiping them is nonsense, which came out of wrong beliefs. And this branch of astrology, the worship of planets, is forbidden, of course, to Jews and non-Jews. And if you look at the books of the nations during the Middle Ages, you see they have many books on this subject, and you see that even in the Western traditions they did it. We see that people in the ancient West also built alters for the planets and tried to appease them in different ways.

<u>Chapter 9</u>

So up to now, we see that there were two sects: One was called 'The founders of the ceremonies', and the other one was 'Those who draw down the powers'. And they perform ceremonies to draw down the astrological powers to earth, at appropriate times, so that the planets would do the will of those worshipers and answer their questions.

"And these two evil sects were certainly idolatrous, and bowing down to strange gods, may they be cursed, and all those that do like them". We can also see a hint here that maybe the Arabic Astrologers of Spain, at the time of Rabbi Avraham, were doing these things. And this is how he knows those Arabic names. "We also find a thirds sect, 'Abael Talezmat', meaning 'the masters of the pictures'. They would study the movements of the planets, and investigate the order of their movements through different pictures in the sky, and when they passed through the place where the image they wanted in this world appeared to them, at that time that they saw the planet pass through that image in the constellations, when it is in the north side or the south side, they would make an image like that image from different types of metals that were suitable for this. If the planet is one of the favorable planets, he increases the strength of that image. And if a destructive planet, he nullifies its power. They know when to stop and when to increase the power of different things in the world. And there remain even to our times all sorts of images from the work of the wicked ones". So if you look around, you will still see those things floating around, and realize how those things were made. These are the 'Masters of the pictures', and they would make the images of the places that the planets pass through in different times, in order to increase the power of a beneficial planet and decrease the power of a destructive one.

"After them is the fourth group, which knows the movement of the planet, on which day and at what hour it is beneficial to collect different herbs from all the herbs, to gather different seeds from all the seeds, to gather honey, beat the olives, to pick grapes and other fruits, to chop wood and collect it. They would know what was gathered on each day and what its nature was and for what it was beneficial. Everything was stored with them, and when they were needed, they would prepare the different gatherings that were stored with them that were beneficial to use at that time and to do their work, to increase the power of one thing or to reduce the power of something else. While they were doing this, when they were gathering from the field, or combining herbal formulas, they would whisper incantations and unclean names and the names of demons. This sect was called in Arabic, 'Atzchav el Hel', meaning 'masters of the capture', and this sect was also called in Arabic, 'Atzchav el Ashar'".

So this fourth group used to do what one can call agricultural astrology. What is amazing is that there is even a group today in Israel, which I have heard about, that has an organic farm, in which they grow organic food. I think it still exists. And originally it was based on the teaching of a German man, Rudolf Steiner. And they picked different kinds of fruit and vegetables at specific times, when it is best to pick the plants. And there is a big argument between the rabbis, if you can give them a Hechsher, to make it kosher. Because even if they follow all the Jewish laws of Trumah and Maaser and the rest of the agricultural laws, the question remains, if you can buy from them, because maybe what they are doing is something similar to worshiping the planets. So you see that these things exist even today. Even in science today, they are working on things like this in a certain way. I was reading that scientists today work on the idea of what is the right hour to give

medicine. They work now on all different times to give different medicines, in connection with the cycle of the person's body. And they found out that there are different ways to give medications that can work better. But this is very different to what the idolaters did because even though these scientists don't believe much in God, they certainly don't believe in idols. They just try to improve science.
So those were the four groups, the four types of astrology which Rabbi Avraham mentions here, and concludes that they are forbidden. Because whether they work or don't, it is not proper for a Jew to get involved, because it is involved with the idea of idol worship. And it is against the fundamental principle of Judaism, which is the belief that there is one God who is in control of everything, and the planets are just agents, without a will of their own. So these four branches can weaken one's fear of heaven and is forbidden as idolatry. And in the next paragraph, Rabbi Avraham is going to go deeper and say when all those four types of people are mentioned in the Book of Daniel. Daniel is a great book for people who are interested in seeing predictions. And one may read Nostradamus, Edgar Casey and all of these kinds of predictors, but the most important and recommended thing is to read the prophets of thousands of years ago. There you read and see that all the predictions which came true. It is amazing, and it is not like a riddle or something like that you can interpret in a thousand ways. It just happened as it had been said in its plain meaning. Like when Moses brought the Torah: 'The Jews are going to sin and mess up, and they are going to be exiled and travel from country to country, and then eventually they are going to come back to Israel'. This is what is clearly written, and it happened, and few pay attention to that. And it very difficult to predict the future even one year from now never mind thousands of years ahead. My astrologer friends tell me that even angels can't see into the future, so obviously people can't, and the more you try to look into the future-the harder it gets. If you are a good astrologer, you see what happens to a person now, and you can tell what will happen to him within a year. But it is harder to say what will happen to him in two years or three years. And then the astrologers become more general and less specific, for it is very hard to predict the distance future. But if you look at the books of the prophets, you see their predictions, and it is amazing. And I recommend this to all astrologers, to bring us some humility. And I think Rabbi Avraham recommends this too, in this letter and in another. And if the astrologers could see everything, there would be no need for the prophets. We need the prophets, because they get the words from above, they didn't get it from the images of the planets like we do. So we see things in a general way, and the further we look into the future the harder it becomes.
"It appears to me that all four (of the forbidden astrological sects) are mentioned in the Book of Daniel in the dream of the wicked Nebuchadnezzar, like it is written: 'Nebuchadnezzar dreamed dreams, his spirit was agitated and his sleep was interrupted. The king said to call the necromancers, the astrologers, the sorcerers and the Chaldeans (star gazers) to tell the king his dream'". This is according to the Storm Edition of the Bible, written in Hebrew with and English translation, and printed by ArtScroll.
So let me first read out to you from the Book of Daniel itself, chapter 2 verse 2:
"In the second year of Nebuchdnezzar's rein, Nebuchdnezzar dreamed dreams, his spirit was agitated and his sleep was interrupted. The king said to call the necromancers, the astrologers, the sorcerers and the Chaldeans (star gazers or demonists-these are different translations) to tell the king his dream".

So he basically dreamed a dream, and was very agitated when he woke up in the morning, and the dream really shook him up, but he didn't remember the dream. So he called all the four kinds of people and said to them: Look, I had a dream which I don't remember. So I want you to tell me what my dream was and to interpret it for me! So each of the four groups didn't know what to do: If the king told them what his dream was, they could interpret it. But they could not be expected to know what was the dream without him telling them! But Daniel came along, and he first prayed to God, and God gave him the ability to tell the king what he dreamed. And then Daniel became close to the king because of that.

"The king said to call the necromancers, the astrologers, the sorcerers and the Chaldeans (star gazers) to tell the king his dream'. And the king said to them, 'I had a dream, and my spirit is troubled to know the dream'. Then the Chaldeans said to the king in Aramaic (most of the Book of Daniel is in Aramaic), 'O king, live forever! Tell your servants your dream, and we will show the interpretation'. The king answered and said to the Chaldeans, 'the word from me is firm. If you do not make known to me the dream and its interpretation, you shall be torn limb from limb, and your houses shall be laid in ruins. But if you show the dream and its interpretation, you shall receive from me gifts, and rewards and great honor, therefore show me my dream and its interpretation'". Rabbi Avraham translates these 4 as: 'Chartumim/capturers (those who capture the time and worship them, in order to increase or decrease the planets' influences), Ashafim/the 'senders of the power', Mechashfim/masters of the pictures, and Casdim/drawers', who are the ones who did things according to their agriculture stars.

Anyway, we find that these four are also mentioned in the Book of Daniel in Aramaic in another place, chapter 4 verse 4:

"I, Nebuchadnezzar, was at ease in my house and prospering in my palace. I saw a dream that made me afraid, as I lay in bed, the fancies and the visions of my head alarmed me. So I made a decree that all the wise men of Babylon should be brought before me that they might make known to me the interpretation of the dream. Then the necromancers, the astrologers, the Chaldeans and the demonists came in, and I told them the dream, but they could not make known to me its interpretation. At last Daniel, who was named Belshazzar after my god, and in whom is the spirit of my holy gods, came in before me, and I told him the dream".

So here, Chartumia, Ashafia, Casdia VeGazria are mentioned. So instead of the Mechashfim, the word Gazria is used. And Rabbi Avraham is going to talk about why the names are switched there: He says,

"We find these four are also mentioned in the Book of Daniel in Aramaic: 'Hartumia, ashpin, cusdi, gezri' (Daniel 4:4). And it is also written: 'Hartumia, ashpin, cusdi, gezri and your father the king made him (Daniel) chief of them'. It is clear that the Hartumen, ashpin and culsdin that are mentioned first in Hebrew, are the Hartummin, ashpin and cusdin that are mentioned a second time in Aramaic". You can see that three out of the four names are the same. "But the Mechashfin that are mentioned in Hebrew, it's possible that they are Gezera in Aramaic", it is possible that they are the same thing, that the Hebrew word, 'Mechashfim' is 'Gezera' in Aramaic, which are magicians, or Baaley Tmunot, the ones who make pictures, "because it is not their way to talk about the future", It wasn't the way of the Mechashfin to talk about the future. "And the four that are mentioned in Aramaic their way is to talk about the future. It is possible that Gezra are those that study the constellations deeply, and they are called Gezra (laws), because their opinion is that the testimony of the planets is fixed and cannot be changed, but that they have permission to decree and establish. This opinion is right in my eyes, because it is said in Nebuchadnezzar's first dream: 'The Chaldeans responded before the king and said, there is no man on earth who can relate the king's matter. That is why no king, lender or ruler, has ever requested such a thing of any necromancer or astrologer or Chaldean'. Of the four, Nebuchadnezzar only mentions three, and leaves out mechashfen (magicians), because it is not their way to make known things like this". So he left them out. So you see that there is a difference between the magicians and the Gezira. On the other hand, one can say that they are the same thing, but once they were mentioned in Hebrew and once in Aramaic, but Gezera comes from the word 'decree', which means that the Gzera, which are mentioned in Daniel, used to use magic powers to make decrees. These people studied the constellations deeply, and made laws from it, because they said that the testimony of the planets is fixed and cannot be changed, but that they have the permission to establish and make decrees for the planets. "Rather their job is to explain the different forces that are on the earth, and when they increase or decrease. In a similar vein, Daniel didn't mention them when he said to Nebuchadnezzar, 'the secret the king requests, no wise men, astrologers, necromancers, nor demonists are able to tell the king'".

Chapter 10

In Nebuchadnezzar's first dream: 'The Chaldeans responded before the king and said, there is no man on earth who can relate the king's matter. That is why no king, lender or ruler, had ever requested such a thing of any necromancer or astrologer or Chaldean'" which means, they were requested to not only interpret the dream, but to first figure out what the dream was because the king forgot. "Of the four, Nebuchadnezzar only mentions three, and leaves out mechashfen (magicians), because it is not their way to make known things like this. Rather their job is to explain the different forces that are on the earth, and when they increase or decrease. In a similar vein, Daniel didn't mention them when he said to Nebuchadnezzar, 'the secret that the king requests, there is no wise men, astrologers, necromancers, nor demonists are able to tell the king'. He didn't mention the magicians, because it is not their way to reveal secrets of the future, but he did mention the Gezran, who ponder the movement of the planets through the constellations, because it is their way to speak about the future which is hidden from the rest of mankind. He didn't mention the Cusdim to Nebuchadnezzar, rather he mentioned the hartumen and ashuf, because the cusdim were not mentioned before the king at that time. Similarly Daniel didn't mention them among the wise men, Ashper, Hartumen, Gezren, because they were students of the Ashpen, and were drawn after them, and they sullied themselves in idol worship more than the Ashpen. And because of this, he saw no reason to mention them. In another place, the hartumen were left out, like it says, 'just then, fingers of a human hand came forth and wrote in the plaster of the wall of the king's palace, facing the candelabrum, and the king saw the palm of the hand that was writing. The king's appearance thereupon changed and his thoughts bewildered him, the belt on his waist opened and his knees knocked one against the other. This king cried aloud to bring in the astrologers, the Chaldeans and the demonists, and the king exclaimed to the sages of Babylonia that only a person who would read this writing and tell him its interpretation would wear royal purple with a chain of gold on his neck and will rule one third of the kingdom'. He didn't mention among them the Hartumen, because it is not proper to ask them about something which requires deep wisdom and understanding, like the writing that was written on the plasters of the wall of the king's palace".

So Rabbi Avraham goes through all different places in the book of Daniel, where all these people are mentioned, sometimes in four names, sometimes in three names, and sometimes their names are changed. And I think you should read for yourself at all these different passages where all these names are located, and get a better idea than you will get from just listening to me. But I think we see that the main idea is that all these different areas are different kinds of idol worship, which are forbidden.

"We find one place in the book of Exodus where all three of these types (as mentioned above in Daniel) were left out, where they were not needed, and only the mechashfim (magicians) by themselves were mentioned. Like it says in the book of Exodus, 'and Pharaoh called out to the wise men and the magicians'. He called to the wise men who were magicians at the time when he saw the staff of Moses turn into a snake. Right away he called the magicians, who know the times when the powers of different forces in the world are strengthened, to see when the power of the form of the snake, or the power of the wood or the power of the staff would be strengthened by the movements of the stars to do this. They took advice together, and agreed that the snake has only the powers to bite, and doesn't have any other power at this time. The wisdom of the magicians is dependent on the movement of the stars and has no power over it. However, the Hartomen, whose work is hidden with them from times past, they hurried to do, and because the magicians didn't protest it, as they were considered partners. Like it says, 'and the Hartomen of Egypt, they also did with their staffs'. It could have said, 'the Hartomen of Egypt did'. However, since it said, 'they also did', we see that the magicians were considered one with them, because they didn't protest". So all these people, the magicians and the hartomen, also made staffs and turned them into snakes.

"We also see here that every plague God brought on the Egyptians in Egypt, none of them were able to be caused by the movements of the planets. In order to make known to the nations of the world their lack of wisdom before God's might. And similarly you can say that all the decrees that God decreed on the evil nations of the world, He doesn't decree them except at a time when the planets do not testify to the decree. And if the prophecy could be learned from the planetary movements, then what is the prophet coming to reveal to us?" this is an important point which Rabbi Avraham makes. That all the miracles that happened to the people of Israel had no indication to it in the sky, and all the decrees that God decreed on the evil nations of the world happen only when they do not expect it. Because if they were expecting it, they wouldn't see His might, and they would say it was because of the stars. So He intentionally does it just at the time when they say everything is going to be alright, and everything looks good. Then the attack comes, and then they get it. And that only comes from the words of the prophets, because the prophets could see higher than the astrologers. Like we have said before: When you read the books of the prophets from 2500 years ago, and look at their predictions, starting with Moses, you see how they predict things so clearly, what happens even in our times, with such obviousness and astrologers can only see things in general, and only in the near future. No astrologer is able to tell what will happen thousands of years from now. So God acted towards the nations intentionally when they were not expecting that, when astrologers didn't see any negative signs in heaven, so that they would know the greatness of God.

"We also see here that every plague God brought on the Egyptians in Egypt, none of these were able to be caused by the movements of the planets. In order to make known to the nations of the world their lack of wisdom before God's might. And similarly you can say that all the decrees that God decreed on the evil nations of the world, He doesn't decree them, except to a time when the planets do not testify to the decree. And if the prophecy could be learned from the planetary movements, then what is the prophet coming to reveal to us? However, it is right that the prophecy will not be in accordance with the movement of the constellations and planets. So that all the wise men of the nations will consult and be confused and shocked in the face of God's might; at the time they see their testimony and thoughts go against them. And similarly, the prophet Isaiah said: 'Where are they? Where are your wise men? Let them tell you now, let them try to know what God, master of the legions, has prepared for Egypt'. To tell you that the decree which He advised to bring on Egypt, the experts in the wisdom of astrology they saw it, but their wisdom was nullified in before God's decree. Like it says, 'Pharaoh's wisest advisers offer boorish counsel'. And the text is not coming to teach that the wise men of Egypt were liars, but rather to teach you God's strength, that He nullified the power of the planets and took away their power, until the wise men will appear fools in their eyes. Like it says, 'I am God... Who abrogates the omens of the stargazers, and makes fools of the astrologers; Who makes wise men retreat and makes their knowledge foolish'. No one except for the astrologers can see the awesome strength of God at these times when they see the decrees of the planets nullified before the righteous and good, and it increases fear and belief". So only astrologers can actually see how great God is, when they see things happening, which, according to he stars shouldn't have happened. So they see a kind of a lower prophetic vision, something which is beyond nature. So let us keep going now:

"From here you can see that this wisdom (astrology) increases fear of heaven and knowledge of God, and it reveals the awesomeness of His name and His might". So in this way, instead of leading people to idolatry, it leads people to fear of God, and reveals to them how mighty He is. "But the other four types of wisdom of the stars we mentioned, they do not increase fear of heaven, and they are forbidden to engage in, because they lead the person to idol worship and cheapen the fear of heaven". So basically, on this point, Rabbi Avraham finishes talking about these four forbidden branches of astrology, which were not God given, but rather they were created by Men. While astronomy and astrology (the general view of what is in the world, and what is going to happen to people and all the planets and 4 elements, etc..) were given from God to Adam Harishon, and handed over, from one person to another, in a traditional way: Adam to the School of Shem and Ever, then to Avraham and then to Babylon and Greece etc. But this line of tradition which holds that the planets are only servants of God, and have no will of their own, is not a tradition which was part of the 4 branches of astrology that are forbidden. Everything is decreed by God, while the planets are used as intermediaries. So due to the sin of Adam, and in order to provide people with free choice, God distanced Himself from the world by having the planets as a kind of intermediarie between him and the world . Like kings who have ministers whom are intermediaries between them and the ordinary people. But it's the king who is in charge. But the other four groups of astrologers later came along, and decided that the planets have a free will, and it is possible to appease them by worshiping them or whatever. And they started making offerings to the planets, and these ideas became popular, and grew into a big business, which could not end. Because once ideas become business, it is very difficult to end them and close down the business.

"There are other crafts like them, and if they are not suitable to be called Wisdom, they are called crafts or cunning, and the text called them, or most of them, divination. Like it says in the book of Smuel 11: 'For the king of Babylonia stood at the crossroads, at the head of the roads, to practice divination, and he shot arrows, inquired of terephim, and looked into the liver'". The arrows mentioned here were possibly sharp arrows, 'I will say to the bad go and find the arrows'. These are the arrows shot from the bow. The king of Babylonia divined with them. It is also possible that the arrows are gravel, like it says in the book of Lamentations, 'He ground my teeth in gravel'". In Hebrew, Chitzim means arrows, and Chatzatz means gravel, so it could be either. "Also 'the bread of falsehood is sweet to men, but afterwards, his mouth will be filled with gravel/Chitzim'. And also we find the Arabs that lived in the Land of Keder, their expertise was to polish stones on the earth, and they would know by this which way to travel, and they would know what to do. And it is possible that this is the meaning of arrows (Chitzim)".

"The terephim were shapes and pictures like visions in glass, many images which they were gazing at, whenever they would try to decide to do something, they would look to

see if it was good and would benefit them, and what they would see in that vision they would rely on. Now we find in these lands something similar to terephim, like those who gaze in glass bottles filled with water, which are placed on something red, and they don't lift up their eyes from it, until the image of that which they asked about appears to them in the water of the glass". Maybe today it would be like reading tea leaves or coffee grains where they could get visions, or looking at a crystal ball or something. "Similarly, they would look at the fingernail, or the shoulder or an egg that was printed by something polished and bright, like pitch or olive oil. All these are similar to asking terephim, it is implied from the word toref, which is the essential part or the root of the thing, and it is translated, 'Tzelamim' – shadows. Rabbi Saadiya Gaon translates these words as images and pictures". So Tzelem can mean a shadow, or an image or picture, of what these people were looking for when they looked at the objects to find the future from them. So these are also forbidden to be practiced.
And Rabbi Avraham goes on:
"It is good for a man to forbid himself from doing all those works, which the king of Babylonia asked through them, because they are called divinations, and the Torah forbids us from divining, like it says (Deuteronomy): 'They shall not be found among you one who causes his sons and daughters to pass through the fire, one who practices divinations, an astrologer, one who reads omens, a sorcerer, or an animal charmer, one who inquires of Yidoni or one who consults the dead'".

I want to go on a tangent and discuss the controversy revolving around whether ancient astrology is relevant today considering the fact that we know that the earth revolves around the sun and not the other way round (sun revolves around the earth). I was told by an astronomy professor who lives here in Jerusalem and taught many years at Harvard, and he is now retired, that the difference between the thoughts of ancient times and today regarding the centrality of the earth, is that it doesn't actually matter whether the sun or the earth is the center of the universe. Astronomy can work this contradiction out using mathematics, and you can figure out everything from either perspective using different mathematical models. Some things would be easier one way, some would be easier the other way, but more or less you can work everything out using the two systems. So what is behind the idea, that people of the ancient times saw the earth as the center of the universe, while modern people see the sun as the center of the universe? So he tried to say that ancient people looked at things from a more spiritual perspective. If you look at the Ari Z"l, at the beginning of "Etz Chayim", the famous book of Kabalah, there he talks about the 2 approaches of looking at the world through the tree of life, where you either have the world of circles and/or the worlds of straight lines. So astrology is the world of circles, because all the planets circle the earth, or the sun. And the circle that is the more outer is more spiritual, for it surrounds and encompasses the circles within it, and it sends forces down to them. And the next circle is higher than the one below it, until you go from circle to circle down until you get to the bottom circle which is the earth, and that was considered the lowest spiritual point. Like the soul coming down to the pit, the Earth, the lowest place possible. And that is why they saw the earth as the center of this spiritual system of circles. So this is looking at things from a very spiritual perspective. But today, everything is measured. And you measure things with physical instruments. So if you look at things from a more physical way, then it comes out that the sun is the center of the universe; but it all leads to the same conclusion.

Chapter 11

"It is good for a man to forbid himself from doing all these acts, which the king of Babylonia asked through them, because they are called divinations, and the Torah forbids us from divining. Like it says in Deuteronomy, chapter 18 verse 10, 'they shall not be found among you one who cause his sons and daughters to pass through the fire, one who practices divinations, a MeOnen, a MeNachesh (reads omens), a MeChashef (sorcerer) etc.'". The Bible in Hebrew uses the word MeOnen, which some mistakenly translate as Astrologer, but it is not so, and Rabbi Avraham does not define a MeOnen as an astrologer, and states that a MeOnen is not a standard Hebrew word for Astrology.

So I am going to quote the full piece from the Bible in Deuteronomy (18:10) using an standard English translation: "There shall not be found among you one who causes his sons or daughters to pass through the fire, one who practice his divinations, an astrologer (MeOnen), one who reads the omens (MeNachesh), a sorcerer (MeChasef) or an animal charmer, one who enquires of Ov or Yidoni or one who consults the dead. For anyone who does these is an abomination to Hashem, and because of these abominations, Hashem, your God, banishes the nations from before you. You shall be whole hearted with Hashem, your God. For these nations that you are conquering , they hearken to astrologers (MeOnen) and diviners (KoseMim), but as for you, not so has Hashem your God given for you". So we learned that all these worlds, the planets, the angels, the sefirot/spheres, whatever, are all intermediaries, which were put in place due to the sin of Adam Harishon, because people are not on the level get things straight from God. And things have to come down through various levels, until a person can receive it. But he is not in the state that he can get things directly from God. And God uses the planets to send things down to people. I have never seen any conventional book that talks about this issue of why was the world made in such a way that the planets/sefirot are used to send energies to people? If it is a given fact that astrology works, then we need to ask the question, why do we need planets to run things down here? This is question that especially those astrologers who don't believe in God should ask. How did the world end up being influenced by planets?

I am offering an answer here, which is not my own answer, but from a famous Kabbala book, from about one hundred years ago, where it is written that the planets are intermediaries, and the world had to be created through intermediaries, and for most people, things couldn't be received straight from God. The exception is the righteous individual, for the goal of the righteous person is to get to that level, where he gets things straight from God with no intermediaries. This is the highest level of the righteous person who is above the planetary influences. One who can, somehow, almost make his will God's will, and become so attached and so connected to God, that he is totally above the planetary influences. This would be the highest state. And this is more than just doing the Mitzvot. It is doing what you were told to do with such fervor and heart that you are intimately attached to God, and God is directing your life. At that level your are above the stars and you get things from the source. But today, I think that most people are getting things via the stars, so that is why we are learning this book.

"It is good for a man not to do all these works of divinations, because the Torah forbids us from divining, like it says, 'they shall not be found among you one who causes his sons and daughters to pass through the fire, one who practices divinations, an astrologer, one who reads omens, a sorcerer, or an animal charmer, one who inquires of Ov or Yidoni, or one who consults the dead'. And you will say all these works are called divinations. But here we have a general rule (not to practice divination) and then the details (astrologer, omens, talking to the dead ect), and you can't judge only on the detail, and you can only say that these specific things, which have been mentioned in the text, have been forbidden under the category of Divination and nothing else". The rabbis had a rule, that when there is a particular rule, like 'one who causes his children to pass through the fire' (particular rule) followed by a general rule ('no Divination'), and them again lists particular rules ('no MeOnen/astrologer' ect.), the general rule (divination) only contains these listed particulars, but no other particulars. So according to Rabbi Avraham the definitions above exclude astrology, for the things which are mentioned here are things of people who supplicate the planets, and not Jewish astrology. "A proof for you that 'divination' is a general rule which encompasses all the details is found in the use of the quote above (in Deuteronomy 18:10) that lists as forbidden 'one who inquires of Ov or Yidoni'. It particularly uses the word 'inquiring' of Ov and Yidoni. and yet in the book of Shmuel (Shmuel I 28:9) it says, "'but the women said to him, surely you know what Saul has done, that he has eliminated the necromancer and diviner of the Ov/Yidoni from the land'. Here in the book of Shmuel we use the word 'diviner' in describing the Ov/Yidoni, and not the word 'inquirer' (as it did in verse from Deutoronomy), to teach you that all of these particular words are included in the general forbidden category of 'divining'. That these arts that are forbidden are called divinations". So in other words, 'divining' in the Ov/Yidoni and 'inquiring' in the Ov/Yidoni has the same meaning, and the word 'diviner' can be used, as a general rule, concerning all divinations listed in verse 18:10 in Deuteronomy (and excludes astrology).

"Another proof (from Talmud, Tractate Sanhedrin, page 65) is that you find that the names mentioned in Deuteronomy 18:10 are clearly mentioned by our rabbis, may they be blessed, in the Tractate Sanhedrin (65), each one what he does and what his work is, and they don't mention among these diviners, because it is a general name which includes all of them". So this second proof is that, in Tractate Sanhedrin, the group of forbidden diviners is listed, and yet it doesn't mention 'diviners' as such. So it is a proof that the word 'divination' is a general description, not a specific one, and therefore it is a general rule.

"They said in Sanhedrin about the term MeOnen (which is loosely translated as astrologer), 'Rabbi Akiva said, this is one who fixes periods and hours". Because the Hebrew word MeOnen comes from the word 'ona' which means 'a season' or a period of time. A season means for example, "Today is a nice day to go out; tomorrow will be a fine day to engage in business, or buy anything to profit from. Or before the seventh year, the wheat is good quality, uproot (not harvest) the beans so they don't go bad and will not spoil'. These people who 'fix periods and hours' rely on their experience, which they experienced during their lifetime and what they learned from it. So this is not Astrology. They didn't learn this from the wisdom of the movement of the constellations, and not from the wisdom of the movement of the planets, because they didn't give importance to one day of the week over another. If Monday this week is good for something, it doesn't mean next Monday will also be good; it's possible that next Monday could be dangerous. Similarly the seventh year is not always good for the wheat crop. Not every year is the same according to the astrologers. The MeOnen, according to Rabbi Akiva, treats the days and years in the same way always, and because of this it was said that the MeOnen's

artistry does not always go along with the wisdom of the constellations and not according to the wisdom of the planets".
So here you see that these things are particulars and not general categories. He continues with showing that particulars are not generalities.
"They described in Sanhedrin who is the reader of omens? It says, 'bread fell from his mouth, his staff fell from his hand, the deer stopped in the path, a snake is on his right and a fox is on his left' (using these signs to divine). And further they say, 'don't make an omen'. And our rabbis say, 'don't read omens'. For example those that read omens using the huldot and birds", 'huldot' is some kind of an animal, I am not sure which. "They speak about what will happen in the world, according to what the see 'in signs' from the planets and animals and birds". Indian astrology seems to use these things, they are big on omens. An Indian astrologer could be reading one's horoscope and you ask a question on pregnancy, and while doing it he sees 2 birds that come along, and then one bird flies away, and then he might say that this is an omen: You are going to have twins, and one of them is going to die, or something. And this is called 'using omens'. And again, this is not based on the laws of astrology, but is something different and additional and based on the laws of omens. So the rabbis didn't like people using that and it is forbidden. "This art is found in the world today mainly among sailors and farmers". They are God fearing people, because their occupation is very much dependent on the environment. Because the sea must have been sometimes very dangerous back two thousand years ago. And the farmers need rain. Without rain, the best farmers in the world can't grow crops. So they always look for signs from the heavens. "Like those who say, if the moon on the first or second day of the month has a black ring surrounding it, it is a sign of much rain during that month, and similar to a black ring surrounding the moon, if the sun shines bright and the air that surrounds it is red, there will be heavy winds from the direction where the red air appears. Similar to this is one saying things like this concerning any of the seven planets, or the bright comets, and also one saying the voice of the raven at night and the voice of chickens at the beginning of the night testify to rain, and the hulda who lifts up its voice and dances testifies to cold weather, and other signs like these, are the ways of the readers of omens from birds and the planets".
Now Rabbi Avraham goes on to sorcerers as listed in Tractate Sanhedrin:
"Sorcerers are ones who do a deed and didn't just hold onto the eyes. And what the sorcerers do we already mentioned above. They know when different powers are found in the world, and also the Chartumim who gather herbs and trees at specific times, these are also deeds, and not just holding the eyes".
Now he goes on to explain the baal Ov as listed in Tractate Sanhedrin:
"Baal Ov is someone who speaks from his joints or under his armpits". "Baal Yidoni is someone who puts a special bone in his mouth and speaks from it. The rabbis said, 'one who asks the dead', this is someone who starves himself and goes to the graveyard so that an unclean spirit rests on him". "On all the different forms of divination, our rabbis explained to us what they are about and how their work is performed. They said, all of them are forbidden to do, like they said, 'don't learn to do'. But you can study them in order to learn and teach. In general it was forbidden to ask of them, because it is written, 'it is an abomination' all who do these, be simple with the Lord your God". So again, this is his proof that 'divination' is a general law, and all these others are specifics to this. But one may learn them in order to learn and teach them, because judges and others have to

know what all these forbidden things are, in order to know what these practices involve, if Jews get involved with them.

From there they saw that you don't ask them, like it says, 'from where do we learn that we don't ask the Chaldeans? From 'be simple with the Lord your God'. And this comes out from this section of the Torah and the Talmud (above), where the rabbis expound all the different kinds of work that are forbidden to engage in and to do. From here they also warned us from seeking them out and asking them". It is not only that you don't do it, but it is also forbidden to try to find the Chaldeans and ask them. "And the word Chaldean here means all those who engage in forbidden works". That is the four types of forbidden astrology and all the diviners. And they are called Chaldeans, because it was the people of Babylonia, the land of Shinar, who engaged in all these arts. "It is known that all the people of these lands are Aramaic, like it says, 'and the Casdim spoke to the king of Aremet, because they spoke in the language of the nation they were from, and the children of Aram, Otz, Chol, Neter and Mash are not mentioned here, not the Casdim and not the Chaldeans. And the people who lived in the Land of Shenar were called Chaldeans, and they were also called Casdim and Soranime and other names. And the name includes all these as false prophets and Chaldeans. And the Casdim, they were from the governmental families in the days of Nebuchadnezzar the evil one. And they had their opportunity to serve their idols, and they were priests in their houses of worship, and from this they were called Casdim, 'those who draw down the forces of the planets'. The Casdim were a specific class of the Chaldeans, they were like the high priests of the Chaldeans. So they can be called Casdim or Chaldeans. But the Chaldeans were generally the regular people, and therefore couldn't be called Casdim according to their class in society". So Rabbi Avraham learns, that Chaldeans means all those groups of people who practice the forbidden astrology or divination. But regular astrologers are not called Chaldeans. "Since our rabbis said, 'we don't ask the Chaldeans', they included among them the Casdim, who drew down forces from above, and all those who engaged in wisdoms like these concerning knowing the future. Their words are to us like we said; we don't ask sorcerers, Chaldeans, readers of the times and all the other wisdoms that are similar to them, because the Chaldeans engaged in all those arts. "Now we have come to distinguish clearly what it means 'we don't ask the Chaldeans', and it has been revealed to us what are the wisdoms that are suitable to learn and practice, and what are those that are permitted to learn but not to practice. It appears from this, that one who practices what is permitted, and his intention is for the sake of heaven, he can be called a truly righteous one even though the whole world calls him misguided. But if he forbids what is permitted and permits what is forbidden, we don't call this person misguided, we call him, guilty and a sinner, because he has left the true path".

"It is enough for us now, with all the reasons we have given, to have shown that the one who was strict concerning the bridegroom, that caused us to write this, he was in fact so strict, that he forbid what was permitted, even though it was known and clear to all, that what he did was for the sake of heaven and he was God fearing".

So now, as Rabbi Avraham finishes the letter, he is going to talk to his teacher, starting by praising him, and then he is going to ask him for a reply, regarding this letter, of whether he agrees with it or not, and what his reasoning is.

"Everything we have brought him until now, from his mouth we have learned, from his water it has been drawn, and all the wisdom that is known to all the people on earth is lit up in him, like the streets of Nehardea". In the Talmud, it is said about Shmuel, who was a famous sage of that time, that he knew the paths of heaven like he knew the paths of the city of Nehardea, which he grew up in. So the same thing he says here about his teacher, that he knows all the wisdom like Shmuel knew the paths of Nehardea.

"If it is suitable before him, if it is strait in his eyes and it is good before him, and if he sees that these words of mine are good and proper, then he will reveal his heart before us, and honor us with an announcement from his lips, and not leave us standing in doubt and walking in darkness. Because pointing out the truth and the proper way is the characteristic of the wise man and the way of acting of the rightous and complete man. It is proper for us and all those who hear his words to thank him and praise him because of his great righteousness and goodness, his humbleness and modesty. And if he will see that my words are riddled with errors and craziness, words of nonsense and insanity, words not proper to speak, words which only confuse, then let his mercy and righteousness grow and open his hand, and show us in which ways my words are broken, and why they should not be relied upon. On that day I will hear his complaints, I will confess my sins and say I recant my words. And I will say about it, 'it is not mine own '. If you don't answer me satisfactory and you don't pay attention to my words to answer one of the questions that I asked, and you will say to me, 'your words don't make sense to me, but I don't have the power to destroy your reasoning', I will say to him, 'far be it from me-until I perish-to say you are right! I will not renounce my innocence from myself'. But if I am mistaken in what I write and in my arguments, I implore my rabbis, don't hold me guilty, for all the words I have spoken, for the Lord of Justice knows, and all hidden things are revealed before him, That I didn't come to teach and expound, neither to adorn myself, nor to build myself up, God forbid, nor to incite. Rather my whole intention was to clear my name".

So what he says is that, in the event his teacher says he is wrong, without giving him any reason, and then he is not going to recant his opinion. But he is imploring of his rabbi: 'If I am wrong, please show me how I am wrong. So I can correct myself and know that I am wrong. But I really truly believe in my heart that I am right'. And the whole reason for him writing this book is to prove that he was right. "Maybe I will be acquitted, for from my youth until this day I was taught the wisdom of astrology and practiced it. I delved into and explored its depth, and I considered myself one who has acquired wisdom and discernment, one who is guilt-free and innocent".

"Now, when I have seen wise men straight in judgment and modesty, who have studied the sciences and are knowledgeable, they disagree with me. They have ruined my work. In my childhood and youth I was judged leniently, because of the honor I received before ministers and kings. And now in my old age I will have this before me as an accuser. It is good that I search for judgment and speak out for my innocence, perhaps until I awaken the anger of those who hate me, who spoke evil about me, and they will tell me my obligations, they will criticize me, and maybe there will be power in their words, to prove to me to follow their way".

"And now you, my rabbis, men of strength and Torah, defenders and mighty ones, who have the power to rule over the wisdom, don't put a stumbling block before the blind, tell me which way to go, put me on the path of the king. Because all of Israel are responsible for each other, and the fat one is obligated to pour out his oil to the skinny one; to light up the eyes and to lead the blind. The one satiated with water will pour water to the thirsty".

This idea, that every Jew bares responsibility for other Jews, is expounded in the Kabbala, where there is the idea that every Jew has a little bit of every other Jew within him. And because of that, every Jew is interconnected, like a holistic system, where everybody has a little bit of everybody else in them. So if a Jew does a good deed, it impacts on everybody else, in all the people of Israel. And on the other hand, when a Jew does something bad, it can have a detrimental effect on everybody else in Israel. This is because the sparks of all the other Jews are within him. And the rabbis compare it to somebody who is in a boat, in his cabin, and drills a hole in the bottom of his cabin. The people in the boat come to his cabin, saying, 'what are you doing! You are going to sink the whole boat!' And he says, 'what do you want from me? I am in My room, and I may do in it whatever I want !!'. And because of that, a person has to look at things with a longer term view. This is the whole holistic idea: You are all independent, but at the same time you are all interconnected. You are part of a group also. "Because all of Israel are responsible for each other, and the fat one is obligated to pour out his oil to the skinny one; to light up the eyes so as to lead the blind. The one satiated with water will pour water to the thirsty, until the day comes, when everyone will be happy in his portion and find his true desire. It should be your will, Lord of Heaven, to honor us at that time and to fulfill what is written in Jeremiah: 'No longer will a man teach his friend or his brother to know God, because all of them will know me, from the smallest to the greatest-the word of God- when I will forgive their inequity and no longer recall their sin'".

So in his letter, Rabbi Avraham Bar Chiya defended the use of astrology according to Jewish Law. And he came to the idea, that basically, astronomy and standard astrology, which is the influences of the planets and the constellations, which the laws of astrology are based upon, all are permitted. But all the other types of astrology and divination are forbidden, because they are all connected, some way or the other, with idol worship, where these people believe that the planet has an independent judgment. But the Jews believe that the planets are only intermediaries of God, who used them to deliver His will to the earth. And the only one who can change the planetary influences is God. The Jews (or righteous gentiles) can influence their planetary influences by their behavior by fulfilling the divine laws and praying to God. The more they do it with integrity, fervor and attachment to God in every moment and circumstance, the more they remove themselves from the planetary influences. A famous Kabbalist from the early 1900's wrote in his book, that the desire of the righteous people is to be directed by God. And thus they become able to go beyond all the things that separate us from God because of our sins, and to attach themselves directly to God.

I remember my teacher, the late great Zoltan Mason, whom I learned with for a number of years. And he said, all of astrology is in the Bible. You just have to know where to look.

The basic model of the Universe

The basic model of the Universe

By Yaakov Kronenberg

An edited transcription of a series of lectures on Torah astrology, detailing where astrology is incorporated in the overall system of Kabbala. The series details the views of our Sages dating back through the millennia; including the Ari Z"l, Rabbi Chaim Vital and Rabbi Moshe Kordovero, and includes references from the Talmud and Zohar and Commentators. The various upper Worlds are discussed, including how the flow of energy descends and is transmitted in the final stage through the Stars and Planets. It also discusses why these planetary influences can be overridden through Torah and Mitzvoth.

Basic model of the universe

By Yaakov Kronenberg

Introduction

A little bit about myself, I was born and raised in New York City, I went to some of the top universities in America, and after that at age 21 I started to work on Wall Street. There I met an old Hungarian Jewish man, Zoltan Mason who was about 70, I guess he lived through the war in Europe and then he came to America. When I met him he taught me a bit of astrology and a lot about mystical philosophy. He also got me interested in Judaism and Kabbala. One day I asked him which country I should go to since I wanted to leave America. I never wanted to live in America; I was always in a rush to get out of America. He didn't want me to go, because he thought highly of me and he wanted me to eventually take over his practice. But I wanted to leave America, so he said to me that the only place where I would make it would be Israel, but the only problem would be that once I went to Israel, I would not come back. And this is how it was. I left America in the summer of 1976, and today it is 2011, and indeed, maybe altogether, except for around 30 days of me visiting in America, I have never been back , and I am very happy here. So when I came to Israel I started to learn Rabbinics as my astrology teacher said I should learn to think like a rabbi. So I thought that since I have to think like a rabbi, the best thing for me would be to learn from rabbis and become like one. And I started studying in a Yeshiva for students who were interested in learning Kabbala and was trained in it, and it was a Yeshiva that had just been opened at that time. And Jerusalem was a little place back then, so I was lucky enough to hang around with the most special rabbis who were experts in Kabbala. I studied with Rabbi Mordechai Sharabi a little and most of my teachers were his students. I also studied with Rabbi Kaduri and Rav Darsi who are no longer with us, and with students of Rabbi Sharabi, such as Rav Tziyon Bracha and Meir Levy. I have also studied with some rabbis of our own generation, such as with Rabbi Mordechai Atia, Rabbi David Batzri and Rabbi Beniyahu Shmueli. I was one of the first students of his Yeshiva. So this is more or less my background.

I have friends, students of Mr Mason, who started, some 20 years ago, an organization called "Project hindsight", and its whole aim was to rediscover the astrology that had been lost. They felt that astrology had become very superstitious and had become very much psychologically oriented; they felt that it had became very humanistic, which ignored the distinction between good and evil because they were value judgments and did not predict the future because everybody could so easily overcome their fate ! This was in the 1960s and 1970s, and also in the 1980s, when it became really psychologically oriented, with predictions minimal where you are heading and what would happen to you, rather astrologers discussed your psychological makeup; it was psychologically oriented, with psychologists, who couldn't make a good living out of psychology alone, so they resorted to astrology. And then a reverse, alternative movement started and grew up in the 1980s. And it aimed towards getting back to traditional Astrology, which is based on ancient wisdom, an astrology that was more predictive, and focused on trying to understand who the person is through what was going to happen to him, what his mission in life is and what does the future hold and where he is heading. So a group of astrologers at that time, most of whom were connected to Zoltan Mason, who was kind of the godfather of that movement. He was probably the only person in America at that time who tried to teach what was called traditional astrology. Project hindsight tried to re-discover the old books which had been lost, and put them together and publish them. Their aim was to rediscover which methods worked in early astrology and which predictive methods worked and which didn't. And so you see how astrology evolved. When you look at all their works you see they re-discovered Greek astrology, Babylonian Astrology, Roman, Medieval and Arab astrology; but what I found interesting is that you can't find any Jewish Astrology which they uncovered, when there is so much! One may ask then, was there ever a Jewish astrology? And if so, what was it all about? They did however cite one book from Jewish sources which is "The beginning of Wisdom", by Rabbi Ibn Ezra, which is a great book, but not a true representation of Torah astrology and it revolved mostly around Western astrology; basically from Western influences as well as Arabic and some Indian astrology, and in some sense it wasn't really a Jewish book. And that seems to be the way the astrology community in the West works; they think that the only book about Jewish Astrology is the book of Rabbi Ibn Ezra, which is about Western astrology! I have a friend who went to the St. John's university (a special educational program of four years' studying the great most prized books of the Western civilization, about one hundred books), and he showed me that that university's approach took a similar line, very few Jewish books. When I looked at the list, I noticed that they had included only two Jewish books: The Bible (Tanach) and a book by Maimonides called "the guide for the perplexed". How can it be that nobody heard of Jewish writers during the millenium? This era which spanned from about the conclusion of the Talmud up to the time of Spinoza and Carl Marx, Sigmund Freud and so on, which is around the 1700s and 1800s, a era when Jews came out of the Ghettos? What did Jews write during the years in between, during the Middle Ages? That you don't seem to hear much about them is interesting to note. Why only 2 books in the university's top book list? Even the Bible, I thought that one reason why the university put the Bible in the list is that even though the Bible is a Jewish book, the Christian religion holds that it was taken away from the Jews and given to them, and became a Christian book. As for Maimonides, people know Maimonides as a great writer, and it is known that many Jews study Maimonides's Legal works such as the Mishnah Torah, so they put one of his books in the list too. But they choose the "Guide to the perplexed", which is a book that basically few religious Jews read and is Western philosophy oriented!

So just as is done at the University, so in the western astrology community. Unfortunately, they think that Judaism only has the Book of Ibn Ezra on astrology! That the Jews have no astrology of their own.

So I want to try to fill a little bit of this gap here and I would like to try to teach some Jewish Astrology, its sources and where it differs from Western astrology. I would like to talk about how the Jewish religion sees Jewish astrology, especially the connection between Jewish Astrology and Kabbala, the question of where does the Jewish astrology fit in with Kabalistic thinking. Then we can talk about Kabbala itself.

When I grew up I had never heard of the Vilna Gaon and the Maharal of Prague, the Ari Z"aL and Rabbi Moshe Kordovero. I didn't know about the existence of their books until I was in my twenties. So we are going to talk about this gap, and try and fill it, as well as about how the Ari Z'L interpreted the Zohar, and about the teachings of Rav Moshe Cordovero and some other great Kabbalists. And we are going to talk about the oriental rabbis, for most of the Kabbala studied today actually comes from oriental rabbis, based on the teachings of Rabbi Shalom Sharabi, who came to Israel from Yemen around the time of the American Revolution, and taught Kabbala. He was a great Kabbalist. So as a start I would like to talk about the basic model of the universe, and the difference between the Kabbalistic model and the Western/Indian models of the universe.

So when you look at old Astrology books, ancient Greek, Roman and Middle age books, you see they looked at the earth as the basic model, with all planets and stars surrounding it: The

Moon above the earth, and then Mercury, Venus, the Sun, Mars, Jupiter, Saturn. They were all surrounding earth as according to those books (we will talk later about why they didn't mention the modern planets, and that maybe they knew about them, but didn't want to mention them. But this is for another lesson). They held that each planet was going around along its sphere. Each sphere was one above the other and one bigger than the other. Above these 7 spheres, there was an 8th sphere, which was the sphere of "the Fixed stars". And above that was another sphere, the 9th, which the Jews called Galgal hayomi ("the daily sphere"), for it actually did a complete circle around the earth in one day. It was also called the blank sphere, there was nothing the 'eye' could see in it, and it was also called the "White Sphere".

There is also a 10th sphere above it, called Galgal hasechel (" sphere of intelligence"), where everything emanates from. We will talk in a moment about all these Galgalim and what they were. But I think this sub-system was taken by the Greeks from the Jewish model, and it became the Greco-Roman system. It also went before that to India via Abraham's children with Hagar who were sent to the east with gifts. This to them was basically the universe. But what was missed is that the full Jewish model of Creation is much much bigger than the sub-model of the solar system and with many more dimensions. In it, there are five worlds with multiple dimensions:

1) World of Asiya (world of Action/Doing), it is the lowest world which we physically inhabit.

2) Above that is the world of Yetzira (world of Formation).

3) Above it is the world of Beriah (world of Creation).

4) Above that is the world of Atzirut (world of Emanation).

5) Above that there are more worlds, such as Olam Adam Hakadmon (the world of Adam, the first man), and then above that Olam Ha Ein Sof (the endless/unknowable world).

The whole Solar System of the planets and stars of our galaxy is in the world of Asiya, which is the lowest world, closest to us. This world of Asiya, is divided into two parts: Earth and Heaven. Both the Earth and Heaven are divided into 7 parts, into seven pieces. The 7 parts of Heaven (in this world of Asiya) are called in Kabbala the 7 Heichalot (palaces). I would like to talk about these 7 Heichalot/Palaces in the next chapter. You will see there that the first 'palace' in Heaven (in the world of Asiya) is called Vilon, which means "like a curtain" and so on.

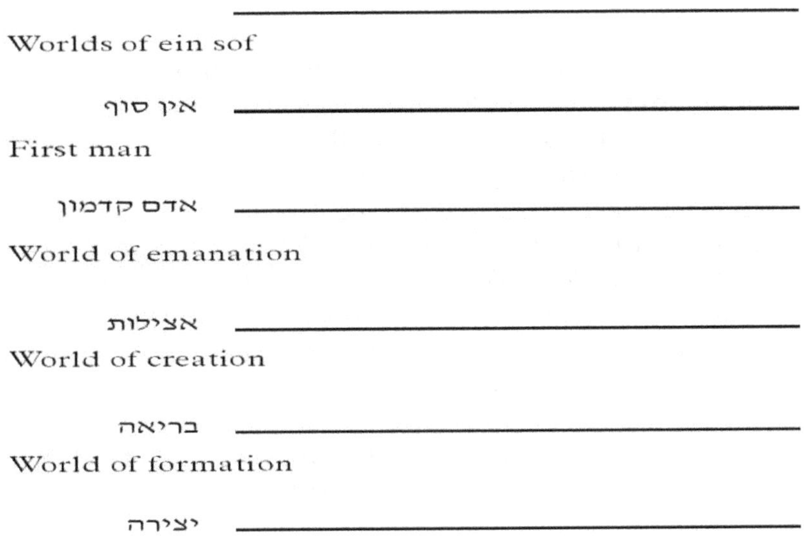

Worlds of ein sof

אין סוף

First man

אדם קדמון

World of emanation

אצילות

World of creation

בריאה

World of formation

יצירה

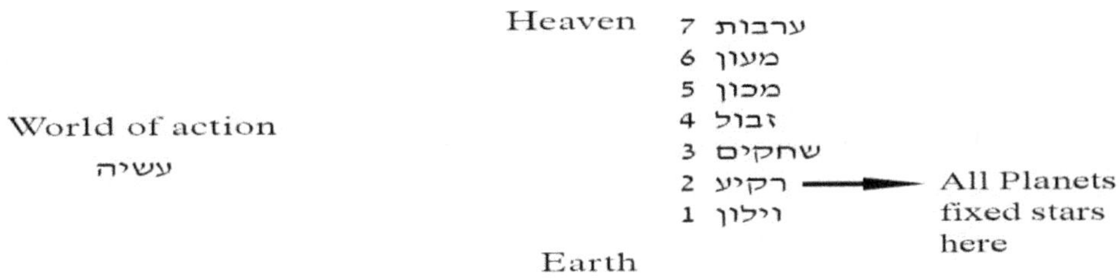

World of action

עשיה

Heaven

7 ערבות
6 מעון
5 מכון
4 זבול
3 שחקים
2 רקיע → All Planets fixed stars here
1 וילון

Earth

Let us talk about the basic difference between Western and Jewish astrology. The Talmud is the primary source of the subject of Heichalot/Palaces. My source for this is Talmud Tractate Chagiga 12b. I have heard that today there are good translations in English to the Talmud. So in the Talmud Chagiga, Rabbi Yehudah and Rabbi Yosef discuss the world of Asiya, and mention that there is the Earth and the Heavens and that the Heavens are divided into 7 palaces: Vilon (curtain), Rakia (firmament), Shechakim (ground up), Zvul (palace, majestic), Maon, Machon (dwelling places) and Arivot (clouds). The Talmud continues with the explanation of the meaning to all these 7 Palaces, but we are just going to see the meaning of the 2nd one, the Rakia (firmament). The 1st palace is Vilon (like a curtain) and is not for anything except going in there every morning and out every evening and renewing the creation. The 2nd palace is called the Rakia, which consists of the Sun, the Moon, the Planets, the fixed stars and the 9th and 10th sphere, within it. So you see that in Judaism, all Planets and stars are in a sub-section of the world of Asiya which is a sub-section of the 5 worlds. Above that palace of Rakia there are 5 more palaces. And even higher than that, there is then the beginning of the world of Yetzira (the world of Angels), and then the world of Beria, the world of Creation out of nothing and then the world of Atzilut, the world of Unity, where the level of spirituality in very high (also called Elohut Gavoha), Adam kadmon and the Endless world.

Jewish astrology is much more detailed about the energies that come down from all parts of Heaven to Earth. Interestingly, Maimonides describes how people in ancient times, came to worship idols: They just woke up every morning and saw the Sun, moon, stars etc., and they didn't realize there is anything above that. So they concluded that those were the sources of power. An interesting question is how did astrology develop the way it did throughout the ancient world? It's a fact that the symbols of astrology are very similar around the world, with the same constellations and planets. So one may ask; how all those countries picked up the same constellations to be used in astrology? Because the zodiac Signs are not so easy to standardize globally and yet they are the same all over the world, how did all the nations all learn to connect the stars in the same way, as there is no real compulsion do so. So where did it all start from, did it start in Babylon? Did the Babylonians draw the imaginative lines, which were picked up and then spread over the whole world? How did everyone agree, for example, on 7 day weeks? There is no place in the world where the week is different than 7 days. So there must have been an original source which originated it and it spread out from there to the whole world.

So the ancient people must have studied astrology, tried one system which didn't work, and moved to another, until the found a suitable one which in most cases involved the planets. So people started worshiping planets and stars, and wanted to change their luck. So this is the way idol worship began. In India, for instance, people believe, even today, that one who has trouble in his life, for example because of a bad Saturn planet influence, has to pray to Saturn, say a special mantra to him, a number of specific times, specific words, and to ask him not to be so mean. And in Western astrology (Greek/Roman), in the time of idol worshiping, they would make offerings and build idols for the planets, and so on, and this is how idol worship developed. The founder of Judiasm, is Avraham Avinu, was born in 1948 in the ancient Jewish calendar (it is easy to remember this year, as the State of Israel was formed in 1948 of the Common Era). So this means he was born over 4000 years ago. He was born around 1700 yrs before the common era. He was an astrologer, the astrologer of his generation, and kings from all over the world came to learn from him, which was unusual. And he wrote the book Sefer HaYetzira (the book of formation) which is the oldest book that talks about astrology, and which has six chapters, at least two of which are almost totally devoted to astrology. The Talmud discusses how Abraham discovered God at a young age, for he was the first monotheist and the founder of monotheism. And he came to the idea of monotheism by watching the planets and stars and their movements and impacts, and realizing that they couldn't do it by themselves. So there must be someone who guides them, and so he came to the belief in one God. So one may ask, if God is running the world, why do you need all of this Kabbala system? And why are energies not sent directly from Him? This is an important question which we will discuss later and it is fundamental to understanding the principles and depth of Kabbala and its sub-section of astrology. So it is interesting to know that the evolution of Judaism was started by the astrologer of his generation, Abraham, and he concluded that the stars and planets couldn't do the job by themselves, but rather there had to be something higher which made them work.

We also need to know that in the world of Asiya/Action (Olam HaAsiya) there are 10 spheres/Sefirot. And the worlds are like a hologram, so each component part also has 10 spheres/Sefirot. So the Palace of Rakia (which is the 2nd Palace of the world of Asiya) there are 10 Sefirot (the Palace of Rakia corresponds to the Sefira of Yesod in Asiya), and these 10 Sefirot in the Palace of Rakia are made up of the 7 planets, the Fixed Stars, the HaGalgal

Hayomi ("the daily sphere"), and the Galgal Hasechel ("the sphere of intelligence"), 10 energies in all.

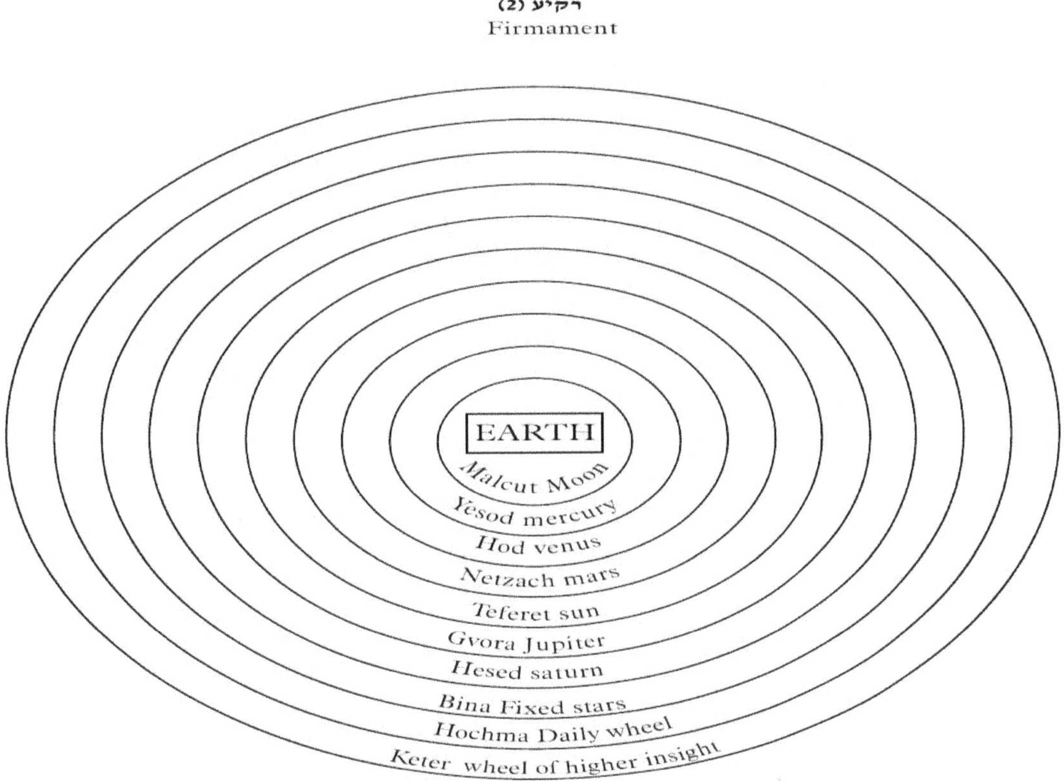

The 10th sphere of Galgal Hasechel (the sphere of intelligence) is not usually discussed and it corresponds to the 10th Sefira of Keter and corresponds to the 10th sphere the highest in the Rakia , and the 'sefira of keter' is where all the energies come through and into the rest of existence.

The 9th Sefira of the 10 Sefirot in Kabbala is called Chochma (Wisdom), and it corresponds to the 9th sphere/Sefira in Rakia, the Galgal Hayomi, the Daily sphere, where it revolves from east to west in one day. Observe how all planets go from west to east, but due to their movement inside the Daily sphere, all planets seem as if they go from east to west.

This 9th Sefira of Chochma/Wisdom, which is similar but different to Keter, which is a Crown, and it sits above the person, and is made of the upper aspect of the lower world and the lower aspect of the upper world, where energy comes from and goes back. The first thing we say about Chochma/Wisdom, is that "all were created from it" (Kulam Bechochma Asita), and it (Chochma) is actually running the whole system. And it is also called the white sphere, for there is nothing in it for us to see. Wisdom is like the beginning, like a male. And like the child starts being seen in his mother, but his father is not known in the same certainty as his mother, so does the visibility of what comes down from above only starts to appear in the next Sefira of Bina (in the palace of Rakia, it is the 8th sphere, the sphere of the Fixed stars, the Zodiac), which resembles the mother.

Actually there is a debate in astrology and astronomy about the zodiac: there is a Tropical zodiac and a Sidereal zodiac. Some people say the world is run by the Sidereal zodiac, and claim the fixed stars are seen as such because they move slowly every 71 years to a degree-

unlike the planets which move faster. Indian astrology uses the Sidereal zodiac, based on the movement of the stars. Western astrology goes with the Tropical system. We will talk about this distinction in later writings.
The Galgal Hasechel (10th Palace) is compared to a crown, and the Galgal Hayomi (9th Palace) is the Daily sphere, is like a Father,... and the Sefira of the Fixed Stars (8th palace) is like Understanding, the Sefira of Bina, and is like a Mother, as we have mentioned earlier. Bina means understanding. Chochma is the pure thought, the seed and is intuitive. The 7 remaining Sefirot below Bina would correspond to the 7 planets. These 7 planets, represent the children of Bina and the fixed stars, the Zodiac. So the Sefirot of Chesed, Gevurah, Tiferet, Netzach, Hod, Yesod and Malchut correspond to the Planets Saturn, Jupiter, Mars, Sun, Venus, Mercury and Moon. Each has a different aspect of an influence (positive and negative) over what happens in the world. The constellations and the Zodiac come from the Mother. And the questions of what kind of person is going to come into the world at a specific time, depends on the position of the Constellations together with the Planets; the Planets' actions are through the stars, through the Zodiac, and they act according to their own placement and that of the Zodiac and stars.

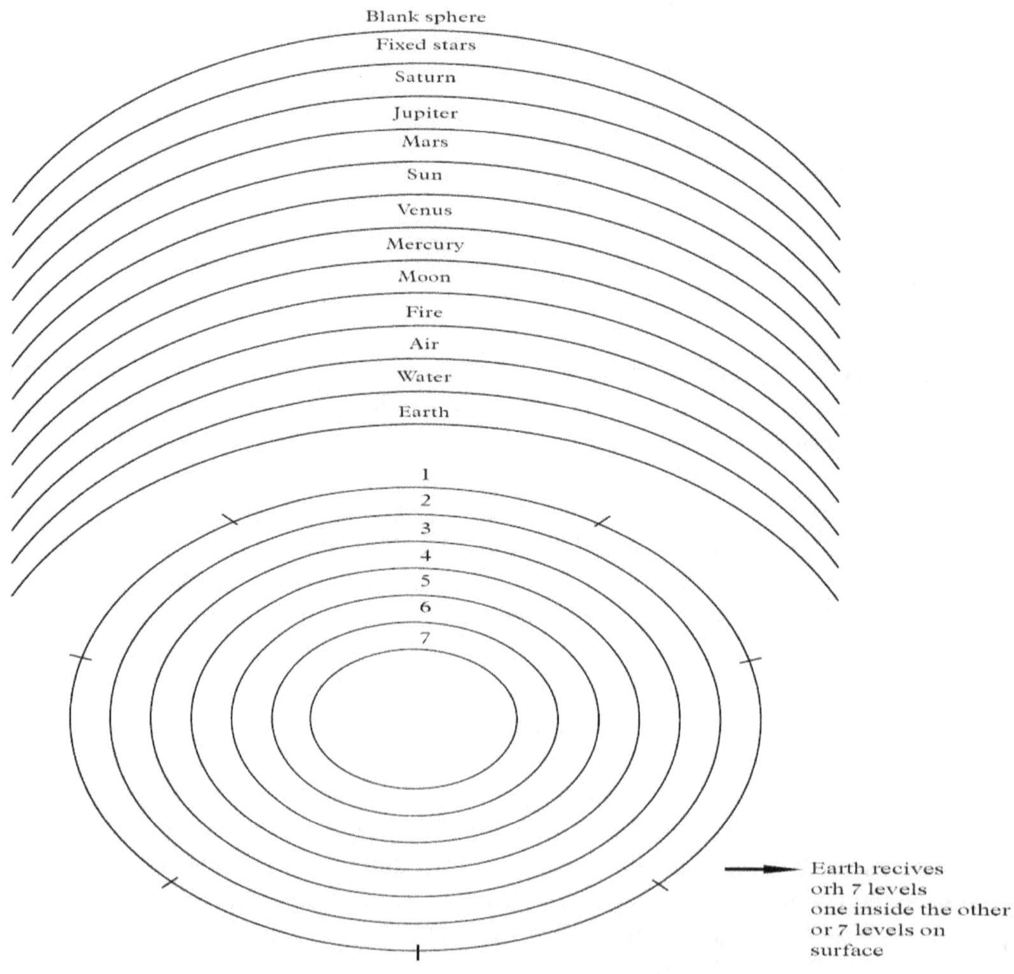

Chapter 1

I would like to emphasize that the Jewish approach to astrology came from Avraham, the Father of Judaism, who was the master astrologer of his generation, and through astrology he came to the revelation of the fact that there is one God. Also Maimonides (the Rambam) brought down the fact that the whole basis of idol worshiping started from astrology too. People saw the planetary influences, and from that they tried to find all different ways to alter the planetary influences for their own advantage and benefits, so they could enjoy a better life, and fulfill their desires. This is what we call in kabbala, "Cutting off the roots". In other words, we say that the level in astrology where all the planets are, is Olam HaAssiya (the world of Action), which corresponds to the Sefira of Malchut (Kingship), the lowest level and yet they never understood this, and seeing the planets they wanted to take the Kingship for themselves, and use it to get what they wanted. So they would worship the planets at certain times of the day, and would make idols in the images of the planets. Hopefully, we are going to talk about all these practices, and exactly what they did, in later lessons.

This is the fundamental difference between Jewish astrology (which is tied in with Kabbala and mitzvoth) and the other forms of astrology. Jewish astrology considers the Planets and Zodiac delivery systems, signs of what is going on above in the upper worlds. Also Jewish astrology can be a very profound learning experience, which can lead you to a deep understanding of the universe. On the other hand, general astrology can take a person way off the true path and lead a person to strange ways and a lack of truth, because it does not have the framework of Torah and Kabbala.

The world of Action, is primarily divided into 'Heaven' and 'Earth', and that 'Heaven' part of the world of Action (Assiya) is further divided into 7 Palaces/Firmaments (Rekeim), and that all of astrology is included in the 2nd Palace/Firmament, which is called the Rakia. Now, the Zohar talks about the fact that in the 'Earth' part of the World of Action, there are 7 Aratzot (lands) just like there are 7 Palaces/Firmaments in the 'Heaven' part. The Zohar also mentions that these 7 Lands are somehow connected to the 7 Palaces/Firmaments. I think there is an argument between the earlier and later Kabbalists about what the seven Aratzot/Lands are. Some say it means climates/continents, and others say it is seven layers of the earth, which are one layer within the other, and each layer is a different "land". The Zohar talks in length about this.

The foundation Palace of the Seven Palaces (in the World of Action/Assiya) is called the Rakia (the 2nd Palace which is also associated with the sefira of Yesod/Foundation), and a little bit of everything from the other Palaces is also in it. The lowest Palace (the 1st one) is called Vilon (Curtain) and corresponds to the Sefira of Malkhut/Kingdom. We also discussed that there are 10 Sefirot in each of the worlds and their subdivisions (like a Hologram). And so each of the Palaces also have 10 Sefirot. In the 2nd Palace called Rakia these 10 Sefirot are specifically referred to as Galgalim (Spheres). These 10 spheres are the moon, Mercury, Venus, the Sun, Mars, Jupiter and Saturn and 3 more upper Galgalim/Spheres (see below), and they all surround the earth which is stationed - in this model - in the middle. Today, though it is accepted that the earth and all planets move around the Sun, it is all a matter of which is easier to calculate mathematically. But both concepts are valid, within their own perspective. We are going to explain things according to the older system, as described above so far.

So, there are 3 Galgalim/Spheres above the seven planets of the Solar system: The 8th sphere in where the fixed stars are, the 9th which is above that is the Galgal Hayomi (the Daily sphere) where everything moves from east to west, and it takes all planets with it, and makes everything in the other spheres look as if they all move in that direction, whereas they actually move from west to east. Above that is the 10th Galgal known as the Galgal Hasechel, which is also called "Crown", and is the intermediary point between the 2nd Palace (Rakia) and the other Palaces above it, namely the 3rd Palace. So as you go up, you see that things are more and more spiritual and less material. This is symbolized by the fact that most of the distant stars can't be seen with the naked eye. Maybe one day we will again be able to see the more abstract spiritual worlds. God told Avraham that his children would be as numerous as the stars in the sky, and at that time people had no telescopes and didn't see stars other than what they saw with their naked eyes about 1,000, so you realize that they realized, already then, that there was much more than they could see. This is an important idea, that they had important knowledge of galaxies and stars, beyond what people could see.

The 7th Palace in the world of Assiya is called Aravot, which is the highest Palace in the 'Heaven' of the world of Action, which is symbolically referred to as 'the clouds'. This 7th Palace of Aravot, corresponds to the three upper Sefirot (of the 10) namely Keter (10th sefira), Chochma (9th) and Bina (8th) in the general scheme of Sefirot in the tree of life. All these 3 are like one, not like arms or legs which work separately, but like a head. The 6th Palace corresponds to 7th Sefira of Chesed, and the 5th Palace to Gevura, and so on with Tiferet, Netzach and Hod. And then you have the palace of the Rakia which is like the Sefira of Yesod.

So why do we talk so much about the Palace of Rakia/Yesod and the lower Vilon/Malchut and not about the higher ones? This is because the earth always gets much more energy sent down from the lower worlds than from the higher ones. Most energy from above is brought down by the two lowest Palaces (1st and 2nd) to earth because they are the roots of this world. Many astrologers are not automatically led to the obvious conclusion of God's omniscience and involvement in our world and our lives. It is possible to read book after book, and see that astrologers ask themselves, how do all these planets, stars and all of astrology reveal the truths that they do? They come up with all sorts of theories except the most obvious which is at the root of Torah astrology, which is that it is God who does this. For example, Carl Jung, a famous psychologist, gives the idea of Synchronicity, which I really don't understand, but its not addressing the main issue of God and his involvement in our world. Other people have their own theories as to why astrology works. But according to Judaism it is not really a question, it is a given that God created and runs the world. And He chose to run it through this intricate model, where he doesn't send things down directly to people, unless he chooses to do so.

So the next question is why did God create the world this way, where he doesn't directly provide things to people, and instead makes it go via many worlds before we get it? The basic answer to this is that due to the sin of the First man Adam, the delivery system was changed. God saw that people would not be able to receive things directly from Him; it would be too much for them, so he created messengers. Its works just like governments work, where there is a king, who has ministers and different agents and messengers. A farmer knows about the king only from the state senator, who knows the governor who would eventually get to the king. So in the same way God created the astrological system to gradually reveal His light through a hierarchy, for the human to slowly and gradually receive it. In the same way symbolically, humans could see what was somehow close to them, and then, gradually, by building telescopes, they discovered galaxy after galaxy, and become able to see more worlds. So astrology can connect you to the upper worlds and to God, and, on the other hand, it can be used by people only for their own benefits and drag them down. Today, many people use astrology to become rich and have more power, instead of using it as a ladder up to the higher worlds. In Jewish astrology, our goal is not to cut off any powers which came down from their sources and use them for our own benefit; one reason is that it makes no

sense to do this since Astrology and the planets are in fact the final stage of a long journey starting much higher up in the upper worlds.
So which Zodiac technique is preferable; The Tropical or Sidereal system?
One of the main arguments against astrology is that when we refer to the 8th Galgal/sphere as the "fixed stars" (the Zodiac), this not a very accurate name, since the fixed stars do move ! But this is not a good criticism since our sages knew about this movement but also knew that they moved very slowly, and are 'fixed stars' in our life time. When a person looks at the stars, they seem to stay at one place, but over 70 years or so, it would be obvious that they have moved. They move a degree over about every 72 years. So after a couple of thousand years, they would move about 20 or 30 degrees. So there are basically two models that address this issue: One model is taking into account the movement of the stars in calculating the Zodiac, and this is mainly used in Indian or Hindu astrology, and according to them, the planets and sun are about 24 degrees earlier than in Western astrology, because they take into account the movement of the stars. But in Western astrology, the tropical zodiac is underlined by a different system which is based on the four seasons and the sun: This is calculated by the two times when the days (night and day) are equal in hours and when the day is the shortest and when it is the longest compared to the night (vernal equinox ect..). So that means it is calculated according to what degree the Sun is in. So this is a major argument in astrology, which is the correct method?
I would like to quote 2 Torah books that deal with this subject. One book is Sefer Hatechuna, written by Rabbi Hayim Vital, and the second is in Migdal Oz, written by Rabbi Yaavetz. In Judaism, there is a problem if you go according to the Sidereal zodiac (Hindu) because Pesach has to fall in Spring time, and it must fall in the month of Nisan. And if you take the movement of the stars into account, I think in the last couple of years, it moved out of the spring time. So Rabbi Hayim Vital deals with this in Sefer Hatechuna, and he mentions that when the world was created, the 8th and the 9th Galgalim (Chochma and Bina) were exactly parallel to each other, they where in perfect sinc. The starting point of each one was zero degrees Aries, and every 30 degrees there was a new constellation: Taurus, Gemini etc, until there was a 360 degree sphere. So that is how it was engraved in the 9th Galgal/Sphere, and that it also why it was possible to see what was in the 9th because it was projected in the lower 8th Galgal (which was incorporated in the 9th); so these two Galgalim/Spheres initially were together in the distant past, and with time they slowly separated and are no longer in sync. We Jews go according to the 9th Galgal/Sphere, the Galgal Hayomi (Chochma), which doesn't move, except for completing it daily circles (and therefore we use the Chart of Adam and Eve). And this 9th Galgal/Sphere is exactly where it originally was when it was first created, and the other people go according to the 8th Galgal where the fixed stars move, which is the firmament of Bina, and this is known today as the Sidereal system. A Rabbi known as the Yaavetz says that during the Flood these two Galgalim/Spheres (the 8th and 9th) were at the same degree of alignment, and from that time on they were separated by a degree each 72 years. And again, he emphasizes that the 9th Galgal is fixed and remains fixed to its original state and energies, and doesn't move at all except for its daily encirclement. This is an important idea, because I see and hear of a lot of people talking about it, saying this is right and the others are wrong, but in fact each doctrine can be explained logically. So Torah astrology works according to the Tropical Zodiac, because the 9th wheel is higher than and encompasses the eighth wheel.

Chapter 2

It important to know where the energies coming down are originating from, but just as important is understanding how these energies are received. How do people receive these energies? How does the world receive them? Why is everybody different? Can you change the energy that comes down from above? The Zohar talks about different entities here on earth receiving these energies that come down, not just people. But let's start with people, who can get good news or bad news coming down, but it is not only the news that counts, but also how the person receives it and what is his current state of consciousness and makeup. Once a teacher of mine told me a story about his grandfather, who was a great Kabbalist, and one day, after giving a lesson, a women, who was not so modestly dressed and not particularly religious, asked him to give her a blessing. So he replied: 'I can give you a blessing, but can you receive the blessing?'

So everything is basically like a two way street, there are energies coming down and there are energies going up, and there is the question of how we receive these energies and deal with them, and what we send back up.

The book of the Zohar, says that the Earth itself has 7 divisions with their unique influences. Up until now we have been talking mainly about the 'Heaven' and its 7 Palaces of influence (in the world of Assiya), and how they are divided and influence below, as mentioned in the Talmud tractate Chagiga where it describes the world of Assiya as being divided into 'Earth' and 'Heaven', and both are divided into 7 parts all of which influence us. So what are the 7 divisions of the 'Earth' part of the world of Assiya/Action? The Zohar give us 2 opinions, it either means seven areas of climate, where the climate is different from one another, and this is because the source of energy it receives is from a different parts of Heaven, from different Palaces, and so you get different people, different animals and vegetation and minerals, in one area and they are different from the people and things in another clime. The second way is explained in that the earth itself is divided into seven layers: There is the Outer Layer, and there are inner and inner layers, until you get to the centre of Earth. And each layer is related to a different Palace above in Heaven.

So the Zohar of Vayikra/Leviticus Daf 9b says: "Rabbi Yehuda opened and began. And he said: "And God said, let there be a firmament inside the water, and let it be between the waters". Come and see (and realize), when God created the world, He created seven firmaments up (in Heaven) and He created seven earths/lands down below (on Earth). And He created seven seas (or oceans) seven rivers, seven days, seven weeks, seven times seven, which are the days between the festivals of Passover and Shavuot, the seven year Shemita cycle of working the Land, and the seven times seven years' cycle of Freedom, which ends with the Jubilee, when everybody is set Free, and the seven thousand years that the world exists. And God is in the seventh of everything, in the seventh level (of everything). Seven firmaments above, and in each are different stars, constellations, objects created as servants, suns, planets and chariots on top of chariots, which belong to the ministering Angels, who rule over different things in the world, so they can receive whatever comes from God's Kingdom, which is above them. Some of the angles have six 'wings' each, some have four each, some have four faces each, some have two, some one. One of these heavenly objects is of hot fire, from the side of Angel Gabriel. Some of them come from water, and they come from Angel Michael. Some are made out of air, from Angel Uriel; as is written: "He makes his Angels like spirit, His servants as burning fire. All these firmaments are one on top of the other, like an onion and its layers, which is divided into different parts. And each firmament/palace makes a tremendous sound, out of fear of the Master (God), who is above everything, and whose sound makes them stand and move, and everything is run by His power and Strength". The Zohar then goes on to propose 2 answers to what the 7 parts of the

'Earth' are; the first theory is that the seven parts of earth are seven lands/climates, and they are like seven different worlds, but all these parts all have people who dwell on them. The difference between these lands is that some are higher and some are lower. And the land of Israel is the highest, and Jerusalem is higher than the rest of Israel. This is meant in a spiritual way even though it is on Earth. But whatever grows in one part is different from what grows in the other (of the seven parts). The arctic area compared to the desert areas, and the people in Africa will look different than the people in China, because every part of those seven lands/climates receives energy from different sources above in Heaven. The second theory is that there are seven layers to the earth. Six of these worlds are all found below the surface of the earth. And there is a firmament that divides each of them from the other. So we humans on the top layer on earth get the full impact of the 7 upper Heavens, and the ones below only get from one above. And the different lands have 7 names. In the middle of all this is the Garden of Eden and Hell and there are different types of 'creatures' in each layer of the earth, just as there are different objects in each of the seven Palaces/firmaments in 'Heaven'. Some of the creatures of the lower layers have four faces, some two and some have one face each, and none of them look alike, creatures of each level look different to those of the other. This Zohar explains that the first man Adam and his children were all on the 1st level of earth, which is called Tevel. The other 6 layers are made from the different Palaces of Heaven and also from the fire inside the earth and the spinning of the planets and the shedim {demons}, which make up the different creatures in the lower world.

In another Zohar called Tikuney HaZohar (another book of the Zohar, by Rabbi Shimon Bar Yochai), it goes further and takes a different approach and says that the first man Adam did in fact fall down to each of the 7 Lands, and in each earth he had seminal emissions, and for each one of these emissions he formed and created, together with a female demon called Lilit, all these different creatures, which inhabit the lands below. So everything down here is influenced by the forces coming from above. So what is the reason that man is at the highest level on earth? It is because just like God is above the Heaven, Man is also at the top of his world. After the 7 sefirot is the Throne of God with the image of the man, and above all that is where God sits, and as it is above so it is below, and in this world too, the human is like a king on a throne of all creatures on Earth/Tevel.

Rabbi Moshe Kordovero explains that Rav Hamnuna, who was a righteous man from the Zohar, actually got punished because he didn't believe the Zohar's teachings of the seven layers, and he became shipwrecked and he then fell down to the lower levels, and saw all different creature and things, and when he came back he repented for not believing in the Zohar's teachings on these creatures. And today even the greatest Rabbis find it hard to believe it. Sometimes things seem impossible to believe, and yet on a certain level you should believe. In any case, one should remember that there are things which are beyond our ability to understand. But we still have to believe these things, because we trust our Sages. And they tell us these things are there.

My teacher Rabbi Mordachai Sharabi, the Rosh Yeshiva of Nahar Shalom, the River of Peace, explained a saying from the Zohar that one should not learn Kabala before the age of forty. That means that up to 40, one should learn the basic models, and after 40, when one thinks more seriously and has self-control and understanding he can then get a bit of a glimpse about what these models mean and why they exist. But we should note that many of the best Kabbalists did not live past the age of 40, so many must have started at an early age. Energies are coming down to earth and affect each area as it reaches it. The Horoscope or Chart of Adam, the first man, has 12 Houses, and each house rules a different area of life and each House is ruled by a specific Planet. Jupiter was the planet of wisdom in the horoscope of the first man, Adam HaRishon, and Jupiter is found in the 9th house and the 12th house. The

12th House is the house of suffering, and the 9th house is the house of higher knowledge, Knowledge that comes from above you, the knowledge you got from your teachers, who got it from their teachers and so on until they got it from God. There are 2 types of Wisdoms, the one that is passed down from generation to generation which is of the 9th house and there is Wisdom from suffering which is passed down from the 12th house; unfortunately, people often learn the most from their sufferings; when things go well, people don't learn as much as they learn from when they suffer; and even Rav Hamnuna learned about his mistakes after suffering. And today too, due to the Holocaust, there was a great loss in our teachers of Wisdom who perished en mass, and our line of tradition was seriously compromised due to the break between the generations. And this may be the reason you see today so many people searching all over the world for Wisdom. Certainly my generation went searching all over the world. People grew up in America for example and saw that things were meaningless and desolate of the Wisdom. So knowledge can be passed down from generation to generation, just like Avraham Avinu, passed it down to his son, Yitzchak, who passed it on to Jacob who passed it on the his 12 Sons, who passed it on the Moses etc.....but knowledge can also be received by the efforts of the individual himself through a tremendous amount of learning. But so much got lost in our past generation in the holocaust, it's a miracle that anything is left.

Astrology is a 2 way street. Two people are born on the same minute and place and can receive those forces differently. For example, I do charts over the internet for clients, and often they are what I call blind horoscopes, where I know little or nothing about the client. So I don't know what they are doing with the energies they receive. How are you using the energies you receive? A person is not influenced only by the stars, or by the land he grew in, but also by his environment and belief system and background. A person who grew up in a rich family is more likely to be rich than a person who didn't, though they may have been born in the same place at the same time. And there are also differences between the ways people receive energies that come to them. People are influenced, to a high degree, by their schooling, by their religious education or a secular influence etc.. If 2 women both have a great chart for children, to the religious one I can tell her she can have 7 kids, and the one with a secular background I would say it differently, something like she could have as many kids as she wants, but it does not mean she will have lots of kids. She could change her mazal by free choice and have few children. So the Zohar is trying to tell us that over and above the energies that come down to us from Heaven, so are there energies that influence us on Earth and it comes down to how people take both these energies and use them; how to properly receive the light. People are different and are influenced differently. My Wife's parents were born in Persia, while she was born in Israel, so there are different mentalities which means its not just what is coming down, but involves working out how to properly receiving that light and improve ourselves and use it properly. A person can change his mazal (his Planetary influences) and improve his life, but it is not easy to change our selves, the way we act, feel and think. But we can learn how to improve our destinies, how to use the energies and lights that come to us in a better way.

You have to know also that, in the system of the Ari Z"L, there is the laws of the Igulim (circles) and the laws of Yosher (straight lines). In Kabbala there are circles and straight lines. Circles represent the world of nature and it's the world that is run by the different forces of nature, elements and the planetary systems. The Yosher system (straight lines) is the Torah and Kabbala system, a system of Divine intervention separate from the Laws of the Igulim. There is plenty of light coming down, but not every vessel can receive all of it. So you have to make yourself a vessel which is able to receive the light properly.

Chapter 3

If you look through today's literature, you cannot see much on Jewish astrology. And, as we have mentioned in the past, this lack is in all areas of Jewish scholarship science and art, so it is not just in astrology. There is a period of about 1500 years in our past history when according to the thinkers in Western world, there are almost no Jewish books of any significance from that period, even though many Jews lived amongst them and wrote many great books. This period started around the time the Talmud up until the time of the enlightenment and the emancipation from the Ghettos, when some Jews gradually became secular, in the late 1700s and early 1800s, then you suddenly see the descendants of all those Jewish writers, from Carl Marx to Spinoza, Einstein and Freud, and all the other Jewish thinkers who 'suddenly came to the world'. But where were all these Jewish writers and thinkers during all that period before the enlightenment, starting from the end of the Talmud onwards? What happened to the Jewish writers during the dark-ages? Who are they? Were Jews only farmers during that time? This is an interesting topic, and when you look into it, you realize that a tremendous amount of Jewish literature had been written in this period, yet a lot has been lost, especially to my generation who do not study them. If you look at Muslim and Christian religious philosophy, none of them really ever denied that the Jews used to be the chosen people, but they all say that they lost this status, and these new religions were chosen later as replacements, after the Jews were abandoned. In contrast, the Holocaust is being denied today by some people, who say it never happened, and that the Jews made it all up. The leader of the Palestinian Authority wrote his doctorate claiming that the Holocaust was a myth. So they are already denying the holocaust and it happened less than 100 years ago, but when it comes to the revelation of God to the Jews at Mount Sinai, nobody of any significance throughout history denied that God revealed the Torah to the Jews. In ancient history, we have no claims that Jews made it up, or were on drugs or anything like that. They just came along, some hundreds of years afterwards, and began a new story that the Jews messed up, didn't behave properly, and therefore God chose others to replace them, but they never denied the truth about the Torah. But in Judaism, religious Jews always held that even though Jews sometimes messed up, and were punished and were exiled, every Jew should still repent and wait for God to redeem us, for God will never completely desert His chosen people, with whom He made an eternal covenant. But not all was lost, and if you look, you will see that there is tremendously profound Jewish literature from all those lost years (the dark ages), and there are great books. When I was introduced to these books I was astounded, to see how many books had been written over this period and totally ignored, and how much of Jewish religious thinking exists through these books reaching back into the middle ages. And just like they were written off from history, so I think the same thing happened when you look deeply into astrology, and you realize that obviously astrology comes from the Torah, from the five books of Moses and from Adam Harishon, whom I would like to talk about today.

Avraham Avinu (Abraham) watched the movement of the stars, and through them he realized that there is one God; so he got to know God through astrology. Seeing the stars he said, look, they move and affect things down here! So why is this? And he came to the conclusion that such a vast universe has to be run by God, and through these intermediaries he communicates with humanity. So the subject and the question of why God chose to run the world through planets and firmaments, is important. And this is a deep subject which the Kabbalists talk about. If you study non-Jewish astrology, you realize that regular astrologers don't even ask the question of why God runs the world through astrology. All that the deep thinkers and philosophers of non-Jewish astrology ask and discuss is the question of why astrology works, but not the questions of Why is there such a thing as astrology? Or what is the purpose of the planets indicating what happens on earth? We should keep in mind that astrology is an idea accepted in the all parts of the world throughout history: The Greeks, the Romans, the Medieval Arabs and all other peoples and cultures all had astrology. And I don't think there is any exception. All grew up with and through astrology.

Academics tell us that astrology started in Babylon. So one may ask; how did astrology start and spread throughout the world? How did people accept it, and how did people realize that the planets have influence over the earth? If you look at the twelve constellations of the Zodiac, we see that it was drawn in symbols/diagrams. So one may conclude that the original founder of these 12 symbols may have seen the stars and drew lines connecting them, and from these lines came the symbols of the constellations/zodiac. Otherwise then, how did people around the whole world come to accept those principles in astrology and these connections of the stars, if they lived in different geographical areas with different views of the skies? And yet astrology all over the world agrees with the zodiac of 12 symbols.

So where does astrology actually came from? I have a hard time with this idea that it is of a Babylonian origin or that a few smart people came along, and drew the lines connecting the stars, made up other principles, and then the whole world just accepted all that without arguing and disagreeing with the fundamental questions. So I would like to give a completely different explanation, which people may not accept, but I would like to show a deep connection between the Bible and Jewish astrology.

My main astrology teacher, was a great astrologer, a very deep thinker and an extraordinary person, whom I met when I was 22 years old. He originally came from Hungary, his original name was Zoltan Schnitzner, and when he came to New York he became known as Zoltan Mason. And he was a preeminent astrologer and book collector in America at that time. He was great in many areas, and I could give a whole lesson about him. But Zoltan Mason once told me that the real source of astrology is the Bible where the subject is mostly concealed. I have found that sometimes in the Bible astrology can actually be found in the simple meaning. Over the years, as I lived and studied in Jerusalem, I came to really see that many things in astrology are found in the Torah.

If you believe in astrology, you have to believe in the Torah; this is what I think, and if you don't believe in the Bible, then many things in astrology will not be available to you, and/or not make sense to you. You might think you have the Truth, but you are off course from the source.

Archetypes are at the heart of understanding the Zodiac, and this universal Zodiac is basically the horoscope of the first human creature, Adam and Eve. When astrologers talk about astrology, they talk about the Zodiac, which starts with Aries which is the first house, which is basically about the personality of the person, and moves to Taurus, which is about money, and then the third house which is Gemini, and how people communicate since Gemini is the constellation of communication. In Jewish mystical astrology everything is learned from the Archetypal Chart of Adam. I think that today all astrologers accept the idea that there is this Archetypal Chart. And I will tell you why? Let us read a little in the Bible, where it discusses the world's creation, and how the first man was created. Regarding the creation of the first man, it is said: “God breathed a soul in man, and then He took one of his ribs and made the first woman, and they were the first couple and were called Adam and Eve”. And rabbis asked some questions, one of which is, why did God start the world with one couple, and not with more? And they explain that the reason God started the world with one couple is so that no one could say, “my ancestors were better than yours”, or “I am from a better source (chart) then you”, a scenario in which there would be no united universality, and where there would not be one science to understand human beings and other creatures and objects. This idea is called the Archetype chart. Without that, there could not be one science, one psychology or any kind of unity for all human beings in astrology. So when astrologers talk about the archetypal chart of the Zodiac, they automatically assume that the human race started with one couple. And the Rabbis explain this as being Gods way of making sure that one could not say to the other, "my Father is greater than yours".

For example, by this archetypal chart, it is accepted that the Aries rising is the idea of the Aries person, a courageous person, who fears nothing and always goes for and achieve what he wants, a strong personality etc., in other words, the ideal male person. A Pisces person (12th house), on the other hand, thinks and hesitates to much before doing anything, so it would be hard for such a person to achieve things, and such a person would have more difficulty in life. So the ideal chart of Adam Harishon was of an Aries person. The word Archetype in Latin means the original man, so indeed Adam Harishon was the Archetype. Even though everyone is different from everybody else there is one universal understanding of man in astrology, irrespective of race or creed, due to the Archetypal Chart. So believing in astrology automatically means and leads to believing in the Bible, or at least in this part of the Torah, where the story of the beginnings of the human race is discussed (in Genesis). Astrology started with Adam and Eve, who were the ideal couple with the ideal horoscope, and it did not start with some Babylonian. Eve's horoscope is different from Adams in that her ascendant is not on Aries but on the other side, Libra, but this is a discussion for another time. When the first man (Adam Harishon) sinned, God decided to use the planetary system to deliver His energies to human beings and the rest of the world. The world started in the Middle East, and later the world migrated to Babylonia, Iraq of today, there all people gathered, tried to build the Tower of Babel, gather all humanity around themselves and become one race. So they made God angry with them, because they tried to rebel against Him, and He scattered them around the world, and mixed up their languages. Until that time, they all had one language, which is Hebrew, but after that, other languages emerged, and people started speaking different languages. There are scientists who believe that all languages started from one original language, though they hold that the original language was Zulu, not Hebrew, but in any case, if you look through the researches of all kinds of scientists, archaeologists, anthropologists, DNA experts, genetics etc., you see that they conclude that humanity originated from one couple. Since they have no other reference point, many call this couple Adam and Eve, though they still debate the question of where Adam and Eve Came from: Africa, or other places. This is the idea of Mono-genesis.

Just like people everywhere have accepted the idea of the week being divided into 7 days, and nowhere is there a week with more or less days. And so is the number ten and all the system of mathematics being divided and multiplied by ten. Though today computers have a system based on two. I think the only logical explanation of everyone accepting these systems is, due to all these being originated and written in the Bible. So the Seven Day Week is an archetypal system. And so is the number ten, for example, 10 times God said: "Let there be" and there was.

Now I would like to read to you the Zohar of Bereshit (Genesis) the First book of the Zohar, page 37, the second side (according to the Hebrew edition) where it says: "Said Rabbi Aba (who was one the students of the writer of the Zohar, Rabbi Shimon Bar Yochai), it is clear to me that a book came down to the first man, and through this book he learned the high wisdom, and this book is given to the children of God, wise people of each generation. And the ones who have the privilege to learn from it and know the high knowledge realize what the whole world is all about, and this book came down through the master of the secrets, who is the Angel Raziel, the chief Angel, who taught this wisdom from his book to Adam Harishon, the first man. Adam Harishon received this book when he sinned and then repented. In fact, there were three angels who were somewhat involved in teaching the first man, Adam. And when Adam Harishon was deported from the Garden of Eden, he held on dearly to this book. And as he went out (of the Garden of Eden), the book flew away from him, so he prayed and cried before the master of the universe, and so he received the book again the same way he received it the first time. The reason he was given back the book was so that this wisdom would not be forgotten from human beings, and they would study it in order to know their master well. So this special book contains secrets of wisdom, which today have been distributed and can be learned. And I think anyone who studies astrology should be aware of the place of the astrological system in the greater scheme of existence. Because with a naked eye one can see only about a thousand stars, and yet with telescopes we know today that there are billions of stars. Learn from the symbolism. And if you look at astrology as having its source in the Torah, you can then better understand how historically the whole world accepted it, along with the 7 day week system, and the significance of the number 10. You can see that all these ideas are all biblical in origin. I think most astrologers today don't see it this way, and this is unfortunate.

Contemporary Rabbis on Astrology

Contemporary Rabbis on Astrology

By Yaakov Kronenburg

A transcription of a short discussion on Rav Yaakov Moshe Hillel comments (Rabbi of Yeshivat Ahavat Shalom) on astrology in an English edition of his work and the strong response and criticism from Rav Yitzchak Kadouri, Dean of Kabbalists in Israel in the 1990's, the oldest living Kabbalist in the generation and considered the master Kabalist of his time.

Contemporary Rabbis on Astrology

By Yaakov Kronenberg

I am going to be talking about the contemporary approach to astrology according to Jewish law and we are going to bring down the opinion of several rabbis, what they hold, concerning astrology in our generation.

I am going to start with the book, by Rav Yaakov Moshe Hillel. He is the rabbi of Yeshivat Ahavat Shalom. He is considered one of the preeminent Kabbalists of our generation. He wrote a book called "Tamim teheyu" and in that book he discusses all the different arts, what is called today, kabbalat maasit (practical application of kabbala). All the different things that a person does to improve their quality of life, or to see into the future... He talks about amulets, is it permitted to use an amulet, something you wear around your neck, in order to find the right girl, or to make money or to cure an illness… He discusses all the matters concerning astrology, palmistry, bringing back the dead to ask them questions. Whatever you want he talks about all of them in this book. I think just about all of them he holds that they are forbidden. The problem with the book is that it was written with the aim of… At the time he wrote the book, there was a big problem in the religious world that all sorts of strange people were coming along that weren't religious. They didn't know Torah or Kabbalah or nothing and they were claiming to be big mystics, big Kabbalists, big rabbis and they were going to help you solve your problems and they were going to tell you what's going to be and all sorts of things like that. And they were basically doing it to cheat poor people out of their money. A lot of religious people tend to be gullible and they are also not very wealthy because they devote their life to learning and praying so they don't have a lot of money. So they were going off to these people claiming to be big souls and they were getting cheated out of their money and worse, sometimes it caused them spiritual damage and things like that.

So the main reason he wrote the book was to try to convince people to stay away from things like this. And in the beginning of the book (the book has been translated into English, I don't remember the name of it) but the Hebrew version after he translated it into English, he wrote a more detailed Hebrew version because a lot of people complained about what he wrote especially about astrology and palmistry because again it was a polemic to get people to not go to these people so people argued with a lot of his conclusions.

Also in the book what was not in the English version are approbations by leading rabbis of the generation approving the book. And in all of their approbations they all say that the main aim of the book was to get people to stay away from these astrologers, but they were also leaning towards forbidding all of these things probably because of the reason we mentioned.

I want to start with one of the letters in the book by Rav Yitzchak Kadouri. He was the Dean of Kabbalists. He was the oldest living Kabbalist in the generation and he was widely regarded as THE Kabbalist and so he argues with Rav Hillel. He says "mah pitom, l you say all these things are forbidden? Look, I write amulets. What are you telling wrong? I have it from my teacher, he has it from his teacher, and I have real amulets that really work. What are you telling me?" And he brings down also from other sources that it is permitted. He also talks about knowing the future and things like that. And goralot which are lots which is also similar to astrology, to know the future.

I'm going to translate it quickly out of the Hebrew. I looked at the whole book "Tamim teheyu" and also the approbations that the big rabbis wrote. And all of them in one voice they forbidded amulets and lots. And Rav Hillel, he brings all of the rabbis, the early rabbis and the later rabbis that forbade all these things and you see how vast his knowledge is of all the Torah. The simple understanding and the Kabbalistic understanding and he talks about how it is forbidden to do things using the Kabbalah. And the punishment that goes with it.

I'm not going to talk about amulets here because that doesn't concern us. And not too much on what he talks about on lots. They also were fixed by the prophets in the time of the 2nd Temple, they were already using things like that because the prophecy was already starting to be diminished. The prophetic voice and the ruach hakodesh, the holy spirit which is a level a little bit below prophecy. And anyway the rabbis at the time, at the 2nd Temple they were already losing the prophecy from God and they were losing this holy spirit which sometimes descended on them. So at times they had to resort to lots and astrology. And these methods of lots that are connected to Ezra HaSofer, to Hezghia HaMelech, to Chamai Gaon, to Rashi, to Ibn Ezra, each had a book, and Rabbi Chaim Vital had a book on it and even the Rashash did and you see Rabbi Shlomo Sharabi, the preeminent Kabbalist of the late 1700s and most of the Kabbalah today is built on his teachings. Even he has a text on lots in his prayer book. And Rav Hillel published that book and wrote an approbation permitting it! So what is going on?

I'm going to skip a little of what he wrote because it's not important to us and go on. Coming back to the book of our friend, my dear friend, the important big rabbi in Kabbalah, Rav Hillel, who no secret is hidden from him and all his intention is to do good, to save his people, Am Yisrael, from these men who are using magic and demons to show their power. And they are tricking the people to come to them and they are requesting a lot of money and they are making them take oaths and sometimes they mix the holy with the profane and demons with the holy angels and sometimes they cause great damage to the ones that ask them and the people they don't even feel the damage done to them. And the amulets that they make are only quackeries and because of this you should stay away from all these people.

And certainly Rav Hillel did a great thing that he wrote this book and I bless him that everything will go well with him in his life etc. etc. So you see from this, I'll tell you what my teacher in America said. Once I asked him why the Rambam was so against astrology. He told me like this. My teacher could say a book in a sentence. He told me that the Rambam wasn't against astrology, he was against astrologers. And that's what the same thing Rav Kadouri is saying here. Look, it's a book of polemics. Really you know. See I have a tradition to do amulets from my teacher Rav Yehuda Fataya who from his teacher the Ben Ish Hai going back generations. And you see that lotteries are cast, I didn't mention, lotte cast 93 times in the Tanach, in the Torah. We have a tradition, but yeah. The problen astrologers, the palmists, who are they. The people who are coming they know nothing, and the people who do know are in hiding. If I remember, I went to a couple of the big rabbis of our generation and they all permitted me to do astrology. Even one big rabbi, the head of a yeshiva, a Lithuanian rabbi, permitted me to predict the future. And it's interesting; in the book a lot of it is more against the practitioners then against the practise. I was just looking in the book and I see there was a little approbation by Rav Sternbach, he was the Chief Rabbi of South Africa, and while I'm pretty sure, I don't have the book with me to reference it but he wrote a book of questions and answers years ago and he permitted people to go to palmists. And now I'm looking at his letter of approbation and in that letter he says the true palmistry has been lost… I remember he permitted palmistry so probably he would also permit Astrology. And I've been to big rabbis who permitted me to practise astrology. So in that letter, in his approbation here he says "from the stand point of Jewish law it is permitted to go to palmists. But it is my feeling that the real palmistry has been lost". You know today the people who practise palmistry don't really know it. If you look in the Zohar, the Zohar teaches palmistry, and they have a whole section of the Zohar that talks about the laws of palmistry, many pages there in the chapter Jethro. So he went back a little on what he said that I guess you can go but the real palmistry has been lost. And I think the Lubavitche Rebbe also had a theory like that. Which I think is also true in astrology; a lot of the real astrology has been lost. And it is work to find it and our work is to find the lost tradition.

The basic model of the Universe

Esoteric Astrology

By Yaakov Kronenberg

An edited transcription of a series of lectures given in Jerusalem on how to determine your fate and how to turn it into your chosen destiny. This system uses ancient techniques to enhance ones strengths and recognize ones weaknesses in his mazal, and begin the process of solving ones problems, not through psychology and mantras, but through the ancient wisdom of Torah and Kabbala embedded in the horoscope of Adam Harishon.

Esoteric Astrology

By: Yaakov Kronenberg

Tonight I am going to start a new series of classes on Jewish esoteric astrology. The main focal point of this series is to introduce to the reader the idea that through understanding and studying the horoscope of Adam and Eve the first man and women, we can tap into the ancient Jewish wisdom that was passed down from the time of Adam, generation after generation, until our time and using this knowledge we can provide true guidance to our clients to help them alleviate their problems. I once saw in a medieval text that the author claimed there are two systems in which are embedded all the knowledge of the Torah, one is the Kabbala and the other astrology. In latter classes I will explain why the need for two systems.

Western astrology today is very psychological oriented; the astrologer tries to flesh out the inner persona of the client using astrology and then proceeds to try to help them using the tools of psychology. It is not concerned so much with predicting the future as helping the person to understand himself. In the nineteen eighties along came a movement to reintroduce ancient astrology and make it more prediction oriented, they began by translating and printing ancient texts which were lost to those who could not read the ancient tongues, and tried to find which predictive techniques worked and which did not. However they did not deal with the question of how to help the client overcome his or her destiny, in a new way.

Indian astrology seems more prediction orientated and when they see bad times coming for a client they try to help them in one of two ways. For less serious problems they give the client jewels to wear to change the energy of the afflicted planet. For more serious problems they advise the clients to say mantras to the planets which is like praying to the planets, supplicating them not to be so destructive. This is very close to idol worship and is probably forbidden according to Jewish law. (see my translation of the letter of Rabbi Abraham Bar Hiya)

So I am going to introduce a new idea, and that is that in Jewish astrology we try to find the answers to people's problems through working with the zodiac. And the zodiac of Adam and Eve tells you all you need to know about the world. And from using it, you can start understanding how to help people with their problems.

My teacher told me that there are two parts to astrology: One is to understand the person, which is not so hard. And the second part is to be able to help the person, and to help the person is very hard.

So by giving you the introduction to the horoscope of Adam and Eve, we will start seeing how to use the zodiac in a way to help people with their problems. And tonight we are going to talk about one subject in the horoscope of Adam and Eve called, in mystical astrology, 'squaring the circle'. And it is based on the number ten. In Kabbala and in astrology, ten is the number for Completion. You count from one to nine, and then ten is the Completion, and you start over again with eleven, which starts the second round of counting. So ten is the completion of everything, and so every house has a completion ten houses away from it. This works both ways, Counter-Clockwise and also Clockwise. Counter-Clockwise is looking at things from the Material perspective and Clockwise is

looking at it from the Spiritual perspectve of the chart. We also often refer to this as going Forward (Counter-Clockwise) or Backwards (Clockwise) in the Chart or Horoscope.
For example, if you start from the first house, which is the person's Ascendant, which is house number 1, then if you go Forward (Counter-Clockwise), its completion would be ten houses away, and that would be the 10th house, which is the person's career, his destiny. Then you start from the 10th house, and we go another ten houses Forward (Counter-Clockwise), and you come to the 7th house. So the 7th house is ten houses away from the 10th house. And then from the 7th house, if you go ten houses, you come to the 4th house. And the 4th house is the house of the home. The 1st house is the person, himself, the 10th house is his career, the 7th is the person's marriage partner, and the 4th is his home. And that is what is called 'squaring the circle'. So that way we have touched all 4 angles of the horoscope, while circling the chart.
And now, let us look at it again. I am going to show you that when you go Forward or in a Counter-Clockwise way you are talking about things manifesting in a more material and physical way, in a worldly way. For example, the house next to the first house, if you are going Forward (Counter-Clockwise), is the 2nd house, which is the house of money. And so already here you can see that the Counter clockwise way reveals the material aspect of life because money (2nd house) is what the person (1st house) needs to make it in this world. In order to have a good time in this world, and fulfill your needs, the first thing you need is money. So to see the material manifestation of the chart, you go Forward (Counter-Clockwise), and from the 1st house to the 2nd, to the 3rd house, to the 4th etc., one by one. Now if you go the other way, Backwards or Clockwise, from the 1st house to the 12th house and then the 11th house etc., you are talking about things manifesting in a more Spiritual way. For example, if you go Backwards from the 1st house, you get the 12th house, which is the house of the secret enemies. My teacher once told me: What is the worst enemy of the person, do you think it is a person's body? No, it's the soul. The body wants the pleasures of this world, and the soul doesn't. It wants to get back to its source in the upper worlds, and it wants to stay pure. And this is one reason it is called the house of the secret enemy, because it is the house of the soul. In other words, the 12th house and the 1st house make, together, a person; the 1st house is the body, and the 12th is the soul. And if you look at each house, with the house before it going backwards or clockwise, you see they make some logical combinations. So if you take the 'squaring of the circle' system and apply it using the backward or clockwise method (which goes after the soul and a more spiritual approach), then the count of ten houses Clockwise from the 1st house brings you to the 4th house, and if you count another 10 you see that the 4th house fulfills itself in the 7th house, and another 10 you see that the 7th house fulfills itself in the 10th house, and the 10th house fulfills itself in the 1st house. So this is another way of 'squaring of the circle'.
So now let us go back to the forward or Counter-Clockwise method: So the 1st house is the person, who fulfills himself in the 10th house which is the house of career, destiny and future. It is through the future that one actualizes his potential and it is in a career that he fulfills himself. I remember that my teacher Zoltan Mason told me that the first thing he did when he came to New York from Eastern Europe, was to spend the first two years, studying in the public library everything he could about careers, so he could help people find the right career. Because the first thing people ask you, especially in New York, is

‘what is my best career choice’ they are really asking what is the best way for me to fulfill my destiny. So the 1st house fulfills itself with the 10th house of career. And then, what happens when you have a career and a destiny? Well, then once you have the career, somebody will want to join you and became your life partner (7th house). So the 10th house completes itself in the 7th house (house of partners) which is ten houses away from the 10th house. So once you have a way in life and a destiny (10th house), then that will then determine who your husband or wife will be. The more your future looks good, the more you are perceived as desirable, this is going to have a major impact on who your life partner will be. So the 10th house influences the 7th. And then the 7th house fulfills itself ten houses away, in the 4th house, which is the home. So if a person has a good life partner, especially if the person has a good spouse, he will have a home and security. This can be seen in the chart of Adam, where the 7th house is the house of his Eve, and from there they get together have a home life (4th house). Like it is said in the Talmud, where a certain Rabbi said that he never called his wife ‘his wife’, rather he would call his wife ‘his home’. This is because if the wife is good, the person will probably have a good home. Later on, we are going to talk about the differences between the charts of men and those of women, the horoscope of Adam and the horoscope of Eve.

But right now, we want to talk about the idea (using the Forward or Counter clockwise method) that the 7th house fulfills itself in the 4th house. If you have a good spouse (7th), you fulfill yourself in the 4th house, of the home. In other words, a good partner would bring you a home, and then you can have children and raise a family. And the fourth house, besides being the home, is also the person's genetics, a person's parents and past etc. And this 4th house fulfills itself ten houses away, which is in the 1st house. If a person was born with good genes, and his parents raised him properly, he is going to be an excellent child and person (1st house). So you see that the 4th house creates the 1st house, from the person's past and from the parents themselves (4th house) they influence who the child will be. (1st house).

So let us say that a person has problems in his career. Where do you look in the horoscope for somebody who has a career problem? So first you go back and look at the relationship between the 1st house and the 10th house, which is a relationship of cause and the effect; the 1st house is the cause, and the 10th is the effect. So if the person is OK, if he has good character traits, and is diligent etc., then his first house will bring him a good 10th house. But if he has psychological and other problems, or bad character traits, it can impede his career (10th house). So in other words, if a person has a bad 10th house, you don't just look at the 10th house like most astrologers; you go back and look at the cause, which is in the 1st house, which is the person himself. If the person himself is OK, then everything will be good with his career. But if he is not OK, then he would have career difficulties. So that means that if a person has problems in his career, he might have some defect in his personality, or psychological problems or bad character traits, or maybe he is not very bright, or maybe he is very shy, and can't put himself forward, or all sorts of possibilities, which you have to try to find out, in order to help the person, following the guidelines and map of Esoteric astrology. You have to look at who the person is, in order to help him improve his career, and help him find himself, so that he finds a better destiny.

It is also recommendable to go through the zodiac in a Backwards or Clockwise way, the spiritual approach to the zodiac. Thus the 1st house would fulfill itself in the 4th house, the 4th in the 7th, and the 7th in the 10th. In other words, if a person has a good spouse or a good partner (7th), that would help his career, because the 7th house is also ten houses away from the house of career (10th) going Backwards (Clockwise). And there is an expression in America: Behind every successful man stands a good woman. In other words, if the seventh house is good, she is going to help the man be very successful. But today it can be the other way regarding gender types; the woman can go to work all day, and the husband would stay in the house, take care of the cleaning, and look after the children etc., so the wife doesn't have to worry about these things. It works both ways, but I am using the standard archetype right now, but you can understand it either way. Later in other lessons, we can talk about the horoscope of Eve and the horoscope of Adam and the differences. So remember that if a person has career trouble, you first look at the first house and then you look at the seventh house. Because these houses are the causes of a person's career, they determine if the person would be successful in his career or not. And the tenth house fulfills itself in the seventh house. That is because if a person has a good destiny, a good career, then he will have a good life partner, which is in the seventh house. Usually, there will always be somebody who would want to partner with a successful person, one who has a good destiny. They know that if you attach yourself to such a person, who has a good future, the marriage partner will always be satisfied. So now you see again, that if a person has some trouble in getting married, where do you look? You do not only look at the seventh house, the house of marriage, but rather you have to look at the house which is the cause of the seventh house, and that is ten houses before that (backwards), which is the 10th house, the house of the career, the destiny. So if the person has trouble getting married or marital problems or whatever, then you have to look at and work on the tenth house, the house of career, and get him to be more successful in his career choice; and then it would be easier for one to get a life partner. So with this material approach (Forward and Counter-Clockwise), it goes 1st, 10th, 7th and 4th house. Now if you switch to the Backwards and Clockwise method (Spiritual) which is the mystical way, it goes 1st, 4th, 7th, 10th house. So the 4th house is really the cause of the seventh house (while in Forwards or Counter-clockwise, Material, it's the 7th that causes the 4th). And this is a big difference. The 4th house is the house of the home, the house of the family. And you see that in very traditional societies, like in Judaism, the first house fulfills itself in the fourth house, not in the tenth house. This is because in the Jewish religion, you have to look at these things by going Backwards and Clockwise with the chart of Adam Harishon. So the first house fulfills itself and its destiny by having a home, the religious person sets a house based on faith in the Nation of Israel; what in Hebrew is called, 'Bone bayit neeman beYisrael'. And having married and having children, his main destiny would be to keep the religious tradition and to raise his children, and to have children and grand children integrated into the people and religion. And that is the main fulfillment, at least in a spiritual way. So if a person comes from a good family (4th house), he fulfills himself by being able to be attached to another good family, by marrying a woman who comes from a good family (7th house). You see that a lot. In ancient societies, they used to make matches, involving the parents. And even today, in some religious societies in Judaism, you see it a lot, that the parents have a lot of say in choosing the marriage partners. And families who come from the same background have more chances of success. The more the husband and the wife are similar in their beliefs and attitudes the more successful the marriage is likely to become. That is because men and women are very different from each other, to begin with. So much so, that the Talmud says that it is almost a miracle to bring them together in marriage. And so, if they also come from different cultures and backgrounds, different countries or different religions, it would make it much harder for them to be successful in having a proper and successful marriage. So in the more traditional cultures, they have the idea that the parents try to play a role in trying to choose life partners for their children. So sometimes they do the arrangements, and the future couple meets once or twice before the wedding, just to be sure that they are physically ok for each other, and then the marriage takes place. And today, you see that marriages which were made after long pre-marital relationship do not last so long, we see that the divorce rate in America is catastrophic, so I think there is something to be said in favor of arranged marriages. And you still see that the Indians do it also. People who go to India, and study the Indian culture and philosophy and stuff, they see that the Indians practice this way of arranged marriages too.

So there are 2 ways of looking in one's horoscope; from the material way, from the first house you create the career (10th house) or if you go in a more spiritual way (clockwise), you decide to build your home first (4th house). And if your career (10th house) and your home (4th house) are good, then you will attract a great life partner. If your tenth house is good, you have money and a good career and power, you are likely to attract a great partner, in the more physical sense. And if your fourth house is good, you are likely to have a very spiritual type of partner. And if both houses are good, your partner is likely to be good and successful in both ways, spiritually and in a physical sense as the fourth house also influences the seventh house. So a good career and a good home cause a good partner. And depending on the partner (7th house), that would determine what kind of a home you have. If you have a good partner, you would have a good home, but a bad partner will give you a hard time establishing a good home and a family. And so, if you want to really know if the family is good, you should look at the seventh house, which is the house of the marriage partner. Because the first house is of Adam, and the seventh is of Eve, so if the Eve is good, the home will be good. This is in the physical way, but in the spiritual way, we said that the man fulfills himself in establishing a proper home. So you see that it really works comparatively with the woman and the man. What for him is physical would be a spiritual task for her, and what is spiritual to him can be physical to her. I remember in my younger days, I used to learn in a Yeshiva where someone paid me to learn with him. He didn't pay me well, but this is the way life is. And in the end of the month, he would always say, my spirituality is your physicality; my spirituality is to help your physical situation. He figured that spirituality and physicality should fulfill each other.

So the seventh house completes itself in the fourth, as we have mentioned. If the husband and wife are good, it would make a good home. And if you see that there are arguments and other problems in the house, or the children don't get along, you don't just look at the 4th house to solve this, and instead you see that the problem is solved ten houses before or after that, in the houses of the man (1st) and the woman (7th).

Another point I would like to mention in astrology is that if a person has difficulty in finding a spouse, instead of using the material approach of helping him find a spouse by improving his career, we go for the spiritual approach and help him improve his home life and not just his career. I remember trying to help someone who had problems in getting married. I told him, look at your genealogy, maybe you came from a good rabbinic family, because that will up your status in the eyes of the women and that will improve your marriage chances. So you see, it is possible to solve people's problems, not through psychology and mantras, but through the ancient wisdom which is embedded in the horoscope of Adam and Eve.

The 4th house will fulfill itself in the 1st house. If the parents raise the kids properly, the child would grow alright. If there is a problem with the child, you go to the fourth house, and try to see if there are problems with the parents, or maybe genetic problems. But for now, let us say that we are talking about the parents. Remember that every house has multiple meanings, and you can interpret everything that I say in different ways within the broad parameters of the various affairs of each house. You don't have to interpret everything the same way I am learning now. But when something is wrong with the kid, people tend to blame the parents. I used to have a learning partner and he was a professor of psychology in one of the universities in Israel. And he was a child psychologist and he would tell me that you never treat a child unless the parents come with and were also treated. That is because the source of the problems that children have is almost always the parents. Or in a more spiritual way, if the person has problems, his career choice wasn't right. That is because the tenth house is the cause of the first house. The direction a person goes through determines who he is. And if he goes off in a bad way, it would have a detrimental affect on who he is. If a person is not alright, it could be, at least in a spiritual way, because he didn't go in the right path during his lifetime. Maybe he went off to a different religion, or to a profession that didn't suit him, all sorts of things, and that got him off the path, and that determined who he is in a detrimental way.

And this is what is called 'squaring the circle'. Because we are talking about the four angles of the circle: The first, the fourth, the seventh and the tenth houses, each one being ninety degrees away from the other; so the four of them together make a square within a circle. So this is called in Jewish astrology, 'squaring the circle'. These are the main areas in life. These are the main Angles of life, because these 90 degree Angels determine the most important houses. And the signs in the angles are all the cardinal signs: On the first house there is an Aries, on the seventh there is Libra, on the tenth Capricorn, and on the fourth Cancer.

Adam Harishon was an ideal person; he had an ideal chart, with his Aries rising. And Aries rising is a cardinal sign, and the nature of a cardinal sign is to be goal oriented, to go after a goal in his lifetime. And the Aries sign is a fire sign, and it is cardinal. This fire sign has a lot of power and energy, one with such a sign desires to go up in the world, and is fearless. The Aries is a Martian sign, and is not afraid to go after what he wants. So again, we have to talk about the question of whether the chart of Adam also applies to women, or maybe women are more from a Libra rising, or maybe they should be a combination of both. We are going to see that the first and seventh houses form an axis, and are really the opposites of each other, and always exchange their energy. The first house is always influenced by the seventh, and the seventh by the first. The man becomes his wife and the wife becomes her husband. If you look at couples at their middle ages, you see they start to look alike. This is because the interchange is ongoing all the time, and one becomes like the other. So it is a deep matter, which we have to spend some more time on, this relationship between men and women. Adam Harishon had an Aries rising, and this is the ideal nature of how a man should be. He should be martial, goal oriented, going after what he wants, fearless, full of fire and enthusiasm and drive. And suddenly a baby boy is born under the constellation of Pisces, which is a feminine sign, which is the opposite of the assertive Aries masculine sign. A male, in astrology, doesn't mean specifically a man. It means the character of a male, the male archetype of being an initiator, one who starts things. A female sign is more passive, more accepting and receptive. But when a Pisces boy is born, it means that he would be more accepting, receptive and passive, so he would have the difficulty of having a feminine ascendant. It is more comfortable for a man to have a masculine ascendant. In the Jewish religion, when a woman is pregnant, you bless her husband that he should have a masculine boy, a 'ben zachar'. How can that be? After all, a boy is masculine!! So I think what they mean is that the boy should be a boy born in a time which gives him a masculine ascendant. That way he will feel more comfortable in his gender type which is masculine in nature. And for example if a male has Pisces or Taurus as an ascendant, which are the most feminine, then maybe he would not feel masculine enough. And the same thing applies with a woman who has an Aries rising; where I have seen that these women with Aries rising could feel that they are not feminine enough. Because they feel they have a Martian sign, being an assertive and even aggressive type of personality. So it makes them feel uncomfortable in their gender, because it makes them feel too masculine. So another way of how to understand the person in their life is to look into the wisdom of the zodiac, which is found inside the horoscope of Adam Harishon. So you look at the ascendant, and understand what your ideal archetype actually is. And then you look at the chart of a person and compare his chart, with the chart of Adam and Eve. And you see how different it is. And from that you can start seeing the problems in the person. So if a male has a Pisces rising, whereas ideally he should have an Aries rising, he feels more feminine/passive and not outgoing enough. He is more a dreamer; he is too sympathetic, too caring. He doesn't go after his own will, and is too afraid of offending people. So just from comparing his chart to that of Adam and Eve, you already start to see all the different problems and how you have to work in helping the person. This is how you try to understand the hidden laws of nature from the horoscope of Adam and Eve. And to understand how to help a person solve his problems from the horoscope of Adam and Eve, and not to have to go off into all other areas; you don't have to do mantras, or wear precious stones, or go to a shrink, but instead go forward using the teachings of the wisdom of Jewish astrology, through the understanding of the horoscope of Adam and Eve.

Chapter 1

Time and Space are key components to our existence, and these form the two major axis's of astrology: you have the Space axis which is between the 1st house and the 7th house and the Time axis is between the 4th and 10th house. Each house is connected to the house opposite it. For example, the first house is connected to the seventh, the fourth is connected to the tenth, and they always interact with each other. For example, the first house is always becoming the seventh house, and the seventh house is always becoming the first house. So if a person is influenced by other people, then other people are influenced by him. He influences his wife, and his wife influences him. In other words, they both influence and change each other. Because if you look at the charts, you see that they are both masculine houses. If you take the Chart of Adam and Eve, the first house was Adam, and the seventh was Eve. So she has Libra. Libra is under the influence of the Planet Venus and it is a good and attractive Sign, but it is masculine. So you see that if the seventh house had a feminine ascendant, then she would always react to the masculine 1st house of Adam. But since they are both masculine, each one has its own control over their own way of life. And really, neither one can change the other. Masculine signs are less influenced by other people than the feminine signs. Feminine signs are more influenced by their environment, while masculine signs are less so. So you see that each one has their own agenda, so to speak, and they have to, somehow, come to a balance with each other. The one is never going to get the other one to totally follow their own way, and they always have to work out something balanced. But they always go through change, and this is the interaction between the 1st house and 7th house which constantly influence each other. This is what is called the Space axis; it is you and the other. The Time axis is between the 4th house and the 10th house, where the 4th house is the past, where you came from and it is also the genetic material you come from and it is the house of parents, that give birth to the 1st house, which is ten houses away (Forward or Counter-clockwise). So the fourth house is the past. And the tenth house is the future, where you are going, where you are heading to, how you construct your life. And these 2 houses are always interchanging with each other. The past causes the future. What you did in the past causes your future. And what you do in the future can, in a certain way, change your past. If a major thing happens to you and you scrape through and later in life, in the future, when you look at the past, you sometimes realize that things that seemed to be bad, were, retrospectively, proven to be good. So you change your perspective on the past. So the future can change the past. So, by looking at what will happen to you in the future, you also look at what happened to you in the past, and see that it was good. So the past is always becoming the future. And the future is always becoming the past, because, once the future happens, it turns into the past. And what happened in the past is going to be influencing the future. So there is always an interchange between the past and the future.

If you look very closely at the connection between the Time axis and the Space axis, you see that there is a ninety degree separation between them. In other words, if you have an Ascendant on 0 degrees at Aries in Adam and Eves chart, then the tenth house would be 0 degrees Capricorn. And if you add it up, the house of Capricorn is 30 degrees, Aquarius is 30 degrees and Pisces is 30 degrees, so Capricorn is at 90 degrees to 0 degrees Aries. So the difference between the 10th house and the 1st house is a Square (90 degrees). And the same thing between the 7th and the 10th house, there will be a square, and between the 4th house and the 7th house there will be a Square too. And if you really look at it, the first house is the person. So the child, when he develops, he really needs a Square between himself and his parents, the 4th and the 10th house, who are the mother and the father. And there should be a square to the child, in order to make some kind of conflict between them, which is usually good. A square is a Martian aspect, one of a conflict. It gives a push to the child, and causes him to brake away from the parents, and start on his own life.

Sometimes I find myself drawing horoscopes from all over the world and so I have to look where they fall on the globe. And sometimes, you would see that there is not a square aspect between one and ten, or one and four. So if there is not a square aspect, if there is a Sextile (60 degrees) instead, like between Aquarius in the mid heaven and Aries in the first house for example, there would be more harmony between the parents and the child, and that would make it more difficult for the child to separate himself from the parents. And that may be not so good. My teacher used to say: 'You like the Squares where Squares should be'. In other words, everything is good within its own context. And one must realize that each thing has a time and a place. So there is a place and time for the squares, in order for the child to have the push.

Another secret of the zodiac is, if you look at the horoscope of Adam and Eve, you see that there are Squares between the 4th and the 10th houses, which represent the Mother and the Father of the bride, with the Groom (7th). Because in many marriages, there are major problems between the parents and the in-laws, who sometime help in marriages, but in many cases, they break up marriages. And you see that in the horoscope of Adam and Eve, by looking at the aspect between ten and one and four and one, and four and seven and ten and seven. You see the lack of harmony between the in-laws and the married couple. And in the Jewish law, it is always said that you should listen to your parents, but the only time you don't have to listen to them is on the matter of getting married. Because your parents have a different view from your own, about what you need. And this is one case where you go more after your own feelings than after what your parents say.

We have so far talked about the Angular houses (1st, 4th, 7th and 10th), now let us talk about the Succedent houses (2nd, 5th, 8th, 11th) which is another way to 'Square the circle'. The first four houses (1st, 4th, 7th and 10th) were Cardinal Signs. Cardinal signs are by nature, the strongest Signs. Cardinal signs are goal oriented, but the Succedent houses (2nd, 5th, 8th, 11th) come from fixed Signs: Taurus, Leo, Scorpio and Aquarius. And they are also 90 degrees from each other. And it is easy to remember, because a 90 degree aspect will always exist between different Elements (Fire, Air, Water and Earth). And also remember that in the 90 degree aspect, it is always between one Sign that is Masculine and one sign that is Feminine. For example, if you take an aspect of Aries (fire) and Capricorn (earth), Aries is masculine and Capricorn feminine. If you take Taurus and Leo, Taurus would be feminine and Leo masculine. There is always the aspect of male and female, which complement and also nullify each other. Aries is masculine, and the sign to its left is Pisces, which is feminine. And the sign to its right is Taurus, and both Pisces and Taurus are feminine. All this is, as we have said, because there is a huge difference between the genders, and they have a hard time trying to understand one another. And as it is said in the Talmud, it is God that holds the man and the woman together like a miracle. And I think what it means is that it is not always so natural for them to stay together. It is hard for them to have common goals in life and they don't think alike or behave similiary.

So if you look at the 2nd house, it would fulfill itself ten houses away, which is in the 11th house. This is in a material world (Forwards or Counter-clockwise). In other words, the money (2nd) brings you friends (11th). Friends are usually from the same socioeconomic strata. You don't often see poor people together with very rich friends and they are usually from the same class of people. Now with the 11th being the cause of the 8th house, I have a problem with understanding how this works, since it's a hard transition. But I will tell you what I have heard regarding this. The 11th house is Aquarius. And I wouldn't say it is a cold sign, but it indicstes someone which is very intellectual and airy. For example, Mr. Obama, the president of the USA, has Aquarius for his ascendant. And he comes across with little emotions; he is like a professor, a school teacher, teaching schoolchildren. He doesn't come across as feeling any emotions inside himself. The goal of the Aquarius is always to become a Scorpio, to become emotionally involved. And yet the Aquarius loves freedom, and because of that, he is very afraid of emotional attachments, because emotional attachments take away freedom. So Aquarius craves to become Scorpio, even though it is difficult and yet that becomes their goal in life. And I think the Scorpio is the most emotionally intense signs, ut this is what the cool aqurius craves.

But in any case, this is one way to see it (11th house into the 8th), and there are other ways to see this.

The 8th house is also the house of pregnancy, which is Scorpio. And the pregnancy fulfills itself ten houses away (forward or Counter-Clockwise), by giving birth to a child (5th house). The 5th house is the house of children, amongst other things. So we went through 2nd, 11th, 8th, and 5th using the Forward or Counter-clockwise method (more material).

On the subject of children you will find that a Jewish astrological perspective would go against what is the common assumption in the Western world today. You find that people in the west don't want to have many children. Because it is an economic burden, for each child costs money, and each kid takes away from the others. And includes elementary schools, and all other aspects of education and raising kids, it costs a fortune. And if a year in school or college costs thirty thousand dollars a kid, then eighteen years of raising them would cost 500 000 dollars each. And if you have 10 children, you would need five million dollars. So people realize this and don't want to have many children. But in astrology the 5th house, that of the child, fulfills itself in the 2nd house, the house of money. So, in other words, children bring money through blessings. This is an important point, if you look how the world changed in the last hundred years or so, since the world became industrialized. Today when a woman becomes a widow, and has five kids, nobody would be too happy to marry her and support so many kids. But in old times, the kids would be the source of support for their mother; the kids would work on the farm or otherwise. And also today, the more kids one has, for both men and woman, the more it motivates one to do things, to have a job and be able to provide them with shelter, money and food. When a woman has many kids, compared to being alone, that would motivate her to find work and support them. But if a person has no children, it holds him back. He can sit around and daydream the whole day. So the 5th house of children, fulfills itself in the house of money (2nd house), because if you have children you have to work and make money. So this is squaring the circle, from the 2nd, 11th, 8th, and 5th house.

And then you can also use it Backwards, and make it more of a spiritual sense: If you start from the 2nd house, going Clockwise (backwards), it will lead you to the 5th house, of children. The more money you have the more desire you would have to expand your family. Money will maybe bring you more romance, since the 5th house is also the house of romance, adventure, sports and things like that. And if you have money, you can do all the adventure you please. And the 5th house would bring you to the 8th house. That is because the desire to have children causes the 8th house to get pregnant. And the 8th house fulfills itself in the 11th by building the society, and then the 11th which goes to the 2nd house of money. Because the 11th house is that of friends, and the 2nd is that of money,

and friends bring you money. That is because sometimes you get things from friends, which are actually worth more than a large amount of money. Besides, friends can cause you to have money: They can make contacts for you, and get you ahead in different areas in the world. So once more, you see the cause and effect apparatus at work here.
And now I would like to go on to the Cadent houses and square the circle with them. These are the 3rd, 6th, 9th, and 12th houses that are the Mutable signs of Gemini, Virgo, Sagittarius and Pisces. We have talked a bit about the fact that there are 3 types of Qualities to the Signs which are, the Cardinal, Fixed and Mutable Signs. Let us give an example to what the differences between these three are: If a person has obstacles in his life, the cardinal way would be to 'go for it', attack and defeat those obstacles. This is what the cardinal signs are about. He is goal oriented, sees an obstacle and goes to defeat it. A fixed person would try to withstand those obstacles. He would always stand on his two feet on the ground. And the mutable signs run away. Somebody told me that when he was in Alaska on a job assignment in , he suddenly saw bears coming towards him. And in Alaska when bears appear the most advisable thing to do is to just stand defiantly, saying I am here, this is my place, and there is nothing for you to do about that. But a mutable sign person, which is the weakest in the group, tends to run away; usually,they don't like to deal with obstacles, and tend to turn and run away. But things always have to be taken with consideration, because there are factors which change things.
So the 3rd house is the house of Knowledge, and it fulfills itself in the 12th house, that of Suffering (going Forward). That is because it is written that "knowledge brings suffering". The more a person knows, the more he starts to suffer from everything he knows. Sometimes innocence is bliss. The 12th house of Suffering fulfills itself in the 9th house of Religion. And the main answer to suffering is to find the answers in religion. Most people come to religion, or their religion gets strengthened, when they suffer. And the 9th house of religion, fulfills itself in the 6th house of service, because religion teaches a person that he has to serve the community, and can't just be there for himself. And I am just giving you here simple explanations of how this works, but there are other ways to explain all these connections too. For example, the 9th house is also the house of ones philosophy, the house of your world view: How optimistic or pessimistic you are, how you see the world, how you see yourself in it. And if your philosophy is right (9th), then it brings you health (6th). The 6th house is also the house of health, how good your health is. And the cause of your health is your mental attitude, which goes 10 houses backwards (to the 9th). This is an idea which is gaining ground in the last twenty years or so. The doctors talk about it and implement it; and the cause of your health (6th) are your thoughts (9th). So again, we see the interconnections between these houses.
And if you go using the Clockwise system (backwards), you can look at it this way: The 3rd house will bring you to the 6th house. For the Knowledge leads people to Service, and helping people. And helping people is a spiritual thing. The 6th house of Virgo always wants to fix itself, and you fix yourself through religion (9th). The Kabbala has all types of spiritual systems of correction, where you can fix yourself. In other words, if you have problems with your mental attitude in the 9th house, if your mental attitude isn't correct, then the correct thing to fix this is to help other people (6th). That is because you look at the cause of the problem, which is in the ninth house. There is the story of young women who felt that she was not liked by anybody. So the advice was that she go to the school cafeteria and asked people who they were and what they needed, and so eventually

people knew and liked her, and she became popular; so things like that would change your mental approach, and you will not be alone anymore and much happier. And now we go to the 9th house, going Clockwise (backwards), which will bring you to the 12th house, because religion brings people to some suffering. Through religion people became aware of their sins, so they suffer, and try to fix themselves. So the 12th house will fulfill itself in the 3rd house of knowledge. Through suffering one acquires knowledge. A person learns most from his suffering. So that is what happens in Jewish astrology when you work with the number 10 on the Horoscope. Remember, the number 10 represents the concept of Fulfillment.

There is the idea in Kabbala which is similar in a way to astrology. Everything in kabbala is looked at in both an Absolute sense and in a Relative sense. And that is why it is so hard to understand the kabbala books, because you don't know if the rabbis are talking in an Absolute sense, or in a Relative sense. And if they are talking in a Relative sense, the question is in which way are they being relative. For example, when they talk about the Sefira of Keter (crown), which is the first Sefira of the 10 Sefirot, you sometimes say it is the 1st Sefira, but in other times you say it is the 10th Sefira. It depends if you go from the bottom up or from the top down. Keter has everything that is below it in itself, and gives to things below it. But it also receives from above itself, so it is Keter when it gives to the lower sefirot, and it is Malchut (kingdom) when it receives from the higher world, because it is now acting as a receiver. So each aspect changes according to the way you relate things to one another.

In astrology, you have a similar idea. Any house really has twelve meanings. Like when we say that the first house is the first house, we mean it is the 1st house in the terms of the horoscope of Adam and Eve. But if you are interested about your money, how much money you will have, or how you are going to make money, you look at the second house. The second house is the house of money, so you make the second house your first house. And then your 1st house will become the 12th house, because it is twelve houses away from the house of money. That house is the secret enemy of the money, and it can make you lose all your money. If something happens to you (1st), all your money is going to go. So am just showing you the idea. If you talk about the 3rd house, then the 1st house will be the eleventh house from the 3rd house. When you talk about the 4th house, the 1st is going to be the 10th house, and when you talk about the 5th house, the 1st will be the 9th house from the 5th house etc. So you see that really each house has twelve different meanings. And each house teaches you something. So if you want to know some more about your wife, all you have to do is to make your 7th house her 1st house, and this is going to become who your wife is. And she will have twelve houses: Your 8th house will become her 2nd house, your 9th house will become her 3rd house, and you can draw a chart for her. So these are called relative charts within the horoscope of Adam and Eve. And if you use all these relative charts you will be able to answer almost all the questions people will ask . This is an important idea, and I wanted to give you this introduction now, before we go on. And once you meditate on these things you will become more familiar with astrology.

Chapter 2

So counting 10 houses Forward (Counter-Clockwise) is where the Fulfillment is. We have explained that the basic fulfillment of the 1st house (you) is in the Career, which is in the 10th house, which is ten houses from the 1st house. This is in the more worldly way, the American way. The first question everybody asks you in America is what is your job? What do you do for a living, how do you make money? But in a mystical way, the Fulfillment is ten houses going Backwards (clockwise), which is the home and the family (4th house). So in Israel, if you live in the religious circle, the first question they ask you is 'are you married'? And then they ask you how many kids you have. So this is the difference between the two countries, two lifestyles and mind-sets. You see right away that America is after the money with the career. I remember my teacher in America who said that when he first came to America from Hungary, he spent his first two years there in the public library, learning about all the different careers, so he could guide people in their proper careers. Because that was what the Americans wanted. And so when I came to Israel I came having being taught the American approach which I was always taught to ask people, 'what do you for a living'? So when I did this in Israel I receiving replies from many people that this was not a question that worked for them (since this is not necessarily their priority in life). It made my task all the much harder to be an astrology here in Israel.

Let's start working with the number 8. There was once a story about the students of the Ari Za"l. The Ari Za"l was the great Kabbalist from the late 1400s and the early 1500s, who lived in Zefat, and is considered the greatest Kabbalist of the last five hundred or six hundred years. And the students came to him and asked him: Now that we don't have the prophets, how do we know what our destiny is? In other words, when the prophets were alive, a person would go to the prophet who would tell him what his work was in this world. But now, that we don't have the prophets, how do we know what are work is supposed to be. So the Ari Za"l told them, simply, like this: 'You should concentrate on two things: One is the thing that you enjoy doing more than anything else, and the other is the thing you find the most difficult to do'. In a general way, this is what you have to work on in this lifetime.

The number 8 is the number for 'death'. This world is all based on the number 7: The seven days of the week, seven years on the Shmita cycles, the sabbatical cycles, the seven planets, the 7 heavens, the 7 colors, the 7 musical notes, the 7 lands etc..... So the number 8 is the number for Transcendence, the number of going into the next world, going above and beyond this world of 7. And in astrology, the eighth house is the house of death. Besides being the house of death, the eighth house can also tell you what the most difficult thing is for a person. It is like where the person 'dies'. Each sign has a house where it dies in, and you see what causes its 'death'. And that is what is really difficult for a person, when he has to experience that house. So let us take a look at it. We will go forward (counter clockwise), and then do it backwards (clockwise). Let us try to experience it in both directions, in the secular/worldly way and in the mystical way. Let us start with the secular way, and try to give some examples. I want to show you something very important. We have talked a lot about the Ascendant being the whole chart. The ascendant is about eighty percent of the chart. But it is more then just the Sign on the Ascendant. Aries in the ascendant is going to have Taurus in the second house. So Adam and Eve's chart is not just Aries in the first house, but also Taurus in the second house, Gemini in the third, Cancer in the fourth and so on. And people don't really look at all the house cusps to learn about each house, what each house teaches you. And then you have to look at the variations of each sign, for example Aries (if you count 8 houses counter clockwise) is going to have Scorpion in the eighth house cusp, then the person is likely to 'die' on Scorpio. Taurus, on the other hand, is likely to 'die' on the Sagittarius. From each house cusp one can learn more and more things about your basic life and mazal. In other words, from what a person is not, you can learn what he is. The count of 8 going either way is about what a person is not. And if you use the clockwise method then 8 houses going backwards from the Aries ascendant will be the 6th house, which is the house of servitude, which does not go down well with the Aries. Adam Harishon had an Aries on his first house cusp. And if you go Counter-clockwise (forward) by 8 you get to the eighth house, whose cusp has the constellation of Scorpio. So it is interesting, Aries and Scorpio have one thing in common, which is that they are both ruled by Mars, the planet of war, violence, and bloodshed. So how can it be that Aries will 'die' in Scorpio? Before I answer that, I want to quote Ptolemy. Ptolemy was a great Greek astrologer. He was the father of Greek astrology and of Western astronomy. And he wrote a book called the Tetrabiblious ('the four books'). That was one of the first astrology texts after the Sefer Yetzira, and it has a chapter of a hundred aphorisms. And I want to read you one of his aphorisms, because you will now be able to understand it. This is Aphorism number 37, it goes like this:

"If a Virgo or a Pisces will be on the ascendant, the native will create his own dignity. But if an Aries or a Libra is on the ascendant, he will cause his own 'death'. The other signs are to be contemplated in the same way".

If you have a Virgo Ascendant, you will have Gemini on the tenth house cusp (count 10 houses forward). And this is because both the first house and the tenth house are ruled by the same planet Mercury. So a person, who has a Virgo rising, is going to be very connected to his destiny (10th) in Gemini. This is because he (himself) is the first house, and his destiny (10th house) will be ruled by the same planet. So he is always going to be destiny oriented, in that direction. So that is what Ptolemy says, that when Virgo or Pisces is on the ascendant, the native will create his own dignity. Because the tenth house is the house of dignity, through career you get honor and dignity and importance. And the same thing with a Pisces rising, which would have a Sagittarius on the tenth house cusp, and both of them are ruled by Jupiter, which is a good planet. So again, the first and tenth houses are going to be intimately linked to the Piscean type of person, and he is going to make his own dignity. On the other hand, using the number 8, Aries and Libra ascendants cause their own 'death', because as we just mentioned, an Aries person in the first house, has Scorpio on the eighth house and they are both Martian, so he (1st) and his 'death'(8th) are very close at hand, they are somewhat combined. The same applies with a Libra ascendant and its 'death' 8 houses later in Taurus, with Venus being the planet for both of them. The Aries and Libra ascendants are uneasy personality types. The Aries is a very brave person, always going fearlessly to his 'death'. And it is interesting that some years back, suicide rates were studied according to the person's ascendant. And the suicide rate was the highest among people with Aries and Libra ascendant. And this is because both of them have the same sign 8 houses away, which are not good for them, whilst Virgo and Pisces also have the same signs but 10 houses away, in a better way. Also Aries and Libra are the archetype signs and being connected with the eight teaches that we were born to die.

So let us go back to the number 8 and the Aries ascendant; When Aries is on the ascendency, Scorpio is in the 8th house. So why would this 8th house be hard for the

Aries? The Aries wants to go forward, it is a Cardinal sign of Fire, always wanting to go forward and have no opposition. And its whole goal is just to move ahead and attack, he is like the warrior, who goes out and fights the battles. And what the Aries doesn't like is to be defensive, he doesn't like to play defense, he is the offensive type of person. And although the Scorpio is a Martian too, he has a different type of Martian personality. It is the defensive Martian, the Martian who waits, and when the enemy comes, he springs all sorts of surprises and attacks that take care of the enemy. But that is a defensive type of fighting using the same Mars, which is not the Aries' thing. The Aries personality feels 'dead' when he has to play defense, he wants to attack. Scorpio is in the eighth house of an Aries person means that he has to learn the patience of the Scorpio, the tactician. The Scorpio person is a much deeper thinker. The Aries knows how to attack, while the Scorpio lays traps, and carefully plans defensive fighting. But this is difficult for the Aries, who desires a quick victory in a fight. I know many Aries people, and when they are involved in a fight, they always desire to have a quick win, and if they don't win quickly enough, they lose, because they don't have the ability of endurance, which people in other Signs have. In a more spiritual way, through the houses of the Aries ascendant personality: If we go eight houses back (clockwise) in an Aries chart, we come to a Virgo, which is a servant, the last thing an Aries would want to be, because an Aries always likes to be a leader. He doesn't want to take orders from anybody. When he has to be a servant, he will feel bad. It is not his task in this world; his task is to lead, not to serve. So you should always look at the sixth and the eighth houses, the bad houses in the horoscope. And in the 6th and the 8th houses from the ascendant, you see what the person doesn't like to be. These are signs of where the person is bothered and troubled, and doesn't function well. So the Aries doesn't function well in Scorpio and Virgo, he hates taking orders or to be a servant. If you remember, Ariel Sharon is an Aries rising type of person. He always got into trouble in the Army, because his superiors ordered him to do one thing and he would do another. He would break his radio, or turn it off so that he could not receive the orders and could then do as he wanted. That is the Aries personality. He doesn't like to take orders, and he desires to do what he knows best and he is going to go and do it. So the Aries dies in Scorpio, and he also dies in Libra.

The next sign after Aries in Taurus; Taurus dies in its eighth house, which is Sagittarius. There is a famous Rashi (most important biblical commentator) about the story in the Torah, where God told Abraham to go out of his land, and go to the land he would show him. And God promised him that he would become rich. So the question becomes, why did God have to tell Abraham that he would become rich? So Rashi explains that because a person usually loses his money when he goes on a journey, and he loses his job, and goes to a new place, where nobody knows him, and has to start over in business, where he has no connections, God promised him that nonetheless he would become rich. So that is the second house, the house of Taurus, and Taurus dies in Sagittarius which is the house of journeys. Taurus is very conservative by nature, the most conservative and feminine of the signs. It is the most laid back, the laziest of all signs, and it doesn't like to travel. And travel is the 9th house of Sagittarius. But a Taurus person likes to stay at home, in his own environment. And Taurus is a money man, who doesn't like to talk philosophy or the higher stuff of the Sagittarius. Taurus gets lost in the world of esoteric ideas, philosophy or religion, and prefers practical matters of the day to day survival. So he dies in Sagittarius. In a spiritual way, you go Clockwise (backwards) by 8 houses, and then the Taurus dies in Libra. Libra and Taurus are different, in the way that a Taurus person is like a bull in a Chinese shop, very clumsy, and not really a social type of person, which is most important to a Libra person who has good social skills. The Libra is a Venusian sign that gets along with people, while the Taurus is a Venusian sign that doesn't. The important thing to a Libra is to make friends, have a harmonious society, a harmonious marriage, and the most important thing for a Libra is marriage. A Taurus doesn't like marriage, because then he would have to give part of his money away, he would have to support his wife, or the wife would have to support her husband, as is common in some societies today. In the religious world, the woman sometimes supports the man. So the Taurus doesn't have the social skills that the Libra has, and in order to make money you sometimes have to not care much about what the other person thinks or feels. Making money is most of the time a win-lose game: You win, and your rival loses, or the other way round. Money is not on average a win-win game. So the Libra doesn't like that; the Libra wants everybody to win; the Libra worries too much about other people. For example, in astrology, the Sun is at its weakest when it is in the sign of Libra, because the sun is the ego, which is not the strength of Libra, and on the other hand, the Sun is exalted in Aries. Libra's ego is an all encompassing one. So some Libra people can become great leaders, because they care about everyone, which can make good leadership; they would do everything for everybody. But because the Libra worries too much about other people, it is hard for the Libra type to do business; they are not good business people at all, because they don't like to take advantage of other people as a rule. So there is a huge dichotomy between the Taurus person and the Libra person.

Gemini is the third sign, and on its eighth house cusp we have Capricorn. Gemini is, in some sense, the most theoretical of all signs. It is an air sign, and a Gemini person would be very interested in the world of ideas, very theoretically oriented. And when he has to go into the real practical world of Capricorn he becomes very unhappy. So the Gemini person tends to 'die' in the sign of Capricorn. And going Clockwise (backwards) 8 houses from Gemini we would be at Scorpio. And the Gemini is the superficial knowledge, of knowing a little about everything, like the jack of all trades and the master of none, without the depth of the Scorpio, which is the deepest and most focused of all the signs. The Scorpio tends to focus deeply on one thing. Scorpio is a fixed sign, and Scorpio persons tend to focus and spend their whole lifetime on one thing. For example, in the study of the Talmud, while some people are good at Bekiut, which is the skill of knowing a lot of the Talmud in a General way, others have the skill of going deep into it. The Scorpio is more of an Iyun kind of person in the Talmud, one who goes deep into every piece in the Talmud, and learns a lot from each little piece. So when a Gemini has to focus and spend a lot of time on one thing, it would be very uncomfortable. A Gemini likes to be able to fly around, to go from place to place and to connect different things. And the Gemini is an air sign, while the Scorpio is an emotional water one. So the Gemini doesn't feel comfortable with deep emotions.

The fourth sign is Cancer, the sign of the home, which 'dies' 8 houses forward, at the house of Aquarius, in the social life, the house of the friends. As soon as a Cancer person gets married, you never hear from him again; he is off in his own world. As soon as he gets a home and a family, he loses his friends. As soon as the man gets married, he needs his wife's permission to go out with his friends; so the Cancer 'dies' in the Aquarius, the sign of friendship. Cancer people tend to be very moody and self enclosed. It is the sign

of carrys the home on one's back. And if they get disturbed, they close themselves up in their home. And a Cancer person always tends to have problems with friendships. If you have a Cancer chart, you should always work on becoming more social, friendlier, and build a friendship type of network. Going 8 signs backwards from a Cancer will bring us to Sagittarius, the house of travel. Sagittarius is the explorer of the zodiac. And a Sagittarius person always tends to be out, traveling and exploring places. Such a person would like to travel around the world, for two years, on his motorcycle. So it would hurt his home life. The Cancer is also a very feminine sign, which is more practical than the philosophizing tendency and exploratory skills of the Sagittarius.
Leo 'dies' in Pisces. Pisces is the sign with the least of ego, while Leo is about thinking of ones self. Leo is the house of childhood, and has a childhood type of nature. It is like the child of the zodiac. A Leo person would feel that the world is all for himself. And Pisces is the opposite of that; it wants to merge with the world. So when a Leo person gets into Pisces, it is like 'death' for him. This is in a worldly sense. Going 8 houses backward from Leo would bring us to Capricorn. Leo is the sign of play, it rules the fifth house: Romance, play, pleasure. Capricorn, on the other hand, is a most serious house, without pleasure, so it is not good for Leo.
The sixth sign is Virgo, and 8 houses away from it is Aries. Aries is a leader type of personality, and Virgo is the opposite. If you put a Virgo type of person in a position of leadership, it will be like it says in Proverbs, 'when a slave becomes a king'; the Virgo doesn't know how to rule. It likes to take orders, and carry out assignments. Again, everything is in general archetypal definition here, because I can show you examples of Virgo type of people who were leaders, so there has to be a big modification based on the chart. And in a spiritual way, 8 signs going clockwise (backward) from Virgo would lead you to Aquarius. Aquarius is the sign of friendship, while Virgo is a sign of being a slave or a servant, and such people usually don't have time for friendship. They always work for their master, and have no time for their own visions. The Aquarius always works towards the goal of changing the world, in a big way, on the macro level. The Virgo on the other hand, is a very much micro type oriented personality. A Virgo person works on a micro level, only for his master, for one person.
The next sign is the Libra, and, as we have mentioned, its opposite sign is Taurus. Taurus is a sign of business, and the Libra person doesn't feel comfortable in doing business. The Libra wants everybody to be happy, a society where everything functions properly, and doesn't feel comfortable in a win-lose situation. Going backwards, the Libra dies on the sixth house, which is the house of Pisces, the least social of all signs, which is off in a world of fantasy. Pisces is more connected in its own fantasies, than being part of society.
The eighth house is the house of Scorpio, which dies at the house of Gemini, the sign of superficial and non emotional level. And going backwards, the Scorpio dies at the sixth house of Aries, because the Scorpio doesn't like to go on the offensive. The Scorpio is a defense type of Mars, the sign of patiently waiting for the attack, and then striking.
The ninth house is Sagittarius, which dies in the house of Cancer. Sagittarius is the one who likes to travel and explore, in the physical sense or in the spiritual sense, and to go to the upper worlds. One man once told me: 'My generation is like the first generation of those who studied Torah at home'. Back in the 1900s, even in Jerusalem, the men used to go away from their homes to study Torah the whole week, and would only come back home for Shabbat. Because once you come home, it takes you away from the upper

worlds. You have the kids crying, the wife telling you about all her problems, and then you start to lose everything you have studied. In a more spiritual way, the Sagittarius dies at the house of Taurus. When the Sagittarius has to go after money, he doesn't feel right. To a really religious person, the money is not so important. If you would like to see how religious someone truly is, then maybe you can somehow see that by the way he deals with money. People who are very religious usually don't go after money too much, and in many cases they don't have so much money anyway. A Western type of person, in contrast, has a lot of money, and has trouble in his marriage or whatever and this is caused by going too much after money and worldly pleasures. But people who are on the spiritual path tend to have financial problems: Big debts, difficulty in helping their children get married etc. I remember that my teacher's teacher in Kabbala was a great Rabbi, Rabbi Mordechai Sharabi. And it is said about him that one night he couldn't fall asleep. He asked his wife if there was any money in the house, she looked all over the house to try to find any money, and finally she found something equivalent to a 50 US cent coin, and he told her to give it to charity. And as soon as she gave it away, he fell asleep. As soon as he had any money in his pocket he would soon distribute it to his students in his yeshiva. And he never had money in his house. Even my teacher in Astrology never touched money. He wasn't very religious, but, according to his level, he tried not to touch money, he held that it wasn't for him. I never saw him touching money. Anyway, the real path of holiness is to turn away from the money. So you go counter clockwise from the ninth house to the second house, where the ninth house 'dies', the house of money. As soon as you get into money, it will take you away from the spiritual world.

The next sign is Capricorn. 8 houses forward is Leo. As we said before, the Capricorn is a sign of working and not playing, being very serious, without knowing how to enjoy life. Leo, on the other hand, is the sign of pleasure. If you put a Capricorn type of person in a wedding, he wouldn't know what to do there. He finds it difficult to dance and sing, and would just wait to go home; and in the spiritual way, going backwards, the Capricorn 'dies' in the house of Gemini. This is because Capricorn is a sign of learning from experience, while Gemini is a sign of learning things theoretically. Experience and practice is for the Capricorn type of person, not theory.

The next sign is Aquarius, which dies in Virgo. Aquarius is the most freedom oriented sign, it likes friendship and being with friends all the time, loving freedom. And Virgo is the house of servitude. Going backwards, the Aquarius dies in the house of Cancer, which represents the home. So Sagittarius women and Aquarius women don't like being too much in their homes. Sagittarius and Aquarius die in the house of Cancer, one in a physical way, and one in a spiritual way.

The last house is the house of Pisces, which, in a worldly way, dies in the house of Libra. Pisces is super emotional, very sensitive, easily hurt, and the most introverted of the signs. And Libra is the most extroverted and social of the signs. And in a spiritual way, Pisces dies in the house of Leo, when it has to build up its own ego, and has to worry about itself. The Pisces type of person likes to lose its identity, in order to merge with the others, and get into high spiritual levels.

My point in going through this exercise was to show you what you can learn just by looking at the cusp of the houses, whether it be 10 or 8 houses away, going either

Forward of Backwards, material or spiritual. The most important part of Esoteric astrology is how people can improve themselves and their mazal in the areas where they are weak.

Chapter 3

I have a friend, and every morning we learn the Zohar together for at least an hour and this is the great mystical Jewish book. And he suggested that I should talk more about the mystical explanation of the 8th house fulfills itself in the 5th house. So everybody has to know that the Zohar (and other sources) explain that there are different ways to understand the holy writings. There is the simple written meaning of the words, and then there are deeper and deeper coded meanings and mystical ways of understanding it, until you get to the real secrets of the writings. So I think that when I talked about the 8th house, the house of Coitus and death, I also mentioned that the 5th house is the house of Children (among other things). And the simple understanding of their relationship is that from the 8th house of Procreation, if you count ten signs (going counter clockwise) you will get to the 5th house, where the child is born. And we explained that out of the 10 houses you count, nine of these houses symbolize the nine months of pregnancy, and the tenth in the count would land on the 5th house, that of Children, which symbolizes the moment when the child is born. And that is really the simple understanding of this relationship between the 8th and 5th house. Before I explain the more mystical meaning of the relationship between the 8th and 5th house I have to give you a basic introduction to the Jewish approach to Procreation, as compared to the Western/Eastern approach. The Western/Eastern approach to sex is to maximize pleasure, to get as much pleasure as you can from sexual intercourse. The more spiritual amongst them in the East even try to maximize the pleasure out of this in order to get into what they call high levels of consciousness. And it is interesting to notice the difference when you look into the mystical Jewish astrology, the archetype chart of Adam, you see that the whole matter of having sexual intercourse is in order to produce children; the 8th house fulfills itself in the 5th. You see that in the West people tend to be more and more interested in the 8th house of sexual pleasure, and less and less in the 5th, in producing children. This is the Eastern approach too, according to which it is more important to fulfill the 8th house, the sexual intercourse, and more and more to get away from the 5th house. Which, of course, is strange in a certain way, because the eighth house is not considered a good house in astrology; it is the house of death. And indeed, our Sages tell us that sex is like $1/60^{th}$ of death, and this is why it is connected to the eighth house in astrology. You see today that there has been a turn away in the Western world over the years, where sexual intercourse became something of a goal into itself, the pursuit of pleasure. And due to that, it is possible to understand how homosexuality, for instance, came to be main stream today. I remember that when I was a kid, some forty years ago, calling someone a homosexual was considered the worst thing one could call another person. Today it is something which is more than OK, and I think it comes from that idea: First Freud came along, and permitted masturbation as a means of getting pleasure without reproducing anything. Then the idea of birth control came along, so you can have sex without pregnancy. And slowly, as time passed by, the act became separated from the purpose, the cause became separated from the effect, and it was no longer inappropriate to alienate the act. And then, what is wrong with homosexuality? The attitude changed and it became permitted, just like other kinds of sex. The Jewish approach is completely different. On the mystical level in Judaism, the reason for sex, besides producing children, is to produce holy children, and this is the whole secret of the 8th house giving birth to the 5th. In other words the way the procreation took place, determines who the child is. Judaism has many sexual laws to help produce a holy child. You want to do this because it will help you fulfill as best as possible the Jewish religion's first command, which is to be fruitful and multiply, and to raise your children to know God, so holiness is important. Without children, which are the next generation, the religion is not able to keep on going. But more than that, one has to try to have children who are on a high level, and can get into high spiritual states, and be excellent people. And that is the whole secret of the eighth house giving birth to the fifth house. This is how you use the eighth house, in order to determine what kind of a child you will have. And this is why there are all kinds of laws in the Jewish law books, connected with the sexual practice: The woman having to purify herself after menstruating; she has to go to the mikve and undergo ritual cleansing, and there are laws regarding the proper time in the night to be together. According to Kabbala, as the Zohar talks about, the best time (for intercourse) is Shabbat after midnight; and if not then, then during the rest of the week after midnight. Or Shabbat before midnight, , or on the new moons and so forth. And there are times when it is not good to have sexual intercourse and other times where it is even forbidden to be together. And there is advice about which positions to be in, and which positions cause certain defects in the child, which positions are beneficial. And how the room has to be, which position the bed has to be in, and all sorts of things. And the deepest secret of all is the intentions and thoughts of the parents at the time of procreation, which has a tremendous impact on the life of the child, and on who the child will be. And all these things together are hinted in the idea of the eighth house fulfilling itself in the fifth. And if you go backwards (from 5th to 8th) you see the cause is the affect, and that in a mystical way, the children (5th) give birth to the 8th house, to death. This is because children bring their parents to the level of developing their new identity as Parents, and stepping up one notch on the cycle of life. For example you see some women, who to their own surprise become, completely devoted to their children, once they have the children. And if they created children who are to become holy people, then the parents should work on themselves, trying to become holy people too, because now they have inherited a new name, Father or Mother. This extra name and title is to remind them that their whole world is now to raise the children. So in a certain way when they have children, they in a sense of 'dying', their old identity dies and they become parents. In the Talmud it is said that a person who is childless is like a dead person. He is not physically dead, but in a way he is because he has no continuation of himself. So we can say that the 5th house expresses itself also in a way that not having children (5th) is like death (8th). And having children is a way of transcending death. So the fifth house gives birth to the eighth, by giving you the transcendental ability to somehow bypass death. So everything has deeper levels, and if you really start to pay attention to everything, I think you can come to understand a lot of different secrets and wisdoms.

Let's look at some other numbers. We basically did the numbers 10 and 8, so lets start with the number 12 and the number 7, because they have something in common, which is that they both talk about enemies. The two houses are the enemy houses of the horoscope. The seventh house knows its Open enemies; the enemies you see. And the

twelfth house is about the Secret enemies. We gave the example of the 12th house as the soul in relation to the 1st house, which is the body, and the soul is the body's secret enemy. The soul always tries to get the body to give up all its pleasures and do its bidding. And the 7th house is the house of open enemy, which sometimes means the wife, and in other times it means other open enemies. Because it is said in the Torah, about Adam and Eve, that "God created him a help-mate against him", which is Eve. This appears to be contradictory, so the Talmud asks: Is the wife a 'help-mate' or is she 'against' the husband? How can you be a 'help' and 'against' the man? So the answer is that sometimes she is a help-mate, while other times she is against him. If he does good, she is a help-mate. But if he does wrong, then she is against him. She is always there, like an open enemy, to always bring him back and correct him, so he doesn't go off too much in the wrong direction. And I guess it works conversely too: If the wife starts going off too much in the wrong way, then she has her husband to contend with. So in a way they are open enemies. So let us start by going Counter-clockwise (Forward):
So for the <u>secret</u> enemy of the 1st house you count 12 houses going counter clockwise (forward). That gets you to the 12th house, that of the soul, and in a more spiritual way, going clockwise (backwards) it gets you to the 2nd house. It's the house of money which causes him to go after the money too much. And in the end money doesn't make anybody truly happy. Money is good, and it is nice to have money, if you have everything else. And it is like somebody told me, that money makes problems seem smaller because if you have money you can deal with your problems in more effective ways. That is why when there are bad times, like now, when people lose their money, they really start going crazy. And in the 1920s, people jumped off buildings after losing their money, not so much due to losing their money but more because suddenly all their problems had become magnified. When they had a lot of money, their problems seemed little, because their money sort of covered up their problems. But their problems seemed to them as something impossible to solve once they lost their money, and that is what made them go off the edge. So that is why, sometimes, the secret enemy of the person (1st) is the money (2nd).
For the <u>open</u> enemy of the person with an Aries ascendant you count 7 houses forward (counter-clockwise) and it gets you to the Sign of Libra. The Aries, by nature, is mostly concerned about himself. The Libra person, in contrast to the Aries person, is interested in social harmony, wanting the Aries person to care more about everybody else, and have a well functioning society, and not everybody just caring about themselves. So the Aries has to see that there is somebody else, according to the Libra, and stop behaving like a spoiled child going after what he wants.

So the number 12 deals with the secret enemy, so for the 1st house, 12 houses away, going counter clock wise (forward) gets you to the 12th house, where the soul wants to go to a spiritual level, while the body (1st house) desires the physical pleasures.
The 11th house, the house of friends, is the secret enemy of the 12th house, that of the soul: What destroys your soul, more than anything else, is having bad friends who pull you away from your goal and values. Although, on the other hand, good friends may help the person maintain his soul. And the secret enemy of the friends, of the Aquarius (11th house), is the Capricorn (10th), which is the house of destiny of a person, his career, which takes him away from his friends (11th). I remember that as soon as we went off to

college, all my high school friends lost touch with everybody else, and it took forty years to reconnect a little bit with each other through the Internet, but it is never the same; you think you can reconnect, but you really can't. People's destinies and careers are what pull them apart. That is the secret enemy of the friendships. People become friends, when they are close together, and live in the same place. And as soon as something pulls them apart, the friendship can't hold.

The secret enemy of the Capricorn (10th) is the Sagittarius (9th), which is the religion, the philosophy, the travel etc. All these things take a person away from his career. The Jewish religion has so many commandments, like praying three times a day, study of the Torah and commentaries, mitzvoth, Shabbat ect.... And many religious Jewish people lost their jobs in America because they refused to work on Shabbat. So, on a simple level, the secret enemy of the career is the religion. On a more spiritual level, many people give up their careers for their freedom to discover new horizons through travel etc.. People with a strong Sagittarian drive do that, like a cousin of mine who was a great lawyer and gave it all up to travel on boats. That was his real dream. On a macro level, the 10th house is the government, and the 9th, the religion, and it can become the secret enemy of secular governments. There are constant fights and disputes between religious and state authorities, as to who makes the laws and who governs, if the law is made by the government or by the religion. So you see that in America, where from the declaration of independence they separated the church from the state. And more than anywhere in the world, you see it in Israel, where there is a tremendous battle between the government and religion, as to who has the authority over the people. So the 9th house is the secret enemy of the 10th. Again, I am just giving you some basic interpretations. But everyone can use this method to interpret the house affairs according to his own understanding, as it says "there are seventy faces to the Torah", which means that things can be understood in at least seventy different ways. So here I am suggesting just two ways of understanding, how the ninth house is the secret enemy of the tenth.

And the 8th house, the house of death and suffering, is the secret enemy of the house of religion and philosophy (9th). The main question against religion is always 'why bad things happen to good people', why do good people suffer, because some of the most righteous people sometimes suffer too. So the suffering is the secret enemy of religion, and takes people off the path sometimes. And many people turned away from the Jewish religion due to the Holocaust, saying that God didn't save all the kids and other innocent people. And these are hard questions to answer.

And the secret enemy of death (8th) is partnership (7th), the person not being alone in the world, escaping death by having his partner. As we said, the person is born alone and dies alone, but shouldn't spend his life alone. Having a good partner overcomes the fear of death. It sort of obscures you to death, so you don't think about it so much.

And the secret enemy of marriage (7th) is illness, which is in the 6th house, that of Virgo, the house of health. For many people, their marriage goes well until one of them falls seriously ill, which destroys the marriage. That is besides the open enemy, of fighting each other and not getting along. But the obstacle which you don't know about until it happens is when one of the partners becomes chronically ill, and the marriage can't function properly.

And the secret enemy of the health (7th) is in the 5th house of pleasure and love. And as the rabbis say, most people fall ill due to too much pleasure, especially sex. So the 5th

house inclination of going after the pleasures eventually leads to ruining the health (6th). Clearly we know that too much eating and drinking, and too much sex, can destroy the person's health.

And the secret enemy of the children (5th) is the home (4th), because the parents are, in a certain sense, a difficulty to the children because they restrain them from breaking free. They sort of hold the child back. I am sixty years old, and my parents still treat me as a kid, because that is how it is. Sometime, in a certain sense, the parents hold their children back from developing the way they should. And the secret enemy of the home, the 4th house Cancer, is Gemini, the 3rd house, which is the house of the neighbors, and also the house of the siblings. Every home has its own path in life, its own way of looking at things and teaching the children. And when children make friends with the neighbors' children (3rd), each may develop ways different to what they were taught (4th). And that is the beginning of the child leaving the home. And the secret enemy of the 3rd house is the 2nd house; the third house, that of Gemini, the twins, is the house of learning the revealed Torah and the secret Torah, all what is worldly and all that is mystical, while its secret enemy is the house of the money (2nd). Because a person has to work in order to earn money. And if he wants to learn Torah the whole day then where will he earn the money from? So the secret enemy of the 3rd house is the 2nd house. And the secret enemy of the 2nd house is the 1st house, the person himself, who may make mistakes in taking care of his money, and has the ability to lose it. And more than that, you can't take the money with you once you die. So the physical body is, in a way, the secret enemy of the wealth.

So now we went through all the twelve signs, going counter clockwise (forward). Let us go through these signs using the number 12 (secret enemies), in a more spiritual way (going clockwise or backwards): So again, we see that the secret enemy of the person (1st) is the money (2nd). Money can cause a person to get off the path. It takes people away from their spiritual goals, so the money is in a spiritual way, the secret enemy of the person. A person who accumulates more and more money usually becomes less and less religious, because he feels more and more invincible and important. The poor person usually lacks the monetary means to go off the path and fulfill his desires. But the rich person can do whatever he wants. And the secret enemy of the money (2nd) is the 3rd house, the desire for knowledge. When a person wants to have more knowledge (3rd), it might take away from his earning powers (2nd). And today you may look at it in another way: The cost of schooling. So the secret enemy of the money (2nd) is the desire for knowledge, and the desire for travel, as well as the brothers and sisters (3rd) and all these are secret enemies of the money too, because what usually destroys the relationship between the siblings is the desire for money. Inheritance usually causes fighting and disputes among them.

And as we said before, the 3rd house is the house of neighbors and the brothers/ sisters, and the secret enemy of that is the home (4th), the Parents. That is because the values of the home are sometimes contrary to the values of the street. The 4th house is also the past, the eternal values and roots of where the person came from and who he is. And if you look through the history, the cruelest and most perverse things had been done, and seemed perfectly normal at their time. That is how the world is, and most people don't think about what is going on. So you really need a strong 4th house, in order to know who you really are and where you come from, and have that as an anchor. And from that, you

will be able to know what is right and what is wrong, and have your eternal values, which can keep you away from the relative and fashionable values of the times. So the 4th house is the secret enemy of the 3rd. And my teacher always used to say that when you do a horoscope, one of the first things to look at is the 4th house. The 4th house is the end of life, and if the 4th house in the horoscope is good, it means that the person is going to be OK, because if the end of his life is going to be good, it means that he got the OK. If he made it through his lifetime, then the way he is at the end really counts. And the same thing is with eternal values, if you have them, it will lead you to a good ending.
And the secret enemy of the home (4th) is the children (5th), because the children eventually grow up and leave the parents behind. They all go off to start their own families, and the parents are sort of left in their empty nest. But that is the way of the world, this is how things are. As said in the Torah, in the Book of Genesis, "the man leaves his father and his mother, and clings to his wife". But in a certain way, when the children leave, it is like the end of the home. And the house of the children (5th) is also the house of pleasures, the secret enemy of which is the house of illness (6th). If you fall ill, you can't get pleasures anymore, you are robbed of your ability to get pleasure. And the 6th house of illness is also the house of servitude, and slaves and servants don't have pleasures either. A slave doesn't have time for his own needs. So the 6th house is the secret enemy of the house of pleasure (5th). And the secret enemy of the illness is the partner (7th), because together they can combat the illness. If you have someone with you, who cares about you, it helps in getting rid of the illness. Besides, a man completes himself by getting married. As a bachelor, he only has the half axis, and is therefore half a person. And houses 1 and 7 always interchange their energies. 1 gives 7 and 7 gives to 1. The older they get, the more they look alike. And getting married also takes away the sins, which also heals the illnesses. So the 7th house is the house of marriage, the secret enemy of which is death (8th). If one of the partners dies, it means the end of the marriage. And all couples worry about the eventual death of one of the partners.
And religion (9th) is the secret enemy of death (8th), because it teaches you about the afterlife. And people in this world that have eyes to see, realize that the purpose of living in this world is not for this world. 99% of the people in this world are suffering and have many troubles, and very few people really pass through this world having gotten much out of their lives. Like it is said, in Judaism this world is a passage way to what you receive in the next world. So the religion is the secret enemy of death, because it is a way to cheat death in a sense. Death is not such a problem for the one who believes in the next world and is not so scared to leave this one. But if a person focuses too much on this world, then his greatest achievement at the end would be becoming the richest person in the graveyard. The secret enemy of religion (9th) is the government (10th), like we said before. And work/career (10th) also is the secret enemy of religion (9th). If one has no career or work that generates income, especially during tough times, he would have to compromise his religion. In Judaism, you should try to study all the time, but if you don't have money to eat, you have to try to earn money first. And religion and governments are secret enemies of each other, because they compete about who has more authority. And many persecutions of religions were done by secular governments and vice versa. So the secret enemy of the religion is the career and the destiny. And the secret enemy of the destiny (10th) is the friends (11th). The more friends a person has, the more it takes him away from his destiny. And the secret enemy of the friends (11th) is the soul (12th), for it

keeps a person from choosing the wrong friends, and makes him choose the right friends, who help him do the right things in this world.
All the secret knowledge is hidden in the zodiac. You can see things on a simple level or in much deeper and more secret level. I wanted to show you that there is much wisdom hidden inside the zodiac and that you can get answers to questions by using and meditating on the zodiac. You don't have to go into psychology or into mantras or wearing precious stones. The answers to the questions appear inside the zodiac itself. The zodiac was a secret wisdom that had all of the principles of Judaism embedded into it. There are really two systems in Judaism which have all its knowledge embedded into it: One is the kabbala, and the other is astrology. In the Kabbala, it is in a more secret way, like inside the material, the Penimi way, the inner dimension of the person. And astrology has all the outer knowledge. But each one interchanges, and each one has all the secrets of the Jews embedded in it. And really, if you can start thinking very deeply about the zodiac and all the signs and everything, you can come to a lot of higher knowledge. And also the other way: When you learn the Jewish holy books, you can try to see how all that is taught actually fits into the chart of Adam and Eve.

Permutations of God's Name

Permutation of God's Name

By Yaakov Kronenburg

A transcription of a series of lectures on the permutation of God's Name and its uses as a powerful tool to reveal hidden truths and realities. The most ancient source for the technique of Permutations is from the oldest astrological book in Judaism called the Sefer Yetzira (the Book of Creation) written by Avraham Avinu, the first Jew who lived 3700 years ago and was also the master astrologer of his generation. The Talmud tells us that people came from all over the world to learn from Abraham and delve into their horoscopes. The Sefer Yetzira is a short book whose depth of wisdom and mystical insight has kept over 100 Sages throughout our history writing commentaries on it. The book discusses subjects such as the 10 Sefirot of Kabala, the 22 letters of the Hebrew Alphabet and the astrology of the Planets and Signs of the Zodiac. In this series we also refer to the writings of the Tikuney Zohar of Rabbi Shimon Bar Yochai, and the writings of the early Kabala of Rabbi Moshe Kordovero (RaMaK) in his master work, the book Pardes Rimonim (Orchard of Pomegranates);

Permutations of God's Name

By Yaakov Kronenberg.

Chapter 1

Let us have a look at the concept of Permutations in Kabbala and astrology. Permutation of Hebrew letters is a deep subject and a powerful tool to reveal hidden truths and realities. Its earliest source is from the oldest astrological book in Judaism called the Sefer HaYetzira (the Book of Creation) written by Avraham Avinu, the first Jew who lived 3700 years ago and was also the master astrologer of his generation. The Talmud tells us that people came from all over the world to learn from Abraham and delve into their horoscopes. This Sefer HaYetzira is a very short book with a couple of pages of data, and yet there have been nearly 100 commentaries on it through the ages by the various leading Sages and Kabbalists, and none claim a definitive grasp of the book's depth of wisdom and mystical insight. The book discusses 3 main subjects;

1. the 10 Sefirot/Spheres of Kabbala,
2. the Hebrew Alphabet and its 22 letters,
3. Astrology with its Planets and Signs.

It is in this book that the principle of Permutations of the Hebrew alphabet is first introduced in writing.

Before we start with the book, let us talk a bit about the chart of the first man Adam (Adam Harishon). Adam has 5 levels in his chart.

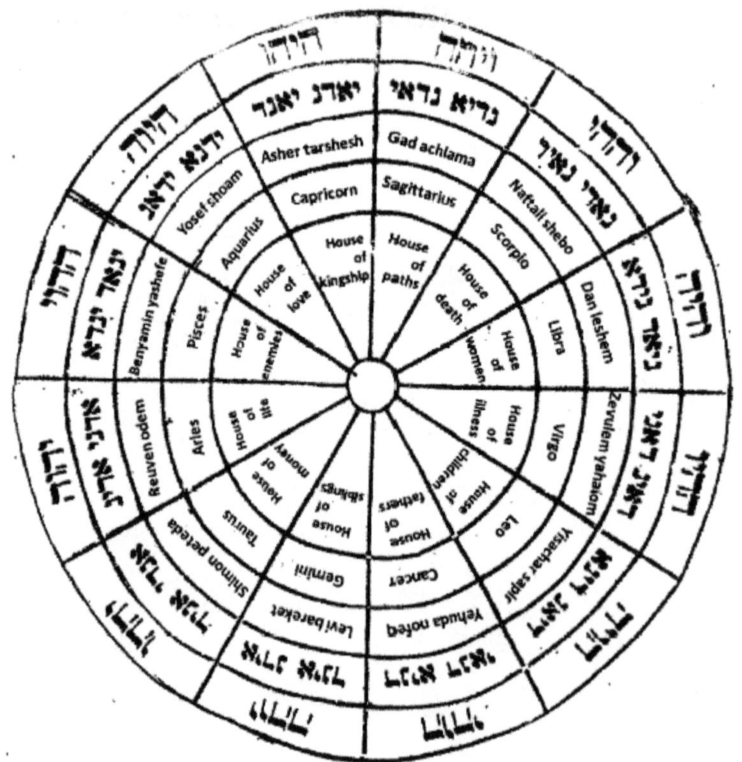

The first 2 levels (starting from the inner circle outwards) is something the nations of the world also have; on the 1st level are the Houses and on the 2nd level are the Constellations/Signs with their respective Ruling Planets. So for example, on the 1st level of the Houses we have the 1st House of life with Aries rising on the East (left side) ruled by Mars. So the first 2 levels basically contain all of Western astrology with the Houses, Signs and Planets. Judaism goes further and includes 3 more levels. We have already discussed and shown (see lectures 'Basic model of the Universe') that in the Torah all the planets, constellations and galaxies in our Universe are placed in the 2nd Palace of the Heavens of the lowest World of Assiya/Action. The World of Assiya/Action is divided into Heaven and Earth, and both are further subdivided into 7 sub-worlds each. The 7 subdivisions of the Heaven part of the World of Assiya are known as Palaces or Firmaments. The 2nd Palace/Firmament is called Rakia and it is there that all of astrology is placed. So there are another 5 Palaces above the Rakia level in the lowest World of Assiya sending down their energies, and above the World of Assiya there are more spiritual Worlds; these are the World of Formation, the World of Creation and the world of Emanation. So this chart of Adam factors in these primal energies flowing down from these higher Palaces and Worlds by including them in the Zodiac. We see in Adam's chart that corresponding to each Sign (2nd level) is a Tribe and a specific Jewel (3rd level). The Tribes come from Jacob who had 12 sons, and each tribe is assigned a Jewel. So Reuven the first son of Jacob and is connected to Aries and the Jewel of Odem, which is red in color like Mars and Odem in Hebrew shares its root meaning with the Hebrew word Adom (red). Taurus represents Shimon, and then there is Levi and then Yehuda etc… We will cover this 3rd level of the Tribes in future lessons and discuss the 2 approaches of associating Aries with either Reuben or the more accepted Yehudah. On the 4th and 5th level of Adam's chart, we get into the permutations of God's names. And on a simple level Adam's chart reflects the important principle in Jewish astrology which is that it all comes from God, and that you shouldn't think that the Planets themselves make the decrees and run the world. Adam's chart distills these higher influences down to 2 major names of God; אדני (4th level) and יהוה (5th level). These names are holy so we never pronounce them outside very specific circumstances. For teaching purposes we use similar sounding names such as:

- For אדני we use the word 'Adnut' (4th level) and,
- For יהוה we use the word 'Havaya' (5th level).

Tonight we are going to concentrate on the 5th level of Adam's chart, the essential name of God 'Havaya'. We are also going to find the sources in the Torah for these 12 permutations. First we must inculcate this basic and profound principle in our astrology, which is that all the energies are coming down from Him first. Each month of the year has its own different energy which flows down to us in a quality represented by the re-arrangement of His 4 letter name; how His name is arranged in each month determines the primal energy which flows down impacting on the lower 4 levels in the zodiac.

I am going to introduce the concept of Permutations through the book Sefer HaYetzira. Our Patriarch Abraham wrote this book and it only contains a couple of pages, so every word counts, and yet he devoted about 10 lines of the book to explaining these permutations, so you have to understand that there is something very important about permutations and it is a very deep thing to connected to. The great scholar and kabalist Rabbi Shimon Bar Yochai, who authored the Zohar and lived about 2000 years ago, wrote a whole book about permutations called Tikuney HaZohar, which was based on the first word in the Torah, בראשית (Bereshit), which would be translated as 'in the beginning'. The word 'Bereshit' has 6 letters (in Hebrew), and we will see that these 6 letters can be permutated 720 different ways, and of those 720 permutations, Rabbi Shimon Bar Yochai explained 70 in his book. These 70 permutations are the 70 Panim (faces) of the Torah. So we need to understand that all the great kabbalists emphasized the use of permutations. Another example is the kabbalist and expert meditator Rabbi Abulafia who used letter permutations extensively in his practice and teachings. Also the book Sulam HaAliya written by his pupil, the great kabbalist who lived in Israel in the 1200's, R. Yehudah Albotini, which deals with how the soul can leave the body and get up to higher levels of consciousness using the power of the permutations of God's names. The book warns the reader that one should only do these permutations together with someone else to ensure that your partner gets you back down fully into your body consciousness, after the meditations. So this is a serious and powerful spiritual tool. So let us learn how it works and see how to use it in astrology, where each month is ruled by a different permutation of God's name.

I am using an English translation and commentary of the Sefer HaYetzira written by Rabbi Aryeh Kaplan, who was an important Talmid Chacham who died at a young age in 1982. Had he been alive today he would be among the top Rabbis of our generation. He was an accomplished Rabbi, mathematician and top physicist with a vast knowledge base. Let's start on page 190 of Rabbi's Kaplan's commentary, Chapter 4:16:

" **2 stones build 2 houses.**
3 stones build 6 houses
4 stones build 24 houses
5 stones build 120 houses
6 stones build 620 houses
7 stones build 5040 houses
From here on go out and calculate
that which the mouth cannot speak
and the ear cannot hear "

This text is written in code, and what is written does not make much sense. How can 3 stones make 6 houses? It means that each house is built from ½ a stone! So you need the key to unlock this code and our sages tell us that one of the ways of building the key is to start seeing the 'stones' as the individual Letters of the Hebrew alphabet, and that these 'stones' come out from the great name of God. With this approach we see that the Sefer HaYetzira is explaining how permutations work and how Letters build Words, depending on how many letters you start with. For example, if you have 2 letters, the letter A and the letter B, one can permute them into words in 2 ways: AB and BA. These are the '2 stones that build 2 houses'. If one has 3 letters (letter A, letter B and letter C), one makes 6 permutations: ABC, ACB, BAC, BCA, CAB, CBA. So '3 stones build 6 houses'. In a similar way 4 letters can be permuted in 24 words, and 5 in 120 etc… And it goes on up to 7 letters that build 5040 words. Throughout this 4th chapter of the book he is talking about the number 7. He then goes on and says, **"from here on go out and calculate that**

which the mouth cannot speak and the ear cannot hear". Over time there have been 4 ways of approaching this book; on a philosophical level, on a kabalistic level, on a meditative level, and on an astrological level. So the book has served different purposes and there are different ways the book has been understood. Rabbi Kaplan's commentary is unique in that it takes a combined meditative and kabalistic approach. For him the stones are letters and with 7 letters you can permute 5040 words of 7 letters each. It would take about 3 hours of concentrated mediation to cover the precise permutations, which is difficult but not impossible. But if you go up to 8 letters you have 322560 words which will take about 30 hours to pronounce and meditate on, which is more or less beyond normal human capabilities. Note that the Sefer HaYetzirah does not start with the number 1, it starts at '2 stones build 2 houses', and this is because in Hebrew, 1 letter cannot build 1 word. The Vilna Gaon comments on this and bases his conclusion on the kabbalistic principles of permutations.

The 5th Level of Adam's chart has 12 permutations of God's name יהוה and yet it has 4 letters. Usually 4 letters would give you 24 permutations, but because 2 of the letters of the name are the same (2 x ה's) we divide the total by 2 and there are only 12 unique permutations of God's name. And these 12 permutations will affect each month, Sign, hour of the day etc.... So for example, the first 3 months in the chart of Adam have a permutation where the first letter of God's name (the י) stays in first place and the other 3 letters (הוה) are permuted into 3 words: יהוה (Nissan/Aries) and יההו (Iyar/Taurus) and יוהה (Sivan/Gemini). So basically the ו switches its position. So the 1st season of the year, spring (3 months), has its energy flow coming from God's name starting with the letter י , and the 1st month of the year is the month of Nisan (Aries), the month in which the children of Israel were taken out of Egypt by God (יהוה). The 2nd season of the year, summer, has 3 permutations starting with the 1st ה in God's name; הויה (Cancer), היוה (Leo) and ההיו (Virgo). So the first ה in God's name rules the summer. The second letter ה in God's name rules the winter, and the letter ו in God's name rules the autumn.

Where is our source for this tradition of connecting the 12 permutations of God's name with the 12 months of the year? We find it in the Tikaney HaZohar written by Rabbi Shimon Bar Yochai. There he shows where each of the 12 permutations of God's name is hinted too in the holy writings of the 24 books of the Tanach (Bible). In kabbalah the First letter or the Last letter of each consecutive word in a sentence are combined to reveal deeper meanings imbedded in the sentence. This is a well established and ancient technique used throughout Torah. For example, in Tehillim/Psalms 96:11 we read; " ישמחו השמים ותגל הארץ " which means, "The heavens will be glad and the earth will rejoice". In this 4 word sentence (Hebrew) we see that by combining the first letter of each word (Hebrew reads from right to left) we arrive at the permutation of God's name יהוה . So there is a strong link here between the meaning of the sentence and this permutation of God's name, which happens to be the permutation of the Name associated with Aries and spring. Permutations can be constructed using either the First letter or the Last letter of each word in that sentence. If the First letters of each word are used to construct a permutation then this indicates energies of Chasidim/mercifulness, and if the Last letters of each word in a sentence are used to construct a permutation then this indicates energies of Din/severity. 12 sources from the Torah make up this tradition and in 6 of these sources the permutations are constructed from the First letters of each word (indicating months and signs that are more merciful) and in the 6 other sources the permutations are constructed using the Last letters of the words (indicating months and signs that are more judgmental and tougher). I am going to list the sources for the 12 months and permutations, and next time we will go into their meanings in more depth.

Nisan	Aries	**יהוה**	Psalms 96:11	ישמחו השמים ותגל הארץ	'The heavens will be glad and the earth will rejoice'
Iyar	Taurus	**יההו**	Jeremiah 9:23	יתהלל◌המתהלל◌השכל◌וידע	'for only with this may one glorify oneself; contemplating and knowing Me'
Sivan	Gemini	**יוהה**	Exodus 26:19/20	ידתיו◌ולצלע◌המשכן◌השנית	'(two) tenons and for the second wall of the tabernacle…'
Tammuz	Cancer	**הוהי**	Esther 5:13	◌זה◌איננו◌שוה◌לי	'(And all) this is worthless to me…'
Av	Leo	**הויה**	Deuteronomy 27:9	הסכת◌ושמע◌ישראל◌היום	'Be attentive and hear Israel this day…'
Elul	Virgo	**ההוי**	Deuteronomy 6:25	וצדקה◌תהיה◌לנו◌כי	'(and it will be a) merit for us if…'
Tishrei	Libra	**והיה**	Genesis 12:15	ויראו אתה שרי פרעה	'When the official of pharaoh saw her…'
Cheshvan	Scorpio	**וההי**	Deuteronomy 26:15/16	ודבש היום◌ הזה◌יהוה◌	'(a land flowing with milk and) honey, this day Hashem your God (commands you…) '
Kislev	Sagittarius	**ויהה**	Genesis 50:11	ויראו◌יושב◌הארץ◌הכנעני	'When the Canaanite inhabitants of the land saw…'

Tevet	Capricorn	היהו	Psalm 34:4	ליהוה○אתי○ונרוממה○שמו	'Declare the greatness of God with me... '
Shvat	Aquarius	היוה	Leviticus 27:33	המר○ימירנו○והיה○הוא	'... if he does substitute for it, then it and its substitute shall be holy'
Adar	Pisces	ההיו	Genesis	עירה○ולשרקה○בני○אתנו	'He will tie his donkey to the vine...'

Chapter 2

Let us focus on the holy name of God (יהוה = Havaya). This Name is permutated 12 times and is placed on the 5th level of Adam's chart. The essence of the message from this 5th level is that no one should think that the energy is just coming from the Planets and the Signs! There are things which are much higher sending down energies and controlling and directing the whole process going on down here on earth, and these higher powers go all the way up to God. The Planets are the lower conduit, they pass down the energy from above, and that's all. They do their jobs but are not directing what is happening on earth! Here is Adam HaRishon's (Adam) chart:

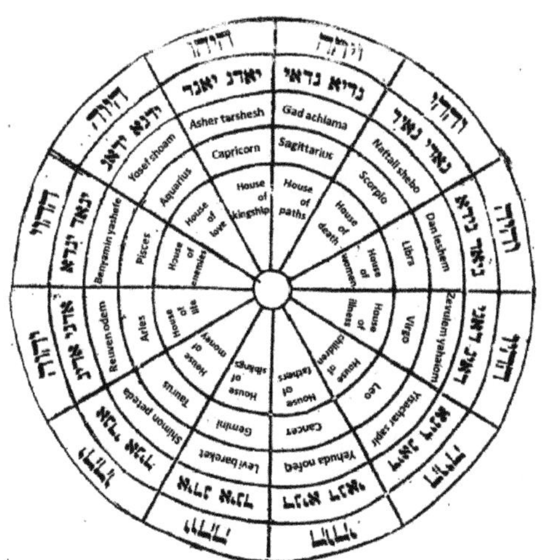

In part-1 we discussed the fact that Adam's Zodiac has 5 levels, of which the first 2 are standard in Western astrology (Houses, Signs and Planets). Above that we have the 12 Tribes of Israel together with the 12 jewels which were on the breast placement of the High Priest in the Holy Temple in Jerusalem. We will cover the 12 Tribes and their influences in future lessons. Above the Tribes are the 2 different names of God, the Name Adnut (אדני) and the Name Havaya (יהוה), which are the 2 main Names. We explained how the highest 5th level name Havaya was permuted into 12 Names. These 12 Names are the source influence of each month and therefore each month is going to have a different characteristic and a different impact on the world. We also mentioned that the permutations of God's name which is associated with the first 3 months (Aries/Nisan, Taurus/Iyar and Gemini/Sivan) starts with the letter י which is the first letter in God's name, and is associated with the time of spring. Then the next 3 months (Cancer, Leo and Virgo) come from the first ה of God's Name and rules the summer. Then the letter ו rules the autumn (Libra, Scorpio and Sagittarius), and the last 3 months (Capricorn, Aquarius and Pisces) are associated with the last ה of God's Name which rules the winter. We also quoted from a Tikuney Zohar (page 9/10) where Rabbi Shimon Bar Yochai connects each permutation of God's name with a passage in the Tanach (Bible). We will talk in the future about the significance to these passages relative to the 12 months of the year.

Before we focus on the meanings of the Name Havaya I would like to give an introduction to 4 key concepts in Kabbala, which will help us get a better understanding of this holy Name:

The 10 Sefirot/Spheres of the Tree of Life:

In Kabala there are 10 Sefirot, each with its own name. The first 3 Sefirot are called the Gimel Rishonot (the first three). They are:

- The 1st Sefira is Keter/Crown.
- The 2nd Sefira is Chochma/Wisdom
- The 3rd Sefira is Bina/Understanding.

The last 7 Sefirot are:

- Chesed/Love or Mercy
- Gevura/Strength and Judgment (connected to the left arm)
- Tiferet/Majesty and Truth (connected to the chest)
- Netzach/Victory and Hod/Glory (the right and left leg)
- Yesod/Foundation
- Malchut/Kingship

Keter is the highest Sefira of the 10 Sefirot, and it is an intermediary between the world above and the world that we are in. Keter is a Crown sitting on the king's head, but it is not part of the king, it is above him. So sometimes Keter is counted with the other Sefirot (as their source) and other times it is not counted with them (excluded as the source).

The 10 Sefirot become the 5 Partzufim (Faces):

The 10 Sefirot are also grouped into 5 Partzufim (Faces). Through these Partzufim the Sefirot learn to do their Tikun (Rectification). Here they are:

- Keter = **Atik Yomin** (Ancient of Days) or/and **Arik Anpin** (Long Face)
- Chochma = **Abba** (Father)

- Bina = **Imma** (Mother)
- The 6 Sefirot Chesed, Gevura, Tiferet, Netzach, Hod and Yesod = **Zeir Anpin** (Small Face)
- Malchut = **Nukva** (An opening)

If Keter is not include in the 10 Sefirot then it is know as Keter, and if Keter is included in the 10 Sefirot it is divided and Keter becomes 2 Partzufim: Atik Yomin and Arik Anpin. This is when it is included as the intermediary between the worlds above the 10 Sefirot and the worlds below the 10 Sefirot; Atik of Keter connects with the upper worlds and Arik of Keter connects with the lower worlds, and the 2 Partzufim together make up Keter. So when Keter is included you then have 6 Partzufim (instead of the standard 5 Partzufim); Atik and Arik (for Keter), Abba, Imma, Zeir Anpin and Nukva.

Havaya, the Sefirot and the Partzufim (Faces):

God's name of Havaya has 4 letters and these 4 letters also represent all the Sefirot and all the Partzufim.

	ה	ו	ה	י
Sefirot	Malchut	Chesed to Yesod	Bina	Chochma (and Keter)
Partzufim	Nukva	Zeir Anpin	Imma	Abba (and Atik and Arik)

Also the Male and Female aspect is represented by י = Male/Abba and ה = Female/Imma forming a pair, and the ו = Male, known as 'the son', pairs off with the final ה = Female known as 'the daughter' (Malchut). As you can see Keter is included in the י (with Chochma/Abba) and this is represented by the tip of the י which has a little curve at the top. Just as Keter is so high up, so that curve at the top of the י is a hint to the inclusion of Keter/Crown. So when we work with the Havaya we don't count the Keter because it is the Shoresh (the root), the source, and is considered a world unto itself. So we only talk about Abba and Imma, Zeer Anpin and Malchut. It is written in the Torah; "Everything You made with Wisdom (Chochma)". God made everything with Chochma because Keter is really above creation, so everything actually starts with Chochma. This is why the Torah starts with the letter ב , in order to show you that everything actually starts with the 2nd Sefira, which is Chochma/Wisdom.

Energy flow of the Partzufim:

Let us include Keter in the count and say in this instance that there are 6 Partzufim; Atik, Arik, Abba, Imma, Zeir Anpin (Za) and Nukva (Nok). Each one of them has a male and a female side (Atik has Arik, Abba has Imma, Za has Nok). The difference between them is that the higher up you are in the worlds, the more unity there is between the male and the female sides. And the lower you come down the less the unity between male and female. For example, Atik which is the highest Partzuf has such a unity that there is no distinction between the male and the female, the one is submerged inside the other. When you get down to the Partzuf of Arik, it also has a very high level of unity and there are no separate entities in there, but there is a distinction between male (which is on the right side) and the female (which on the left side). With Abba and Imma, the Zohar tells us that Abba and Imma are always stuck together, and yet they are 2 separate distinct Partzufim, one male and one female. They are two separate faces which are stuck together and are always Face to Face. So you see that as we go down there is more of a split and separation between the male and the female. And when you get down to Zer Anpin and Nok, which is the lowest level, there you see that sometimes they are together and sometimes they are separate. In other words, sometimes they face each other, they stand Face to Face and sometimes they are Back to Back with no real connection.

Now that I have given these basic introductions let us try to better understand the permutations of the God's name and their associations with the months. We are using material from the early Kabbala which is found in the writings of Rabbi Moshe Cordovero (RaMaK) in his master work, the book Pardes Rimonim (Orchard of Pomegranates). The RaMaK was an important Kabbalist in Zefat before the Ari Zal. And in that book he summarizes and synthesizes all the Kabbala that was written and studied before his time. In fact the Ari Zal based his studies and relied upon the writings of the RaMaK to build his deeper insights. So when the Ari Zal taught the top rabbis of Zefat, he already knew the system of RaMaK and he assumed that everyone else also knew it, so he did not repeat it. So often we have to go back to the early Kabbala to learn the basics because the Ari didn't teach the foundations of the Kabbala, but rather its development into deeper worlds. The Vilna Gaon said that where philosophy ends Rabbi Moshe Cordovero begins, and where Rabbi Moshe Cordovero ends this is where the Ari Zal begins.

The 1st month is Aries, which in Hebrew is the month of Nisan. And the word 'Nisan' comes from the Hebrew word for ' a miracle'. That was the month of miracles when God took the children of Israel out of Egypt with all those miracles and wonders. And God said about the month of Nisan; 'this month is the first of all months for you'. In other words you count the 12 months starting from Nisan (the year is counted from Tishrei and the months from Nisan). And God's name for the first month is read in a straight way יהוה (see Adam's chart), in its proper order (the way we write it), with י as the first letter followed by ה and ו and then the last ה. When the 4 letters are in the proper order the energy flow is one of complete unity, love and mercy, and it is the secret of what we call קרבן ליהוה ('an offering to God'), where God is referred to as יהוה (his attribute of unity, mercy and love), as apposed to the name אלהים (Elohim), which is a Name of God depicting an attribute of Judgment. Also in Hebrew the word קרבן (Korban-Offering) refers to the word קרב (Keruv) which in English means 'to bring things closer together'. When you make an offering to God, you bring the upper worlds and the lower worlds together. And this unity is depicted in the form of the 2 male letters and the 2 female letters in their correct order; first the male י and then the female ה , and then the male ו and the final female ה. We mentioned before that the Partzufim of Abba and Imma are a set of a male and a female, which correspond to the י and the first ה of Gods name, and Zeer Anpin and Nok are another set of male and female corresponding to the ו and the last ה of God's name, as is explained in many places in the Zohar. So this permutation of God's name enables the flow of energy to come down in the best possible way, in the proper way, according to the proper arrangement. This order of God's name is associated with Aries, and Aries is ideally the best Ascendant. It is ideal for a man to have an Aries Ascendant because it is associated with the normal, proper and straight sequence of God's name. It is what God wanted as an ideal for Adam. All the other permutations and months are variations to this 4 letter name in different sequences, and they do not have the ideal balance of mercy, unity and love which is indicated by this normal name of God. There are many other hints and secrets about this first name but that is for another time.

The second permutation יההו (Taurus and the Hebrew month of Iyar) also starts with the י (for the first 3 months of spring), and the last 3 letters (הוה) are the ones to be permuted. What happens is that the last ה (Malchut/Nukva) is now going to go up next to the י where you now have י which is Abba, followed by ה of Nukva giving you the relationship of Abba with the Daughter. The first ה (Binah/Imma) moves to 3rd spot to be a Mother to the Son ו (4th letter). This is the 2nd 'Havaya', the 2nd energy which flows from God expressed through His Name permutations. Sometimes the Malchut goes up and unites with the Chochma and then Bina comes down and unites with the Tiferet, which is with the Son, the Zeir Anpin, the ו . The RaMak comments on the "Book of Proverbs 3:19:'God (יהוה) with Wisdom He founded the Earth'. The Earth is a hint to Malchut (Kingship), for the Malchut is in the secret of the Wisdom (Chochma) and it continues…'And (God) prepares the Heavens with Understanding'. For the Tiferet is propelled by the Bina (Understanding)." So he is connecting Chochma with Malchut through 'God created the Earth through Wisdom', and Bina with Zeir Anpin (Tiferet) through 'God preparing the Heavens (Zeir) with Understanding (Bina)'. The RaMaK continues…"and that is the secret of the יההו permutation of God's name, where the י followed twice by a ה and then by a ו. The first ה that unites with the י is the Malchut, and the ה which is next to the ו is the Bina. And it has to be this way for two reasons: The first reason is because it is impossible for the first ה to be Bina (in the permutation יההו). This is because if it was, then Chochma and Bina would be uniting while Tiferet/Zeir Anpin (ו) and Malchut/Nukva would not be uniting (since they are out of order with Malchut above Tiferet) and this is impossible". So if the י and the first ה (Abba and Imma) are working in correct order and unity and the ה and the ו (Nok and Za) are out of order and unable to work, that is not possible. In other words if you would have the י and ה in unity this must cause unity in the lower Partzufim of the Son and the Daughter (ה and ו) and this cannot be since they are out of synch. So you have to say that the first ה is the Daughter which is Malchut, and is together with the י Abba (Father); and the second ה is the Imma (Mother) and she is together with the Son ו. "The second reason is that from the perspective of the Son which is Tiferet, Malchut should always be lower than him and therefore the ה which is higher than the ו has to be Bina and not Malchut".

The 3rd permutation which also starts with the letter י is יוהה , and is the last month of the 3 spring months, which is Gemini and the Hebrew month of Sivan. The RaMaK explains this permutation as follows; " Here you have the Males (the י and the ו) inclining to the right side, for the nature of the Male is to go to the right, and the nature of the Female is to go to the left. And because of this it is necessary for the Tiferet (ו) to go up by way of Chesed to Chochma (י), and the Malchut (ה) will go up by way of Gevura to Bina (ה)".

One way of depicting the Sefirot is with the 3 pillars of the Tree of Life which the Sefirot stand on. This Tree of life has a right pillar (Male), a left pillar (Female) and a central pillar balancing in the middle. The right pillar has the following Sefirot; **C**hochma, **C**hesed and **N**etzach, which are abbreviated to **ChaChaN**. The left pillar has the following Sefirot; **B**ina, **G**evura and **H**od, abbreviated to **BaGaH**. The central pillar has the following Sefirot; **D**aat, **T**iferet, **Y**esod and **M**alchut, abbreviated to **DaTYaM**. And it is also possible to add Keter on top of that central pillar. So he is saying that the Tiferet (ו) which symbolizes the chest in the middle is going to go into Chesed which is on the right side and from Chesed it is going to go straight up to Chochma (י). In other words 'now the Males are going to be together on the right'. Also the Malchut is going to go up by way of Gevura, which is on the left side, and then from Gevura it is going to go straight up to Bina (ה). So now you have the Males on the right side which are Chochma and Tiferet (י and the ו) and the Females on the left side (ה and the ה) which are Bina and Malchut. "So Tiferet which is ו is uniting with the י which is Chochma, and then the last ה which is Malchut is uniting with the first ה which is Bina. And this is the permutation with י at the beginning, followed by ו and two ה 's. Concerning the Chochma and Tiferet being together it is said that 'the Son is drawn from the intelligence of the father'. And another explanation for this permutation is that it teaches about the exile of the Shechina, the Divine Presence, in both the higher and the lower worlds because it has been separated from its place because the males יו are separated from the females הה, as if divorced from their husbands".

The 4th month is going to start with the letter ה which represents Bina. This permutation הוהי is Cancer and the Hebrew month of Tamuz. The RaMaK teaches us that this is a permutation of strict and powerful Judgment, because the Feminine (הה) is ruling over the Masculine (וי). The first ה (Feminine) rules over the ו (Masculine) and the second ה (Feminine) also rules over the י (Masculine). The Zohar says that this is the secret of the returning light. There is a light which goes from the top down to the bottom (Masculine down to Feminine), and there is a light which goes from the bottom upwards to the top (Feminine up to Masculine) which is called 'the returning light' (returning from the bottom to the top). And this is due to the power generated by the 4 letters being turned around into the opposite of the 1st permutation of Havaya (יהוה). Instead of the י being first, it is now last, and instead of the ה being last, it is now first. This 4th permutation הוהי is the opposite of the 1st permutation of יהוה. So this causes Judgment and severity. So to get back and to turn this around to mercy and love instead of strict judgment, we have to climb back up using this opposite permutation of the Name, like it says in Psalms; 'The despised stone of the builders will eventually became the foundation stone'. Because the energy flow of the הוהי can be turned around and started from the bottom to generate the energy flow of the original name יהוה .

So in summary the Zohar teaches that when the Name permutations starts with a י it is connected with the Right side; Chochma, Chesed and Netzach, and are connected with the first 3 months of spring, generating unity and love. When the Name permutations start with the first ה it is connected with the Left side; Bina, Gevura and Hod, and are the 3 months of summer, whose heat generates strict Judgment. When the Name permutations start with the ו it is connected to the Middle pillar; Keter, Tiferet and Yesod, and are the 3 months of autumn, generating mercy from a balance between Chesed and Gevura (Love and Judgment). And when the Name permutations starts with the last ה it is connected to the bottom Sefira of Malchut, and are the 3 months of winter, which can generate energies from either one of the 3 pillars; 1 month to the right to Chesed (Love), 1 month to the left to Gevura (strict Judgment) and 1 month to the middle to Tiferet (Mercy).

Chapter 3

In chapter 2 we talked about the first 3 permutations of God's name יהוה starting with the י which covered the first 3 months of Nisan/Aries, Iyar/Taurus and Sivan/Gemini. We also covered the first permutation of 3 which starts with the ה (Tamuz/Cancer). These permutations are from the 5th level of Adam HaRishon's chart. Here is Adam's chart:

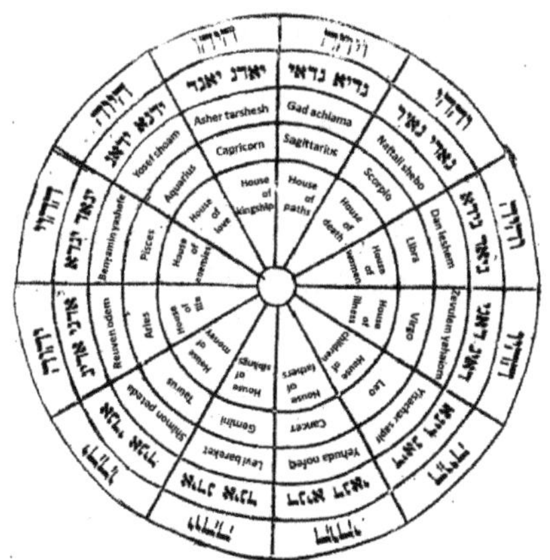

We discussed a kabala principle in Jewish astrology where we have 3 Pillars or some call it 3 Lines (3 Kavim) which form the basic template of the time of the Tikun. Tikun is fixing, fixing the world on a micro and macro level. Before the Tikun, before the 3 Pillars, everything came out in 1 Pillar of energy, and this could not be sustained and broke. That was one of the reasons why there was a breakage in the original Creation which lead to the time of Tikun, where everything came into the world one after the other, and so broke, which is called in the Kabbala 'Chad Samcha'. So it broke and resurfaced as the time of the Tikun, and everything became 3 Pillars. In other words, all the Sefirot/Spheres which are connected with the Chesed/Love went to the Right side, and all the things which are connected with Gevura/Strength and Judgment went to the Left side. This Left side is depicted in kabala as **B**ina/Understanding, **G**evura/Judgement, and **H**od/Glory abbreviated as **BGH**, and the Right side is depicted as **C**hochma/Wisdom, **C**hesed/Love and **N**etzach/Endurance abbreviated as **CCN**. The middle Pillar is the balance between the Right and the Left side; these are the Sefirot of Keter/Crown, Tiferet/Truth and Yesod/Foundation abbreviated as **KTY**. Malchut goes into each one of the Pillars and is underneath them and covers them all.

So we learned that the first 3 months are connected to the י of Gods name and י teaches about the Right side (CCN), which are the months connected with love. We also learned that the 12 months are divided into 4 seasons, 3 months per season. The first 3 months are the Spring and connect with the Right side (CCN) of love. The next 3 months are Summer and connect with the Left side (BGH) of strength and judgment. The middle column is going to be Autumn which is the ו which is connected to the Middle pillar (KTY) of Mercy and Truth. And the last 3 months are the Winter, the Malchut, the Kingship and sovereignty which can attach to any of the 3 Pillars above it. We will now continue with the 5th month of Av/Leo (summer) and complete the remaining months and associated permutations of God's name. The main point here is to meditate on these permutations and their significances, and intuit a deeper understanding of the months and Signs. The energies are not generated by the Planets and Signs, but rather these Planets and Signs are conduits for a much higher source (5th level) depicted through the 12 permutations of the holy name of God. It is these 12 Holy names that are running the world, with each name directing a specific energy into each month of the year. So if you can really start to understand these Permutations you can get more in touch and connected with the energy of each month that you are in. In the practice of Kabbala, Kabbalists pray with a special prayer book whose main difference is that it guides the user in using the appropriate meditations on the names of God during the various sections of the standard daily prayers, and with the correct concentration and experience, they are able to draw those energies down from the higher worlds. So for example in the prayers on Rosh Chodesh (the monthly prayers on the day of the new moon/month) when they recite the extra prayer of Musaf for the upcoming month, they have special Kavanot/Intentions in the prayers specific to each of the 12 months which are based on the 12 permutations of God's 4 letter name which we are studying now, each name with its own unique energy appropriate for each specific month's work. So these permutations are very important. This prayer book is referred to as the Book of Kavanot, and was compiled by the Rashash.

Let us continue with the 5th permutation of Leo. This material is coming from the writings of the RaMak (Rabbi Moshe Cordovero) who was an early Kabbalist and the master Kabbalist of his time, before the arrival of the Ari Zal. Remember that the Vilna Gaon said that 'where philosophy ends the RaMak begins, and where the RaMak ends, the Ari Zal begins'. So the RaMak was a very important rabbi, and he synthesized all of the Kabala that came before him into his master work, the book of Pardes Rimonim (Orchard of Pomegranates). That is the book we are learning from tonight.

So the 5th permutation is הויה , which is the month of Av which is Leo, and that teaches us that the Son ו is going to go up to be with the Mother ה , which means that Tiferet ו is going to be together with Bina ה, which teaches us that the Mother is comforting the Son. And the Father י is going to go down to the Daughter ה. This 5th Havaya הויה is the opposite of the 2nd Havaya of Taurus יההו where the Daughter ה went up to the Father י and the Mother ה was the one who came down to the Son ו. But here in Leo it is the exact opposite: The Son is going up to the Mother, and the Father is coming down to the Daughter. There is another explanation where we can talk about this Name coming as units, with the 1st unit being הוי followed by a 2nd unit being ה only, like Rabbi Shimon Bar Yochai explained in the Zohar. The ה which is Bina is joined by the ו which is Tiferet and is also joined by the head of the righteous person (the Tzadik) which draws the blessings which is the י making up the הוי unit, leaving the last ה alone. We see that the ה is more about strict Judgments when compared to the י which is more about mercy, and the permutation which start with a ה is the season of Summer and Av/Leo can be very hot.

The 6th Permutation is ההיו which is the 6th month of Elul and the Sign of Virgo. This teaches us about the Exile. It teaches us about the Exile of the 2 Sisters, 'that the 2 of them will go together', the Bride ה and the Mother in law ה; Naomi and Ruth. And the Father י and Son ו will go together and the 2 ה's are going to be separated from them. So the 2 Female ה's are going it alone, and the Masculine י and ו are together, but separated from the two ה's. But on the other hand יו are in the proper order (when compared to the prime יהוה); 1st the י and then the ו , but the 2 ה's are above to teach us that there is not much energy coming down in that month.

The 7th Permutation is a והיה for the month Tishrei which is the Sign of the Libra. This order of the ו followed by a ה and then a י and a ה teaches us about the energy when the Right side rules over the Left side; the Masculine ו is 1st and then the Feminine ה and then again the Masculine י and the Feminine ה , so the Masculine Right side leads the way and turns the Left side into becoming more merciful. The וה are in their proper order (when compared to the prime יהוה) and the ו coming 1st is to teach you that the Right rules over the Left and turns the Left around to mercy. And this is for good and is a beneficial thing because a וה is the energy of Receiving while the energy of the יה is to send down, to give. So in this Month we have the receiver וה first and then the giver יה. And the יה is the mercy, while the וה is judgment. And they are in the secret of the giver and the receiver. So in other words והיה is similar to the first prime Name יהוה (the 1st Permutation Aries) except for the fact that the 2nd group of the prime Name וה became the 1st group and the 1st group יה became the 2nd group. Here in והיה we have the receiver וה first and then the giver יה while the Permutation of Aries has the giver first and then the receiver. The והיה is a masculine energy because both halves start with a masculine part of the 4 letter Name: The 1st group is וה which starts with the ו which is masculine and the 2nd group is יה which starts with the י which is also masculine. Compared to the prime Name the only difference is that the Son and the Daughter went up to be 1st as the Receivers, and the Father and Mother, the Givers יה, came at the end. So this turns the Left (which is normally the receiver) into being the Giver, which is as the Zohar above.

The 8th Permutation וההי is the month of MarCheshvan (or Cheshvan) and the Sign of Scorpio. It falls in October/November in the regular sun calendar. The Permutations for the more gentle seasons of spring and autumn, start with the masculine letters י and ו which are more merciful, while the Permutations for the more severe seasons of summer and winter start with the feminine letters ה and ה, which are more judgmental. The Permutation for the month of the Scorpio is וההי ...and this is teaching us again about the Right ruling over the Left. The וה which is on the right side rules over the second הי which is on the left side. So here the וה which are the Son and the Daughter came first. But in this month of Scorpio the 2nd pair/unit which are the Father and the Mother appear here with the Mother coming 1st (while in the month of Libra the Father come 1st). So therefore it is not complete mercy like the previous permutation, because there the right one ruled over the left, and turned the left to mercy, while here although we have the same וה from the right side but the 2nd pair is הי which start with the judgment of the feminine ה so the ה rules over the י which leaves an aspect of strict judgment here in Scorpio.

The 9th Permutation is ויהה for the month of Kislev which is the Sign of Sagittarius. This Name is going to teach us about the exile of the High Shechina (the High Divine Presence of ה), and also the Low Divine Presence of ה. And both of them were divorced from their place. So the Father and the Son went up as וי and the feminine ה's separated and went down. Another way to learn it is that both of the ה's were divorced. So the Father י went down to be with the 2 ה's but from a distance, to guard His children while they are in exile. And that is what is said in the Zohar of the Parasha of Ki Tetze, on page 288, that the Abba י goes down from the righteous ו to guard the Shechina which is in exile.

The 10th Permutation היהו is the month of Tevet with is the Sign of Capricorn, the Sign of the goat. By now the winter months are starting and the months which are connected with the middle column ו have ended. The Permutations begin now with the letter ה again, which are more difficult months. So the Permutation for the month of Tevet היהו teaches us about the י which is the Father who goes down to be with the ה which is the Daughter, and the Daughter goes up to meet him in the middle, both of them are there in the middle of the Name, which means they both left their place. They are the Chochma (Wisdom) and Malchut (Kingship). The Abba (Father) came down and instead of being before the Imma (Mother) he moved down to be after the Imma. And the Imma ה went up and the the ו Tiferet came down. And this also teaches us about Din (strict judgment), because now there is no Yichud (co-joining of Masculine/Feminine energy) because they are out of order. The Feminine ה's are coming first in both pairs in this Permutation, its הי and הו. When there is no Yichud it teaches us about a time when there is no energy coming down. There is a principle in Kabbala which states that energies come down from the upper worlds only when there is a Yichud down here below, when there is a relationship between the Male and the Female. So when this relationship does not exist, there are no energies coming down, so it is a time of strict judgment. The ה which is normally on the Left takes over the Right (which is normally the י) to הי and the strength of this causes the ו in the 2nd unit to move down and let the ה go up to make הו which cause the block in the energy flow and brings about strict judgment. And this is similar to the 4th Permutation of הויה of the Sign of Cancer which is more about total strict judgment than is the month of Tevet. The היהו of Capricorn is not as much about a total strict judgment as the הויה of Cancer which turns everything completely around (when compared to the prime Name יהוה). In each of the sub-units of 2 letters in Capricorn (הי and הו) the ה's rule so there is a lot of judgment there, but not as much as when the letters in each of the sub-units are themselves turned around like in the month of Cancer. This is because in the month Tevet (Capricorn) the sequence is היהו which is Mother ה and Father י, and then Daughter ה and Son ו, so its still the parents up top and children below which is less of a mix up than the month of Tammuz (Cancer) הויה where the sequence is Mother and Son, followed by Daughter and Father. All this teaches us about the important concept in Kabala called Or Chozer (Returning Light). There is the Or Yashar (the Straight Light) which is the light coming down from above, from Keter/Crown to Chochma/Wisdom to Bina/Understand, and then you have the Returning Light, which is the light that goes up from below, which starts from Malchut/Kingship and goes up to Bina. This happens because Bina ה is sending to Chochma י, and this is mirrored below with Malchut ה sending to Tiferet ו. This teaches us about the Or Chozer, the light which goes back up.

The 11th Permutation היוה is the month of the Shevat which is the Sign of Aquarius, the water carrier. In this month the Father goes down to the Son. In the 3rd Permutation יוהה of the month of Sivan, the Son ו (Tiferet) goes up to the Father Chochma, but in the Permutation of Aquarius of היוה the Father (Chochma) goes down to the Son ו and the Mother comes 1st. The Son and Daughter are in correct order, but the Father and Mother have switched roles with the ה coming before the י. So the real movement is the Father going down to the Son. Another explanation is that the 2nd unit of וה which is Masculine because it starts with the Masculine ו is therefore said to be coming from the side of the Right (which is Masculine) so that **וה** fits into the Name **אלוה** which is another name of God known as the Shem Elohut, which is made up to the holy Name אל followed by the letters of וה. The 1st unit of **הי** start with the Feminine ה so it is associated with the Left side and the name of God **אלהים** with the name of God אל followed by the הי. So that teaches us more about the strict judgment because the name אלהים is a more judgmental name. But when it is a וה then everything is in balance and the name **אלהים**, which is strict judgment, turns into the word **אלוה**, which is mercy.

The 12th Permutation ההיו is the month of Adar and the Sign of Pisces, the sign of the fish. This permutation also teaches us about the exile of the Upper and the Lower Shechina (Divine presence). Here the 2 ה's, Bina 1st and then Malchut, go together and are separated from the 2 Masculine's of the Son and Father and there is no Yichud here, no coming together between the Males and the Females causing judgment.

These 12 months are allotted slightly different letter combinations in the 12 Permutations by the different schools of kabala, with the famous Moroccan Rabbi, Rabbi Lavi, teaching it one way in his book the Ketem Paz (which is a commentary on the Zohar) compared to the writings of Rabbi Moshe Cordovero, who does a slightly different arrangement of the 4 letters. They are in agreement with respect to the order of the י and the ו while the discrepancy arises with how the ה's are arranged, but the principle is the same. This we will go into more details in future lessons.

Chapter 4

So far we have learned that there are 12 ways to permute God's name, where God's name has 4 letters, and 4 letters can normally be permutated in 24 ways, but because the letter ה in God's name appears twice, you have to divide 24 by 2, and so the name of God can be permutated in 12 ways only, one permutation for each of the 12 months of the year (see part 1). We also studied how the Ramak (Rabbi Moshe Cordovero, the chief rabbi of Sefat before the Ari Zal) learned how each of these permutations/months is different from the others in terms of the energies coming down. We also covered the archetypal chart of Adam HaRishon which has 5 levels to the zodiac. We also clarified how Western astrology only includes the 1st level of the 12 houses and the 2nd level which has the Signs and the ruling Planets. The 3rd, 4th, and 5th levels of energies coming down in Adam's chart (the Tribes, the Permutations of the name Adnut, and the Permutations of the name Havaya) are not part of Western astrology.

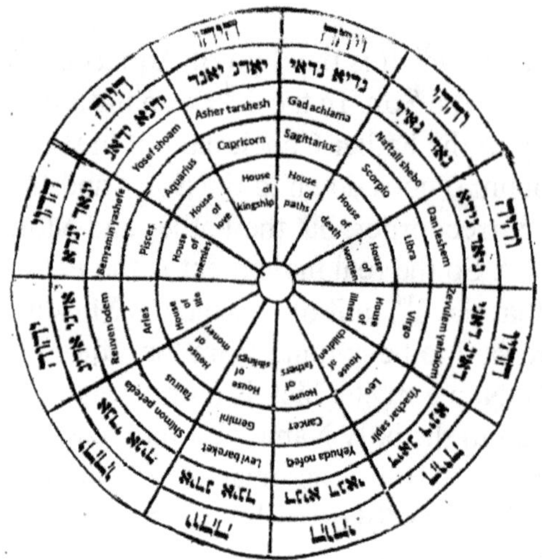

The basic lesson of Adam's chart comes to teach you that you shouldn't think that all the energies are coming from the Planets or the Signs only, as if they are the ones who determine what is happening down here on earth. They are the conduits of much higher influences. Everything really comes from God, and it comes, among other things, through the permutations of His names. So through these different permutations of God's name the energies coming down are different in each month.

Let us talk about the letters of the Hebrew alphabet. The 22 Hebrew Letters are important because according to our Torah, God looked into the Torah, and using the Letters He created the world. The book Sefer HaYetzira (book of Creation), which is the oldest book in Jewish literature, written by Avraham Avinu, categorizes the 22 letters of the Hebrew alphabet into 3 groups: The 3 Elemental Letters, the 7 Double Letters, and the 12 Simple Letters. The 3 Elemental Letters are א מ ש and represent Water, Air and Fire (the Sefer HaYetzira does not include the 4th element of Earth). The 7 letters are ב ג ד כ פ ר ת and represent the 7 Planets (Saturn, Jupiter….Moon) and are summarized by the acronym of BaGaD KaFRaT. All these 7 letters are called 'Doubles', because they can be pronounced in both ways: hard and soft. For example, the letter ב can be pronounced as Bet or as Vet, depending on where the dot is in the word. And ג can be pronounced as Gimel or as Jimel depending where the dot is, and so on. So these 7 letters have a side of Chesed/Love and a side of Din/Judgment; soft or hard. And those letters represent the 7 Planets and indeed each Planet can be good or bad depending on its circumstances.

Then you have the 12 Simple Letters. Why are they called Simple? One reason is because they don't have a hard and a soft side. But we will see that the Ramak is going to give other answers to this question which we will deal with latter. The 12 Simple Letters represent the 12 Signs of the Zodiac, the 12 months of the year, the 12 hours of the day, the 12 hours of the night and the 12 boundaries of a cube (a cube has 6 sides, east, west, north, south, up and down and it has 12 boundaries; on the top there are 4 boundaries, on the bottom there are 4 boundaries, and there are another 4 boundaries connecting the top with the bottom). Just like the 12 permutations of God's name each are connected to the 12 Signs in the Zodiac, so are they connected to the 12 Simple Letters; the Simple letters are ה ו ז ח ט י ל נ ס ע צ ק. So these 12 letters of the Hebrew language are each connected to one of the 12 months. And our tradition is that God used these 12 letters to create the energies of the 12 months. You would think that because these letters do not have a Hard or Soft sound (like the 7 Double Letters), that they are neutral and are not sometimes Merciful and other times Judgmental, they just go one way. But the Ramak says that, "we don't say that they are called 'Simple' because they neutral and are not made up of Mercy and Judgment, like many of the commentators say, because that it is not true. Why? Because it has already been explained that of the 12 Permutations of God's 4 letter Name (יהוה), some begin with the letter ה, whether before the י or before the ו, and when the Permutation begins with the Feminine ה it causes Judgment". Like we have learned in previous lessons these 12 permutations have either a Mercy or Judgment energy flow, so if it is a strait way of permuting Gods name (יהוה), then there is more of a Chesed/Mercy energy flow, but if it permutes in a backwards way (הוהי) then it is completely about strict Judgment/Gevura; and all the other 10 permutations are different degrees of Judgment and Mercy. So the difference between the Double and Simple letters is not that they do not have Judgment and Mercy.

"Also these 12 Simple Letters are connected to the Partzuf of Zeir Anpin (which is represented by the Sefira of Tiferet) which is made up of the 6 Sefirot of Chesed, Gevura, Tiferet, Netzach, Hod and Yesod (where each Sefira has a Masculine and Feminine side making up the 12 sides) and there is no doubt that these Sefirot have Judgment and Mercy. So the Simple letters do have Judgment and Mercy even though they do not have a hard and soft sound each". The Ramak gives another explanation as to why these 12 letters are called Simple/Peshutot (instead of assuming incorrectly that they are named as such because they are neutral in nature); "We can also say that they have a Dagesh, a dash, on their sound. So even though they are not letters which can be pronounced in different ways, their sound is harder than the other letters. Also they are called Simple Letters because they are branches that break off from the Sefirot, and they are not the Sefirot themselves, as opposed to the 3 Elemental letters (ש מ א) and the 7 Double letters of BaGad KaFRaT which together make up the 10 Sefirot. So these 12 Simple letters are like branches which come out of those 10 Sefirot. And behold, you should also know that it was these 12 letters which created the 12 Signs of the Zodiac and the 12 months of the year and the 12 limbs/organs of the body".

Let us now go to the Sefer HaYetzira, the Book of Creation, and look at Chapter 5;

"12 Simple Letters are ה ו ז ח ט י ל נ ס ע צ ק and their Foundations are Speech, Thought, Motion, Sight, Hearing, Action, Coition, Smell, Sleep, Anger, Taste, and Laughter. Their Foundation are the 12 diagonal boundaries: The east upper boundary, the east northern boundary, the east lower boundary, the south upper boundary, the south eastern boundary, the south lower boundary, the west upper boundary, the west southern boundary, the west lower boundary, the north upper boundary, the north western boundary and the north lower boundary. And they extend continually until eternity of eternities, and they are the boundaries of the Universe. Their foundation is that He

Engraved them, Carved them, Permutated them, Weighed them and Transformed them, and with them He formed 12 constellations of the Universe, 12 months of the year, and 12 directors over the soul, male and female".

The Sefer HaYetzira teaches the principle of 3 Worlds which work, at all times, in parallel to each other, and are called in Hebrew Olam (Space), Shana (Time) and Nefesh (Consciousness), and they are all inter connected; whatever happens in one of these Worlds happens in the others at the same time. These 12 letters work in the Olam/Space World by creating the 12 constellations, and these work in the Shana/Time World by creating the 12 months, and they work on the Nefesh/human soul (consciousness) by making the 12 organs of the body that are directing the body. For example, the Religious holiday of Yom Kippur (when Jews fast for 24 hours), we find that the religious rituals for the day are structured around these 3 Worlds; The correct rituals of Yom Kippur as described in the Torah, have Olam/Space since they are supposed to take place only in the holiest place in the world, which was the Jewish Temple in Jerusalem, where the highlight of the ceremony takes place in the Holiest Place in the Temple, The Chamber of the Holy of Holies. The rituals had to take place on a specific date and time, so we have Shana/Time since this was the High spiritual time of Yom Kippur in the month of Tishrei (Libra). And the Nefesh/Consciousness is reflected in that the rituals must be conducted by the man with the highest spiritual status (consciousness) of the Jewish people of that generation, the Cohen Gadol, the Jewish high priest; Space, Time and Consciousness a perfect alignment on the Day of Atonement.

The Sefer HaYetzira continues; "There are 12 constellations in the universe: Aries, Taurus, Gemini, Cancer, Leo, Virgo, Libra, Scorpio, Sagittarius, Capricorn, Aquarius and Pisces.

There are 12 months in the year which are (in Hebrew) Nisan, Iyar, Sivan, Tamuz, Av, Elul, Tishrei, Cheshvan, Kislev, Tevet, Shevat and Adar.

The 12 directors in the soul, male and female are: the 2 hands, the 2 feet, the 2 kidneys, the gall bladder, the intestine, the liver, the Kurkevan (Stomach), the Kivah (colon) and the spleen.

He (God) made the letter ה as a king over speech, and He bound a crown to it and He combined one with another, and with them He formed Aries in the universe (Olam), Nisan in the year (Shana), and the right foot in the Soul, male and female (Nefesh).

He made the letter ו as the king over thought, and He bound a crown to it and He combined one with another, and with them He formed Taurus in the universe, Iyar in the year, and the right kidney in the soul, male and female.

He made the letter ז as the king over motion, and He bound a crown to it and He combined one with another, and with them He formed Gemini in the universe, Sivan in the year, and the left foot of the soul, male and female".

So up to now the Sefer HaYetzira talks about the 12 Simple letters and in particular the first 3 Simple letters of ה and ו and ז and connects them to the Signs, the Months and the internal organs. These first 3 Simple letters also correspond to Spring, and the next 3 letters to Summer, and then to Fall and Winter.

So let us go on: "He made the letter ח as the king over sight, and He bound a crown to it and He combined one with another, and with them He formed Cancer in the universe, Tamuz in the year, and the right hand in the soul, male and female.

He made the letter ט as the king over hearing, and He bound a crown to it and combined one with another, and with them He formed Leo in the universe, Av in the year, and the left kidney in the soul, male and female.

He made the letter י as the king over action, and He bound a crown to it and combined one with another, and with them He formed Virgo in the universe, Elul in the year, and the left hand in the soul, male and female.

He made the letter ל as the king over coition, and He bound a crown to it and combined one with another, and with them He formed Libra in the universe, Tishrei in the year, and the gold bladder in the soul, male and female.

He made the letter נ as the king over smell, and He bound a crown to it and combined one with another, and with them He formed Scorpio in the universe, Cheshvan in the year, the intestine in the soul, male and female.

He made the letter ס as the king over sleep, and He bound a crown to it and combined one with another, and with them He formed Sagittarius in the universe, Kislev in the year, and the keiva/intestine in the soul, male and female.

He made the letter ע as the king over anger, and He bound a crown to it and combined one with another, and with them He formed Capricorn in the universe, Tevet in the year, and the liver in the soul, male and female.

He made the letter צ as the king over taste, and He bound a crown to it and combined one with another, and with them He formed Aquarius in the universe, Shevat in the year, and the stomach in the soul, male and female.

He made the letter ק as the king over laughter, and He bound a crown to it and combined one with another, and with them He formed Pisces in the universe, Adar in the year, and spleen in the soul, male and female.

He made them like a trough, He arranged them like a wall, and He set them up like a battle/palace".

The 12 Signs and their Affiliates								
Letter	**Sign**	**Quality**	**Organ***	**The Name**	**Month**	**Tribes Shmot**	**Tribes Bamidbar**	**House**
ה	Aries	Speech	R Foot	יהוה	Nissan	Reuben	Judah	Life
ו	Taurus	Thought	R Kidney	יההו	Iyar	Shimon	Issachar	Property
ז	Gemini	Motion	L Foot	יוהה	Sivan	Levy	Zebulun	Attraction
ח	Cancer	Sight	R Hand	הוהי	Tammuz	Judah	Reuben	Ancestors
ט	Leo	Hearing	L Kidney	הויה	Av	Issachar	Shimon	Descendants
י	Virgo	Action	L Hand	ההוי	Elul	Zebulun	Gad	Health
ל	Libra	Coition	Gall Blader	והיה	Tishrei	Benjamin	Ephraim	Coition
נ	Scorpio	Smell	Intestine	וההי	Cheshvan	Dan	Menashe	Death
ס	Sagitarrius	Sleep	Kiva	ויהה	Kislev	Naftali	Benjamin	Travel
ע	Capricorn	Anger	Liver	היהו	Tevet	Gad	Dan	Government
צ	Aquarius	Taste	Korkovan	היוה	Shevat	Asher	Asher	Friends
ק	Pisces	Laughter	Speen	ההיו	Adar	Yosef	Naftali	Enemies

* According to Gaon of Vilna

So we just did all 10 paragraphs of Chapter 5, and I have to emphasize that every paragraph is very deep and conveys many secrets using many methods of concealment. This book of great wisdom is condensed into a few pages that will take you 30 minutes to read, and it describes how God used the Hebrew alphabet to create the World. So we have to realize that Avraham Avinu condensed all of principles of Creation in this very short book, so everything he wrote there is tremendously important and today we only have the ability to grasp a little part of what Avraham Avinu is trying to tell us there. The main lesson is that God created the world using the Hebrew letters of the alphabet.

Regarding the early Kabbala of the time of the Ari Zal, it should be known and remembered that the Ari Zal had many students before Rabbi Hayim Vital came to him and become his main student. There were rabbis from Europe who visited him in Safed, and he taught them what is called 'Rala Shearim' or 'the 231 Gates'. And these rabbis, went back to Europe and taught others what the Ari Zal taught them and wrote those ideas in their books. They wrote that there was a primal world, which existed before Adam was created (Adam Hakadmon/Adam Harishon). This primal world was run by the Permutations of God's name and the rearrangement of the letters of the Hebrew alphabet to create Space, Time and Consciousness onwards. With the first Emanation came the whole Universe and since then the Creation through re-arrangement of the 22 Letters has been flowing down. So you see how important it is to get an idea of how these Permutations work. As an example, if you want to make a golem (animate an image to reality), this is the book, because the golem was created using the Permutations of the Sefer Hayetzira.

The Tribes in the Desert						
Sign	**Tribe**	**Element**	**Hot/Cold**	**Wet/Dry**	**Gods Letter**	**Sefira**
Aries	Judah	Fire	Hot	Dry	ה	Gevura
Taurus	Issachar	Earth	Cold	Dry	ה	Malchut
Gemini	Zebulun	Air	Hot	Wet	ו	Tiferet
Cancer	Reuben	Water	Cold	Wet	י	Chesed
Leo	Shimon	Fire	Hot	Dry	ה	Gevura
Virgo	Gad	Earth	Cold	Dry	ה	Malchut
Libra	Ephraim	Air	Hot	Wet	ו	Tiferet
Scorpio	Menashe	Water	Cold	Wet	י	Chesed
Sagitarrius	Benjamin	Fire	Hot	Dry	ה	Gevura
Capricorn	Dan	Earth	Cold	Dry	ה	Malchut
Aquarius	Asher	Air	Hot	Wet	ו	Tiferet
Pisces	Naftali	Water	Cold	Wet	י	Chesed

A great Kabbalist from the 1200's, Rabbi Abulafia, whose Talmid/Student was Rabbi Abdini, who was the chief rabbi of Jerusalem at the time, wrote a book called 'Sulam HaAliya' or 'The ladder for climbing up'. And there he talked about in detail how one can get out of our body consciousness into other realms, like what is called today out-of-body-experiences. These techniques and moral codes can get you into high and holy levels of consciousness and have a lot to do with regular meditation and doing things like that. All these meditations were built on the Permutations of God's name.

Chapter 5

Let us look at where these 12 Names are coming from in the Kabalistic model of creation. A while back I did a course called 'The basic model of the universe', in which I gave you a basic outline of the Kabbalistic view of how the universe is run, and we learned there that there are a number of different worlds, one on top of the other, with the lowest World being the World of Assiya/Action, which is where we find the Earth, Planets, Stars and Constellations. Above our World of Assiya is the World of Yetzira/Formation which is the world of Angels and above that we have the World of Beriya/Creation and above that we have the World of Atzilut/Emanation, and above that we have the 5th World of Adam HaKadmon/the first Human Being, which is the interface between the 4 lower Worlds and the Endless Ein Sof/Infinity.

The Baal Shem Tov used to say that it is not that there is no Mazal to Israel (there is no planetary influence on the People of Israel), but rather that the Mazal of Israel comes from the letter Ayin (nothingness), which is the highest Sefira of Keter (World of Adam HaKadmon). Keter is the Crown, the highest world which transcends all of existence and all 4 Worlds below it. So the Keter of Atzilut is the highest part of the Atzilut and above, and that is where the influences on the Mazal of the People of Israel come from. Rabbi Moshe Cordovero (Ramak), in his commentary on the Sefer Hayetzira gives us new ideas in our understanding of these 12 Names and their Permutations. He deals with these 12 Permutations in his explanation of the 13 divisions of the Beard of Adam HaKadmon (12 + the 13th as the interface), which are very high up, on the top of the World of Atziliut/Emanation, and are connected to the Keter, the crown of the World of Atzilut, to the Ayin which the Baal Shem Tov talked about. The source of the 13 divisions of the beard is called the 'Moach Stima VaRik', the 'Concealed mind'. This is where the whole universe is being directed from. It is from this one place which is called 'the hidden mind'. There is a very famous story of Moshe Rabenu (Moses) who was on Mount Sinai, receiving the Torah. He had a vision where he saw all the people in the future who would study the Torah and his teachings, and God showed him Rabbi Akiva, who would be a great sage in the future. And in his vision Moshe Rabenu saw Rabbi Akiva expounding on the Torah, and Moshe Rabeinu saw that he didn't understand what Rabbi Akiva was explaining; even Moshe Rabeinu found it hard to understand Rabbi Akiva! To cut a long story short Moshe asked, 'what will his reward be? And God showed him Rabbi Akiva being tortured to death by the Romans by having his skin peeled off with metal combs one layer at a time, and he died in excruciating pain. So then Moshe asked God, 'this is the man and is this going to be his reward? And God said to him 'be quiet! This is what went up in my will, that is what went up in my mind'. In other words, we can't understand, and even Moshe couldn't understand this higher mind of God which is high up above, running the world so to speak. Because there is God's Will, and when He created the world He created it in a certain way with a specific purpose. He had everything below attached to the Mazal, which are the planetary influences. So Moshe was shocked and upset to see the Fate that was awaiting Rabbi Akiva and he said to God 'is this is the man and this is his reward'. If a person does good, he should get a good reward, and if he does bad he should get punished. But it isn't always set up that way, God didn't always set it up that way because there is also what is called the Planetary influence, which is the influence of the planets and stars. There is that part of nature where everybody has a particular destiny and a particular challenge in this world. So things are different to what we would expect an ideal world to be. Every person has particular things that they came into this world to fix, and sufferings that they have to deal with. And all this comes from what we call 'the hidden mind'; this is the true source of all the planetary systems and their influences. The planetary system is the system through which God directs His will, which is unknown to people. So the righteous do not always receive good, and the wicked do not always get bad; the wicked are being rewarded in this world and sometimes we see the righteous suffer. So this is the source of the 12 permutations of the HaVaYaH. This is the higher mind and the source of the 13 divisions of the beard. Remember that there are 12 divisions, with the 13th one being the central one, with all 12 wrapped up into it emanating the 12 Permutations of God's name. This is the source of the permutations and of the planetary influences on the People of Israel. Like the Baal Shem Tov said, 'Ain Mazal LeYisrale', it is directed from up there, from the 'Ayin' ; and then it goes down from the Ayin, through the beard, to the 12 Permutations of God's Name.

The beard has 13 divisions, and you can see that if you look at the beard very closely. The beard and what it symbolizes is an important Kabalistic matter and is connected with astrology. There is a famous rabbi who lived about 120 years ago and was the chief rabbi of the Baghdad Jewish community, the capital of Iraq, and his name was Rabbi Yosef Chayim Ben Ish Chai, and his famous book was the 'Ben Ish Chai', the Son of a Living Man. So the Ben Ish Chai said that a person who is really knowledgeable, and really understands all these 13 divisions of the beard, he can look at a person and at his beard, and from that he can know all about that person. In those days every man had a long beard, the divisions of which one could see and learn from. It is like the ancient art of palm reading or reading the forehead. So what are these 13 divisions of the beard? These 13 divisions, which are the 12 Signs plus the source, which are also called the 'Yod Gimal Midot Harachamim', the 13 attributes of mercy. I think that is the essential meaning of these 13 divisions of the beard. And the highest place is Keter, and that is where we find the Arich Anpin, the Ayin. And this source is only doing good, it is sending down the mercy. One could say that the Mazal Elyon, like Keter, is the Orh Makif (transcendant) and therefore the concealed Will of God which transcends the lower worlds (Atzilut down). While the Mazal Tachton is the Orh Pnimi/Inner Light which is our natural mazal as we receive it here coming down from Atzilut to Assiyah, the Mazal Elyon is the macro Mazal, the Will and Purpose of Hashem which transcends the lower Worlds. In other words in Jewish astrology, if I want to go beyond my Mazal (Mazal Tachton) as depicted in my chart (hour, day, week, month, year and place of birth) I need to connect to the Mazal Elyon through Mitzvot (which are the transcendent will of the Creator) and line up my will with His Will; I take my natural inclinations and predispositions and mold them around the Mitzvot, study Torah and practice it, thereby transcending my Mazal through the pursuit of the Creators Purpose. These are the 13 attributes of mercy which are connected with the division of the beard. These are the 13 divisions of the beard:

The 1st division is called אל ('El'), which is a name of God. This is the first part of the beard, which is called the sideburns. It is like the first form of a beard which a young boy gets. It is at the top of the ear, or a little bit into the ear. And from there the sideburns come down until the area of the jawbones. The 2nd division is the mustache, which is also part of the beard. And those are the first two parts of the beard that you see in a young boy. The 3rd division of the beard, is in the middle of the mustache, where there is a bridge underneath the nose, where there is no hair (but you can't see it in every man, just in some men). And that divides the mustache into two distinct parts. And it is known that people who have that empty space there are very intelligent. The 4th division is underneath the lower lip. There is some hair that runs parallel to the lower lip and is very close to the lower lip and is called the lower mustache. The 5th division is a line in the middle of the lower mustache, which divides it into two pieces (just as the third part of the beard divides the mustache into two pieces). The 6th division of the beard is underneath the sideburns, where the sideburns end. The best example for that is found in America, where people go around with what is called a 'lamb chop beard'. The only divisions of beards they have are the sideburns, and what comes out of the sideburns. It is called 'Rav Chesed'. The 7th division of the beard is the part of the face where there is no hair. Like between the ear and the nose, the area of the cheek. The 8th division of the beard is what is called HaMazal HaElyon/the upper Mazal. 2 divisions of the beard have the name of 'Mazal'; they are the Mazal Elyon and the Mazal Tachton. Up to the 8th division the divisions come in pairs, like 2 sideburns, the 2 parts of the mustache, 2 parts to the lower mustache, 2 cheeks, 2 lamb chopped beards. The 9th to 13th divisions are single parts. So the main division is the 8th and 13th division, the Mazal Elyon and the Mazal Tachton. A beard that grows to its full length reaches the heart area. And like the bottom hair that comes out of the chin, there is also a similar part of hair coming down, and it also grows down to the heart, and these two eventually meet there. So these two pieces are called 'Mazal Elyon' and 'Mazal Tachton'. These are the 8th and 13th divisions of the beard, and they are called the 'Mazalin', or 'Mazalot'. These Mazlin take all the energies of the beard and send them down to the lower worlds. The 9th division of the beard is between these two parts, like in the middle of the hair which comes down to the heart area. The 10th division of the beard is going to be all the little groups or units of long hair underneath the chin, underneath all this hair coming down from the chin to the heart. The 11th division is the underneath the long hair where there is the smaller hair, the smaller groups of hair. The 12th division is the mouth. The 13th division of the beard is the part underneath the chin, which is next to the heart, and is called 'Mazal Tachton'. These two Mazlin, the 'Mazal Elyon' and 'Mazal Tachton', are going to meet, and they are like a male and a female. They are going to have some relationship, and thus, by doing that, they are going to send energies to the lower worlds. I think this is what Rabbi Moshe Kordovero, the Ramak, means when he says that these 13 divisions are the source of the 12 permutations of God's name. In other words, the source for these 12 permutations of God's name come from this beard in the upper world, on top of the World of Atzilut. And the starting point for the whole system of the 13 divisions of the beard is the Moach Stima/the concealed brain, the hidden mind of Keter/Crown, which is the Crown of Atzilut. And this is the high world which nobody could understand, not even Moshe Rabenu; when the future of Rabbi Akiva was shown to Moshe, he asked God, how can that be, how can such a great man receive such a cruel death as a reward? And God said to him, 'be quiet', because this is something that no human being can understand. Everybody in the world has a different challenge and a different purpose, and we don't really know why, it is hidden. When we see the manifestation of this hidden energy we don’t understand it, and it is somehow the opposite of what we would consider fair. We would expect that good happens to the righteous and bad happens to the evil doers. But sometimes it is not like that, and sometimes you see that the wicked thrive and the righteous suffer. This is a difficult reality and a hard concept to accept, and some people have a challenge accepting this as taught in our religion, because that is indeed the fundamental question: If God is good, then how come good people sometimes suffer and bad people sometimes don't?

Now let us go back to the Ramak and his commentary from where we left off last time; “So we have learned now, that the 12 Simple letters create so to speak, the 12 months and the 12 constellations, as well as the 12 limbs. All, as we said, according to the secret of the Universe/Space, the Year/Time and the Soul/Consciousness. And they all hint to very deep things. And now we want to say, that people who were experts in the laws of nature, state that the 12 Signs in the Zodiac (the way they are arranged, with Aries first, followed by Taurus, Gemini, Censure, Leo, Virgo, Libra, Scorpio, Sagittarius, Capricorn, Aquarius and Pisces) are themselves divided according to their actions. And each one is connected to its Flag, according to its Signs and Deeds”.

The Ramak is going to teach you how it works according to the flags of the Tribes. But first let me tell you that there are 2 places in the Torah where it talks about the 12 Tribes;

1) The Book of Shmot/Exodus 1:1-4, where the tribes are listed according to the 2 wives and 2 concubines of Yaakov/Jacob. First it lists Lea's 6 sons, and then it lists the sons of the other wives.

2) The Book of Bamidbar/Number 2:1), where God commands that the order of the 12 Tribes take on a different order and content.

In the Book of Bamidbar/Numbers listing it says; "And God Spoke to Moses and Aharon, Saying: The Children of Israel shall encamp, each man by his banner, according to the flags of their Fathers' households, at a distance, surrounding the Tent of Meeting shall they encamp".

"And those who encamp at the front, to the East, are the flag of the camp of Yehuda/Judah, according to their legions, and the leader of Judah is Nachshon, the son of Aminadav. Its legion and their account is seventy four thousand and six hundred. Those encamping near him are the tribe of Yisachar, and the leader of the tribe of Yisachar is Netanel, the son of Zuar. Its legion and their account is forty five thousand and four hundred. The tribe of Zevulun, and the leader of the tribe of Zvulun is Eliav, the son of Cheilon. Its legion and their account is fifty seven thousand and four hundred. All those counted for the camp of Judah are one hundred and eighty six thousand and four hundred, according to their legions, they shall be the first to journey". So that is the first camp, of Yehuda, Yisachar and Zevulun. And they are in the East.

The 2nd Encampment is Reuven and his encampment is to the South: "The banner of Reuven's tribe's encampment shall be to the South with all their legions, and the leader of the tribe of Reuven is Elitzur, the son of Shdeur. Its legion and its account is forty six thousand and five hundred. Those encamping near him are the tribe of Shimon, and its leader is Shlumiel, the son of Tzurishadai. Its legion and its account is fifty nine thousand and three hundred. And then the tribe of Gad, whose leader is Elyasaf, the son of Reuel, with its legion and its account are forty five thousand, six hundred and fifty. All those counted for the camp of Reuven are one hundred and fifty one thousand, four hundred and fifty, according to their legions, they shall be 2nd to journey". So this is the second encampment to journey, and this is the encampment of Reuven, Shimon and Gad.

And the Torah then lists the 3rd Encampment which will be to the West: "The banner of Efrayim, according to their legions, to the west, and the leader of the children of Efrayim is Elishama, the son of Amihud. Its legion and their account is forty thousand and five hundred. Those encamping near him are the tribe of Menashe, and the leader of the children of Menashe is Gamliel, the son of Pedatzur. Its legion and their account are thirty two thousand and two hundred. And the tribe of Benjamin, and the leader of the children of Benjamin is Avidan, the son of Gidoni. Its legion and their account is thirty five thousand and four hundred. All those counted for the camp of Efrayim are one hundred and eight thousand and one hundred, according to their legions, and they shall be third to journey". This is the third camp, which is on the West, and it consists of Efrayim,

Menashe and Binyamin/Benjamin (Although Efrayim and Menashe are the 2 children of Yosef, they are included in the 12 divisions in place of Yosef. Even though they are the Grand children of Jacob, and not the children of Jacob, God appoints them as the part of the 12 Tribes).

Then the Torah mentions the 4th Encampment: "The banner of Dan to the North, according to their legions, and the leader of the children of Dan is Achiezer, the son of Amishadai. Its legion and their account is sixty two thousand and seven hundred. Those encamping near him are the tribe of Asher, and the leader of the children of Asher is Pagiel, the son of Ochran. Its legion and their account is forty one thousand and five hundred. And the tribe of Naftali, and the leader of the children of Naftali is Achira, the son of Einan. And its legion and their account is fifty three thousand and four hundred. All those counted for the camp of Dan are one hundred and fifty seven thousand and six hundred, and they shall be the last to journey, according to their banners".

And then the Torah goes on: "These are the counting's of the Children of Israel, according to their father's households, all the counting's of those encampments, according to their legions, are 603 550 ". And then the Torah goes on about the Levites: "And the Levites were not counted among the Children of Israel, as God commanded Moses. And the Children of Israel did everything that God commanded Moses, so did they encamped according to their banners, and so did they journey, each man according to his families, according to his household".

So the Children of Levi were not counted in this arrangement. So the difference between the Shmot/Exodus listing of the Tribes and this Bamidbar/Numbers listing is substantial in both order and content; The order of the Tribes is reset and both Joseph and the Levi tribe are not included in this listing by God in the desert, as the Jews set off for Israel.

In Exodus where the Tribes are first mentioned, it reads: "And these are the names of the Children of Israel who came down to Egypt, each man and his household came with Yaakov: Reuven, Shimon, Levi and Judah, Yisachar, Zvulun and Benjamin. Dan, Naftali, Gad and Asher. And all the persons who have emerged from Jacob were seventy souls, and Joseph had been in Egypt". Joseph is mentioned (last), because he already was in Egypt when the other tribes came down. So Joseph is mentioned but his sons Menashe and Efrayim are not, and we also see that the Tribe of Levi is mentioned as the 3rd Tribe.

Now the Ramak is going to explain the 12 Zodiac Signs according to the Elements; "This is the arrangements of the flags of the camps: The flag of the camp of Aries is fire, and with them are Leo and Sagittarius. And these are the 3 Signs which are connected with Fire. And the second camp is of Taurus, which is earth and with them are Virgo and Capricorn. They are the 3 Signs connected with Earth. The next camp is that of Gemini, which is Air and with them are Libra and Aquarius. They are the 3 Signs of the Element of Air. The 4th camp is that of Cancer which is Water, with them is Scorpio and Pisces. They are the 3 Signs connected with Water." The Water Signs are the deepest Signs which are the hardest to understand. Water is the emotions, which are often hard to understand. "And this arrangement, according to the way we have explained the 12 Signs, that were created from the 12 sides of the rectangle, and the 12 Simple letters".

Chapter 6

Let us summarize where we are holding so far. We have looked at the 12 Permutations of God's name in a general way, and we were saying that they show that it is not the stars or planets themselves that decide the names, but the Rulership over the planets comes from God, and that is the reason that each month gets a different name and permutation of the name of God. And we are not going to talk about Jewish philosophy. Of course, in Jewish philosophy, there is clearly only one God. But in Jewish Kabbala you don't really talk about God, because God is unknowable, and it is beyond our ability to grasp Him. And the Vilna Gaon even said that it is forbidden to even think about Him in this aspect, because then you make a place where God isn't, God forbid, and this can't be, and it is a big problem, because you can't say anything which is limiting anything about God. And so we don't really talk about God in the Kabbala; this is one of those things we don't talk about. And we realize that there are things we don't know and we can't know. But what we can know is the manifestation of God in the world. And He has different names, and in fact He has masculine names and feminine names. And all those names are different ways in which God reveals Himself to the world and influences the world through His actions and deeds. So this is not actually what we are talking about here. Here we only talk about the general sense of the twelve permutation of God's holy name of Havaya. And we have had a whole lesson about all these different permutation, and how each one is different from all the others. We have already said that each month of the year the energy that comes down from heaven is a little different from the energy that comes down during the other months. And the way the world is directed is different during each month, depending on the different kind of permutations. So during the last lesson we tried to show, in a more detailed way, where all these permutations come from. And we even attributed it to the thirteen parts of the beard, which is represented in the highest partzuf of the highest world, which is the world of Atzilut. And there we see that there are thirteen divisions to the beard, and that the two bottom ones are also called Mazalot, and these are the eighth and the thirteenth parts of the beard. These parts of the beard send the Mazalot down to this world. As for the question of how they come down to this world and influence it, we will talk about it in another lesson. But in any case, they are called the two Mazlin, which are the two main influences on the Mazalot, and they influence the world. And we also said, that the root of the beard, the place where the energy of the beard comes from, is the Moach Setima, the Hidden Mind, which is in Arich Anpin. And that is the point which is running everything in this world, and the way it works is completely hidden from us, and we talked about that, mentioning Moshe Rabenu when he saw the future of Rabbi Akiva, and how the latter was teaching the Torah in a way that even Moshe Rabenu couldn't understand, so Moshe Rabenu said: 'This person is so great, please show me his end'. And then Moshe Rabenu saw that his flesh had been pealed layer by layer off his body, during his execution at the hand of the Romans. So Moshe Rabenu said: 'This man is so great, and is this supposed to be his reward? And then God said to him: 'Be quite, because you can't understand what I am doing'. And that is the concept of the 'hidden mind', and accordingly you can't understand why God does what

He does and what happens in this world. You can't understand why the righteous people sometimes suffer, while sometimes they don't, and why sometimes evil people have a good time in this world, and why sometimes evil people suffer in this world. So everybody has a different experience in life, and the source of those experiences in everyone's lives is from a place beyond our understanding.

And the tribes are mentioned at the beginning of the Book of Exodus according to the order of how they were born, with the children of Leah being mentioned first, followed by the children of the other mothers, and this list doesn't list Joseph and it doesn't list Efrayim and Menashe. But we see in another place, in the second chapter of the Book of Numbers, it is mentioned that there were four camps each with three tribes, one in each direction. And there it is somehow connected more with the four elements of earth, fire, water and air.

So tonight we will be starting the lesson by going deeper into these four elements. This is where we left off, saying that the first four months of the year, the constellations of which are Aries, Taurus, Gemini and Cancer, represent these four elements, which you can see if you pay attention. So Aries represents the fire sign, Taurus represents the earth sign, Gemini represents the air sign and Cancer represents the water sign. And then it starts all over again, with the following four months of the year representing these four signs in the same order. So Leo is a fire sign, Virgo is an earth sign, Libra is an air sign and Scorpio is a water sign. And this is followed by the last four months of the year, which are represented by the remaining four constellations in the Zodiac, and represent those four signs in the same order. So the twelve months of the year and the constellations they are represented by form four groups. Aries is fire, and it is going to take Leo and Sagittarius together with it, and form one camp which is the camp of the fire signs. Taurus is earth, and it is going to take Virgo and Capricorn together with it, and form one camp which is the camp of the earth signs, which are the second house, the sixth house and the tenth house. These are the houses of career, of money and of the work place and servitude. But the first houses are connected with the person himself, his religion, his children etc. And then you have the third group, which is Gemini, and it takes Libra and Aquarius , which are the third house, the seventh house and the eleventh house being combined, forming the element of air sign, which is the sign of social matters, which are connected with air and communication. And the fourth camp is that of Cancer, which takes also Scorpio and Pisces, they are the fourth, the eighth and the twelfth houses, which are connected with emotions. And the hardest thing to understand is the emotions. So it is sometimes very hard to understand people who have a lot of water signs and how to help them.

In any case, this is a brief summary of what we learned last week. And tonight let us go on and continue with our discussion regarding the four elements. And I think tonight we will go on to the four elements themselves, and break them down into qualities.

So I would like to read to you a little bit more from the writings of Rabbi Moshe Cordovero: “And you have to know that the world of Atzilut has boundaries, in the north, the east, the west and the south. And each one of those boundaries is connected to one of the four elements, of air, earth, fire and water. And they are the four letters of God's name”. This is another way of breaking down the four letters of Gods name, into air, earth, fire and water. And now Rabbi Moshe Cordovero is going to tell you that the water is connected to the south, and it is the ruler of Chesed. So now he is going to connect the elements with the directions and with the Sefirot.

So the element of water is going to be in the south, and it is going to be connected to Chesed. And remember that in Kabbala there are three columns: The left column is that of Gevura, which is strict judgment. The center column is Rachamim, which is love and mercy. And the last column, the right column, is Chesed, which is righteousness, loving kindness. So the left side is Gevura, judgment it is connected to the element of fire, and it is in the north. And the element of air is in the east, and it is the aspect of Tiferet, majesty, and the element of earth is in the west, and it is kingship, Malchut.

So let us review this again, so we will not forget it: There are four directions, which are east, west, north and south. Those four sides are connected with the four elements (air, fire, water and earth) and with the main four lower Sefirot, which are Chesed, Gevura, Tiferet and Malchut. And they are connected to the four letters of God's name, and that means that each letter is going to be connected to a different element.

And now you have to know the connection to all the different constellations, because they are connected with what is going on in the upper worlds.

And Rabbi Moshe Cordovero goes on to explain, that each of these four elements has dfferent qualities. For example, fire is going to be hot and dry, because the nature of fire is to dry things. Because it is so hot, it burns out all moisture, all liquid, in anything. So it makes things dry. And earth is dry too, but it is cold. And water is cold and moist. And air is hot and moist. So each element has two qualities, and these two qualities switch within each one: Fire and air are both hot, one is dry and the other moist. Water and earth are both cold, but again earth is dry, while the other, water, is moist.

There is a big idea in Kabbala, which I want to explain. The idea is connected to astrology, which we have already talked about, and I would like to base it on the Torah. In the Torah there are two different types of commandments, which a person has to fulfill in this world: One type of commandments is what is called positive commandments, while the other type is called negative commandments. In other words, a positive commandment is to do something positive, to do a Mitzva, to do a good deed. And the Torah, and after that the Talmud, lists all the positive commandments, as well as the negative commandments, and there are plenty of them, plenty of each. So for example, a positive commandment can be the deed of visiting someone who is sick, or the deed of giving a person a proper burial, or putting on Tefilin in the morning, all sorts of things, which are positive commandments, that you have to go out and do them. So this is one type of commandment. And on the other hand, there are negative commandments, commandments which forbid something to you, and you have to try to refrain from doing them. For example, you shouldn't commit adultery, you shouldn't steal, you shouldn't kill, and you shouldn't eat non-kosher food. And all commandments of this kind are what are called negative commandments, where you have to refrain from doing something which is forbidden. So, regarding the nature of fire, I would like to say that some of those commandments are connected to fire and air, which are the hot elements, while some other commandments are connected to the cold elements, which are water and earth. So for example, the fire people have horoscopes which are very hot. So what is going to be their main problem? Such a person's main problem is going to be, how to refrain themselves from doing something which is forbidden, from transgressing and doing a forbidden deed, because such a person is more heated up. Such a person has too much heat in their body, and they are too much of a hot headed person, which means that they act before they think. In other words, their nature is to do something right away. They don't like to think about things, and when something comes into their head they just do it. So when they get angry, for example, they are likely to express their anger by harming someone. So what I am trying to say is, that when somebody has too much fire in him, for instance, that is if he has a lot of fire signs in his horoscope, then it will be very hard to hold him back, and very hard for him to control himself . So many times, when they get into contact with something, and there is a commandment to refrain from doing that thing, it would be very challenging for them to withstand it and refrain from doing that thing. On the other hand, it would be very easy for them to do something which is positive, that is to say that it would be very easy for such a person to fulfill a positive commandment. This is because their nature is heated up, and they live an active life and want to do things. So the idea of going out and doing things would not be much of a challenge for them. And in general, in this world, such people are likely to be active, outgoing and doers.

And in general, such people don't have much of a problem going out and doing things, not only regarding the positive commandments, but generally they like to initiate things. But regarding refraining from doing things, this is very difficult for them.

And there is also going to be a difference between the hot elements of fire and air, because of course the fire is going to be hotter. So a person who has more fire elements within him would find it more difficult to refrain from doing things. Because there are always different degrees and you always have to look at things in terms of degrees. So, for example, the air hast some degree of heat to itself, but it doesn't have the same degree of heat as the sun, for instance. So a person who has more fire signs within him is expected to be more into this nature of wanting to go out and do things. So he would like to go out and initiate more then somebody who has everything in the air signs. And we will talk about this.

And again, the same thing applies when you talk about the cold signs. The cold signs are, of course, earth and water, and they are feminine signs. The masculine signs are hot signs, and the feminine signs are cold. And again, the colder the signs are the more opposite the person will be from the one who has the hot signs, because the nature of the cold signs and the cold planets are the opposite from the hot ones. So people who have the cold signs strong have more of the ability to restrain themselves from doing things. They have the power of self-restraint, the power of holding themselves back. And what do we say in English? There is an expression stating that a person freezes up. And "a person who freezes up" means a person who can't act.

So a person who has everything in earth and water is expected to have a problem, which is similar to the problem of a person who has everything in fire and air, but is the exact opposite, they will not have the ability to act. So they will have difficulty in doing the positive commandments. Such a person would often be too lazy or to tired, or would not feel like acting. Because such people just 'freeze up', they are too cold by nature, they don't have that warmth, that tendency to do things. But on the other hand, they would find it easier to hold themselves back, and refrain from doing what one is commanded not to do. They hold themselves from transgressing what we call negative commandments, they hold themselves from doing wrong deeds. And the same thing is going to be in regular life. People who have all their signs in earth and water are not likely to do anything; they are likely to be too lazy. And of course, with earth signs, which are colder, it is expected to be more so than with water signs. The earth is very cold by nature, more than water, because it is cold and dry. So it has more of a cold nature then the water.

So let us keep going now, and let us get back to the text:

So in the text it says that "fire is hot and dry, because the nature of fire is dryness, because fire consumes and evaporates all the moisture within something; the heat takes out all the water. Earth, on the other hand, is dry and cold, water is cold and moist, and air is hot and moist.

And you have to know that fire and water are opposites; and that is from two aspects: Water is cold and fire is hot, water is moist and fire is dry. So, in other words, fire and water are opposites from two sides: Fire is hot and dry, and water is cold and moist".

So how can they (fire and water) be joined together? This is an important secret now, in astrology and in Kabbala, which Rabbi Moshe Cordovero is going to teach you now. So the question is, of course, how are they connected? So the answer would be, that "in one way they are connected by air, and in another way, they are connected by earth. How does that work? He is going to explain. And also air and earth are opposites from two sides: The air is hot and the earth is cold, and also the air is moist and the earth is dry. And they are joined together through water and fire.

And how does that work? How do they join together? The air completes and joins together these two completely opposite things: water, which is wet, with fire, which is hot, because it (the air) is hot and moist. So you see that air is equal to fire on one side, which is the side of heat, and it is equal to the water from the other side, in that it is wet".

So let us summerize: In other words, we have fire and water, which are total opposites. This is because one is cold and wet, while the other is hot and dry. So they can be united by way of the air. Because the air has one side which is connected to fire; it has heat. And it has another side which is connected to water, because it has moistness. So this is what connects them together. So we see that the fire and the water are connected together by air. And now, let us go on with the text:

"And similarly is another way water and fire can be connected; they are connected and made compatible through earth. Because we see that earth is dry and cold. So it is connected to fire on one side, that it is also dry. And it is connected to the water from the side that it is cold. So the earth can connect them also".

"And similarly it works the other way, in which fire and water are the ones which complete and make compatible air and earth. How does this work? Water is equal to air in one way, which is that both are moist. And it is equal to earth because both are cold. Because the earth is cold and the air is moist they are united through water. And similarly, fire is equal to the air from one side, that they are both hot. And it is equal to earth from the other side, which is that they are both dry. So it comes out that earth and air is united through fire".

So let us summarize: we say air and earth are opposites from two directions, because air, by nature, is hot, while earth is cold, plus air is moist, while earth is dry, but the two of them can be united through fire and water. In other words, fire is like air in one sense, that both are hot. And in another sense, fire is like earth, because it is dry. So fire unites air and earth. And in the same way, water unites the two, because water and air are both moist, and water and earth are both cold. "And this is how the elements are united. And this is also the way the constellations are united with one another. And similarly, this is how the Sefirot are united in Kabbala".

Before we continue with Rabbi Moshe Cordovero describing the way the Sefirot in Kabbala unite, let us talk a little bit about the way all this works in astrology. Planets which are of the same element, such as fire, are obviously going to be similar from both sides because they are of the same element. All planets in fire signs are going to be hot and dry. But of course, there are going to be different amounts of heat and dryness. But the only difference is going in quantity. That is to say how hot and how dry every planet is, but that is their nature. But let us say, you have two signs, which are sextile to each other. Let us say, you have Aries and Gemini, which are 60 degrees apart, and they have a sextile, so they are going to be similar to each other in one way. And any signs which are 60 degrees from each other are going to be similar in one way. They would have the same gender. So here is Aries, which is fire, and fire is masculine and hot. And Gemini, which is in the air, is going to be hot too, and Aries and Gemini are 60 degrees away from each other. So they are similar to one another in the sense that they are both masculine and hot. But in the other sense, the fire sign is going to be dry, and the air sign is going to be moist. So these two signs, Aries and Gemini, are similar to each other in one sense. But if we take two signs which are 90 degrees away from one another, such as Aries and Cancer, which is fire and water, then they are going to be different from one another on both sides, which means in two ways. So in a sense, that is going to be a very hard aspect (the aspect which two signs, such as Aries and Cancer, which are 90 degrees away from each other, make). When two signs are 90 degrees apart, they are different from one another on both sides. And if they are a hundred and twenty degrees away from each other, then they become of the same element again, and then they are going to be similar to each other again from both sides. And then you have the one hundred and eighty degree aspect, where the two signs are going to be similar to one another from one side. In other words, the two signs may be in fire and air, so they are both going to be hot, but there will be a difference, in the sense that one will be moist, while the other will be dry. In other words, let us say that you have Aries and Libra, both will be hot, but one, Aries, which is in fire, will be dry, while the Libra will be moist. And I guess it will be the same thing in a sextile, which is when there is a 60 degree difference between one sign to the other. So this is the way the signs are divided, and they can be united through the planets and influences. So this is the idea of how it works in the constellations in the sky. And now, Rabbi Moshe Cordovero is going to explain, how the same thing works between the Sefirot. So let us take a look at that:

So you have Chesed, which, as we said before, is water; the side of mercy is in the element of water. And the side of judgment is in the element of Fire. The right side is mercy, while the left side is power and judgment. And they are joined together through Tiferet, which is air. So again, here, in the Sefirot, we also have the same thing, where the right side is the water, and the left side is the fire. These two sides are joined together through the middle column, Tiferet, which is the air, the air joins them. And sometimes, those two sides are going to be joined together through Malchut, which is in the middle too, and is earth.

So on the right side we have Chesed, which is water; the left side is Gevura/Judgment, which is fire; and the middle column can join them in two ways: Either through Tiferet, which is air (and has one side like fire and the other side which is like water), or through Malchut, which is earth, and is lower down, but nonetheless in the middle too, it will unite them, because it works like earth; it is dry like fire, and it is cold like water.

So don't be surprised now by the fact that we have explained that the Malchut (not only Tiferet) also balances between Chesed and Gevura; between mercy and judgment! Because originally, at a certain point, before the moon got diminished, it was higher up and was able to balance between them.

But in any case, there are going to be differences, in the sense that the higher up the middle column is, the more it will pull them to the right, in balancing them. So Malchut would balance between the fire and the water, but it would be leaning towards the left." So Rabbi Moshe Cordovero is now talking here about balancing, but he is now going to give the major examples to the different degrees of the balancing. Just like not all doctors are equal; there are some doctors who are really good doctors, while there are others who are really bad doctors. And there are also others, who are kind of in the middle. And the same thing goes about anything. For example, there are lawyers, some of whom are the best, while some are the worst, and there are those who are in the middle. So the same thing is with the heat; you have different degrees of heat. You can have different degrees of cold, different degrees of moist and different degrees of dry. And so you always have to take this into account when you are trying to modify things and try to join them. In such cases, it is going to change a little bit, because of the amount of quantity. This is not about the quality. I mean, I call the two sides of each element qualities. The qualities are either 'hot' or 'cold', or 'moist' or 'dry'. But they also have different degrees, of how hot they are, or how cold, or moist or dry.

So let us go on and see how the Tiferet and Malchut unite. Because Tiferet and Malchut are both in the middle column; one is air and one is earth:

"And they, Tiferet and Malchut, unite by what they receive from the fathers. In other words, they unite through Chesed and Gevura. Chesed and Gevura unite Tiferet and Malchut."

But Rabbi Moshe Kordovero doesn't explain here how it works. So let us leave this matter for now. But again, it is the same idea.

Now Rabbi Moshe Kordovero is going to go back to the matter of the planets and constellations, and this is important for us:

"And when you meditate on the different seasons and the elements that are within them, and the order of the months, you will find out that there are some little differences between them. There are going to be opposites within them." And Rabbi Moshe Kordovero is going to explain these differences now, and how it works:

"For example, the season of Nisan, which is the Spring time, and contains three months (April, May and June, the constellations of which are Aries, Taurus and Gemini. In other words, the Hebrew months of Nisan, Iyar and Sivan), are the letter 'Yod' of God's (Havaya) name, and it is the element of water. So the letter 'Yod' in God's four letter name represents water. So the first three months are going to be water months.

And then the second season, which is the summer, and contains the Hebrew months of Tamuz, Av and Elul (in the civilian calendar, it is July, August and September, the constellations of which are Cancer, Leo and Virgo), represents the first 'He' in God's name, and it represents the aspect of strength and judgment, which is the element of fire."

In other words, the first season is the period of the year when everything starts to grow and blossom, which is the 'Yod', which is water. This is the nature of water.

Then the second season is the first 'He', which is going to represent the element of Fire because the summer is when the sun is at its peak of strength and heat. So the summer is hot and dry, like fire. "And then you have the autumn, which contains the months of Tishri, Marcheshvan and Kislev (in the civilian calendar, it will be October, November and December, the constellations of which will be Libra, Scorpio and Sagittarius), represents the letter 'Vav' in God's name, which is represented by Tiferet, which is in the element of air". And again, the air is the milder time of the year, which is the opposite of the season represented by the 'Yod'. It is going to be an airy time, when there is a lot of air, and the leaves are blown off the trees due to the wind, etc.

And Rabbi Moshe Kordovero continues: "And the final three month season is the season of Tevet (which is the fourth season of the year, the winter. And it contains the three Hebrew months of Tevet, Shvat and Adar, which are January, February and March in the civilian calendar, the constellations of which are Capricorn, Aquarius and Pisces), is represented by the last 'He' in God's name, which is represented by Malchut, the element of which is earth. And earth is the coldest of the elements, so it is the element of the winter, which is the coldest season in the year".

So this is how the Ramak, Rabbi Moshe Cordovero, explains why each of the three month periods of the year starts, permutations wise, with a different letter in God's name, and why it is that specific letter for that specific period. So he says that the three months of spring start permutation wise, with the letter 'Yod', because the letter 'Yod' represents water. And the first three months of the year are the months of the spring, which is the season of growing, and crops grow with the help of water. All the ripening and fruition come through water. And the second three month season is the summer. And the permutations of the three summer months are going to start with the first 'He' in God's name, because that 'He' indicates heat, it indicates fire. And the months of summer are fire months, when the earth is the hottest, in comparison to all other seasons of the year. And then you get the letter 'Vav', which begins the permutations for the three months of the autumn, which are the third period and is in the air element. This is the season when everything starts to cool off. There is already going to be some water in the air. And in fact, in Israel it doesn't normally rain in the summer, and that is why everything is dry in summer. So in the autumn, the moisture is going to begin, and the heat eases a little . It is still going to be hot, but not as hot as during the summer. The air, which is heated by the fire, which means that it is heated by the sun, is now going to cool down a little . So these three months of the autumn are ruled by the letter 'Vav', which is in the element of air. And air also connects between the summer and the winter, just like it makes a connection between the fire and the water, and just like the spring connects between the winter and the summer too. And then you get the last season, which is winter, and it consists of the last three months of the year. And permutation wise, the three months of the winter start with the last 'He' in God's name. The winter is represented by the element of earth, and earth is the coldest of the elements. And that is why the permutation for each of the three months of the winter is going to start with the last 'He' in God's name. And the last 'He in God's name indicates coldness. And then you get to the spring again, but then it is not as cold as it is in winter, because the cold of the spring is the cold of water, which is not as cold as the element of the earth. And since the earth is dry, things are going to get a little moist in the spring, and crops are going to start growing.

And now Rabbi Moshe Cordovero is continuing: "And know, that this is not the order of the months!" In other words, up to now he was talking in terms of seasons, and not in terms of months. In other words, when Rabbi Moshe Cordovero divided the year into four, he was talking about the seasons. And each one of the four seasons consists of three months". But now Rabbi Moshe Kordovero is going to speak about the months:

"And this is not the months, in term of the elements because if you talk about the period of Nisan, which is the spring, then you are connecting it to the element of water, which is represented by the letter 'Yod'. But as for the signs of the months, fire is the sign of Nisan (the constellation of which is Aries), and the sign of Iyar, element wise, is earth, because its symbol is a bull, and then Sivan, the constellation of which is that of the twins, Gemini, is represented, element wise, by the air. And here it is not like the seasons. The elements for each month are different from the elements of the seasons. So in the spring it is all in water. But in the term of the months, one is in fire, one is in earth and one is in air. And the same thing when you get to the season of Tamuz, which is summer, which is fire, and permutation wise, it is represented by the first 'He in God's name. So month wise, since the constellation of Tamuz is Cancer, Tamuz is represented, element wise, by water. Av is in fire, since its constellation is Leo, which is a lion, which has a lot of the element of fire in it. And Elul has the constellation of Virgo, which is a virgin, and its element is earth. And it is not like the whole season, which is summer, and summer is in fire. But month wise, they are in water, in fire and in earth. And then you get to the fall, the autumn, and we said that the autumn is in air, which is the letter 'Vav' in God's name. However, in term of the months, since the constellation of the month of Tishri is Libra, this month is going to be in air. And the month of Marcheshvan is in water, because its constellation is scorpion. And since the constellation of the month of Kislev is Sagittarius, this month is going to be in fire."

And again, you have one season, which element wise, is going to be air, but month wise, it is going to break up into air, water and fire.

And the last Tekufa, the last season, is the season of Tevet, which is the earth, and by the last 'He' in God's name permutation wise.

But in terms of the months, Tevet, the constellation which is Capricorn, is represented by the element of earth. And the month of Aquarius, which is a bucket, is in air. And the month of Adar is represented by the water, since its constellation is Pisces, which are fish. And again, the three months are all one season, but they are with three different elements for each month."

spring			
months		***season***	
April	Fire	***April***	water
May	earth	***May***	
June	air	***June***	
summer			
months		***season***	
July	water	***July***	fire
August	fire	***August***	
September	earth	***September***	
winter			
months		***season***	
October	air	***October***	air
November	water	***November***	
December	fire	***December***	
fall			
months		***season***	
January	earth	***January***	earth
February	air	***February***	
March	water	***March***	

Chapter 7

Let us summarize what we have learned till now: We have talked about the difference between the way in which the tribes were listed in the beginning of the book of Shemot (Exodus), according to the mothers and the way they were listed in the book of Bamidbar (Numbers), according to the order of their camping in the desert. And we have said that the order of the tribes was broken up according to the four seasons and 12 months of the year; so each one of the seasons has three months. And we said that the permutations for the months of the spring start with the letter 'Yod'. And we have learned that they (the months of the first season, which is the spring) are all connected to the element of water. And the season of the three months which have the permutations starting with the first 'He', which is the summer, are connected to the element of fire. And then we have the season of autumn the next three months, the permutations for which start with the letter 'Vav'. That season is connected to the element of air. And the last season, which is the three months of the winter, has the permutations for its three months, which begin with the second 'He', and is connected to the element of earth.

But then we had a problem towards the end of the lesson, because that is in contrast of what we have learned up to now. Because according to what we have learned in the book of Bamidbar (Numbers), there are four groups, which represent the four seasons of the year. And each season has three months, which are all connected to the same element: The months of the spring season are all connected to the element of water, the second three months are all connected to the element of fire, the third group of three months are all connected to the element of air, and the fourth group of three months are all connected to the element of earth. And this, of course, contradicts what we have been learning up to now. Up to now we have learned that each month is connected to a different one of those four elements, and that they rotate: Each month of the spring is connected to a different element, making three elements together: The first month of the spring, which is the month of Nisan, will be connected to the element of fire, the second month, which is Iyar, would be connected to earth, and the month of Sivan will be connected to air. And then the next three months, which are the months of summer, will also be three months which are connected to three different elements: The month of Tamuz will be connected to the element of water, the month of Av will be connected to fire, and Elul to earth. And then you get the three months of fall (autumn). And the month of Tishri will be connected to the element of air. Cheshvan will be connected to water, and then Kislev will be connected to fire. And then come the last three months: And the month of Tevet will be connected to earth, Shvat will be connected to air, and Adar to water. So here we see in this system that in each season there are three months, each of which has a different element. And this is also the way we have learned it in Sefer Hayetzira. It is mentioned in Sefer Hayetzira that each of the seasons has three different elements. So we see a contradiction here, between Sefer Hayetzira and what we have learned in the Ramak. And one of the commentaries on the Ramak, Rabbi Menachem Azariya of Pano wrote a book called Asis Harimon, which means 'the juice of the pomegranate', asks the question I am asking now. Because I thought about this question before, and I didn't know the answer for it, so I said: Let me look at what Rabbi Menachem Azaria wrote regarding this. So he asked the same question which I asked myself, but he gives an answer, which is that everything must be in each season.I think he wants to say that each season has all the elements in it, but each season relative to the other season's one element predominates. In spring that element is water but the spring itself has three months which are the beginning the middle and the end of the season and each one has a different element.

In other words, what is explained here is, that as always in Kabbala, everything is interconnected, and everything has a little bit of everything else within. So if you say that the spring is all in the element of water, then you say that there is nothing else in it, and that there is no fire earth or air as in other seasons, which is obviously not correct in Kabbala. So you have to say that there is everything else in it. But the only thing that is meant when we say, that the spring is the element of water, is that in spring what sticks out is water, but all the other elements are in it too. There is going to be air, there is going to be fire, and there is going to be earth too, but there is mainly water, hinting to the time of growth of spring, because water is needed to grow things. And the same thing is with summer, there will be all three elements too, but the fire will stick out. Because everything is going to be very hot in summer. And then, when you get to the fall, everything is going to cool down, because the wind is going to blow now. So the element of air is going to stick out. All of a sudden the dry hot summer is over, and now you have some more of the cool air, so you can take some more of a breath of fresh air. But even though the element of air is sticking out, all three elements are actually there. So in any case, this is the answer which is given by Rabbi Menachem Azaria of Pano. He says that everything is included in everything else, just that one thing sticks out in each season. And we talked about this before. We talked about it when we discussed the time periods. And it applies in everything in Kabala. This is what the Ari Zal calls 'Hitkashrot Haolamot', which means 'the interconnection of the worlds'. It means that, at a certain point in creation, everything became included in everything else. And through this interconnectedness, God directs the world. And when everything is interconnected, then everything has an influence on everything else. If everything is interconnected, then everybody has a little bit of everybody else in them. And all periods of time have everything in each, which means that each time period has a little bit of other time periods in it. And I will give you an example for that: The famous Kabbalist of the late 1700s was Rabbi Shalom Sharabi of Yemen. And he said that if a minyan of Jews (which means 10 Jewish men) said one prayer properly, exactly the way it should be prayed, the Messiah would come instantly. And why? Well, his idea was that all time is included in each moment. So even in one moment, like if each and every one of the minyan prayed properly, the way they are supposed to pray, everything would have been fixed. And why is that? Because, as mentioned above, all time is in each and every moment. So if you do one moment correctly, the way it should be done, then all time is fixed. And the same idea applies in life as Rabbi Shalom Sharabi also used to say, everyone's life is actually just one test and all his or her life is just a preparation for that test. And that one test, that one moment when you act the way you act, determines your whole life. And again, it is the same idea; because all his life is a preparation for that moment. And that moment has one thing and also everything in it. And therefore, if you passed that one test, then you fixed everything in yourself. Anyway, this is a big idea, which we will come back too when we do some more serious lessons in Kabbala. And this great idea is called 'Hitkashrut Vehitkallelut Haolamot', which means, all the worlds being united and included in each other. So all the worlds are interconnected, and everything has everything else in it. I only wanted to give you this idea, because the Rama (Rabbi Menachem Azarya) of Pano already used that idea here, in order to answer the contradiction between the two ways of learning the twelve months of the year and the four seasons they form. So anyway, this was a brief review of what we have learned up to now, with a little addition. And now I would like to keep going on with what we have been learning up to now, I would like to move on to another book, which is also going to explain a lot of what we have been talking about. And I think this book is going to make a lot of sense now, with all the basic introductions we have had. And I am using this book as an example for the next class, when I want to take some time and talk about the tribes and the flags, especially about the flags that each of the tribes had in the desert. And I would also like to talk about the tribes themselves. And this lesson is going to be a lead in for the next one. So this lesson is going to be based on book called 'Shaarey Ora', which means 'the gates of light', and it was written by Rabbi Yosef Jaqtilia, who also lived before the Ari Zal. And he was very special, because the Ari Zal said that there were three rabbis before him who understood the Kabbala, And Rabbi Jaqtilia was one of them. Those rabbis, including Rabbi Jaqtilia got the seal of approval from the Ari Zal.

And the Ari Zal said, that he was taught the same system as Rabbi Jaqtilia , but he was not allowed to reveal it at that time. So the works of Rabbi Jaqtilia are tremendously important. And when you read his books you see that he was a tremendous genius. And he was a great explainer of Kabbala, and all his books are highly recommended. But I am going to talk about a piece from 'Shaarey Ora'. And 'Shaariy Ora' is a book which actually has the aim of connecting the Bible to Kabbala. It basically takes the words from the Bible, and shows you which Sefirot each of these words is connected to. In other words, every time the word 'well' is used, or every time the word 'river' is used, or any other word, this book tells you which sefira it is connected to and why. So it is a big introduction, to understand the Bible according to the Kabalistic tradition. But in any case, he actually wrote a number of books, and was very prolific. He also wrote a book called "Ginat Egoz", which talks about all God's names; all the different names of God which are used in the Bible, and there Rabbi Jaqutilia explains why God has so many names and what is the meaning of each name; why sometimes the bible uses the name Elohim and why sometimes Adnut, Eheye, Havaya etc. So, in other words, what Rabbi Jaqtilia explains is, why sometimes the Bible uses one name, while other times the Bible uses other names. So he has a book on that, and he has a number of other works, which are all very important and are great pieces of work, which I highly recommend. And I think there is some kind of an English edition to the book I am quoting now, but it is out of print, so you have to make some effort in order to find it (the English edition). As far as I remember, I found it once in a bookstore. But if you look carefully, I am sure that you can find one too. But I have a Hebrew edition, which is more common. There are many Hebrew editions to this book, 'Shaarey Ora', and the edition which I have includes the 'Beit Shaar', which is a special explanation to it, written by Rabbi Burnstein, if I am not mistaken, who is an important Kabbalist of our generation. He is still alive, and the book came out only recently, about two to three years ago and his notes on it can be very helpful. And he refers you to other places for more information. But in any case, let us start with Shaar (gate) number five, towards its end. But before we start reading from the book, I would like to inform an you of one more thing; Just as Abraham and Yitzchak were part of the chariot of heaven-they were God's chariots sending energy down from heaven, one was the right side, while the other was the left side (Avraham was the right side, and he corrected the right side of Chesed. And Yitzchak was the left side and he corrected the attribute of strength), Yaakov the third wing in that chariot, he is the middle column. So let us go on. "So is it with Yaakov too. He represents the middle column. And he is the secret of the name Havaya, may He be blessed, which stands in the middle". Here the names of God for the right side and the left side are not mentioned. But I think it had been mentioned earlier, that the right side is for the name 'El', which is the name for Chesed (mercy), and the left side will be for the name 'Elohim' which is the name for Din (strict judgment). "And just like the name of Havaya, may He be blessed, is in the middle of the signs and all the other names all those names cling to that Havaya name of God". Because he is in the middle, and all the other names and Sefirot cling to the middle, So this is similar to the Children of Israel all coming out from Yaakov, who is the center of the energies from God: "And just as Yaakov is the source of all 12 tribes who came out of him (which is the secret of the 12 boundaries), they all cling to the name of God. And the secret to this is written in the Torah, as it says, 'He placed the boundaries of the nations, according to the number of the children of Israel'". In other words, just as we get the energies directly from heaven, without the need of an angel as a mediator (which is unlike the 70 nations around us, each of whom needs a particular angel, who act as their own minister in heaven, to get energies from heaven), so do the 70 descendants of Yaakov, whom are mentioned at the end of the Book of Genesis and the beginning of the Book of Exodus, stand for the angels who act as ministers for the 70 nations. Because, as we know, Yaakov had 12 sons, but by the time they came to Egypt, they became 70 people in all.

"And therefore you can find all the chariots in the secret of Israel. And just like the main name of God, the Havaya name, carries all the chariots. And how is that? It is due to the fact that the name of Havaya stands in the middle, between the name of 'El', which is on the right side, and that of 'Elohim', which is on the left side. And the three of them together attach from here and there". In other words, these three become one piece. "And similarly, Yaakov has three characteristics, which are against the three sides, and they are the Cohen, the Levi and the Yisrael". In other words, the children of Israel, which means the descendants of Yaakov, have sub divisions; they were divided into Cohen, Levi and Yisrael. These are the group of priests, among the Tribe of Levi, who also had some functioning (to a lesser degree then the Kohanim, the priests) in the temple. And then there were the regular children of Israel.

"So the Cohen is in parallel to the right side, the side of the name El, which represents mercy. The Levi is in parallel to the left side, that of the name Elohim, which represents strict judgment. And the Yisrael is parallel to God's name of Havaya, which is in the middle. And so you see now, that the chariot of Yaakov is built like the chariot above. And just like all the names are attached to the name of Havaya, so are all the fathers included in Yaakov and his children: The Cohen is included in the place of Avraham, the Levi is included in the place of Yitzchak, and Yisrael in the place of Yaakov." So you see that the children of Yisrael, even though they have three separate fathers (Avraham, Yitzchak and Yaakov),are all included in Yaakov. Because when Yaakov came along he completed the chariot, and Avraham and Yitzchak, which are Chesed and Gevura, are included in Yaakov, and they became the Cohen and Levi. "So now, isn't it true, that you see that everything is balanced? Because God arranged that Yaakov and his children became the complete chariot for the true name of God. And now I am going to teach you secrets which you actually already know: You know that the constellations are twelve (there are 12 constellations)." This is our main topic and the main reason I came into this subject tonight. What I read up to now was an introduction. So now we are going to learn a secret. But you already know that the number of the constellations is 12, "and that the 12 months of the year come from them. And each constellation was made separately for its month. And though the 12 constellations, which are in heaven, where the sustenance to all the creatures below come from, they receive their power from all the 12 permutations of God's name according to each constellation, that is connected with it, in the great name of God, the name of Havaya, may He be blessed." In other words, each month has a name, which goes into that month and, so to speak, it contracts itself into that month and gives out the power of that month. "And each of the 12 permutations is bound to the four directions of the encampment of the Children of Israel in the desert. And you also find four seasons (of 12 months altogether) in the year. And you also find that in the encampment of the 12 tribes of Israel in the desert, there were four flags. All have 3 permutations of God's name on them. How is that? The letter 'Yod' rules over three permutations, because there are three permutations which start with the letter 'Yod'. And it is similarly with the first 'He', similarly with the 'Vav' and similarly with the last 'He'", so each of them rules over three permutations. Because, as we said before, if you have a four letter name, two letters of which are the same, it would be twenty four divided by two, and so we get 12 permutations. So each of these four letters is going to rule three months, the permutation of each is going to start with that letter. So the letter 'Yod', and the permutation which starts with it, rules three months, and so does each of the other three (out of these four) letters and the permutations which start with them, rules three months. And now Rabbi Jaqtilia is going to present a diagram, which I am going to talk more about in the next chapter.

The twelve names divided into the four flags:			
Flag A:	יהו"ה יהה"ו יוה"ה	***Flag C:***	והי"ה והה"י ויה"ה
Flag B:	הוה"י הוי"ה ההי"ו	***Flag D:***	היה"ו היו"ה ההו"י
The twelve tribes divided into the four flags:			
Flag A:	Yehuda Issachar Zebulon	***Flag C:***	Ephraim Menasha Benjamin
Flag B:	Rueben Shimon Gad	***Flag D:***	Dan Asher Naphtali
The twelve months divided into four seasons:			
Season A:	April May June	***Season C:***	October November December
Season B:	July August September	***Season D:***	January February March

But in any case, you see that the order of the tribes in the desert was a little different from their regular order, as we saw in the last lesson. So in the desert, the camping order in the eastern side was the tribe of Yehuda, together with the tribes Issachar and Zebulon. And then to the south were the tribe of Reuben, together with the tribes of Shimon and Gad. To the north, the third camp was the tribe of Ephraim, together with the tribes of Menasha and Binyamin. And the fourth camp, to the west, was of the tribes of Dan, Asher and Naphtali. And remember that the tribe of Levi was taken out of this order, so the tribe of Levi formed a camp unto itself, and wasn't part of the four camps. In fact it was placed in the middle of the four camps. And in place of Joseph, there were the tribes of the sons of Joseph, Ephraim and Menasha. So let use keep going:

"And we see the four flags of the camps, are connected with His holy name. Because the letter 'Yod' has three permutations, and it is the first letter in God's Havaya name. And the letter 'He' has three permutations. And similarly each one of the four letters has three permutations. And you can see that each letter in God's name has three permutations. And you can see that each of the four flags is similar to each of the four seasons, because just as each of the four flags has three tribes, so does each of the four seasons have three months within it. And a lot of it depends on the holy name of God, may He be blessed because you see that the months and signs and the permutations of God's name are all interconnected. And the twelve tribes of Israel, which are set into four groups, four flags, are from the power of the permutations of His name. And this is the secret of the verse, 'that your name is called on your city and on your nation'. This is the name of Havaya, and all His planning and His flags. All of them are called on the name of Israel. And therefore, we see that Yaakov gave birth to 12 children, which stand against (represent) the 12 permutations of God's name, which He is attached to. In other words, Yaakov is like the name of God. And just as from the name of Havaya comes the 12 permutations of this name of, so Yaakov permutated himself 12 ways, and had 12 sons. So against each of the permutations of God's Havaya name, one son was born to Yaakov. And remember this, because this is a great principle, which is very important to remember." So let us keep going: "So now, after we have taught you all this we have to inform you another thing. And this is, that the 12 signs in the Zodiac, which are in heaven, can't have any effect on earth by themselves. Rather it is through the power which each and every sign receives from the special name of God, because each of the 12 constellations receives the power from a different permutation of God's name. And each sign receives its power from a certain permutation. Because the three constellations, which are parts of the season of the spring, which are the signs of Aries, Taurus and Gemini, receive their power from the three names of God. These are the names which consist of the letters 'Yod', 'He', 'Vav' and 'He'; 'Yod', 'He', 'He' and 'Vav'; and then 'Yod', 'Vav', 'He' and 'He'. Because 'Yod' (which stands for Yehuda) is in the beginning of the four flags according to the camping in the desert, as it is the beginning of the permutations. And therefore, the first three months of the year are all one season. And that is to say, that the seasons receives its energy from the 'Yod' of the holy name, which in itself has three permutations. And three constellations complete the season of the summer too. They are Cancer, Leo and Virgo (the months of which are, more or less, July, August and September, or the Hebrew months of Tamuz, Av and Elul). And they receive their power from the three permutations of God's name which begin with the first 'He'. They are the permutation of 'He', 'Vav', 'He' and 'Yod': 'He', 'Vav', 'Yod' and 'He'; and 'He', 'He', 'Yod' and 'Vav'. And there are the three constellations, which are connected to the fall, which are those of Libra, Scorpio and Sagittarius (The Hebrew months of Tishri, Cheshvan and Kislev). And they receive their energy from the three permutations of God's name which start with the letter 'Vav', which is the head of the flag. These permutations are, the permutation of the letters 'Vav', 'He', 'Yod' and 'He'; 'Vav', 'He', 'He' and 'Yod'; and 'Vav', 'Yod', 'He' and 'He'. And also there are the three signs which are connected to the winter. These are the constellations of Capricorn, Aquarius and Pisces. They receive their power from the three permutations of God's Havaya name which begins with the second 'He' in His name, because that last 'He' is the head of that last camp. These permutations are those of the letters 'He', 'Yod', 'He' and 'Vav'; 'He', 'Yod', 'Vav' and 'He'; and 'He', 'He', 'Vav' and 'Yod'. And so you see, that all the constellations above do not have their own power but rather it is because of the permission they get, to take from the name of Havaya, so each one takes the permutation which is proper for it. And regarding this it is said, 'according to God they shall carry on with their journey and according to God they shall camp'". In other words, it is only if He gives you the energy then can you move. But otherwise, the planets and constellations can't do anything. "And therefore, open your eyes and see, how the name of Havaya rules over all of the powers above and below! And everything is in service under that name, may He be Blessed". So this is very important, and it makes things clearer now than in other lessons we have done up to now. True, a lot of this is a review, but I think Rabbi Jaqtillia gives it from a slightly different perspective. And he says a lot of things which are clearer then we learned from the Ramak. So even though the Ramak basically learned and said the same thing as Rabbi jaqtillia, here we learn from a different angle, how all the constellations for the months only receive their power from the permutations of God's Havaya name. In other words, we now clearly see how the planets and constellations get their power from God. So let us keep going a little more:

"And now, that we have meditated on this, that God's name, may He be blessed, was handed over, with the permutations of His name, to Yisrael, and so Yisrael stands against the permutations (represents these permutations), we realize that from these permutations the 12 tribes of Israel were born; each one from a different permutation".

So that is what I want to work on next. I think with this we are going to open up new ideas in understanding the Zodiac. So we are doing theoretical stuff right now, but I want to get to a more practical level, where we can learn how to interpret horoscopes from a lot of the information we started learning. And you can also see, that Rabbi Jaqtillia gives a very important principle, which is, that all the tribes of Israel get their energies from the permutations, with each one getting it from a different permutation. And we had one lesson, where we tried to explain the differences between the permutations and the orders of the letters in them. That lesson was not very practical, but it did explain the differences between each month in a mystical sense. And now, what Rabbi Jaqtilia tells us here is that we learn from the tribes, that each tribe is connected to a different permutation. So in truth, if you learn what each tribe is all about, and what the flags which rule the tribes are about, then you get a really good idea about each of the constellations. And the following is important; so Rabbi Jaqtillia carries on:

"And this is the blessing that Yaakov blessed his children before passing away". It is a well-known fact that Yaakov blessed his children close to his death, but he also rebuked them. And it is known that when you rebuke someone, that person may hold it against you. So being a righteous person, Yaakov waited until the time he was close to leaving this world, and only then did he rebuke his sons. But in any case, even when Yaakov rebuked his children, he actually blessed them in a way. So Rabbi Jaqtillia carries on, saying: "And each son Yaakov blessed according to the permutation (the permutation of God's name which was dedicated for that son) that was applicable to him, out of the different permutations of God's name. And this is the meaning of the verse, 'all of these are the tribes of Israel, which are 12 in number'". So the question becomes, why did the Torah have to say that the tribes of Israel were 12 in number? It is obvious, we know how to count? It is obvious, that if you count Reuven, Shimon, Levi etc., you will get 12 tribes. So what is the Torah teaching by saying that the tribes of Israel are 12 in number? "It means that each of the 12 tribes is according to each of the 12 permutations which are well known. And when Yaakov blessed them, he blessed them according to the permutations, each one of which was applicable to a different son, a different tribe of

Israel. And that is the meaning of what is said, 'and this is what their father said to them and blessed them. Each one, according to his blessing did he bless them'". In other words, each tribe was getting its blessing from a specific permutation of God's name. And therefore Yaakov blessed each tribe differently; he couldn't bless every tribe with the same blessing, because each tribe was getting from a different permutation of God's name. And because of that, he had to bless each tribe in the way which that tribe was meant to receive the blessing, because each tribe was born with different abilities and different characteristics and functions, so that the whole group of 12 become characterized in a way as a whole, as a group of different individuals. Because you can't have everybody as a teacher, or a politician or anything else, you can't have everybody the same. The world contains different types of people, it wasn't made otherwise. You need a world where everybody is different. So Yaakov had to bless each tribe in a different way. You can't have everybody being the same, and similarly it was with the tribes; each tribe had to be different. Each tribe is connected to a different month and a different constellation. And those months and constellations were each connected to a different permutation of God's name. And each tribe was built from a different permutation; it got its characteristics from a different permutation. So Yaakov had to bless each tribe according to the permutation which was applicable to that tribe. And Rabbi Jaqtillia goes on: "And what does it mean, 'each one, according to his blessing, did he bless them'? That is to say that, to each one of them, he gave the blessing that was suitable for them, according to the permutation of God's name. And similarly, according to this secret, there were 12 stones in the breast plate of the Kohen Gadol, the high priest, which, again, is a remembrance to the 12 tribes, of the children of Israel". And later we will also talk about the 12 stones, which are also connected to the chart. So each tribe had a different stone representing it on the breastplate of the Cohen Gadol. And maybe we will talk later about the characteristics of the different stones and what they mean. "And there were four columns of stones on the breastplate; three stones to each and every column; and just like God's name is divided into each of the four camps and permutations according to each letter, against the four camps of Israel; three tribes in each camp. And the end of the matter is this: That there are four camps for Israel, and each camp or flag of them carries a sign, it carries a letter out of the four letters of God's name. And each letter has three permutations, against the three tribes of each that camp, of that flag. And now we have explained many secret things to you, which now became clear to the eye. And we have already explained how Yaakov is the middle column, and he goes up to the Ein Sof, and he inherits what is without boundaries, as we have explained above". But this is something we didn't talk about. That is not applicable to us right now. But in any case, to summarize what we have learned here, we see a big thing. We see that Rabbi Jaqutillia makes it clear, how all the 12 tribes, the 12 constellations and all the 12 months, all get their energies from the same source, these are the 12 permutations of God's name of Havaya. And each of those permutations is different, because its letters are arranged in a different order. So the energy of each month, the energy which comes into each constellation and to each of the 12 tribes, is different. So now, we will have to talk some more about the tribes and about the flags in the desert. We are going to go deeply into it, and we will bring you more places where it talks about the flags and what was written on the flags. And then we are also going to find sources about the different tribes and what there characteristics were. And I hope this will give us a great introduction to the months and to the signs of the Zodiac, how each one is different from the other and what the meaning of each of these is.

Chapter 8

In the chapter 7 we talked about how you order the tribes. In other words, what is the proper order according to which the tribes should be counted? Know there are a number of different texts of Sefer Yetzira, we will be using the Gaon of vilna- Arizal version which is considered the most accurate.

So we had a problem, and I have been thinking about it a lot. Because if you look at the text of the Ari Zal, which is the text of the Vilna Gaon, and Rabbi Jaqtillia (whose writings we began studying in the last class, and we will come back to him later), it seems to be the accepted text which is used today. And I am going to read the first Mishna in it, because we have done it and looked at it before. And it says the following: "There are 12 simple letters, which are 'He', 'Vav', 'Zayin', 'Chet', 'Tet', 'Yod', 'Lamed', 'Nun', 'Samech', 'Ayin', 'Tzadik', and 'Kof'". And now, the text will go on, explaining how each of these letters is connected to a different sense, a different power of the soul.

"The first of these letters, which is the letter 'He', represents the sense of speech. The second of these letters, which is the letter 'Vav', represents the sense of the thought (thinking). The third letter in this group, which is the letter 'Zayin', represents the sense of motion, or walking. The fourth letter in this group, which is the letter 'Chet', represents the sense of seeing. The fifth letter in this group, which is the letter 'Tet', represents the sense of hearing. The sixth letter in this group, which is the letter 'Yod', represents the sense of action. The seventh letter in this group, which is the letter 'Lamed', represents the sense of intercourse, or cohabitation. The eighth letter in this group, which is the letter 'Nun', represents the sense of smelling. The ninth letter in this group, which is the letter 'Samech', represents the sense of sleep. The tenth letter in this group, which is the letter 'Ayin', represents the sense of anger. The eleventh letter in this group, which is the letter 'Tzadik', represents the sense of sipping and drinking. And the twelfth letter in this group, the last one in it, which is the letter 'Kof', represents the sense of laughter".

So now, the Sefer Hayetzira is giving us the order of the letters and how they are connected with a set of sense functions of the body, or actions of the body. And so, in the next couple of Mishnayot, these letters are going to be connected to three different things. And you have to remember, that Sefer Hayetzira is based on the following three things: Olam, Shana VaNefesh; which means world, (or universe, as he calls it), year (or time) and soul. It is everything that happens in the universe, everything that happens in the year (in time), and everything that happens inside the person.

So in the next couple of Mishnayot, it is going to be explained how these 12 letters are, in terms of the world of time, the 12 months of the year. It starts with the first month of Nisan in the Hebrew calendar, in other words, it starts from the spring time, and it goes forward: Nisan, Iyar, Sivan and so on.

And in the world of the universe, these 12 letters represent the 12 constellations, from Aries, through Taurus, Gemini, Cancer etc., to Pisces. So each month has a particular constellation.

And the third is the characteristics in the soul, what they call 'the senses' or 'the directors of the soul'. And as we have seen before, they are 12 different senses, and they are inside the soul. And they start with the sense of speech. And therefor, the first month of the year

is the month of speech. Because there are Olam, Shana and Nefesh, which means Universe, Time and Soul, and they are all connected to each other.
So the first month of the year, which is the first month of spring time, will be Nisan. And parallel to that you have the constellation of Aries in the universe, and the sense of speech is the sense in the human body which is connected to the soul.
But it is interesting, that the Sefer Hayetzira doesn't mention the 12 tribes of Israel. We don't see any mention of the 12 tribes in Sefer Hayetzira, the Book of Creation. So when the time came to acquaint these functions with the 12 tribes, there was a problem, regarding the question of what the order of the tribes would be. Because the standard order, the order according to the first time we see the listing of the tribes, is in the beginning of the Book of Exodus: "These are the names of the Children of Israel who came to Egypt". And there the order is given according to the four different mothers. Because in Judaism, the three fathers are: Avraham, Yitzchak and Yaakov. The four mothers are Sarah, Rivka, Rachel and Leah. Avraham gave birth to Yitzchak, but he had other children who went off. Yizchak gave birth of Yaakov and Esau, and Esau went off. And Yaakov had two wives and two concubines. So the tribes of Israel originated from one man, Yaakov, and from four women. So these four women were: Leah and Rachel as Yaakov's wives and who were two of the mothers, and their servants were Bilha and Zilpa, who gave birth to four of the tribes of Israel. So that is how we have the 12 tribes of Israel from one man and four women. So in the Book of Exodus, the 12 tribes are listed according to their mothers. It obviously starts off with the children of Leah, because the first children of Yaakov were birthed by Leah.
So I would like to quote from the beginning of the Book of Exodus. "And these are the names of the Children of Israel who came to Egypt, with Yaakov, each man and his household came there: Reuven, Shimon, Levi and Yehuda, Issachar, Zebulon and Binyamin, Dan, Naphtali, Gad and Asher. And all the souls who were born from Yaakov 70 people in all, and Joseph was already in Egypt". So we see here, that it looks like they were listed here according to their mothers.
So if we look at the order of the tribes here, we see something which is very interesting. We see that the tribes are listed here according to the wives and concubines of Yaakov. Basically it is according to the order of the time the mothers gave birth, but it is different regarding Rachel. This is because Rachel was a wife of Yaakov, not a concubine, so her son, Binyamin, is mentioned here before the sons of the concubines. So Reuven, Shimon, Levi, Yehuda, Issachar and Zebulum were the sons of Leah. And they are listed according to the order of their births. Then Binyamin is mentioned, because he was the son of the other mother, Rachel. This list leaves Joseph the other son of Rachel out, because, as mentioned later, Joseph had already been in Egypt, and therefore he is mentioned at the end. And mentioning Binyamin here, together with the sons of Leah, also emphasize here that Joseph belongs in this place too, in this order of birth. And actually Joseph was born before Binyamin. So had Joseph been mentioned here, he would be mentioned just after Zebulon and before Binyamin. And that would be the proper order for the two children of Rachel. So the number of children which Lea and Rachel gave birth to, is, altogether, eight. And then the Torah lists the four children of the concubines: Dan and Naphtali were the children of Bilha, the servant girl of Rachel, and Gad and Asher were the children of Zilpa, who was the servant girl of Lea.

So we see here that the order, in which the 12 tribes are listed here, is according to their mothers. And this is very interesting, because when you go to the other place in which the tribes of Israel are mentioned, in the Book of Numbers, Bamidbar, you see that the order in which the tribes are mentioned is different.

And we saw in 'Shaarey Ora', written by Rabbi Jaqtilia, that he lists the tribes according to the order in which they are mentioned in the Book of Numbers. And there, the tribes are listed differently than they are listed in the beginning of the Book of Exodus.

So let us look again at how the tribes are listed in chapter 2 of the Book of Numbers. And it is important, because the Rabbis want to use that order in Sefer Hayetzira. In any case, let us briefly see the text because I would like to introduce a new idea which I found before we go deeper into the text.

So it is said, that the people who camp in the east are all under the banner of the camp of Yehuda, according to the hosting tribe. And the prince of the tribe of Yehuda is Nachshon, the son of Aminadav.

So here it is going to be explained, what was the order of the tribes according to the way they were placed in the desert. So the Torah here lists the names of the tribes, plus the name of the head of the tribe, plus the hosting tribes and the sides of the camping they were placed on.

So Nachshon, the son of Aminadav, was the head of the Tribe of Yehuda. And the Torah goes on to specify the number of men who were members of the Tribe of Yehuda and the other tribes of Israel. But after the camp of Yehuda is mentioned, the Torah goes on to say, that the camps of Issachar and Zebulon were part of the camp, which the tribe of Yehuda hosted. And the prince of the tribe of Issachar was Nathaniel, the son of Tzuar. And then the Torah goes on to say how many men were in the camp of Issachar. And then the Torah mentions the camp of Zebulon, and the prince of Zebulon was Eliav, the son of Chelon. And then the Torah goes on to tell you how many men were in that tribe. So the Torah goes like that through all the tribes, telling you the name of the prince of each tribe, and how many men were in each.

So we see two different ways of counting the Tribes of Israel: One in the Book of Numbers, and the other, the more simple way, in the beginning of the Book of Exodus, which is according to the mothers of the tribes.

So ideally, everybody would really like to use the order of the tribes of Israel, as written in the beginning of the Book of Exodus. But there is a problem using this order in Sefer Hayetzira because Reuben, for example, is clearly connected with the sense of seeing. Because when Leah gave birth to Reuben, she said, 'for God saw my misery, and now my husband will love me more', and therefore she gave him the name Reuven. Because the truth is that Yaakov loved Rachel more, and wanted to marry Rachel. But her father tricked him and gave him Leah instead. And only afterwards could he take Rachel. So in any case, Leah felt undeserving. So when she had her first son, and that was before Rachel had any children, she said that God saw her misery. But in any case, the name Reuben comes from the Hebrew word for seeing. And then, when she gave birth to Shimon, she said, 'for God heard that I am unloved, and therefore she gave him the name Shimon. So we see that the name Shimon comes from the Hebrew word for hearing. So Shimon is connected to the sense of hearing. And if you look at the order of the senses, according to the Vilna Gaon and the Ari Zal, you see that it starts off with speech, and then comes the senses of thought, motion, and only then come the senses of seeing and hearing. So only the fourth and fifth senses are connected to Reuven and Shimon. And only the fourth and fifth months are connected to seeing and hearing. So you are going to have a great problem if you go according to the order which is given at the beginning of the Book of Exodus. Because if you go that way, it doesn't work out properly, for according to that order, the months which represent Reuven and Shimon should be the first two months of the year, and in reality they are the fourth and fifth months of the year. So I think this is the main reason that the order of the tribes in Sefer Hayetzira doesn't go according to the order of the tribes in the Book of Exodus. So there might be some other text where the order of the months is different, and there might be an order of months according to which the first month is the month of seeing and the second is the month of hearing. But according to the common texts, the texts we know, I think that it is agreed by all sages, and certainly it seems to be agreed by the Ari Zal and the Vilna Gaon that the order of the months begin with the month of speech, like the order of the senses, and that only the fourth and fifth months become those of seeing and hearing. So I think that due to this, we come to the idea which we saw in Rabbi Jaqtillia's book, Shaariy Ora, that everything goes according to the camps. So we go according to the camps. And then, if you learn according to the camps, then it comes out that Reuven and Shimon become the fourth and fifth months. So other months come before, and there are some months which come after, but Reuven and Shimon are connected to the fourth and fifth months. So you start with Yehuda, Yisachar and Zvulun, who camp in the east. And only then come Reuven and Shimon, in the fourth and fifth places according to this order. And in the Zohar, as well as in Sefer Hayetzira, the senses of seeing and hearing are regarded as the fourth and fifth senses. So I think this is the reason for them (The Ari Zal, the Vilna Gaon etc.) saying that you have to use the order of the tribe as specified in the Book of Numbers, regarding the order of the camping.

And I would like to come back now to another idea, which may be a deeper level of understanding why they are doing this, why this is the order of the tribes, and why they are learning it from the story of the camping in the Book of Numbers. So you have to know, that in Judaism there are two principal rules: First of all, you have to know if the person is Jewish or not. And how do you decide if a person is Jewish? The answer is simple: It goes according to the mother; if the mother was Jewish, then the child is Jewish. And if the mother was not Jewish, then the child is not Jewish; the father does not matter here, as far as the definition, of whether the child belongs to the Jewish people or not. It all depends on the status of the mother. But as far as the order of the tribes is concerned, we go according to the father. So if the father belongs to the tribe of Reuben, for instance, and the mother belongs to another tribe, then the child belongs to the tribe of Reuben. And so it is with any other tribe. The child is a member of whatever tribe the father is a member of, even if the mother is a member of another tribe. And therefore, all the Children of Israel are called so, because they are children of Yaakov, who was also called Yisrael.

And here, we should also mention, that Israel was also divided into three groups' the members of the tribe of Levi had the task of working in the Temple, and among them were the Kohanim, the priests. And the Kohanim are represented in a way by Abraham, the Levites by Isaac, and the Israelis by Jacob.

And the laws for the Kohanim, were more strict then the law for the other children of Israel. And the Kohanim had to bless the children of Israel in the prayers of the Temple, and they would not be allowed to go to the graveyards, and there were other rules connected to marriage regarding the Kohanim, the priests. All these rules were connected to the Kohanim. And how do you determine if a person is a Kohen? It goes according to the father. In other words, if the father is a Kohen, then the child is a Kohen, even if the mother is not a Kohen. But if the father is not a Kohen, even if the mother was a Kohen, then the child is not a Kohen. And so it is with a Levi, as it is with a member of any other tribe: If the father is a Levi, even if the mother is not, then the child is a Levi. And if the father is not a Levite, even if the mother is, then the child is not a Levite.

And the way this is learned, regarding the tribes, is very peculiar: In the Book of Exodus, where the tribes are on the order of the mothers, then it talks more about the months of the year. But if you look at the order of the tribes in the Book of Numbers, there we go, according to what Rabbi Jaqtillia said, according to the seasons of the year. And if you remember, Rabbi Jaqtillia explained how it goes according to the seasons and not according to the months. So there he started with the season of spring, and then he went on to summer, the fall and winter. And he connected these seasons to the four elements, of earth, water, fire and air.

And if you think about it, you realize that the idea of seasons is connected to the sun, which is masculine. So the sun is masculine, as opposed to the moon, which is feminine. So the order of the months is a feminine order, because the months are defined according to the moon which is feminine. And the months are counted, as we have mentioned before, from Nisan, as it is said, 'this month for you will be the head of the months, it is for you the first of all the months of the year'. So we start with the month of Nisan and do the counting, and all this is based on the moon. It is based on the way the moon travels: the moon orbits the earth every twenty eight days, and that is the order of the moon and the months. But the Tekufot, the seasons of the year, are fixed according to the sun: Each time the sun turns through heaven, so to speak, there is a new season. Because the sun makes a circular motion, so to speak, of 90 degrees each season. So each time that the sun completes a 90 degree motion it becomes a new season. So the seasons go according to the sun, and therefore they are masculine.

So I think you can say, as I want to say, that a deeper reason for the use of the seasons and the order of the camps is, because the camps are connected to the seasons of the year, they are broken up into four seasons, and the seasons are masculine, because they are dependent on the sun. And if you look at the order of the camps, as written in the Book of Numbers, you also see that the Torah is talking there about the masculine head of each tribe. So we see, for example, that the head of the tribe of Yehuda was Nachshon, and so in each tribe, the Torah gives you the name of the head of the tribe, who was masculine. And this is as opposed to what we saw in the book of Exodus, that everything, namely the order of the tribes of Israel, is feminine, because it goes according to the mothers of the Nation of Israel. So I think this is a deeper reason for Sefer Hayetzira using the order of the seasons, instead of using the order of the months, because here the masculine element should be used, because here we are talking about the tribes. Because the mother just determines whether the child is Jewish or not, but the one who determines what tribe the child is a member of is the father, not the mother. This point is determined by who the father of that child is. So therefore, in the Book of Numbers, the male head of each tribe is mentioned. And again, this is why the order of the months is used through the order of the seasons of the year. Because the order of the seasons is masculine too, for it depends on the sun. So I want to say, that this is the deep reason for why everybody learns that you go according to the order which we learn in the Book of Numbers, the order of the camping of the tribes of Israel in the desert. So I think that this is a good explanation, and then everything makes sense. And this way you can perfectly explain the order of the Vilna Gaon and the Ari Zal, as found in Sefer Hayetzira, and all that goes according to the order of the camping of the tribes in the desert. And then you see that each tribe is connected to a different quality.

So, to summarize everything, I really think that it answers everything, and this is tonight's idea. But I still have to show it to a great rabbi, to see if he agrees with me. And I also think there is a very important matter to study the tribes. Because you have to remember that our Bible is also an astrological text; it teaches you astrology too. And if you read the Bible thoroughly, and follow the history of each tribe, and try to work out which tribe each person in the Bible came from, I think you can then learn a lot about each of the different signs of the Zodiac, and about each of the different months of the year. So I would like to go through that now. And I have a few things which I want to show you regarding this. And we are now going to get into a deeper idea about who the 12 tribes were. So we are going to learn this in terms of astrology, and soon we are going to get into the idea of the signs, because we want to get into practical use of this material. We would like to use in the real world what we learn in a theoretical way. So one goal we have here is to become better astrologers, through the assistance of the holy writings, and deeply understand what goes on in each of the signs in heaven, by knowing better who and what are each of the different tribes. Because we learn that each tribe is paired off with a different month and a different sign, as explained in Sefer Hayetzira. So you know that each tribe has certain qualities to it, and a certain history which you can learn about, regarding each of the signs.

And so, remember, that the first month we are going to talk about, will be the month of Yehuda. And from now on, we are going to learn about the months like this, in this order, and not like in the chart which I have initially gave you, which I think starts with Reuben. In other words, now we are going to go according to Sefer Hayetzira, which starts the order with the tribe of Yehuda. And later on, we are going to talk about the question of why it is the tribe of Yehuda which comes first in this order. Because we still have to see, why is the tribe of Yehuda connected to the first month of the year and to the astrological sign of Aries, and why Yehuda is connected to the sense of speech. So we are going to work on this.

But first of all I would like to talk about something else, which I found in the Book, Chesed Leavraham. And we have taught the subject of 'Time Lords' from it. This is a book which was written by a great Kabbalist in Sefad in the 1600,s, and I think he wrote a whole commentary on the Zohar. And he also wrote a book, which is called 'Chesed Leavraham', and it is a tremendous book. That book is not a very long book in the world; it is 300 pages. But it is a whole introduction to, and a wide view of, the Torah. So each little piece which he has in his book, is connected to a number of ideas which are all throughout Judaism. And so, it gives you a collection of fundamental ideas in Judaism. And it is a tremendously important book, in my opinion. And I found one piece in this book which I want to show you, because it is going to go through a variety of subjects too. This goes according to Rabbi Jaqtillia, and the Ari Zal, as well as the Vilna Gaon. So we start with the sense of speech. And he has many pieces here, but this is a small one. It is called the fourth well in river number 13. And he is going to explain the special characteristics of each tribe.

"And though there are 12 special characteristics which were created in the world, and each of them was given to a different tribe, and these are them: The first special characteristic is speech, and that was given to Yehuda, and he had an advantage over all other people in the power of speech.

The second special characteristic was the thought, the thinking process, and the process of understanding the Torah in depth. And it was given to Issachar, and he had an advantage over all other people in this regard".

So you see right away now, that he is going according to the order of the tribes which was specified in the Book of Numbers, regarding the camping in the desert. And he is telling you that each tribe had a special Segula, a special characteristic.

And today we don't really know who belongs to which tribe. So maybe you can say that each person had a special ability, so they could figure out which tribe they were born from. But when we read the Bible, we see that every person has a special genealogy, and from that we could learn which tribe he belongs to. We could learn things from it. So let us go on:

"The third special characteristic was the motion, which is going or walking, weather we are talking about motion by sea, or by land. And this was given to Zvulun, and he had an advantage over all other people in this regard.

The fourth special characteristic was that of seeing, and that was given to Reuven. And he had an advantage over all other people in this regard."

And we will have to look if everyone who is born in the fourth month, which has the constellation of Cancer, may have a better sight then other people, who were born on other months.

"The fifth special characteristic is hearing, and that was given to Shimon. And he had an advantage over all other people in this regard.

And the sixth special characteristic is action, and that was given to Gad, in warfare and in all other actions. And he had an advantage over all other people in this regard.

The seventh special characteristic is intercourse, and that was given to Ephraim".

Because the name of Ephraim comes from the word of "Pru Urvu", which means "increase and multiply". In any case, let us continue with the text: "And he had an advantage over all other people in this regard.

The eighth special characteristic is smell, and that was given to Menashe. And he had an advantage over all other people in this regard.

The ninth special characteristic is sleep, and that was given to Binyamin. And he had an advantage over all other people in this regard.

The tenth special characteristic is anger, and that was given to Dan. And he had an advantage over all other people in this regard.

The eleventh special characteristic is wisdom, which was given to Asher. And he had an advantage over all other people in this regard.

And the twelfth special characteristic is laughter and good will, and that was given to Naftali. And he had an advantage over all other people in this regard".

So you see that this is written in the book of 'Chesed Leavraham', which listed each tribe according to the order in the desert, starting with the tribe of Yehuda. And he shows you that each tribe got a special different characteristic over the other tribes which made each one unique. So it is like we see, that each person, born in a different planetary sign, is going to have a different set of characteristics over other people. And the interesting thing is, that when the Sefer Hayetzira learned this, it didn't go according to any of the known astrological systems. Sefer Hayetzira does not explain how you connect speech to Aries, for instance, or thought to Taurus, walking to Gemini and seeing to Cancer. Nor does it explain how you connect hearing to Leo, and the other characteristics to the other constellations; it is something which we don't really have. So this is an important point which we will have to come back and work on.

But before we do this, I would like to take a break and go into a famous book, which explains in depth the topic of the tribes in the desert, their banners and what pictures were on them. And this is the only place I found where this topic is discussed in depth.

So I would like learn this first, and after that we are going to get deeper into this subject which we started now. And I am going to introduce some material from the Vilna Gaon regarding that. I would like to go with you through the ideas of the Kabbala and astrology of the Vilna Gaon. However we are going to start with the Rabenu Bechayey, after which we will start studying the writings of the Vilna Gaon.

So let us start off with the writings of Rabenu Bechayey. But first of all, I have to explain to you, that he was an important rabbi. In fact he wrote the famous book of ethics called 'Chovat Halevavot', which means 'the duty of the hearts'. And you can get this book in English too. It is called 'Duty of the hearts', and it can be found among classical ethical books, because it is a book on the subject of ethics. And Rabenu Bechayey also wrote a commentary on the five books of the Torah. And also there, he summarizes all the ideas that are found in the Torah. And just as the writer of the book 'Chesed Leavraham' had that ability, so does Rabenu Bechayey. He could briefly explain all the main ideas the Torah speaks about.

But I would just like to briefly go into the idea of the tribes and their flags. And I don't know what his source is, because he doesn't mention it. But in any case, people mention that there were flags in the desert, and that each tribe had a different banner. But nobody talks about what was on those banners, or about the question of whether there was anything on them or not. Because there are a few questions regarding those banners: Did they have anything written on those banners? Were they empty? Did they have any pictures on those banners? Did each tribe have a differ banner?, and from that we can get a glimpse of ideas about each of the tribes of Israel, and what their abilities were. And this will be a kind of an introduction into the writings of the Gaon of Vilna, and the way he understands and explains, what each of the tribes' special abilities were. And thus we will be able to see how we can connect them with the different months of the year and the seasons of the year. And of course, the main thing we would like to do is connect all of this to the constellations of the Zodiac, because we would like to understand the forces which are coming down from above. And again, we work on the idea that everything comes from the different permutations of the Havaya name of God. Because there are 12 different permutations, and we want to say that they really come from the upper worlds, like the world of Atzilut, from the two parts of Arik, which is in the beard of high above. And they come from a higher source, which is from the Moach Stima, the hidden mind, which is on top of the Atzilut which sends all the energies down. So the energies come down from there, through the two Mazalot (constellations) in the beard, and eventually they get down to the constellations and to our planetary system, and from there they go down right to the earth and thus they affect us. Because before the energies go down to us, there are a few circles above, through which they come. So the outer circle is that of the 12 permutations of God's Havaya name. And then, in the circle which is in it and is surrounded by the outer circle, are the names of the 12 tribes of Israel. And then the energies come down to the signs and then to the planets.

So if we properly understand the 12 permutations of God's name and the 12 tribes, it is going to give us a much more detailed understanding of the constellations and the houses, which are the most inner circles. And this is why we came here tonight to study the writings of Rabbi Bechayey.

Now we will quote Rabbi Bechayey

So I will start off with a verse from the Torah portion: "Each man, with his banner, according to his sign".

So now, Rabbi Bechayey proceeds to explain what the meaning of the words 'his signs' is. So he says:

"Their signs mean that each banner had a different sign on it. So the banner of Reuven had a picture of a man on it, which was a hint to the Dudaim". The Dudaim were a kind of a special fruit, which was given to women who couldn't have children, and they were then able to conceive. And the dudaim had the form of a man.

So let us go on:

"And it was the banner of Yehuda, which had the picture of a lion on it. Because the father of the tribe was referred to as a lion, by the verse which states that 'Yehuda is like a baby lion'. And the banner of Ephraim had a picture on it of a bull. As it is said in the Book of Deuteronomy, 'He is the first born of the bull, which is an honor for him'. And the banner of Dan was in the shape of an eagle. Because they looked like the angels which are describes in the Book of Yechezkel; these are part of the angels which Yechazkel saw".

So in any case, the flags are called 'signs' because they have signs on them and because each tribe had a different picture on its flag, which is very interesting. And Rabbi Bechayey gives us a couple of examples, but he doesn't go through each of the tribes and their banners.

So another time we are going to come back to this subject and go more thoroughly into this subject. But for now, we will quote another few lines:

"And there is another way of explaining the meaning of the word 'Otot', which initially means 'signs'. This is by connecting the word 'otot' with the verse 'with all the desires of your soul'". Here Rabbi Bechayey learns that the word 'Otot' come from the Hebrew word for 'desire'; because the People of Israel desired those banners. Because when they stood on Mount Sinai, they saw that the angels above, who served God, all had banners.

And now I am going to skip a few lines, because they are not relevant here to what we are doing. So in any case, the main idea here is, that the children of Israel desired those flags, which were similar to the flags the angels had.

So let us carry on:

"And this is the idea of the banners, according to what we found in the writings". And I guess Rabbi Bechayey had some writings with him (maybe certain old texts, which were written by rabbis, maybe even from the Talmudic time), where it talked about these banners. And as you already know, there were 12 tribes, which were devided into four main flags, three to each direction. "And this is just like the 12 tribes are divided into four

camps, which are three to each side of the world. And they are called the four camps of the divine presence. And they had 12 Mapot (Flags or maps)".
So in any case, each tribe had its own flag. "And the forms and colors of each flag were different from the other. Just like the flags above, which the children of Israel saw on Mount Sinai, were of different colors".
And the text goes on:
"Yehuda, Issachar and Zebulun were on the east. Yehuda had a flag, the color of which was like the color of heaven. And on it was the picture of a lion. Issachar had a flag which was blue". But I guess it was a darker blue color then the flag of Yehuda. "And on it were the pictures of the sun and the moon because they were the experts in understanding the seasons of the year and the constellations. Zebulun had a flag, the color of which was white, which is a sign of wealth. Because silver is white. And on it was a picture of a ship". This is because members of this tribe traded around the world, and merchandised through shipping.
"And Reuben, Shimon and Gad were in the south. Reuven had a flag, the color of which was red. And on it were the pictures of the Dudaim, the fertility herbs. Shimon had a flag, the color of which was green, and on it was the picture of Shechem". I guess the city of Shechem, Nablus, where there was a whole story connected to Shimon. "And Gad had a flag, the color of which was white and black, and on it was a picture of a battalion, a group of soldiers".
And so we are getting into the matter of the flags and what is drawn on each flag. And then we will take it from there, and go deeper into these 12 tribes, the 12 constellations of the year and the 12 months and the 12 divisions of the soul. We are going to get deeper into all this. And hopefully, all this is going to make us better astrologers, and help us understand the depth of the Torah, also from the perspective of an astrology book.

Chapter 9

In the last few chapters we have been working on the order of the tribes of Israel, and on the different ways we connect these tribes to the zodiacal signs. We are going to continue learning about that, and also the flags each tribe had; because, as we have already mentioned each tribe of Israel had its own flag, when the Children of Israel were in the desert. And this had been written about in detail in 'Midrash Rabenu Bechayey', which is a lengthy commentary on the Torah, and is a very important book, which contains all the basic principals for understanding the Torah. And there is a lot of mysticism in the book of Rabbi Bechayey, there is a lot of Kabbala, and it is a highly recommended book. For he is one of the only Rabbis I have read, who talks about the flags of the tribes of Israel. So I think we should try to learn as much as we can about each of the Zodiacal signs by understanding the flags. Because, since each of these flags is connected to one of the 12 Zodiacal signs, we can get a clearer picture, through the flags, who each tribe was, and then it will reveal to us more and more about the Zodiacal signs, since they are connected to those tribes and flags.
So for example, if we can understand the tribe of Yehuda, we can have a better idea of what the sign of Aries is. So it is a very important thing for us to understand. And it is not only important for understanding astrology; it is also very important for understanding the Torah, because if the Torah equates Yehuda with the sign of Aries, and we read the story of Yehuda, then we can learn more and more about the Arian character. So from

learning the stories of Yehuda in the Bible, you also learn about Aries. And since the tribe of Reuven is connected to the sign of Cancer, if you learn the stories of Reuven, you learn more and more about the Cancerian personality and get a better idea about him or her. And of course, there is Sefer Hayetzira, which was written before the Bible; it was written by Avraham Avinu. So I think this is the reason that the tribes of Israel are not mentioned in Sefer Hayetzira. Because it was written before the tribes were born. But even so, you are going to see that all the great rabbis, including the Ari Zal, the Vilna Gaon and many other great Rabbis would connect the 12 tribes of Israel with the 12 Zodiacal signs. So by learning and understanding the characters of each of the tribes, you can understand the 12 Zodiacal signs better. And so can you understand them better by looking at the pictures of the stars in the sky. And we will be start to talk a little about the Gaon of Vilna and explain how he approached astrology from Sefer Hayetzira.
So it is a duel thing. Because, of course we learn astrology from the Torah, but on the other hand, from learning astrology, we can have a better understanding of the Torah. Because when you learn about Reuben, for instance, you actually also learn about the sign of Cancer. And when you learn about Yehuda, you learn about the sign of Aries. And the same way, when you learn about Issachar, you also learn about the sign of Taurus. And they all had descendants, so when you learn about them, you follow the history of the tribes. And then you are likely to get a deeper appreciation of the Torah too, and a better and deeper understanding of astrology, from all of this interconnection between different people and things. Because it is not for nothing that the sages had pointed out to the connections between the twelve simple letters, the Zodiacal signs, the 12 tribes of Israel, the 12 months of the year, the 12 permutations of God's name, the 12 limbs which rule the body, the 12 senses and everything else. And in any case, from all these divisions we see that the number 12 is a very important number. So the more we study and understand all this, the more we can understand and know the world better. And thus we can understand astrology better and understand the tribes better, and understand the Torah in a deeper better way.
So I would like to start off at the point we stopped at the end of the last lesson, and to go over that paragraph, from the explanations of Rabbi Bechayey regarding the flags of each of the 12 tribes of Israel. Because he brings up this idea, that each of those tribes had its own flag. And this is an idea we haven't seen anybody mentioning before. And I am not sure where his sources came from, and he doesn't tell us his source. But he is going to bring down and list all the 12 tribes, describing what their flags looked like. So again, from this we can gather more pieces of information. And from each sign or symbol in each of the flags of the 12 tribes of Israel, we can get some more information about the 12 signs in the Zodiac.
So let us go back to Rabbi Bechayey's text regarding the flags of the 12 tribes. Because last week we didn't do too much; we only did a few lines. So let us go back and start again from where he talks about what the flags looked like, and then we will push on and continue:
"Yehuda, Issachar and Zebulon were on the east. Yehuda had a flag, the color of which was like the color of heaven and on it was the picture of a lion. Issachar had a flag which was blue, and on it were the pictures of the sun and the moon, because they were the experts in understanding the seasons of the year and the constellations". Members of the tribe of Issachar were experts in astronomy and astrology. And I guess that this is the

reason for the color of their flag being blue, which was similar to the color of the flag of the tribe of Yehuda, which was the color of heaven. And for this reason, images of the sun and the moon appeared in that flag too. "Zebulon had a flag, the color of which was white, which is a sign of wealth, because silver is white. And on it was a picture of a ship". I guess this is because members of this tribe sold around the world, and merchandised through shipping. Because Zebulon was a merchant, and he made a deal with Issachar, according to which, Issachar would learn the Torah and Zebulon would support him. And Zebulon used to travel on the sea; he travelled with his merchandise from country to country on his boat. So therefore there is a picture of a boat on his flag. And the background of the flag is white, which is the color of silver; the color of money and wealth.

So these three tribes, Yehuda, Issachar and Zebulon, formed the first camp, which was on the east. The second camp was that of Reuben, Shimon and Gad, which was on the south. So let us carry on with Rabbi Bechayey's text:

"And Reuben, Shimon and Gad were in the south. Reuben had a flag, the color of which was red. And on it were the pictures of the Dudaim, the fertility herbs". And as we said before, this picture was due to the story of Reuben finding the Dudaim and giving them to his mother, so she can become pregnant again. And you also have to think about the question of how it is connected to the constellation of Cancer. So on first glance, it is not clear, why the red color and the Dudaim are connected to the sign of Cancer more then other colors and pictures, and how they are connected to the sign of Cancer. So we have to figure out this matter. "Shimon had a flag, the color of which was green, and on it was the picture of Shechem". I guess the text is referring to the city of Shechem, Nablus, where there was a whole story connected to Shimon. So maybe the picture was of the city, or of the people whom Shimon, along with his brother, Levi, killed. Or maybe it was a picture of the man, Shechem, who raped their sister, Dina. But in any case, let us go on: "And Gad had a flag, the color of which was a mixture of white and black, and on it was a picture of a battalion, a group of soldiers". This is because Gad was a warrior.

So now we have finished the text describing the flags of the first two camps. So now, let us go on the third camp, which was made up of Ephraim, Menasha and Binyamin. And they were in the west:

"Ephraim and Menasha, along with Binyamin, were in the west. Ephraim and Menasha had flags, the color of which was like the color of the Soham". The Shoham is some kind of a precious stone, and I am not sure what color it had; what the color of the Shoham was. "On the flag of Ephrayim was a picture of a bull, and on the flag of Menashe was a picture of a bison. And on the flag of Binyamin, which had all the colors , was a picture of a wolf".

So that was the part of the text, discussing the tribes and banners of Ephraim, Menasha and Binyamin, who are represented by the signs of Libra, Scorpio and Sagittarius. And again, we have to think about all these things and realize what they mean.

And now, let us carry on with this text. And now Rabbi Bechayey is going to talk about the camp of the tribes of Dan, Asher and Naphtali, who were in the north:

"The camp of the north was that of Dan, Asher and Naphtali. Dan had a flag, the color of which was similar to that of a Sapir". A Sapir is a precious stone, which reflects all the lights in it. "And on it was a picture of a snake. Asher had a flag, the picture of which was similar to the light of oil, and an olive tree was drawn on it. Naphtali had a flag, the color of which was that of clear wine. And a picture of deer was drawn on it.

And now, understand well! And I will arrange all these flags according to their names and their tribes. And there are tribes above and below.

The flag of Yehuda was the one to travel first, and it was in the east. And because he was a strong man, he was compared to a lion, as it is said, 'a baby lion is Yehuda'. And together with his tribe were the tribes of Issachar and Zebulon. And this set of tribes would travel first. And this camp was the first, as a hint to Chochma (wisdom). As it is said, 'the beginning of wisdom is the fear of God', which can be read as follows: 'The beginning is wisdom' etc. And it is true that all these three tribes were masters of Torah. As it is said, 'Yehuda, my law giver' and in the Book of Chronicles (Divrey Hayamim) it is written, 'and from the children of Issachar, one can find those who know the understanding of the times'". So again, we see that the tribe of Issachar was connected to astrology and astronomy. And the text goes on:

"And it is also written, 'and from the tribe of Zebulon are those who write with the stick of the writer'. And therefore they were suitable to sit together (in one camp)", Sso all three of them were called the camp of Yehuda, because they were all bright students. They were all scholars. And therefore they were placed together, and this is the connection with the first three signs. And the text goes on to say: "And in the upper worlds, they are similar to the camp of the angles Gavriel, Azriel and Shemiel. They were placed in front of the Divine presence, and the three of them were called the camp of Gavriel". And again, the name Gavriel comes from the Hebrew word for Man, which is referred to as the strong one. And this comes back to the idea, that the forefather of the first tribe in this order, Yehuda, was a very strong person, and therefore he was called a lion. "And a number of camps and a number of colors belonged to them (these three tribes), and they were connected to these angels who were ruling over them. Just as in the camps of Issachar and Zebulon there were thousands and tens of thousands of Jews". I think the meaning of the last sentence is, that also in the upper world, the three angels who were mentioned above had many other angels, maybe of another kind, standing with them in front of the Divine Presence. In other words, there were many other angels underneath them.

"And now you can understand the meaning of the hint in the Book of Divrey Hayamim (Chronicles), 'Yehuda was the strongest of the brothers'". So it is said that 'Yehuda was the strongest of the brothers' (the sons of Yaakov). And it is a hint to us, that the camp of Yehuda was similar to the camp of Gavriel, which was, above, because the name of Gavriel, as we said before, is similar to the Hebrew word 'Gever', which means a man, and comes from this word. And it may also come from the word 'Gibor' which may mean a hero or a strong man. And this equates Gaviel to Yehuda.

"And the camp of Reuben was on the south. And he was a repentant person; he was what is called a Baal Tshuva. He repented after sinning. And that was something which granted him and his tribe the great mercy from God that He has on His creatures. The great mercy of God towards His creatures is expressed by the fact that He lets them repent". And I guess people make mistakes in this world. And I guess there are instances when one mistake can set a person 10 years back, or even 20 years or 30 years. And I have seen people making big mistakes in my lifetime. And I have even met a man who when he was young, and he jumped into the pool, performing a beautiful dive in order to impress the women there. But the water was shallow, which he didn't realize, so he broke his neck. And I met him when he was about forty years old so he had spent the last 20 years in a wheelchair. He became paralyzed from his neck down, and this is a terrible tragedy. So you see that in this world, there are sometimes cases when one makes a mistake, and there is no real way to go back on it and correct it. There are cases in which if you did it, then you did it, and there is no way of changing what you have done. And all the tears of the world are not going to wipe it away. But in the spiritual world, God has a great mercy on us, and in a spiritual sense, we can change our past. And that is a tremendous opportunity for a person, that one who has sinned has this God given ability to do what is called repentance, and change his past. Because a person can change his bad deeds, and even turn them into good deeds. This is if his repentance is with love, as it is described.

In any case, let us go on with the text written by Rabbi Bechayey:

"So Reuben starts this group with mercy and rescue, as it is said, 'and Reuben heard and he saved him (Joseph) from them (his brothers)'. And together with him and his tribe was the tribe of Shimon, who was born after him, and the tribe of Gad, who was the oldest son of Leah's nursemaid, Zilpa. And about them (the tribes of Reuven, Shimon and Gad), 'and they would be the second ones to travel'. And this is similar to the Bina, the understanding (which is represented by Reuben), being second to the Chochma, the wisdom (which is represented by Yehuda). And this is the way we have said before, that 'the wisdom comes first', and it is also said, 'and the second group would travel'. And why did the Torah use those words, 'and the second group would travel'? Because the second group is connected to Bina, so the Torah gives a hint to that. So also in the order of the camping we see that Bina is second to Chochma; understanding is secondary to wisdom. And these three tribes (Reuven, Shimon and Gad) together are called the camp of Reuven. So in the upper worlds, the camp of Reuven was similar to the camp of the angels Michael, Cochviel and Adiel, from the right of which was the Divine Presence. And the three of them together were called the camp of Michael. And that is what Moshe hinted to, when he said, in the song of the sea, 'who is like you!'. And he concluded the Torah with the words, 'there is no one like the God of Yeshurun (Israel)'. And that is the name of Michael. Because if you take the word 'Mi' (who) and the word 'Chael' (the God of), two words which contain the letters 'Mem', Yod', 'Chaf', 'Alef' and 'Lamed', you get the name of Michael, which contain these letters. And this is similar to the words 'Mi Chael' (who is like God!). And we know that Michael is the angel of mercy, of peace and healing, while Gavriel is the angel of strength, of might. So the first camp in heaven is called the camp of Gavriel, while the second is called the camp of Michael. And this is similar to the camps in the desert: the first camp, the camp of Yehuda, was the camp of Gevura, the camp of strength and strictness, because Yehuda was known to be a physically strong person. And the second camp was the camp of Chesed, the camp of mercy. And this is similar to the camps in heaven: The camp of Gavriel is the camp of Gevura, while the camp of Michael is the camp of Chesed, the camp of mercy. This is because Reuben (the second camp in the desert was the camp of Reuben) was a Baal Teshuva, a person who repented. He repented his misdeeds.

So let us go on:

"And afterwards, as for the camp of the Levites, they travelled in the middle of the different camps. And we know that the number of the Levite men was twenty two thousand, as it is said, 'all males, from the age of one month and above, were twenty two thousand'. And this number of the male members of the tribe of Levi, of these twenty two thousand, is similar to the number of angels who came down at mount Sinai, when the children of Israel received the Torah. As it is said, 'the chariots of Elohim (God; this name is the name of God from the perspective of strict judgment) were twenty two thousand'. And these twenty two thousand were close to the Divine presence".

But I am going to skip over the tribe of Levi, the Levites, for now. Because, according to the system we learn, we are now interested in the order of the 12 tribes of Israel (which is besides the tribe of Levi) and the way they were divided into four camps. And the Levites were not really part of the camps, because they were in the middle. And instead of counting the tribe of Levi, or the tribe of Joseph as one tribe, we took out the tribe of Levi, and we divided the tribe of Joseph into the tribes of Ephraim and Menasha. And Ephraim and Menashe were the two sons of Joseph, so in any case we have 12 tribes of Israel.

So now we are going to move on to the camp of Ephraim, which was on the west: "The camp of Ephraim was on the west side. And regarding that, you have to know the story of King Yerovam, who sinned and caused the masses to sin with him. And he was from the tribe of Ephraim, and therefore he needed a kind of medicine, a way of healing, some kind of a medical doctor's care, to heal what he broke. So therefore the camp of Ephraim existed, in order to heal the sins which King Yerovam would do many years later.

And with the tribe of Ephraim were the tribe of Menasha and the tribe of Binyamin. And this is what it is said, 'before Epraim, Binyamin and Menasha, they have awakened the strength'. And they camped in the west. And our rabbi said that the Divine Presence is in the west. And about them it is written, 'and that group was the third to travel'. And it is suitable and desirable to attach the Torah and the repentance to the strength, in order that the person would return to his or her right place and position by repenting, and will become strong over his (or her) evil inclination. And those three tribes together are called the camp of Ephraim. And his camp was similar to the camp of Raphael above (in heaven), which included the angels Raphael, Zavdiel and Achziel, who were behind the Divine Presence, and the three of them were called the camp of Raphael. And this is what Moshe Rabenu hinted at when he said, about Miriam when she needed healing, 'El (a name of God), please heal her, please'. And when you combine the name 'El' with the Hebrew word for heal, 'Refa', you get the name Raphael, which contains the letters 'Reish', 'Fe', 'Alef' and 'Lamed'. So here the letter 'Alef' appears once, while it appears in both the name 'El' and the word 'Refa'. And Raphael is the angle of healing". So you see that the camp of the angel of healing was represented, in the desert, by the camp of Ephraim. And this was to create a spiritual form of healing the incorrectness of King Yerovam, who would be a notorious sinner in the future. Because the tribe of Ephraim really needed some kind of healing for the future, because of the mass sinning which King Yerovam (who was a member of the tribe of Ephraim) would cause later. And I guess the other two tribes who were connected to it, the tribes of Menashe and Binyamin, also needed this somehow. And they were connected above to the angel Raphael, who is the angel of healing. Because they needed this kind of healing, in order to heal themselves and the other people they would later cause to sin.

And now let us go on to the fourth camp, which was the camp of Dan, and which was on the north:

"The fourth camp was the camp of Dan, and it camped in the north. And it is known that the tribe of Dan received the two golden calves which King Yerovam made. And it is said, 'the one he put in Beit El, and the other one he put in Dan'. And this should have been indeed in the north, because the wealth comes from there to the whole world. And Dan caused the bringing of the darkness to the world by doing idol worship. And it is said in the Book of Yeshaayahu (Isaiah), that there was darkness because of their deeds, because the sun in the east goes out from there".
So I would like to start over again with the tribe of Dan, and we have already said that the tribe of Dan, as well as its whole camp, was on the north. And it was known that the tribe of Dan received the two golden calves which King Yerovam made. And this is written, 'the one he put in Beit El, and other one he put in Dan'. And it was suitable for him to be in the north, because the wealth comes from there. The wealth comes from the north and goes out to the world. And the tribe of Dan would darken the world with its idol worship, as it is said in the Book of Isaiah, 'and it was when he darkened their actions'. Because you have to know that the east is where the sun goes from in the morning. And also, the south is where the sun is while it is on its highest position, when it is the highest in the sky. And therefore, the Hebrew word for south, Darom, is made out of two words: Dar Rom, which means, dwell in the high place, because the south is where the sun is at its highest position during the time of the day. This is to say, that the sun dwells in the height of the sky. And it goes also into the west, because it sets there; it goes in that same direction, the same way. But as for the side of the north, the sun never rises there at all. The sun never shines brightly from the north, and that is why the Hebrew word for north is Tzafon. The word 'Tzafon' is similar to the Hebrew word for the word 'hidden', which is 'Tzafun'. This is because the sun is kind of hidden in the north. The sun is concealed when it is on the north, and it becomes darkness. And that is suitable for the tribe of Dan, which darkened the world with its idol worship. "And therefore the tribe of Dan needed to do Tshuva, it needed to repent, so God would forgive its members for their sins, and He would light up to them, as it is written in the Book of Micah, 'for even when I sit in darkness, God would send me light'. And together with the tribe of Dan were the tribe of Asher and the tribe of Naphtali. And this was in order to lighten up the darkness, as it is said in the Book of Devarim (Deuteronomy), 'and he dipped his legs into the oil'; this was written about the tribe of Asher. And the oil is called light. And it is written about the tribe of Naphtali (The same place in the Book of Deuteronomy), 'Naftali is full of good will, and he is full of the blessings of God'. And it is written about them (the tribes of Dan, Asher and Naftali, which make the camp of Dan), 'and they would travel the last'. And here the Torah changes from all three other instances, where it describes the order of the travelling according to the camps, and instead of saying 'and they would be the fourth ones to travel', it says 'and they would travel the last'". Because about the camp of Yehuda the Torah says, 'and they would travel the first', and about the camp of Reuben, 'and they would travel the second, and about the camp of Ephraim, 'and they would travel the third'. But about the camp of Dan the Torah says, 'and they would travel the last', instead of 'and they would travel the fourth'. "This is to hint to the name which is on its head. And the tenth is the last 'He' in God's name. And the three of them are called the camp of Dan". I guess 'the three' mean the three tribes of Dan, Asher and Naphtali. And this camp, of the tribes of Dan, Asher and Naphtali, was in comparison of the camp of the angel Oriel above (in heaven), which included the angels Oriel, Daniel and Ramiel. And

this camp was on the left of the Divine presence. And the three of them together were called the camp of Oriel. And this hints to what King David said about the atonement of the offerings, the animals which were sacrificed to God, 'and He would light us up'. And because of that, the angel is called Oriel (from the Hebrew words 'Ori El', which mean 'God is my light)".

So to summarize, it seems that we went through the 12 signs here, which are represented by the 12 tribes of Israel. And we talked about each of the flags of the tribes. And then we talked about which direction each camp was, and how that was connected to each tribe. And I think there is a lot to meditate on all these things. And you should really start, as kind of homework, reading a little bit of the Bible, and try to see where it talks about the different tribes and the different characters mentioned in the Bible. And you should try to see which tribes these characters were connected to. And they you should try to understand the symbology of the different tribes: Where they were, where their placement was, which direction, what was the flag of each tribe like. And see if you can come up with anything. I remember my first teacher, and that was many years ago, in fact it was about thirty five years ago. And it was before I even knew Hebrew. He was a very great Rabbi, who passed away since then. And his first advice to me was to read the whole Bible , kind of a first thing to do. Just to read the whole Torah, Neviim (Books of prophets, but not only those that are called 'Book of Prophets') and Ketuvim (other holy writings). Even if you have to read it in English at the beginning, you should just read it in order to get an idea about what it is all about. And I really think that it is a good idea for all the people who are listening to this lesson, and who try to tune into it a little. And then you can try to understand all the lessons which are going to be coming up. And since we are already in Sefer Hayetzira, I think I would like to stay here (in Sefer Hayetzira) for a while, and work a little bit more on the 12 simple letters, and how they are connected to the 12 months and the twelve signs of the Zodiac. And in the next lesson or two, I would like to go through some materials which were written by the Vilna Gaon, who was one of the great geniuses in Jewish history. Just hearing his name puts me in awe, because he had such a tremendous mind and intellect. And the way he could make connections between every different part of the Torah and unite them is amazing. And actually, most of his existing writings are on Kabbala, believe it or not. And one of the major works of the Gaon of Vilna was a commentary on Sefer Hayetzira. And so, there is a lot of interesting material, which has not been translated into English. And I would like to bring some of that material. And again, all this has the aim of helping us understand the 12 simple letters, which we are working on right now, and which I hope will bring us more and more into an understanding of what the 12 signs in the Zodiac are, and how they function. We should also understand what the purpose of those signs is. And then we can get deeper and deeper into astrology, as soon as we can really start understanding each of these signs. Because in fact, the signs are out there, though I think that in Jerusalem you can't see the stars so clearly anymore. This is because Jerusalem became a great and huge city. But you can always go into the country and see the stars at night. And that is a very important thing. It is extremely important to meditate and look at the constellations. And really, if we can really start looking and understanding the constellations, as well as the 12 tribes of Israel and the 12 simple letters, then I think we can really have a much deeper understanding of the universe. And because of this, I would really like to go into the writings of the Gaon of Vilna next time, and see how he understood the fifth chapter which we have just been going through in Sefer Hayetzira.

Chapter 10

During the last few chapters we have been working on other groups of things which are divided into 12. For how do we get to those other groups? Because we have learned that each of these permutations of God's name is connected to one of the 12 months of the year; each month of the year has a different permutation of the main name of God, which contain the letters of 'Yod', 'He', 'Vav' and another 'He'. This is how it is spelled. And then you take these four letters and permutate them 12 ways. And each of these permutations rules over a different month and determines what is going to happen during that specific month. And so we talked about that. And then we got off from that into the topic of the 12 tribes of Israel, and this topic took us into other topics and subjects, which are divided into 12. But actually before that, we also studied the 12 simple letters in the Hebrew Alphabet. And we learned that there are twenty two letters in the Hebrew Alphabet, but they have three divisions; the letters of the Hebrew Alphabet are divided into three groups: Three letters are called 'elementals', and they are connected with the elements which are mentioned in Sefer Hayetzira. Because in Sefer Hayetzira, only three elements are mentioned, which are fire, water and air. And then there are seven letters, which are called 'Bagad Kafrat', and they are the letters of 'Bet', 'Gimal', 'Dalet', 'Kaf', 'Pey', 'Reish' and 'Tav'. These seven letters are called 'doubles' because they can be pronounced either in a hard way or in a soft way. And then there are 12 simple letters, which are pronounced only one way, so to speak. And those 12 letters are connected to the 12 tribes of Israel, with the 12 months of the year and with the 12 constellations in the Zodiac. And so we came to Sefer Hayetzira, in order to learn the chapter which discusses these 12 letters we have mentioned, and how they are connected with the months of the year, with the constellations in the Zodiac, and with the 12 tribes of Israel.

So tonight I would like to carry on with this text in Sefer Hayetzira. Because last week, we took off and had a break from Sefer Hayetzira, and studied a piece from Rabenu Bachayey about the flags the tribes of Israel had, because each of the tribes of Israel had its own flag.

So again, we always want to get more and more information as we can on the different tribes of Israel, and what their relationship is to the Zodiac and the constellations, and how we can learn about the Zodiac from the tribes, and how we can learn about the tribes from what really goes on in the Torah.

So tonight I would like to start with one of the major commentaries to the chapter we are studying in Sefer Hayetzira. And indeed, this is one of the major commentaries on the whole Sefer Hayetzira, and this commentary was written by the Gaon of Vilna, who was a great genius. And everybody in the Jewish religious world has heard about him. But unfortunately, not so many secular Jews heard about him, and if they did hear about him, they probably have not read anything written by him. So while we are here, why don't we bring down some of the Gaon's writings! We shall quote some of his writings on this chapter, and we might bring some of the other commentators too, and try to add more to our information about what we have been learning so far. So I am not going to literally translate what the Gaon of Vilna says here word by word, but I will give the main ideas of what he says, using some commentaries on his writings.

So let me start now. And first of all, I would like to read the first Mishna because the Gaon of Vilna is going to talk about the first Mishna of the fifth chapter. So this is what the Mishna says:
"There are 12 simple letters, and these letters are: 'He', 'Vav', 'Zayin', 'Chet', 'Tet', 'Yod', 'Lamed', 'Nun', 'Samech', 'Ayin', 'Tzadi' and 'Kof'. These are the 12 simple letters. And their manifestations are according to the following order:
Speech, thinking, walking (or motion), seeing, hearing, action, intercourse, smell, sleep, anger, eating and laughter, these are the 12 senses of the body (or the soul). And each is going to be connected with one of these letters. And each one is connected with a different month too".
So now we are going to read a little bit of what the Gaon of Vilna says. And he says: "These 12 simple letters are called simple, because they don't have a hard and a soft sound". Because, as we said before, the elemental letters, which are called Bagad Kafrat, have a hard and a soft sounds each. Like the letter 'Bet which can be pronounced 'Bet', which is a hard sound, and it can also be pronounced 'Vet', which is a soft sound. And the letter 'Gimal' can be pronounced that way, or it can also be pronounced like the name of the Latin letter 'G' is pronounced in English. In other words, a hard 'Gimal' is the way the letter 'G' is usually pronounced, and a soft 'Gimal' is the way the name of the letter 'G' is pronounced in English.
So now the Gaon of Vilna is going to ask a question. Because "even the letters 'Alef', 'Mem' and 'Shin' are also simple letters actually, because they don't have soft and hard sounds for each either. So how comes we have only 12 simple letters and those three letters are not included? In reality there should be 15 simple letters, so why are only 12 considered as such? But in any case, these three letters, 'Alef', 'Mem' and 'Shin', are called 'Mothers', because the rest of the twenty two letters came out of them; these three letters are the source of the remaining letters of the Hebrew Alphabet, which are the double letters and the simple letters. So they all kind of came out, somehow, from these three mother letters, even these three letters themselves. So these three letters are called 'Imahot', which means 'Mothers', and they are the elementals; the elemental letters, the three elements of water, fire and air. Everybody has the element of earth too, but in Sefer Hayetzira, the earth is not considered as an element, but as a combination of different elements.
"And these 12 simple letters are the secret of the three times which God's Havays name is mentioned in the verse, 'God is the king (or God rules), God was the king (or God ruled) and God will be the king (or God will rule) for ever and ever'. And these three times stand for Keter, Chochma and Bina (crown, wisdom and understanding). And there is a 'Yod', a 'He' and a 'Vav' in the first Havaya, a 'Yod', a 'He' and a 'Vav' in the second Havaya, and a 'Yod', a 'He' and a 'Vav' in the third Havaya. And the last 'He' in each Havaya is the Malchut (kingship), which is the fourth to all other three Sefirot. And then you have these additional three letters, which make 12 letters, when they are counted together with the other nine which were mentioned above. In other words, the letters which represent Keter, Chochma and Bina, are nine, and Malchut completes all of them, and thus they become 12, so now all of them will have four each, if these 12 letters are still divided into three".

So the Gaon of Vilna wants to connect these 12 letters to the three times in which the Havaya name of God is mention in that verse which talks about God's kingship, which is three times the four letter name of God, so all together it makes 12 letters.
But let us go on now:
"And these twelve senses of the body (or the soul, which are: Speech, thinking, motion, seeing, hearing, action, intercourse, smell, sleep, anger, eating and laughter) have no opposites; they are not like the Bagad Kafrat letters. They don't have themselves together with anything which we see as their opposite, such as love and hate, war and peace, or life and death and things like that. So they are not like the seven double letters; they are similar to the 12 simple letters. And indeed in the last chapter, we discussed the seven double letters, and soon we shall learn the fourth chapter too, which discusses the seven double letters and how they are connected to the planets. So we really have to start understanding, what the difference between the planets and the constellations is. And this is something which most of the astrologers don't really talk about; the fundamental difference between the planets and the constellations, which we are going to talk about later. In other words, this chapter is connected to the constellations, while the seven double letters are connected to the planets.
But in any case, those seven double letters, which we talked about in the last chapter, each has something opposite to it, for example, there is wealth and poverty, life and death etc. But, as we mentioned before, these 12 senses which are discussed in this chapter, do not have anything which is opposite. "And even though you can say, for example, that sight indeed has an opposite, which is blindness, and that the opposite of hearing is being deaf", as the Gaon of Vilna continues explaining in this text of his, "this is not really an opposite but the lacking of the sense. So blindness is the lack of sight, and not the opposite of sight, and being deaf is the lack, not the opposite, of hearing. In other words, a blind person or a deaf person is missing the organs from which the sight and hearing go out, from the potential to the actual. In other words, the blind person is missing what actualizes the sense of seeing, and the deaf person is missing what actualizes the sense of hearing, but they still somehow have the senses of seeing and hearing in them, though these senses don't reach their potential. And further more: The opposite is not thought of as an opposite, unless it is a subject by itself. And this is just as we have war and peace, where war and peace are two things which are opposite to one another. War is one thing and peace is something else. So things like poverty, death and war, are things upon themselves, and they are indeed the opposites of wealth, life and peace, which are things upon themselves too. War is not peace, death is not life, poverty is not wealth, but they are all things upon themselves, even though they are the opposites and lacking of each other. And these things also have the quality of having a little bit or a lot of each; like a little bit of war, or a little bit of wealth. But that is not the case with the 12 senses. As for the 12 senses, all they have is existence or absence, it either exists or it is missing, which means that they are in a situation in which they are either established or they are not established. In other words, they have no opposite; if they are not established, they are not thought of. In other words, the non existence of one thing (among these 12 senses) is not necessarily its opposite. So, for example, blindness is not the opposite of seeing, in the sense that it is not an exchange of seeing; it is just the absence of seeing. But war, on the other hand, is the opposite of peace. But being deaf, for instance, is just the absence of the sense of hearing, but not the opposite of it". And this is what the Gaon of Vilna

wants to explain; which is the fundamental difference between the doubles, which are the planets, and the simple letters and constellations of the Zodiac.
So let us go on:
"And out of these 12 senses that exist in every speaking person, ten exist even in animals. And two of them, which are thinking and laughter, exist only in human beings. And there is a similarity to that in the 12 constellations, for ten of them exist in animals too, while the other two, which are Gemini and Virgo, exist only in human beings". In other words, what the Gaon of Vilna says here is, that if you look at the pictures of the constellations in the sky, you see Gemini, for instance, which means twins, and this is a constellation which has the shape of two boys in the sky, or Virgo, which is the constellation the shape of which is similar to that of a virgin, which is a young maiden. And these are pictures, or shapes, of human beings. But the other ten constellations are of shapes of animals and inanimate objects, but not the shapes of people. And the Gaon of Vilna further explains, that "the constellations of Gemini and Virgo are connected to Mercury, and Mercury is the planet of speech, it controls the sense of speech, and speech is what differs the human being from everything else. The special thing about human beings is, that they have the ability to speak. And due to that, Mercury and these two constellations had been given a human sign, because they represent speech, which is the highest attribute of a human being. And this is what separates the human being from animals, because animals are not able to speak".
And now the Gaon of Vilna is also going to explain the difference between the three letters of 'Alef', 'Mem' and 'Shin' and the seven double letters and the 12 simple letters. So let us go on:
"The letters of 'Alef', 'Mem' and 'Shin' represent the essence of a thing, which is called in Hebrew 'Etzem Hadavar'. And they are the foundations of the world which are mentioned in Sefer Hayetzira: Air, water and fire".
In other words, the idea in Jewish philosophy is that anything you take away from something, so that thing loses its meaning by the thing which had been taken away, is considered an 'Etzem'. For example, if you take away the tip of a pen which you write with, and by doing that you actually break the pen, then it is not a pen anymore; it is just a stick now. It looses its essence, because you broke its tip from it. And without the writing tip, the pen is not a pen. But on the other hand, if you pealed off the color of the pen or scratched it, it is still a pen, but you have just changed it incidentally. So "this is the idea of the letters of 'Alef', 'Mem' and 'Shin', they are the essential letters and represent the essential things, which are fire, air and water. And in the soul, they represent the head, the body and the limbs. But the 12 senses are not essential, but they are attached to their essential. For example, the senses of seeing and hearing are attached to the head. And without the essentials, it is impossible for the senses to exist. For example, without the head, it would be impossible for the senses of seeing and hearing to exist. So the senses are attached to the elements.
And the seven double letters, which represent wisdom, wealth, war and things like that, are incidentals. They are not essentials. So if you are a person, and you are wise or dumb, wealthy or poor, it doesn't change the fact that you are a person. And these letters, as well as what they represent, do not cling to the essence itself, and can exist without it".
So the Gaon of Vilna says that there are three different stages: There is the stage of the three letters of 'Alef', 'Mem' and 'Shin', which are the elements. They are the elemental

letters, and they are the 'Etzem, the essence of the thing. And if you take anyone of them away, the things they are the essence of don't exist. And then you have the 12 simple letters, which represent the senses, and they are attached to the essences; they are attached to the fundamental elements of fire, air and water. So it is possible to exist without those senses, but not without the essences. And on top of that there are double letters, which represent things that are not attached to the elements; they are not attached to the essences. And they talk about, and represent, things like wisdom, wealth and things like that, which are incidentals. In other words, you can be with these things or without them, and they are not going to change the question of weather you exist or not; they are not going to change your existence. So the Gaon of Vilna gave us another explanation about the difference between these three, seven and twelve letters in the Hebrew Alphabet.

So now I am going to skip a little, and move to the part where the Gaon of Vilna talks about the tribes:

"And the tribes are also twelve, and behold, they are: Reuben, Shimon, Levi, Yehuda, Issachar, Zebulon, Joseph, Binyamin, Dan, Naphtali, Gad and Asher.

Reuben, Shimon, Levi and Yehuda are parallel to the four senses which are in the head; the senses of seeing, hearing, smelling and speaking. And Zebulon is connected to the sense of walking (or motion), as it says, 'rejoice, Zebulon, in your getting out'. So Zebulon represents the sense of motion, while Issachar, which is a tribe known for its engagement in the study of the Torah, represents the sense of thinking. And the tribes of Joseph and Binyamin, who were the sons of Rachel, represent the senses of sleeping and intercourse. And this is like the verse in the Torah, which says, 'He slept with her, and he slept'. And the tribes of Dan and Naphtali represent the senses of anger and laughter, which are the good and bad of the soul and spirit. And the tribes of Gad and Asher represent the senses of action and swallowing (or eating)".

And now, the Gaon of Vilna is going to quote the Zohar and explain it. So let us go on:

"And the Zohar says that there are eight senses, which stand against (represent) two names of God, as written and as pronounced (in other words, in many cases, the Havaya name is written, but it is pronounced as the name of Adnut), four (senses are) in the head and four in the body. But here, in the Sefer Hayetzira, there are 12 senses".

So the Gaon of Vilna is asking now, how come there are only eight senses mentioned in the Zohar (four in the head and four in the body), while in Sefer Hayetzira it is said that there are 12 senses (eight in the head and four in the body)? What is the difference in the way the authors of each of these books learned and understood the number and calculation of the senses? Are they arguing with each other, or what are they actually talking about, because here, in Sefer Hayetzira, it is said that there are 12 senses, plus another four, which represents God's name of Eheye. So there are actually three names of God which have four letters in each: The Havaya name has four letters, the Adnut name has four letters, and the name Eheye has four letters. And all these letters in these names of God represent eight senses in the head and four in the body of a human being.

So the Gaon of Vilna now explains, that "all of the limbs are doubled in their senses: So you have the eyes, and the eyes include the senses of seeing and sleeping. Because when you sleep, you also see things in your dreams. And these senses represent the two aspects of the eyes, which are seeing during the day and dreaming during the night. Just as it is said in the passage in the Book of Numbers, Chapter 12 verse 6, 'when I appear to him, I make myself known in a dream' (or 'in a vision shall I appear to him, in a dream shall I speak to him'). So you see that a person can see even during his sleep. And the sense of sight may include the sense of sleep, as it is said, 'if I shall give sleep to my eyes, and rest to my eyelids'. This verse is in the Book of Psalms, chapter 132, verse 4. And the ears include two senses too, which are the sense of hearing and that of thinking. And these are actually the two aspects of hearing: There is the aspect of hearing without paying attention, and there is the aspect of hearing with paying attention, and understanding, or trying to understand, what you hear. And this is like the passage goes in the Book of Job, Chapter 12 verse 11 and chapter 32 verse 3, 'My ear shall choose the words it hears'. And another verse from the Torah, the Book of Deuteronomy, chapter 28 verse 48, states, '(a nation) the language of which you shall not hear'. So there are two aspects to the sense of seeing: the aspect of seeing when you are awake, and that of kind of seeing, while you are dreaming. And there are two aspects to the sense of hearing: One is just hearing, without paying attention, and the other aspect is hearing and paying attention, which is listening. And the difference between the senses of seeing and hearing is, that while the sense of seeing comes from the eyes, and you may close your eyes and not see, you can't shut your ears; the ears are always there, and they get messages all the time. But sometimes you pay attention to what you hear, while other times you don't". So the Gaon of Vilna says, that those two 'ears' stand for the two aspects, of hearing with paying attention, and of regular hearing.

"And there are two aspects to the nose too. There is the aspect of the sense of smelling, and there is also the aspect of the sense of anger. And how do you know that anger is connected to the nose too? Because a Hebrew word for 'anger' can be 'Af', which means nose. And the mouth represents two senses too. It represents the aspect of speaking, as well as the aspect of eating, which are the mouth and the tongue; the mouth eats and the tongue speaks.

And the four senses that are in the body represent the throat, the hands, the feet and covenant, which means the reproductive organ. And they are in parallel with the senses of laughter (which is in the throat), intercourse (which is in the sexual organs, which are connected to reproduction), action (which is in the hands) and walking (or motion, which is in the feet)".

So you see that the Gaon of Vilna explains and answers the question, of how come in one place it is said that there are eight senses, while in another place it is said that there are 12. And the answer to this question is, because in Sefer Hayetzira, the four senses which are connected to the head are taken and doubled, while in the Zohar, these four senses, which are connected to the head, are referred to as one sense, or one level, each. So the two eyes (which represent the senses of sleep and dream) are considered one, the two ears are considered one, the two nostrils are considered one (and they make one nose) and mouth is one.

And now, I would like to move to another part of this text of the Gaon of Vilna and read it out to you. So he says the following:

"And the rabbis (the sages) attributed those 12 senses to the 12 tribes of Israel: The sense of seeing is attributed to Reuben (Because the Hebrew word for 'seeing' or 'sight', Reiya, sounds like the name of Reuven), like it is said in the Book of Genesis, about Leah's reason for calling her first son Reuben, 'for God saw my poverty'. Because Yaakov really loved Rachel, and he didn't love Leah that much, and he was sort of tricked into marrying her. So now, she gave birth to a son before Rachel did, and said, 'God saw my poverty', and therefore she gave her first son the name of Reuben. The sense of haring is attributed to Shimon (Because the Hebrew word for 'hearing' is Shmia, which is similar to the name of Shimon), like it is further said, at the same place in the Book of Genesis, 'for God heard'. And the sense of smelling is attributed to Levi". In other words, the Gaon of Vilna is bringing proof, from passages in the Torah, to the matter of how each of the senses, which had been mentioned above, is attributed to a different son of Yaakov, who was a father to a different tribe of Israel. So "the sense of smelling is attributed to Levi, as it is said in the Book of Deuteronomy, chapter 33 verse 10, 'they shall put the incense in your nose (or under your nose)'. And it is also written, 'a fire offering, which has a beautiful smell'. And the sense of speaking is attributed to Yehuda. As it is said, again in the Book of Genesis, regarding the story of Leah giving birth to her children, 'this time I shall thank God'. And thanking God is part of speaking (and also, the Hebrew word for 'thanksgiving', or 'thanking', is Hodaya, which sounds like the name of Yehuda). The sense of thinking is attributed to the tribe of Issachar. Like it is said, 'Issachar shall be like a donkey', which talks about meditating on the Torah. And the sense of laughter is attributed to the tribe of Zebulon. And this is as it is said, 'rejoice, Zebulon, when you go out'. He would make money in his business and would be happy with it. And happiness is similar to laughter. And the sense of anger is attributed to the tribe of Dan. And this is learned from the verse, 'Dan shall be a snake lying on the road'. And the snake waits for the right moment to strike, which is similar to being angry and wanting to take revenge over something. This verse is also taken from the Book of Genesis, but it comes from chapter 49 verse 17. And the sense of walking (or motion) is attributed to the tribe of Naphtali. And this is like it is said, on the same chapter 49 in the Book of Genesis, verse 21, 'Naftali shall be like a dear who had been sent'. And the sense of action is attributed to the tribe of Gad. And this is like it is said, in the Book of Deuteronomy, chapter 33 verse 20, '(Gad shall be as a baby lion who) grabbed the pray, hands and head (or with his hands and head)'. And the sense of eating (or consumption) is attributed to the tribe of Asher. And this is taken from what is said, 'from Asher, there shall be fat bread (or bread which is dipped in oil)'. And this verse comes again from chapter 49 in the Book of Genesis. And the sense of intercourse is attributed to the tribe of Joseph. And this is taken from the verse, 'Joseph is a fruitful son', which is in the same chapter of Genesis, chapter 49. And it is also said, about the tribes of Ephraim and Menasha, which came out of Joseph (in other words, the tribe of Joseph is actually divided into two tribes: That of Ephraim and that of Menasha), 'and they shall multiply and increase in their numbers like fish, but this shall be on ground'. And the sense of sleeping is attributed to the tribe of Binyamin. And this is learned from the verse, 'and between his shoulders shall he dwell (or rest)'". So we saw now how the Gaon of Vilna connected all the 12 tribes of Israel with the different 12 senses. Or, to be more precise, the Gaon of Vilna connected the whole order of the 12 tribes of Israel to that of the 12 senses. And he connected them with one another, by bringing a verse for each of the 12 tribes, connecting it with one of these 12 senses.

Now I would like to go on, and show you a quote from the Raavad, who is another commentator. And he (the Raavad) was one of the early rabbis, before the Ari Zal. But nobody really knows which Raavad that is, because it is not the famous Raavad. And by the way, Raavad is the acronym for Rabbi Avraham Ben David, Rabbi Avraham, the son of David. And there were many rabbis who had the name of Avraham the son of David. So I am not really sure which one it was. But we are sure that it is not the famous Raavad, who wrote the commentary on the Mishne Torah, which was written by the Rambam (Maimonides), and argued with the Rambam a lot. This is a different Raavad.

But in any case, the Raavad here wants to show you that there is another interesting thing here, which is, that all these attributes are also connected to different attributes of God. I think it is something interesting. In any case, the Raavad is going to list the 12 verses, which connects all those 12 senses and attributions to different attributes of God. And besides that, when you hear these things, you also have to think which planets they are connected to, which constellations, which months, and then you can really start understanding things. And the Raavad says as follows:

"All these 12 characteristics are also attributed to the actions of God. Like it is said about the sense of seeing, 'and God saw'. So it is an action of God that He sees". And you always have to remember, that when things like this are said, there is more to that, and it is always in a spiritual way. In other words, God doesn't have eyes, but He sees better then anyone else. When God is referred to as having eyes, it only means that He watches things. This is referring to the power in which He controls things. "And it is said about the sense of hearing, 'and God heard'. And it is said about the sense of smell, 'and God smelled the good smell of the offering'. And it is said about the sense of speaking, 'and God spoke'. It is said that God spoke with Moshe, and that He spoke with all the righteous people. And it is said about the sense of eating (or consumption), 'His tongue is like fire, which consumes (consuming fire)'. And it is also said, 'for the Lord, your God, is (like) consuming fire'. And it is said about the sense of intercourse, 'and I (kind of, in an illusion for) had an intercourse (or intercourses) with you'. And it is said about the sense of work, or action, 'all the actions of the great God'. And it is said about the sense of anger, 'and God became angry'. And it is said about the sense of laughter, 'And Elohim (God) laughed'. And it is said about the sense of walking (or motion), 'and Avraham walked with Elohim (God)'. And so it is said about Noah. And it is said about the sense of sitting, 'the one (God) who sits in heaven shall laugh'. And it is said about the sense of thought, 'God thought (and considered the option) of destroying it'. And it is said about the sense of sleep, 'And wake up (or awaken thee), why should you sleep, God'".

So you see all of these 12 characteristics, all these 12 senses, as being attributes of God. And that goes back to the idea of us having the 12 permutations of God's Havaya name. This is with each month having a different permutation of God's name, and each month God is going to act in a different way, as He has all these 12 different attributes in Him. In other words, the sense, or attribution, of speech, is going to be the first one, and that is going to be working through the simple permutation, of the letters of 'Yod', 'He', 'Vav' and another 'He', on this order, the straight order, which is the permutation for the month of Nisan. And that is going to go down to the tribe of Yehuda, the sense which it is connected to is speech. And then it will come down to the constellation of Aries. And so we see the connections between all the different groups of things which are divided into 12 each.

And now the Raavad is going to go on, and say what I said just now, that "you may find in the Torah, or in the books of the prophets or in the other holy writings, that there is always one of these adjectives being used concerning one of the characteristics of God. And you should know that we have a tradition, and according to it, we need all those

characteristics. And this is according to the standard explanation, from mouth to mouth. In other words, this is a tradition, which the Kabbalists learned and taught from mouth to mouth; one Kabbalist taught it to his students and the students to their students and so on. And those attributions are just parables, so to speak, because in reality, we speak here about the cause of causes. And God forbid! We shouldn't really give Him one of these attributes; we just explain His ways in a way we and other can understand".
So in any case we went through the commentary of the Gaon of Vilna, and I thought a it was interesting to see what he has to say, and shed some light on this topic. And we saw a little bit of the commentary of the Raavad on this topic too. And I think next week we are going to go on and talk about the planets for a while. In other words, we have spent a number of weeks talking about the months and the signs, as well as the planets, as all those topics are explained in Sefer Hayetzira. And now we are going to talk about the planets. And we would like to slowly get a picture of the way in which Sefer Hayetzira looks at astrology, which is interesting. Because you don't see a lot of the things we talked about in any other text on astrology, where it gives these 12 senses, connecting each one of them with a different Zodiacal constellation. I really haven't seen this anywhere before, and we will talk about it a little more in our next class.

Conclusion

We have discussed the five levels in the Zodiac, and we know that in Western astrology there are only two levels: We see the houses, and we know that there are 12 houses in each person's chart, and each house is about a different area of life. And the first house is the ascendant; it is the house of the person himself, or herself, their appearance, their nature, their characteristics, their looks etc. the second house is the person's wealth, the third house is the siblings, the fourth house is the family, the fifth house is the children, the sixth house is service and servitude, the seventh house is the partner in life, in other words, the seventh house is marriage, the eighth house is death, the ninth house is religion, the tenth house is the person's career, the eleventh house is the person's friends, and the twelfth house is the person's enemies. And all this was the first level. And the second level is that of the twelve constellations in the Zodiac. Those 12 constellations are: Aries, Taurus, Gemini, Cancer, Leo, Virgo, Libra, Scorpio, Sagittarius, Capricorn, Aquarius and Pisces. And each of these constellations is connected to different houses in the chart. And each one is ruled by a different planet. But the planets are not discussed here, because they are so much connected to the signs of the Zodiac. But in any case, you already see two things which are based on the number 12. So the number 12 is really a very important number. And this whole series of lessons had been constructed around the number 12, which we shall come back to. And we also came to study the idea, according to which they are also based on what is called the 12 simple (Pshutot) letters in the Hebrew Alphabet. And we shall come back to that too.
So, in any case, the level of the constellations in the Zodiac was the second level. And these two levels are the levels which the non Jewish astrologers focus on. And that is where their system basically ends; they have the houses, the planets, the constellations and the stars. But there is basically no more then that in non Jewish astrology; the Western astrological system, and basically the non Jewish astrological system, goes as far as that. And that also includes the system of Eastern astrology. So in this series of lectures I didn't really discuss these two levels. But I talk about these two levels in other

places. I give a series of lessons, which are shorter, and in fact, they are 10 minute lessons (each lesson is a ten minute one), and there I talk about standard astrology. Those lessons are based on the Jewish tradition, of course. And indeed, according to the Jewish tradition, we hold that every kind of astrology, which is known today, had been passed down from Adam Harishon, who was the first man in history, who passed it on to other select people, who passed it on to yet other people and so forth. And then there was the time of the dispersion, when it had been sent cast out to all the different parts of the world. And that explains how the knowledge of astrology got to all the civilized lands, and there are no arguments among them on the particulars of astrology. For example, and as to the question of how they chose all the different constellations this can be the only logical explanation. Because there is no logical reason to draw the pictures of the constellations the way they were drawn. And it is not logical to say that each country came to this logic independently. And it is also difficult to prove that somehow it passed from one country to another, without any changes being made to it. Because if so, if it passed from one country to another, without any changes being made to it, then the question arises, how come everybody accepted it, without arguing or making any changes in anything regarding it? This is far fetched too, because you all know that game in America, where one whispers something to another person, and he, or she, is supposed to whisper the same thing to a third person and so on. And at the end, there is no connection between the words the last persons whispered to one another and what the first person whispered to the second. So it is very hard to expect things to be passed properly, from one civilization to another, without seeing any changes made. And indeed, the Jewish astrology holds that the principles of astrology were passed down, from Adam Harishon to the next generation, and from that generation to the following generation, and then from teacher to student etc. Because if you don't believe and hold that it had been passed down this way, then it would not be logical for the Jews, for Jews don't believe in things which were invented by a man in a cave, who just decided that this is day and that is night, and then he and his friends just decided to make constellations and stuff of that kind. That is not the Jewish way, because we have a tradition, and we hold and believe in things that were traditionally handed over to us. And anything else is not really for us. So in any case, that is how I see it.

But in any case, in terms of the first two levels, there are many similarities between the Western astrology and the Jewish tradition, because it all really came from the same source. But of course, there will be differences in it too, between Western astrology and Jewish astrology, and we shall talk about those differences over time. And if fact, all these lessons are, in a way, talking about these differences, and for example, I talk about the higher three levels in the horoscope, which nobody among the other nations talk about. Maybe the reason for that is due to the amount of secret wisdom which is connected to the three higher levels in the horoscope, or maybe the reason is because those three levels are connected to the Hebrew Alphabet. Because, as we see, the permutations of God's name are all based on Hebrew letters. And this may be the hidden wisdom, because the knowledge of those three levels in the horoscope is all based on the Hebrew Alphabet.

In other words, let me give you an example: In the Zohar, where it talks about the time of the dispersion, just after Noah, when all the people of the world gathered in one place, as you see if you read the Bible there, and they built the tower of Babel and a city (as it is

said, 'a city and a tower'), and they wanted to gain control over the spiritual forces, and the whole world gathered there and, as it is said, they spoke one language and said similar things, it is explained (in the Zohar) that the language they spoke was Hebrew; at that time, the whole world spoke Hebrew. And this is another interesting thing. Because really, the anthropologists and linguistics came to that idea too, which is, that all languages came from one primary language, but they are just not sure as to what was the language which all other languages developed from. They are still working on it, but we hope they will come to the right conclusion at a certain time. But in any case, there is a book from the 12th Century, which was written by the famous Rabbi Avraham Abulafia, who was a Kabbalist, and he showed in that book how the Greek and Latin languages came from Hebrew. So there is some concrete proof for that. So in any case, where the Torah talks about the dispersion, the Zohar asks a question. Because if you read about the dispersion, you see, that the reason for all the people, trying to rebel against God at that time, and being so successful, was the fact they knew the language of the angles and spiritual levels in the higher worlds, which is Hebrew. Because indeed, the whole world, or almost the whole world, gathered at one place, and they all spoke one language and were very powerful, and there was a danger of them taking control over the spiritual forces. And then, what did God do? He came down and confused all their languages, and He also sent all those people to different areas in the world. So instead of all of them being together, He dispersed them all over the world. And then, instead of one language they had up to then, they had many languages from that time on, so it became hard for people from different countries to communicate with one another.
So the Zohar asks, why did God have to do both things, wasn't it enough to just disperse the people? If some are going to be in Honolulu, Hawaii, and others in Africa, they can never get together again and build a tower and try to gain control over spiritual powers. And the answer to that is, that indeed, it wasn't enough to disperse them, because there was something special in the Hebrew language. The Hebrew language was the only language that the angles knew, and which all the spiritual beings in the upper worlds understood. So when all people were together at that time, they all spoke Hebrew, and because they knew the Hebrew language they were so successful in building the tower and everything, because they were able to force the angels to take oaths, according to which they pledge to do their will; the angels were made by to vow to do their will. And due to that, they were able to build the city and the tower. So you see that it wasn't enough to disperse them, because they could still use the holy names. So God had to confuse their languages too. And once He did that, then they couldn't get up to the higher levels anymore, and they couldn't ask other people, because they were dispersed. So in any case, and due to their dispersion and their languages being confused, they couldn't influence the angels and the higher powers anymore, because they didn't have the knowledge of the Hebrew language anymore. And that was the only language which the angels know.
And coming back to where we are, you see now, that the next three levels which we are going to talk about, which are the three higher levels, and which are all connected with the Hebrew permutations, names and letters, cannot be understood in the non Jewish world, and this is the reason astrologers, other then Jewish ones, don't talk about these levels; because, as we said, the third level is already the level of the tribes of Israel. And we discussed the different ways of counting these tribes. And if we go according to the

order of the tribes which is based on chapter two in the Book of Numbers, where the Torah talks about the camps in the desert, then we are talking about the order of the tribes as it was from the point in which the tribes began, because in the beginning of the Book of Exodus, the tribes are listed according to the order of their mothers, who were the wives and Yaakov. Because Yaakov had two wives and two concubines, and the children of each one are listed (in the beginning of the Book of Exodus) according to the order of their birth, more or less, and according to the order of the mothers; which one of them gave birth first, who are the wives and who are the concubines. So the order of the tribes there is according to the chronological order of their birth, with one exception. But there they were not tribes yet; there they were just individual people. The Torah didn't really discuss them in the terms of tribes yet. But in the Book of Numbers, they are already discussed in terms of tribes, and in terms of how many people were in each tribe at the time. So there it is already a matter of tribes. And so we talked about the tribes, and about each of the characteristics which are connected to each tribe, as well as the flag of each tribe, and how we use the tribes in order to understand astrology better, and actually to use it as a key to the finding of the hidden wisdom in the Torah. And that is done by using each of the tribes as an astrological symbol, and thus, by understanding that each of them came from a different place in the upper worlds.

And then, after that, we saw that there are two more levels (the fourth and the fifth), which are based on the names of God; the first of these two levels is based on God's name of Adnut, which contains the letters of 'Alef', 'Dalet', 'Nun' and 'Yod'. But we didn't really talk so much about that. But in general, I think it is connected more with the hours of the night. So that is not really what I wanted to get into here so much; I wanted to get more into the other name of God, which is connected to the most outer circle, which is called the name of Havaya, and contains the letters of 'Yod', 'He', 'Vav' and a second 'He'. This can be considered the real name of God. And the order of the letters, 'Yod' followed by a 'He', which is then followed by a 'Vav' and another 'He', is the standard way of spelling this name of God, and this order of letters in the name of God stands for the first month in the Jewish Calendar, which is Nisan, where everything is going in a straight order. And then we went into all the other different permutations, and thus we have explained all the twelve permutations of God's name. And, as we explained many times before, a four letter name can be permutated in twenty four different ways, which is four times three, times two times one. But since this name of God has two letters which are the same, so we divide twenty four by two, and thus there are 12 permutations to this name of God we are talking about. And each month has a different permutation. And those permutations are the real key to determining what kind of energy is coming down to the world. And I hanged a picture of those permutations here, for you to see, that the sources of the energies are rally not the planets or the stars; energies really come from a higher power, which is the power of God. And so we see the 12 permutations of His name. And since His name has 12 permutations, each of the 12 months has a different aspect of God directing the world. In other words, we can't really think about God or talk about Him, because God is really unknown, and you are not even allowed to really and truly think about Him in the Kabbala, believe it or not. This is a fundamental principle; as far as you can help it, you are not allowed to even think about God. Because once you think about Him, it is as if you make a place for Him outside of Him, and He is everywhere. He is above everything, He is inside everything and He consumes everything. So you can't really make a separation between you and Him, in a sense that you can investigate Him, which you obviously can't. It is just the sense of you thinking of what is called, in quotation marks, God, that you are not allowed; you should regard God as something you can't even think of really understanding. And this is how the Gaon of Vilna explained why it is actually forbidden to even think about God (in the sense that you are kind of picturing Him). But what we are allowed to do, which is the highest we can get in Kabbala, according to the Kabbalists, is learn the conduct of God; God's will, so to speak. In other words, we are allowed to, and we should, learn how He directs the world through the Torah, which is the special book He gave us. And through that we can start understanding how God directs and runs the world. And this is the work of the Kabbala, to try to understand how God made the world and put it together, how history operates and how God directs and manages everything. This is the Kabbala, and this is what it is about.

And so, when we look at these names, which are permutations of God's Havaya name, we see that each of these permutations is different from the other, as if they are different names. And we see how the way God directs the world in each month switches in the following month. And this is due to the different permutations which are used for each month; the different order of the letters in the permutation which is connected to each month. And this indicates the different energies which come down in each month. And for example, you see in in the different temperatures for each month. And you can see it in the growing of crops, the animal reproduction and in all different sorts of things. You see that everything changes, depending on when it is in the year.

So we went into all this, and we saw how each of the permutations, for the different months of the year, works. And we have spent a lot of time on that. And I would like to add one more thing tonight regarding that. And if people remember, we already saw in the earlier lessons, that there are 12 senses in the human being, which we have also connected to these 12 permutations of the Havaya name of God and to the 12 tribes of Israel. We said that the senses include that of speech, thought, action, sight, hearing, cohabitation, smell, sleep, anger, taste, laughter, walking (or motion), things like that; all different qualities, all different senses. And we connected them with the 12 tribes of Israel; we connected each of those senses with each of the tribes. Each of the tribes is connected to one of those senses, as we saw in the Book of Chesed Leavraham, where its writer mentioned that each tribe had a special quality in which it was better then all the other tribes. And this was based on which of the senses were strong in each of the 12 tribes.

But now I would like to show you something, which I don't remember weather I showed it to you last time or not. If I showed it to you last time, then I am going to add on to it now. So just like those 12 characteristics are connected to the 12 tribes of Israel, we also see that all these senses are used in connection with the name of God and its permutations too. And again, don't thing that God really has these senses in the same way we have them! Don't think that God thinks and smells or sees the same way we do! because this is not true, and God is above that. He gave us all those abilities, which He has in a much higher way, in a much higher sense. And we are using it when we describe God, in other words, we are attributing all those senses to Him, in order to figure and explain His actions in a way which would make sense to us, according to our understanding. So if we say that God sees, we mean that He directs things, but we don't mean that He sees as a visible body with eyes. But in any case, all those actions, or senses, are also mentioned in connection with God's name. Just like they are connected with the tribes, all of these actions, or senses, or whatever, are connected with God's name. For example, whenever it is said 'and God saw', or 'and God heard', 'and God smelled (or sniffed)', 'and God spoke', 'His language is like a consuming fire', (as God says) 'I had an intercourse (or intercourses) with you', 'all the great actions of God', 'and God got angry (or was angered)', 'and God walked', 'the one who sits in heaven (God) shall laugh', 'And God thought of destroying (or how and when to destroy)', 'wake up! Why would you sleep, God', and other attributions of that kind. So you see that all these attributions, these senses and actions, are connected with God. So just like each of the 12 tribes of Israel is connected to one of these attributions, so are the 12 permutations of God's name connected to it. So you really have to understand each month, and how the energies come down from these permutations of God's name. So we see that all these senses are also attributed to God Himself, and He Himself already uses each of those senses, so to speak, and this is what connects each of those senses to each of the permutations of God's name. And for example, the permutation which laughs is connected to a tribe which laughs. And the permutation which walks is connected to a tribe which walks, or, to be more accurate, which has a great ability of walking and travelling. So we see how all these different attributes come down from the names of God; they are already in the names of God. So if you really look in the Torah, or indeed, in any place in the Bible, you see that there attributions of senses to God. So when you see a passage in the Bible which attributes the action of laughing to God, you know that it talks about the sense of laughing in a much deeper aspect. And the sense of laughter is connected to the constellation of Pisces. So whenever God is described and laughing, you know that the passage is talking about the aspect of Pisces. And so, you can thus start learning more on how that sign works. And you also see how the tribes behave, but not only that; you also see, so to speak, how God behaves. So you start connecting everything with the months and the tribes etc. So, in other words, you start connecting each month with the tribe it is connected to, and with the permutation etc. And then you get much deeper into astrology, and also into the Bible. And thus you become able to learn the Bible on a secret level; on a mystical level. And in fact, there are two ways of learning the Bible mystically: One is the astrological way, and the other is the Kabbalistic way, because all the secrets in the Bible have been concealed in the Kabbala and in astrology. And therefore, if you know Kabbala and astrology, you can start understanding the Bible on a much deeper level.

So again, as we said, in the chart we have the 12 permutations of God's name, the name of Havaya. And we also asked where those 12 permutations come from. And we have learned that their source goes all the way back to the highest level of the world of Atzilut, which is called the Partzuf of Arik Anpin, in the mind of Arik Anpin , from the hidden mind of the Arik Anpin. And even more then that we can say about the source of the 12 permutations of God's name; we can say that it goes back, all the way, to the hidden mind of the world of Haadam Hakdmon, who was Adam Harishon, the first man in history. And this source, of the mind of the Adam Kadmon, is, in fact, the first revelation. And more then that; as we said before, the whole world is run from there, because out of the Hidden Mind come the Upper and Lower Minds, the Moach Elyon and Moach Tachton. And they are the upper and lower Mazalot of the beard. And they are really the ones which direct the world; the source of whatever ways the world is directed is there. All the forces come down from there. And by the time we see or feel it, all the energy had travelled through all that distance and through all the upper worlds, before it gets to the planets and eventually to earth. So again, in Kabbala, the whole system and essence of praying is the idea of being able to go all the way up, to the upper worlds, and bring down the energy, and use it properly.

And I want to start a series of lessons soon, on how it is possible to change the influences of the planets, which I think is what many people really want to learn. How can you change the energy? How can you change what is coming down to this world? How can you change the way the planets work? So these questions are going to be answered in the series of lessons which I would like to give. And in Western astrology you maybe go through psychoanalysis for this purpose, of changing the energies and influences of the planets. And through psychoanalysis, the psychoanalysts try to correct your attitude, and in fact your destiny; they change you and the influences you get. And again, in Western astrology, what the experts are able to understand is the person's chart . But they don't really have the ability to help the person. And if they had it, it has been lost. And today, most of the astrologers are very connected with psychology, and for that purpose, indeed, they use the system of psychology. They use astrology for the purpose of trying to figure out what is wrong with the person they are treating, and what that person's problems are, in order to prevent those problems from functioning. And then they go off with psychology, maybe in order to try to help that person. And there is another system of astrology, which is that of the Indian astrology. And the Indian astrologers use mantras, which they say to the different planets. And this is what we call dumb, and it is close to idol worship, because it is like saying prayers to the planets; like praying to the planets. And for example, it is about asking the planet Saturn, twenty thousand times, to be nice. And then, maybe Saturn would be nice. And if the planet is really bad, you even get a bunch of priests; you get ten or 12 priests together, and they would go around the whole day, praying for you, which means saying mantras to the planets or to a specific planet, in order to halt their influences. But in Judaism there are many ways to alter the influences of the planets, but, of course, the whole Jewish system is based on Torah and Mitzvot (good deeds), and there is no prayer, or mantra or anything, which is said to the planets or the stars themselves, God forbid. In Judaism, there are Mitzvot which a person has to do; there is a certain amount of commandments which a person has to fulfill. Jews were given a certain number of commandments, and according to an ancient Jewish astrology book, they were given in a way, that if you fulfill them, you would overcome the planetary influences. And hopefully I will be translating that book. And in fact, I have already translated one third of it up to now, and I am still working on it. I hope it will be finished in the next couple of months. But in any case, that book talks about how all those commandments, if you do them and practice them, nullify the planetary influence. And for example, in the Torah it is written, 'though shall not steal', and indeed, if one doesn't steal, and he, or she, has a nature of steeling, they can overcome their nature in a deeper way.

But we are going to go on another level now. And due to the fact this is an astrology lesson, we should learn more about a level which is connected to astrology. And indeed, I would like to talk about the Mitzvot, and how they are connected to the planets, and if you practice certain Mitzvot, they would alter the planetary influences. But I would also like to talk about the fact that it is not only about how the planets send the energies down, but also about who the person receives the planetary influences, and the energies in general. And if the person receives those influences properly, then he, or she, can use that energy better, in a better way. So it is not only about what comes down; it is also about how it is received. There is always a sender and a receiver, and things depend on both of them. So a lot depends on our ability to receive; it depends on the question of how we are able to receive, and in what way. It depends on the question of who we are, and if we really have the vessels to receive the energy which comes down to us. Because, indeed, there is a law in Kabala, according to which, God sends down the energy and the amount of energy according to what a person can receive. So if He sends down too little energy, then the person would be lacking energy, he may be weak, he may be depressed and things like that. But on the other hand, if He (God) sends down too much energy, then it may cause the person to explode, and it might be too much for them; it may be too high in spirit or otherwise, and things like that, until the person would get too much energy, which might brake him, or her. So God has a purpose in sending down the amount of energy He sends; He always sends down energy which relates to the body, in quality and in quantity. And then it may improve your body, but I don't mean in the sense of going out to the gymnasium and things like that. But if you improve your ability to receive, then you will be able to get more energy down, you will be able to get more of the sustenance from above. So we are going to be talking about that in the coming lessons.

But there is one more thing I would like to talk about before we conclude this series of lessons, this series of lectures. And that is going to be the connection between the senses and the different parts of the body, which we haven't focused on until now. And so I would like to spend a little bit of time on that, and once more I am going to quote from the ancient book called 'Sefer Hayetzira'. So these body parts are called the 12 directors of the human body, and the connection between them and the 12 senses, which are also called the 12 Peulot, the 12 actions of the soul, should be discussed before we conclude this series of lessons. And if you take a look closely at the matter, there seem to be no connection between them.

So I am going to read a few paragraphs, which show us the main points of what we are now interested in learning, from Sefer Hayetzira, which is the Book of Formation. So this is how it goes:

"And He (God) made the letter 'He' king over speech, Aries in the universe and the right foot in the soul". So the question becomes, what is the connection between speech and the right foot? And this is an obvious question, because speech and the right foot, though they are both connected with the sign of Aries, seem to be totally different things, because a person doesn't speak through his right foot; a person speaks through his mouth? So what is going on here?

And then, if we go on, we read: "He made the letter 'Vav' king over thought, Taurus in the universe and the right kidney in the soul". And again, this is the same idea and the same question, what does the right kidney has to do with the sense of thought? Because it is well known that thought is a brain function, and not a function of the right kidney.

And again, we go on: "He made the letter 'Zayin' king over motion, Gemini in the universe and the left foot in the soul". So ok, that has a little bit of a connection, because motion is caused by the feet of the body too, and it includes the left foot. So let us go on:

"He made the letter 'Chet' king over sight, Cancer in the universe and the right hand in the soul". And again, the question becomes, what is the connection between the sense of

sight and the right hand? Sight is in the eyes; people see through their eyes, and not through their right hands. And we can go through all of this. In fact, let us go through it, as long as we are here:
"He made the letter 'Yod' king over action, Virgo in the universe and the left hand in the soul". And again, I don't know exactly where action is connected, but there is a little bit of connection between action and the hands. So that is not much of a problem like some of the other ones. So let us go on:
"He made the letter 'Lamed' kind over sexual intercourse, Libra in the year and the gall bladder in the soul". So again, the question becomes, what is the connection between sexual intercourse and the gall bladder? The gall bladder is not really the place where the function of intercourse is found. And let us go on in the text:
"He made the letter 'Nun' king over smell, Scorpio in the universe and the intestine in the soul". So what does the sense of smell got to do with the intestine? The sense of smell comes and functions from the nose.
"He made the letter 'Samech' king over sleep, Sagittarius in the universe and the Keiva in the soul". And I am not sure what Keiva is exactly, and in fact there is an argument regarding the question of what Keiva is. Some people say it is the suffices, some people say it is the pancreas, or a hormonal thing; there are a number of approaches to the word keiva and we don't know exactly what it is. But in any case, we don't see such an apparent connection between that organ and sleep. But in any case, let us go on:
"He made the letter 'Ayin' king over anger, Capricorn in the universe and the liver in the soul". So again, what is the connection between the liver and anger?
"He made the letter 'Tzadik' king over taste, Aquarius in the universe and the Kurkevan in the soul". The Kurkevan is basically the stomach. But again, what is the connection between the sense of taste and the stomach?
And now the last passage: "He made the letter 'Kof' king over laughter, Pisces in the universe and the spleen in the soul". And so again, the question becomes, what is the connection between the spleen and the sense of laughter? There is no apparent connection here.
And so I want to turn again to the great rabbi, the Gaon Mevilna (the Gaon; the genius, of Vilna), and see what he has to say about this. And he says the following:
"The connections between these actions, or senses, and the limbs, are not about the limbs being the vessels of these senses, because they are not. These limbs are not the vessels through which these actions are performed. Rather the power of these senses is somehow found in limbs; these limbs somehow have the power through which these actions are performed. So what does it mean, for example, that the sense of speech is connected to the right leg, or that it is connected to a leg? It is said, 'He walked and spoke', or 'He walked and had a conversation'. And it is also said in 'Pirkey Avot', the Ethics of the Fathers, that one who is learning while walking, and then he interrupts his learning, due to some beautiful tree he sees, and says, 'how nice is this tree', or, 'how nice is that gathering of wheat or barley', is obligated to death, because one shouldn't stop himself from speaking the words of the Torah while he is on his way. And it is also said, that if two people are on their way, and they don't learn Torah with each other, it is suitable for them that they should be burned. Like it is said about some people who walked together and stopped and didn't say anything about the Torah to each other, and they got burned. And in many places in the Zohar it is said, that you need to light up the way (when you

walk) with Torah, with the fire of the Torah. So we do see that the power of speech is somehow connected to the leg and has something to do with it. We see that if a person speaks the words of the Torah while walking, then it is good for his legs. And the power, or sense, of thought, is in the kidneys, as it is said, 'the kidneys give him life', and like it is said, 'even at night my kidneys will guide me in the proper way'. And the night is the time of meditation; the night it the time of thinking. So you see that there is some connection between the kidneys and the sense of thinking; even though a person thinks with his, or her, head, there is somehow a connection between thinking and the kidneys. There is some power in the kidneys which is connected to the sense of thinking. And also the power of sight is in the hand, because the action of seeing is in the hand (most kinds of actions are done with the hands). And this is like it is said, 'He saw all of His deeds'. In other words, He saw all of His deeds, and deeds are dependent on, and connected to, the person's hands. So again, through action, there is a connection between the sense of seeing and the hands. And it is also said, 'I saw all of their deeds'. And similar things are said in different places. And all of these senses are on the right side, because on the right side there are things which are more spiritual. And for example, seeing, hearing, thinking, are all spiritual actions; those senses are senses of spiritual things. And that is because the right side is more hidden and concealed; it is the secret light. And similarly the Abba, who is the father, is hidden and concealed within the mother, the Ima. And this is like it is said in the Zohar".

So let us go on:

"And now, walking with the left leg, or actions which are connected to, and dependent on, the left side, are more physical and are things which have to do with more physical senses, so the left leg is more connected with walking, which is a more physical process", as the Gaon is explaining. "The right leg is more connected with the sense of speech, which, in itself, is also connected to walking, but is a more spiritual type of quality. It is a more spiritual quality and less of an earthy one. And hearing is more connected with the left kidney, because wisdom is connected to the sense and action of hearing, like it is said, 'pay attention to wisdom! Incline your ears and your heart for understanding'. And it is said in the Talmud that the kidneys are the ones who give advice". So again, it looks like the left kidney is more connected to the sense and action of hearing, which, I guess, is more physical then the sense and action of thought, which is more connected to the right kidney. And the Gaon of Vilna also gives the reason to the question of why it is so: "Hearing is more physical, because, after all, hearing is more connected to a voice. In other words, hearing works when you hear a voice, which is not the case with thinking. And therefore, the sense and action of hearing is listed on the left side, because the hearing is more of a physical action then thinking. Thinking is just in your mind, and it can happen when you close yourself out from the voices you hear. You can think when you close yourself from the outer world (even though you don't necessarily have to close yourself from the outer world in order to think). But hearing is done by picking up the sounds and turning them into words, which is more physical. And action is in the left hand. And intercourse is in the Marah, which is the gall bladder. And this is like it is said in the Talmud, that a person's bed should be situated between the north and the south sides. Because in the Jewish law, there is even a rule regarding the question of which direction the bodies of a couple should be placed, in order to bring down and conceive the most spiritual child. Again, in Judaism, the main purpose of intercourse is to bring down the best spirits in order to conceive and enlighten the future children who would be born as a result, because children can receive the highest and the best spirits under the proper conditions. So there is a kind of a law, stating the right direction in which the bed should be placed; where the head should be placed". And in fact, here it is said 'between the north and the south'. And actually, there is an argument between the Kabbalists on the question of what exactly it means; weather the head should be placed and directed to the east or not. And I think that the general Kabbalistic view is that the head should be placed and directed to the east, and then you would have Chesed (mercy) to the south and Gvura (strict judgment) to the north. In other word, you would then have the right arm placed on the north, and the left arm placed on the south. And that seems to be the position of the AriZal. So we have explained the reason for why it is desired to place the bed between the north and the south. So let us come back to the Gaon of Vilna, and he explains the reason for that as follows: "So it (the bed) would not be too cold, and nor shall it be too hot, because going to the extreme in any direction is evil (or a cause of evil), because if the heat is too much, then it might cause the giving birth to a child who shall be an angry person. And the result of it being too cold might be the giving of a birth to a child who might be too simple, in other words an idiot. And therefore it is said in the book of Proverbs (in Hebrew: Mishley), 'with much heat comes much anger'. And it is also said, 'every Mamzer (child who came out of a forbidden sexual relationship) is clever'. That is because if a child came from a forbidden relationship, he or she has the potential to be more clever then normal children, because it is more exiting and more pleasurable intercourse. And the Mamzer is somebody who comes from a relationship which is forbidden by the Torah, in other words, such a person comes from a sexual relationship which is Biblically forbidden. For example, if, God forbid, a father has sexual relationship with his daughter or a man with a married woman who is not his own wife, the child who comes out of those relationships is called a Mamzer. And in many cases, a child who comes out of such relationships is very clever. And that is because such sexual relationship is so called a very hot type of a thing. So the best time is when everything is mixed; not too hot and not too cold. And also, therefore, the right time to have intercourse is the middle of the night. This is, again, because such time is considered balanced, for it is not daytime and it is not really night, it is something in the middle. So therefore the best time to have sexual intercourse is a little bit after midnight. And this is on the same principle. And this is the same reason that, as we saw, the sense of intercourse is connected to the sign of Libra. Because the month of Libra, Tishri, in the beginning of the fall; it is the time when it is not too hot and not too cold; it is not summer anymore, but on the other hand, it is not too cold like in the winter. So it symbolizes the right time for cohabitation. Because that is the right time when things are balanced, when the weather is fair, like we said, it is between 'hot' and 'cold'. And similarly, that is the sign of Libra, which is the sign of scales, which is about wanting everything to be balanced. Because one would like things to be balanced; to have some balance. And similarly, there are four humors in human beings: The gall bladder is white, which stands as a symbol for the sense of sight, and it is cold. The liver is warm and red, the spleen is balanced, and I don't see what the forth humor is. But in any case, the forth humor, whatever it is, is green, and it is balanced between the colors (in other words, the green color is somehow balanced; it forms some kind of a balance between the colors of white, red and some other color, which is the color of the spleen). And due to that, intercourse is connected to it".

And let us keep on with the study of what the Gaon of Vilna says:

"And the sense of smell is connected to the Dakin". And again, what is Dakin? There is actually an argument between the Kabbalists as regards to the question of what Dakin is. But in any case, let us just call it Dakin. I don't think we have to relate to what it is exactly right now. But in any case, I think most people relate to the Dakin as the intestines. So now we say that the intestines are connected to smell. "And you have to know, that all those parts of the body are, somehow, connected to the upper chariot. And it is said in the Zohar, that all the limbs (here the word 'limbs' refer to different parts of the body, and not only the hands and legs) of the human being are connected to the upper chariot".

But in any case, I would like to check now if there is anything which we didn't do and study. It doesn't seem so. So the Gaon of Vilna goes on to show us how each of those senses is connected with each of the 12 months of the year. I don't know if we have enough time to go through all of them. But we will go through a few of them, just to give you an idea in that regards. This is the connection between the senses and the months:

"Like the sense of speech is connected with, and symbolizes, the month of Nisan. And why is that so, because in the month of Nisan there is the holiday (or holy day; Jewish festival) of Passover, when you have to use the sense of speech, and tell the story of the children of Israel going out of Egypt. You have to tell your children the whole story of how the Children of Israel came out of Egypt. So you see the connection between speaking and the month of Nisan. And it is also said in the Hagada, that the more a person tells and discusses the story of the redemption of the Children of Israel from the Land of Egypt, the more he is praised. And meditation is in the month of Iyar, and therefore the sense of meditation is connected to that month. Because that is the month in which desire awakens, and which is a symbol for Gvura (strength). And therefore, the sign of the month of Iyar is a Bull, for Taurus is a bull. And the sign of the bull is on the left side of the chariot. And seeing is in the month of Sivan. In other words, the sense of seeing is connected to the month of Sivan, as it is said, 'and all the nation (of Israel) saw the voices (of thunder) and the lightening' on Mount Sinai. And the sense of walking is connected to the month of Tamuz, as it is said about the angel, when he hit the sensitive part in the leg of Yaakov, that it happened in the month of Tamuz, according to the commentators. And the month of Tamuz was also the month when the 12 spies were sent by Moshe and began their journey to the Land of Israel, where they were supposed to walk through the Land of Israel, see how strong the inhabitants are and tell the Nation of Israel what they saw. So you see that the month of Tamuz is connected to the sense of seeing. And the sense of hearing is connected to the month of Av. Because in the month of Av, the spies came back from the Land of Israel, and told the Children of Israel what they saw and heard there, and what impressions they got from the Land of Israel and its inhabitants, regarding the question of whether they would be able to conquer it. And in that month, all the people who heard that became upset and were condemned by God to die. And the sense of action is connected to the month of Elul. And this is as it is said, 'and in that time God told me, for yourself, write two new tablets… and I wrote two new tablets'. And that happened in the month of Elul. And the sense of intercourse is connected with, and symbolizes, the month of Tishri, the constellations of which is the sign of Libra. This is because, as we said, it is a balanced month. It is not too hot and not too cold, and it is also the best characteristic for a child; not to be too hot and not too cold. And the sense of smelling is connected to the month of Cheshvan. Because after Noah came out of the ark in which he had been during the whole period of the flood, and offered the sacrifices in the month of Cheshvan (according to the opinion that the flood ended, the earth became dry again and Noah came out of the ark, in the month of cheshvan), 'God smelled (or sniffed) the nice smell', as it is said in the Book of Genesis regarding that story. And the sense of sleep is connected to the month of Kislev, which is the month of Chanukat Hamizbeach, which is the ceremony of the consecration of the alter in the Temple. So maybe because the Hebrew word for 'they camped', which is somehow similar to the words 'they settled and rested', is Chanu, which is similar to the word 'Chanuka. And the sense of anger is connected to the month of Tevet, because that is the month during which the king of Babylon began the siege over the city of Jerusalem. And we are going to explain later on, that the month of Tevet is one of the three difficult months. During a later lesson we are going to explain why it is a difficult month. But we will leave that for now.

And the sense of eating is connected to the month of Shvat. And this is as it is said, in the Book of canticles, 'I ate my fruits where the honey is, together with my honey'. And this verse talks of trees in forests, and the month of Shvat marks the beginning of the growth of trees. That month is when the trees start growing. And the sense of laughter is connected to the month of Adar, for the Jewish festival of Purim falls in Adar. And we have to be happy during the Festival of Purim; all the Jews have to drink and be merry during that festival.

So again, in the writings of the Gaon of Vilna we see all the connections between the different parts of the body and the 12 senses, as well as the connection between the 12 senses and the 12 months of the year, according to the Jewish Calendar.

And with that I think we shall conclude the series of lessons on the subject of the permutations of God's Havaya name. And just remember; whenever you see the number 12 and any order of 12 things, remember that they are all connected with each other. In other words, all those things which are divided into 12 are connected with one another. And now I remember one more thing which is divided into 12 too, but we shall talk about that, and how it is connected to the other things, for another lesson in the future. And remember, the Gaon of Vilna said that there is the number 12 in 'Olam, Shana Vanefesh', which means, in the universe, in time and in the human body and soul. And you shall see parallels in other things, but the bottom line is that all three systems are parallel to one another. It is found in the world, it is found in the person and it is found in time, and you shall find many other different things which are divided into 12 too, and whenever you find them, pay attention to them, because you can be able to make a connection between them and the months of the year, the permutations of God's Havaya name, the limbs (in other words, the body parts) which direct the body, the 12 senses and all other things which are divided into 12.

Philosophy and the History of Jewish astrology

Philosophy and the History of Jewish astrology

By Yaakov Kronenberg

A transcription of a lecture on the astrology of prediction as compared to the astrology of psychology; how Torah astrology is more Mazal orientated when compared to Western astrology; also how Torah astrology differs from Indian astrology.

Philosophy and History of Jewish Astrology

By Yaakov Kronenberg

a talk about really the Philosophy and History of Jewish Astrology because I think I'm the first person, at least that I know of, that is really going in to Jewish Astrology. Until now, really, if you look around, in the last say 20 to 25 years in the Astrology World there has been a movement back to ancient texts. It started on one hand from a lot of guys from America, women too actually, and they went off to India, and they learnt Indian Astrology, which was until then, I remember in the early 70's I tried to learn Indian Astrology books by myself and even with a translation it was impossible to understand. You couldn't understand it. And so these guys, they went off to India, they had long hair and who knows what, and they went off there and they grew out of the America of the 60s and the early 70s and they took off to India and they went around until they found teachers. In India a lot of the people are English speaking, the educated class especially, because at one time it was ruled by the British so it was like the second language there, English, the Queen's English. And so they went around and they were able to find really top teachers that really knew their mareial and they took that knowledge and the brought it back to America and they wrote books and really they opened up Indian Astrology for Americans. You know for Western speakers. So that was on one hand. On the other hand, they have a very rich tradition in Astrology in India, I don't want to say much but I can show maybe a little later on the connection between Vedic Astrology and Jewish Astrology. There is a tradition that a lot of the stuff from the East came from Jews. But we will wait on that for now because I first want to give you a little bit of introduction about what's leading me to do what I'm doing today.

So anyway, these people they all came back from India, they wrote books and brought down all these new techniques, a lot of which nobody knew about, the dashi system, time periods, and all different things. Different ways of interpreting the Chart… Anyway I don't want to get into that now, my job is not to teach Indian Astrology. I think if you want to learn Indian Astrology there are better people to learn it from than me. But I'm here to talk about the differences between Indian Astrology and Jewish, and Western Astrology. What they have in difference and what they have in common. So anyway I want to give background material first and show how there was a movement really to bring back the ancient Astrology. Because what happened in the early 1900s with the advent of Freud and psychology, psychoanalysis… SO anyway the Western Astrology became very psychoanalytically oriented in the early 1900s and later on, really till the 1970s even. It became totally like psychological Astrology. The Astrologer would spend most of the time dealing with peoples psychological problems and giving him a psychological profile, you know and not too much talking about prediction because they didn't really know how to predict and they had a philosophical idea that people had total free will and in a certain way it was you know not good to predict. You're taking away the persons free choice, I don't know whatever and it became very psychoanalytically oriented, psychology oriented. And then there was naturally a revolt against that because really the job of the Astrologer has always been to try to predict the future. He's not 100 percent and he never will be 100 percent. If he was 100 percent there would be no need for prophets. So a good Astrologer maybe 70 percent of the time he could be right, he could make good predictions, he could be very good at seeing trends and things like that. But he's certainly no prophet. If you want prophecy you go to the Bible, that's where it was just full of prophecy and you see it all came true. And they were predicting things 2000 years ahead of the time. Look in the Jewish Bible, it says the Jews were going to be exiled, they were going to live all among the nations of the World, and then eventually they were going to be brought back to Israel. And in our generation you see it before your very eyes. A prediction that was made 2000 years ago, not in cryptic language like Edgar Casey or Nostradamus, that if you want to play around with it you can come to any understanding that you want but they predicted things really out in the open in the Bible. And look that's going out on a limb… If you're just starting a religion and you want to get followers you need to be careful not to make predictions that don't come true. And really if you look through the Jewish Bible you will see prediction after prediction that they weren't afraid to make and you see it all came true. But again, that's not my job, if anyone wants to go places where they can talk about things like this, I'd be happy to direct them, just send me a letter or an email and I'll answer them and maybe later on we can do a series on Jewish prophecies, I think that would be an interesting idea. We can talk about all the different prophecies in the Bible and show you how they came true and how they were on the mark. But we will come back to that also.

In any case, besides all these guys going off to India to learn Indian Astrology, there was also a lot of people in the West who decided to look back into their tradition you know, they went back to a movement, a movement which was trying to revive old Astrology books from Greece and Rome and from the Middle Ages, Arabic, Persian, you name it they were looking for it, Babylonian even, lately they have been coming out with Babylonian texts… And they have been trying to go back into the early history and coming up with new old techniques to try to explain what was going on in the World of Astrology back then and try to use these techniques in today's World. But of course it's very interesting that there was nothing, or very little, on Judaism actually, on the Jewish approach to Astrology. And I think tonight I want to show you really all of … I think it is going to be a short piece but very interesting , I want to answer a lot of problems of the Western approach to Astrology, to the History of Astrology… But in any case you see they also came back. But in Jewish Astrology there is very little, almost nothing let's put it that way, there is almost zero on Jewish Astrology. On one hand it's maybe a dearth for people who have knowledge of Judaism and Jewish religion because Astrology is… Well all books on Judaism, any book on Judaism up until maybe a 100 years ago, 200 years were by rabbis, religious rabbis, Orthodox rabbis, some of it or part of it in old Hebrew, some of it in Aramaic. A lot of it isn't even in Hebrew, it's in Aramaic, which itself has a few different dialects. So there weren't too many people that were conversant in Astrology, that knew these ancient languages and also knew their way around the Jewish religion and could learn the Jewish sources so there was almost no revitalisation of Jewish Astrology to any degree and really the only thing that I've seen really are one or two basic texts, there are books by Ibn Ezra, great rabbi, a tremendous genius, a tremendous scholar, but his Astrology is very much Western Astrology. It's more or less Ptolemaic in origin, similar to Greek Astrology and I'll show you why later in my talk. And why it is that way because you see they really have one source and they just got split off at a certain point. But we will talk about that. But Ibn Ezra has been translated, there are a few different people translating it now actually, I forget their names though. There is a professor from Bar Ilan University who has been translating a number of his books recently, maybe 4 or 5 of them, but he is selling them at university prices, small books and quite expensive. But in any case, Ibn Ezra I don't think encompasses the whole field really of Jewish Astrology. I would guess it is basically a Western textbook on Astrology. Very well written, very knowledgeable, very good, but he doesn't cover a lot of the ground work in Jewish Astrology. And besides him there is really almost nothing. So I felt that it is my job to bring back some of the old stuff and try to teach it on the website. And it's a little bit hard because the rabbis didn't really engage per se in Astrology. You know they are rabbis and their job is to teach Torah. Their job isn't to teach Astrology. So they dealt in it but they dealt in it in a not so much systematic way. Maybe I have 10 or 15 books that are dealing totally with Astrology, some of them very old going way back, and then most of the stuff is all hidden here and there and you have to really look around to find it because there it's like they knew medicine back then, the rabbis knew medicine but they didn't write medical books, it wasn't their avodah, it wasn't their job. The same way they knew … Botany or they knew other sciences, say Astronomy, they wrote a little about it but they had to know Astronomy, because a lot of the Jewish religion, the times of the Jewish religion, the times of the holidays, depended on knowing Astronomy. So they knew Astronomy but per se they didn't write a whole lot of Astronomy books over the years. They wrote a few but mostly in order to teach people the basics of Astronomy so they could use it to figure out the Jewish holidays, the Jewish years, things like that... And so it was the same thing for Astronomy per se it wasn't a topic that they were keenly interested in writing about.

But anyway there is a lot of rich literature on Astrology in Judaism and I want to bring back a lot of it, and we will talk about it over the next… you will see on my site there will be lots of classes and I hope people will read them. SO let's now start to get back into the lecture tonight.

I guess the aim of this lecture is to give a short introduction to the history and philosophy of Jewish Astrology. King Solomon, the wisest of men said "Of books there is no end" and of lectures there is no end. A person can talk and talk… So I am going to try concentrate on one thing oo talk mostly about where Jewish Astrology differs from Western and Vedic Astrology and a little bit why these differences do exists. And even show how certain to try to show how Vedic and Western concepts are rooted in Jewish Astrology. But for the most part I'm going to try and stay away from trying to talk about what they have in common, except for one main idea which I think they do have in common and we will come back ro.

In the Biblical story of the creation of the World, G-d created one man. Out of the Earth was created his body and G-d breathed the living soul into his nostrils. Then G-d took one of his ribs and made for him a help mate. They were called Adam and Eve. That's the original creation at the beginning of the Bible. So our rabbis ask, they have what are called midrashim which are rabbinical explanations of the Bible, the rabbis ask there a simple questio

 ask, why did G-d start the World with one couple? Why didn't He make many couple did He start with Adam and Eve and nobody else? So they answer, He did it in this way so that no one could say his ancestors are better than mine because we all come from the same source. When you look back and do your genealogy and if you trace it back far enough, if you use an expert in genealogy to do your genealogical history, every person he does if he knows his job really well in the end he will get them back to Adam and Eve. Unbelievable but true. So that is the answer of the rabbis. He did it in this way so no one can say his ancestors are better than mine. We all have the same genetic material, so if you messed up it's because you wanted to mess up. So in any case, this man's Chart or this woman's Chart, was the Astrologer's archetypal Chart, called the Chart of Adam HaRishon, the Chart of First Man, that's what's called the archetypal Chart. In other words, we have a Chart with Aries on the Ascendant and then Taurus on the 2nd House, Gemini on the 3rd, you'll get the Libra on the 7th House, the House of marriage, and if you start from there that will be Eve and she will have her Chart starting from the 7th House. So you will have the Chart of Adam and Eve. And this is what is called the Archetype Chart and from the Chart we build all of Astrology. In other words, all Jewish Astrology, all of esoteric Jewish Astrology is based on an understanding of this Chart, the Chart of the First Man, that in Hebrew we call him Adam HaRishon, the First Man.

To understand this better, if there were many couples created, there would have been many Archetype Charts. Each with different characteristics and natures and there would have been no universality to man and no one science to understand him. In other words if the World was started with all different couples and each one came into existence on his own, however you want to learn it, if they were created by G-d or if they came from a monkey or whatever, however you learn it, we are not going to get too much into evolution today because you will see in a little while this class is not connected to evolution at all, what I'm going to be talking about. But let's just say if there were many different couples there would be many different types of Archetypal Charts. And then there would be no universality to man. People came from different sources and they maybe would have been different, one from each other. And there also wouldn't have been a science to understanding them. Each creation would have had to have been of its own understanding, and in truth by definition there cannot be more than one Archetype. In Latin "archetype" means "the original" and by definition there cannot be more than one original. So really when Astrologers talk about the Archetypal Chart, it assumes that the human race started with one couple, which brings us to the biblical account of creation. So really you see the Astrologers, when you get back to original assumptions, I don't think people really paid attention to the original assumptions. When you use Astrology, and most people do, most Astrologers do, to one degree or another, they use the Archetypal Chart but you see you're really going back to the Jewish Bible where the World was created with one couple, because if you had more than one couple it would be imossible to do Astrology. By the way, today almost all, if not all, anthropologists, linguists, geneticists agree to this and accept what is called mono-genesis. Mono is one, genesis is creation, one creation. In other words everything was started with one couple. There is still arguing over who this one couple was. Was it in Africa? Where did they start from? Was it in Africa or in the Middle East or here and there. But in any case it seems to be more or less agree today that it was started by one couple and the anthropologists even call the couple Ad

Eve. And it has no relevance, as was mentioned before, it has no relevance to the question of evolution. If there was evolution or if there was Godly creation or things like that, it just says that however it was started, it just started with one couple. Whether it was started by evolution or by G-d making man and blowing a life force into his nostrils, however you want, it's not a question that concerns us at this moment because it seems to be agreed upon that there is this idea of monogenesis.

There is another question concerning Astrology that I've never heard anyone talking about, except the Jewish Astrologers, and that is why G-d created the World in such a way that everything that happens on Earth is dependent on the planetary positions, and relationships in the sky. Another way of asking this question is why didn't G-d just send down His energies from above directly to man without passing through all these intermediaries such as the constellations, the Planets, the Angels and travelling through all these diverse Worlds? This is a deep question which I will talk about incidentally because I am only using the question as a stepping stone to understanding the Jewish approach Astrology. I don't want to get into the details of this right now because it's not the aim of what we are talking about, we are talking about why G-d created the World and why He did it in the way He did. Ideally G-d should have sent his largesse to man and Earth directly. But because of the sin of the first man, who is no longer worthy of enjoying a close, direct relationship with G-d, He created all these intermediaries between Him and man. In other words, man couldn't have a close relationship anymore with G-d, it had to be broken down and there had to be some sort of separation, just like you see in the World today. You have a king or a president… let's give the idea of a king, which is the way we used to understand things. There is a king but how many people talk to the king and met the king? The king had ministers for each different area of the government and if you had a problem in that area you talked to one of the ministers and that is if you were worthy to get to the ministers, the minister had all these emissaries and officers in each city and each town. And so you went there. And really to get to the king was not so easy. The same thing in the Heavens it also happens that way. Originally G-d passed everything down straight but then afterwards because of the sin, man couldn't be connected directly anymore so He built up this whole system of intermediaries.

According to the Kabbalah there are 5 Worlds. The lowest is the World of action, this World is broken into 2, the Earth and the Heaven, Heaven itself has 7 palaces, which I think are spiritual, these 7 palaces I don't think they can be seen. All the Planets, Stars and Constellations are in the 2nd palace. Only in the 2nd palace that's where all the Stars and Constellations are. And above that was the 3rd, 4th, 5th, 6th and 7th palaces which I guess only the Jewish Kabbalah talks about. Above them are 5 more palaces above the 2nd one. And then the next World is the World of formation, all of that was in the World asiya. Asiya itself had the Earth of World of action and the Heaven of the World of action. The Heaven broke in to 7 pieces, the 7 palaces. All of what we call Astronomy and Astrology is found in the 2nd palace, then there were another 5 palaces above that and then we went up to another World above that called the World of formation. And above that is the World of creation, there's even another World above the World called the World of emanation. Above that is the World of the supernal man, which is the World of Adam HaRishon, the first man, and above th never-ending light which illuminates all the Worlds, which we call the Ein Sof. But in any case, we see that the planetary systems and the Constellations are only a low level, according to the Kabbalists. They receive their powers from the Worlds above them. So really in Jewish Astrology we see that the Astrological system is really in a very low place. It's just down into the… again, we saw that it is in the Heavens of Asiya and only in the 2nd of the 7 palaces, 2nd from the bottom of the 7 palaces. And above that were many other worlds and many other influences. We will see later on when we are talking about Jewish Astrology that we don't limit everything to the Planets. Above the Planets are causes, more and more causes and much higher than you can get there and that can influence the Planetary movements, the Planetary effects and eventually you will see that it comes back. I think in the next class I am going to talk about the names of G-d. In Jewish Astrology each of the 12 Signs was connected with a different name of G-d. G-d has really one name but it permeates itself into 12 combinations. I'm going to talk a little bit about that in my next class.

But you will see that in the picture. I'm going to put up the picture for this class also and you will see that behind every Sign there is a name of God and that is what it really wants to show you that everything is really coming from God. Don't think it's just coming from you know the highest you can get is the Milky Way, is the Planets, the constellations, the stars and maybe a little behind that. But there are really worlds among worlds and much higher levels. And I think that by putting those 12 permutations there it's just to show you that don't take things in such a limited way, that the Planets are controlling your life. You have to understand that eventually it's God that is controlling your life and that's always the approach of Jewish Astrologers.

Going back to Abraham, Abraham was the oldest Astrologer, actually the oldest extant book on Astrology today is a book called the Sefer Yetzira which is written by Abraham. But we will come back and talk about that in a few minutes. In any case, we see the Planetary systems and the constellations are only a very low level according to the Kabbalists and they receive their powers from the worlds above them. In ancient times many civilizations saw the power of the stars and said they were the source of all life. This was the beginning of idol worship. When people started to pray to the Planets and do all sorts of divinations to change the planetary forces, in other words because that was really the known world till then. That was really the only thing you could see, the Planets and about a thousand fixed stars. There weren't telescopes or anything. And so people decided for whatever reason that the Planetary forces were ruling their lives and they didn't see anything behind it. Or maybe originally at one time everything was connected to a higher source and then it broke off from the higher source and then all they saw was the Planets and they made a separation between the Planets and what's above them because they are much more spiritual entities as opposed to physical entities.

Anyway it is related in the Talmud, that Abraham, the founder of Judaism, was the master Astrologer of his generation. He was born 3823 years ago and is the author of the oldest extant book on Astrology called the Sefer Yetzira. So in other words for Abraham it is easy to remember his birthday because the Jewish state of Israel was founded in 1948. In the calendar, we have a 6000 year calendar, Avraham was born 1948 years after the creat years before the 2000th year. And that would make him 3823 years old and he is the author of the oldest extant book, the Sefer Yetzira. As far as I know there is no older book on Astrology. Most of the book is on Astrology, part of the book is Kabbalistic. It talks about the 10 Sefirot, it talks about the Hebrew alphabet and it talks about Astrology. But I would say about 3 out of the 6 chapters of the book they talk about Astrology. It's a very difficult book, very concise, if anyone wants to understand it maybe we will try talk about it later on, maybe have some classes on it. Anyway how did he become the first person to believe in one G-d? He was meditating on the Planets and he said to himself that there must be a higher force behind the Planets. It's not possible that they are directing the world by themselves. In other words, through Astrology, he came to the realisation of G-d. How can the Planets run history? How can the Planets determine what is going to happen? He saw behind everything and came to a really deep conclusion that maybe once existed or got lost but whatever… He came to the realisation of G-d. The founder of Judaism was an Astrologer who came to the realisation of G-d through Astrology. Wonder of wonders. But that is what is written in the Talmud.

The next point I would like to talk about is how Astrology originated. The accepted wisdom, Astrology started about 2000 years before the common era in an area which today is Iraq. It was about the time of Abraham. In that area, and Abraham also lived in that area. How it started and developed is very hazy and there is no adequate explanation for how the images of the Zodiac came to be, and the other star clusters. How did all the people all over… Who connected the stars to form images? If there was no logical reason for these images, how did a consensus come about and they were accepted in Iraq and then spread throughout the world with no disagreement? If there is no logical reason for something why should everyone accept it? Even when there are logical reasons for something nations and peoples disagree and here something was universally accepted for no apparent reason. So again, it's a very ancient question. How did the… I was always bothered by this… How did it happen that the whole world accepted that if you look at the stars at night, you look at picture books of the constellations how they look and you ask yourself how everyone in the world made the same connection between the stars and formed the same pictures? It just does not make any sense to me at all. It was always something that bothered me very much. Why do all the nations agree? And it's a big question on Astrologers. How did it spread out? There were other things that spread throughout the world and were universally accepted for no apparent reason. In other words why do all the nations use a counting system based on 10? Wherever you go there is a counting system where everybody counts to 9 and then you start over. Why? Well we will talk about that someday because you know… 10 Sefirot. The world was made on 10. And why do all nations accept the 7 days of the week? How come every nation in the world has 7 day weeks? Maybe there is somewhere in the world that doesn't but as far as I know just about anywhere you go in the world they are going to have 7 day weeks. And again, that is also from the Bible. Where do we get the idea of 7 day weeks? It's from the Jewish Bible. And then if you accept that 7 day weeks comes from the Jewish Bible then you have to accept the whole planetary hour system comes from the Jewish Bible. All of a sudden you have a 7 day week and each day is ruled by a different planet and each hour of the day is ru
different planet. And you see it is all based on the idea of seven and so you hav

yourself why it was created with 7. And also you know in the Bible, the world was created with the 10 statements of G-d, why do we have the number 10, counting till 10? It also comes from the Bible. G-d said "let there be light" and G-d said "let there be this" and he said 10 utterances and the world was created. So we have a counting system of 10. And we have 7 days of the week. So you see that all of this is found in the Bible. And you see that really everything comes from the Bible. And I want to say that really the Jewish rabbis would never have accepted… You have to understand that the Jewish rabbis would never have accepted Astrology. In Judaism Astrology is believed, in other words there is an idea in Jewish religious law that Astrology works. Maybe there are arguments over whether you can practise it or what the Jewish approach is to practising Astrology or to following Astrologers advice… But the Jewish approach to Astrology in the Jewish Law Book, (The Jews have a Jewish Law Book called the Shulchan Aruch), they have a law book that they follow and in that law book says that Astrology works. And they would never have accepted Astrology if it was developed by the people of Babylon, some people who just sat around, some tribal people who sat around campfires and drank beer they connected the lines to the stars and drew the constellations. The Rabbis are not like that. They would not have accepted something man made. They just don't do that, it's not accepted if it can't be proved. So in any case, there are sources that show that really Astrology to answer all these questions what you really have to say is that certain wisdoms, certain things were started with Adam HaRishon, the first man. There was one man created and he was given secret knowledge. And to answer these questions you really have to come to an idea like this. That really the laws of Astrology began with Adam HaRishon. An angel of G-d taught Adam HaRishon, the first man, Astrology and then he passed it onto his sons and they passed it on until it reached to the Tower of Babel. What we call the story of the Tower of Babel which was somewhere in Iraq, I guess, in that area in the Mesopotamian region. And that was where Abraham also had his place before he came to Israel. And that became the hot bed of Astrology. At that time the whole civilised world was there. And then when the world got dispersed at the time of the Tower of Babel, everybody got spread out. Everybody got different languages and they spread out to different areas of the world. And that is how Astrology became spread but it was spread from this original teaching that was given over to Adam HaRishon. It was given over to Adam HaRishon, the first man, and then he passed it on and then when the dispersion came, people took it to all different places of the world and it got spread out. And we see for example in India, the Brahmans. The Brahmans a lot of it was from Abraham. Abraham was A Brahman, say the Brahmans they came from Abraham. It says in the Torah that Abraham had a concubine that he sent to the East with gifts. And the Torah, they had a major commentator on the Torah at that time he says, what kind of gifts would Avraham, send He's not going to send diamonds and beautiful clothing, he was a great spiritual master. So he sent them over with special names and a lot of special things that he sent over to India. And I think a lot of their teachings are built on that. But that is for another class.

But in any case, what I'm saying is, I came on this idea a lot on my own over the years but lately I've been seeing it in a lot of different places. There is a book on Jewish Philosophy called the Kuzari and the Kuzari, he talks like this, that there was secret knowledg over to Adam. And just now I was talking to a great Astronomer, a professor of Astr and he told me my idea is found in a book by a Jewish historian from the time of the Roman period that lived in Rome that wrote a book on the History of the World back then. His name was Flavius Josephus. And he calls his book "History of the world" and in there he said Adam HaRishon had a son and he passed that on until it reached Noah at the time of the flood, and Noah passed it on to his son, Shem, and Shem was the original Astrologer. He taught everyone Astrology. And you know you see it came from the sources where it shows, not just me, there are sources from History, the Kuzari, Flavius Josephus... The Kuzari was written by Rabbi Yehuda HaLevi, it's a very interesting book and there are good English translations of it available today, it's eminently readable. Also Josephus there are translations in English, you shouldn't have any problem getting it. And they talk about this idea that there were certain secret wisdoms that were given over to Adam HaRishon and they said that one of them was Astrology. And because of this Jewish rabbis accepted Astrology. Not because, G-d forbid, they would never accept it from a teaching that was started by some Neanderthal men, sitting drinking in a cave by a campfire and watching the sky and writing down what they saw. No they would never have accepted that, that is for sure.

Anyway, to close, I remember my first teacher of Astrology, the great teacher, the godfather of all traditional Astrology of today, I think almost all people who went off into traditional Astrology were at one point or another his students, Mr Zoltan Mason. He once told me that all of Astrology is hidden in the Bible. Only the person needs for his eyes to be open to see it. In other words, all of Astrology is hidden in the Bible, if you can find it. Later on the famous rabbi, the Gaon of Vilna, a great genius who lived in Lithuania in the 1700s said that all of science and all of mathematics is all also hidden in the Bible but it got lost and the tradition of how to find it all got lost. The Gaon of Vilna brought back a lot of it but a lot of it got lost, unfortunately.

Prophesy and the End of days

Prophecy and the End of days

By Yaakov Kronenberg

This is a transcription of a short discussion on the difference between Prophets and astrologers and their predictions about our times.

Prophecy and the End of Days

By Yaakov Kronenberg

One of Rabbi Avraham Bar Chiya's favorite sayings was that if the astrologers knew everything, then there would be no need for the prophets. I've been talking about why people look at these prophets, so to speak, like Nostradames, and I remember in my university days it was Edgar Casey, and people believe in all sorts of weird prophets, when they could look back on the ancient books, especially on the Jewish ancient books of the prophets and you see that prophesies were given thousands of years ago, so clearly written. Or even going back into the bible, just reading the five books of Moses, and you see all the prophesies there, and how they have all come to be fulfilled over the course of history. And if people really want to see the end of days and what's going to happen then I believe that is where they should be looking, and not at these weird prophets so to speak. I want to read a prophecy that comes a bit later than the main prophets. It's a prophecy from the Talmud which is after the prophets. The Talmud was redacted about 2000 years ago, and it was written by the Rabbis of the *Knesset ha Gedolah*. The great Rabbis of that time wrote down the Mishnah which was the oral tradition, because the Rabbis knew that the Jews were eventually going to go into exile, and they were afraid that all their teachings and all their wisdom would get lost, so at a certain time they wrote it all down and they called it the Mishnah. Today I want to talk about a Mishnah that is discussing the end of days. And this is hopefully going to lead to something that eventually I am going to do a whole series on, which is that the great Kabbalists divided up the world's history into 18 periods. This is a class primarily for astrologers because most of the people that are interested in this are into astrology, so to give an example, in India they have a time system called the *Dasha* period, and in Ancient astrology they have something called time-lord systems where they take a persons life and divide it up into 120 years or 80 years, there are different systems. And each period of life changes depending on what Planet is ruling that period of the person's life. So you can say the first 15 years will be this Planet and the next 10 years will be this Planet, and the third 10 years will be that Planet. And then they sub-divide each period with other Planets helping the main Planets etcetera.

In Judaism we believe in that with history. We believe there is a beginning to history and that there will be an end to history. So they broke up the 6000 years into different periods. Actually there are two ways that they broke it down, the first way they broke it down was that every day of the week was 1000 years, they learned that from a passage in the psalms: 1000 years in the eyes of G-d is like one day for us, or something like that. So we learn that 1000 years is equivalent to a day, so each day of the creation is 1000 years. We learn that in the first 1000 years the Sun had an influence, the second 1000 the Moon, etcetera.

That is not my concern today; we can spend a lot of time on that later on when we discuss Planetary systems. But on top of that they broke up the history into 18 periods and in each of these 18 periods, the way G-d ran the world changed, so he managed the world differently. In order to be a good astrologer you have to be able to tune into these 18 different periods where the direction of the world is different and where G-d is running the world differently from how he ran it at another time. We are going to be learning about this more, but I want to read you what they write in the ancient book of the Talmud on what it is going to be like in the End of Days. It says: with the footsteps of the *Mashiach*, insolence will increase. In other words it's talking about the footsteps of the Messiah. And the Talmudic commentaries explain that at the end of the exile, just before the coming of the *Mashiach,* so we are talking about our times now, with the ingathering of the Jews, we are talking about the last 50 years, the Jews have slowly been making their way back to Israel, from just about everywhere except for the last outpost which seems to be America. I don't want to go into it too much because this is just a short class, but let's just get a feeling for it. It's as obvious as it is written that I don't think I have to explain it too much. 'In the footsteps of the Mashiach insolence will increase and inflation will soar' everybody knows that inflation soars, everybody sees it everyday, the inflation is getting more and more. 'The vine will give its fruit and the wine will be dear' even though there will be plenty of wine being produced, there wont be enough because everybody will be getting drunk. 'And the government will turn to heresy' I guess you don't need much to understand that. 'And there will be no rebuke' what does it mean there will be no rebuke? It means that there won't be anybody high enough to give rebuke to anybody else. If someone gets rebuked he sits back and says: look, you are no better than me with what you are doing! 'The meeting places of sages will be used for immorality' 'and the Galil will be destroyed and the boarder towns will be desolate' anyone who lived in Israel in the last war saw what happened to the Galil and the destruction of the Galil. 'and the border towns will be desolate' remember all the people in the border towns where the rockets were falling in the south and the residents all came to the middle of the country and no one really cared about them. 'The boarder dwellers will wander about from city to city but they will not be pitied'. 'The knowledge of scholars will be lost, and those that fear sin will be despised'. 'And the truth will be hidden' just look at the Torah and all the Jewish knowledge that has been hidden; only now it is starting to come back. 'Youth will shame old men and old men will stand up for youngsters', you see this especially in America where everybody wants to be young, the old people are despised and they are trying to figure out how to get rid of them and everything is about the youth. 'There will be times when a son shames his father and a daughter rebels against her mother and a daughter in law against her mother in law and a man's enemies are the members of his household'. 'the face of the generation will be like the face of a dog', there are a number of explanations to what that means, one is that the rich people have no compassion for the poor people, just like dogs which gather their meat and then they keep it for themselves. Another one that I heard is that just like a dog that goes out with his master for a walk he runs ahead and he looks like he is really leading, but when the master changes direction and the dog sees him and runs back to the master. So it is the same way with the politicians today, they don't really lead and they don't really guide people towards living in a better way, they just lead the people in the direction that the people want to go so that they can get reelected. 'The son is not ashamed before his father, on whom can one rely only on the father in heaven' the commentary here says that no social institutions will remain intact and only faith in G-d will provide any stability. And that is really happening today. I have a site where I predict the future and over there two years ago I predicted that there were going to be revolutions all over the world for the next eight years, and that there are going to be wars between countries and revolutions and upheavals within the countries. And most of it is going to be because of the economic crisis, and inflation soaring and no food etcetera, and because there is no social cohesiveness anymore. And all of that you see in this little piece that was written 2000 years ago talking about the End of Days.

4

The 10 Commandments and the 10 Planets

The 10 Commandments and the 10 Planets

By Yaakov Kronenberg

An edited transcription of a lecture on the writings of Rabbi Avraham Ibn Ezra on astrology.
Ibn Ezra (1089 – 1164) was a prolific writer and he was one of the most distinguished Rabbi's in the Middle Ages; writing numerous books on Torah, Halacha, philosophy, astronomy, astrology, mathematics, poetry and linguistics. In his famous commentary on the Torah he reveals many astrology sources. This lecture delves into his comparison of the 10 Commandments to the 10 Firmaments in the sky bringing down his classic approach to Torah Astrology.

The 10 Commandments and the 10 Planets

By Yaakov Kronenberg

Tonight we are going to do a class on a piece that Rabbi Ibn Ezra wrote in his commentary to the bible where he compares the 10 Commandments to the 10 Firmaments in the sky (the 7 Planets; Moon, Mercury, Venus, Sun, Mars, Jupiter, Saturn and the 3 Firmaments above them). But first let me give you a brief introduction to the Ibn Ezra and tell you a little about who he was. The Ibn Ezra was one of the great commentators on the Bible; he wrote a classic commentary on the Bible that is published in almost all of the Jewish Bibles. In that commentary he actually talks a lot about astrology. Hopefully one day someone will translate and put all his astrological writings on the Bible into one book. I'm going to take one piece where he talks at length about astrology. It's a very interesting piece. So he was a Bible commentator, he was also a Hebrew grammar expert; he wrote many books on Hebrew grammar, he also wrote about 7 other books. I remember when I first started astrology, one of Ibn Ezra's books was translated into English, it was titled in Hebrew Reshit Chochma, which translates as 'the Beginning of Wisdom'; I read that book in 1972; it was translated by a professor from John Hopkins University, Mr. Levy. Since then there have been other translations of Reshit Chochma into English, including the translation by Meirah Epstein, which she translated for Project Hindsight. So that is about the only book in Jewish literature on astrology that has been translated into English, and I hope to correct that and to start translating many books on the Jewish approach to astrology. The Ibn Ezra's book is based on Ptolemy's teachings, and in the book he also quotes astrologers from the Indian tradition and astrologers from the Arab world; so he knew all the astrology of his time and he condensed it all into his book which is very compatible with the rest of the Western astrology tradition. If you look at Jewish history and Jewish writing you will see that there was no Jewish publishing on a large scale from the time of the redaction of the Talmud in about 400 or 500 CE until the Enlightenment period, which was about 200 years ago; so there was a large time period where Jews were writing books but none of them where being published beyond their immediate circles. So for about 1300 years there was nothing available, and the only Jewish astrology book was 'the beginning of wisdom', and that was basically a Western book. Many of the books translated in that period from the Torah world were not books that were Jewish at all in nature. Like the Rambam for example (Maimonides), the main translation that was made of his writings was the book,' A Guide for the perplexed' which is based on Aristotelian philosophy, and yet amongst the observant Jewish people only 1 in 10 000 would read that book. Most of the observant Jews do read the writings of the Rambam extensively, and many study them every day, but the books of the Rambam that they study are his commentaries on the Talmud, on the Mishnah, and other books about Jewish law, not the Guide for the perplexed! So you see that there was a disconnect with the Jewish tradition and the Western world over that period, and that was only rectified in the last 15 or 20 years, when Jewish literature began being translated and published on a large scale for the first time. That is because in the late 60's or early 70's a lot of young Jews started to return to their religion and their Jewish roots, and they became good scholars and they started translating and bringing back a lot of the lost works that were never really published. So in the last 20 years we are seeing books that are being published by writers that we have never really heard of; the Vilna Gaon's books are being translated and so too are the Maharal of Prague's books, Rabbis who were both great geniuses. Even the Talmud has been translated and explained properly for the first time with the ArtScroll translation in English which makes it really understandable for people who don't know either Hebrew or Aramaic well enough to learn in the original. And there have been many good translations and commentaries on the Bible that make everything accessible for people who don't have much background. That's what I would like to do too but in the field of Jewish astrology.

The Ibn Ezra went along with Western astrology only because he knew that it came from a divine source based on the tradition of the Torah. Recently I was reading an astrology book by a secular professor where he asks the question, 'how did astrology start'? And the answer he gives is that cave-men used to sit around with nothing to do, and they would drink around the camp fire and they would look up at the sky and ponder things, and that's how astrology began. Now it's very hard to believe this, and if it was true, then I can assure you that the Jewish Sages would not have accepted it as true, and yet they wrote extensively on astrology and Jewish law accepts astrology as true. So there must be a divine source to it, or they would never have touched it. You can find the Jewish approach to the history of astrology from many ancient Jewish sources, including the well-known Josephus in his 'history of the world', and also Yehudah HaLevi, who was a great Jewish philosopher of the Middle Ages, in his master work 'The Kuzari', both explain that astrology started with the first man, Adam Harishon (Adam) who was taught the secrets of astrology by an angel of God, and this tradition was passed down until it reached Avraham, who lived after the great flood and during the period of the Tower of Babel; and then from the times of the dispersion, after the Tower of Babel, when the people of the Mesopotamian basin got dispersed throughout the world, this tradition went with them throughout the world.

What I want to do now is read you a piece from my first teacher in astrology, Mr. Zoltar Mason; he was a practicing astrologer in New York City between from1950 till his retirement in 1993. He was the great astrologer of America during this period, and most of the top astrologers of today learned with him. I was his assistant for a while and I used to meet all the big astrologers at his office because they would come to see him to have their horoscopes done by him. He was the astrologers' astrologer back then. He was a tremendous genius, and unfortunately he did not publish much at all. When I was learning with him he was working on a book on astrology that he was going to publish. I went away to Israel and I came back after about five years hoping to buy his book and I asked him about his book; and he said that the world wasn't ready for it and people would misuse the knowledge. He said he ripped it up and he wasn't going to publish it and that was it. So there are very few of his writings around today, but there is one piece that I'd like to read tonight that he wrote for a book called 'The Coffee Table Book of Astrology'; his article was on spiritual astrology, and he makes an interesting remark which is worth reading. He wrote; 'The most important part of an astrologers study, is the spiritual side of the human nature. A person's goals are viewed in light of the relationship in his horoscope between the Sun Sign, the Moon Sign, and the Rising Sign at birth. Man's nature is three fold, the Sun represents his relationship to the Divine Spirit, the Moon is related to his own soul, and the Ascendant Sign is his physical body. So the question has to be asked: Must man believe that everything is pre-destined and that he cannot escape his fate? Does he have freewill? And is it possible for his nature to change? Hindu astrology cannot endorse freewill since it is based on the theory of reincarnation. The Hindus maintain that man must continue to reincarnate on Earth until he has paid for mistakes that he has made in previous lives. Westerns astrology does not accept this fatalistic attitude. It is true that in the book of Ecclesiastes (Kohelet), the author King Solomon said; 'To everything there is a season and there is a time for every purpose under the heaven; there is a time to be born and a time to die, etc..', which appears fatalistic, but already in the early Middle Ages the following teaching was found in an astrological treatise by the Ibn Ezra: "The beginning of wisdom is the fear of the Lord. That is the starting point for when a man refrains from following his eyes and his heart and the tendency to satiate his concupiscence; then knowledge comes to rest within him. Further more, the fear of the Lord protects him from the decrees of the heavenly bodies and from their sway as long as he lives". So the Ibn Ezra is telling you here how to get beyond the Planetary influences which other people in astrology really did not talk about much. When he says "the beginning of wisdom is fear of the Lord"; he means that first you have to believe that there is a God and that he is running the world; that is the starting point. Then he says; "When a man refrains from following his eyes and his heart from tendencies to satiate his desires", he is clearly not saying that man is compelled to do this, rather that he is inclined to do it and should and can refrain. That's one point that I think he wants to make here about fatalism, don't believe it. The Ibn Ezra says that there is a tendency, people have a struggle. Everybody is born with bad characteristics, nobody is born perfect, everyone is born with defects and everyone has some kind of problem, and that's the whole purpose of this world, to fix yourself. The Gaon of Vilna in his major book on ethics starts with the idea that the work of man in this world is to correct his character defects, that's why people come into the world. And everybody is drawn after certain things in this world. That is they have tendencies. And everybody has different tendencies. One person is lazy, so he has to overcome his laziness. Another person is rushing too fast to do things. He acts before he thinks. Other people are greedy; they have to work on their greed. Other people have too much pride, another person thinks too highly of himself; so there are all different types of character defects. You see it today in homosexuality. I don't want to get into politically incorrect opinions here, but homosexuality is a good example because today people want to say that it is genetic, in other words there is nothing they can do about it, so you just have to deal with it, accept it, live and let live. But if you come out and say that, then at what point does all this end? Can we say that pedophilia is also genetic? They can say they were born like that, that they can't restrain themselves from liking kids that are 3 years old. It's genetic, what do you want to do with me? How can you lock me up? I was born that way; there is nothing wrong with me, that's just the way I was programmed. And you can say that about anyone. A person who is a criminal or a thief can also claim that it's genetic!

That's what the Ibn Ezra is trying to say here, people are born with good inclinations and bad inclinations and everybody has to work on different character defects and problems that they are born with. Just like everyone's face is different, so is everyone's character different. So we have to respect that principle and understand it, and nobody is perfect and everybody is here to try to fix themselves, that's what the Ibn Ezra is saying; you have a choice and you can change your natural inclinations. And you will see this in his essay on the 10 Commandments; they are telling you what to do and what not to do. If they are telling you not to do something it means you have an inclination to do it. There is no reason to tell you not to do something if you don't have an inclination to do it and the capacity to over come it. So that's a major point here. The Bible is teaching you what things you must do and things you must not do, and through that, how to get above your instincts and above your physical desires which could lead you astray. When you go after the body you are under the planetary influences, like he says: 'when you go after your eyes and your heart and your tendencies, to fulfill your desires'. Today in the Western world there are a lot of people who go to psychiatrists or doctors or psychologists or life coaches or even astrologers, and basically they are going to them because they can't get their bodily desires fulfilled. They feel something is wrong with them, they can't make enough money, they can't get enough love, they can't succeed in life, and they fell like losers. People consider themselves losers because they can't get their physical desires, and so they go to people to help them and that's what the astrologers function is today, to help a person fulfill their physical desires. And the Ibn Ezra is telling you a big point here, which is the whole idea of Judaism; which is that actually the goal is not to go after you physical desires, but rather to restrain them, otherwise they will put you under the planetary influences. You will never be able to get beyond the Planets. And a person who is under the Planetary influences is going to have good times and they are going to have bad times; but mostly bad times because that's the way the world is made, that's the way of nature, nature can be very tough and ruthless. That is the big disconnect today between Judaism and the whole of Western psychology, which is that I need to get my pleasures now, get it while you can, life is short and get as much fun as you can, be merry and drink because soon we die. And that is their philosophy. Today we live in a tremendously hedonistic time in history where all the philosophies of the last few hundred years have been nullified and the only thing is; "eat and be merry because tomorrow we die". The Jewish approach is really the opposite. It says that this world is really just a testing ground, and if you get through this world and pass the test then you will get your reward in the next world. But there is no real reward in this world; here the pleasures are like saltwater the more you drink of them the thirstier you become. So the whole point is what the Ibn Ezra says: 'a man who refrains from following his eyes and his heart and his tendency to satiate his concupiscence, then knowledge comes to rest within him', but only then, once he can get beyond his eyes and his heart, can he come to have the knowledge rest in him. Furthermore, the fear of the Lord protects him from the decrees of the Heavenly Bodies and from their sway for as long as he lives. That is because he is not running after his body any more. If you are going after your body you are basically out of control. Like my Teacher said in the beginning: 'the Sun represents his relationship to the Divine Spirit, the Moon related to his soul and the Ascendant to his physical body'. So a person who goes after his physical body is separating himself from the higher forces and he comes under the Planetary influences. And the whole Jewish approach is to be able to get beyond the Planetary influences. And you do that by following the Commandments.

So the Ibn Ezra is going to talk about the 10 Commandments and their relationships to the 10 Firmaments in the sky. So let's start with the 10 Commandments, and the Ibn Ezra's commentary:
God spoke all these statements saying:
1) I am Hashem your God who has taken you out of the land of Egypt, from the house of slavery.

2) You shall not bow down to other gods in my presence. You shall not make yourself a carved image nor any likeness of that which is in the Heavens above or the Earth below or in the water beneath the earth, you shall not prostrate yourself to them nor worship them for I am Hashem your God, a jealous God who visits the sin of fathers upon children to the third and fourth generation from my enemies. But who shows kindness for thousands of generations to those who love me and observe my Commandments.
3) You shall not take the name of Hashem your God in vain for Hashem will not absolve anyone who will take His name in vain.
4) Remember the Sabbath day and sanctify it. Six days shall you work and accomplish all your work but the 7th day is the Sabbath to Hashem your God and you shall not do any work. You, your son, your daughter, your slave, your maidservant, your animal, a convert within your gates, for in six days Hashem made the heavens and the earth, the sea and all that is in them, and He rested on the 7th day and therefore He blessed the Sabbath day and sanctified it.
5) Honor your mother and father so that your days will be lengthened upon the land that Hashem your God gives you.
6) You shall not kill.
7) You shall not commit adultery.
8) You shall not steal.
9) You shall not bear false witness against your fellow.
10) You shall not covet your fellows' house; you shall not covet your fellows' wife, his manservant, his maidservant, his oxen, his donkey, or anything that belongs to your fellow.

So those are the 10 Commandments and the Ibn Ezra says that the 1st Commandment, "I am the Lord your God who took you out of Egypt", is connected to the 1st Firmament and we don't talk much about the 1st Firmament as it is incomprehensible to us, we do not have capacity to comprehend this level. This Firmament is connected to the Sefira of Keter which is beyond man's understanding and comprehension.

The 2nd Commandment, 'that there should not be for you another God, just me', is connected to the Daily Galgal , which is the 2nd Firmament, which makes a circle in one day, and it goes East to West and it causes all the other planets and stars, which normally go from West to East, to be pulled along by this higher firmament and to go from East to West. It causes all the other Spheres to go in the opposite direction of their natural movement and moves them from East to West every 24 hours. And he said connecting that to, "you shouldn't have any other Gods besides me" to teach you that it's the strength of God that is moving all of the Firmaments. You see the 2nd Firmament is moving everything and you have to know that that is the Prime mover, its moving all the other Firmaments to go along with it. "You shouldn't have any other Gods" is saying: I am the one doing the moving. He wants to compare the 2nd Commandment to the 2nd Firmament. Many people thought that this 2nd Firmament was actually God himself, the Creator himself, because it doesn't have a body, but it's teaching you that no there is only one God and it's not the force that moves the Planets to go in this direction. That's just a physical manifestation, it's not God himself. So that is the 2nd Commandment and Firmament.

The 3rd Commandment: "You should not take Gods name in vain" is in parallel with the 3rd Firmament, which includes all the Fixed stars, which are all the celestial objects (Zodiac) besides the 7 Planets. You have to know that when God surrounds all of these bodies with 48 constellations or star-groupings in the heavens (the naked eye can only see about a thousand stars and the Ancients had these 48 forms in the sky) and it appears as if the power of God is being seen. There are places in this 3rd Sphere were there are a lot of Stars, and there are places where there are no Stars. And man himself can't know the secret of why there are 48 forms in the sky visible to the naked eye and why they are arranged the way they are. And he goes on to say that a lot of people who don't have any knowledge or were lacking in knowledge on the subject thought that God did this for no reason. He created the stars the way he did just randomly, with no specific reason to why he created them in that form and in those shapes. And so that is like taking the name of God in vain. If you believe that the stars were created in a random way then it's like saying that you don't believe in a Creator, its like saying that God doesn't exist which is like taking Gods name in vain and that all of his works were random and there is no real reason for them.

The 4th Commandment is talking about Shabbat, guarding the Sabbath. And that is connected to the Planet Saturn, the Planets that is furthest from the Earth. The wise men with great experience said that each of the different Planets rules a different day of the week. Through the day of the week you see the power of that Planet. The Planet that rules that day is the Planet that rules the first hour of that day. The day has 24 hours and each hour of that day has a different Ruler. And it switches and goes on for 7 days so each day is going to have a different Ruler in the first hour of the day. The Planet that rules the first hour of the day is going to be the day Ruler and the Planet that rules the first hour of the night is going to be the night Ruler, and they are going to set the tone for that day or night. We are going to talk a lot about this and the source for this is in the Talmud in Masechet Shabbat, on page 156, and I have a whole series on the letter of Rabbi Avraham Bar Chiyah, which discusses planetary hours in detail. There are two Planets that are considered Malefic, Saturn and Mars, that cause damage. Whoever starts work or starts a journey when one of those two Planets is ruling, he is putting himself in danger. And similarly our Rabbis say that on those days; on the 4th night of the week and on the Friday night (the beginning of Shabbat), it's dangerous, because the destroying Angel has permission to damage. And you will never find in all the other days of the week that a bad Planet rules at the beginning of the day and also that a bad Planet is ruling at the beginning of the night. The only day where the two Malefic Planets are ruling, one at the beginning of the day and one at the beginning of the night is on Shabbat. And therefore the Rabbis made a rule that on the Sabbath a person doesn't work and spends his day praying, studying and eating with his family and friends; because it's a bad day for starting anything. So you see a connection between the planetary energies and the rule that God made that we must abstain from mundane activity on the 7th day. He wanted us to rest on that day so that people would remove themselves from the Malefic influence of that day. And you see all over the world that that is the day where the most people suffer. So Hashem made it a day of rest because of the bad mazal, and it always been for the Jews a day of happiness by refraining from all worldly affairs.

The 5th Commandment, which is to honour the parents, is connected to Jupiter. The attributes of Jupiter are peace, justice, mercy, to pay what you owe, and to honor who ever you are obligated to. So Jupiter is talking about righteous behavior and the main thing is to recognize the good that people do to you. It's what we call in Hebrew *hakarat hatov,* which is the recognition and appreciation of the good people did for you. So you have to honor your parents, if for no other reason than they created you and gave you life, and they supported you at least when you were young. So that is what he is saying here, you have to recognize the people that are good to you, and its only natural. So that is parallel to Jupiter.

The 6th Commandment is not to murder, which is against Mars, which rules blood letting. You have to realize that he is trying to show you the secrets of how to get beyond the Planets; he tells you Saturday is the worst day of the week to do anything. And most people, astrologers included, don't keep Shabbat. And here it is telling you how to get over it and above it, you give the day to God, either you are studying, or having a meal with the family or praying, and being happy and you are not supposed to even think about anything in a worldly way that whole day. So in that way you get above the planetary influences. It's the same thing with Jupiter, to honor the parents, people who don't get along with their parents suffer. And when you fight with your parents you never win. If you win you lose and if you lose you lose. So there is no point in fighting with them because you can't win. So he is telling you here that you have an essential obligation to give them honor because they created you and they gave you life and they supported you so it's only natural to give them honor and to respect anyone who helped you so much in life. So again, it's another way to get above the Planetary influences. There are endless problems between children and their parents, I know so many people whose biggest problem is suffering because of the parents and they can't get over it. And he is telling you a great wisdom here to get along with your parents and to honor them. So Honor your Parents because it will lengthen you life upon the land that Hashem your God gives you. So he is teaching you a life extension technique. If you want to have a long life, honor your parents. And not to murder to work on violent tendencies to overcome the planet Mars.

The 7th Commandment is not to commit adultery. Adultery is the Sphere of Venus, the action of Venus is to teach about all types of sexuality. So if you don't commit adultery you are already setting yourself up on the road to fixing yourself up from sexual troubles. So adultery is the worst because that's the one that gets most people into all sorts of troubles, and many people fall for this, and its very bad because you want to know parentage, you want to know who everybody's father and mother are. Although the heading is adultery it also includes many other types of sexual deviancy. It causes all sorts of real problems in life. So if you can get above that it will make your life better. So you see from these commandments that everyone has inclinations and animal desires and in some people they are more pronounced, but everyone has tendencies toward certain things. If people weren't able to overcome them then there wouldn't be a point in having a commandment and teaching people not to do it. People say they can't stop themselves, but they can, if they really try.

The 8th Commandment is not to steal, that is in the Firmament of the Sun, which teaches about force. The Sun takes away the power of any Planet that is connected to it, any planetary body in the area of the sun is hidden because the light of the sun hides the planet. In other words a Planet is Conjunct or in the same place in the sky as the Sun, the Sun sort of eclipses that Plane. In astrology it's called Combustion, there is a state in astrology where a Planet in Conjunction with the Sun is not considered good, because when the Sun is so close it burns up the other Planet. If you look up at the sky when Venus and the Sun are Conjunct, you won't see Venus, because the Suns rays wipe it out. And that is what he means by force, it's the Planet of force because it takes away the strength of that Planet. And that is like stealing. A person who steals takes away what the other person has. That is like the Sun being Conjunct to a Planet, it takes away all the strength of that Planet. The Rabbis say that when you steal, it is like you are killing that person. You are taking away who he is and his power.

The 9th one is that you should not bear false witness; there is a Commandment not to testify falsely about somebody. And that is like Mercury which is the power of speech. You have to learn to use your speech properly. Most people's biggest transgressions are in their speech because it's very easy to transgress in your speech. So what it's telling you is don't testify falsely, which is about Mercury, and you must watch your language.

And now the 10th Commandment is don't Covet. You shall not covet your fellows' house; you shall not covet your fellows' wife, his servant and his maid servant, his oxen and his donkey, or anything that belongs to your fellow. Against that is the Moon which is the lowest of all the Spheres, and it teaches about desire. The Moon is where the desire is and where you covet things that other people have because it is so close to the Earth.

Judaism is based on commandments and if you practice them and take them seriously and it almost becomes impossible for you to transgress them, then you are going to be above the planetary influences to a large degree. So you learn in the Torah that people have tendencies to do wrong, but you can rise above it, its not genetic, you have free will, it's only a tendency built into you and everybody is different and has different tendencies. But everyone can overcome these tendencies. As they say, different strokes for different folks, that is what has to be overcome.

So you see tonight that the Ibn Ezra is giving you an introduction that explains why the Torah was given to the Jews to help them overcome the planetary influences, and rise to high spiritual levels . And really the whole role of every *tzaddik* or righteous person is to be directed straight from God and to not be directed by an intermediary or the Planets. Its only because the sin of Adam HaRishon that there was a big separation between us and God; in other words God had to distance himself from us and He sent His energies down to us through the angels and the Planetary systems and the Kabalistic worlds, all different screens and filters until it gets down to us. And what we want is to get to that level where you can get you flow straight from God without any intermediaries, by correcting our tendencies and rising above our nature and individual planetary influences. And that is what the Ibn Ezra is talking about, that you can get beyond your eyes and your hearts and really connect with the Creator.

The Ascendant and our Character traits

The Ascendant and our Character traits

By Yaakov Kronenberg

A transcription of a series of lectures given in Jerusalem on some of the character traits which are found in the 12 Ascendants; by knowing your Ascendant you can focus on what part of your personality you can develop with natural success and what parts you need to watch out for and constantly reign-in until you master them and rise above your astrological inclinations. This series is based on the following texts:
1) An old Jewish ethical text called "Or HaTzadikim" – The Way of the Righteous, written about 450 years ago by an anonymous author.
2) "Sha'ar Kedushah" – the Gates of Holiness, written by Rabbi Chaim Vital, the great Kabbalist from Tsfat, in the middle to late 1500s.
3) "Archot Yosher" - Straight paths, written by a contemporary Rabbi of our time, Rabbi Chaim Konefsky.

The Ascendant and our Character traits

By Yaakov Kronenberg

Chapter 1 - Truthfulness

How to help a person overcome the planetary influences is a basic learning experience we all have to study. Throughout our talks, we have said that we can do this by doing the mitzvoth, the commandments. God gave the Jews 613 commandments. Some of them were negative commandments, not to do certain things, and some of them were positive commandments, to do certain things, and this is what we will be talking about; how to actively and consciously do something to rise above our mazal. It is our tradition, that by doing these commandments you are able to overcome the force of the Planets and rise above the planetary influences. No other nation was given a system like this. In a sense it was like a blue print to living. Everybody is, or should be looking for the blueprint to life, how to live life, what life is about. In Judaism this is spelled out in detail, and these are called the commandments. The Jews live by these commandments and by fulfilling them they were able to overcome the influence of the Planets. That is one thing that we have talked a lot about. Also, we have talked about Esoteric Jewish Astrology and through that you could learn how to guide yourself; to guide yourself to solve your problems by understanding the deep wisdom of the Horoscope of Adam HaRishon and his partner, Eve. Through this the person is able to understand the mystical Astrology.

One of my listeners asked a very deep question: Where do character traits fit in? We talk about doing the commandments and the mystical Astrology of Adam HaRishon but we never really talk about the person himself, and how the psychology of the person and the character traits fit into this system. If the person has bad character traits is that going to turn things around for him and make things difficult in life? Will that interfere with his Mazal? And if he has good character traits isn't that going be an advantage in life? That is a very good question. So I want to talk, in essence, about character traits, and what their place is in Jewish Astrology. This class is based on 3 different books. One is an old Jewish ethical text called "Or HaTzadikim" – The Way of the Righteous, written about 450 years ago. The second book is "Sha'ar Kedushah" by Rabbi Chaim Vital, the great Kabbalist from Tsfat. It is his famous book on Ethics, and was written in the middle to late 1500s, in Tsfat. The third book that I'm using is written by a contemporary Rabbi of our time, Rabbi Konefsky. Rabbi Chaim Konefsky wrote a book called "Archot Yosher- Straight paths" which is an Ethical book about the main Ethical problems in our time; because each generation has their own different problems that they have to deal with.

The Talmud was written over 2000 years ago, it is the Oral Tradition that was given over at Mount Sinai and was passed down. At a certain point in history it was written down out of fear that it would be lost. The Sages saw that they were heading for exile so they wrote it down so it would be saved.

In the Talmud there is one tractate called "Pirkei Avot – The Sayings of the Fathers" and there, all the ethical teachings are written down. And that book starts off "Moses received the Torah on Mount Sinai and then he passed it on to his disciple, Joshua and then Joshua passed it on to the Elders. And it goes through the whole tradition of how the ethical teachings were passed down. The commentators explain that the Talmud is unique and there is really nothing similar in Western literature; except for the ethical book of the Talmud, called The Sayings of the Fathers, which Western secular and religions thinkers have also produced. So the book Pirkei Avot (The Sayings of our Fathers) starts off with the idea that Moses got it on Mount Sinai from God and then it was passed down. With all the other nations, it was their philosophers, historians, ethicists and all different kinds of people who wrote their books on ethics. So Pirkei Avot started like that to show that the ethics of the Rabbis was not something that was made up but rather it was something that is coming down through tradition. It's not man made, which is the first point I want to make. The second point I want to make is to start off with an answer to the question "where do character traits fit in?" We have to look at Rabbi Chaim Vital because he asked basically the same question. He said something like this: "the character traits are not counted amongst the 613 mitzvoth because they are the basis of all mitzvoth and without them it is impossible to fulfil any of the mitzvoth." And because of that they didn't count them among the mitzvoth. In other words, what is Rabbi Chaim Vital trying to say here? He is trying to teach us that the middot/character traits, in a certain sense, are above the commandments. Because depending on the person's character, on his or her character traits, they will either be able to have an easier time to do the commandments or a harder time to do the commandments. In other words, the more the person perfects the character traits, the more he will be able to fulfil the commandments that God gave him to fulfil.

So for example, in Judaism there are positive and negative commandments. A positive commandment is to do something. A man has to wear Tefillin every morning or he has to go pray in the morning. So if a man is lazy, if he has the characteristic of laziness, he might not get up. He might be too lazy to get up early and go to the synagogue and he might not have the energy to put on the Tefillin. So because of that bad character trait of laziness, it impairs his ability to fulfil a certain positive mitzvah; and the same thing for a negative mitzvah, for example sexual commandments. A person has the negative commandment to not be with a woman who is menstrually impure. But if he is lustful by nature, he has the bad character trait of lasciviousness and lust and because of that he has the strong tendency to transgress these negative commandments. And the punishments for negative commandments, as a general rule, are much greater than the punishment for positive commandments, so if a person will have certain bad character traits, it could cause him to really mess up big time, at least in certain spheres of life. It could even cause him not to be able to fulfil the commandments. Rather the opposite will happen, because of his bad character traits he won't be able to fulfil the mitzvoth and sometimes he will transgress even the negative commandments because he or she can't overcome his or her essential nature. A married woman for example could be very lustful, very lascivious and she might end up with another man while she is married, which is adultery, which is very serious. There are all sorts of types of things. Say a person has a nature to steal. One of the major commandments is not to steal, so if they can't overcome that and they steal it is going to prevent them from fulfilling the commandment and they will become more under the influence of the Planets. In other words, the more the person can't do the commandments, the more he or she is going to be knocked down by not being able to fulfil the commandments.

Even though I said in the beginning that the commandments are one thing, and the character traits are another thing, there are certain places in the Talmud where they mention examples where character traits are also, to a degree, forbidden and they exaggerate the punishment for indulging them. A good example is somebody who has a character trait of inciting discord amongst people; he is transgressing the negative commandment of "don't be like Korach and his congregation". (They were wicked people who incited against Moses). So you see there it mentions a specific character trait, someone who incites to arguments. Another example it says "kedushim t'hiyu – you should be holy people" and the Rambam learns that that is a warning that you shouldn't use bad language. Also our tradition counts modesty as one of the positive commandments because it says all of your congregation should be holy and all of your camp should be holy.

We find a lot of places where they really exaggerate the punishments. A good example of that is someone who is excessively proud. It's like he denies the existence of God. They exaggerate it because they want to show you how the character traits are more important, to a degree, then the commandments. In other words, the trait of ga'eva (excessive pride), is a tremendously bad character trait it can cause you to transgress many commandments, negative and positive. And because of that they say it's like somebody doesn't believe in God. And not only that, she doesn't believe in God, she will be cut down like a tree of idol worship (a tree that is used to worship). And also, someone who gets angry, it is like he does idol worship. Once again, to be angry is a tremendously bad trait. A person who gets angry can't teach. If you have a teacher or even a parent who is angry, they can't teach their children. As soon as they teach them they start to yell at them and they just don't have the ability to teach. Just like we say a person who is excessively shy can't learn because he is afraid to ask questions. The opposite is a person who gets angry and he or she can't teach because they don't have the patience and the ability to teach. It says about someone who is angry, he does idol worship and all sorts of hells rule over them. And on jealousy it says his bones will become rotten. Jealousy, desire and honour they take a person out of the world. And on hatred it says that it is as if the person did idol worship and sexual immorality with a relative, and spilled blood. So they exaggerate the importance of the character traits, because a person who has bad traits, he or she will come to do all these things, from idol worship, to who knows what.

The fundamental thing really is to work on the character traits and I have made a table of many of the basic character traits and related their influence according to Signs of the 12 Ascendants. Here is the Table:

Character traits that need to be worked on by the Ascendant													
	Aries	Tauru	Gemi	Cance	Leo	Virgo	Libra	Scorp	Sagit	Capricc	Aquar	Pisces	
1 = Strong inclination 2 = Medium inclination 3 = Weak inclination													
Arrogance	1	3	3	2	1	3	3	1	1	2	1	3	Arrogance
Frivolity/Clowning	2	2	1	2	1	1	2	3	1	3	3	3	Frivolity/Clowning
Hatred	1	3	1	2	2	1	3	1	3	1	1	2	Hatred
Vein	2	1	2	2	1	2	1	2	1	1	3	3	Vein
Naivity	2	2	3	1	2	3	2	3	1	3	1	1	Naivity
Curiosity	1	3	1	2	2	1	2	1	1	3	2	1	Curiosity
Audacity	1	3	2	2	1	3	2	2	1	2	2	3	Audacity
Compassion	3	2	3	1	2	2	3	2	3	3	3	1	Compassion
Joy	1	2	1	2	1	2	1	3	1	3	3	1	Joy
Diligence	1	3	1	2	2	1	1	2	3	1	2	3	Diligence
Shyness	3	1	3	1	3	1	3	2	3	1	3	1	Shyness
Cruelty	1	2	3	2	1	3	3	1	2	2	2	3	Cruelty
Sensitive to others	3	2	3	1	3	1	1	3	3	2	2	1	Sensitive to others
Courageous	1	2	2	2	1	3	3	1	1	2	2	3	Courageous
Worry to much	3	1	3	2	3	1	3	3	3	1	1	2	Worry to much
Capacity for Remorse	3	2	3	1	2	1	2	2	3	2	2	1	Capacity for Remorse
Love	3	1	3	1	1	3	1	2	1	2	3	1	Love
Jealousy	1	1	3	1	1	3	1	1	3	2	3	1	Jealousy
Appeasement	3	1	2	2	3	1	1	3	3	2	3	3	Appeasement
Caution	3	1	3	2	2	1	2	3	3	1	1	2	Caution
Anger	1	3	3	2	1	3	3	1	1	2	3	3	Anger
Generous	2	2	2	3	1	2	2	3	1	2	2	1	Generous
Laziness	3	1	3	3	2	3	2	2	3	2	2	2	Laziness
Miserly	3	2	3	3	3	2	2	1	3	1	2	3	Miserly
Forgetfulness	2	3	3	3	3	2	2	2	2	3	3	2	Forgetfulness
God Fearing	2	2	2	2	1	3	2	2	1	2	1	1	God Fearing
Exaggerates	1	2	2	2	1	3	1	2	1	2	2	1	Exaggerates
Patient	3	1	3	2	2	2	3	1	3	1	3	2	Patient
Silence	2	2	3	1	3	3	3	1	3	1	3	1	Silence
Depression	3	2	3	2	3	2	2	2	3	1	1	2	Depression
Truthful	2	2	1	2	2	2	2	3	3	2	2	3	Truthful
Torah study discipline	1	2	1	2	2	2	2	1	2	2	2	2	Torah study discipline
Lying/Manipulation	1	2	2	2	2	3	2	1	3	2	2	1	Lying/Manipulation
Desires/Lust	1	1	3	1	2	2	1	1	1	1	3	1	Desires/Lust
Pride/Honor	1	3	2	2	1	3	2	1	1	3	2	3	Pride/Honor
Materiality	2	1	3	2	1	1	2	2	3	1	3	3	Materiality
Revengeful	2	2	3	2	1	2	2	1	3	1	3	3	Revengeful
Gossip	3	2	1	2	2	2	1	2	2	2	1	2	Gossip
Humility	3	2	2	2	3	1	2	2	3	2	2	1	Humility

A person who is religious and has good middot, he exalts God's name. If you see you have a person who is religious but has all bad middot, people are going to see him and say "Oy, woe to the father and the mother that gave birth to him, woe to the teachers that raised him!" and it is a desecration of God's name because the person can't fulfil the commandments as he has all these bad character traits and he is seen as a desecration of God's name. This, in Judaism, is possibly the most serious of all offenses. It says in the tractate of Yom HaKippurim, "Love the Lord your God that the name of Heaven will be loved because of you". In other words, you should teach Torah and learn Torah, be together with the wise men, practise your business dealings properly, engage with the people with good speech, conduct yourself with nice manners… And then what do the public say? "BLESSED is this guy's father; blessed is the teacher that taught him Torah! Woe to them that didn't learn Torah. See how pleasant are his ways, how sweet are his deeds!" And then the opposite is said about someone who has bad character traits. Someone who learns and reads Torah, serves the wise men but doesn't carry his business dealings in good faith and he doesn't speak pleasantly with people. What does the world say about him? "Woe to this guy that studied Torah, woe to his parents that taught him Torah, woe to his teacher that taught him Torah" or "See this guy who learns Torah, see how much he destroys through his actions, how despicable are his ways!" And about him it says that he disgraces Gods name, and so you see there again, the fundamental importance of the character traits.

The Gaon of Vilna says that the main way of serving God is fixing your character traits and that is why we came into the world. The hardest thing to do is to fix your character traits. There is a famous rabbi, Rabbi Yisrael Salant, and he taught that it is easier to learn all of the Talmud, which is thousands of pages of complicated learning, than it is to change one character trait. I know, I'm 60 years old today and I have been working for 40 years to change different character traits, or improve my character traits, and I can tell you it is harder than learning Talmud. For learning Talmud you just need a pretty good head, but to change a character trait you need to really want to do it and to work hard at it, because it is very hard work.

The Gaon of Vilna said that is why we came into the world. In other words, why do you want to change the character traits? Because all of the sins that someone does, the root of where they come from are these bad character traits. In other words, if a person had all good character traits he would be a much freer type of person. And the Gaon of Vilna says "if he didn't come in to change his character traits, why did he come into the world?" You see in Astrology, I learn how the planetary influences are, and from that in a certain way, I deduce what we came into the world to overcome. We came into the world to overcome our mazal. The mazal is who the person is, if you look at the Horoscope, you can see what their character is. And that is what they came to work on in the world. Everybody has different problems; there is nobody who came into the world who didn't come into the world with things they have to work on. If not, they have no reason to come into the world. This world is to fix. You came into this world to fix yourself. What do the Kabbalists explain about coming into the world to fix yourself? That it's so that you can earn yourself a reward. When you go into the next world and receive a much higher light you will say, if you didn't fix yourself, "I'm not worthy, why am I getting all this goodness? I don't deserve it." So God brought people into this world so that we work to fix ourselves, so that we will be worthy to get the reward in the next world and we won't feel embarrassed. And so that is what the Gaon of Vilna means that that is the main work of a person in this world.

There is one other idea, besides fixing your own middot; there is an idea to work to accept other people's bad middot. It says somebody who forgives the bad middot of somebody else; it is as if all his sins are forgotten. The Torah works on a principle of midda k'neged midda. How you behave that determines how other people react to you. And how you behave is how

 God relates to you. So if you have the ability to overcome how other people acted badly towards you, then in a sense you can also be given forgiveness for a lot of things wrong that you do. Just like you forgive them and accept that, then you are accepted also. It's a 2 way street. So you have to look at it from 2 sides. From correcting your middot and having the patience and understanding to know that other people are in the same boat as you. Even if they acted badly against you today, it wasn't because they really wanted to do it, it was because their bad middot overcame them and they would have liked to have acted better toward you. So there has to be an understanding also of the side of other people.

So in a sense the first part of the class we talked about the character traits. And so we see for a conclusion, that the character traits are coming from the side of the Planets. They are what a person is born with and what a person is engraved with in this world. There are traits he is born with and traits that are acquired with repetition. It is tremendously important not to get bad habits because eventually the bad habits become character traits. So you have to fight them so they don't become institutionalised in you. And then also the person's thoughts and philosophy could also influence his character traits. By growing and understanding the person can also modify his character traits. In Astrology that is the 1st, 5th and 9th House. The 1st House is a forward House that is what you are born with, the middot that a person comes into the world with. If you're a Capricorn you are going to have the Capricornian nature. The 5th House is the natural House of the Lion. The Lion is what becomes second nature to you. The first Sign is the Sign on the Ascendant. Let's say you have Aries on the Ascendant, which is the ideal Ascendent of Adam HaRishon; so you are going to be born with the Arian qualities. And if you're a woman you will be born with the Libran qualities. But then you will also acquire through habit other things and they are connected to Ariyeh, which is the Lion, they become eventually second nature and they rule over you. And then you have the 9th House too. The three Fire Houses which were each connected to each other by a good Aspect which is the mental plane (philosophy, higher religion...) and through that you can also have the ability to alter or change the character traits.

So let us take one character trait and show a little bit about what Judaism has to say about it and how it can affect your life to a very high degree; this is the trait of "truthfulness". To speak the truth, it is something simple; it is something you don't see. It is interesting, in the Western world people go to school, to universities… But in school and university they don't really talk to you about proper behaviour. They don't talk about character traits or anything like that. It's not a part of the curriculum because it is multi-pluristic or something so it is not part of the curriculum. They just teach you the sciences and the courses you need to learn to get a high school degree. And then you go to college to get a better job. But they just teach you a career. But it is not to teach you the proper way to live. That is never really taught. So you don't have ideas like this, like the idea of a character trait, like truthfulness. What is so special about truthfulness? Well first of all, a person that speaks the truth, it is so important that it is said that God's signature is truth. Because the truth is so important, in fact it is said that God created all the character traits except for lying. In other words, every bad character trait can sometimes have a positive usage. For example, anger. There is a proper time to be angry, like when someone desecrates the Torah. You have to be angry at them. You have to defend the Torah; you have to use your anger. Like in the story of Pinchas, he was angry for

God and he killed the Midianite woman and the man because they were desecrating holy places. So for that he was rewarded with priesthood and from that you can see that there is a proper time to be angry. There is a famous story about a guy that goes to a rabbi, a Chassidic master, and asks how can atheism ever be considered a good character trait? And the rabbi says "That's an easy question! When someone comes and asks you for charity, don't tell them God will help you. Make believe there is no God and give them money." So you see character traits are not exclusively good or bad. They are relative. And it is how you use them. So even the worst character traits, no matter how bad they are, there is a positive connection for it. There is a time where it has its proper place. But lies, no. God didn't create lies. The only reason people lie is because people did things wrong and they have to cover their tracks by lying. So if people did everything right, in essence, there would be no reason for them to lie. So lying wasn't created. It only came about because people perverted their ways and they stopped speaking the truth. Why did they stop speaking the truth? Because they started doing improper behaviour and then they had to cover up and lie. So in truth there shouldn't have been lying. And even more so, someone who speaks the truth is never going to get in trouble. There is a very famous story in the midrashim, in Jewish literature, of a man who was very controlled by his desires. He was from the village of Eitanim and when he was young he was ruled by his passions and desires and had many bad character traits. He went off the path but then one day he decided to repent. The spirit of God entered into him and he decided to repent. So he went to Rabbi Shimon ben Shetach, one of the great Rabbis of the Talmud. He cried before him and told him all the things he had done wrong and asked that he should heal him. Rabbi Shimon said "don't worry that is an easy one, we will find the right medicine to heal you of everything. But I want one thing from you. Promise me you will never lie". The man thought "all he is asking from me is that I never lie. What's the big deal?" so he said "yeah yeah I won't lie." And Rabbi Shimon made him take an oath that he would never lie. So he took an oath that he would never lie. But a couple of weeks later his desires overcame him. He was in someone's bathhouse and then he got into their house somehow and he saw all these precious ornaments inside the house and he packed them up and he took them. On his way out he started to think "what is going to happen if the police see me and ask me if I took these things? I'm going to have to lie! And if I lie I am going to transgress the oath of Rabbi Shimon ben Shetach! What a wise man Rabbi Shimon ben Shetach is! If a person takes on himself never to lie, he is never going to come to any transgression because he won't be able to cover it up." There was a story of Richard Nixon, they did a burglary and the actual burglary wasn't so bad but it was the cover up that killed him. It's what got him impeached; they did this big cover up. So whenever you do something wrong it leads to a cover up which leads to more problems and bigger headaches and eventually it can bring a person to his downfall. But if a person always speaks the truth then he will never get in trouble because he is always doing what he should be doing.

I want to talk about something in the Talmud. There was a city called Kushta (it means truth in Aramaic) and a rabbi went there once, he wandered in there. It was a place where no one told lies. And in that city nobody died before their proper age. Everybody lived to their proper age. In the Torah it says that everybody is born with a certain number of years given to them. If they did good they can extend it. If they do bad it can be shortened. But in Kushta, since everybody spoke the truth, nobody had their life shortened. In the Western world, it's a big thing, alternative medicine; we talk a lot about life extension principles, ways to extend one's life. So here is a classic example of something that we talked about in an earlier class like if you honour your parents it is going to extend your life. So here is another example of something the rabbis say will extend your life. If a person speaks only the truth it is going to extend their life. You can understand it in a simple rational way that if a person has all sorts of lies and cover ups, it messes up his mind and he becomes stressed. Or if he lies it could lead him to do all sorts of sins which could damage his body. The rabbis said that on a spiritual level, for longevity, it is a tremendous advantage to be truthful. In any case this rabbi chanced upon this town of Kushta and he decided to stay. He married a woman from the town and he learnt not to lie. They also had 2 sons. One day his wife was taking a shower and washing her hair and someone knocked on the door. He answered and said "who is it?" and she answered "the neighbour, I want to talk with your wife." He was embarrassed to tell the neighbour that his wife was taking a shower, shampooing or whatever, so he said "she is not here in the house". So the next day his two sons died. Everyone in the town came and asked "how did your sons die so young? Did you tell a lie?" so he said "well I was embarrassed to say my wife was in the shower so I said she had gone out". And so the people immediately kicked him out of the town. He was not suitable to live in the town called "Truth".

You would think that there are certain situations when the rabbis tell you that you are allowed to tell a fib or a lie. For example, to keep the peace or not to embarrass, like by saying his wife was in the shower. But even in those cases where it is permitted to lie, it's not really permitted to lie but you have to say something which can be understood in 2 ways. Like for example, he could have said "she can't come to the door right now" which was true but wasn't embarrassing her and saying she was in the shower. A classic example was Yaakov. When Esav came he said "don't worry I'll meet you at the mountain in some future time". Esav understood it would be in this lifetime. But there was a tradition that Yaakov would meet Esav by this mountain in the world to come. So Esav could understand it in one way and Yaakov could explain it in another way. So even to lie to keep the peace or save your life (in Yaakov's case he wanted to escape from Esav who was a bloodthirsty type of man) you can't mamash tell a lie, rather you have to say something that can be interpreted in two ways so it's not really an untruth. Our rabbis were very cautious about getting accustomed to lying. There is another story about a man and his wife who was very contrary, very difficult. She would ask him, for example, what he wanted for lunch and on the day he said he wanted lentils she would make him beans. And when he said beans she would make him lentils. So the poor man never got to eat what he wanted. So one day his son said to him "Father I have a great idea for you! Next time Mother asks you what do you want to eat, so if you want to have lentils say you want to have beans and then she will cook you lentils which is what you really want to eat!" And he said "Oh that is an interesting idea but I could never do that because then I would accustom myself to not telling the truth" and all the commentators asked how could this be that this big rabbi never thought of that himself? It never went into his mind to say the opposite? To tell his wife, when she asked him what he wants, to say what he doesn't really want so then she will make him what he wants? That is simple, why did he have to wait 20 years for his son to grow up and come up with it and tell his father? But they explained that the man was so embedded in the characteristic of truth that it never even entered his mind to do such a thing and lie in that way.

Of course there is one mitzvah that you have to work on your children, if you want your children to have good mazal, is to teach them to be truthful. If you teach them to be truthful then they will be good in everything. Once they can't lie, you don't have to worry what they are going to do. They aren't going to run around on the internet or go off into all sorts of weird directions because they are going to have to lie.

There's a story about a famous rabbi, called the Shla (Shtei Luchot HaBrit – the Two Tablets of the Covenant). There was a Sephardi rabbi who would come to him and he said that for all the money in the world, he would not tell an untruth because when he was younger his father used to tell his children if they did something wrong "If you admit that you did something wrong, I'll forgive you and I'll even give you a reward, if you really did it and you confess. But if you say you didn't do it, and I found out you did then you will get a heavy punishment." And he trained them in that way, so this man came to never tell an untruth when he was older. Once you always speak the truth, when that becomes engrained in you, then your character is going to take on a whole different aspect to itself than you would have thought. It can make a major change in who the person is just by being truthful. Because really you can't do anything wrong because anything you do wrong you are going to have lie to cover it up. So the minute you decide to only speak the truth, than you're not going to do anything that is really bad. So I encourage all parents to teach their children to be truthful and it will save the child a lot of difficult problems in the course of his lifetime.

It is a very important thing this idea of truthfulness and you will see in Astrology I talk about which Signs have more of an inclination. I would say probably Water Signs have more of an inclination especially when it comes to emotional things because they are over emotional and it messes them up. Like if you stick a rod in the water, it looks like it is bent; they can bend the truth a little. Air Signs have a tendency to duality. Really everybody has a tendency to lie, some Signs more, some Signs less. But it's a general thing that everybody has an inclination but I would say the Air and the Water more. But everybody has an inclination because of their different types… Maybe each Sign will have a different reason why they lie but I think in all of the Signs there will be a sense of lying. So if you decide to tell the truth that already is going to be a major change in the person. So if you want to overcome the planetary influences, the first character trait that I would work on is the trait of truthfulness. And for that you don't really need to go to a psychologist, it's not something like an addiction or a deep seated psychological problem or trauma. It's something that the root of it is very simple. The person messes up so he needs to lie. So as long as you speak the truth it can work both ways, if you act good then you're going to automatically speak the truth because there is no need to lie. On the other hand, if you train yourself to speak the truth you can overcome all your bad character traits because you won't have them anymore because you have to be truthful. So I think that is the starting point for all of the character traits. That in a sense is the most important one.

It says in the Torah, “give truth toYaakov”, Yaakov the main father, who all the 12 holy children came from. Remember the Kabbalists teach that Avraham had two sons, a good son and a bad son, because he had to get out the bad side of mercy so he had Yishmael and the good son Yitzchak. And Yitzchak had two children, Esav and Yaakov and Esav was the bad side of judgment. But Yaakov, all his children were good. The twelve tribes came out of him. And you can say because it says “give truth toYaakov” that Yaakov was the truth speaker and he engrained in his children the idea of speaking the truth. And if you speak truthfully, in a way you are home free.

I think I covered a lot of material on two themes. First of all we talked about the middot, the character traits and the utmost importance that they hold in deciphering a Horoscope. And in the future, maybe we can talk about different ways to find and correct different character traits which is a big study and would take a lot more classes than just this one class. But on the second part of the lecture I talked about one main character trait because I considered it the main character trait, so if you have one character trait to work on, it should be this one because it can correct everything, work towards the Truth in everything you do in your life.

Chapter 2 - Fear and Worry

In this series of classes on character traits, we are going to be talking about all sorts of character traits in people, especially the ones that are most prevalent in our generation. I want to focus on things that are connected with our times. As you know, in each generation there are different problems and different challenges so I want to talk about the character traits that are so influenced by our society.

Last week I spoke about what I considered to be the main character trait, that if a person has that then they will never come to misfortune in life. And that character trait is the aspect of truthfulness. We live in a society of lies, based on lies. There is so much politics and what do we say about politics? Politics is the world of lying “olam HaSheker”. And why is it the world of Sheker of lying; because today, at least in the Western world, all of society is based on democracy. In order to win an election you have to convince as many people as you can that you want what they want. And to do that you have to be a great liar. So everybody is lying through their teeth and that permeates into the rest of society. So pretty soon everybody is lying left and right. But Truth is one of the big pillars of the world, the world is based on truth and the Torah is truth and that is what keeps the world functioning, that there is an element of truth in the world, as a basis for the world to be established. They say in the Torah that “the lies have no feet”. If you look at the letters of the word “sheker”, the first letter, the shin, has a solid foundation but then the kuf and the resh, they are letters that fall over, they don’t really have legs. So the big lie eventually brings everything down with it.

We talked about it, that if a person is truthful, if a person is guarding truthfulness then he can’t come to sin. Once he starts to sin then he is going to have to lie to cover up. And sometimes the cover up is worse than the sin. We gave an example of that last week, when the father exhorted his children that if they did something wrong but they were honest and told him about it, then instead of punishing them he would give them a reward. But if he catches them lying to cover up, then it would be double the punishment. He did that in order to get the concept of truthfulness into them, so that they would never come to sinning. So I want to talk about that for another couple of minutes before we go onto a new character trait which is called worrying.

On the element of truth: Today, in the world, there is this idea that you can make what is false true. We see that in the world of homosexuality, today the whole movement to legalise homosexuality. Why do they want to do it? First I should say, the Gemara, the Talmud and the midrashim, they explain why Sodom and Gemara were destroyed. It says that they were destroyed because they legalised homosexuality. It's interesting, they didn't say they destroyed Sodom and Gemara because homosexuality was so prevalent there; rather they destroyed it because it got institutionalised. In other words, the people legitimised it. They made it from being a bad character trait to a good character trait. And once you legitimise something, it becomes so engrained in the system that you can longer escape or get out from it because it is ok to do. So we see that it became institutionalised in America, or now that it is on its way to becoming institutionalised, that it has reached a new level of getting away from the element of truth. There are a lot of people in the world who can't change their bad behaviour. So what do they do? They make it into a good behaviour. They say "look I'm not a clean person, but there's a good side to not being clean" or "I get angry but…" or "I like to steal but I only steal from rich people, and I'm going to give some of the money to the poor". So everybody legitimises and once the government legitimises it, it's very hard to reverse it. And once it becomes institutionalised, the truth is lost. When the truth is lost then society is in free fall. I have columns I write in different newspapers where I give predictions and one of the predictions I've been making… well, I write a lot about economics and if you look at America, it is in a much better shape, economically, compared to the rest of the world. America has lots of big problems, but the rest of the Western World is much world. America still has a positive demographic rate because of the immigration. They tend to get better immigrants, highly educated and all that. Especially from Asia, the leading source of emigration to America is from Asia, more than from the Hispanics. And they tend to be a highly educated class with a strong work ethic. If you look at Europe, however, they tend to get the dregs. Mostly from Arab countries with no education, and a lot of children with a different cultural bent. And there is no natural growth there except from the immigrants and the people don't like it there in the Western countries. Japan doesn't allow immigration, they have a less than zero reproduction rate. America has a tremendous amount of land and they just discovered a massive amount of oil. In fact they could be the biggest oil producers in the next 40 years. They have tremendous farm land and they are just a very rich country. But even with all that I tend to be more negative towards America because America is destroying itself from within. "The careless ease of the wicked will lead to their destruction" and that is America today. The people there, with the tremendous wealth and stuff they just went a little bit crazy, or more than a little bit crazy, because of the legitimisation of homosexuality, where we see that Sodom is going to be destroyed because of the institutionalisation of it. Once again, we see that is worse than the sin. The sin, ok it's another sin, there are plenty of sins there are 613 negative commandments to transgress. There are all sorts of things that you are forbidden to do. You can talk about how to overcome it. But you can't make everything just into genetics, "I was born that way". What's the difference? You can be born to be a homosexual or born to be a crook… Eventually people are going to say "what do you want from me? I got the genes of a crook!" or "I've got the genes of an angry person, how can I change who I am? How I can stop being angry? Let me rejoice in my character traits!" or "I like women, lots of women, what can I do? It's genetic!" and so eventually it will come to someone saying "I like to kill, it's in my genes. I can't change myself". So eventually things will go that way. People are saying that the next generation is going to be the age of genetics. They are going to try change diseases through influencing the genes and they are going to get into research on the character traits in genes. It's a big field. If someone wants to get into a growing field, I'd highly recommend genetics.

Anyway that is enough on truthfulness. Really, sometimes the truthfulness is more important than the sin itself. We see that from what it is said about Sodom, that the institutionalisation of homosexuality is the downfall of Sodom. And probably could be the downfall of America too, because they were the ones that started it. The first person to do something, his punishment is big. The second person to do it, already it's no big deal. We see with Naomi, in the story of Ruth. Ruth and Ofra, they were two people from a foreign nation that the sons of Naomi married. They both died young. The oldest one, who married Ofra, no one remembers him. They both committed a big sin by marrying someone outside of the tribe but the other son who married Ruth, in the end, they did libum which is leverite marriage, which she did with Boaz and eventually from will come the messiah. So the son of Naomi, who married a goya, even though he married a non-Jewish woman, eventually because of this leverite marriage, which according to the Kabbalah, is connected with reincarnation (it tends to be a reincarnation of the soul of the original husband) and eventually from him came the Moshiach. He was in the list of the descendants of the messiah. So they talk about that a lot. Why was it different? Why was it that the older boy got lost but the second one from him descended the Messiah? They explained that the older son, he married out first and since he did it first, he led the way so he got a bigger punishment. But then the second kid comes along, and it's already institutionalised, "my big brother did it and other people are doing it so why not me?" In other words, he thinks its ok. So it's the same idea. He thought already its ok and he didn't know it was wrong so his punishment wasn't as bad. So he wasn't really punished because it was "permitted".

IN any case, now I want to talk about a new character trait and we will get into the character traits plus we want to see which Signs tend to be connected with which character traits. You have to know that there are some character traits in a generation which everybody has them. You can say that they are the traits of a generation. But even so, there are some particular Signs that have it more than others. Tonight we are going to talk about worrying, fear and worrying. That is one of the big problems today that people just worry. It's the generation of anxiety, stress and worry. We will talk a little about that tonight and causes of worrying and stress. Today there is a big health movement because people realise today that one of the big problems in health is that the deterioration of health comes from worrying and fear. So in all the natural health programs of today one of the components in the cure is to deal with the stress and the worrying. So because of that I want to talk a little about the roots of this problem, this character trait which can be very bad.

I'd say that it is going to be more in our generation, than in other generations. Let me give you an example. Let's say a person has the ruler of the 5th House (which is the House of love and romance) in the 6th House (which is the House of ill health) it says that that person could catch a sexually transmitted disease. Why, because love brings them illness; the ruler of 5 in 6. Years ago I used to look at that, I always used to check that for clients, to forewarn them that they have to be really careful. But today it is so prevalent, sexual diseases, that it is not going to come from just one Sign, it's also going to come from all sorts of other causes. I was reading that today 30% of people who are sexually active have sexually transmitted diseases. So its everywhere now. There are people who have a tendency towards it but even so it became institutionalised. It became part of the world that you're going to have to deal with sexually transmitted diseases at one point or another in your life (if you are sexually active, or if you have sex outside of marriage or more than one partner, things like that...). I'm lucky I deal with the religious world so I don't see too much of that but I get clients from all sorts of backgrounds and we deal with things like that.

So we see that sometimes there are specific things that symbolise it, other times there are generational effects. And that's why I want to talk about worry tonight. It has a generational effect. It's part of our fabric today that people worry. We are going to talk about the real two reasons for it but before that I want to give you the more superficial reason before we get into the deeper mind-sets of what leads to worry. One thing is that we see all the different possibilities. There is a famous Zohar, Rabbi Shimon says: "if a person could see all the destroyers in the room, they would die from fear". In other words, there is a state between good and evil. Even in the body, there are all sorts of bacteria, viruses growing in it and something goes a little bit off and all that disease is released. People turn on the radio, TV or read the newspaper and they see that a new disease was found here, that it's antibiotic resistant... Tuberculosis is making a comeback; Iran is ready to shoot nuclear weapons at Israel and America and so on and so forth ad infinitum. So people get up and finish reading the newspaper, and they are already stressed out people. They see all the destroyers in the air. On one level, it's the media that is playing on the fears of people that sells news. You don't really read very much good news in the newspaper. I try not to read the newspaper. In fact I haven't listened to radio or television for 30 years. I try as little as possible to look at the newspaper. In fact, the only newspaper I read is a financial paper because it's just business news and I don't have to read all the nonsense that is in the paper. I just have enough to run my business, my investing and to make predictions on the economics.

Anyway let us talk about worry; I think worry is an important topic. Later we will come back and connect it to all the different Signs, as we go along.

Certain types of people always worry. They're afraid of all different types of misfortunes. They are worried about bad health, war, evil people and all the days of their lives they are fearful and shaking and worrying that this will happen or that will happen. There are even people who worry so much that they are afraid to travel form one place to another. There are people who don't want to go on busses, people who don't want to go in cars, and people who don't want to move from fear! And there are other people who are even afraid to leave their house, which is very bad behaviour. There is a story brought down from the Gemara about a student who used to walk in the back of his teacher Rabbi Yishmeal because of fear. So Rabbi Yishmeal said to him "the sinners were afraid in Zion". In other words, if a person sins, it causes fear. This is a big idea, a breakthrough and if people could understand it that what really leads to fear is sin. And the possibility of getting punished for it leads a person to become fearful. The Kabbalists say that when a person sins they create all this negative energy. And then what happens in the repentance process? There are 2 ways a person can fix he can repent or he can suffer. Sometimes he needs a little bit of both to get rid of things. So when a person sins they create all this negative energy and this energy needs to get burned off. The way it gets burned off is through suffering. And so a person who sins he feels as if the suffering is coming to him and that causes him to worry. In the world today it's a little different; to get free of their worry they sin. They sin in order to get free of their worry. Like masturbation, that's a big thing. It became legitimised by, as far as I know; Dr Sigmund Freud was one of the first, as a tension relieving device. It became a medical way to reduce tension and stress. In the end, it's a very severe thing because you are doing something wrong. You are releasing sperm which has a certain life of its own and now it's not going to be fertilised and grow into a baby. Now it's going to go out into the sitra achra, the forces of evil, and they are going to take it over and use it for their own twisted purposes. And so in the long run it is going to cause tremendous sorrow to the person. But today, in the Western world, sin is a stress reliever. It's a way around worrying and it is antithical to the Torah approach to life which is that if you really want to be worry free you have to lead a clean, wholesome life. You need to know what's right and what's wrong and know to do what's right and not to do what's wrong. So that is one of the secrets of worrying, that sin leads to worry. And today people don't believe in sin, there is no such thing as good and evil, everything is relative. So the people are stuck, they don't know what to do. Is this wrong? Is this right? There is no morality whatsoever anymore, it's all relativistic. So it becomes very hard for a person to escape their predicament and because of that the worries today are so much. People can't shake off the worrying.

Let us go forward now and talk a little bit more. There was a contradiction in the Gemara. It said in another place "Blessed be those who are always fearful". What's good about being fearful? The commentators explain when it's good to be fearful. It's when you are worried about forgetting the Torah. So the person then is always reviewing his learning and that is a positive form of worrying. They want to be over right. But then today, you get the opposite. The world is so twisted; you get people who have repetition diseases. Like you get religious people who have to wash their hands two hundred times a day because they are afraid they didn't do it properly. That's not what they were talking about in the Gemara. But there it is also a sickness that needs to be dealt with.

In any case, the Zohar also says that someone who has sin is always afraid. They learn it from the pasuk "You are afraid night and day". And it teaches there in the Zohar, that before a man sins other man respect him and are fearful of him and all creatures are worried by him. But after the person sins everything is turned around. He becomes fearful of other men and creatures worry him. When a person sins, according to the holy Zohar, it totally changes his mind frame. He goes from being someone above other men to someone who is very lowly. He becomes lower than the animals; he becomes worried by the animals. Instead of ruling over the animals and forces of nature he is ruled by them. He is controlled by them, in their pockets so to speak. Rabbi Chanina, the assistant to the High Priest, he taught in Pirkei Avot "if words of Torah don't go up in his heart, thoughts of hunger, thoughts of destruction, thoughts of foolishness, thoughts of sin all enter in to the person". The worries destroy the body and cause all sorts of illnesses. Like it says in the Gemara in Sanhedria, "Don't allow worry to go up in your heart because it gets stronger and stronger and then it kills". So even 2000 years the Gemara was talking about that, the idea that worry is bad for your health. We spoke about that in Astrology; we had a number of classes on cause and effect in the Chart of Adam HaRishon. Let us talk about that, about the Signs, before we go back and deal with the problem of the character trait of worrying.

The Signs that are most prevalent to worrying are the mental Signs. Like the 2 Signs that are connected with Mercury, Gemini and Virgo and the 2 Signs connected with Jupiter, Pisces and Sagittarius. And those Signs rule 4 Houses in the Horoscope. The Jupitarian Signs rule the 9th and the 12th Houses and the Mercurial Signs rule the 3rd and the 6th Houses. The 3rd and the 9th Houses are connected with the thoughts. Higher education, religion, philosophy, mental outlook… Now say if you start at the 9th House and go forward 10 Signs, it leads you to the House of ill health. So the mystical Jewish Astrologers learnt there that the cause of illness is impure thoughts, from bad thinking, from worrying and a not right approach to life and sinning. Also if you go from the 3rd House and forward 10 Houses, the 3rd House is also a House of knowledge and understanding, you will reach the 12th House, the House of imprisonment, and the House of suffering and long term illnesses. So you see that the thoughts lead to the illnesses. And also the illnesses they intensify things. Just like the cause makes an effect, the effect can turn around and become the cause. So if a person becomes sick it could make them worry more and ruin his outlook on life even more. So these are the 4 main Signs, the 4 main worriers of the Zodiac, especially the Virgo. The Virgo is the chief of all worriers. It's an Earth Sign and... I'll tell you the truth, what really leads to worry; we haven't quite gotten to it yet. One we just talked about it, we'll talk about it a little bit more and that is the idea that sin causes the person to worry. And the second thing is that it's a lack of faith, if a person has a lack of faith that causes him to worry. When a person has lack of faith… That's the Virgo. The Virgo is born with a certain type of lack of faith that they have in them. If you look at the Chart of a Virgo, you put Virgo on the Ascendant and then you have Gemini on the 10th House cusp. So the person sees that he and his destiny are connected. He makes himself. In other words, the Virgo thinks that everything is in his hands and he has a hard time accepting that there is a God that is running the world and not him. I know I have a lot of Virgo and I'm always thinking that I'm running the world but that is just not true. Especially when you get older you realise just how limited your abilities are if the world depended on me to run it then the world would be in bad shape. But in any case, the Virgo tends to see everything as in their hands. And because of that they don't have the Emuna the faith The Virgo you always have to encourage them to pray. They are great learners but they have a difficulty praying because they have a hard time accepting something above themselves. And that is the Virgo type of person; they see everything as in their hands. Pisces or Sagittarius which are Jupitarian Signs, when in the 10th House, they also think everything depends on them. Pisces by nature also like to suffer. Anyway Pisces and Virgo they tend to be the chief of all these people that suffer from worrying. But you will also find that Gemini and Sagittarius also worry. Fear is an important Element in their Charts. But like I said before, even though those are the 4 main places you will find the worry, because its such a generational effect today that people are so stressed out, because they just have to turn on the TV and they are connected with the whole world, they know what is going on everywhere and it can make them a stressed out. There are lots of reasons to worry today, I guess.

I remember I used to live on a street one street away that 7 or 8 years there were bombings all the time. A friend of mine comes to visit from America and asks "do you know you live on one of the most dangerous streets in the world?" I guess I didn't know that. I mean, I knew it but I didn't know it until he told me that it is difficult to live in an area where every day they are bombing you. You read the newspaper and you see what is going on and it's a scary place you live in. But the real cause of worry, like I said before, is two things. One is that sin causes worry and the other is lack of faith. Those are the roots of fear and worry in a person and they drive a person to be lower than animals when really he should be the crown of creation.

But let us go on... One other thing I just wanted to say: Because of this it's so prevalent today that all the Signs are going to have an element of worry in them. But each Sign, for the most part, is going to worry about what they really need. Like the Signs that will worry the least will be the Fire Signs, especially Aries. Aries, in a way, they have a lot of faith and belief. They rule 1 and 8. Life and death are in the hands of God. It's not us who determine how long we live. So they do what they know they have to do and they don't worry about the consequences. But everybody worries about what is important to them. A Taurus, for example, will worry about financial security. Maybe he won't worry about other things but financial security is so important to him that he will worry about that. Or another example, a Libra woman will always worry about her relationships, her marriage because that is so important to her. So the worries will focus on specific things. The Virgos and the Geminis however will tend to have general worries. Like a person who thinks all their problems come from their nose, their nose is not right. So they get a nose job but then after a couple of months they realise it wasn't their nose that caused the problems, it was their double chin. So they get a chin operation. But then after a couple of months again, they see it wasn't their chin that was causing the problems but something else, maybe it was their bad personality. So they go off to the psychologist and then to this and then to that and so it goes on... They have general anxiety and it just tends to move from one place to the other. It latches on to a place and that place is different for everyone. In our generation you have to see where each person's worries are, where they are coming from. So even though all the Signs will have it some more, some less, some will be general anxiety that will be to many areas of life and other Signs, where it is less prevalent (for example the Fire Signs or the Air Signs) the worries will be more focused in a limited area of a life.

All of these are because of a lack of faith. If a man believed always in Hashem, if he doesn't lift even his pinkie finger unless it was announced first in the Upper Worlds, then what is there to worry about? If he knows everything is coming from God then he has no reason to worry. It's all holy, it's all for his benefit. God only does things for a person's benefit. If he is to suffer, there is a reason for his suffering. So, on the one hand, if everything comes from God then why should you worry? And if it is decreed by God then no wisdom or understanding can go against His will. And if there is no decree then why worry? And if there is nothing decreed against the person also he shouldn't worry. So there is really basically no reason to worry. Every minute we are in God's hands, in times of war, in times of peace and He has many ways. There is only fear from God. Fear that we will transgress one of His commandments, or not fulfil one of His commandments, or go against one of His negative commandments. Fear that he will do something that is forbidden or fear that he will not fulfil something he is obligated to fulfil. That's the only thing really that he should fear in this world, is to be righteous, because that is divine protection. We have been talking about it in our books, how the 10 commandments were given to overcome the Planetary influences.

If you want to overcome fear, worry, stress and all these things, well then you just have to do 2 things. Firstly, you have to not sin. You have to do the positive commandments and stay away from transgressing the negative commandments. And then you have to come to have belief that God is running around the world. You have to realise that nature is one thing but it's not the main thing. The problem is today in Physics and Science; they learn that nature is the essential thing. In the Torah, the Kabbalists teach us the exact opposite. They teach that the natural system is subservient to the supernal system where God is really running the world. It just looks as if nature is running things. But really the world is being run by above nature, by divine commandment. So if a person can come to that, by studying the works of Kabbalah, especially the Ashkenazi kabbalah (we are going to have some books on this in the near future) by the Gaon of Vilna and other people, the rabbis that came after him in Europe, he will understand that God is running the universe. The Kabbalah based on the idea of how God created the world, how He is running it and directing it every minute. And so if you can really tune into that and see, on a deep level, how everything is being run from above then you're going to automatically lose that fear of nature. The fear of the natural world, the fear of the Stars, and the fear of all sorts of things and you are going to come to believe in a higher sort of life.

Even though we say caution is required, we are going to see some places in the Torah where we see that the person is going to require caution. Like we see in Sanhedria again, if pestilence comes into the town, then you should hide yourself. You don't want to go out in public. I remember in the 1950's when polio was very present. They told the parents never to let the children out where there was a group because they didn't want them to catch polio. So the children tended to stay at home, to lock themselves up. So that caution is required, like when there is pestilence to hide. And when there is famine then you should flee from your town to try find a place where there is food. So don't think that's a question that you should just trust in God. You should also make an effort. There's another part of the Torah that says you have to also make an effort. But it's not a contradiction in terms that if you have to make an effort it doesn't mean you are a person of little faith. You're a person of faith but you also have to make the required effort.

There is a pasuk in Proverbs: "All his days poverty and misery" that refers to somebody who has a short mind, a little mind, who is always worrying about what will be. And the pasuk goes on "good news is always feasting" that person has a large mind and worries about fulfilling Torah, and so really when it comes down to everything, the thing is to pray to God that all is good and no more than that. You pray every day to Hashem, three times a day, that everything should go well and don't worry so much. Our rabbis praised those who were happy and those who made other people happy. In other words, people should be happy. God saw it as a sign of true faith when people were happy. They were in the right frame of mind, free of sin, because they were happy. A happy person is someone who is free of sin and doing good deeds. The rabbis praised that and all the more so they praised those who made other people happy, people who went to weddings, who cheered people up, who brought joy to the bride and groom and things like that, people who went around raising other people's consciousness so to speak, bringing them up to happiness. It's a big thing. You see today, in the streets people look so dejected. Everything is permitted but nobody is happy. People permit themselves all sorts of things to do but yet they are not happy.

So I think one of the things I wanted in this class, besides showing which Signs tend to be most connected to worrying (the natural prevalence it's going to be the mental Planets, the Signs connected to Mercury and Jupiter) as well as we talked about the generational effect. That's something you always have to look for, the generational effect. In this case it's that worry is going to be prevalent in every person's Chart even if they don't have a big significance for it, just because it's so prevalent. We talk about finding the disease of cancer in a Chart. Today 1 out of every 3 people is going to get cancer in their lifetime. It's just so prevalent. You maybe won't find it in a Horoscope, every 1 in 3 people you're going to see has cancer written in the Horoscope? It used to be not so prevalent. It used to be one out of every 20 people or 50 people. Ok that you could maybe find factors for it in the Horoscope; but one out of every 2 or 3 people? That is too much. It's generational. Something to do with the air or smoke, I don't know what. So the point I wanted to make in this class was that you also have to look at generational effects. They will affect everybody but some Signs to a higher degree than others. Especially the mental Signs will have free floating anxiety. It just goes everywhere. Other people will worry about one thing or something else. We could do a whole class on what people worry about. Which Signs worry about which things, which interconnections worry about different things. But tonight we are talking about it in a more general way. The point I wanted to make tonight was that some problems are more generational. Maybe a hundred years ago people weren't worrying. Today people worry about why they are worrying. People's lives were much simpler, they grew up in a little town, they knew everybody there and they had a support system. Life was different; they just didn't worry so much. But today is different. Today everybody is on their own.

Chapter 3 - Anger

So far we did 2 character traits, let's do a quick summary, we did truthfulness. That was the first character trait which I considered the main one, really if a person is truthful in my opinion he is going to have a pretty good life because if a person id truthful he is not going to come to do anything wrong. He is afraid of doing something wrong because then he is going to have to lie to cover it up. And if you don't have to cover up something then you are going to be ok and all your deeds will be good deeds. So if I had to work on one character trait to perfect it, in the sense of doing a good character trait, then I would choose truthfulness. And really the world stands on the truth. You see the world today is just full of lies; wherever you look everything is lies and more lies. The truth is something that has been lost. People don't even believe that there is truth. They say today that "everything is relative". There is no absolute truth, only relativisms. What is true for one person is maybe false for someone else. We have come to the point today where people have even given up on the idea of looking for truth. It's a non-existent. So that's a big problem and that's why I started talking about truthfulness. And then I talked about another character trait, fear and worry, because it's so prevalent in our generation. Everybody is so worried. If you look at all the health programmes today, one of the main components of them is to relieve stress, to take away worry. People are tremendously overburdened by worry. So because of that, I chose to talk a little about worry, what causes worry, how to overcome worry in one's life and how to get more to a state of natural feeling good and rested and not really worrying. Today in our generation that's called a very high level when a person can get above the worrying about so many worries in the world. You just turn on the radio, the TV or the internet and there are all the worries of the world! People are so interconnected to everybody else that they are interconnected with the worries too. So that was the second week. Now the third week I want to talk about a character trait and I'm going to talk about it because it's such a difficult character trait. Maybe it's the most difficult of all the character traits a person can have. A person who has this character trait, their life is miserable. I don't think I've ever seen anyone with this character trait that had any sort of happiness. And to uproot it, it is also very difficult. The person has to be willing to make a big attempt to overcome this character trait. But if they can do it, they can get to a very high level. This character trait is called anger, rage... To be incensed... it's just such a difficult character trait and it's very hard to overcome. You'll see when we start to talk about it, the difficulties that come with it.

So we are going to talk tonight about anger, the usual approach, how the rabbis looked at anger, how they saw it, what the defect of anger could do, what it could cause to the person and then we are going to talk about if there are ways to overcome anger. And then we will take a look of course in astrology at which Signs cause a person to be more angry and which Signs are more likely to have a more mellow approach to life so that the person doesn't get angry.

The first thing I want to say about anger tonight is that it says in the Gemara, in the Jewish Talmud, in Pesach, the laws on the holiday of Passover it says "three people God loves. One is a person that never gets angry..." It's a big level never to get angry. I remember the first rabbi I learnt with. I stayed with him for one reason: he never got angry. I saw that as a very high level. And he had a natural inclination to get angry, I think. He had lots of Fire Signs, all

Fire Signs, but we will talk about the problems with Fire and anger later. But he worked very hard to overcome it. I don't think I saw him get angry the whole time I was at the yeshiva. So any case, it's a very high level, a person who doesn't get angry. I remember I once went to visit Rav Kadori. Rav Kadori was one of the big rabbis of the last generation. He was an incredibly giant in Torah, kabbalah and Middot. He could see from one end of the world to the other. I remember once my bank got robbed and I had a lot of money in the bank so I went to see Rav Kadori and he said "don't worry, in 60 days you will get everything back". And in exactly 60 days I got everything back. I remember my wife had a couple of miscarriages before we had children and he said "don't worry you will have 4 children". And that's what it was, I had 4 children!

I'll tell you a story about Rav Kadori and anger. Whenever somebody in my wife's family, whenever they had a problem… Actually let me put it this way. Every Friday afternoon my wife's father used to bring hilbeh (a type of Temani sauce dish) to Rav Kadori as a gift for Shabbat. And if somebody in the family at that time had a problem then he would bring it that week and then they would have a chance to ask Rav Kadori about the problem. This was years and years ago, maybe 35 years ago, when you could still get to see rabbis. Then it was a very small community and it was like that. Then you could go up, knock on his door, bring him some hilbeh and face to face talk with him. So I remember one week I had a problem, I don't remember exactly what the problem was, maybe it was concerned with miscarriages probably… So I went there with my father in law actually and we went in there and for some reason Rav Kadori's wife was really angry at him. I think she didn't want us to be in there, I don't know. They were speaking in Arabic together or Iraqit or something. She was yelling and screaming but he was just sitting there smiling as if nothing was happening. Eventually she stopped yelling and he talked with her for a few minutes. He had such control over his anger and on that day I knew he was a great rabbi because I saw that he had to ability to rule over his emotions. I mean anybody who has somebody yelling at them is inclined to react but he was able to overcome who he was and to restrain himself. And at that time I knew he was a great rabbi and I knew it was important to try get close to him because he worked so hard on himself to perfect his character traits. I mean what happens in the real world? The woman yells then after a few minutes the husband starts to yell back and then pretty soon they are throwing things at each other. And pretty soon they end up in a divorce court. So he had the ability not to do this.

A little idea of what his ability to overcome anger is… Anger is a tremendous thing. I've seen a lot of people in my life that have in their nature to be angry and they all suffer so much. I'll give you some examples later on, astrologically, to pinpoint anger.

The Talmud says they wouldn't give the 42 letter name, the secret name of 42 letters that was passed down rabbi to rabbi, the name which they could do big things with, to someone who has anger. It was forbidden to give to someone who had anger. If the person had anger then it kept them away from the highest, most sublime levels of Torah and mitzvoth. It says in the Gemara, in Taanit, that a person must train himself to speak softly. In other words that's one of the great means t overcoming anger. A person has to learn not to raise his voice, and especially a person who has anger in him. The main thing he has to do is just train himself not to raise his voice. If you don't raise your voice you can't be angry. A person has to learn to train himself (or herself- there are lots of angry women out there too) to speak softly. I've seen a lot of women that also get very angry. I have a friend whose wife's parents were Holocaust survivors and that did something to her brain and she never speaks in a soft voice. She is always yelling, she never stops yelling and then when she get angry it is really bad. But it's hard to train somebody not to talk in a loud voice. And the rabbis considered an angry person as someone who was practising idol worship. They considered it such a bad thing that they compared it to idol worship, to a person who doesn't believe in God or believes in false gods. They said "the one who rips his clothing in anger or smashes his vessels in anger or gives away his money in anger will be in your eyes as if he is an idol worshipper". So you can see how much the rabbis didn't like the character trait in itself.

It also said in Nedarim, another tractate of the Talmud, that anyone who gets angry, all different types of hell will rule over him. His life becomes a misery, in other words, the person gets trapped by all different types of bad situations. All the lower creatures rule over him, in other words, he becomes ruled over; his life is no longer in his hands when he gets angry. Even the shechina, the Divine Presence, does not have any importance against him, it can't help him. He forgets his learning and it adds to his idiocy and it is known that his sins are much greater than his merits. It also says in another place in the Talmud "don't get into a rage and you will not sin". Raging or getting angry leads to sin. It also says the people who get incensed, their lives are not lives. They don't have a real life. It says "anger in the house destroys the house like a worm that destroys the food that you're eating". Once you see that worm eating away at your food, you can no longer eat it. And it also says that the anger causes the light to leave. Anybody who gets angry, if he is a wise man his wisdom leaves him, if he is a prophet his prophecy leaves him. And even if they guaranteed him that he would get to this high place of honour, they take him down from there because of his anger.

And they say even about Moshe Rabeinu. There are 3 places where he got angry and in all 3 places he ended up making a mistake. It says "in an angry person the only thing that goes up in his hands is anger". An angry person can't accomplish anything; it's very difficult for an angry person to accomplish anything. To illustrate it, there is a story in Beit Yosef, he gave a very famous story there, concerning the Well of Miriam: The Well of Miriam existed in Tiberius. There is a legend that there is a well of Miriam in the Kinneret and it says that every Saturday night, that this well of Miriam is always moving and all the different places where they draw water and anybody who was sick and he chanced upon this water and drank it, even if his whole body was covered in tremendous sores, instantaneously he would be healed. That was this power of the well of Miriam, it talks about it in the Gemara. And it is known that, for example, the Arizal's main talmid was Chaim Vital one day didn't understand the learning so he took him out into the river, the Ari, in the Kineret and told him "draw water from here and drink it" and after that he never had problems learning. So it was a tremendously important merit to drink water from this well, so if you were able to get water from it, from the well of Miriam, then it was a big thing.

Let me tell you a story, I have a lot of stories tonight, about when I learned at the Yeshiva maybe 35 years ago, just to give you an idea of what the Well of Miriam was. Don't think it was so easy to get to, there's a Gemara that says, for people who know Tiberius, "If you stand on top of where Rabbi Meir Baal Ness synagogue is, sometimes you can see it moving (the well)". There's a tradition like that. In any case, I was learning in a Kabbalah yeshiva many years ago, maybe in 1980, and one day a bunch of guys came in who I had never seen before. There were maybe 3 guys and they asked if they could sit in the class, they wanted to learn a bit of Kabbalah. So the Rabbi said "sure, come sit, join us…" and it turns out that these 3 guys were from the Syrian community in New York and they were learning with a very big rabbi, Rav Katzin, one of the big Kabbalists of the last generation. So the Rabbi asked what these guys were doing in Israel. So the guy said that they came to look for the Well of Miriam. He said that was their task and they came prepared to get to the Well of Miriam. So the Rabbi asked "how are you going to do that?" and they said "We came here with special equipment…" (You know Americans, that if you throw enough money at any problem you can solve it) "…US army binoculars, so you can see an ant at 100m, we are going to have a guy up at the Beit Knesset of Rabbi Meir Baal Ness with these binoculars, and he is going to be able to overlook the Kineret and see where the Well of Miriam is. And also, we came equipped with the best walkie talkies in the world, the best American US Marine walkie talkies, as soon as our man on Rabbi Baal Amir Ness sees the well he can direct his compatriot in the boat and tell him exactly how to get to the well." This was, of course, before cell phones, it was 1980. So they had the top walkie talkies and the top boat from the US Navy, a super speed boat and it could move really fast. So they were going to go there, they had all this equipment and money was no problem to find the Well of Miriam and drink it to get these super revelations. So our rabbi at the time said "please if you find it, bring us back some water to drink too" and they said "sure! We'd be happy to do that". But unfortunately the guys never came back. It's not so easy to find the Well of Miriam! But if you can find it, if you get lucky, if you are worthy of it… (I shouldn't say lucky, its more if you are worthy of it) then you can make a big move in life. But anyway that was just an introduction to the story that Beit Yosef brings about the Well of Miriam moving around on Saturday night. If you are worthy of it then you can even cure somebody who is just full of tremendously bad skin diseases, even just drinking a little bit of that water can cure it. So the Beit Yosef brings the story of a man who had this tremendously bad skin disease. His skin was all red, full of infection and pus, he was a walking nightmare. His wife went one motzei Shabbat, one Saturday night, to draw water and she was delayed more than usual but while she was delayed she was also given, it came in to her possession, some water from the Well of Miriam. So she filled up her vessel with that water (of course she didn't know it was that water) but she filled it. When she came back to her husband he became very angry with her and because he was so angry with her, the jar that she put the water in fell from her shoulders and broke. But when it fell and broke a little bit of the water splashed up and touched his body. And every place that this water touched his body, his wounds were miraculously healed. And that's what our rabbis meant when they said "an angry person, the only thing that goes up in his hands is anger". He couldn't even get the Well of Miriam. He lost his chance to be healed because of such a difficult burden, his angriness.

The Holy Zohar also teaches that if a man gets angry, he uproots his soul, his higher holy soul and it is replaced with the sitra ackra, the forces of evil, which come in and inhabit his body.

That shows you how bad it is. That's why it is so hard to overcome this anger, when a person gets angry he loses his soul in a certain way. The forces of evil, the sitra ackra, sitra means side and ackra means other, the other side comes in and takes possession. And certainly it's like a guy who rebels against his master, it's forbidden to draw close to him because he damages his soul with anger and a foreign god takes over. Somebody who is friendly with him it is like he unites with idol worship, in truth, (Because the idol worship dwells inside him). You can't even look at a person like this. It's forbidden to even look at an angry person. And about this it is also written "don't turn to other gods" and all different types of impurities can be purified except for this one of anger because his body becomes taken over by it and it becomes all impure. Even if the man comes and uproots this foreign god from inside him he is still always going to have worry and be on guard that he doesn't get angry. Because if he does get angry, right away he will lose everything again and the forces of evil will come back in. The Arizal's commentary on that the person who gets angry makes his soul impure and there is no cure for his anger. Even if he does teshuva, even if he repents, even if he increases his Torah study and good deeds as soon as he gets angry again everything will leave him. His soul, his nefesh, will leave him and his soul from the "other side" will come again. He will lose everything again until he is tremendously on guard that he won't get angry at all. And then he can return finally in teshuva. So we see that to get over anger there has to be complete repentance, there can't be any fall back. Like the people who drink, they tell you "one drink and you are finished!" Once you get on the wagon, once you get off drinking, one drink is like life and death. As soon as you drink a little bit of alcohol that can set you off and bring everything back. So that is what the Ari is saying, something like that. Anger is such a difficult emotion; it really messes up the whole body of the person. It causes in some way for the pure soul to leave and a soul of impurity to take its place. So if a person has one little setback and gets angry he can lose all the work he did to try repair this evil trait. So it's like drinking almost, if you go off once you're finished. So it's a thing a person really has to work on his whole life. If a person is born with this character trait it is very difficult. That's why I wanted to talk about it tonight. It's not a character trait that is not found very often, a lot of people have it and we will talk about it some more as we go on.

The Rambam, the great Jewish expounder of the law, wrote "Even though in all the character traits, the person should strive to find the middle path. He should never go too much to one extreme." A person shouldn't be too loose with his money, nor too tight, he should be somewhere in the middle, and similarly with the other character traits. But anger is different. Anger is such a bad character trait that it's important for a man to get as far away from it as possible and to train himself never too get angry. And even for something that he should be angry for he should train himself to not get angry over it. If he wants to instil fear in his children or the other people in his household or on the community, (if he is a community leader) and he wants to get angry with them in order that they return to the right path, he should make believe he is angry. He shouldn't do it but rather in a situation like this he should make himself as if he is angry. He should appear before them as if he is angry but in his heart and his mind he is relaxed and in a proper frame of mind. In other words, you can't heal or correct a person when you are angry. It's just not done. The same thing as when you see an angry person you can't talk to them. It's something very important that I've learned in life; if someone is angry don't try to calm them down, or reason with them, or try to talk to them. It does not work. You can talk with an angry person. They are in a very bad way. So in a situation like that the best thing to do is to be quiet and to let the person calm down on their own. You can't deal with an angry person. The same thing if you are an angry person, you can't fix people by being angry. Nobody ever cured their children of problems by yelling at them. When they see you with smoke coming out of your ears and yelling at them, the kids think that there is something wrong with the father or mother. You can't cure a person with anger. So that's what the Rambam is saying. You have to make believe as if you are angry but you have to be completely relaxed inside in order to affect something positive, a positive type of healing.

So in other words you have to make yourself as if you are angry, but you're not. And the early wise men they said, "whoever gets angry it's as if he did idol worship. If he is a wise man his wisdom leaves him, if he is a prophet his prophecy leaves him and an angry person his life is not a life". Therefore you are commanded to get as far away from anger as possible until you don't feel any anger inside you even with stuff that should really make you angry. In other words you have to try get as far away from this character trait as possible. Today there is a lot of anger in the world, everybody is getting angry and we will talk more about it. So the way of good and righteous people is if someone does bad to them they do not respond. If they hear people speaking badly about them, they don't answer back. And they are happy with their suffering. The ones who love me they go out like the sun in its full strength. So the thing is you have to be happy with the suffering that you get. One of the reasons a person gets angry is because they think they shouldn't suffer. No one gets angry for no reason. They get angry because bad things happen to them or people don't treat them right or they have misfortunes that they think they don't deserve. And really a person has to learn that there is suffering in the world and they have to be able to face that suffering if they want to get to high levels. So one of the things is to really work to overcome anger is to not think "it doesn't come to me." You have to get to a level where you realise that all of this world is just a test to get you into the next world. If you think you are just here to make a lot of money, to get a lot of pleasure, and to have really good food and all the best things in life, all the best things that money can buy, to do all the sins you can do, get everything in while there is still time then you are always going to get angry because you want stuff. And the stuff that you want isn't going to come to you. Not everybody gets what they want. People want to be rich but how many people are rich? People want the best food, the best wine, the best love, and how many people have it? Most people it just wasn't given to them. Until you realise the whole work of this world is to get to the next world then you are still going to be in the situation where you can get big anger. But really the work of this world is to prepare you for the next world. You handle the challenges down here and then you are worthy to get the rewards of the next world then it is much easier to overcome that anger that is inside the heart.

One more story and then I want to talk about some of the Astrological significances of anger. There was a famous book called Sefer HaChassidim, written in the 1200s by Yehuda HaChasid, one of the tosfots. He told a story of a boy who honoured his father as much as possible. And his father once said to him "honour me in my life and honour me also when I die, in my death. I command you that whenever you start to get angry don't do anything for one night. I command you that you should suspend your anger for one night and delay your anger and your words so that you don't speak." So after the father died, the boy went overseas to make money and he left behind his wife who was pregnant. And for some reason this man who went out overseas didn't know his wife was pregnant. And he got delayed on the way for many years and when he returned to his city and he came back home at night and he went up to his room where his wife was. His wife was there and she was lying down and he heard the voice of a young man talking. And he was kissing her. So this man drew his sword and he wanted to kill both of them, the boy and his wife. But he remembered what his father commanded him and he put away his sword. He heard his wife talking to that young man that was her son, that already it was many years since the father had been away and if he knew that a boy was born to him, he would already have returned home to find this boy a proper wife. And when the man heard this he said "my wife, thank God that I overcame my anger and blessed is my father that commanded me to hold back my anger for one day. Because of that I didn't kill you and I didn't kill my son." He rejoiced and made a big feast for all the people in his town and they were all very happy. Blessed is the person who can overcome anger all the days of his life. So you see here you can get a little taste of what anger can do to a person. What they say is "an angry person, his life is just not a life". I was looking at Horoscopes over my career and first of all, there tends to be the Signs that are most inclined to anger have been the Fire Signs, especially Aries which is ruled by Mars, the Red Planet, the Planet of heat and anger, too hot. And Martians are too hot by nature. All the Fire Signs have big egos, they think they are better than other people and they want to rule over other people. So when people don't do what they want they get angry. In other words, they want to be listened to and respected and they can't take it that other people don't listen to them. It's a difficulty in Fire Signs but I guess it would also be difficult in Scorpio too. Even though it's a Water Sign it is also by its nature a Martian Sign. So they also have a tendency to get very angry. They are very afraid of trouble. They are the people that see trouble everywhere. They see under every rock and every pillow an enemy out to get them. There are always people out to destroy them so they are always in this very defensive position. So they can also get very angry by nature. On top of that I have seen a lot of people… You have to look at the Horoscopes and see the different things, the different combinations that cause a person to get angry. One of them like I said is a person who wants things from this world. Like a person who has a lot of water, he has a tremendous desire for food, drinking and sexual relationships. So when they don't get it it can make them very angry. Or Earthy people when they don't have money, it's so important to them to have financial security in their lifetime, in this world so they can also get very angry about money, especially a person who has a bad Mars. Mars is the Planet that can get angry. If you have a Mars, say, in Taurus, I've seen a lot of people with Mars in Taurus that can get very angry because they have such desires… Taurus is pleasure and Mars is the ego so they want money and relationships and things like that so when they don't get it they get very angry. Also I've looked at a lot of Charts and the rulers of the Charts. I just did the Chart of a woman actually, years ago and she was a Sagittarius Rising, which is a nice Ascendant, with Jupiter in Honour in Sagittarius but she had Mars in Gemini exactly opposite the Jupiter. Jupiter is religion and Mars is anger so she was very angry for God. She was the type of person that always had to criticise people and try to get them to change their ways. So she would go out in the street and see women who weren't dressed modestly and she would start to yell at them. And she told me she couldn't get any of her friends to want to go out with her into the street because she would always go out in the street and get into fights and arguments with other people because of her anger for God. She just wanted all the women to dress modestly, but it's just not the way to do it. You don't get people to change their ways with anger. Nobody made someone a righteous person by being angry with them. It just doesn't happen. I've seen a lot of cases like this. So you always have to look if Mars is going to make a bad aspect to Jupiter, like religious anger, fanaticism… There are probably a lot of people in the Arab religion with this Jupiter Mars type of behaviour. The whole religion is like that type of Jupiter Mars bad aspect. So you always have to look where Mars is Aspecting to see which area the anger will go. So if you have Mars aspecting Saturn, Saturn by nature is the career, the person wants to get ahead and they will try using their anger to get ahead, which is a big mistake. But any case wherever the Mars is very strong it could be a tendency towards anger. So the main thing we learnt tonight is that it's a condition and if you have it you have to do everything in your power to get it under your control. Don't let it run your life but if it's in your nature to get angry then the thing to do is to learn not to raise your voice, to realise this world is a test, we are here to get to the next world, to get accustomed to the fact that suffering comes to heal a person to make them ready for the next world. Then you can start to deal with it. I've also seen in Horoscopes that people with a lot of anger in their Horoscopes, if they can overcome it they can make their Horoscope into a very beautiful Horoscope, because it's such a bad character trait that their life is not a life. If they can overcome it however, they can totally turn their Horoscope around. So because of that I wanted to teach about anger. So if you see that people have anger, especially if you are an Astrologer for other people look at their Chart and see if they have anger there. Ask them if they have anger. Say "I see that you have this Aspect, all this Fire, so there must be a lot of pent up emotion, you have a bad Mars here or Mars is aspecting 4 or 5 of your Planets and you can get very heated up, you can become a religious fanatic or you can speak bad language, you have the bad Mars Mercury aspect, you have foul language you use, you curse and your curse people…" So you can see it in the Charts of people and then you can start to work with them and make a big change in their lives. That's really why people come to Astrologers. Most people think that Astrologers are coming to help people get to all their evil desires. Astrologers think they are there to help people get to what they are having a hard time getting. Maybe to a certain degree… I mean you want to help someone who is not married... or someone who has money problems, you want to help them. Btu really what people want to be is they want to get to high levels. They want to be calm and content in life. They would rather give up a lot for contentment. I was reading up on Medicine. They have pills for people, stuff like Prozac, and things like that. Prozac is a calmer; it takes away your worries and things like that. But at the same time it has the tendency to decrease your sexual desires, and other things like appetite, but even so people crave it. They are willing to give up all these pleasures in order to get the contentment that comes from this pill. So really you see what people want more than anything is contentment. And contentment, in the Torah way, comes from proper living. It comes from what we always learned, learning Torah and doing mitzvoth. Doing the positive commandments and staying far away from the negative commandments as you can. And through that then you don't create any of this negative energy and anger that will lead you to sinning.

Jewish world view of the 7 Planets

Jewish world view of the 7 Planets

By Yaakov Kronenberg

This is a transcription of a lecture on the Torah world view of the 7 Planets and their influences; focusing on the ancient book, the Sefer Yetzira (book of Formation). The series blends Kabala and Astrology into a holistic world view of the energy influences on humanity.

Jewish World View of the 7 Planets

By Yaakov Kronenberg

Chapter 1

Tonight I'm going to start a new series of classes on the Jewish world view of the 7 Planets using the Book of Formation (Sefer Yetzirah – Written by Abraham Avinu over 3500 years ago) as my source and benchmark. We have in previous talks learned from the Book of Formation, especially chapter 5 of the book; and there we talked about the 12 simple letters. The twelve simple letters are the twelve Houses, and the twelve Signs and the twelve tribes, and the twelve organs of the body that direct the body. We used these letters to try to understand the constellations (Zodiac) better. We also talked about the two highest levels, which nobody else really talks about, which are the twelve tribes and the twelve permutations of Gods names, and that comes from a very high place in the Kabbalistic worlds. And that is really what is running the twelve different Mazalot (Zodiac). Each Mazal is a different permutation of Gods name. So now I want to move on to chapter 4 of the Book of Formation.

Chapter 4 talks about 7 more letters of the Hebrew alphabet. In the Hebrew alphabet there are 22 letters. There are 12 simple letters and 7 double letters and 3 elemental letters. The 3 elemental letters are Air, Fire and Water. *Aleph*, *mem*, and *shin.* The 7 doubles, which we will talk about below, are connected to the 7 Planets.
The Gaon of Vilna talks about these 3 sets of letters (12, 7 and 3); where everything in the world has this pattern of the 3, 7 and 12. For example take the Square cube: the square cube has three dimensions, length, width and height. That is parallel to the 3 simple letters. It has seven directions, it has six sides, East, West, North, South, up, down, and it has a middle point which unites and holds everything together, which is the 7th. And then the square has twelve boundaries. Each side has four boundaries, so each of the six sides makes it 24, and then you divide it by two because each boundary is shared by two sides, and there you have 12 boundaries. And you can find that in everything in the world, and in Time and in a Human.

So let's start with the 7 double letters by reading the whole 4th chapter in the Book of Formation, its very short. It starts:
"The seven doubles are the *bet, gimmel, dalled, kaf, peih, reish* and *taff.* Those are the seven letters in Hebrew. They direct themselves with two tongues. *Bet* and *vet, gimmel* and *jimmel, dalled* and *dallef, kaf* and *chaf, peih* and *feih, reish* and the soft *reish,* and then there is *taff* and *sav;* a structure of strong/hard and soft/weak". We are going to come back and spend some time on this first *Mishnah*. But it's just saying here that there are seven letters that are double; they are double because they can be pronounced in two ways. They can be pronounced as a hard sound or a soft sound. For example the letter *bet* can be pronounced as 'bah' which is hard, or 'veh' which is soft. *Gimmel* can be pronounced as 'geh' which is hard, or 'jeh' which is soft; and we are going to come back to that and talk about what that means and why its connected to Judgment and Mercy, each letter having in it the ability to be merciful and judgmental.

To save time they combine all the 7 letters together into a 2 word acronym, which they call *BaGaD KaFRaT*.

"Their foundations are Wisdom, Wealth, Seed, Life, Dominance, Peace and Grace". So he is telling you that each of these 7 double letters is connected to an aspect of life. One is connected to wisdom, one to wealth, one to seed, one to life, one to dominance, one to peace, and one to grace. "The seven doubles, B*aGaT KaFRaT,* represent speech and the transposed position. The transposed position of wisdom is folly, the transposed of wealth is poverty, the transposed of seed is desolation, the transposed of dominance is subjugation, the transposed of peace is war, the transposed of grace is ugliness". So we see now that he is adding a new point that even though the *bet* is wisdom, it also has its opposite, which is folly; depending on whether it is going to be a hard sound or a soft sound. "The seven doubles, B*aGaD KaFRaT,* they are Up and Down, East and West, North and South and a holy palace precisely in the center, which supports them all". So there are the six sides; and the 6 sides are what we call in Kabbalah the Small Face.

"Seven doubles B*aGaD KaFRaT,* seven and not six, seven and not eight. Examine them, probe them, make each thing stand on its essence, and let the Creator sit on his base". So here he is showing that there are seven, not more and not less. So maybe he is trying to show that there is an idea that there should be eight and not seven, or six and not seven. How can that be; and again, we will talk about that later.

"Seven doubles, B*aGaD KaFRaT,* a Foundation, he Engraved them, he Carved them, he Permutated them, he Weighed them, he Transformed them, and with them he formed the 7 Planets of the universe, the 7 days in the week, the 7 gates of the soul, Male and Female". That brings us back to the idea that we saw in chapter 5. For example, over there he taught you that there were 12 constellations in the universe, and then he said that there are 12 months in the year, and there are 12 directing organs in the body, Male and Female.

"Seven Planets in the universe; Saturn, Jupiter, Mars, Sun, Venus, Mercury, and Moon, seven days in the universe, seven gates of the soul, male and female; 2 eyes, 2 ears, 2 nostrils and a mouth". He is now telling us that there are 7 days in the universe which means that the year is broken up into days and each day is ruled by a different Planet. One day is ruled by Saturn, one day by Jupiter etcetera. We will see later that he is working on the 3 states of being; Universe, Time and Person or Space, Time and Consciousness. Clearly this system of astrology in the Book of Formation has nothing to do with the system of Western astrology. This system here is called the planetary hour system, each day of the week is parallel to a different Planet., and that is not Western astrology. Western astrology is about plotting the Planets at a particular moment in Time, not fixed embedded Time energies set from the moment of creation in perpetuity, which is the Book of Formation system. Also, the parts of the body that he talks about are all in the head. Two eyes, two ears, two nostrils, but the mouth only has one opening so that makes seven; and we will come back latter and talk about why there is only 1 opening to the mouth. But the main point here is that its all 7's.

"He made the letter *bet* king over wisdom, and He bound a crown to it and combined one with the other, He formed the Moon in the universe, Sunday in the year, the right eye in the soul, male and female". So he is connecting the letter *bet* with the Moon and with Sunday and the right eye.

"He made the letter *gimmel* king over wealth and He bound a crown to it, and combined one with the other. And with them He formed Mars in the universe, Monday in the year,

the right ear in the soul, male and female". So you see that Mars is connected to *gimmel,* it's Monday in the year and it's the right ear of the soul.
"He made the letter *dalled* king over the seed and He bound a crown to it and He combined one with the other and with them He formed the Sun in the universe, Tuesday in the year, the right nostril in the soul, male and female". So he is connecting the *dalled* with the Sun, Tuesday and the right nostril.
"He made the letter *kaf* king over life and He bound a crown to it and He combined one with the other and with them He formed Venus in the universe, Wednesday in the year, the left eye in the soul, male and female". So now we move on to the fourth day, which is Wednesday and its Venus and the left eye, all related to the letter *kaf.*
"He made the letter *peih* king over dominance and He bound a crown to it, and He combined one with the other and with them He formed Mercury in the universe, Thursday in the year, the left ear in the soul, male and female". So *peih* is Mercury, Thursday and the left ear.
"He made the letter *reish* king over peace, and He bound a crown to it, and He combined one with the other and with them He formed Saturn in the universe, Friday in the year, the left nostril in the soul, male and female". So he is connecting the letter *reish* with Saturn, Friday and the left nostril.
"He made the letter *taf* king over grace, and He bound a crown to it and he combined one with the other and with them He formed Jupiter in the universe, the Sabbath in the year, the mouth in the soul, male and female". So he is connecting the letter *taf* with Jupiter, the Sabbath and the mouth.

That is the 4th chapter of the Book of Formation, and you see what a small book it is, in maybe 15 minutes we read the whole chapter and gave a brief explanation of it, and all the other chapters are about the same length so you could probably read the book in an hour, and you can spend the rest of your life trying to understand it. It's a short book, this is what is called the short version, which we use today and it was accepted by the Arizal and the Gaon of Vilna. So before we go through this 4th chapter in detail we need to learn a few concepts in astrology and kabbalah which I think will help people understand this chapter better.
You have to know that there are 3 basic levels in astrology, there are Houses, Planets and Constellations (Zodiac); the Houses are the receivers, they receive the energy. If the Sun comes down, depending on which House it falls in, that House will direct the solar energy. For example, if the Sun will fall in the persons 1st House when he is born, that Sun will be directed toward the person himself. That Sun will give him leadership abilities, it will give him authority, it will give him power over other people, it will give him honour, because it is being directed toward that House, that House is what receives the energy of the Sun. If the Sun falls in his 5th House, it will give him Children who will be solar in quality. There will be a tendency to have boys, his children will have leadership abilities. It will give him authority in that area in life. The 5th House rules speculation, so he might become an authority in an area of speculation, or authority in the area of someone who gets famous from the theatre or art, because the 5th House is connected with the theatre and the arts. So it becomes a leadership ability in those areas. It will be directed to that area of life. We call it the ruler of the Affairs of the House. The Sun energies will be directed more on to his children than on himself. So maybe he won't have leadership abilities but his children will. So you can go on and do that with all the

Houses. The Houses are the receivers. They don't give off energy themselves. They just take the energy and direct it. On top of that, there are the Constellations, which are the senders. They send down the energy. In other words the Sun travels around the belt of stars and that belt of stars is called the Zodiac. That Zodiac is divided into 12 portions and each portion is a different Constellation with a different energy, like what we talked about in chapter five, with different permutations. So each month has a different energy that is going to be sent down. They are always sending energy, and that is the energy that is coming down from *shamayim* or the heavens. Then there is the 3rd level. The 3rd level is the Planets which is what we are talking about in this chapter. The Planets are the intermediaries. In other words they take from the Constellations and they send down to the Houses. If you are doing individual horoscopes, which is based on the time a person is born, each Planet is in different House for each individual. It's never the same for any person, because each moment the Planets are moving. For example, if a person is born with Mars in Aries, that means that the Mars is going to work using that Arien energy to express itself, and it's going to use it in whatever House it falls in. If it falls in the 1st House, the person will be a warrior. Mars in the 1st House with an Arian energy makes it a double Mars because Aries is also a Martian energy. So they will be a very powerful war-like individual. So everything that happens here is expressed through the Planets. In other words the Planets are the ones that transfer the constellations down into the Houses. So what the Book of Formation is really trying to say is that the Planets are really the cause of what events happen here on Earth, and they have a range. They can either be doing things from the extreme side of mercy to the extreme side of judgment and in between, and we are going to talk about what that means later.

In Kabbalah there are ten *Sefirot.* There are three in the head and seven in the body. And then you can add the twelve internal organs. We said before that if you have a square there are three dimensions, seven sides and twelve boundaries. Same thing in a person. Three *Sefirot* in the head, seven limbs of the body, and then there are twelve internal organs that rule over things; 3, 7 and 12; The 3 Sefirot in the head are called *chochmah, binah and da'at.* In the human body there are also three sides. A right side, a left side and a middle. The right side is the side of mercy, the left side is judgement, and the middle side is the balance. It's called the *machriah* in Kabbalah, someone who decides between the left and the right. The right side has three *Sefirot, chochmah, chesed* and *netzach,* which is the side of mercy. And then you have the left side which has 3 Sefirot called, *binah, gevurah* and *hod,* which is the side of Judgment. And then you have the middle which is the balance, and the Sefirot there are *Keter/Da'at, Tiferet, Yesod* and *Malchut*.
So in Kabbalah the right side is called El; which is one of the names of God from the side of *chesed,* the side which he does good and has mercy. The left side is *gevurah,* the side of judgment and punishment. And that is the name *Elohim*, the judge. And then there is the middle which is *Hashem*, the main 4 letter name that balances between the left and the right and decides which one rules between the left and the right. We will discuss this in more detail later. If you look at the head, there is *chochmah, binah* and *da'at. Chochmah* is the right side of the head, which is wisdom; *Binah* which is on the left side is understanding; and *da'at* is the lower middle part of the brain which is actualized knowledge. And it is always that the middle part breaks in two, because the middle has to resolve the pull between the right and the left. In other words the right side is sending down mercy and the left side is sending down judgment, so the middle has to have both

mercy and judgment in it, and it then has to decide which to send down and how to send it down to the 7 lower Planets, which will determine how they are going to act, and how you are going to modify the energy; which direction are you going to go.
So those are the two introductions for now, hold them in the back of your mind because in the next class we are going to use them.

So let's talk about the letters of the Hebrew alphabet and their pronunciations. The Book of Formation is the oldest book in the Jewish library. And today with the ingathering of the Jewish people from the Exile to Israel, the Book of Formation has played an important role in helping to standardize the revival of the Hebrew language, especially the pronunciation of its letters. As you know Jews came from different countries all over the world; from Europe to the Middle East to South and North America to Africa and Australia. Some of these Jews already knew Hebrew, some Jews didn't, and many spoke with different accents and pronunciations. So this had to be standardized. How you pronounce the letters in Hebrew is important, especially when you pray; it resonates in the universe, so if you pronounce the words wrong, it could have a very different effect to what you would like it to have. So now you have to ask how did they agree on the standard pronunciation. So that is where the Book of Formation (Sefer Yetzira) comes into to play as a benchmark; because the Book of Formation breaks the letters up into which area of the mouth they are pronounced from. In other words, there are five areas of the mouth where the sounds come from and each group of letters comes from a different part of the mouth. Let's go through them and see. There are the Guttural letters, which are the *aleph, hay, chet,* and *ayin.* Then there are letters that come from the Palate, and these are the *gimmel, kaf, koof* and *yud.* And then there are letters that come from the Lips which are *Bet, vav, mem,* and *taf.* And then there are the letters that come from the Tongue which are the *daled, lamed, tet, nun* and *taf.* And then there are the letters that come from the Teeth which are the *zayin, samech, shin, reish* and *tzadi.*
So if a person pronounces a letter using the wrong part of the mouth, then he is not pronouncing it right. In Kabalah it is known as the 'five comings out of the mouth'; the throat, palate, tongue, teeth and lips, going from the inside out. And then each of these breaks down further, so for example with the Lips, the *bet* is the most outer, you pronounce it with the outside of your lips hitting together. Then the *vav* will be a little bit more towards the middle of the lips, and then the *mem* is more towards the inside of the lips, and the *peih* is even more toward the inside of the lips. It is the same with all the divisions of the mouth. So now that you know that there are the five openings of the mouth, you need to know that there is one problem, and that is with the letter *reish (Teeth)*. There is no hard *reish* pronunciation anywhere in the Jewish world today, no nation pronounces the hard *reish* according to the rules of the Book of Formation. Rabbi Ariyeh Kaplan wrote a great commentary on the Book of Formation, and I briefly want to quote an idea he said in his book. Ariyeh Kaplan wants to say that because of the mystery of the pronunciation of the *reish*, there is no peace in the world. That's because the hard *reish* is connected to peace, so since its is missing, that is why there is no peace. He also explains that the letters are the body of the scripts and the vowels are its soul. The Kabbalists note that the *dagesh* and *rafeih* are neither vowels nor letters, but intermediary between the two. It is this intermediary stage in essence that man must perfect if he is to enter the domain of the soul.

So let's explain that because it's very cryptic, before we start with a detailed look at chapter 4 of the Book of Formation. We say that the Torah has 4 levels. They are called *TaNTA: Tamim, nekudot, tagim* and *otiot.* In English these are the Musical sounds of each letter, the Vowels (like the a, e, i ,o, u, in English), the Crowns on top of each letter and the Letters themselves. So these 4 aspects of the written Hebrew represent the 4 levels of Understanding of the Torah, and for now we are only going to be talking about the Vowels (nekudot) and the Letters (otiot). The letters are like the body, and the vowels are what move the body. So Ariyeh Kaplan explains that in the Sefer Torah there are either hard or soft sounds to the 7 double letters *BaGaT KaFRaT;* there is either a dot inside the letter which makes them hard, and there is also a mark that indicates a soft sound. So there were symbols for hard or soft sounds, and that is not a vowel, so in other words, they are not part of the body and they are not part of the soul. So what are they? So he says that they are the intermediary that man must perfect if he is to enter the domain of the soul. So what does that mean? (This is a great book, Sefer Yetzirah by Ariyeh Kaplan, I recommend it to everyone, it was written about twenty years ago, and I see now that they have just translated it into Hebrew. It's a really important book; its one of the few works that was written by a Rabbi in English and then translated into Hebrew. He was a very brilliant scholar and some of his stuff is hard to understand, if you don't have a background in it). So what does he mean by this intermediary essence that man must perfect if he wishes to enter the domain of the soul? A very famous Kabbalist once asked a question like this. This is from Rabbi Shalom Sharabi, a Rabbi from Yemen. Most of the Kabbalah learned today is learned by his system of Kabbalah. He asked, 'what is the work of man in this world? Why did he come into this world?' If he came in to this world to work on the body, then it is a hopeless task. The body, no matter what you do, is eventually going to decay and die. So it can't be the work of the body.

And if you say a person came into the world to work on his soul, that's also difficult to say, because the soul is a little piece of Godliness, and it's perfect. How can you improve it. So that isn't the work of man in his life time either, because the soul is perfect. So if that is so, then what is the work of man? So Ariyeh Kaplan answers it like this. In the Zohar there is the idea of the *chalukah de rabanan,* that is the garment of the Rabbis, what that means is that in this world the garment of the soul is the physical body. But when the person dies, their soul goes up into the next world, or the world of the future, it doesn't have a garment to enclose itself with. So it is going to feel naked. So the Zohar learns that the way to go into the next world of the spirit is to fashion a spiritual garment here on earth while we live, through acts of righteousness and kindness. When it goes up into the next world, its garment is going to be made from all the mitzvoth and all the commandments and all the good deeds that the person fulfilled in this world; that is going to be the garment for his soul in the next world. So the Zohar and also Rav Sharabi learn that that is the work of man in this world, to make these garments for the soul for the next world. So here the Kabbalists say that the *dagesh* and *rafeih,* the hard and the soft notations, they are hinting to this. Because that's really the work in this world, where you are dealing with these Planets and you are trying to take the planetary effects and do good deeds with them and fulfill the commandments. And sometimes you succeed and sometimes you don't, it's always a struggle. So the battle of life is always here, and the Planets are what you can use here to make the garments of the Rabbis. Or not, if God forbid you don't fulfill your purpose, what will you go into the next world with? My teacher once told me that if you don't do the commandments properly today, in the next world the garment for your soul will be missing pieces or stained. I know that today its in fashion to have parts of your garments missing, you see people going out with part of the knee in their pants cut out, or different parts cut out, or they have stains on it and things like that. But in the next world, the perfect world of the spirit, it will probably be a little bit embarrassing that you have a spiritual garment that is missing pieces. So this world is a battleground for doing mitzvoth and good deeds or not being able to; there is always this fight between the hard and the soft sounds.

Chapter 2

This will be my second class in my new series of classes on the Jewish world view on the Planets. the first thing I would like to is to start to summarize what we did in the first class, so that we have a good basis to go on in the second class and so that we can go a little bit deeper. In the first class I gave two basic ideas, two simple introductions. One was an introduction in Kabbalah, and one an introduction in astrology, and both of them are very connected and we will be using them tonight. So let's go over them and try to add a little depth to them.

I want to start with the Kabbalah. We always know that there are ten *sphirot.* Three of them are in the head: *ketah, chochmah* and *binah.* And they are parallel to the letters *aleph, mem* and *shin,* they are the elementals. And then there are the seven *sphirot* that are connected with the body, *chessed, gevurah, tiferet, netzach hod, yesod* and *malchut.* Which are connected with the basic characteristics of the person in their body, what their drive is and what they want to achieve in this world. Those seven *sphirot* are connected with *bagad kafrat,* which are the seven double letters which have a hard and a soft sound. So each of the seven *sphirot* down there in the basics, they have themselves and their opposite. In other words, *mercy* is going to *hesid,* and it will also be connected with its opposite which is foolishness, which is the opposite of wisdom. But they are both in the same *sephirah,* and it will depend on how that *sephirah* is working and how it is receiving its energy, which we will talk about in a minute.

So we said that the first *sphirah* of the body is *chessed,* and we said that it has wisdom in it, and the opposite, foolishness, in it, and it is connected with the letter *bet.*

After it comes the next *sphirah, gevurah,* on the left side, it rules wealth and poverty. Sometimes a person with a good *gevurah* will have wealth, or sometimes they will have poverty. Sometimes you see that it is not black and white, you can have varying degrees on the spectrum which we will talk about in a little while adding the ideas of the Vilna Gaon. Afterwards there is *tiferet,* which is connected to the *daled,* and that is the seed, the ability to reproduce, to produce vegetation, etcetera. And the opposite of that is barrenness. After that comes the *kaf,* which is *netzach,* which is on the right hand side and that rules life and death. Then there is the *peih,* which is rulership, or slavery, which is parallel to the *sphirah* of *hod.* Then comes the *reish* which is peace and the opposite which is war, and that is *yesod.* And then finally you have the *taf,* which is grace and I guess you could say clumsiness, or unattractiveness, the opposite of grace, but I'm not too sure how to translate it. And that is *malchut.* So those are the seven *sphirot,* and each of them in itself can be one or it's opposite. So you have to know that there are three upper *sphirot; chochmah, binah* and *da'at. Chochmah* is the right brain, *binah* is the left brain, and *da'at* is the back side and the middle of the brain which sends all the energy down the spinal column and into the body, so you have to know that the *da'at* itself has two parts to it. The middle column always has two parts. Why? Because it receives from the right and it receives from the left. So it has to have a part that can receive from the right and a part that can receive from the left. So when it receives from the right it is called *rachamim* and when it receives from the left its called *gevurot. Gevurot* is, let's say, judgmental. And *rachamim is mercy.* So then the *da'at* itself sends down these seven actions that happen in the world.

I once had a teacher that said that all books can be classified as only seven types of stories. And each one of them is some how connected to one of these *sphirot.* Everything in life can somehow be put under one of these different categories.

So the whole thing is, is that *da'at* takes the energy that is coming from above, and sends it down to the lower seven *sphirot,* which are *bagad kafrat,* and if they are sent from *chassadim* then they are going to be sent from the stronger, good energy, and you will get the good side of the qualities that are coming down. If they come down from the side of *gevurot,* then they are going to be very judgmental energies that are coming down, and they may be working in opposite ways to how the person would want them to work, in other words, the bad qualities of the *sphirot* tend to be produced.

So that is one introduction that I wanted to give you, to give you an idea that this may be a cause in the shift of the energy that is coming down.

The second introduction is going to be very similar, except its going to be given in terms of astrology. In astrology there are three levels. There are the Houses, which are the receivers, the Houses are a different area of life, and when the energy comes from above, and the Houses take that energy and use it according to the House that it is coming in to. For example, if you have the Sun in the persons 1st House. The 1st House is the person himself, so if the Sun is good in his 1st House, it's going to work toward himself. It will give him a certain honour, people will respect him. if the Sun falls in the 10th House it means he is going to be very respected because of his career but not necessarily because of who he is, he could be a miserable person who everybody hates, but they might give him a little bit of respect because he is really good at his career because he has the Sun in his career House.

So the Houses are the receivers, they receive the energy. On the other hand, the energy is coming from above, from the Constellations, so they are the senders, they are sending the energy down. And then you have a middle point, which are the Planets. The Planets are the intermediaries between the Constellations and the Signs. In other words, the Planets only work through the Signs, the Planet takes the energy of that Sign, the one the person was born in, and it uses that energy and sends it down to the Houses. So it is a receiver in relation to the Signs and it's a sender in relation to the Houses.

Lets take the same idea again, we are working with the Sun, so now the Sun is coming down and its coming down in Aries, and its falling in the 1st House, so its going to give him a very domineering type of personality, because the Sun is very powerful in Aries, its Exalted. So the person could be a very well honoured person, because of his qualities etcetera, depending on how the Sun works in his chart. Or he could be a megalomaniac, or he could have a tendency to think too highly of himself, he could have too much pride or things like that. Everything has to be judged but on the whole it's pretty good if the person can use it. If it is in his 10th House, he will be very well honoured in his career, and he will have a very successful career energy, with the Sun Exalted in the 10th House.

So that is taking the Sun, and the Sun is working through the Sign. Since Aries is a Martian Sign, the person will be very strong, very aggressive, very outgoing, they will go after what they want. In the 10th House it will be toward career fulfillment and in the 1st House it will be toward personal fulfillment.

So in any case we see there are three levels. And that is the same idea that the energy is coming down, and the Planets take that energy. And how they use that energy and throw it down here in to that world determines how good or bad things are going to be.

So those are two introductions that are very similar and I think people should keep them in mind. Because really, the two great systems that teach all of the Torah in them, are Kabbalah and astrology, some how in Kabbalah and astrology, Hashem managed to put all the messages and hidden things in the world in to Kabbalah and astrology.

So that is how we started the last class, with this general idea of an introduction to them, and then we went on to talk about the five openings of the mouth, we said that the letters can be pronounced from five places in the mouth. And then we learned that the *reish,* according to the Book of Formation is pronounced using the teeth. And we spoke about that now in books, people have examined all the different ways that you can pronounce the *reish* sound. And it turns out that all of the different Jews of the world from different countries, when they came to Israel, the way they spoke Hebrew was examined by grammatitions, and they discovered that not one of the people from anywhere in the world could pronounce the *reish* properly, like it teaches in the Book of Formation. I saw that some people say that that is because the *reish* rules peace and war, and since there is no true peace today, and there hasn't been for thousands of years, since the temple of Shlomo. So because of that there is no real *reish,* because the world is never at peace. So that's one interesting idea.

The other thing that I talked about was the idea that the symbols for the hard and soft sounds. Everyone knows the symbols for the hard sounds, for example when you have the letter *bet* and it is a hard sound, then it will have a dot in the middle. And when it doesn't have a dot in the middle, then it is a soft sound. But you have to know that about a thousand years ago, in the old Torah scrolls, they used to have a symbol that indicated that it was a soft sound. Like on top of the *bet* there would be a symbol that indicated that it was a soft sound. So you had these symbols for hard and soft sounds, but there was a problem with that. What was the problem? We know there are four levels of the Torah, there is *tanta: tamim, nekudot, tagin, otiot.* There are the letters, that's the lowest level, they are like the vessels. Then you have the vowel underneath the letter, that's like the *ruach*, that's what moves the letter. Then there are the *tagin* that are attached to the letter, they are something like the *nefesh* of that letter. Then there is the *tamim* which is the higher level, the *neshamah.*

So lets just learn it simply, lets say there is a body. There are vowel signs and letters, the letters are the body and the vowel signs are the soul. So then what are these hard and soft sounds signifying? The Zohar explains something very interesting, it asks the question, what is a persons life all about? What is his work in this world? They answer the question that it can't be talking about the body, because the body is something physical, and no matter how much you take care of it, eventually it's going to get old and decay and fall apart. And it can't be talking about the soul because the soul is a part of God, which is perfect and can't be improved upon. So what is the work in this world? So there is the answer that the work in this world is called *chalukah derabanan.* What is the *chalukah derabanan?* The translation means the garments of the rabbis. And it means that the whole work of a person in this world is to weave for himself a garment for his soul in the next world. In other words all the work of a person in this world, learning Torah, and doing mitzvoth and the Commandments, and he perfects for himself a garment for his soul in the next world so that he wont be embarrassed over there. the real work of this world is to prepare yourself for the next world. The whole *avodah* of this world is to prepare yourself for the next world so that the reward you get, you have earned it. So you will be wearing the garment that you made and you will be comfortable with who you are and what you did down here. And if you didn't do the work then you will be embarrassed in the next world with your garment, it could have holes in it, it could have things spilled on it, who knows? So it gives the idea that the whole *avodah* of this world is to prepare yourself for the next world. So this world is really just a preparation for the next world. So going back to *bagad kafrat,* what does that say to us? It says that this test is carried out through these seven Planets. through these seven Planets it looks like the world is being run not by God, and not by higher forces, but its being run by the Planets, and its being run by the Constellations, and sometimes in this world the bad people get good things and the good people get bad things, and everything is basically just *mazal*. Its not according to who is righteous, or who is wicked. If you look at things it really looks to be that everything is run by nature, it looks like its being run by Planetary forces, and that is the whole test of this world and it comes through these seven Planets, and that's what I think they are trying to say. Something that Areyeh Kaplan said, I forget his exact language, but he was referring to the idea that through the Planets, that is how we really get our rewards, because if we didn't have the Planets there would be no reward or punishments. If everybody knew that the good people got good and the bad people got bad then everybody would act good. But if it looks like everything is just coming by chance through the Planets and its all *mazal,* then the whole world becomes a different game, there are believers and non believers, there are people hedging there bets and all sorts of things like that. And even more than that, when all the Planets are working its like you are being tested all the time, if you're put in a place where everything is always calm and comfortable, and relaxed. You could do things or you could not do things, just like the Planets never stay in the same relationships, even for a second, the same thing with a person, his life is always moving. Its one of the main ideas of the Kabbalists, its that life never stands still, its always changing, some people want to say stop the world, let me rest a little bit, but that just doesn't happen. A person is always changing, everybody is always changing, every second the forces change. The people born the one second are different to the people born the second after them, so the universe is always changing, every minute and every second. And it's another main idea that these symbols of these hard and soft sounds hint to the idea that the whole world is built on the system of preparing yourself and your garment for the next world. So that's basically a review, and I think I went a little bit deeper into the idea of the basic ideas. That's always my direction which I teach these things, I try teach things one way and then I try teach it a little bit differently the next time and so the ideas sink in. if its worth learning once then its worth learning a second time, and I think the second time you start to see it more clearly and more deeply.

Lets go on, I want to start something different, I want to read a new commentary which I think everyone will enjoy. I think what is special about this commentary is that first of all it's a very old commentary, its one of the oldest commentaries written on the Book of

Formation, it was written in about the year 1000 by a very important rabbi. He was a rabbi, he was a doctor, and even more important than that for us, is that he was a professional astrologer, a master of astrology. So I want to read you the introduction to his book. First of all his name is Shabtai Donolo, he was from the area of Italy, we will see in the introduction that he talks about where he came from. And like I said he was a doctor and a rabbi and at one point in his life he became very interested in astrology and spent maybe twelve years learning astrology very seriously, and we will talk about that tonight. So what I want to do tonight is first of all before I read you the introduction to Shabtai Donolo, I'm going to start with something interesting in his commentaries. In his commentaries, for example, if you look in chapter four, it has sixteen mishnahs. sixteen very short pieces, the first fifteen are all tremendously connected, they are all talking about the seven double letters, *bagad kafrat,* how they are connected with the Planets and how they are connected with the different openings of the mouth and the different days of the week. And that's basically the whole chapter. But the last mishnah of the chapter all of a sudden talks about something different. It talks about permutations. We touched on permutations once, but lets just look at them again for a second. We said that it was a very deep thing, its one mishnah in the Book of Formations, but there are books and books and books on this one mishnah. If you read *Tikun HaZohar,* you see that it is built on these permutations. If you read the books of Rabbi Abraham AbuLaffiyah, or the books of Sulim HaAliyah, you see that there is a meditative system that is built on the permutations of Gods name, but we will come back and talk a little bit about that. But in any case, the last mishnah of this chapter, all of a sudden it goes off and talks about permutations.

And he says like this: "two stones built two houses. So what that means is that two letters can build two words". So for example you have the letters A and B, and they make two words: AB and BA. Three stones will build six houses, three letters will make six words. ABC becomes ACB and then BAC and then BCA and then CAB and then CBA. There is a mathematical formula for it, these are called factorials. It works with any number you are working with. So if there are 4 stones you can get 24 houses, and you work it out by doing 4 x 3 x 2 x 1 which is 24 combinations. 5 stones build 120 houses, 6 stones build 620 houses, and 7 stones build 5040 houses. "From here on go and calculate that which the mouth cannot speak and the ear cannot hear." After 5040 you get a much bigger number which is very hard to permute, the human mind wasn't built to permute it. But the question becomes, what is the difference between the permutations here and the whole chapter which seems to have no connection? The only connection that I see between this mishnah and the whole chapter is that here it also works on the idea of seven. The highest number is 7 stones that build 5040 houses., so again its also built on the idea of 7.

So anyway, in Shabtai Donolo in this chapter on the Book of Formation, he starts the chapter with this mishnah, the last mishnah. He explains the permutations, and then he comes back and explains the chapter. And we will see in a little while why. But first, before we get into these problems I want to go back and read you the introduction to his book because I think it is tremendously interesting. I would love to translate his book, I once heard that someone did translate his book, a professor or a Rabbi at Yeshiva University. I don't know if it was actually a translation or just something similar about his life and times, but in any case, when I looked on the internet on Amazon, I couldn't really find it. But I will do some more looking because it is a very interesting book.

Tonight, Ill give you a basic translation of at least the beginning of the book. You can see how he got into astrology and how he compares Western Astrology with Jewish astrology etcetera.

So lets take a look: "all of this I strived for wisdom, I said I would chase wisdom and it is far from me, Shabbtai, the son of Avraham, with the family name of Donolo, the doctor. With the help of the eternally living God, who gives knowledge and wisdom and understanding, and always request from him to grant me these things, and I was careful to make many books. And I gave my heart to enquire and explore for wisdom. And of course I was exiled from the city of Orse, my city of birth, by the Arab armies on the second day of Shabbat, (he wants to show you exactly the day and the time of when he was exiled, and you see that he is into the Planetary systems), so Monday, in the 4th hour of the day at the time of the Planet of Mars, on the 9th day of the month of Tamuz, in the year 4685 from the creation of the world, in the 11th year of the 247th cycle, so each cycle is about 28 or 29 years. And at that time they were murdered, ten Rabbis, wise and righteous, their memories should be blessed. Rabbi Chaftai, the son of Rabbi Eli ben Chanel, the great one, the tzaddik. Close to my relative Rabbi Yoel, and Rabbi Amnon and Rabbi Oriel and Rabbi HaTzaddik, and Rabbi Menachem and Rabbi Chayeh and Rabbi Tzadok and Rabbi Moshe and Rabbi David and Rabbi Yermiyah and Rabbi Nuriel and many other elders, the righteous ones from the congregation, and leaders of the generation and students of the Rabbis, may all of their memories be blessed for eternal life in the world to come, amen. I, Shabbtai, was redeemed in Toronto with money of my father when I was twelve years old. And my father and my relatives were exiled from the land of Balarmo, and from the land of Africa, and I stayed in the lands underneath the rule of the Romans. And I turned myself to all of these things that my ancestors did, and all of my work that I worked to do, because there was no work that my eyes saw that my hands did not try. And everything is nonsense in vanity and evil spirit, and nothing is better than anything else under the sun, but I saw that there is an advantage of wisdom from foolishness. Like the advantage that light is to darkness. Because in the shadow of wisdom and the shadow of silver, the increase of knowledge from wisdom gives life to its owner, just like Hashem, the one who gives wisdom. All of these things I struggled very much to learn, to understand medicine and to understand astrology. I copied many books of the wise men of Israel that came before me. And I didn't find any wise men of Israel for any of these lands that understood these things (I think he means medicine or astrology or maybe just astrology). Only a few of the wise men of Israel (here he is talking about astrology) that talk about astrology that is in the hands of the Jews, but they are not really true, because the people that wrote them down did not understand them. and they said that the books of wisdom of the stars are scattered among the nations of the world and they are not written in the same way that the books of Israel are written. And because of this it awakened in my heart, to know and explore and search out the wisdom of the Greeks and the wisdom of the Arabs and the wise men of Bavel in India, and I didn't rest until I wrote down many books of Greece and Mastadonia and their writing and their language, and explained them and also with the books from Bavel and the wise men of India. And I found these books equal in wisdom to the books on the Planets that are in the Jewish books. And all of their knowledge is equal. I also understood that all of these books and everything that is written in them is hinted at in the books of Shmuel HaDoresh."

Today the book is called the Brieter of Shmuel HaKatan. Lets just explain what the words mean. Doresh means the one who gives the talks. Breiter comes from the root word which means bar, which means outside. When Rabbi Yehudah NaNasi connected the mishnaot, he went to all the rabbis and they gave him all the teachings so that he could learn from the rabbis in the past and so that he could write them down and codify them because he was worried that they were going to get lost in exile, and so not everything that he had was written down in the Talmud. What was written down in the Talmud was what was called mishnaot, and later on other rabbis came along to explain the mishnaot, because people already started forgetting them. but besides for the mishnaot there were other teachings that were also very important, but they weren't included in the Talmud for what ever reason. And they are called Breitot, the language meaning from outside. In other words they stayed on the outside. But they are all very important. One of these is called Breiter of Shmuel who was a very early rabbi, it was said that he knew the path of the skyways like he knew the streets of the town of Nahadriyah where he lived. He was a master astrologer. Doresh also means someone who gives ethical talks where people come to listen. But today it says the Breiter of Shmuel HaKatan, katan is diminutive, he calls himself katan out of humility. But in any case, Shabbtai Donolo had it as Shmuel HaDoresh. If you read his book its much more similar to Western astrology than the Book of Formation. The Book of Formation is very hard to relate to Western astrology. I don't really know how Rabbi Donolo sees it as so equal. But I don't think its very surprising that you will find a lot of equality in the Jewish and the teachings of other nations because it seems like it all came from one source, and that source was Adam HaRishon. In other words, astrology was one of the wisdoms that were passed down at the time of creation, and it was continued down into the time of the flood, and when the people got dispersed, then so did astrology get dispersed around the world. But originally it started with the Jews, it was passed down from Adam and eventually it was given to Shes, his son, and then it got given to Shem, the son of Noah, and then to Avraham, so it's a Jewish tradition, that with the dispersion, everyone took it with them to wherever they went. And you will see that that answers many problems that the academics of astrology have. How do you have astrology all over the world? How does everybody have the same 12 Signs? It also answers questions as to how everybody has the same numerical system, numbers are based on ten because the Kabbalah has ten *sphirot,* and the days of the week are seven because God created the world in seven days. So its not such a surprise that every system in astrology is very similar. I can show you also that there are a certain branches in astrology that weren't given over to the nations of the world which I will talk about later in upcoming classes. So don't be complexed that there isn't necessarily a distinction between the Western and the Asian astrology or the Indian and Babylonian astrologers compared to the Jewish astrologers. And its all hinted in the book of Shmuel HaKatan, which maybe one day we will translate. Its not such a long book, but the shorter books are often harder to translate than the longer books, because the shorter books have so much hidden in them, every word has hidden meaning and things hidden in them and its very hard to do the book any sort of justice when you are translating it. I think I may have translated a little bit of it in one of my previous classes, but we will come back to that.

So let's go on. It says "it all built on the work of Breiter of Shmuel HaDoresh, and also the wise men of the nations agree with the Breiter of Shmuel, but Shmuel concealed very much in the book". So what you have to remember is that the Jewish rabbis had a very different approach to life, they held a lot of secrets because things aren't meant to be revealed to everybody, they say: not everything you think you should say and not everything you say should you write down, and not everything you write down you should print. If something is real you don't want to give it to just any body. If you have real knowledge you just don't give it over very easily. Nobody is going to give away millions and millions of dollars and nobody is going to give away stuff that he has been working on for years. Nobody is going to give away real knowledge especially if it can be very powerful. You don't want a very powerful tool to fall into the wrong hands. So it can be tricky reading Jewish literature because they put seals on it, a lot of the books were written for the initiates, and so the initiates had the keys, and then when they got the book, they could understand the book because they had the keys to it. But people who didn't have the keys they couldn't find their way into it so it became a lost thing. And it's the same with magic texts in Judaism, so they took stuff out and they couldn't really use the incantations unless they had the keys. It's also sometimes for the protection of the person. I remember when I was first starting in Israel, I was in a Kabbalah Yeshiva, under a Rabbi from Yemen, and he learned astrology. He learned a special *goral* , which is like a casting device, it's a way of casting in order to answer your questions. It's a way of asking your questions and getting them answered using a Torah divination system. And he used to say that every time he would use it, one of his children would become deathly ill. So after that he said he just gave up, he couldn't use it. So sometimes certain things aren't meant to be used, that's what I think he was trying to say there, that he was being warned.

Lets continue: "After I wrote down all these books, I traveled to different countries to find them, I found myself among the wise men of the nations that knew the wisdom of astrology. I found myself one or two to study with, and then afterwards I found myself a very wise man from Babylon, and his name was Bagdash. And he knew a tremendous amount of astrology. And he knew how to do the calculations, to know in truth that what was and that what will be, he could understand the Planetary systems, and all of his wisdoms agreed with the Breiter of Shmuel and with all the books of Israel, and with all the books of the ancients Greeks and the Macedonians. The chochmah of this wise man was opened and revealed more than any other place that I found it, and after I experienced many tests with him and with the wisdom of this man because he would say, using the calculations and the science of astrology and the Constellations, things that would happen in the future. I offered him money and a big amount of presents in order to teach me the tradition of astrology of the Planets and he taught me to recognize the Firmaments and see the 12 Constellations and the five Planets. and he taught me about the rising Signs, and the Sign at the bottom of the horoscope, and the setting Sign and the top of the chart, and the Midheaven. He taught me the four angles, and how to look at the Planets and the relationships between the Planets and the Signs and he taught me about the stars. Which ones are good and which ones are bad. He taught me to fine the Shadow of the hollowed out wood, (I don't know what that is, it is written in the book of Breiter of Shmuel so I will have to look in there to find out myself what it means.) and he taught me to learn the mazal of the hour, and the Planet of the hour, and he taught me how to answer any and all questions. And after he taught me this wisdom I realized that I had learned tikkun (a fixing), and then I decided that I would explain all the books that came in to my hands, and I gathered together all the knowledge together with the knowledge of the Babylonian and his teachings, and I wrote the book in explanation, which is the book that I am presenting before you, which is the book of the one who searched out wisdom."

Lets read one more paragraph and then I have done the whole introduction to his book.
"and he taught me the cycle of the Planets and of the Nodes, and of the Constellations, in his time which is the year 4706 away from the time of the creation of the world, to know which mazal it was, and which part of which mazal it was, and which Sign all the different Planets and the Node was. And know that each Sign has thirty divisions, and the later astrologers broke them up further into sixty divisions. There thirty degrees and each has sixty minutes. And he taught me the days of the month, which are called in the language of Israel of the Book of the month of the moon. And the month of Israel is the month of Elul, which is the last month of the summer. It is the month of Iran and the month of Egypt. And the days of the week are the Sun, the Moon, Saturn, Jupiter, Mars, Venus, Mercury, the Node, Virgo, Libra, Leo, Cancer and Pisces."
I don't know what he wanted in those last couple of lines.
But any way, we spent a long time tonight doing the introduction, so we are going to stop here for tonight, and next week we will pick up with why Shabbtai Danlolo decided to start the fourth chapter with the last mishnah of the chapter, which is the mishnah on the permutations. Why did he put that first and not leave that for last?

Chapter 3

We are going to be continuing in our series of classes on the Jewish point of view on the seven Planets. I think this is going to be a very interesting class.
We are going to start off with a couple of ideas from the Vilna Gaon, and we are going to build on his ideas on the *perush* of the commentary of the Gaon from Vilna on the Book of Formation. The way of the Gaon from Vilna is to speak very concisely and with hints, he doesn't really explain things fully, although in his commentary on the Book of Formation, he talks a lot more than in some of his books where he is truly cryptic. Here he gives a little bit of a hint as to what he is talking about. And we are going to see if we can try to expand a little bit on the ideas of the Gaon from Vilna. We are going to be talking about how you can influence the Upper Worlds and how you can change the way you receive the influences of the Planets, which I think is something that everybody wants to talk about, its of big interest, how to change the influence of the Planets. if you couldn't use astrology or the Kabbalah to change the way you receive the influences, there would really be no point in learning it. The whole idea is that a person has free will, they can change who they are and they have the ability to modify, at least in some way, the influences they receive. Over the course of time we are going to be talking a lot about the different ways that a person can change who they are and how they can change how they receive the influences of the Planets. the ideal way, which I actually have a book on from the 1500's, where he actually says that all the Torah and mitzvoth were given to the Jews just to overcome the Planetary influences. In other words if a Jew follows the path of the Torah, and does the Commandments to what ever degree, the more that he or she follows the Commandments that are imposed on them, the more that they will over come the influence of the Planets, which is a big deal. I have already talked about that in a number of talks, if people are interested they can go take a look at my lectures on the questions and answers of Rabbi Avraham Barchia, where I talk about this a lot. And soon

I am going to have another book on how through the Torah and doing the Commandments you can change the influence of the Planets which is a big thing. It's a tremendous statement to say that the Torah was given to us just to over come the planetary influences. So you see that people who don't follow the Torah and don't do the mitzvoth, to a certain degree, are slaves to the planetary influences, its much harder for them to over come the planetary influences almost impossible. They don't have a guide and a direction, the person is clueless on how to over come the influences, its much more challenging.
Avraham Barchia goes as far as to say that the only difference between the Jewish and Western astrology, in other words he holds that they came from the same tradition, a tradition that was carried down from Adam HaRishon, which came down to the present day, is that the Jews were able to overcome the Planetary influences. That's the whole difference, we were given the keys to overcome the planetary influences. So when the non Jewish astrologers saw that the Jewish astrologers could overcome the planetary influences, they would be shocked to see that it doesn't apply so much to the Jews. The Jews had this uncanny ability to overcome the planetary influences, and the non Jewish astrologers were stupefied by it.

But that is not the subject matter for now, instead we are going to talk about some other ways, more magical ways, it's connected to astrological magic I guess you could say, although I don't think that it is permitted for a Jew to do, but we will talk about that. And then we will talk about more mystical ways, or more Kabbalistic ways, to change how a person receives influences.

Before we start with the Gaon from Vilna, I want to start off with where we left off last week, an important question. We were looking at the writings of Shabbtai Donolo, the question was, why did he start his writings on chapter 4 on the Book of Formation with the last mishnah first? The last mishnah is about how permutations work, remember 2 stones build 2 houses, 3 stones build 6 houses, until you get to 7 stones which build 5040 houses. Stones and houses here are really letters and words. So there he is talking about the combinations and how you can permute them. so Shabbtai Donolo starts with that, and the 14 mishnahs before that are talking about something completely different, it talks about the seven Planets and how the seven Planets are connected with the seven days of the week, and the seven openings of the head, and they are connected with the seven year *shmittah* cycle and how everything in the world is built on this idea of seven. And then suddenly it goes off and explains permutations. it only does the permutations up to seven which I think is the connection between the two things. but Shabbtai Donolo starts his chapter with permutations, so we ask the question, why did he explain them out of order? Remember in the first couple of mishnahs he talks in general about the Planets, starting from mishnah 8, he goes through each Planet one at a time. He takes one of the letters of *bagad kafrat* one at a time and connects it with a Planet. So let me just read the beginning of mishnah 8. it says: and now it ruled that the letter *bet* which is connected with wisdom, and He attached to it a crown, and He permuted it, one with the other, and he made with them the Moon and the world, the first day in the week and in the soul he made the right eye, and everything male and female.
So I think what Rav Shabbtai Donolo wants to do here is explain the beginning: he gave *bet* to rule over wisdom, and he attached to it a crown, in other words he made it the first

letter. And then he rotated it and with all the other letters he permuted it. That's how I think Rav Shabbtai wants to learn the beginning there. with them he formed the Moon and the world, the first day of the week of the year, and the right eye of the soul. Remember everything is built on the idea of *olam, shanah* and *nefesh,* every thing is happening on three distinct levels and they are all parallel to each other.

I just heard an interesting thing on what the word *mazal* means in Hebrew, its made of the letters *mem, zayin* and *lamed.* It goes something like this: if you are in the right place, the *mem* stands for *makom,* the word for place, and if you are in the right time, *zayin* which stands for *zman,* time. And the *lamed* is for *lashon,* if you speak the right thing, then you have *mazal.* In other words its *olam, shanah* and *nefesh.* You see it happening on all three levels. If you are in the right place, that's the world, at the right time in the year, and you speak the right things from your soul. Then you have *mazal.* So that is an interesting idea.

Rav Shabbtai wants to explain something very deep. Remember we have been talking about this idea that the permutations is the way to get out of body experiences, which in Judaism is how to get beyond your self. It's a way to get up out of your body and get to a higher state. I don't know if I recommend this to anybody off hand, I imagine you have to prepare yourself for it. If you look in the famous book called *Sulam HaAliyah,* the Ladder of Elevation. And there he says that if you do all these permutations then you have to have a special room and you have to wear special garments, you have to purify yourself, you shouldn't really do it alone, you should have a friend with you that if you cant get back into your body he should be able to help you get back. Its not a light thing to do that a person can just jump in to, its a refinement process. It has to do with who you are, what kind of level you are on, what you are capable of doing. But we will come back to that in a minute. We will talk about that with the Gaoni Vilna. But first we are talking about Shabbtai Donolo. He says that there is this idea that if you want to meditate, he gives the example of starting with the first letter which is *bet* and *bet* rules the first say of the week, and it rules the right eye and its connected to the Moon. So what he says here is that you take the first letter which is *bet,* and then you have six letters that come after that, *bagad kafrat.* After the *bet* comes *gimmel, dalled, kaf, peih, reish, taf.* So when you want wisdom you always start with the letter *bet,* because it is a representation of wisdom and you crowned it with that. And then you take the other six letters and you permute them, in other words you rearrange their orders in how ever many ways you can rearrange them. and here since it is seven letters, and you are always going to keep the *bet* first, so then you are only going to rearrange the six letters. And we know that six factorial is 720, so that means that there are 720 ways to permute these letters starting with *bet.* So I give an idea that each Planet could be in one of twelve Signs, and they interact with one of the six Planets, so 6 x 12 is 72 and each of those 72 breaks down into 10 because everything subdivides into 10 which is 720, which is an astrological *remez* as to why there are 720 permutations.
So in any case you see that these letters can be rearranged in 720 ways. So the Gaon fromVilna is going to start off and ask a simple question, what is the difference between the simple letters and the double letters? The double letters are something and their opposite. But the simple letters are just something and that lack of something else. That's how he wanted to explain it initially. But you can also say that there is life in the doubles, there is life and death, and you can say that death is an absence of life. So the Gaon from

Vilna is also going to go a little bit further and say that things run along a spectrum. There is an intermediary point and gradations along the way. For example with the *bet* you see that there will be 720 permutations.

What Shabbtai Donolo said, is that if you want to take the *bet* and permute it, is you have to take the first letter and then permute the rest in 720 ways.

I have to give a class on how to permute because its complicated. I think I will eventually devote a whole class to how to permute things, I'll give you a simple way to do it so that you wont get confused. So for example, lets start with four letters, A, B, C, D. we want A to be in the first position, so the first thing you do is keep the B and you switch the order of C and D. so you have A, B, C, D and then you have A, B, D, C. then you take the 3rd letter and put it in the 2nd position, so you take the C and switch it with B, so you have A,C,B,D, and you also can get A,C,D,B. then you take the D and put it 2nd, so you have A,D,C,B and then you can switch the C and B to get A,D,B,C. so there you have six permutations with four letters, because one letter is not changing, its always staying as the first letter. So that is the idea of how basic permutations work, I gave an example with four letters, and you can expand on that with more letters, but I am going to try give a class on an easy way to do that.

So what he says is that if you really want *chochmah,* you have to go sit and meditate on these permutations starting with *bet.* and if you want lets say, wealth, then you do the same thing, but now you start with the letter *gimmel,* because that is the letter connected with wealth. There are all 720 combinations because there is a continuum, which is what I want to get into with the Gaon from Vilna. First I want to finish off with Shabbtai Donolo, who says you can do it with each letter. He says that any time you want something, for example if you want wealth, then you start with the *gimmel* and its 720 permutations, and you do it on a certain day at a certain hour that is favourable for bringing down wealth and an hour that is connected with Mars for example, which is connected with wealth if I remember correctly. So if you do it at the correct time then the permutations will be more effective.

So now I want to start with the Gaon from Vilna, I'm going to paraphrase a little bit of what he wrote here, he is talking about mishnah number 3, which I will just read quickly: there are seven double letters, *bagad kafrat,* and all of these seven have an opposite.

Lets read mishnah 2 quickly which says that the seven letters are parallel with wisdom, wealth, seed, life, rulership, peace and beauty. In the second mishnah he doesn't tell you the opposites of what they are because really, we should only be experiencing good. But because of whatever sins there are, we get a combination. So now in mishnah 3, its going to tell you that there are also the opposites, even though you don't want the opposite state, because it is not a natural state, it seems like it is more prevalent today than the good states. So it says: there are seven doubles, *bagad kafrat,* in speech, them and their opposites. There is wisdom and against wisdom there is folly, the opposite of wealth is poverty, the opposite of seed is barrenness, the opposite of life is death, the opposite of rulership is servitude, the opposite of peace is war and the opposite of beauty is unattractiveness.

So lets read a little bit from the Gaon from Vilna now. He asks what it means by speech. It is that it either has a hard sound or a soft sound. The hard sound is the thing in itself and the soft sound is the opposite. And that happens in all of the seven ways that the world is directed, in the seven areas of life that we are talking about, that each Planet or *sphirah* influences. And similarly in the seven *sphirot* they have them and their opposites, where you have mercy or judgment. And now we have the main important thing, which is what he says now. In every thing there is a middle point, like it says in Masechet Brachot, that what you want to be is not wise and not a fool.

Lets see what the Talmud says on this, because the Gaonfrom Vilna doesn't quote the whole thing, his way is to bring everything very concisely. 'When Rav Dimi came, he said, a person shouldn't be too tall and he shouldn't be too short. And he shouldn't be too thin or too fat, And not too white and not too black. And he shouldn't be too wise or too stupid."

So the question is, why shouldn't he be too wise? Rashi answers like this: So that we wouldn't be a wonder in the eyes of the people, because they will start talking about him and how wise he is, and the evil eye will rule over him.

My teacher always used to say that when you examine a chart you always look for the too little and the too much. And that is where the troubles in life come from, either too little or too much. There are places like America where too much has destroyed people, and there are places in the world where there is too little, and people get destroyed from the too little. My experience growing up is that it tends to be the too much that is the biggest challenge. A person who has too little doesn't really have the means to go off into a life of dissolution. If you look at the Americans today, they were so wealthy and they went off into a life of total immorality. People in poverty tend to not go off so far. But they both bring troubles, that's what the Gaon from Vilna is trying to say. There is a continuum. For example with wealth, on the continuum you start with poverty, where a person has nothing, he doesn't even have food for the day. And then on the other side you have wealth, for example the richest guy in America, say he is worth 100 billion dollars, I don't know exactly, maybe more, but just the money he makes in one day can be more than what some people can make in a life time, and he can make more in a minute than what a lot of poor people can make in a life time, just from interest accrued on the money he has. And then in between that, you have varying amounts.

I think this is also a big idea in the Talmud. I've always been teaching that the Book of Formation is a three page book. You can write the whole book on three pages with all the wisdom of Avraham our Father in it, all the words, every idea, is giving you the basics of a lot of things, so I think here in this mishnah, don't take things as being so simple. In other words, when he is saying that you break things up seven ways, he is giving you a deep meaning into the secrets of the universe. If you look at the Talmud, it always starts with extreme cases, it will look at all the cases from seven different angles, and then it will narrow it down until you get to the more relevant cases. But you always want to first look at all the different possibilities. And I think that us what Avraham Avinu is trying to tell us here is a round about way, which is what the Gaon from Vilna is hinting at. There is always a continuum, there is complete poverty and complete wealth and then in the middle there are all sorts of variations. You have a person who has food for one day, or a person who has food for a week. And you will see that there are laws pertaining to poor people, you see that there are always laws for the extremes. There will be laws as to which person can collect money, how much money he can collect, who is considered as a poor person. And then on the other side you have the laws for a rich person, which may be different from the laws for the people in the middle. So you just have to be aware that there will always be a continuum. Maybe eventually I would like to do a whole series of classes on this, on how you move through the spectrum, and how the spectrum changes according to Judaism, and all the different laws you will see as you get to the extremes.

Like life and death for example, like a child who is first born, he has full potential but no actuality, he is very frail and very fragile and he has special laws to take care of him. can you break the Shabbat for him? maybe it is easier to break Shabbat for someone who is a little baby because of the laws of him being somebody who is always in danger, so you can be more lenient with the laws of Shabbat with that person. also with an old person, when you get closer to death you have the law of the *goses,* a person who is on his deathbed, he is allowed to make oral statements to change his will in order to settle his mind. But you will see all sorts of things in the middle, in other words each age as a person goes along his life span, slowly the action becomes potential, and the person reaches his potential, and his energies come out over his life time, so the spectrum is the age of the person and each stage of life.

If you look at war an peace, the extreme case would be total war. The rabbis say that in the time of war, the Angel of Death doesn't distinguish between the righteous and the wicked. In other words he just has permission to kill and he doesn't discriminate. I guess that would be the worst case scenario. The best case scenario would be something like total peace, where there is no more evil inclination and there is no evil in the world and everybody lives in peace and harmony which maybe will be some time in the future. So those are your two extremes. You can also have the extremes in a persons life, what kind of internal peace he has.

All the seven areas of life that we talked about are going to flow on this spectrum.

Then the Gaon from Vilna goes on to talk about a book that King Shomo wrote called *Kohellet,* and that book has 12 chapters, I think each chapter is connected to a different Sign, but lets leave that for now. In the third chapter he talks about 28 time periods. And the Gaon from Vilna is going to explain that. He says that there are 28 time periods or 28 camps of the Moon, there are 28 days in the lunar month which means it takes the Moon 28 days to go around the Earth. Half of them are when the Moon is getting bigger and half of them are when the Moon is diminishing. The Moon itself has seven against the seven Sefirot, and each Sefira has four letters of Gods name, which makes 28. In other words you have seven days where is it increasing, it and its opposite makes it 14 and then you have seven 14 days where it is decreasing. All together you will have 28.

So he explains here the idea of the seven Planets and that each one rules a different area of life. For example one rules life, one rules fertility, one rules wealth. Lets go over it again with the Planets. He made the letter *bet* and gave it wisdom, and with that He formed the Moon in the universe, Sunday in the year. With the letter *gimmel* He gave wealth, He made Mars in the universe, and Monday in the year. With *daled* He gave it fertility and made the Sun in the universe and Tuesday in the year. With the letter *caf* He gave life and with it made Venus in the universe and Wednesday in the year. And then He made *peih* and gave it rulership and that was Mercury in the universe. And He made *reish* rule peace and He made Saturn in the universe. And then He made *taf* over grace and beauty, and he made Jupiter in the universe. Each of them have a spectrum, so if you want to really understand the Signs then you have to look along the spectrum. If you are analyzing a chart for wealth you have to look in exactly where it fits in according to the capabilities of the person, and there are many components of that, and you will see it along the whole spectrum.

The Gaon from Vilna says that the *bagad kafrat* leans toward one end of the spectra or the other. He says that if the recombining of the letters is in a straight way, in other words *aleph bet gimmel daled,* then it leads toward the good side of things. If the letters are reversed, *daled gimmel bet aleph,* then they would be backward and that wouldn't be so good. So everything depends on how the letters are rearranged. I did a class on how you rearrange Gods name in twelve different ways. So now he has done the same thing with the permutations, every time you change a permutation, depending on which permutation you have, there is an alteration in the way the energy is coming down to you and how it will influence you in this world, and how you can use the permutations to influence how the energy is coming down. I don't know if I should advise anyone to go and do this, but it might be interesting to try, but it is something that has to be taken very seriously.

I will give you a story, to show you what level a person is on, and the preparation that one must take. There used to be a Tzaddik living in Jerusalem, 30 or 40 years ago, named Areyeh Levine, he was know as being on of the 36 Righteous Men that the world stands on. There is an old tradition of the Gaon from Vilna, that if you have a question that there is no answer to, there is a special way to ask the Bible and to get an answer. And it is based on sevens, we saw earlier in the chapter that Hashem loves sevens. I forget exactly how it works, but you have a special Tanach with columns on each page. First you open it up to whatever page you want, and then you go seven double pages, then seven single pages, then seven columns, then seven paragraphs, then seven sentences, then seven words and then seven letters. Then when you get to that last letter, you find the first sentence in the Bible that starts with that letter. And that will give the answer to your question. And that question is only something that you can't answer through the process of logical reasoning.

There is a famous case, there was a submarine of the Israeli army. There was an accident and everybody onboard died. And when they brought up the submarine, all that was left was basically the people's bones. And they really didn't know how to bury each person, the families wanted a Jewish burial and a grave where they can go visit. The army didn't know what to do, so they asked Areyeh Levine, and the chief rabbi of the army decided to use this device of asking the Torah called the *gorel hagra*, and they brought Areyeh Levine to do the asking because he was a big tzaddik, and he got another nine men, also big tzaddikim, and they got up at midnight and spent the whole night praying special prayers. They also went to the mikvah to purify themselves and then after they spent the whole night praying, Areyeh Levine did the goral 35 times 35 *passukim,* and each one had a hint in it to a different person who died and that is how they found out which bones were connected to which person. But Areyeh Levine was on a tremendously high level to begin with, people recognized him as a very righteous person, but even so, he got another nine people to pray with him, they stayed up all night praying, and only then did they feel like they were on a level to do what is called the *gorel hagrah* and to ask the Torah what to do. Today you see so many people that just come along and ask a question without any preparation, they open the Bible and they put their finger somewhere and they think that God is talking to them. Everyone wants instant enlightenment and instant answers but it doesn't always work that way. A lot of it is dependant on the preparation, that's why I am giving you this story. If you want to permute things then first you should get to the right state of mind, so that you are ready to do it. Because it's not so easy, like it says in *Sulam HaAliyah,* it can be dangerous. You might leave your body so you need someone there who knows the rules and how to bring you back down if you can't bring yourself back down. So it's not something to take lightly, because it's very powerful. And anything that is very powerful can be a healer but it can also be dangerous. This is a warning to the wise.

So in any case, that's what we see now in the Gaon from Vilna. So what we see here that the wisdom can be permuted in 720 ways, so you have to see the distinction between the wise and the total fool. On the one side you have the genius and on the other side you have the autistic and then you have all the other stuff in the middle. There is always this continuum and you are going to see it in everything in life. You really have to see all the possibilities and all the variations. I think it is a way to open up a person's mind, to look at these seven ways of life and the seven ways that the word is directed. Is it a time of war or a time of peace? Is it a time of wealth or a time of poverty? Is it a time of expansion or fruitfulness or a time of barrenness or emptiness? Is it a time of beauty or is it a time of ugliness? Then you have life and you have death, rulership or slavery. All of these things are challenges, and I think that if you look at them and start to permute them you might start to see all the variations along the spectrum. You must always first isolate the extremes on each side, and then you work toward the middle, and then you can see exactly where everybody is holding, it's a judgment call. And that is the whole point of astrology, to be able to see where there is too much or too little in a person. You want to see where there is an excess and where things are balanced.

Ideally you want to balance the chart. The person could have great things in an unbalanced chart but can be an unbalanced sort of person. Because wherever there is too much, there is too little, and wherever there is too little, there is too much and things are going to be out of balance.

So we talked tonight about how there are seven Planets, and each one rules a direction of life. In other words the Moon is connected with wisdom and folly, Mars is connected with wealth and poverty, Saturn with peace and war, the Sun with fertility and barrenness, Mercury with rulership and slavery, etcetera. With each of them you will have to examine, in each persons chart and also in the chart of the world, how much each one is running their direction. And I think when you start to look at the permutations, you start to see that everything is very subtle, because it is always a judgment, you want to see how much and how little is there, and then you can start to get an idea of who that person really is, and what they have to work on and how they can start to change.

In the next class I want to go off and talk about another piece in the Gaoni Vilna and how he talks about colours and how each Planet has a colour. And then we are going to talk about Rav Moshe Cordovero and what he says about how colours are used in Kabbalah, and also in astrology to affect changes. And we will see exactly what it means when you talk about colours in the upper world and in the Planets, so I think that is also going to be a very interesting class.

I really think that you should try meditating on the permutations just to see the spectrum of possibilities. And to think about all the possibilities, to first understand all the end points, all the extreme cases, and then from the extreme cases to work toward the middle. Again talking about what the Gaon from Vilna brought down from the Talmud: not too wise not too stupid, not too long and not too short, not too skinny and not too fat. So think about that and I think you will have a lot of revelations.

Chapter 4

I am going to be doing the 4th class in a series of classes on the Jewish viewpoint of the 7 Planets. Tonight we are going to talk about an interesting topic, once again the starting point will be the Gaon from Vilna and his commentary on the Book of Formation. As we have said before he speaks in a very concise way. After we bring his ideas, we will take a look at Rabbi Moshe Cordovero who was one of the great Kabbalists of all time, he was just a little bit before the Arizal, and he died when the Arizal moved to Tzvat. Rabbi Cordovero wrote a book called *Pardes HaRimonim,* where he summarized and condensed all of the teachings of the Kabbalah up until his time, it was profound work. The Gaon from Vilna actually said about Moshe Cordovero and the Arizal: where philosophy ends, Moshe Cordovero begins. And where Moshe Cordovero ends, the Arizal begins. Today, everybody learns from the Arizal, but remember that you have to have legs to stand on, when the Arizal taught, he taught to all the top Rabbis of his generation, he wasn't teaching a beginners class, he was teaching the top students. It was a tremendously powerful generation of extremely smart people, and his students were all the top people of that generation. The Arizal assumed that you knew Rav Moshe Cordoveros work, and he built on that. But today we learn the Kabbalah from the Arizal, but we don't really have that foundation that is needed if you haven't learned from Rav Moshe Cordovero. I'm teaching the classes over the internet, and we aren't examining every word, but I want to give people a general introduction, so that afterwards they can use it everywhere. If they know Hebrew then they can open up any Jewish writing and they will be able to use what I am trying to teach here as some of the foundation to what they are learning. My main objective is to teach astrology and also a bit of Kabbalah, but also how to look and see the multiple complexities of the universe. It's interesting, there is a phrase in the Talmud that says: just how everybody has a different face, everybody has different thoughts. So that is an important idea, everybody thinks differently. You are going to have your way of thinking about how you want to live, but don't think that everybody is going to run after you and do as you say, so don't think you can attract the whole world. Just like your face is different than everybody else's face, also your thoughts are going to be different than everybody else's. That's just how things work. So if you want to capture the world, it's not so easy.

It's like in politics when you have a dictator. A dictator is someone who wants everybody else to think like him, so he wants to take away peoples free will, he wants to change their minds and he wants everybody to think like him. You also find that with cult leaders, they want to change you to become like them.

On the other hand you have a person who will come along and captivate everybody, they realize that everybody thinks differently, and they see the world differently, but he can give a vision, and even though everybody lives and thinks differently, they will all see his views, and even though they all have different faces, they can all unite his vision and go with it. That is a different type of leader with a totally different idea.

One of the rules of Kabbalah is that there is tremendous variety in the world, it's another idea that you have to factor in. just like everybody has a different face, and everybody will think differently. Everybody will want to have a different profession. Imagine if everybody in the world wanted to be a doctor? We would have no other professions, if everybody didn't think differently, we wouldn't have all these professions. You need a multiply varied universe in order to have a complex universe. God didn't create the world without multiplicity and without everybody being different. Only through everybody being different can you have all these interactions and all these different things happening. You can have people fulfilling different professions and functions and that's how you build a universe, its all built on multiplicity. It can never work to have everybody thinking alike, eventually it will crumble, like with dictatorships because you can't have everybody being the same. It's a falsehood when people don't have free will, and you can't have a world with no free will.

I think this is a bit of a continuation of what we did last time, when you start to do permutations, you start to see the complexities of things. The 720 permutations, and

The variations you see along the spectrum and you start to see the complexities of the world which you have to factor in. I am trying to give you some of the view points from the Kabbalah and how you have to look at the universe, and how you deal with that and how you deal with people and clients. To pick a profession for a person is challenging, you really have to think about it. I remember my teacher used to say that when he first came to New York he spent two years in the library researching every profession. He said that Americans want professions. The first question in America is: what is your career? So he spends two years familiarizing himself with the careers. But it is a tremendous complexity with many different variations in the world, so it's quite a daunting task to be an astrologer.

Tonight I would like to go into something called colours. I will read you a little piece on this chapter by the Gaon from Vilna about the Planets. And he will associate the Planets with the different colours. It's the same concept, we always say there is *olam, sha'ah,* and *nefesh,* there is the world, there is time and there is the soul of man. They are all running parallel to each other. And you can add the colours into that. You can add all sorts of things. You can add the seven rivers or the seven mountains, the seven continents, what ever you want, and you can always parallel them. So now we are going to take the different colours and associate them with different Planets. So that will be out starting point tonight. And then we can talk about how the Kabbalah uses the different colours, and then we will talk about astrology and what you can know about different clients and how they are influenced through colours.

Let's start with the one sentence from the Gaon from Vilna: He created the *bet* in wisdom, and he gave it a crown and he performed all these permutations and he formed with them the Moon and the World, the first day of the week, the right eye, male and female.

The Gaoni Vilna starts with the stars, according to their proper arrangement with the Moon and then Mars and then the Sun and Venus, Mercury, then Saturn and Jupiter, I guess according to the days of the week. And this is how they use the seven Planets, but that explanation does concern me so let's leave that for now. And they are also connected to the seven *sphirot.* It's interesting to see, Rabbi Shimon Bar Yochai wrote two main books, he wrote the Zohar, and the Tikkunai HaZohar. And the whole book of Tikkunai HaZohar is an explanation of all the different permutations of the first word of the Torah. In other words, the first word of the Torah is *bereishit* which has six letters, and it can be permuted in 360 ways. Rabbi Shimon Bar Yochai takes 70 of those permutations and talks about them, and that is the Tikkunai HaZohar. So you can see already that the Rabbis back in these Talmudic times were already using these permutations. Rabbi

Shimon Bar Yochai built a whole book around the permutations of the first word of the Torah.

So in any case, in the Tikkunai HaZohar it says on the seven *sphirot,* that the Moon is the colour is white, that's why one of the words for the Moon is *lavanah,* which means white. And we are going to talk about what the colour white symbolizes. It says here that it is *chessed,* or mercy. The colour of Mars is red, and that is *gevurah* or strength. The Sun is green which is *tiferet* or majesty. And Saturn is black, which is *sod.* Jupiter is sky blue, and that is *malkut* or kingship. Mercury and Venus are parallel to *netzach* and *hod,* and they are purity. I don't know what he means by that, maybe they are pure and you don't see a colour. I'm not sure.

I want to go off and see what the Ramak is saying and how he expands on the Gaon from Vilna, he is going to explain *netzah* and *hod* a little differently, so let's just keep that in mind. The Gaon from Vilna says that their colour is pure, whatever that means, and we are going to work on that.

So now I want to talk about Rabbi Cordovero, some of this class is going to be taken from his book, *Pardes Rimonim,* the translation is literally "Pomegranate Orchard". We are talking now about chapter 10 which is the chapter on colours. I don't think we will do the whole chapter, but I would like to do the first part where he gives you a general overview of colours, and how he relates them to astrology and to kabbalah and he talks a little bit about their uses. It's a very interesting chapter and I think it will also open up some ideas for a person in their Jewish astrological practices.

So let's start now with Rabbi Cordovero, he gives an introduction as to what the whole chapter and idea of colours is all about, he is going to explain all the different colours according to the different commentators and according to the Zohar based on Rabbi Shimon Bar Yochai. He is going to explain the colour of every *sphirah,* and the reason for this. And he is going to explain it in a very short way, so nobody will get tired out by listening to too lengthy an explanation.

This is one of the ideas in Talmud, which is to try and say everything as concisely as possible. This is because the rabbis are worried about the people that will come and read their books, there are so many books and so much is written that the way that many rabbis wrote is to try to condense things and say everything in the shortest possible way. So sometimes it can be very cryptic, if you read the Ibn Ezra, he was known for being so concise that at times he was completely not understandable in his commentary on the Torah. So there is this idea that you try to condense everything, people don't have time to learn everything, today especially with so many different variations in this world. This is getting on to the idea of complexity, in the secular world they say that the last person who knew everything was John Stuart Mill, he lived about 200 years ago, around the same time as the Gaon. And it was said that he knew everything, because at that time you could still learn everything, there wasn't so much complexity in this world, like there is today. Today there are so many people around and there is such an expansion of knowledge that you can spend your whole life on a narrow field. For example if you are a heart doctor today, maybe all you can do is keep up with the literature on the heart, but you cant keep up with all the literature that is coming out every year for all the different parts of the body. So there is a break down in wisdom and you get to a situation today where nobody can know everything any more. Maybe you can know the general rules of the universe, and then from them you can try to figure out the ways of reasoning. That is possible, but to know everything about every subject is too daunting a task. So you can say that John Stuart Mill was the last person who knew everything, because in his time there were a limited number of books. Today, more books are published every year than there were in his time. So today you can't know everything, it's too hard.

I had a teacher that used to say that the world was created through contraction, and today the way to go when you want to know about something is that you have to devote all your time to that thing. Only through this process of only learning about one thing, can you really develop it. But again, we are going off the beaten path here. It is also another idea that there is a limit to what you can know. For example, the astrologers in the ancient times used to be known to have the highest form of knowledge, because the astrologer really had to know everything in his time. The astrologer was somebody who synthesized everything, and he had to have all the knowledge of his time and only then could he practice astrology, because he had to be able to answer anything and everything. It was the highest profession to have in that time. But today with astrology you just can't know everything. So you have to approach astrology from a general way of understanding things. That's why I'm trying to give you a general understanding of the universe so that you can figure out answers to different questions without really knowing everything, because it's just not possible.

Let's just get a little bit of an understanding of this idea of colours, and what they are about. We are going to read a little bit of Moshe Cordovero, and then I am going to explain it for people who don't know Hebrew. This is a book that hasn't been translated to English yet, and I imagine it is an incredibly daunting task, because it is a complex book. But we are going to do a simple translation, and we will talk about it while translating. If there is someone that does know Hebrew and has the book available to them they can look at the chapter on colours, which is chapter 10, and its on page 150.

Let's start, he says that a lot of the time there is a student of Kabbalah that is going to read the Kabbalah books or read the Zohar, and in those books they are going to make the connection between the different colours and the different *sphirot.* And we can add that it is also going to be connected to the Planets. It is important that the student be careful, and it shouldn't go up in his heart or his thoughts to understand this in a simple way. Because the colours are only connected to something that is physical, and something that is physical has a colour. And that is why part of the description is something that is physical. You say that a person has a white complexion or a red complexion, or you say that the dress is red, or the colour of the table is brown. It is an adjective that describes a noun and its something that is incidental, its not the main feature, its usually that the colour is not the main feature of something and the colour can change, but the thing can still be the same, it wont lose its identity. We call that random, non essential characteristics, and then we have essential characteristics too. An essential characteristic is something that if it changes then the thing isn't the thing anymore. For example if you have a pencil or a pen and you break the tip, then it is not a pencil or a pen any more, it can't write. But if the colour of the ink changes a little bit, it will still be a pen. So colours are usually something that is incidental.

Colours are always connected to an object, so with something that is not physical, it's not really suitable to give it a name that is based on something that is physical. So somebody that thinks that the *sphirot* has colours, he is going to destroy the world. It is almost like he is trying to give certain characteristics, in a way, to God which is something that is not permitted. It is prohibited to give any physicality to God. The s*phirot* themselves aren't God but it is the same idea, that you can't really make something physical out of the *sphirot* . So you can't understand in a simple way, you can't think that *hesder* is going to be white, and *gevurah* is going to be red, that majesty will green, etcetera. Like the Gaon from Vilna said, which he brought down from the Zohar. But that is not what the Zohar wants to say, that's what Moshe Cordovero has been telling us up until now. So let's see what the colours really do mean.

Therefore it is important for the student to be careful in this matter, and know that the colors are a parable for the actions that are coming from the root above. For example, *gevurah,* the *sphirah* of Mars. It is connected with strict judgment. *Gevurah* gives you the power to win in battles. And therefore it is suitable that you connect this Planet and this *sphirah* to the colour red, because the nature of this Planet or *sphirah* is to spill blood, which is red. The redness also teaches about cruelty and anger and violence, so in other words, when you say that the *sphirah* of *gevurah* is red, it doesn't mean that it's actually going to be red. The red Planet is not necessarily going to be red, and the same is true even more so when you look at a *sphirah* which you are not even allowed to give the name of a colour, so how can you call it red?

So Moshe Cordovero is telling you that its not really red, but it is telling you about how that *sphirah* behaves and how it influences the world, and the way it influences the world is that is causes war and violence which leads to blood spilling and the color of blood is red. It talks about people who are merciless and violent and rage and blood spillers and things like that, and that is what we mean when we say it is red. Its talking about what the Planet or *sphirah* is capable of doing, that's what it means by these different colours.

Because of that, when we are talking about strict justice, you attribute to it the colour of red. There is no doubt that when we talk about things that are red, it is drawn from the power of its source. In other words, when we are talking about blood spilling over here, you look to the *sphirah* of gevurah or the Planet Mars if you are talking in astrological terms.

Similarly white is teaching about mercy and peace, and the way of the people who are white is to be peaceful people, like old people. Their way is not to go out and fight in battle. What does it mean when you call old people white? As people get older their hair turns white. There is a joke that says why does old people's hair turn white? It's to remind them that their time is running out! If you don't act now, you won't get another chance.

So in any case, when people get older, their hair turns white to show you that they are becoming merciful. The highest stage that a person can reach in the Kabbalah is when he gets to mercifulness. It's a higher level even than wisdom. Wisdom is the second highest level, and above that is becoming merciful. And that is found in older people. They have been through a challenging life, and they learn to really care about other people and appreciate the struggles of other people, and they learn to be merciful. You see that in people that are older and have become white. And therefore whenever you want to talk about peace or mercy or love, we call it by the term of 'white'. And there is the idea again that all of the things that are white are drawn from their source which is white, like we already explained. The *sphirah* is *chessed,* which is attributed to white, and the Moon is going to be attributed to white.

I remember when I first came to Jerusalem, all the old Kabbalists used to wear all white because they wanted to draw *chessed* down to themselves. When you are wearing white clothing it is very easily to get the clothing stained if you don't behave properly, so it made them behave in a certain way. Wearing white also gave them the ability to draw down merciful things, they wanted to bring down mercy into the world. I remember my teachers' teacher wore all white all the time. He spent all his days in prayer and teaching and helping people. Today you don't see any Kabbalists that dress all in white. You see some kabbalists dressing all in white on Shabbat, because Shabbat is a day of *chessed,* and a day of mercy, and you symbolize that through wearing white. Today people don't really know, they say wear anything but just not black, because they say that black is not so great to wear on Shabbat, but people don't really take these ideas so seriously in the religious world. They should because its Jewish law, but some things got lost along the way.

Let's continue, so you see that the colours are only a parable to the *sphirah,* and its talking about the actions of the *sphirot* or the Planets that are drawn down according to their essential nature and the things that they rule over. We can only talk about this in terms of parables.

All the colours will multiply and the boundaries of the colours will divide. They will be higher and more increased according to the strength of the different colours. Each one compared to its friend. And therefore we talk about the Upper world in terms of colours.

And you will see that each colour is going to break down too. You will have the seven essential colours, but then you will also have a break down of that. For example you have pure white, you have off white, and all different variations, like what you have with house paint. It used to be that you would go to hire a house painter, he would come and give you seven colours, and you would choose the one you want. I remember maybe three years ago I painted my house, and the painter came and gave me a whole book. About twenty different variations of white, thirty different variations of yellow, and by the time you have looked at all of it you have one giant headache!

That's the way the world is today. It's the same with book stores, I remember when I was in America I went to Barnes & Noble and they have four stories with tens and thousands of books. You can spend your life there, it's just too much. That's the way the world is today, there is a tremendous breaking down into variations. But you can think about that here too, don't think that there is only one *gevurah* coming down, or just one type of red. There is a range, Stalin killed 20 million people, Hitler killed 15 million people, there are people who have only killed one person, and there are variations. So there are different shades of each color.

But in any case, let's go on.

So there is no doubt that the colors are like an introduction to the *sphirot* and how they act, and how their energy is drawn down. So he is going to tell you now that you can use the colors to draw down energy, and this is important for practical reasons. And because of this reason, for example when someone want to draw down love in this world from the Aspect of mercy, he should imagine the name of the *sphirah* written in the color of the matter that he wants to draw down according to the color of that *sphirah.* If he wants to bring down complete mercy, then he should think about pure white, and if he wants something that is not completely mercy, but majority mercy, then he should think of the *sphirah* in a color that is similar to plaster which is off white, it's not exactly white but it is close. And similarly if you want to draw judgment down into the world, you should imagine the *sphirah* to be in red. Usually when you are drawing energy down, its only drawing down names of God, you aren't really drawing down the *sphirot,* but each *sphirah* is actually representing a different name of God, and when you bring down that name you should imagine it in that color, and that will intensify the power of that name. And similarly the actions that you do when you draw down the colors, whether you need mercy or love, then you should wrap yourself in white. We have a very good example of this, which is the *Kohanim,* they were the High Priests that performed the services in the Temple, and they need to have the quality of mercy, and their garments were white garments to teach about peace, and that is the idea that the High Priest on Yom Kippur would take off his golden garments and wear pure white garments, because on that day you want mercy, you want all your sins forgive. So on that day all his clothes would be white to indicate the idea of drawing down mercy. And similarly the idea of amulets which they don't use too much today. One of the famous Kabalists wrote that people don't have the knowledge to write amulets any more. They can only partially work because people lost the ability, they don't have the spiritual strength to make an amulet that will work properly and draw down certain powers.

When a person makes an amulet for mercy, he will write the name of God in a white that is a very pure white. Because then it will increase the strength of that name. So for example say you want to draw down *chessed,* so you use the name that is connected with *chessed,* and you draw it in white, so that it is intensified. Here is an example, I used to have a problem with my jaw, so I would get acupuncture and it helped for a while, and then one day I went to a different acupuncturist who used an electrical device that was about ten times stronger. And that is similar to the idea that if you are drawing an amulet and you draw the color that is connected with the characteristic that you want to bring down, then it is intensified. So when you are making amulets you want to have a connection to that color. And similarly with judgment, you want to take that name that you are drawing and you want to imagine it in red. It's similar to something that the Ramak says, that with each day of the week you should imagine a different colour. Say it's a Monday which is connected to Mars, so that is the day that when you pray, all the letters should be red. On another day, Sunday for example, you should imagine white it's the day of the Moon and of *chessed.* On each day you want to be in tune with the world, so although you can't have seven different prayer books, each day of the week you imagine the letters in a different colour and it will intensify the prayers if you are in the right frame of mind. Again the same idea of intensity is what he is talking about and how to draw down the intensity of the influences. And his main idea here is using the example of the High Priests on Yom Kippur wearing special all white garments, and this was the only time of the year that they wore these special garments. All of these things are known and they have been explained by the people who write the amulets, but I personally don't have any connection with amulets. It was a Kabbalah idea. You want to get the angels to somehow submit to your will and do what you want. A lot of Kabbalists say that that is forbidden, and that's what Rav Cordovero is saying, that he doesn't like to use amulets. He believed that trying to force the angels to do what you want is going a little bit too far in his opinion.

He says that he has seen the amulets that teach about judgment which are written in red, and the ones talking about mercy are written in white. And on love it is written in green, and it is all according to what the different amulets want to effect.

So all of this is an introduction to the colors and how their actions and how the energies are drawn down from above. But you don't really think about the *sphirot* being those

colors, but more about how those *sphirot* are acting. But you can't say that *chessed* or mercy is white because it is not a physical thing so you can't give it a colour.
Now we are going to go a little bit into astrology, he says: similar to this were the people who worshiped the stars. If you read my class on Avraham Barchia, he talks about the areas of astrology that are permitted and forbidden. One of the areas that are forbidden is to pray to the Planets or to supplicate the Planets. And that is why he calls them worshippers of the Planets, because they forgot that there is something higher than the Planets so they are putting all their energy into the Planets and supplicating them. Their work was to offer incense to the Planets in order to try draw down the energies of the different Signs, and they used to dress in clothing that was similar to the actions that they wanted to do. In other words they would also use this idea of the colors to intensify the effects of what they were drawing down.

So we are getting into the colors now, eventually we are going to talk about it in a practical, rabbinic way. For example, just understanding the Sign of a person, let's say their Sign is Cancer. Cancer is connected to the Moon and the Moon is white. So a person with Cancer rising, you can often see those people with extremely white skin, almost pure white. So if you see a person like that you know almost immediately that they are Cancer rising. If you see a red head with a little bit of a reddish color skin, then you think that they are more of a Martian type of person. Most of my astrology today is done over the internet. I don't even see the people. It used to be that you would see the person and get clues from that. For example if a person comes to you dressed in black it may be a person who is under the influence of Saturn. If a person comes dressed in white you know they are under the influence of the Moon. So you can learn something about them, but today you don't have that anymore. Most of my business is over the internet, I don't see them , I just have their horoscope. So I don't get the clues of how they dress, or with women you can also look at their jewelry and how their hair is styled. All those different things give you clues to how the person is holding what level they are on.
But we are going to talk about that more in the upcoming classes, this is just an introduction. We will talk about how you can look at the client and what you can see and how you can tell what the persons Ascendant is. You look at what they are wearing, what their skin is like, how they hold themselves etcetera.
So now Moshe Cordovero gives you another example of the breastplate of the High Priest. He used to have a breastplate that was made up of twelve different stones. And they were also what you drew down from the twelve tribes of Israel from above. In other words each stone on the breastplate was a different color. And when that stone lit up it would draw down from that tribe that was connected to that characteristic and that was connected to that stone.
We haven't really talked about stones yet but we will, they are also on that chart that I always use. Remember that it is all parallel; there are twelve stones, twelve sides to a square, twelve Signs, twelve months of the year. All of these things are parallel. So don't go too far away from this idea. There were scientists that said that if a man looked with his eyes at flowing water, it would increase in him the white humour in his eye. In ancient medicine they had all different humours in the body. Four humours and each one had a different colour. But let's not go into that too much, right now they are talking about white, and if you look at flowing water it had the ability to increase this humour. Today I think we would say the humour is something like a hormone. So the water would

increase this humor in the body. So much so that a sick person who was very unsettled in his mind, and whose sleep wouldn't descend easily on the mind, they would have him imagine flowing water, in order to raise up the white humors, or these hormones, and these hormones would decrease the other hormones in his body and they would allow him to sleep. So you see even the doctors back then used the ideas of colours awakening different hormones in the body in order to effect changes in the person.

Chapter 5

We are going to be continuing in our series of classes on the Jewish view point of the 7 planets. In the last class we started talking about colours. We saw that each Planet is connected to a different color, and we also saw that all the *sphirot,* and the Upper Worlds are also connected with the colours. And then from that we went into the Ramak, Rav Moshe Cordovero, he was one of the great Kabbalists and he has a whole section on it. He wrote his master work called *Pardes Rimonim,* the Orchid of Pomegranates and in it he has a chapter on colours. We started to learn that, we did the first chapter, the section on colors is about three or four chapters. He started to say how when you talk about the Upper World, it really has no colors, color is only an attribute to physical things. Physical things have colours, but with something in the Upper World, spiritual things, you can't really use the idea of colors. But he explains there that the colors indicate what kind of energy the *sphirot* give. They are the source of the energy of what happens in this world. And by knowing the color of each *sphirah* is, it can give you a hint as to what kind of energy it is sending down. For example *gevurah,* the *sphirah* of war, and battle and things like that, its red, because red is the colour of blood. But don't think the *sphirah* itself is red, it's just and indication to show you that it is the source of where all the energy is coming down from. We learn that it is similar with the Planets. I want to learn a little more from Rav Moshe Cordovero who writes and explains about all the colors, then I want to come back and use it in astrology and show you what you can learn from it. Because it works two ways, let's say you have Mars and red. So you know that Mars is the source of violence. But what you also learn is that what you can learn about red, is what you can learn about Mars. So if you want to learn about what Mars is then you study the colour red: you study blood, you study all the things in the world that are red. And that comes to give you a greater appreciation as to what Mars is. And we are going to do that with a lot of things, not only colors, I want this to be a general introduction to a lot of things in astrology and also in Kabbalah.

There are also the seven metals and each one is connected to a different Planet, so we are going to talk about why that is, and we are also going to talk about each day of the week, we are going to spend a lot of time on that, and why each day of the week is connected with a different Planet. And I want to teach people to experience the day of the week by looking at the Planet that rules that day and to really see if you can come into this feeling for each day of the week. And then you can also take the Kabalistic *sphirot* and do it the same way. So I really want people to start getting a feel for everything. And that is important because then you start to see the world really differently. If you see something that is red, you can go back to its source which is *gevurah,* or you go back up to Mars.

What is really the difference between Kabbalah and astrology? There was a famous Jewish rabbi in the Middle Ages that said there is two ways to understand the universe through the Torah. And in the Torah all the secrets of the universe are hidden in two different types of studies. One was Kabbalah and one was astrology. And the two are quite similar. I think astrology is what the Arizal said is the Outer World, or the World of Circles or the World that the energy is coming down from and running nature. Kabbalah is talking more about the spiritual way the universe is run. God gave the Jews the Torah, and by living by the Torah and doing mitzvoth they can overcome the Planetary influences and change the stars. To be a Kabalistic astrologer, you have to know both. You have to know the physical causes of everything and you have to know the spiritual causes. Its not enough to know just the physical, you also want to understand things on a spiritual level and how everything is being influenced by the Kabbalah, the "innerness" of the world, which is higher than the "outerness" of the world. In other words the whole astrological system becomes dependant on the Kabbalah and the system of the Torah and the Commandments. And that is why in astrology we always talk about the main thing being the Ascendant. Why? Because the Ascendant is the receiver, its not only about the energy that is coming down, it's about how you take the energy and use it. That depends on who you are spiritually and even more so who you are physically. It's also about how you view the world, what kind of environment did you grow up in, what sort of education did you have? All of these things impact how a person receives the influence of the Planets or the *sphirot*. So it's not just the stars, it's also the man and how he receives the influences of the stars. So that is an important idea, and that is why the Ascendant is so important, because there you can look to see how a person receives the influences. And that is how a person can change his identity. So I want to do a little bit of Kabalistic astrology. We haven't really talked about this yet, so I want to talk about the spiritual causes of things. And then at the end of this class we will come back to the colours, because I want to show how everything in the world, each day of the week, each month of the year. We say *olam, shanah, nefesh*, in the universe, in time and in the person, everything is connected to a Planet or a Sign or a *sphirah* in a spiritual way, and we want to start to look at things in a way that we can connect it back up to its source, either Kabbalistically or astrologically or even the two together.

So I want to talk about spiritual causes. This week in the Torah reading we start with the book of Shemot, the book of Exodus, which is the second of the five books and it starts with the Jews in Egypt and how they gradually became enslaved, and how God chose Moshe and Aharon to lead the people out of Egypt and into the desert and to receive the Torah. But in any case, there is a book that explains the Torah on a very high spiritual level, the name of the book is the Zohar, it's a rabbinic literature that is attributed to Rabbi Shimon Bar Yochai, who lived in the second century. His master work is the Zohar, and there he talks about the spiritual causes of things. It's a tremendous book that I highly recommend to everybody. When I started learning Kabbalah, it must be 35 years now, I learned with some of the top old Kabbalists of that period, and they all said something which is important for practicing astrologers, that if you have children and they have a tough time spiritually like having a tough time in school, either getting along or understanding the material or concentrating or having a spiritual crisis, the thing to do is to get them to read the Zohar, it doesn't matter if they don't even understand what is written because the book is on such a high level that just by pronouncing the words, it changes who you are. I'm not a kid any more, I have an old man's body but a young man's mind. So I still have my problems, I try to read the Zohar every day, but when I feel like I'm losing it then I try to read it even more,. And I always find that it is like the best drug. It really has an important effect and it changes how you receive the forces, so I think it's an important tool that should be in the Kabbalistic astrology toolbox. So when someone needs it then it is a certain type of medicine that you can give out.

I would like to read a little bit about spiritual causes from the Zohar, about how they work in this world that are caused by things going on in the Upper World. Maybe it's not so apparent to people, but really if you want to be in astrology you have to be able to see everything. The astrologer and the Kabbalist are both telling you the way of the world and nature, and how the world is run physically and also spiritually, and they are both connected and both are considered the highest profession, the top Jewish scholars were the Kabbalists. And the top Western master was an astrologer, he knew everything that was going on, he knew everything and how to explain and interpret things properly. So we will talk about spiritual causes and then how to connect everything down here on Earth to the Planets and the different Signs and what can be learned from that. We will also finish off Rav Moshe Cordovero where he talks about colours, and we want to learn what each individual colour in itself means, which we will learn Kabbalistically and then we will transfer it to astrology and then we will go on and see some other things, like different minerals, different plants, different grasses, different days of the week, different hours and different parts of the human body, and we will start to work on all of that.

We will start off with a piece about Egypt and what happened to Egypt when the Jews came into Egypt. Just like the Jews came into Egypt and things happened to them in Egypt, things also happened to the Egyptian people. So that is what I want to start talking about, and then I want to relate it to all of history. The giving of the Torah was about 3300 years ago and they were in Egypt about 3400 years ago, and we will learn a little bit about history from then until now. So I will read and translate, just because we say that the words of the Zohar have a powerful impact on people. So let's start, we are going to examine one paragraph from the Torah. "A new King went up over Egypt and the new King did not know Yosef" so in other words he didn't remember all the good that the Jews brought to Egypt and he made all these decrees. That is the standard way of looking at it but here, Rabbi Shimon Bar Yochai is going to learn it in a completely different way.
"A new King went up over Egypt…."
"There was a book by the Rabbi Habdunah, the old man, and there it says, what does it mean that a new King went up and ruled over Egypt? Come and see"
It is interesting that the Gemarah and the Talmud always say 'come and hear' and the Zohar always says 'come and see'. I think that is because seeing has a much bigger impact than hearing. But we are talking about different levels. We always see seeing as a higher level than hearing. Hearing is *binah* and seeing is more *chochmah* which is a higher level.
"And so it says, all the nations of the world and all the kings of the world, their kingdoms did not get strengthened, except because of Israel"
Here we are learning a major spiritual principle, it's incredible, and you can see that this book was written almost 2000 years ago, and you are going to see this principle all throughout history. Let's go on and explain that.
" Egypt was not ruling over the whole world until Israel came there and entered into exile."

In other words, until the Jews came into Egypt and the exile began, Egypt was a nothing nation.

"And then it became stronger than all the nations of the world"

It's an amazing principle, only when the Jews came into Egypt and became subjugated, did Egypt become the strongest nation in the world. And he goes on: "Babylon didn't become the strongest nation in the world, except when the Jews were exiled there."

So you see that he is starting to show that wherever the Jews get exiled, that country becomes the strongest country in the world. You can think about it now. Where are all the Jews? In which countries? We will come back to that.

" The Romans didn't rule over the whole world, except for when the Jews were exiled there. These nations were known for being despicable nations"

And he is going to bring you passages to show you that now. So in other words before the Jews were there they were nothings, and you will see now that after the Jews left they went back to being nothing.

"They were lower than all the nations, and because of Israel they became strong"

"It is written, they were called the House of Slaves" in other words they were low-lifes, they were slaves.

You see that Egypt was on a lower level than all the other nations at the time.

We see what is written about Babylon: "the land of the Cosdine, this nation was not" they weren't even worthy of being a nation, it was a nation of simpletons until Hashem picked them up, which we see is because of the Jews.

What does it say about Rome?

"I made you smaller than all the other nations, you are despicable"

So you see that each of these three countries was the lowest countries around in their time, and as soon as the Jews got there they became lifted up.

"And none of them became strong, except because of Israel."

"because when the Jews go into exile in that country, right away the country becomes stronger than any other country in the world.:"

What is the reason? This is the question, why do all of these nations become strong when the Jews are exiled there?

"because Israel is against all the other nations of the world"

I think what he is trying to say here is that the Jews were 70 souls when they went down into Egypt, and we say that there are 70 nations of the world (the *goyim)* and each nation has a minister that rules them in the Upper World and it rules whatever is happening in that nation, and whenever the Jews go into a specific nation, the minister of that country becomes powerful and stronger than all of the other ministers in the sky.

What is the reason? It is because the Israelis are against all the rest of the world.

"When the Jews went into exile in Egypt, Egypt started to be established, and their government became more powerful than all the other nations."

"A new King ruled over Egypt, and it was established"

Why didn't it say that the old King died and his son took his place? Why did it say that a new King ruled over the country? In other words it is saying that the minister in the Upper Worlds suddenly got a tremendous boost of energy from God and he became stronger than all the other emissaries of the other 69 nations. And that is how he wants to learn about the new King coming over Egypt, that the minister of that country in the Upper World became stronger than the ministers of all the other ministers of the 69 nations.

"and he became powerful and he got up and his country, Egypt, became the strongest ruler"
"and he was given strength and rulership over all the other ministers of the other nations."
"The first thing that happens to a country is that its minister becomes strong, and afterwards, the nation which is below."
In other words first the emissary of Egypt becomes stronger in the upper world, and then the emissaries of the other nations in the Upper world, and then down here on Earth the nations becomes more powerful. So that is what it means when it says that a new king ruled over Egypt.
"And they said that the ruler of that country in the Upper Worlds also became new,
"until the Jews came there, it didn't have any rulership over the other nations, but now it became more powerful that all the other nations of the world".

It says in the Book of Proverbs, that there are 3 situations in which the world shakes. One of them is when a slave will rule. I guess that is talking about what we said in the beginning, that they were a nation of slaves.
"When God brings a judgment upon one of the nations, first be brings judgment upon the ruler of that nation in the upper world. The first thing he does is he visits the ruler of that nation in the Upper World, that is to say that he makes low the ruler of that country that are in the Upper worlds, and then after that he brings his judgment down here, and then on the rulers of that country."
"And what kind of judgment is he judged on, this ruler above? He takes the ruler of that country of the Upper World, and he gets passed through a river of fire and he goes all the way down to *gehenom*"
"and then right away the rulership of that country down here is taken away, right away they make an announcement in the upper firmaments that the rulership of this emissary from the Upper Worlds has been removed until this voice reaches all the different firmaments, until it comes down and gets heard down here. A voice goes out and announces to the whole world, until it gets heard by the birds and the young children and to the stupid ones down here who don't know anything."
I skipped a little piece in the Zohar here because it wasn't really relevant, where he talks about the different types of prophecy. When the world is on a low level the type of prophesy gets announced through problematic people. Today we ask autistic children what is going to happen in the world. We don't ask big rabbis or big scholars, you ask autistic children. And everybody takes it as the word of God. So you see this today, that when the world is on a low level then the prophecy comes through lower people or from children. When the world is on a higher level then it comes through people who are on a very high spiritual level and can affect the changes and modify the risk of the Jewish people.
So that is what he is saying here, that once they knock down this emissary of the Upper World, the Egyptian emissary, then it gets announced to all in the Upper World that it has been removed and put through the river of fire and that he has been removed from his rulership, and then it comes down here and everybody knows about it.
Let's keep moving, this is important stuff, and you can think about it in terms of America, which we will come back to, but now we are talking about Egypt, Babylon and Rome. But you could say that the American exile is a continuation even of the Roman exile that still hasn't ended. But we will come back to that.

I'm going to skip another little piece because I don't think it is relevant for us right now. "Rabbi Eliezer and Rabbi Abba and Rabbi Yossi were traveling from Tiberia to Tziporah and on the way while they were traveling they met a Jewish man, and he started to talk about the prophesy of the destruction of Egypt: Hashem rides on a fast cloud and comes to Egypt and all the idols of Egypt were moved out of the way. Come and see, all the kings of the world and all the people of the world, they saw that they were nothing before God. All of the residents of Earth are thought of as nothing before him. and whatever God wants he does in all the firmaments." even though all of the strength and all of the might that Hashem showed, and his Mighty arm that he raised up in Egypt, only in the end, when he came to the last punishment, to kill the first born was where God Himself came to Egypt.

"Why was it different to all the nations of the world?"

It's asking, what is the difference now? When ever Hashem wants to make something happen in the world he just makes a decree and then it is established. So what is the difference here that in Egypt it is as if God rode on a fast cloud and came to Egypt and he killed the first born by himself. That is what the Zohar is asking.

So the Zohar will now bring an answer to why does God go down to strike the first born himself? So it says: "because the King is coming out to bring the Queen". He explains that when the Jews went into exile the Divine presence went down with them, and now when Hashem takes the Jews out He will take the Divine presence with them. So He will take out the Queen that was there, the Divine presence. Because of the dearness and importance of the Divine presence, that is why He came.

"And He had to come to pick her up, and He gave her a hand to lift her and straighten her. Just like God will do at the end of the exile of Rome"

"Rabbi Yossi asked: is it true that because the Divine presence was there, then why wasn't it similar in Bavel, that the Divine presence went down there? why didn't God come down there to take out the Divine presence?"

" we say that in Bavel it was because of the sins that the Jews did there, that they married foreign women"

"and they put their holy circumcision in a foreign place, and because of that all the miracles and wonders were taken away that should have happened when they were taken out of Bavel. This wasn't the case in Egypt"

In Egypt people guarded the Covenant and they didn't marry foreign women so they were taken out with big wonders and miracles.

"they were all the tribes of God, the children of Israel went in and the children of Israel came out"

In other words they didn't damage themselves spiritually, so they were suitable to be taken out by wonders and miracles. God Himself, so to speak, came down to take them out.

"and at the end of the exile of Rome, when God wants to make known His power and His glory, then even though Israel is not suitable for them to have a revelation of God"

Like it says about the last generation, a generation where everybody is guilty, you just look around at the tremendous immorality in the world. It's almost impossible to believe and its not getting any better, it looks like things are getting worse but that is another topic.

"because of the glory of the *Shechina,* Hashem is going to come down by Himself, to pick up the Divine presence and to lift Her up from the dust"

So the end of the exile is going to be special, in Egypt, everyone was taken out with wonders and miracles and that Hashem Himself is going to redeem them and take out the Divine presence because they guarded their spirituality and they were worthy of these things, in Bavel they came out by way of nature, it looked like it was non miraculous, especially because the sexual immorality was rampant, so they came out without God coming to take them out.

But even though it is much lower than Bavel, the End of Days could be with a generation where everybody is messed up, and God Himself is going to take them out because He wants the whole world to see His glory. The time has come to reveal who He is, and who His people are, so He is going to do it with wonders and miracles again.

"Woe to that King and woe to that nation when Hashem will come down and say to the Divine presence: wake up and lift yourself up from the dust. "

Meaning that he is trying to say that the Divine presence is trying to lift herself up from exile and from dwelling among the impurities.

"get up and go to Jerusalem, take off the ropes around your necks, who is the King and who is the nation that can stand before him"

That's what we are saying now in the world. Who would have believed that Russia would disintegrate and that all the Jews would leave. Did anyone believe it? Did anyone believe it was imaginable, Rabbi Shimon wrote this about the 2000 years ago, how was he able to predict the future? Most people can't see in front of their noses, some astrologers can predict up to a year in the future, some can see up to ten years into the future, maybe the top ones can predict 20 years into the future. But Rabbi Shimon wrote this 2000 years ago, he is telling you what is happening right before your eyes. He is telling you clearly in the Zohar that in the End of Days, the Jews are going to be brought out and who is going to stand before them? Even though they are not worthy. They are going to be taken out and none can stand before them. Not the Russian government, not the Arab nations, all of whom kicked the Jews out when the Jews started moving back to Israel.

So why are people reading all these nonsense books like Nostradamus, and the prophecies that you can read into them however you want. Look at how clearly Rabbi Shimon is telling you 2000 years ago what is happening today in front of your eyes. It is a clear prediction, it's not written in esoteric language or anything. He says "shake off the chains around your neck, who is the King and who is the nation that can stand before him? Let the idols of Egypt move aside"

When it says the idols of Egypt it doesn't mean stones or trees, its talking about all the emissaries of Egypt of the Upper World and all the Planets and the stars that the Egyptians worshipped.

"all of them are going to shake before the fear of Hashem when he comes to redeem the Jews"

I could go on, but the main point he wants to make here in the whole point he is trying to ask is why is it that when the Jews go to a nation and become subjugated , the nation becomes strong? Because it seems like it is an embarrassment for God. Because when the Jews go down into subjugation, the Divine presence goes down with them to protect them and watch over them. So it would be embarrassing for the Divine presence that is down with the Jewish nation and protecting them to be in a lowly nation that was being ruled over by other nations. So as soon as the Jews go down into a nation, that nation becomes exceptionally strong, stronger than all the other nations of the world, and you see this happening throughout history. It's a spiritual law, you see this throughout history, even though he wrote this 2000 years ago, you see that where ever the Jews went, they took over, and that country became the preeminent nation of the world, if you are talking about Babylon, or if you are talking about Persia, and then Greece, and then Rome, and they all took over the world. And it's going on until today. If you look at the early 1900s in Europe, that's where the Jews were congregated, and it became the cradle of civilization at that time until the Holocaust. And now today, where are the majority of the Jews? They are in Israel and America, so you ask which is the strongest nation of the world? You have to count how many Jews there are in America. They say that the Jews have 4 million people and America has 400 million people and they are fighting over who is going to knock out Iran. And the only reason that America is so strong is because the Jews emigrated there and like Rabbi Shimon said, the Divine presence is there with them, and that nation became strong. So that is where the majority of Jews are today besides for Israel. and just like from this story you can get the idea that even in this generation there are also going to be miracles and wonders, not because we are worthy, but because it is time for God to make himself known.

But you can read the whole history of the world like this, think about Spain, when the Jews lived there it was the top country of the world, but since they left has anybody heard about Spain since 1500?

What happened to Russia after the Jews left? It broke up into 15 pieces and its power in the world is minimal now. You can do that throughout history, where ever the Jews were that nation became a super power of the world, and when the Jews left it lost its power. Rabbi Shimon Bar Yochai explains this phenomenon and he explains why it happens and he explains why it ends.

As an astrologer you have to understand the spiritual causes of things, especially if you want to be a Kabalistic astrologer. An astrologer has to understand the outer aspects of the world. When you add the word Kabbalist, then the astrologer also has to understand the inner aspects and spiritual workings of the world.

In the next class there is one more piece from the Zohar that I would like to read, and then we will go back to colours.

Chapter 6

In this class we are going to continue our series on the Jewish viewpoint of the 7 Planets. We took a detour, we went into colors, and we are going to come back to them. But before I go back into colors, last week we looked at the Zohar, about the spiritual laws of the universe and how the universe is teaching us the Jews get exiled, and where they are exiled that nation becomes the most powerful nation in the world, and when the Jews leave that nation, then that nation disintegrates. And we have mentioned that we have seen that all over in history, we saw it with Russia; and we saw it in Spain, and where did we not see it? We have not seen it yet in America but it looks like the Americans have been good to the Jews in certain respects. People say that it is because of the Holocaust and that people needed to rebuild so G-d sent them to places where they knew they would have an easy existence, and they can rebuild and we can see a tremendous amount of rebuilding of the Jews in America and in Israel, the re-blossoming of the Jewish people after the war, the rehabilitation period but sooner or later the rehabilitation period is going to end and the Jews are going to be in trouble once again. When G-d thinks that time is right nothing, no government, no people can stand in his way. We saw Russia open the doors and then just let all the Jews out. And if you look throughout history we see can all these principles. Wherever the Jews went that country became super and when the Jews left then the country disintegrated. Do not expect anything different in America, just how and when it is going to happen is the only question. We saw that the first thing is that either it gets transmitted to the wise man or it gets transmitted to the birds and the fools and the young children. We can already hear the whispering that the great days in America are over. And you know it is a nation in spiritual and military unravelling. And so we are just watching from a distance to see how it is going to crash.

But in any case let us go on. Of course we want to see how the Jews get out, will they get out, how will they get out, something to look forward to. So let us go on, I want to talk about one more thing as long as we are in the Zohar and Parsha Shmot, I was reading from Parsha Shmot, the exodus, I think it was on page six of the Zohar in the original paging system, today I want to go back and start looking at some other stuff that is also sort of contemporary, in the news and you will also see other spiritual laws that are brought down by Rabbi Shimon in the Zohar. And then again it is stuff that astrologers don't need to know but Kabbalistic astrologists need to know. Because the real cause of things are happening on a very high spiritual plain. You can see that if you look at today, everyone goes to modern medicine or modern natural medicine, but that stuff is only really working on a very low level, they say it is working on the spirit and not the body, but it is not 100% true what they are saying. It really only works on a very low level, the Kabbalah says it is working on a very low level of the soul. It is working on maybe the lowest level of the soul where there are some changes that can be effected but the real changes you have to go to the Kabbalah to see how to make the deep fundamental changes in the person. Because that is where all the spiritual laws are contained is in the Zohar and so it is a tremendous book to read. So let us do another page or two in the Zohar.

Let us talk also about other spiritual sins that can affect the person and their destiny and a whole nation's destiny. We touched on it a little bit last class when we asked what was the difference between the Babylonian exile and the Egyptian exile. We said the Egyptian exile, the Jews came out with miracles and wonders and the Babylonian they just came out in a natural way without any signs and miracles. What we said is that G-d went down to Egypt to knock out the first borns in Egypt and bring the Jews out, and that did not happen in Babel, he took them out from a distance. So we have explained that the difference was that the Jews in Babel, they intermarried. That was their big mistake. They intermarried and it lowered their level and because of that they were not suitable to have miracles and wonders.

So let us start with this and then we will go back to colors, which is also a very important subject matter.

"There are three types of people that push the divine presence from the world, cause God not to dwell in the world." In other words Hashem leaves and it is as if he is not here. He takes away from looking at the things and directing them, he leaves them open to nature. Not only is it that Hashem sort of leaves the world but also: "The people cry out because of their sins, because of their suffering and their voice is not heard." That is even the righteous people; their voice is not heard because of these three sins. What are they? Someone that has intercourse with a woman, who is *niddah* the technical definition is a woman who has a menstrual cycle, and after it ends, after seven days if the blood stops she can go to the Mikvah and then ritually immerses herself and then she becomes pure.

But if someone, if she has not gone to the Mikvah yet even if the blood has stopped she is still ritually impure and it would be forbidden and when a man has intercourse with her, it is a very harmful thing. The Zohar is going to explain:
"This is no impurity in the world stronger than the impurity of a woman in *niddah*"
Especially back in those days it was much more powerful the more than today. " The impurity of the woman who is *niddah* it is more difficult than all of the other impurities in the world." because the person who has intercourse with the *niddah* he becomes spiritually impure and whoever comes close to him, and touches him, also become impure.
"Where ever he goes he pushes away the divine presence from before him."
"And not only that but he brings bad things onto himself." " And also he brings bad things to the children he gives birth to." A man that has intercourse with a woman that is impure at the time, and they have a child, that child is spiritually impure. He brings on to his children spiritual evil, bad illnesses on himself. In other words, a person that has intercourse with a woman is spiritually impure brings illnesses, on himself and on to his offspring that he gives birth to, from this woman.
"Since the man draws close to a spiritually impure woman, this spiritual impurity jumps on to the man, and attaches itself to him, it stays in all the limbs of his body, and the child that is conceived from this union, brings a child that is spiritually impure. And all his days will be in impurity", this child that is born from this union. So you see how important it is, the principle of the women going to the Mikvah here. Again we always say the idea of Jewish law, sexual laws, is to produce a spiritually elevated children. That is the whole purpose of sexual union. The Jewish Rabbis and the Torah, conceived it as being connected with procreation. It seems obvious that the whole reason to have intercourse is to have children. Today, you know that today a separation has been made. Sex became like an indoor sport and the one thing you keep in mind is doing everything you can to prevent having children and maximising pleasure. In the Jewish religion there is an idea that the whole idea of having sexual union was so important and if they did it in an impure way then such a way that would bring down spiritually impure children. If you study the law, that is really the goal, it is to create spiritually high children, to keep the religion going and the world going, and to purify the world and it was not to maximise pleasure at all. Today the whole idea is to maximise pleasure, people go off into all sorts of things, this and that because they really want to get as much pleasure as they can while they are here. So if the person does have intercourse with this woman who has not gone to the Mikvah yet, then the child that is produced, you can see from that union is spiritually impure and he has tremendous difficulty to get to a high spiritual level in life. It does not mean he cannot do it, they say that nothing stands before the person who does Teshuva, repentance. There are plenty of people today that do not know what type of union they came from but they can do teshuva and overcome it, it is just very hard.
Let us go on. "because all of his foundation of the person, it was an impurity, a tremendous strong impurity because of all the impurities of the world, as soon as a man draws close to a *Niddah*, that impurity jumps on him. Like it says in the Torah, her impurity will be on him." That is to say that it jumps on him.
"It is the covenant is also the secret of G-d's name. The secret of G-ds name is the establishment of the malchut which is the truth" and so G-d was very angry at people who did not guard their Covenant.

It says in the Torah in the Midbar, desert, that the Jewish people began to do sexual impurities with the daughters of Moav.

"And right away G-d became angry with the Jews. The leaders of the Jewish people, that knew what was going on and they did not protest"

"Take all the leaders of the people and bring them before Hashem and in the sun." In other words they blamed the leaders because they did not protest, so the leaders got punished first.

Rabbi Aba asked: What does it mean opposite the sun? It is because of the sin that they did with their covenant which is compared to the sun. That is because the Sun and the guard is the holy Covenant "just like the sun lights up and shines on the world, similarly the Covenant, the circumcision of the man, it lights up and shines on the whole body of the man."

And what does it mean by the Guard? "It protects a man, the man who guards his covenant, his circumcision, than he is guarded from above."

"Similarly the holy covenant, guards the man and somebody who guards his covenant, he has no damage in this world. Somebody who guards it does not have any damage in this world and he is able to draw close to it." And even somebody that guards their Covenant, he draws close to a wild animal, nothing is going to happen to him. That is what it means when he is taken out against the sun, because of the sin that he did to his circumcision, which is called the sun.

And now he is going on to the second one that we talked about it before, Someone that takes the holy circumcision into another place. "It says do not have another G-d before me, do not bow to them, and do not serve them. I am your G-d a jealous G-d. And it is all one jealousy, and then the *shchina* is pushed from its place. If someone who lies to the circumcision, it is carved on the skin of the man, it is as if he lies to the name of G-d, somebody who lies to the seal of Hashem, as if he lies to the king. There is no portion of the G-d of Israel if he does not do continual repentance for what he did" ,

because if the person wants to correct himself he needs a tremendous amount of repentance to get back to the holiness. So you can see people that do all of these things which is rampant in America today because of the total immorality of the society there. The people that are inside the country do not see it but if you look at it from afar, at the level of immorality is just unbelievable, I can talk about it but it is hard to talk about it because it is just so bad. And so you can see with the person that does all this immorality, that it does tremendous spiritual damage.

And today we can see two things that are happening that are a problem. The first is for a man to be with a woman who is spiritually impure and second that a Jew should not be with a non-Jew. And that is also very difficult. These unions will cause tremendous suffering on the children born from them, according to the Zohar. We saw before that Rabbi Shimon could predict what is happening today 2000 years ago and we can see just how accurate it was and how clear his prediction was that we have to maybe start to believe it, maybe he does know what he is talking about here as well, so it is an important thing.

The problem today with astrologers and psychologists and even these so called Kabbalah books, they are all about how to get pleasure in this world, they all really against Jewish philosophy. Especially the so called Kabbalah groups in America that are teaching Kabbalah to the masses, they are just like the psychologists.

There is a guy I know, and he is a nice guy. He wants to influence people and so he wrote a book, it is called "Kabbalah, how to get wealth, love and happiness through the Kabbalah." And that is not what the Kabbalah is about. It is but it is not about getting your worldly desires. Why do people go to psychologists or astrologers? They go because they want to know how to get their worldly desires, how to get love and wealth and happiness, everything that they want to get. And most of it is things that are going to in the end going to bring evil on to them. But for the astrologers and the psychologists today, that is not their concern. The person wants to get this so let us help them to get it. But it really is not for the persons good in the end.

In America everyone is having a tremendous pleasure meanwhile a very big percentage of Americans have been mentally ill. How many people are on Prozac? America it is called the Prozac nation because they are all on medication. They are all going to their psychiatrists and their astrologers and the psychologists and their life coaches and their massage therapists and their acupuncturist and there tantra teachers and whatever, but why are they not happy? Why are they on medication? Why are 30% of them mentally ill? Why is half the country on anti-depressants? Why are they not happy?

So somebody is doing something wrong. You have got to start to question the ability of these psychologists and psychiatrists and all these people, the life coaches, whoever you want. You have got to start to question that maybe they are not helping people and they are actually messing people up. And that is what I want to teach people in astrology, especially Kabbalistic astrology, you want to teach the person to be happy and the happiness comes from doing things properly, doing the right things in the world even on a spiritual level. It is more than being a good person, how can you be a good person if you do not know how to be a good person? What does it mean to be a good person? Everybody thinks they are a good person. The head of the mafia, if you ask him are you a good person, he will tell you I am a good person. Ask the head of Syria are you a good guy,? sure he is a good guy he will tell you he is a good guy. The thing is what makes a person good? And so it is a thing that we have to come back to if you want to be a Kabbalistic astrologer and really help people. And that is what we want to teach here, How to really help people so that they will have true happiness in this world. Kabbalist also want people to be happy, it give rules for living in the end of days, like the time we are living in. It says two things, it says you have to study Torah and you have to do good deeds. So you have to learn, you have to learn what a good deed is and then you have to start to do good deeds. And then you will be protected from tremendous disintegration in the world today. Certainly by trying to maximise your pleasure it is not going to help, just like he says you are getting more and more into the impurities of the world and more these impurities jump on you the harder it is to escape them and the more damage they do to you.

Let's go on. "And they forgot their Lord our G-d, what does it mean that they forgot? They pushed away from the holy covenant." He says here that they did not do the brit properly when they did circumcision they only did half of what was asked of them to do in the circumcision. "And they did one part of the circumcision"

I will not get into the technicality of the circumcision, but one part of it they did and one part they didn't.

"Until Deborah the prophetess come, she prophesized to all of Israel like it is written because they did not do the stage of the covenant of the circumcision. As soon as they did the proper circumcision then Hashem blessed them."

And now let us go on to the verse. We see there are three things that push G-d away from the world. When we say to push G-d away, we mean He hides his light from certain people. And when he hides his light from people then they become under the influence of the stars. The whole call of astrology and Kabbalist astrology is to teach people how to get above the Planetary influences. What is true freedom? It is to get above the Planetary influences. You want Hashem to direct you. You want to be connected to Hashem. G-d is telling you what to do and not the Planets. and so in order to do that He gives you direction, you can already see here three things bring you under the Planetary influences instead of taking you above them.

And now let us go on, we said that the first one was having intercourse with a woman, a *niddah*, the second one was somebody who has intercourse with a non-Jewish woman. Of course all of this works on the women too. A woman that does not guard the laws, of course she is also obligated and if she is with a non-Jewish man then it is all the same thing. At one time it was more prevalent from the man's side, that the man would go off more than the women. Today it is probably about equal I would guess so just because it was more prevalent with the men, they use it in the masculine but everything is also has the feminine side too and we see it today, I do not think the immorality among women is less than among men.

The third one is someone who kills their children.

"the foetus that a woman becomes pregnant with, and she does something to kill the baby in her stomach."

Back then they would give the women a special drug that would kill the baby. today they have stronger medicine. They have birth control pills and that prevents pregnancy but now if the person gets pregnant she can take the morning after pill as they call it now. The morning after pill that if she is unlucky and got pregnant she can kill the kid. So that is another thing that causes the Divine presences to leave the world.

To me I understand that if the Divine presence leaves the world then one comes to be directed by nature. You become directed by nature, by the Planets and you are not a free person any more. You are a prisoner. What is so bad about it? The Zohar says that if the woman kills the foetus then she destroys the building that Hashem made and his true work. he or she kills the foetus that was made by G-d in the woman's stomach and that he did it with this tremendous artistry. He made a new child, a little world, and a person comes along and kills it. It says in the Gemorrah, that Hashem he makes the woman pregnant, He designs something inside of something else that he designed. And he puts inside it a spirit and a soul. Nobody can build or design like Hashem.

"somebody who kills the person, and somebody that kills his own children." is a tremendous thing if you think about it.

With regards to Israel, when I tell people the Arabs kill us, maybe it is understandable on a certain level, you are at war, they hate us, and there is all this propaganda against us. But why do people, why do Jews kill their own children? It is a serious thing. If you do not have mercy on yourself why should others have mercy on you?? You do not want to raise the kid, you do not have time, you want to go out and have a good time all your life. It is the first commandment in the Torah, to be fruitful and to multiply. you can see the whole world suffering today because they do not have children. It is going to be the cause of the economic downfall of the world today, in the next couple of years, because the western world does not reproduce, it is going to kill the economy of the world, it is even in China! China has a one child policy they are really vicious about it. They are only allowed to have one kid to a family and if a girl is born the parents come and kill the girl because they want a boy. This is happening in the 20th century and China has become the new world power so to speak. I do not know if it really will be but they are definitely overtaking America in economic output and military life. So it is fearsome to even think about what is happening in the world today. So he is telling you how bad a thing it is. G-d made this person inside another person imagine a scientist trying to do that? And then a woman that comes along and takes the morning after pill to get rid of it. Rabbi Shimon says that this is one of the three things that cause the Divine presence to leave the world. And that is very serious.

I had a friend years and years ago, he is actually Jewish and he married someone Jewish and the woman got pregnant and they did an abortion. They were not ready and did not have enough money, they were going to school and they did not have time to take care of the kid so they aborted the kid and then they got a dog. As if the dog would be a replacement and then a couple of months later they got divorced. A dog is not a replacement for a child, it is not why people get married. it seems the main reason to get married is to have children. If you do not want to have children than what is the point of it? The marriage is not the happiest institution in the world.

How could a person kill their own flesh and blood? It is overwhelming to contemplate. Anyway, let us go on.

"Why should a person kill their own son?" "the foetus that the woman became impregnated with, and kills it from her stomach, destroys the building of G-d, what G-d built." And then " like a person that kills other people, this woman kills her own child." "and these are three evils that the whole world cannot bare, and because of this the world starts to dissolve, little by little and people do not even pay attention." So America is going to get destroyed, do not think it is because of the economy or because of who the president is, if he is going to be democratic when he is running because of that, or if you do not like the republicans then it is because of them. It is because they are doing all these sins, immoralities that are going to destroy it.

"because the world starts to dissolve a little by little, and people do not even pay attention. And they do not even know why the world is falling apart." Everyone says America is falling apart and Europe, but they do not know why. The psychologists cannot teach them, their astrologers, and their life coaches can't teach them, why is everything disintegrating before my eyes? And then there is nobody to teach them.

"and this one who kills his child, he destroys the building of G-d, and he pushes away the divine presence that goes and flies around the world, and it does not rest any more in its place. And because of this, the spirit of G-d cries. And the world is judged for all these three things. Woe to the person who does any of these three sins, woe to him. It would have been better for him if he was never born"

"Israel is worthy", even though the Jews were in the subjugation, they were slaves in Egypt, and they had no free will, they had no money, and there was a law against the Jews. Anyone who would not kill their child would have to give their child over to be thrown in the river, and sometimes they killed their children themselves. And there were laws passed to kill all and any children that you gave birth to. But even though they were living in this tremendous period of darkness and slavery and there were all these laws against them to reproduce, even so they did not pay attention to any of these laws.

and they guarded the laws of the ritual impurity and regarded the laws of being with foreign women, and they did not abort their children" even though there was a judgement against the people, if you brought a child into the world they would be killed. The child would be killed and you would be killed. And even so they still reproduced.

"the Egyptians made a decree that any boy that was born has to be thrown into the river, they did not find one person who aborted their child and all the more so after the child was born, they did not dream of killing it. And because of this the Jews were worthy to come out of Egypt, to come out of the exile. Not only did they come out but they came out with wonders and miracles."

he goes off now and explains the three things and how we know that the Jews guarded them in Egypt. I am not going to bring down the proofs as to how we know it, I am just going to read the last line, "from all these things that Jews guarded themselves when they were in Egypt, they were children of Israel when they went in and was as children of Israel that went out."

"they guarded themselves from all of these impurities and it is written: these are the names of the children of Israel. And they went in as the children of Israel and they came out as the children of Israel, because they guarded themselves as they should have guarded themselves.

So you see again, the tremendous importance of the spiritual understanding of the world and the spiritual causes of things in the world. He is explaining what is causing this dissolution of the world today. He says it is the gross immorality and especially the immorality of the Jews, they are supposed to be the light unto the nations and unfortunately a lot of Jews they practice these things, they are bringing tremendous difficulties to themselves and to the world. If you want to be a Kabbalistic astrologer the whole thing is to really make a person happy, and the person becomes happy when they are living properly. When they are doing things that are right in G-d's eyes and they are guarding themselves, they are guarding their purity and guarding their high level. And if you go off into immorality, like we have seen today, it just brings more and more impurity on the person, he or she becomes enslaved to their desires which is another way of saying the Planets. They become enslaved to their desires and they lose their free will, they have no influence over what they do and eventually they come to do tremendous immoralities they even come to kill their own children.

But in any case, the whole idea is how to guide them as an astrologer or as a Kabbalistic astrologer. These are things that we are going to go into in the future, questions such as: how do you fix people and how do you help them? That is the main point of astrology, We want to help people get above the Planetary influence and that is what we are going to teach in our class to make people become Kabbalistic astrologers.

Chapter 7

We are going to continue our classes on the Jewish view point of the seven Planets. We went off on a tangent last week when we started to talk about colours and their connection to the seven Planets and the *sfirot,* so we are going to continue learning about the colours, because I think it is an important issue. Even though we are going to be leaning from the Ramak, who talks more about how the colours are connected to the *sfirot,* you can extrapolate from that what you can learn about the Planets and the seven colours, and more than that, after that you can learn more than just how the Planets are connected to the colours, you can also see all sorts of different things that are connected to the seven Planets. There are seven days of the week, every hour there is a different

Planet that rules, and every hour they switch the ruler ship, which also goes in sevens. You will see that there are seven grades in the land of Israel, and seven rivers, and there are seven types of metal that they connect to the seven Planets, and if you pay attention to all these things and you listen to the Ramak, in the book *Pardes Rimonim,* the Orchard of Pomegranates, you will see that you can really learn a lot from what he is saying about the colours and you can extrapolate it to astrology and all different areas and you can see how much you can learn about why the colour is connected to that particular Planet.
We will start to talk about it in this lecture and if not, then the next lecture. I also want to talk about how you extrapolate and use this information from the Ramak as it is very important.

Let's just summarize what he said in the first chapter. In the first chapter he talks about the colours in general and he wants to explain first of all that you mustn't think that in the Upper World there are colours, there is no such thing as colours in the Upper World. The Upper World is not corporal, and if something isn't corporal it doesn't have colours. But what he wants to explain is that everything that happens in the Upper World is a root for what happens down here. And he is telling you that when you attribute a colour to one of the *sfirot* in the Upper World, you are actually talking about how that *sfirah* is the root for things that are happening down here that are connected with what is happening with that *sfirah.* For example you have the *sfirah* of *gevurah* which is connected with the colour red. It's not because *gevurah* is actually red, it is because red is the colour of blood, and down here *gevurah* is violence and warfare, its cutting and it's all sorts of blood spilling, so because of that they attributed it to the colour red to teach you how it manifests itself in the Lower Worlds. He also is going to talk about it a little bit in terms of astrology. For example he teaches about how when the Ancients used to do ceremonies to bring down the influences of the Planets, like if they wanted to bring down Martian energies, the red Planet, they would wear red clothing and all sorts of things like that to help bring down that energy during the ceremony. It's not because the Planet is red, it's because it is symbolizes something. They would also do it on a day of the week that was connected with Mars.
We are going to learn about when a client comes to you all dressed in red, what does that mean? Or when a client comes to you all dressed in black. You can learn all sorts of information from the colours. So he talks about that a little bit, and he talks about how when they used to make amulets, if they really wanted to intensify the energies coming down to the amulet they would use colour to intensify it. For example if they wanted to bring down the energy of kindness they would make an amulet with white. For example, old people have white hair and beards so it indicates that they are more gentle and kind.
But he talks about how if you want to bring down kindness and intensify the amulet then you make it white, and the names you use you write in white so then it makes the energies that you are drawing down even more powerful.
So in the next chapter he is going to talk about each *sfirah* and which colour is attributed to it, which the Kabbalists attributed to each *sfirah,* then we will connect it to astrology and then we will branch off into other things that the astrologers brought down and connected with the Planets.

Let's start now, the Ramak talks about each *sfirah* by itself and he starts with the *sfirah* of *keter*, which is the highest *sfirah* of the ten *sfirot.* There are a couple of different opinions which he talks about now. The first of which is that *keter* doesn't even have a colour, because it can't capture the actions of what it does because it's so hidden. In other words it's so high up that you can't see what it's doing. Remember he told us in the first chapter that the colours are not really in the Upper World, they are just teaching you about the actions of the *sfirot* and how they cause what happens down here. And if you don't know what *keter* is doing then how can you attribute a colour to it? So that is the first opinions that he wants to give, in other words you can't give it a colour because you can't see what its actions are. So they called it a light that was hidden, to teach that its actions were hidden from view. But there are other Kabbalists that come along and say that it is proper to attribute a colour to *keter,* and the colour they attributed to it was white. And they have proof for that by using a quote from the Book of Daniel: 'the Ancient of Days sat on His chair, dressed in a garment the colour of white snow.' And the Ramak explains that the Ancient of Days is actually *keter.* This is something that Rabbi Shimon Bar Yochai explains in many places in the Zohar. The Arizal explains that the Ancient of Days is actually the higher part of *keter,* and *keter* itself we say is made up of two pieces, there is the Ancient part which is the highest part of *keter* and the lowest part of the Upper World, and then you have the second part which is the highest point of the world under it. So it is the lowest point of the Upper World uniting with the highest point of the Lower World and together that makes *keter.*

So in any case, the higher part of *keter* has the colour white attributed to it. It is given the colour of white according to its mercy.

But the Ramak says that you don't have to buy this explanation that it is white. Why? Because you could say that it is just talking about the garment of *keter.* So the garment of *keter* is white, but not *keter* itself. Or you can say that the hair of *keter* is white, but not *keter* itself. But you don't have to say that these two opinions are differing with each other. In the one place it says that you can't give it a colour and in the other place it says that its colour is white, but they are not necessarily contradictory. You can answer that by saying that when the energy of *keter* is in the Upper World and it's not coming down, then you can say that it doesn't have any colour. But when the energy of *keter* is coming down into the world, then you can attribute to it the colour of white.

Shimon Bar Yochai gives an example of the two aspects of *keter,* that on the one side it doesn't have a colour and on the other side it is white, he brings down the opinion of the Zohar who says that *tal,* which is dew in English, is droplets of water that come down and when they are on their way down they really don't have any colour, they are unseen. But once they come down to the Earth, then they reveal themselves as being white. So he wants to say that just like how *keter* is still up there and you don't see its actions, it doesn't have a colour. But when it comes down and it acts in this world and you can see what it is doing, you can see the kindness and the mercy coming down, and then you can attribute to it the colour white. Because it is so hidden, you can't even attribute to it the aspects of mercy because it is so hidden. But when it reveals itself and it is revealed through the other *sfirot,* then it becomes pure white. You'll see that there are different shades of white. There is pure white, there is snow white, there is off white, there is cotton white, there is plaster, there are all different shades of white, and *keter* is the whitest of the white. Why is it the whitest of the white? Because it is pure kindness and mercy. And in the Book of Daniel when it talks about the clothing and the hair, it's an example of what it going on in the Upper Worlds where things are hidden and that's why keter in the Torah is also called machshov halavan, in the story of Rachel and Yaakov, it's like white magic. Which is also, machshov is like to reveal something. Revealing the white. And that is also the same idea, the revelation of the white, after it is revealed down here the keter it comes down here and is revealed. And that's talking about after it's revealed to the sfirot and it comes down. Like we already explained. So that is the first 2 perushim, the explanations of the colour that is connected to keter. One is that it doesn't really have a colour because you can't really see its actions and how it acts down here. On the other hand, other Kabbalists say it is white and attribute it to white because it is kindness and mercy. Pure kindness and mercy and pure white. They even have a proof from Daniel. So the rabbis answer it up and it's not really a contradiction because one is talking about where it doesn't really have a colour and keter is still not really revealing itself. So you don't know what its actions are so you can't know what its colour is either. On the other hand when it comes down it reveals itself already and you can see that it is acting down here as pure kindness and mercy, pure white. And they also bring a 3rd opinion. There is another opinion that keter is black! A completely different idea now. They are going from unseen to pure white and now to black! This teaches you again on its hiddenness. The light in it is hidden and its complete hiddenness. Darkness that completely conceals itself. And this opinion also doesn't contradict the first 2 opinions because keter is called darkness from the attribute that it is so high up and completely hidden that you can't see it. It's all completely dark and you can't grasp it. Even the sfirot that are under it can't know anything about it. And that's talking about the Aspect where it is attached to its creator. In other words, keter is the first sfira, so you have a stage where it is still inside the original emanator. In other words, keter is the first emanation and the time where it is still attached to the emanator, when you are talking about that aspect of keter, then you have to use the term black. It's completely hidden and you can't know anything about it. You see it's sometimes like Saturnian people are like that. Saturn is the colour of black (we will talk about that later on). And just like keter is the highest sfira in the Planets, the highest Planet farthest away from the Earth of the original Planets was Saturn. It was considered slow because it had the slowest orbit. It took 30 years to make an orbit. The next closest Planet was Jupiter which took only 12 years to make an orbit. It was so far away that they may be attributed the colour black to it because it was hard to see. You couldn't know about it. There are certain characteristics about Saturn that you can't know about them. They are very… they hide themselves tremendously. There is a certain type of Capricorn that hides itself. They are very taciturn, they don't like to talk, and they feel because they are somehow connected to keter, they have this aspect in them. The really strong Saturnian people, like the deep thinkers, are all the time up in the Upper Worlds and they never send things down. They are always in the aspect Air, lost in space and their thought are contemplating high things and they are unknowable. And so there is going to be a connection between the aspect of keter and Saturn. But we will come back and talk more about the colours connecting with the Planets. But you will see, for example, if a client comes dressed all in black. Right away you will think of Saturn because Saturn is black and if you're an Astrologist or Kabbalist you will also think of keter where it's totally concealed in the emanator and already you start to think of things because of that colour.

Anyway let us go on. You can't know anything about the keter at this stage where you call it black because at that time, in a certain sense, there is no difference between the emanator and what was emanated. Except that there are certain higher things on the emanator than on the emanated. But at that stage they are still one within another. So it comes down that there are 3 colours we give to keter. The first one is when it's connected to the emanator and that is called darkness/blackness. The second aspect is when it is inside itself. It's not together with the emanator but it is inside itself, not revealing itself. And then you can say it doesn't have any colour. It exists but it doesn't have any colour because you can't see its infactions. And then you have the 3rd stage which we call white. And that is like the example of the dew that gets thickened and turns into ice as it comes down. And that is when it's already appearing in the lower sfirot. And now the Ramak also wants to go on to explain that the darkness/blackness itself has 3 different stages/3 different kinds of blackness which is very interesting. The first stage of blackness is when you take keter itself. Keter is tremendous light, like we said before. But because of that, its light is so blinding and high, we can't see it up in its high place where it doesn't come and get filtered. So we call it blackness because of that. But now he wants to say something different. He wants to say "this giant light of keter, this high white light in relation to the emanator it is like it is nothing. And because of that we call keter black. We call keter black in relation to what is above it. In other words, in Kabbalah everything can be judged in 3 ways; in relation to itself, in relation to what is above it, and in relation to what is below it. I think that is what he is getting at here when he wants to say there are 3 types of black. The first type of black is going to be in relation to what is above it. Keter is called black in relation to the emanator which is above it. Even though it is a big light and the sfirot underneath it can't experience keter in itself, keter in relation to what is above it is like nothing. In that sense we call it black meaning like it is nothing like zero. He is going to bring a quote from the Zahar. He quotes Rabbi Shimon Bar Yochai (I will read it in Hebrew, actually Aramaic, as it is only one line "********" The high keter, even though it is pure, refined light, it is called black in relation to the cause of all causes. So the first way of looking at black is looking at it in terms of what is above it. Everything that is black in terms of what is above it. Everybody has parents. However old they are. Today I am 60 and my parents still look at me as if I am black. Whatever you get to, they still see you almost as nothing. Always in relation to what is above you can look at what is below as being black. In other words, the big light of the emanator wipes out the light of keter no matter how big it is because it's nothing in relation to what is above it. In other words, you are comparing this high white light to the one who gives out the light to all the things. The second way of looking at it is that it is called darkness because it is so high up. And here we say it is the opposite reason. Here it is called black because it itself is such a big light. It is called black because it is so big, so high and so hidden. Its light is so refined that even the other sfirot can't grasp it. I'd say here we are talking about keter in relation to itself, in other words before it comes down but when it is already separated from what is above it, from the emanator. Here we call it black because it is so high up. In terms of itself it is a big light and what is under cannot receive it. And then there is a third stage, which we are not going to talk about so much. But we somehow talk about the female side of keter as being black. I guess the bottom part of keter, the malchut of keter as somehow ebbing black. And I guess you can say that is in relation to what is below it. There is a certain element of... I don't know, he isn't going to explain it here, we have to look somewhere else. The bottom piece of keter is black in relation to the other higher pieces. Because somehow it is going to separate itself off from its essence. SO you can't call it this pure white anymore, its unattainable. But we will wait on that. So there are 3 types of black; one is called black in relation to what is above it, because everything is nullified in relation to the big light that is above it, then in relation to itself because it itself is this tremendously high light, and then because the bottom piece of itself is separating itself off, that bottom piece is called black.

So we have finished more or less with keter now and I think we are starting to get a little idea of different colours. It is a very important subject and you can expand it with so many things, if you just start thinking about it. For example, this week try think of every day of the week in terms of colours. The first day of the week is Sunday so imagine yellow that day. The second day is the Moonday, so think silver. There's this place where the Ramak talks about the amulets. When they wanted the amulets to be extra strong they would make the names of God in colours to make it come down more powerfully. There is a place where it says "each day when you pray you should imagine the colours of the prayer book differently. So on Sunday you should see all the letters of the prayers yellow because it is a solar day and Monday you should see all the letters silver. You then start to get into the rhythm of things and you start to feel what all the Planets are, what all the energies are, what the sfirot are… You start to connect to yourself. I was actually thinking today, maybe I should have 6 different prayer books? But there is a limit in size, in space, it would probably take up a lot of space and cost a lot of money and then you would have to remember which book to take with you etc… But then someone was telling me today that on the iPod you can get a prayer book put in and you put it in on a particular Hebrew day and then for the next hundred years each day it will give you the exact prayers that you need. I was thinking that you could also probably colour it. You could tell it on Sunday to make all the prayers in yellow and on Monday in silver and Tuesday in red… It works out well too because on Saturday, when you can't use your iPod, the colour is black. And so you can use the regular prayer book which has black letters and everything will work out fine.

So again you can see this idea from the Ramak that you can use it also for say the days of the week, when you are praying you can visualize the colours coming down on that day because that is the main energy coming down on that day.

Let us carry on and start with the 2nd sfira, which is chochma. He starts off by saying that some people who attribute it to the colour of red but he doesn't like that. They attribute to the aspect of judgment and he already nullified that idea somewhere else in his book. He doesn't like the idea of it being red. That's how we learn in Kabbalah that there are 3 sides, the left, the right and the middle and the left side is judgment. Chochma is the side of mercy so how can you connect it to red? He says that other people gave it the colour of sapphire. Sapphire is a colour that receives all the other colours in it. Somehow when it is shined upon, you can see all the other colours in it. Others still gave it the colour of tchelet. We will talk about what that word means in Hebrew in a little while. Tchelet is like sky blue, the colour of tzitzit. Tzitzit were all white, except for one which was this like special blue, sky blue, and the blue of the ocean. Anyway sapphire receives all the different colours in it. There is another perush where it is tchelet because it is the final purpose, the tachlit, using the other language now tachlit for tchelet, of all the colours or all the colours are included in it. Like from lishon kol, kol means everything. In other words, in Kabbalah when energy comes down it sometimes comes down from keter, which has all the other 9 sfirot in it but you don't see because keter is so big. Then keter keeps the light of keter and sends everything down to chochma. Chochma has itself and the other 8 sfirot included in it. Then they send it to bina and bina distributes it to all the children. So he wants to say something like that is the tachlit or the kol that has everything in it. He is going to say "I made everything with chochma" and we said that all of the actions had a different colour. So, if everything is made from chochma then it has to have all of the colours in it by definition. If all the actions are in chochma then all the colours have to be there, whether they are hidden or revealed. I think he wants to say something like that. So he wants to say the original is black and then after that, the colour to come out of it is tchelet. In other words, just like the first colour to come out of this blackness is blue, the first thing to come out of keter is chochma which they attributed this colour of blue. Going back to the original idea that it receives all the colours, you can't really use that idea because really you are talking about yesod and malchut. Yesod gets everything, all the sfirot send down to yesod and then it receives all the energy and gives it over to malchut. So then you can use that idea there. But here, when you are talking about chochma, chochma is going to *send* everything down. In other words, we are not talking about the side that is receiving all of the colours but actually it is talking about chochma from the side that it is sending down all the colours. As a sender we are saying it has everything and chochma will be the source of all colours. Again, this is what appears in the Zohar. That could be the idea of the rabbis when they attributed it to tchelet, the lishon kol which has everything in it and also from the idea of the sapphire, which when the light shines on it you can see all the colours in the sapphire because that is the opening of all the colours. Where it is coming form no colour at all, from the blackness to the idea of colour. And from there all the colours will branch out. Each one, in its own particular time to reveal itself in its own particular sfirot and its own brightness and combination that it is supposed to reveal itself. And similarly, the chochma is also the source of all the actions that it sends down to bina. In other words, inside the chochma, the father, it is going to give the seed to bina. In other words, the inside of chochma, inside that seed is all the actions and then the bina is going to develop it to give it form and grow it. But the original idea is that all the peulot/actions are contained in chochma. Just like all the actions are there, then all the colours have to be there. But we are also going to explain later that there is a 3rd explanation of the word tchelet which means to destroy. Kalei, kalei is like to burn up, to destroy something completely. There is another primary use of tchelet which is a symbolism for judgment but the tchelet in that respect, that has no connection to the tchelet with the blue that we are talking about here.

And we say that it's the purpose of all the colours, because all the colours are going to be sent down from Him, the *chochmah,* and in the end, everything is going to go back to *chochmah,* where it becomes the *taglit,* which is the final purpose. In other words all the action is to bring it back to its original state, to go back to the *chochmah.* Its just like a wheel, there is a starting point of something and then when you go around and get back to where you started, then that is the end, the starting point becomes the end point.

So I would just like to talk about one thing that we talked about a second ago, we talked about the idea that *techelet* is also judgment from the word "to destroy" so that is going to be different, that's talking about *malchut,* which is sometimes called *techelet,* it's the lowest s*phirah* in *atzilut,* and sometimes they call *malchut* the lower *chochmah.* You don't count *Tet* because it's so high up, it's really the persons crown, so *chochmah* is really the first *sphirah* and it sends everything down. And *malchut* being the last *sphirah,* it receives everything, and then it sends down to the lower worlds, so there is a connection between *malchut* and *chochmah,* and sometimes *malchut* is called the lower *chochmah.* There is a Zohar that says that all dreams of colours are good, except if you dream of *techelet,* because *techelet* is the throne of judgment, it is an indication that the person is going to have judgment placed on them. So that's not talking about *chochmah,* that's talking about *malchut* which is the lowest *sphirah* and it has the ability to wipe things out. So that is just an aside which we also have to consider.

There is another opinion that says that *chochmah* has the seven colours in it, just like the seven colours of the eye. And in *chochmah* we that there is, and in *keter* we say that there isn't, you don't see it because it is hidden. So it is the same idea here, in *keter* everything is hidden and then *chochmah* is the revelation of everything. He brings a long Zohar in here but I don't want to go through the whole Zohar, because it's a long Zohar and that's not really our purpose here, our purpose is to talk about the different ways of looking at the colours, so just keep that in mind. And he compares it to the eye, that the eye has seven colours in it. Another reason that I am skipping this is because Rav Moshe Cordovero doesn't particularly understand the explanation, and he has problems with how it attributes the eye to *chochmah.* So we will skip that for now.

There are 3 ways to look at it, and it seems that the Ramak liked the first two ways more, it's more or less the same idea. That the *chochmah* is attributed to the colour *techelet.* Here he is using it in two senses, one that it has everything in it and it's going to send it down to everything. And the other idea is that it is the final purpose of everything, that all the activities bring it back to *chochmah,* like a circle where the starting point becomes the end point when you go all the way around. So he is attributing to it the two ideas, the first that *techelet* has all the other colours in it. It's the first colour to come out of black some how, and then all the other colours are contained within it, and then there is sapphire which is a similar idea. It is this translucent colour that when it gets light on it, you see all the other colours in it, it is going to be the revelation of all the other colours. So that is what he is saying, that from *chochmah* all the other colours are going to come out. As well as with actions, like it says in the Torah, "Everything I made, I made with *chochmah*" . So if everything was made with *chochmah* then all the colours are going to be contained in *chochmah.* So I think it's a similar idea if you learn it as *techelet* or if you learn it as sapphire.

And now he is going to start the third *sphirah* which is *Binah.* There are people that explain that *binah* is red, which leans toward the colour white, so its not pure red, it's red with a lot of whiteness in it. He nullifies that opinion somewhere else, but what he really holds is that it's like the colour *yarok,* which today is the colour green. I don't know if the *yarok* in the Talmud is exactly like the colour green, but any way it's not really green like grass, I think later on he is going to say its more like the yolk of an egg.

So he says that that is the green line that surrounds the whole world. I don't know exactly what that is about. I think he wants to say that the intention here is that the green is the green of grass. And what is the explanation of that? The commentators explain by saying that all of the fruit of the world, what ever colour they will eventually be, their earliest stage is going to be green. All fruit before it becomes ripe is green, and then when they become ripe they become their own colour. So because of that they are attributing this colour green. So because of that, green is the colour of *binah.* Because the idea now is that *binah* really is going to come into revelation, in *chochmah* the colours are still hidden, you don't see them yet. But in *binah* you see the colour green and you see that all the other colours are going to be coming out of it. Just like green comes before all the fruit of the world, this *sphirah* proceeded all the lower *sphirot.* Like it says in the Torah, Elokim came, which is *binah,* and He made everything. And God said, Let there be light. Each day there was a different saying of God which brought something out, so you see everything comes out from the *binah.* But he says that this isn't a good enough reason why you can attribute *binah* to the colour green. He says this because you can't learn from something physical about something that is going on in the spiritual world. In other words you cant say that *binah* is green because the fruit down here is green when it is not ripe and then everything is going to come out from them, because that's like learning cause and effect backwards, you are trying to learn about the Upper Worlds from the Lower Worlds. But it's really the opposite, you want to learn about the Lower Worlds from the Upper Worlds. Rather he wants to do now is give a different explanation. When the *techelet* or the *chochmah* which is this bluish type of colour, when it comes and mixes with this green, which is kind of like the green of an egg yolk, then you will get the green like the colour of vegetation. And that is why we say that *binah* is like judgment but it's not really judgment, that is why it is not red. It is on the side of judgment but it's not really judgment itself. Therefore we cannot attribute it to the colour red, because it is not really in itself red. But it will be green, which is like a mixture of red and white. So it is not really *din* or judgment. But you have to understand that in the Kabbalah *binah* always has two parts to it, its really part of the mind, and it is unite by *keter* and *chochmah,* just like the brain is working as one unit. And really the main part of *binah* is that it is up there and unknowable, and that you can't really speak about it as being an aspect of judgment, because judgment only starts down in the lower *sphirot.* But when you talk about the children that emanate from *binah,* then since the children are in the women's stomach, we talk about it as that *binah* starts from her. But *binah* itself isn't judgment so you can't attribute to it the colour red.

So he wants to say on one hand you can talk about it being *techelet*, a bluish colour mixing with a yellowish colour that is like egg yolk, and that makes green and then that green is going to give birth to all the offspring.

Or somehow he has this idea that *binah* is red with white and that somehow makes this greenish colour. Or maybe that the red and the white together mixed with the blue which is *chochmah,* then you get this combination which is green, or *binah,* which is a mixture of sky blue and white and red.

And that is all known to the people who work with colours, if you go speak to a colour expert they will tell you about the primary colours and how they mix to create secondary colours. And there is a third idea that the next thing that comes out from *binah* is going to be white which is *chessed,* and red is going to be *gevurah,* and if you take white and red then they come out as green, and that is going to be *tiferet.* So you have coming out of *binah: chessed* which is white, and red. And then you have *tiferet* which is the combination. And *binah* is a conglomeration of these three together. And therefore when these three colours are put together it will make a green like an egg yolk. And then when you mix the *techelet* with it, then it will become green like grass. And that is an idea as to why *binah* will be green, and it is the same idea why fruit will be green before they give birth to all the different colours of fruit. Green is a representation of *binah,* and then all the fruit that comes out is a representation of the other six *sphirot,* each of which is a different colour. And that is why we attribute to *binah* green which is like the colour of unripe fruit, because it a combination of *chochmah,* and then the three lower *shpirot*

which are *chessed, gevurah* and *tiferet,* white and red and yellow, and they join with *techelet* which is blue.
So tonight we did three *sphirot, Keter, Chochmah* and *Binah,* and I hope this is starting to give people ideas on how to see colours and how to use colours. And we will talk more about this next week. I thank everybody for listening

Chapter 8

I am going to be doing probably the last class in a series of classes according to the Book of Formation. For the last couple of weeks we have been working on the colours and their connection to the Planets, and what we can learn on the colours from the Planets, and what we can learn on the Planets from the colours, because you can learn important things on each from the other and how they impact each other. I wanted to show you an example from the Kabbalah to show how colours work. We said that in the Upper Worlds there are no real colours, because it is a spiritual world. But when we talk about colours in the Upper World, we are not saying that there is actually red there or green there, but it is more that the colour is indicating what the root of the particular *sphirah* is and how it works down in this world. For example, *gevurah* is red, and red is the colour of blood, so *gevurah* is connected with blood and violence. So when you see a colour in the Upper World you have an idea of how that Planet or how that *sphirah* works. But it's the same thing when you talk about a Planet. Mars is called the Red Planet, but that doesn't mean that the Planet is red, it's called the Red Planet because its actions and the way it works is in a red-like way or in a violent way. So when ever you see red, you know that the person will have a connection with red and with Mars and it will teach you how Mars works. So if you have a client that comes to you, and he or she is wearing all red clothing, then you know something about them right away, you know that Mars is very strong in their chart and then you can figure out how Mars is going to work depending on the person. So you see that everything that is red is going to be connected to Mars in some way.
In a similar way, black is connected to Saturn. I live in a religious world and here everybody dresses in black to symbolize that they are removed from this world in a certain way. So if you get a client that wears all black you can tell certain things about then right away because they are very Saturnian, so you can pick out Saturnian qualities in them and see it in their horoscopes just from their appearance. Saturnian's have long faces, we haven't really talked about face reading yet and how to see the Planets in a persons face. People with Saturn tend to have a longer face, Mars is a smaller face. But in any case, when you see a person wearing black you know they have a lot of Saturn in their chart. A group of people wearing black will be a very Saturnian type of group that are pleasure denying, abstinence, and a very serious type of group, and very responsible.
So you can see that it works in both ways. For example let's take yellow. Yellow is the Sun, it's a solar type of influence. So gold is connected to the Sun because it has a yellowish type of colour, and you can learn that gold and the Sun share some characteristics, they can be used interchangeably. So if a person wants to invest in gold they will look to the Sign of Leo, you check how Leo is in the sky and also how Leo is in your chart. So if you have Jupiter in your 2nd House in Leo. Jupiter is a sign of good fortune and Venus in your 2nd House in Leo. Jupiter and Venus are the Planets of good fortune, and Leo is the Sign of gold and it is in the House of money. So maybe you can make a lot of money investing in gold. So you can learn from the Planets about gold.

You can also learn about the Sun from gold. Gold is something that everybody wants, gold is important. It is status seeking, not many people have it, it is not always available, its number one, it's always the centre of attention. Not everybody has leadership qualities like the Sun. people with the Sun are special because they have that leadership ability so they work about interchangeably. From gold you can learn about the Sun and from the Sun you can learn about gold. But we will talk about it later as we go on.

Tonight I want to finish off with the inner *sphirot.* We did the outer s*phirot, Keter, Bina Chochmah,* the three highest *sphirot* and we discussed what colours they are.

Tonight we are going to talk about the bottom six *sphirot* and we will try and tie everything together and show you how to use the symbolisms used in anthropology. and you will see just how there are seven colours that are connected to the seven Planets, and you see that the seven Planets are connected to the seven continents, and all the nations have Planets that rule them and all the different metals have Planets that rule them, and each day of the week is ruled by a different Planet. And slowly you can use all these correspondences and you can start to understand the Planets and the Signs, and you look at it both ways. You look at how the Planet influences colour and how colour influences the Planets, and that way you can really start to have breakthroughs in your astrological understanding. You have to try to put everything that you see together. You see that everything starts to fall in place.

Say for example you go into a shoe store, and you see immediately what type of person will own a shoe store. You would think Pisces, because Pisces rules the feet, so you would think Pisces or maybe Libra will own the shoe store, because Libra likes clothing and beauty and likes to be attractive. So you start to think and you know that when you see a shoe store it is a Pisces. If you go into a bank, what kind of store is a bank? You think that that is a Taurus because that is the Sign money, and you look at the people working there and you see that they have a Taurus type of personality.

The main point of what I have been doing while talking about colours going off into the idea of the seven Planets in the Book of Formation, is to show you that everything is connected, everything that has seven is interchangeable. So you can start to use the Planets with everything that has groups of seven. Like the seven days of the week, the seven colours, the seven continents, the seven main rivers, the seven grains of Israel, its almost unlimited. You can put everything into a category and learn from that. You can take countries, each one is connected to a Sign. Britain is Aries, so when you see British people you start to think about Aries. I know when I first started doing charts in American I used to think everybody was a Gemini before I would do their horoscope because America is a Gemini nation. So the impact of Gemini will influence all the people of America even if they don't have Gemini in their charts because they are a subset of a country that is Gemini.

So if you look at a person in a Gemini country, like me for example, and I have a Capricorn Rising, it just doesn't fit there. Capricorn falls in the 8th House, it dies in Gemini. Gemini doesn't like to go deep and serious and so it dies there. So I left the country, I went for a much more serious type of place. But you can start to learn things by looking at each country and what their Sign is and you can start to pick up that a lot of people have those qualities. A lot of the time you will see qualities in a person that they pick up from their country or their city that aren't in their actual chart.

So it is very important to improve yourself in your understanding of astrology. So everything you see, try to relate it back to the Planets and the Signs.

In the Middle Ages they used to build memory palaces for the Planets and the Constellations, they used to take everything that they would learn down here and they would store it in different Planets and different Signs, and Constellations and Aspects. They would put everything in the Upper World and then when they needed it they would know exactly where to go to retain their memory. And so it was a super memory device, and that is something that you could use today.
Each Planet is also connected to a limb of the body. Or each Sign has parts of the body that it rules. And from them you can learn more about the organ or about the Sign, its all about making connections. It's what we have been learning the whole time from the Book of Formation, *olam, shanah, nefesh,* the soul, the time and the place, and all three are interconnected and parallel.

So now after that long introduction, let's try going through the final six Planets. most of this lecture I am taking from the book Pardes Rimonim, from the chapters on colour, and tonight will be mostly from the third chapter, which you can also learn astrology from it. So up until now we have learned about the colours from the three highest *sphirot; keter, chochmah* and *binah.* And now we are going to go on and learn about the bottom *sphirot.* We will start with *Gedolah,* the big *sphirah.* The Kabbalah before the Arizal, called *Chessed* the *Gedolah.* So we will call it *chessed* for now.
There are people that say that *chessed* is white, and there are others that say it is sky blue that is becoming white. And the reason is because *chochmah* is sky blue and *chessed* is the sky blue that starts to turn white. That is the revealing of *chessed* which is hidden inside *chochmah.* In other words, there are three columns in astrology, there is the right column which is *chochmah,* and under that is *chessed* and under that is *netzach.* So *chochmah* as we said is sky blue, and the other two, the lower two, *chessed* and *netzah,* are usually hidden inside of *chochmah.* And when *chessed* comes out, which by itself is white, but when it is coming out of the blue it is going to be sky blue becoming white. That is the first *perush* that we said and now this is the second one; so he says that it is sky blue turning to white and not actually proper white. To make a distinction between the white that is in *chessed* and the white that is in *keter elion,* remember that we said that *keter* is also white, so we have to make a distinction, because the white that is in *keter* is completely white, but *chessed* is not complete white, its white that turns a little bit blue. In other words, *keter* is so high up that you can't see it, and for that reason it is counted as white. But here it is talking about it more as a manifestation of *chochmah,* doing *chessed,* and so it is a white that is coming out of the blue and turning towards white with a bluish shade. So it's blue turning towards white. And then when you go a bit further into this colour, you also find that is can even be silver-like. It's like the colour of silver which is connected with this *midah* which is mercy.
For example, why do you have to marry a woman? We talk about it in marriage, that you have to give the woman a silver ring. This is because silver is the colour of *chessed* and you are showing her that you want to do *chessed* for her, and that you want to be good to her. If you take the letters of the word for *kesef,* money, the letters are *kaf, sameach peih.* And if you use the numerical value for each letter, *samech* and *peih* is 100, *mem* and *kaf* is 120, and *peih* and *heih* is 305 which is also the numerical value for *ishah,* or woman, to show you that a woman is acquired with silver. So ideally according to the Kabbalah, the marriage is made with silver.

And then you can understand more deeply the Planet that is connected with that colour, in this case silver which is the Moon.
In the Zohar it says that *chessed* is connected with money, or silver, because money isn't exactly white. Because it is white that is connected with a little bit of blue, so it comes out as silver.
But in any case, we sometimes do say that *chessed* is white. For example when we talk about milk we say that it is connected with *chessed,* because the mother gives the child milk. And that could be because it is showing that there is an increase in light coming from *keter*. In other words, when the woman is giving the child milk, in those years that she is breast feeding, you get a special light coming down from *keter,* which is pure white, and it increases the white of *chessed,* so because of that we sometimes talk about *chessed* as being pure white when we talk about milk. So you see sometimes the connections between things and how it can become more complicated. But it is also very fascinating because you can learn so much when you start to make these connections.
There is a big connection between astrology and being able to make connections within the world and to see things holistically and to see that everything is interconnected with everything else. And all the systems tend to be working the same way, so if you know one system, for example Kabbalah, you can work out how everything else works. The same thing for astrology, they have this tremendous ability to increase your perceptions of the world.

Let's go on to the next *sphirah* which is *Gevurah.* Everyone agrees that the colour of *gevurah* is red. Because red teaches you about the power of judgment so red symbolizes judgment. Rabbi Shimon Bar Yochai says in the Zohar, that *gevurah* is connected to red. And sometimes they also call *gevurah* black in the Zohar, and sometimes even sky blue. Our Rabbis also said in the Talmud, that whoever sees sky blue in a dream, it is not a good sign, and so they say there that they are interpreting the word *techelet* from the word *killah,* which is a word for destruction so they are learning it there as a symbolism for destruction. It's not always, but they say that when *techelet* is connected to *gevurah* then it is talking about its aspect of destructiveness.
So we see that these three colours are connected to *gevurah.* Why is that? One is because *din* draws close to *tiferet.* So it receives power to decide and it is closer to the white and the mercy. And that is to say that it is red that is yellowish, which is for *simchas* and joy, so that is good judgment which awakens love and happiness. So the Ramak is trying to explain to us here that *tiferet* is in the middle of *chessed* and *gevurah.* So it is between the side of mercy and the side of judgment, it is in between red and white, and so it is going to be the balance. It leans a little bit more toward *chessed,* but it is the balance. We see that the middle one is always the balance pole. There are three columns in kaballah, the right column is mercy, the left column is judgment and the center column is a balance between the two of them. So the higher up you are, the more the middle column goes toward the right, and the lower down you are, the more the middle column goes toward the left. So here we are fairly high up, we are in *gevurah* and *chessed* so *tiferet* will lean toward *chessed.* When you look at *netzach, hod* and *yesod, yesod* will lean more toward the left which is toward *hod.*
So that is why we say here, that it is leaning toward the right, that it is going to be a joyous *din,* because it is between judgment and mercy, but it is going to be a happy type of judgment, because it is leaning toward the side of mercy which awakens love and joy.

So that is a yellow colour, which is awakens love and joy and that is the nature of the Leo which rules the 5th House which is the House of pleasures.
In India, Leo is called *simcha,* which is the Hebrew word for joy, so you see a little bit of a connection between the Indian astrology and the Jewish astrology.
The second aspect is the strong *din* which makes people unhappy and causes death, and that is black.
Why do we say there are three different colours to *gevurah?* We said there is red, a yellowish colour, and black. So the yellow we explained is in the middle column, so it is leaning toward *chessed,* but it still has *din.* And now we are going to explain that black makes the face of the creatures dark, it is the fire of *geheinom,* of Hell. And that is why it says in the Talmud that black is a red that became bad.
My teacher always used to ask what the difference is between Saturn and Mars. Mars likes to be violent, Saturn doesn't want to be violent, but when it does turn violent, it wants to wipe everybody out so that they won't come back at a later stage to get revenge. If Saturn wants to kill, they want to kill everything.
So that is why they say that black is a red that became bad. That is another concept that is applied to *nidah,* if a woman sees blood that is blackish in colour, so she becomes ritually impure, because black is red that became bad. You also see that in people that get cuts, that the red blood becomes black when it starts to heal, so black is symbolizing a worse red than what red is.
The rest of the tape (15 minutes) was damaged and could not be transcribed. Woe to the Teachings that have been lost.

The Outer Planets in Astrology and how they work in the Houses

The Outer Planets in Astrology and how they work in the Houses

By Yaakov Kronenberg

A transcription of a lecture on the Torah astrology approach to Neptune, Uranus and Pluto; and their influences on the Horoscope

The Outer Planets in Astrology and how they Work in the Houses

By Yaakov Kronenberg

Chapter 1

What is the Jewish view on the Outer Planets (Neptune, Uranus and Pluto) in Torah Astrology? Tonight I want us to learn from an old Jewish book. It was written about 15 years after the discovery of the Planet Uranus, which was the first outer Planet. Uranus was found in 5541 in the Hebrew Calendar and today we are in 5772. So that is about 230, 231 years ago. So that would make it about the year 1780 that it was found. And this book was published in about 1795. I don't know when he wrote it, how much earlier because in those days it took a while to write, set it up and get it printed. So it is probably not too far after the discovery of the first Planet Uranus. And this rabbi wrote this very famous book, it is called Sefer HaBrit and we are going to learn one perek, one chapter in it. It is made up of one chapter which has 3 divisions. We are going to learn from this book and then go off and learn more about the Outer Planets. But I want us to learn from Sefer HaBrit to give a general introduction to the Jewish view on the Outer Planets. Actually the first edition of Sefer HaBrit was published anonymously. A lot of rabbis over the course of history used to write books without a name, for modesty, or they didn't want to get honour or kavod... They wanted to stay away from it. So they ran it and printed it without their names, but here somehow his name was revealed and in the second edition he published his name. His name was Rabbi Pinchas Eliyahu from the town of Vilna. Vilna was a very famous city in Lithuania where a lot of the major rabbis lived in that period. The Gaon of Vilna was from there and sometimes it was called the Jerusalem of Europe. He, in his day, decided to write a book to synthesise all of Science up to his time, no rabbinical authority had done that. There were a lot of advances; it was a time of a lot of advances. The Chatam Sofer, one of the great rabbis of Europe said, "thank G-d for Rabbi Pinchas, because if not for him, I would have had to write the book". It was a book that its time had come. It's a very interesting book; he talks about all of science. And in the second half of the book he tells you how to get to what we call Ruach Hakodesh, how to get to divine revelation, a very high meditative state. So that is something you can actually get from higher knowledge. So that was the 2 parts of the book. And it is a very interesting book, you can just pick it up and open it wherever and there is always something interesting. It's interesting, Rabbi Pinchas writes in the introduction of the 2nd edition of the book, "in the 1st edition I wrote it anonymously. Afterwards somehow my name got out so I'm writing with my name this time". When it was originally published nobody knew who the author was. There were people speculating that there was no possibility that it could have been written by one man. It must have been written by a team of experts in all the natural sciences and medicine, only a team of group of writers could write such an encyclopaedic work, such a deep work. It would be impossible for one man to do.

I want to talk about the Torah approach to the Outer Planets. In other words, there is going to be a lot of questions. Uranus, Neptune and Pluto, they make a big philosophical question for Astrologers, especially Jewish Astrologers, ancient Astrologers. This is because the Ancients did not use the Outer Planets. They didn't have the Outer Planets. In other words, they are all unseen to the naked eye. You can't see the Outer Planets with the naked eye. When Rabbi Pinchas came along, in the late 1700s they finally had a telescope that was powerful enough that they could see Uranus but they still didn't have a telescope powerful enough to see Planets farther out. So since it was unaided to the naked eye, nobody saw it. So it comes down to the question, but the Sages knew everything, they had Ruach Hakodesh, the Holy Spirit, they were given the Torah at Mount Sinai and besides being given this, they were given an understanding of the sciences which are a handmaiden to the Torah. We always say in our books that Astrology was one of the sciences given over to Adam HaRishon and that is how we have an understanding of it. So if so, how come the rabbis never talked about the Outer Planets? It becomes a serious question. In other words, if you look in the rabbinical books, the Mishna, the Talmud, they only talk about the 7 basic Planets, the farthest out being Saturn, the closest to the Earth being the Moon. The Moon is not really a Planet, it's a satellite that travels around the Earth, but for all purposes we consider it a Planet. So you come to the question, how come they never mention the Outer Planets? And today do the Outer Planets really have an influence? Maybe they don't have any influence on the Earth? Or do they have an influence on people's actions? If they do have an influence on peoples actions how come the rabbis didn't talk about it? So these are some of the questions we are going to deal with. If they do have influence, what kind of influence do they have? And so these are the things we are going to try to talk about a little over the next one or two classes, these particular problems..

I'm going to start from the beginning of Sefer HaBrit, from chapter 1 and what we really need is the 2nd chapter, but I will talk on both chapters because there is a lot of interesting material in the first chapter. I have a series of classes on the Basic Model of the Universe. In there I talk about a fair amount of this material that he is going to mention here in Sefer HaBrit. But it is always good to review. When I wrote the basic model I didn't take it from Sefer HaBrit, I took it from the most part from the Arizal.

Simply put (and you can get the full details and explanations in my eBook 'Basic Model of the Universe') there are 4 worlds and the lowest world is the world of Assiya/Action. In this world of Assiya, there is an Earth and a Heaven, and the Heaven of Assiya has 7 firmaments, which become the 10 Sefirot. Out of those 7 firmaments, the 6th firmament working our way down, is called the Rakia Firmament. In other words it is the 2nd Firmament closest to the Earth. Remember that these Firmaments are spiritual in nature. This Rakia Firmament has in it all the astronomical things that we see in the heavens, and we look up to it. All the Planets and all the Stars and whatever are going to be there. So that is what he is talking about now. Know that the 6th firmament is also called the Yesod, like the Sefirah of Yesod; it is the Yesod in the Heavens of Assiya. In other words, the Heavens of Assiya break up into 7 firmaments but the highest firmament has 3 Sefirot in it. So another way to say it is that the 6th Firmament is the 9th Sefirah coming down, which is the Sefirah of Yesod. In the Rakia are all the Galgalim/Wheels. The ancients hold that the Planets were inside these Wheels and they circled around inside these wheels. And there were always questions, did the wheels do the circling and the Planets were affixed? Or do the Planets circle while the wheels are fixed? The ancients held that there were 10 Galgalim, 10 wheels. 7 of them were the Planets, the 8th one was the Fixed stars, the 9th one was what was called the daily Galgal, the daily wheel, and then there was the 10th Wheel of higher intelligence, and he is going to talk about them now.

So inside the 6th firmament were all these wheels, stars, and the Planets are, the 10 wheels which we know, the 10 sefirot of Yesod. In other words, the 6th firmament is called the Yesod of the Heavens. And inside the Yesod itself, the Yesod is subdivided into 10 Sefirot. And those 10 Sefirot are the 10 Galgalim, the 10 wheels. And this is who they are: the highest of the wheels is called the wheel of Higher intelligence, which is a wheel unto itself and that's the Keter of the Yesod. The 2nd wheel is called the Galgal of the Surrounding wheel, the wheel 'that goes around in one day'. And it's a wheel that goes around from east to west, which is the opposite direction to the other Planets and Stars (their orbits are from west to east) and he turns them all as if they are going from east to west, the opposite of their real motion. So therefore it appears that the Sun, the Moon, and all of the other Planets, that they are going from east to west. An example of this is a fly that is travelling in a wheel and the wheel is circling around in its direction from east to west and it takes the fly with it. So even though the fly is going from west to east, it appears as if the fly is going from east to west because the wheel is going from east to west. You have to know, inside this wheel, the 'daily wheel', there are no Planets, no stars, nothing and it is the Chochma of the Yesod. In other words the first one, the wheel of higher intelligence is the Keter of Yesod, the daily wheel is going to be the Chochma of Yesod. The 3rd wheel is called the Mazalot. That is the one with all the fixed stars, and corresponds to the Sefira of Bina. The stars are divided up into 12 different formations in the sky. We are talking about the Zodiac, the 12 different constellations, and their names are based on the type of form that they took in the sky. We call them taley which is the sheep, the shor which is the bull, teumim which is the twins, sartan is the crab, arieh is the lion, betulah is the virgin, mosnayim is the scales, akrav is the scorpion, keshet is the bow and arrow, gedi is the goat, dali is the water carrier, dagim is the fish. This galgal/wheel is the Mazalot. This wheel of the stars is called the Fixed stars, because the move so slowly from our world point of view that they appear Fixed. And the Zodiac goes from the South to the North, it travels around the Equator which goes from East to West and 7 of the names of the constellations; Aries, Taurus, Cancer, Gemini, Leo and Virgo are in the north, and the other 6 others are in the South; Libra, Scorpio, Sagittarius, Capricorn, Aquarius and Pisces. Remember that all this is in the 6th Firmament, the Yesod of the Heavens of the lowest of the 4 worlds, the world of Action/Assiya. And these 10 wheels are the 10 subdivisions of that 6th Firmament/Rakia. You have to know further that there are another 36 constellations on the 2 sides of the belt of the Mazalot. In other words the 12 constellations which make up the Zodiac, are centred around Equator, and these 36 others are to be found above or below this Zodiac belt. The Sun is seen moving in a year through the 12 Zodiac Constellations and what he wants to say is that besides that, there are another 36 Constellations that are also seen in the night sky, on either side of these 12 Zodiac constellations. And all together that will give you 48 different forms or constellations. The Gaon of Vilna has a piece on these 48 formations, but now is not the time and place to talk about it.

So back to the question, why did the ancient sages not mention Uranus in their planet count? If you look in the Bible, in the 3rd chapter in Genesis called Lech Lecha, God says to Avraham, "look up into the sky and know that your people are going to be as numerous as the stars in the sky". So for a modern person, when he first reads it, he does not think about it much, because he thought that there are billions and billions of stars, so God is telling Abraham that the Jews are going to be as numerous as there are stars. They say there are as many stars as grains of sand, but at that time there was no telescopes and Uranus was not visible and in fact only about 1000 stars were visible to the naked eye. So if you think about it, in the times of Abraham, that wasn't really much of a blessing! I mean, what is God blessing Abraham with? Look up into the sky, the night sky, and you are going to have as many kids as there are stars! And what do you see? A 1000 stars. And so you have to really see that there was this understanding, in fact it's one of the proofs, that they already knew that most of the stars that existed where invisible to the naked eye. Today we have telescopes and every day they are finding new planets and new constellations, and new milky ways and dark matter and all sorts of things.

We said in this 2nd Firmament that there were 48 different forms, the 12 Constellations that the Sun travels through plus another 36 constellations on either side. And then after that there are 7 Wheels/Galgalim, and in each wheel represents one Planet. Which are called the 7 Planets that orbit the Sun. We learnt today that they orbit the Sun so let us just go like that for now, that they orbit the Sun. Back then they held that everything orbited the Earth, you can learn it that way too, it doesn't really matter. But their names were Saturn, Jupiter, Mars, the Sun… See here we are learning like the Earth is in the middle and everything is surrounding it and then you have after The Sun, Venus, Mercury and then The Moon. And then we have the abbreviation which is what is called "shatsan chamkal", for people who know Hebrew, shatsan chamkal. Which is the abbreviation, the first letter of all 7 Planets. And this is their order from above to below. In other words the farthest one away s Saturn and the closest one is the Moon. So eventually you get a second question. A lot of the Astrology was known from the naked eye. You could learn things about the Planets from the Ancient Astrology but from where the Planets were. For example they held that Mars was hot because it was above the Sun and the rays of the Sun went up and hit it. And you have that Saturn was considered cold because it was the furthest Planet away. And Jupiter was considered a benefic because it was between the hot and cold Planets, Mars and Saturn. And Saturn was considered heavy because it was the slowest moving and all sorts of things like that. So if you are going to talk about the outer Planets, How are we going to talk about them? They weren't even seen. So in a way you can't really know anything about something that is unseen; which is another question. Anyway these 7 Planets are considered the 7 Sefirot, chesed, gevurah, tiferet, netzach, hod, yesod and malchut and this yesod . The yesod of … they want to say chesed, gevurah, tiferet, netzach, hod, yesod and malchut. And each one of them has an angel that's the soul of the Planet. And here are the names of the angels: Saturn, Shabtai, his angel is called Kapsiel, Jupiter, its angel is called Sidkiel, Mars angel is called Samiel, the Sun's angel is called Rafael, Venus' angel is called Aniel, Mercury's angel is called Michael and the Moon's Angel is called Gabriel, Like it says in the book "Etz Chayim" by the Arizal in a chapter called Short explanation of the 4 Worlds. And this is the opinion of the Kabbalists and the Philosophers agree with this, that the Malachim, the Angels they move these wheels. And on each of the 7 Planets, they rule 2 Signs. And this is again important for Astrology. Each of the Planets has Rulership over 2 Signs, except the Sun and the Moon which only rule 1 each. And that is how you get 12, five Planets, Saturn, Jupiter, Mars, Venus and Mercury, each of which rule 2 Signs, that is 10 Signs, and the Sun and Moon rule 1 each. I think why the Sun and the Moon each rule one is because really the Sun and Moon should have been together one planet just because of the sin of man somehow they got split up and one rules the day and one rules the night but really they are like one, they should be treated like one piece. And then they split up into two. So because of that each of them rules one sign. And now I'm going to explain how it works. The Sun rules over Leo and the Moon rules over Cancer. Mars rules over Aries and Scorpio. Venus rules over Taurus and Libra. Mercury rules over Gemini and Virgo. Saturn rules over Capricorn and Aquarius and Jupiter rules over Pisces and Sagittarius. Now each of these wheels and the Planets, Constellations and the fixed Stars all of these you have to remember are in the 6th firmament, which is called rekiya, which is a firmament. And it is the 6th one going from up down, like we explained. And it says there in Torah God put them in the rekiya of the Heavens" . So there it is an allusion already in the beginning of the Torah that they were all going to be in the firmament called rekiya. Like our rabbis said the rekiya is a Gemara in hagigas, the Talmud hagiga. The rekiya, in it is the Sun, the Moon, the Planets, the Stars... And these 10 wheels are the 10 sefirot of this yesod. And they're against the 10 sefirot which are the 7 rekiyim. In other words the 7 rekiyim are 10 sefirot , Now I'm going to tell you how the rekiyim work.

The highest rekiya, regiot, has 3 sfirot which is... Now it's going to show you how the aravot has the 3 sfirot rishonim, which is the wheel of higher intelligence and the wheel of the day and the fixed stars. And then machon which is the next and samon and zevul, the other 3 firmaments. There again Saturn, Jupiter and Mars. And against the sechakim there is going to be 2, which is the Sun and Venus. Sechakim is the grinders, plural. And against the rekiya is going to be Mercury and against Zvilon is going to be the Moon. In other words there are 7 in general rekiyim and in the last rekiya, the 6th rekiya, which is called rekiya in itself has 7 rekiyim inside it, in itself divides up into 7. Because whatever is in the whole is in the part and those 7 also break up into 10 sfirot. So you can do it either way. The big ones are called the 10 sfirot and the little ones are also.

So that was the end of the first chapter. Let us start now with the 2nd chapter. And now we are going to start to get into what we came here for, to talk about the Outer Planets. If you will say in your heart, how did the ancient ones know, all the wise men of the nations of the world, all the wise men of Israel, that the number of Planets was 7 and the numbers of the wheels was 10? Isn't it true that now the wise men of Astronomy say the number of Planets is 8? And if so it becomes reasonable to say that the number of wheels will become 11 and not 10? And this is because in the year 5541, one of the wise men of the Astronomers from

England by the name of Herschel, he found by looking through a big telescope, another star. A star which is orbiting above the Planet Saturn and it was going around the Sun. And he called it Uranus. And the size of the Planet is 80 times the body of the Earth. It has an orbit of 82 years. It goes around the Sun in 82 years and it is about 19 times further away from the Sun that Earth is. And Hashem put 2 Moons around it, just like the Earth has one Moon going round it. And with this telescope we can see Uranus and its 2 Moons. We can follow its orbit and track it exactly. And so on this now I am going to have to answer it and say, no my brothers, that you have to know in the place between where the fixed stars are and the 7 Planets begin, in that empty area Hashem created many many Planets. All of them are travelling in orbits, just like the 7 Planets that we know, that we can always see. They are not standing like the fixed stars. In other words, fixed stars aren't really standing but they are moving very slowly, they move a degree in about 72 years, so in relation to the Planets which travel quite fast, its considered as if they are fixed. And for that reason we call them the fixed stars. We could have called them the very slow moving Stars but we rather give it a relative name. There are real names and there are names in relationship and so it's called a fixed star in relation to the moving stars, the Planets that move. And they also go around the Sun, these Planets in the grey area between where the old Planets, the Planets you can see with your naked eye, ended and where the fixed stars, a lot of them also, at least a thousand of them or more which you can see with your naked eye, because they are so much bigger than these other Planets. They look small to us but it's because they are so far away that we see them as being small. And they are one above the other just like the 7 Planets that are known are also one above the other. All of them are higher than Saturn in their orbit and we know this also from the 2nd group of Stars that are also in this grey area, this area that is between the Planets and the fixed stars, and we also know this from what our rabbis called the comets. They knew already from the comets that their orbits are starting out there and then they have a time where they draw close to the Earth and then they move far away again. But where they come from is somewhere in this grey area. The area between the 7 basic Planets that are seen with the naked eye end, and where the fixed stars which are much farther away, where they begin. So he wants to say that in this vast empty space that right now we see Uranus, and we also know that there are comets originating from that area, which is also a proof, and that there are many more objects that are out there in that area.

So let us go on and we will read some more from Sefer HaBrit: I want to say that this new Planet which was discovered, called Uranus, is from the first type of objects in the sky that we see. In truth it's one of the Planets. Don't say it's a star, and it's not some other object but it's also a Planet. And not only this, but also all the other objects that you are going to find in this area are also going to be Planets, just like it, just like the 7 Planets that are known to us. And know that there are going to be other Planets above this Planet Uranus, and they are going to be higher up and farther away and they will be gevoah meal gevoah, higher and higher away, farther and farther away. But we haven't seen them yet because we can't see them with a naked eye and we don't yet have a telescope that is big or strong enough to see them with. But it is possible that within a generation or two generations, they will discover new Planets that will be found when they have new and better, more improved telescopes that are going to be bigger and better than those that are in our hands. And it will be in the end of days that they will know many more Planets. And know that the rabbis, the wise men of Israel, the ancient ones, they all knew of them. Don't think that the rabbis didn't know of these other Planets. This is always one of our ideas throughout the book, that Astrology and Astronomy, it was all secret knowledge taught to Adam HaRishon and passed down and then it got sent out to the other nations of the world. You can look at my other lecture series, the earlier ones. If not there would be no other way to figure this out with the human mind to construct it. You see there all the proofs we have brought. Let's go on, he wanted to say that the wise men of Israel, the early ones, they all knew of these other Planets and they grasped them and saw them but not with a physical eye and not with a telescope. Rather they had special insight, what we call ruach hakodesh, they had the Holy Spirit resting on them or it somehow was given over to them by tradition from the ancient fathers. He wants to say that either they obtained it from the Holy Spirit or something like that. Or that it was a tradition that was passed down from Avraham, Yitzchak and Yaakov. They got it going all the way back from Yaakov studying in the yeshiva of Shem and Ever, the sons of Noah and Noah traces back to Adam HaRishon, from his youngest son Shet and then going back to Adam HaRishon. But they never mentioned it, but so how come they didn't talk about it? If they knew about it, why didn't they talk about it? But they never mentioned it and they never discussed it because the Planets that are above Saturn, they don't have an effect on the Earth, except for a very little. They have very little effect on the Earth, and only in periods that are far away. In other words, they are not working all the time, these Planets. They have a little bit of influence and they are also not working all the time. I want to come back and analyse these words. I think from these words that he is saying here you can get some kind of idea of what these Planets are. I'm going to try conjecture in any case in a later class, in the next class. Ok but these are important words that he is saying here. These Planets, their influence on the Earth is very slight, and only from time to time. They're not always working; and only for particular matters. It seems like they have special missions. In Hebrew, it says b'dvarim pratiim, in particular reasons they come. But the 7 Planets, the lower ones, all of them from Saturn and below, since they are closer to the Earth they influence the Earth that we sit on with full force. And that their actions are felt continually.

Look I think we are going to take a break here. It took a little longer than I thought. But I think it's a very interesting subject matter. I'm not enough of a historian to know if he was the first to speculate on the Planet Uranus and the other Outer Planets. And if people came before him I don't know exactly when he wrote this. I know when it was published but I'm sure the book took a while to write and till it got printed, but anyway its very interesting material. I don't know if I've ever seen anyone from that time period talk about Uranus, to really speculate on it. If anyone has any material from that time period and they would like to send it to me or write me a letter and tell me about it, I'd love to see it. But here he is speculating, from a Jewish perspective, he's asking the simple question: How come our rabbis didn't know about it? How come there are not more Planets? How come they didn't consider it? We've used up the 10 galgalim which is already the 10 sefirot. There are no sefirot left for these other Planets so what is going on here? You have big questions. We're going to continue next week and I hope everyone liked the class and we will go further into our investigation into what are the Outer Planets.

Chapter 2

Last week we were working on the writings from Sefer HaBrit, its one chapter in Sefer HaBrit where he talks about the discovery of the Planet Uranus. So that was a major thing. There were no Planets discovered for thousands of years. Everybody knew there were seven Planets so nobody ever knew there was an eighth until the year 5541, 230 years ago about. And at that time this was a big thing and so Sefer HaBrit asks a fundamental question. Didn't the Ancients know about all the Planets? Especially the Jewish sages, didn't they know about it? So how come they didn't talk about it? So there are different opinions on the subject matter. What about the modern Planets? Do they influence the Earth or not? And if they do influence it how come the earlier rabbis didn't talk about it? So tonight we are going to talk about these questions and go deeper into it. But first, I just want to read a little bit more. We have a couple more lines that we didn't read, in the Sefer HaBrit. Well let us read again the main lines. The main line I came for is the answer here. He says "the chochmei Yisrael..." again this is quoting the Sefer HaBrit, I'm just quoting the last 3 lines I read last time. And then we will go forward a little bit more... the wise men, the ancient ones, they all knew and they all were able to grasp and see, to obtain the intention and to experience the Planet Uranus, not with their physical eyes, not with their physical eyes and not with a telescope but rather they appertained Uranus through some kind of vision, or some kind of holy spirit or they had a tradition from the fathers of the world. I guess from Avraham, Yitzchak and Yaakov, the forefathers of Judaism. Yaakov is known that he studied in the Yeshiva of Shem and Ever. And it goes back they were the sons of Noah and Noah was connected with Shet, who was the son of Adam HaRishon. So they have a tradition going all the way back to Adam HaRishon's days on these ancient Planets. So if so, he is going to ask, how come they didn't talk about it? So let us go on. Where were we? But they never mentioned it (meaning the rabbis) and they didn't go into detail about it because these Planets, which were above Saturn, their influence on the Earth is very slight; and only occasionally. In other words, they are not influencing the world all the time; they're only influencing the world occasionally, and in slight types of ways and in particular cases. Not always for the whole world, only in specific cases, in specific instances. But … that one sentence from Sefer HaBrit to me is very significant. And I think in there are all the secrets that he wants to give us over, to have more of an idea of what these Planets are... what Uranus is... and like he says in the text that sooner or later there will be more Planets.

Let us go on a little bit more. But the 7 Planets, the ancient ones, all of them from Saturn and down, they are close to the Earth. And they are influencing the Earth on which we sit, and we know their actions and we know that they are acting on us continually just like the Sun and the Moon that are acting on us, causing the grass to grow and fruit to ripen. He's going to bring down a few passages to show you, I think I'm going to skip them for now, and also the other 5 Planets that are known to everybody, that they also have an influence on the Earth and on all the things in and on the Earth. Then there are the 7 types of metals that are connected to the 7 Planets, which is the world of minerals, and then also in the world of vegetables, and then the animal world and the human world… And because of this the rabbis, the wise men of old didn't mention them because they are not relevant to us here. And because of this they also didn't mention their wheels. Each of these Outer Planets is going to have wheels. They didn't mention them. However, the wheel of the fixed stars, where the stars are fixed in them, they are established and they are lighting up the Earth and all the people living on it at night, which are called the fixed stars. They do come into account because of their actions that they have on this world. Just simply they give light at night. If we just had the Moon maybe that wouldn't be enough to light up the sky. They work in conjunction with the Moon to light the sky up at night. That's already one of their actions and of course they are seen, not like the Outer Planets which aren't seen. The fixed stars are seen. And the next wheel, the yomi, the daily wheel, it cause all the actions of all the wheels below it. And the wheel of the intelligence it gives power to everything in order to do what they do. Therefore they also come into account when we count these 10. And therefore the rabbis counted them and the number of wheels is 10 not more. And the number of the Planets is 7, not more. So until we have read Sefer HaBrit and he's explaining that really there is nothing left, there are only 10. There are 10 galgalim, there's no place for the Outer Planets. You can't add more sefirot than 10. And we learnt last week that there are 22 letters in the Hebrew alphabet; 3 to create the elements, 7 for the Planets and 12 the Signs. So again there are no letters left for the Outer Planets, for Uranus... Pluto… So what is going on? So it's interesting, he wants to say their influence on the Earth. He wants to say first that their influence on the Earth is very minor.

So let me go first. We will go back in a minute to Sefer HaBrit. There is a rabbi today, Rabbi Arieh Kaplan who wrote a commentary on the Book of Creation, Sefer Yetzira, the oldest book in Judaism. And there he also talks a little about the Outer Planets and he wants to say they have no influence on the Earth. I'm sure he has read Sefer HaBrit, I think he brings it in in his footnotes. He goes and says that they have no influence on the Earth and he brings his proof from the asteroids. He says the asteroids are much closer to the Earth and they don't have… he says if you are going to count the Outer Planets and say that they have influence then you should also say that the asteroids, which a bunch of them are fairly big, not all of them, should also have influence because they are much closer to the Earth. That's his proof that they don't work. It doesn't mean that… Maybe he was writing for a different type of audience … He could have held like Sefer HaBrit, maybe they worked a very little bit and only at specific times and that. But he didn't want to get into that so he just left it in a general way by saying that they don't have any influence. But I can see that that is his answer, he was writing for a more contemporary generation. And he was writing for people that didn't necessarily have a good knowledge of the Torah or the sciences. So he just said what he said in a modified form. That they don't work. But I don't think that it means he is disagreeing with Sefer HaBrit.

So coming back to Sefer HaBrit, he gives 3 statements that are very interesting. He says that their influence is felt only a little bit, only felt occasionally and only felt in specific instances. Unlike the other Planets which are working all the time. That's the one thing he wanted to say. And the other thing we see again is that there is no place in the yesod of the Heavens, we said that everything is in the yesod of the Heavens in the 6th firmament which is called the yesod of the Heavens and in there is all the 10 sefirot. But we saw already that all the 10 sefirot are used up. So another problem is where we are going to fit the Outer Planets in, there's no place left for them. So I want to say that these Outer Planets that fall between the fixed stars and the 7 major known Planets, they are somehow connected with a different system. In other words, everything he has listed here is connected with what we call in Kabbalah, "or pnimi". In Kabbalah there are 2 types of light. There is or that goes inside a vessel... Or is light, and that is called or pnimi, pnimi means inside and inside light. It's the light that goes into a vessel and that means it's a light that can be received. Vessels can receive it. Not all light can be received. If you bring in too much light into something you can break it. Some light just can't be contained. You can't package happiness. If someone gets very happy you can't put it in a container and save it and take it out later. There are lights that there are no vessels for or there is a vessel for a little bit of light and then it leaves. In Kabbalah there is an idea, that there is light that goes inside a vessel, and there are lights that go outside and surround a vessel. Actually there are 2 lights that are surrounding lights. In other words there are lights that go inside and there are lights that surround a vessel. And they are against the 5 levels of the soul. In Kabala the soul has 5 levels and they are called, from the bottom up, they have names according to their first letters from people who know Hebrew, they are called nornachi. The first letters for each one, nefesh, ruach, neshama, chaya and yechida. Those are the 5 levels of the soul. Three levels are what we call light that goes inside a vessel. There's the nefesh which is the lowest level and its dwelling place is inside the liver, there's the ruach which is also an inner light and its dwelling place is the heart and then there's the neshama whose dwelling place is inside the brain. And then on top of that are the 2 Outer lights. One of them is called the chaya, it goes in and then goes out and surrounds the person or the partsuf, whatever you're talking about and then there's a second makif which doesn't even go in at all it just surrounds from the outside. And they are called the chaya and the yechida, the 2 highest levels. And they are what's called or makif, surrounding light. And the surrounding light is very special. Maybe next week we will take a detour, maybe, I have to look up and see if I can find a good place to teach it, what the function is of the surrounding light. But I'll just talk a little about it now, off the top of my head, not bringing it from a book. But there is a difference that the inner light, since we learnt that it goes into a vessel and fills it up, therefore that inner light has to relate to the vessel. What do I mean by that? The inner light if it doesn't put enough light into the vessel, then the vessel will be very weak and run down, like a person who doesn't get enough energy, he will be run down and weak and he might get depressed, stuff like that. And the same thing in the spiritual world, even the physical world, when we're talking about a vessel, if the light comes in too little then the light is not relating properly to the vessel. In other words there is not enough light in that vessel to keep it functioning as it should. And on the other hand, if the light comes in too much, then the vessel maybe won't be able to handle all that light and it could get damaged, it could break even, it could shatter into pieces. So we have to worry again on that side. So this light, this inner light, it has to run in a certain way according to nature. In other words, it always has to deal with a body. It has to adjust itself to the fact that it is inside a vessel. And it has to relate to that vessel, whether it's a rock or a flower or a sefira... or whatever... that it doesn't put too much or too little light in it because in that way it will make trouble. But if we talk about the orot makisim, the surrounding light, since they don't go into a vessel they don't always necessarily have to adjust themselves and act according to the vessels. And because of that when Hashem directs the world, He has 2 different lights, the or, the inner light, which must adjust itself to the vessel and act with them. And then on top of that there is this Outer light which doesn't necessarily have to work together with the vessels. In other words it can act above nature. In other words, the Outer light is the source for all the miracles that happen in the world. There are revealed miracles and hidden miracles, it's a whole study in itself. And on top of that there's God and we believe that there is a purpose to history. That history is being run in a particular way to bring the redemption at a certain stage in history and that the Jews are going to be redeemed. And these Outer lights they work to direct the world in the proper direction to go to bring the world to its proper conclusion. So whenever G-d sees that the world is going off in different directions, that it's pulling it away, then He'll have these surrounding lights to operate, to bring it back on course, and also use these lights to bring miracles. And these lights they don't always work, especially today, we don't see too many miracles. And how many people see miracles in their lifetime? And certainly not every day. It's only every now and then that it happens and the world too it sees miracles. It happens in war , the 6 Day War, the miracles! But how many times do you see that? I guess that many people didn't see that as a miracle, a hidden miracle... But in other words, there are things that are happening in the world that can't happen through the regular light, the inner light, because the inner light needs to work together with the vessel. But then you have these super vessel lights, called the surrounding lights, which can act on things without having to relate to the vessel. And therefore they can do things which the other lights can't do and they can redirect the energy to where it has to go to reach its final conclusion. And so its power is not always felt ans only sometimes is it felt, it's not felt that often and sometimes people miss it. For example the 6 Day War, they managed to defeat all the Arab countries in 6 days, with hardly any casualties and the Labour Party, the socialists, said that it was because of the might of the army. So again, they missed the point, or at least they saw it as something within nature, they saw it as something that happened within the vessels not something that was coming from outside. And in a person's life too, there are things that happen that transform him or her. And they're also supra, they can be outside of... people can realise that they are miracles for what they are, that something special is happening or they cannot even feel it, they just miss it. So I want to say the "little bit felt", when he uses the language only felt a little bit, and not everybody can pick it up. Some people pick it up… It's like a high frequency sound. Dogs can hear it but humans cannot. There are things that some people pick up on and things that other people don't pick up on. So it's not always felt and it happens only occasionally. And only in particular instances, in other words, it's not always happening, it's only when you really need it, only in particular instances, to set a person straight or to set the world straight. So things happen… I know so many people who became religious who said something happened to them. That suddenly got them to... An event, or something that got them to change their lives. And its why them and why not somebody else? So again, these Outer lights are connected with a whole different system in Kabbalah. We say that all these Planets we have been talking about now, the regular Planets and the fixed stars, the other wheels, they are all connected to the inner lights. But these Outer Planets they seem to be connected to what we call this Outer light. Which is a whole different system, the light is much different. It's a light that doesn't have to necessarily relate to a vessel. Maybe sometimes it does, I don't want to go into detail. There are different types of Outer light and surrounding light, it's not the proper place here to go into it. But there are definitely Outer lights that don't have to relate to vessels. And I think this is the area where then you can say that the Outer Planets fall in this area. And that's my take anyway on Sefer HaBrit that he's hinting that these Planets are connected with supernatural types of things. With things that are primarily to change the world, to move them in the proper direction, and to get things and to keep the world always going in a way that it will bring the final redemption, and bring the people who have to get to the final redemption,to get them all to the proper place at the proper time. So that's how I want to learn Sefer HaBrit.

And using that I want to start talking about some of the contemporary views of the Outer Planets and actually some of them don't use the same language. But some of them are a little bit in that area. For example there are all distinctions. Some people who hold that the Outer Planets have no influence. Nobody mentions outer planets in Vedic Astrology, the Astrologers in India; they never talked about these Outer Planets so they have no meaning. You've got Neptune, which functions like the South node and then you've got Uranus, in its place is the North node which acts functions like uranus. And also a lot of what we call traditional astrologers today they also, because it wasn't known to the Ancients and therefore there is no relevance today. That's one theory, one shita, one approach. So that's the first approach that the Outer Planets really have no impact on us. They are too far away, too far away as a Planet to have any influence on the Earth. Even now, contemporary astronomers want to say that Pluto isn't really a planet, maybe it's a mini planet, or something. But they want to take away even its distinction as being a planet. So that's one explanation. Another approach is that it works in a general way. It doesn't work on individuals but it only works on society as a whole. Only on the world, it has an influence on world trends and world events but it doesn't work so much on individual lives. That's the 2nd approach. My teacher, he had a different approach. He wanted to say; also you can compare it to Sefer HaBrit. He wanted to say that the modern Planets are higher octaves of some of the lower Planets. For example Uranus is a higher octave of Mercury and Neptune is a higher octave of Venus and Pluto is the higher octave of Mars. And each of these Planets he wanted to say they don't work really on the body. In other words they work in a more mental way. They don't really influence the physical body, in other words the Sefer HaBrit say they don't cause day to day actions, they influence the person more on a psychic level. IN other words like the Sefer HaBrit would say, they are surrounding lights, they're not light that's inside but they're surrounding the person to some kind of a degree. In other words he would say that a person who has let's say all the Outer Planets very strong in his horoscope then they would be very speeded up, and would lead very unconventional lives because all the Outer Planets they are not connected with the normal things of this world, they are all higher octaves of this world. So a person who would have these Planets very strong in their Chart, on the Ascendant or the mid-Heaven or in exact conjunction says to the Sun or the Moon, or something along those lines… Then that person will be very unconventional. It will be hard for him to live a conventional life. The person wants to do big things and feels like he has a big destiny, things like that. A person who has the Outer Planets strong because he's not so much connected to the conventional. These Planets don't rule the conventional 7 areas of life. They don't rule the 7 days of the week, they rule the 8th day and the 8th day is in the air. They rule things that don't have vessels so to speak. So in a sense they take a person out of the body sometimes. They speed him or her up and they can really get very moved by it, and it's very hard for them to lead a conventional lifestyle because of this, a person who had got the Outer Planets strong, they want to do big things. And so he held something along those lines that the Outer Planets are again what we call higher octaves. And what exactly does that mean? They work more on a psychological level. They work on a higher level. For example Mercury is the Planet of the intellect. So if the persons got Mercury on the Ascendant, Mercury is an intellectual Sign, the Sign of reasoning. If you look at the symbol of the Planets, maybe one day I'll do a class on the Symbols of the Planets. If you look on the symbol, all the Planets have one of three things, or a combination. They have the Moon, the Sun and the Cross. If you look for example at the Sun, it's just a Sun, a circle. The Moon has a half Moon sign. If you look at Venus it has the Sun with a Cross sort of coming down from it underneath the Sun. Mars has a cross above the Sun. Saturn has the Moon below the Cross and Jupiter has the Moon above the cross. So it comes out every Planet, each of the 6 Planets has either a cross and the Sun or the cross and the Moon, sometimes above sometimes below. The only exception is Mercury. Mercury is if you look at it, a Moon and it's a Sun and a cross underneath. I remember my teacher used to say Mercury should be… the Sun is masculine and the Moon is feminine... and Mercury should be both because it's got a Sun and a Moon. In traditional Astrology they don't give Mercury a gender, because it can be either gender depending on certain situations. That's why they put a Moon together with a Sun. So my teacher used to joke, he said that most Mercury people should be both, they should have masculine and feminine but instead they usually have neither, because the Mercury again is the Planet of reason. It's hard to be in love if you have too much reason and Mercury is the Planet of reason. But Uranus is again, its super reason. It's a higher octave of Mercury. It's like a super computer type of thing. The person is going to be really way above, even more detached from emotions than Mercury, Mercury in the end has the Sun and the Moon, and in the end it has this emotional capability. Uranians sometimes are more computer like in a certain way. And Neptune is the higher octave of Venus. Venus is the Planet of love. It wants communication, it wants to make connections. To lose itself with its partner, to be united, to be one with another person. Neptune is more than that. Neptune wants to be one with the whole universe. You see Neptunian people, they're drug addicts or there are different type of Neptunians. There's good Neptune and there are bad Neptunes. The bad Neptunes are easier to understand. They want to lose themselves but maybe in the wrong way. They don't want to be caught up in themselves, Just like the Venus wants to be caught up in another person. They want to get even more than that. It's not enough for them another person. They want to become one with the universe or something like that. So they will go out and sometimes they will take drugs, sometimes they'll take alcohol or they'll be meditators and things like that… So the bad ways are the drugs and things like that which shortcuts are but there are other ways that maybe are better, like meditation or things like this. Certain religious practises in Judaism too, people do to get oneness with G-d. To be able to sort of attach to Him and feel like we are connected to Him, which is the high ideal state; this is the true Neptunian type of vision. So these are much higher states of consciousness that are connected with that.

Pluto is the higher octave of Mars. Mars is the Martian Sign, Mars likes to fight. Mars is a fighter, a warrior, its breaks things down, it destroys, and it leads into battle. And Pluto is more than that. It's like in the prayer; the Jews have a prayer that they say every day, where they talk about the ceremony in the Temple. When the Temple was established they used to cut up the ketoret, the offerings, they used to break it down and then offer it up. They'd have to chop it up to make it easier to burn. They said on Yom Kippur they chopped it up even more, finer and finer. And that's like Pluto. Pluto is… Mars likes to just destroy but Pluto likes to mamash totally destroy and build something new in its place. It wants to do some kind of regeneration. Pluto has this idea to regenerate things. They want to tear down and rebuild. And they think they can rebuild things in a better way. And that's the higher octave aspect of Mars. All these Planets they don't function, the Outer Planets if you look at what they do, they don't really function so great in this world. You don't have success in this world if you go around like a Neptunian who wants to lose yourself in G-d. And you're not going to make it in this world if you are a Pluto who wants to destroy things in order to rebuild. Or a Uranian who wants to bring change, it's a super mind, it wants to bring change and it doesn't worry so much about the established order also. It says let's forget about the established order. The Uranian is the guy who comes into the room, comes into somebodys house, it happened to me in Jerusalem, in Jerusalem years ago, people you hardly know the neighbour would come into your house and start talking to you. He'd start opening up your drawers and looking in your drawers to see what was in them and he'd start to rearrange your furniture, stuff like that… that's the Uranian. The Uranian is the guy who comes into your house and restarts everything; he rearranges your furniture without asking. They want to bring change. They don't really care about the emotions so much. They want to… it's not that they don't care, Uranians have emotions, but, in other words, they're willing to sort of leave the emotions for a while, while they do what they have to do, to transform the world. To make the world more like how they think it should be. S all these Outer Planets they don't function so well in this world. They again, if you learn Sefer HaBrit, they are things that shouldn't be happening all the time. You don't want all the time having your furniture rearranged or having things being broken down or all the time merging with G-d. So it's things that happen occasionally. Like Sefer HaBrit says, they only function a little bit. They're only felt a little bit. And I think there are only certain people who can pick up on these aspects, the people who have them very strong in their Horoscopes. In other words, I don't use their Aspects like the old Aspects, even 6, 10 degrees apart, some people even more as long they're in the same Sign; they say they are connected aspectually. Of all the Outer Planets you have to use a much smaller degree of contact if they are going to work. I would only use Uranus Neptune or Pluto if they are very closely conjoined to another planet or if they're very powerful in the Chart for other reasons then I would use them. Otherwise I would deemphasize them. The problem is that modern Astrologers, most of them they don't really know Astrology. So what they do is they use the Outer Planets because they can't find things using the 7 major Planets. And there is an advantage to the Outer Planets, that the Outer Planets move so slowly. In other words, if you're looking at Aspects, where the Planets are in the sky to where they are when you were born, you'll find that, say a Moon Aspect within 2 hours it happens and its gone. A solar Aspect will travel and will be gone in a day. So the Ancients placed more emphasis on a Jupiter or Saturn Aspect because they lasted a longer time. A Saturn Aspect could go back and forth for a year over a Planet. A Jupiter Aspect could go for a couple of months, sometimes 3 months over a Planet. So they used them more than the earlier Planets. But then you get to the Outer Planets and you can get Planets that can influence and go over your Ascendant and it can take 2 years for Pluto to cross your Ascendant. So it gives the modern day Astrologer a field day of action happening in the Horoscope that he can find easily even though I'm not necessarily sure it is always going to work. But there is a strong tendency to use these modern Planets and not to see them as being higher octaves or Planets that work on a psychological level or on the level that Sefer HaBrit calls bringing history to its proper conclusion. They use these Planets they get pulled down and say these Planets are in your everyday life and they use them like regular Planets. Sometimes even more because their Aspects are felt for such a long period of time that they will use them. So to go back and look at it, these are the Outer Planets, so if someone has Uranus that is very strong in their Chart, they are going to want to bring about change, revolution the idea of change. Also the Uranian doesn't live so much in time. He can be very far into the past or very far into the future. He doesn't necessarily live for the now; he's above a lot of things. He can visualise the world like it's going to be in the future and try to bring things there, that they'll be like that. Again the Neptunian wants to merge, to bring peace to the world, to bring unification, the ideal. The bad Neptune false illusions and the real Neptune which wants to see himself as an integral part of the Universe totally interconnected with every piece. Like in Judaism, Judaism is so difficult because it's based on the idea that everything a person does influences the whole Universe because the whole Universe is interconnected. So it comes out that everything you do is going to influence the whole Universe. And that's a total Neptunian type of vision, that you're one with the Universe. And that's a very high state; it's very hard to get to that state. I think if a person felt that all the time and he wasn't ready it could destroy him. But it's a very high ideal to strive for, like everything you do… I think the scientists say today this idea that if a butterfly flapped its wings one extra time it could change the whole course of history because it would change the wind currents and it would do this and that and the whole world would be different. And so here it's even more of an idea, they don't want to use it in human terms but in human terms every person's action, I mean you can derive it from what the scientists are saying, if a butterfly flapping its wings can affect the whole world then imagine what a word coming out from a person's mouth can do, or an action that a person does, how it can change the whole course of history sometimes, how it can have a tremendous influence on the world. So that's a very Neptunian type of vision. And then the Plutonian of course he also wants in his own way to rebuild the world. All these people they want to rebuild the world, to change, to make a difference. In other words they want to work beyond the system so to speak. They want to get to these really high levels. And Pluto wants to knock things down. But not for… they want to knock things down in order to rebuild. Their idea is to knock things down in order to rebuild. In other words their knocking down has a purpose. They also see the world as being made a better place. So all these people that are ruled by the 7 Planets who don't have these Outer Planets they have a very hard time handling these people, that have the strong Outer Planets and are of course always trying to put them down. And again, it is an interesting subject, the Outer Planets. And of course, they help... A lot of people say the Outer Planets they tend to work more on world events. Which again would be somehow like Sefer HaBrit, that the Outer Planets are coming to bring the world to its final conclusion and to get things back on track, so to speak, and to bring things toward its final conclusion. Sometimes it has to use these Outer Plants, this energy to get the people to make the changes necessary to bring things back on the fundamental path.

I hope these 2 classes were enlightening, I think I learned a lot, you know I didn't really know, to tell the truth when I started to talk I didn't really know what I was going to talk about and I think I got some ideas from this. And I'm sure there's a tremendous amount more that can be talked about connected to the Outer Planets. But I gave this as a general introduction to see how to look at and how to use the Outer Planets and b'ezrat Hashem we will come back some day and deal with it more in detail.

Chapter 3

The Outer Planets are fundamentally different from the Inner Planets, and we have already talked about it a little, but people who really want to know well the difference between the two, I have a two part series on the Outer Planets according to Jewish astrology and I highly recommend it. It brings down the teachings of a very famous Rabbi, Rabbi Pinchas from Vilna. He wrote a book called *Sefer HaBrit* and he was around when the first Outer Planet was discovered, Uranus, or back in those days it was called Herschel after the English man who found the Planet. So he talks about it and he gets into it and why the ancient Jewish astrologers never talked about the outer planets. If they really knew everything then they should have known that these other Planets exist. So we are going to talk about it a little but not too much because I don't want to review information that I have already put up in other places, because you can just go there and find it. What I would rather do is talk about something new.

In the Torah, the five books of Moses, they talk about Abraham. It says that God said to Abraham, look into the sky, you are going to have as many offspring as there are in the sky. So that is a very difficult thing to understand. Avraham lived about 3700 years ago, and in that time there was no telescope. The telescope was invented by Galileo, if I'm correct, about 2000 years later. So there were no telescopes and it was known that with the naked eye you could only see about 1000 or so stars. So what was God promising to Abraham? That he would have a thousand offspring? Or was it a hint already in the bible that the Rabbis knew and Abraham knew that there was an infinite number of celestial objects. So it would be like the offspring will be like the stars and there are a tremendous number of stars. And really only recently with very modern telescopes have we been able to see the unlimited number of stars and how giant the universe is and how many stars there are and how it really is an unlimited number. So over there already you can say that there was knowledge of all the stars. But they only talked about a thousand, and I guess the reason is that on one hand they only dealt with Planets and stars that were visible, because it's hard in a way to talk about something invisible. Uranus wasn't discovered until about the late 18 hundreds, and if you talked about it maybe people wouldn't believe you. So things were different in those times. And then there is the idea, does everything influence things down here on Earth? Maybe what you don't see doesn't influence things, or it influences things in a different way. That's what

Sefer HaBrit talks about. He teaches that the Outer Planets are not always working, that they are not really connected with physical things; the Rabbis didn't see them as being connected with events down here on Earth. They see that events down here on Earth are only connected with the 7 Lower Planets or what we call the 7 Ancient Planets, that each day of the week was one of those Planets. The Outer Planets seem to be more connected with states of mind. My teacher used to call them the Higher Octaves of the Lower Planets. in other words Uranus was the Higher Octave of Mercury, so Uranus is the thinking mans Planet, its very connected with the though process, which we will talk about later on. Neptune is the Higher Octave of Venus so it's connected with the idea of love and unification and things like that. Pluto on the other hand is the Higher Octave of Mars so it is more of a warrior type of Planet. So we will talk more about that as we explain the Planets.

I have a gripe with the modern astrologers who, in my opinion, pay too much attention to the Outer Planets. A lot of the modern astrologers today, if you look at what they are writing, they give more importance to the Outer Planets than to the Ancient Planets. because the Outer Planets move so slowly, they see Uranus for example can hang out on a persons Ascendant for a year, Pluto for two or three years. So the longer a Planet stays in a certain place, you can say that the effects are going to be stronger. It's known for example that Saturn, which is the slowest moving of the Ancient Planets, the astrologers gave more attention to their transits because they were much slower. So it has more time for its effects to build up. The modern astrologers say that going on Saturn which goes around the globe in 30 years and has such a strong effect compared to the Moon which goes around in 28 days, then Uranus which takes 84 years to make an orbit, its effects will be even stronger. And Neptune which takes well over 100 years will be stronger, and Pluto even more. So the modern astrologers build it like this, but I don't really think it's a fair thing to say because astrology is a science based on what is seen. A lot of what we are taught is based on what you can see, how the Planets move etcetera. So according to Jewish opinions it is fundamentally different, and the Lower Planets affect the Earth. They affect what is going on down here and their influence is stronger. The Outer Planets which are unseen to the naked eye, I don't want to get into the Kabalistic explanation right now so you will have to look at my tapes on the Outer Planets, but in any case, their influence down here is more psychological and more mental. In other words if he or she has a strong Outer Planet they are going to have a tendency toward unconventional lives. That seems to be the main thing, that it is very hard for them to lead conventional lives because their minds or their emotions or their obsessive natures is going to pull them away from leading a normal life. Let's put it this way, just as these Planets are unseen, they cause people to go after the unseen worlds.

Chapter 4

We are going to be doing the second class in the series of classes on the Outer Planets in the different Houses. Before we start to go into specifics about each of the Planets in the different Houses, let's talk about the significance of these Outer Planets. So last week we said that you have to know that the Outer Planets are unseen, and we wanted to argue with the modern astrologers who sometimes place more importance on the Outer Planets than on the Inner Planets, because they think they can see long term things from the Outer Planets. I also agree in a certain way but I think the Outer Planets only work sometimes. They don't always work and they come along to make changes to the world in a big way. But again, I don't know if they influence each and every person as much as they influence what is going on in the world. I think maybe the influence is more important there than the individual influence. The individual influence is only going to work at certain times and maybe only with certain people who have the power to transform the world through the use of the Outer Planets.

Even today in contemporary Indian astrology they don't use Uranus Neptune and Pluto, and a lot of traditional astrologers don't use the Outer Planets. And more than that, if they do use the Outer Planets they don't consider them as connected to a Sign, they will say that it's really unconnected to a Sign. For example how can you say Uranus is connected to Aquarius if it is already ruled by Saturn? My teacher would say to use both of them, and that Uranus has some kind of a connection with Aquarius. But some people argue with that and say you can use the Outer Planets but don't connect them with a Sign. And they will bring reasons as to why you don't connect them with a Sign; they don't think that the correspondences fundamentally agree.

Today with the idea of using long term predictors, they have different Planetary Lord systems, where you can see an overview of the person's whole life by using the Planetary Lords, where there are different periods for each Planet that is ruling. And of course there they don't use the Outer Planets, it's a specific system with the older Planets, and they can get an overview of the person's whole life. So there is not really a need to try to fit in these Outer Planets. Contemporary astrologers place so much importance on these Outer Planets because they didn't have long term predictive tools and because of that I think that's why they put so much stress on these Outer Planets. But in my experience I haven't seen the Outer Planets being so accurate. I find much more accuracy using the older Planets, the original Planets, and the Planets seen by the naked eye or the Planetary Lords system. I see those as being much more reliable than the use of the Outer Planets.

In any case, let's talk a little bit about the Outer Planets anyway, we can talk about some of the tips, or the more important indications that I have found with the Planets. I think they do work some of the time, I just wouldn't place that much emphasis on them, certainly that they are less important than the Planets visible to the naked eye and not more important. I think the people that do say that are wrong in the sense that they can't come along and change astrology and say that the Outer Planets are more important than the Planets that you can see. In other words what is unseen is more important than what is seen. It's very hard to come along and say that.

You see from the Torah that the Rabbis knew about the stars and I assume they knew the outer Planets existed and they had their reasons for not talking about them. Probably because they didn't consider their influence on the Earth strong enough to talk about or, like I want to say in my classes, that they are coming around for special purposes and they are not always working. For that you can listen to my tapes on it.

Before we start on the Planets in each of the Houses, let's talk a little bit about each of the Planets themselves. Uranus is the Higher Octave of Mercury, so it's a mental Planet and it speeds things up. People who have a very strong Uranus tend to live way in the past or way in the future, its hard for them to live in the present. That's why a lot of inventors can see what other people can't see, they have this grasp of the future. It's a Planet that is strongly connected with freedom, it was discovered when the world was going through a lot of revolutions, and it's connected with freedom, individuality. A person with a strong Uranus has a desire for individuality. It's a Mercurial influence; it's not an emotional thing. Mercury is a mental Planet so it doesn't have an emotional attachment to things, and Uranus even more so, it can become very mental in a certain way. So sometimes that can be difficult unless there are other considerations, such as a lot of Water, it can cause a person to be emotionally distant, because they like to keep their freedom and when you get involved with things that are emotional it tends to take away your freedom and you tend to become attached. That takes away your freedom and your ability to think clearly and logically.

Neptune on the other hand, is a little different. Neptune is the opposite. Neptune is the Higher Octave of Venus. Venus is the Planet of love, unity, emotions, and the pleasures of this world. And if a person has Neptune, which is the Higher Octave of Venus, then they are even more emotional. People who have Venus have simple needs, they just want to merge with one other person, have a big love affair and be totally in love with the person. Neptune gets so carried away that they want to be in love with the whole entire world, they want to merge with the universe. So people who have a bad Neptune try to merge in the wrong ways, using drugs or using alcohol or all sorts of different things where they can lose touch or get outside of themselves. They want to break boundaries and merge. Uranus on the other hand has a strong identity and doesn't want to lose their identity. Neptune has the urge to merge; their whole idea is to merge.

The third Planet there is Pluto, which is the Higher Octave of Mars. Mars tends to want to destroy. Pluto wants to totally destroy and then to start over, to rebuild into something better. Mars will break something down into big pieces, Pluto wants to disintegrate it. So Pluto comes along and wants to change everything and rebuild. It has a tendency to be connected with obsessions. A person with a strong Pluto has a strong power drive, and a strong obsessive nature.

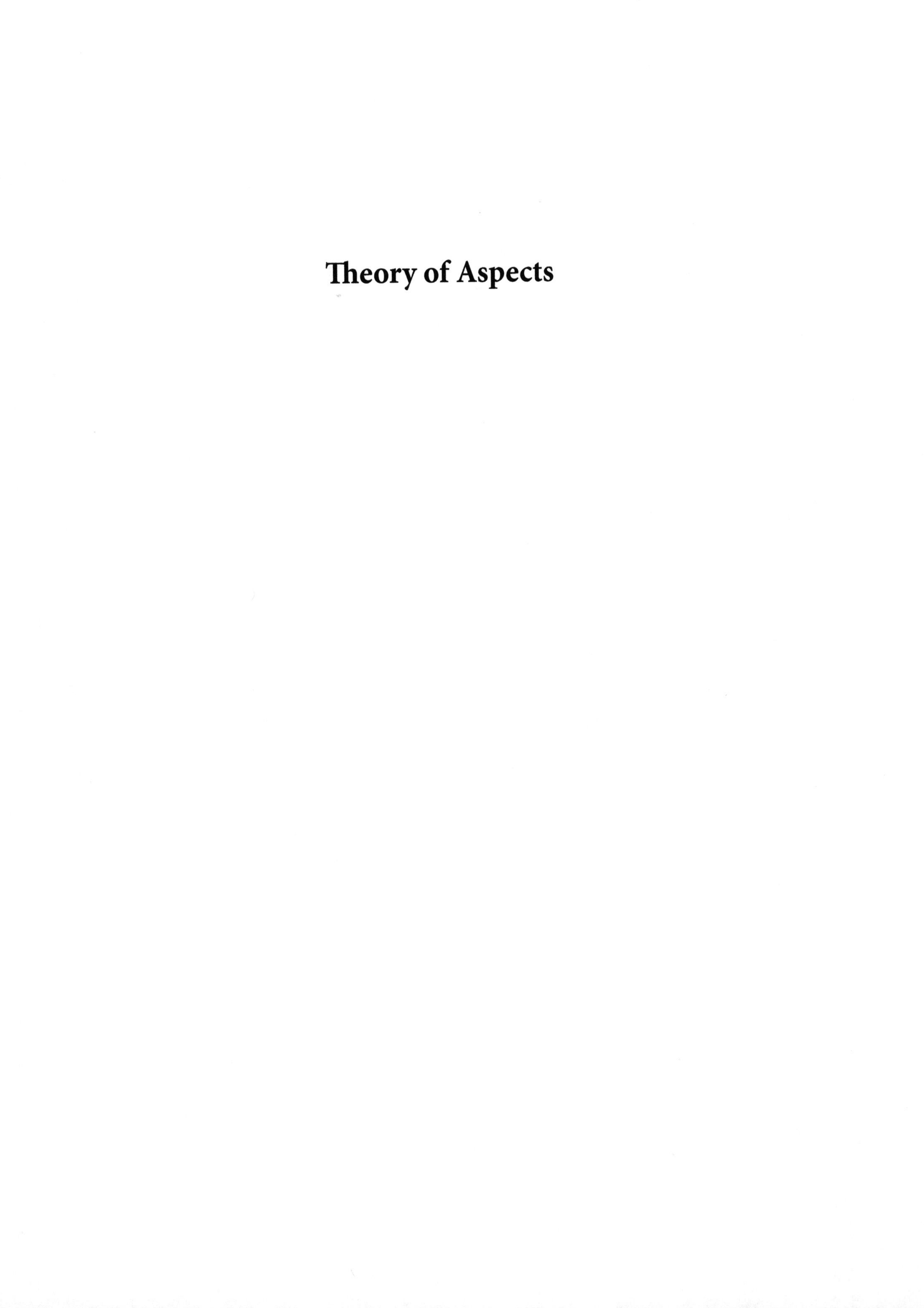

Theory of Aspects

Theory of Aspects

By Yaakov Kronenberg

A transcription of a short discussion on the Angles made between Planets. Angles enhance or deflect the energy, and are known as Aspects. Aspects are one of the most interesting topics in astrology and we discuss here their core effect.

Theory of Aspects

By Yaakov Kronenberg

This is a short class on the theory of Aspect analysis. Aspects are one of the most interesting topics in astrology, it's the relationship between two Planets that look at each other in a certain way and they combine the meaning of the two Planets together for good or bad depending on the Aspect.
According to the Ancient system there are only a few Aspects, there is a 60 degree Aspect, a 90 degree Aspect, 120 degree Aspect, 180 degree Aspects and a Conjunction if you want or a 0 degree Aspect. Besides these, today there are astrologers that use all sorts of extra different Aspects; they say there are also a 30 degree, 150 degree, 210 degree and all sorts of aspects like that. I'm going to stick to the ancient basic system which has 5 Aspects and I'm going to explain how to derive the meaning of each Aspect.

If you remember, we always go back to derive the meaning of things in astrology from the chart of Adam HaRishon. If you look at Adam HaRishon's chart at the bottom of the chart, the 4th and the 5th Houses, the 4th House Cusp is Cancer and the 5th House Cusp is Leo. Cancer is ruled by the Moon so lets put the Moon in the 4th House. And in the 5th House Leo is ruled by the Sun so let's put the Sun in the 5th House. Now if we go one Sign over each way, for example if we go from Leo to Virgo or from Cancer to Gemini, in other words if we start from Leo we are going to go in a counter clockwise direction and if we start from Cancer or the Moon then we will go in a clockwise direction. If you move both of them one Sign over then they both come to a Mercurial Sign. The Sun comes to Virgo which is ruled by Mercury, and the Moon comes to Gemini which is ruled by Mercury. That's a 0 degree Aspect or a conjunction. We say a conjunction is a Mercurial type of Aspect. Later on we will have classes on these types of things.
Mercurial by nature means that it combines the planets in an intellectual way and the meaning between them depends on a certain amount of factors connected to Mercury which we will talk about later on. Now if you go another 30 degrees over, so if you start from Leo you go two Signs over, you get to Virgo and then you get to Libra. So 60 degrees away is a Venusian Aspect, because you have a Libra there which is ruled by Venus. The same thing if you go 60 degrees clockwise from the Moon you get Gemini and then Taurus and Taurus is also ruled by Venus. A 60 degree Aspect, a sextile, is a Venusian Aspect, which means that the two Planets that are 60 degrees away from each other work in a harmonious and loving way, and they want to help each other, and that is why it is considered a good Aspect. Whenever there are two Planets together you always consider that there is a third Planet there; let's say the Sun and the Moon are 60 degrees apart, so you say that Venus is also there, so the relationship between them will be Venusian. The Sun is always the Sun and the Moon is always the Moon, but it is the way that they relate to each other that will be different.

If you move over another Sign, to 90 degrees, so in this case you start from Leo, Virgo, Libra, Scorpio. A 90 degree Aspect is Martian, because Scorpio is ruled by Mars, and it's the same thing if you go from the Moon, you will get Gemini, Taurus and then Aries, which is also Martian. So a 90 degree Aspect by nature is Martian which means that the relationship between the two Planets is a fighting type of relationship. They are squared to each other and they are in conflict with each other, each one wants to defeat the other one so you have a relationship of conflict. If you have two Planets at 90 degrees to each other, let's say the Sun and the Moon: instead of being in a loving and harmonious relationship they will be more in a fighting and discordant relationship with each other.

My teacher used to say that all Aspects between Planets are the same, the only difference is that the timing is different. If you get a square Aspect it means that there is a struggle and they are pushing against each other and they are trying to heat things up.
The Venusian Aspect is more harmonious, the timing is more proper.
If you go 120 degrees, you get Jupiter. If you start from Leo you go Virgo, Libra, Scorpio, Sagittarius; the same thing starting from Cancer, you get Pisces, and you get a 120 degree Aspect which is also harmonious, it's a Jupitarian Aspect, in other words each one helps the other one because they are expansive from one to the other.
If you go one more Planet over then you get Capricorn, if you go Leo, Virgo, Libra, Sagittarius, Capricorn, 180 degrees, and the same thing going the other way from Cancer, you get to Aquarius. 180 degrees is a Saturnine Aspect because you get Aquarius and Capricorn which are ruled by Saturn. A Saturnine Aspect is an Aspect of delay, each one holds the other one back. They are pulling against each other and each one is telling the other not to do what they want to do.

The planets always act according to their nature, Mars is always going to act in a Martian way and Saturn is always going to act in a Saturnine way. But when they are in a Martian relationship they are going to fight each other and push each other, so the timing can be off, they are going to act before the time is ripe. In the Saturnian way they are pulling against each other and delaying each other so the timing is all off there too. The one is trying to do things too fast, the other too slow. The sextile and the trine are much more smooth and balanced, and therefore they are working in harmony with each other so you get a better Aspect. A conjunction has its own set of rules which is beyond the scope of this short lecture to talk about, but I would just like to say that this was a very quick introduction to the Theory of Aspects; later on I will have a number of longer classes on it. I think people will enjoy it, explaining in a deep way how Aspects work.

Time Lords in Human history

Time Lords in Human history

By Yaakov Kronenberg

This is an edited transcription of a series of lectures on the Time periods of Humanity from the Kabalistic astrology perspective, focusing on the Macro time periods of history. The 18 Time period system is based on the teachings of Rabbi Moshe Kordovero, and is found in a book called Chesed LeAvraham, written by Rabbi Avraham Azulai. Both Rabbi Kordovero and Rabbi Azulai were major Kabalists who lived in Zfat in the 1400s, which was the time of the end of the early kabala, and the beginning of the Lurianic kabala. This series explains in depth the Torah teachings of the 18 Time periods of the 7000 year long history of Humanity, as we have know it through our history and as it will evolve in our future.

Time Lords in Human History

By Yaakov Kronenberg

Introduction

Time lords in Jewish astrology is not the Time lords that people are accustomed to; it is a completely different Time lord system, based on Kabalistic astrology and its approach to the Macro aspect of the Human history, as opposed to the general approach of using Time lords in an Individual's history. Knowing the historical world Time lord system helps the astrologer get a better view of the Macro context of what is happening to individuals in their Micro dimension. These Time lords for the Individual (as opposed to what we will cover in this series – Time Lords of the whole of Humanity) is a very old idea which was, in a certain sense, rediscovered in the last fifteen years by Western astrologers. The Indian astrologers have always been using something similar to it. Indian astrology actually has many time lords' systems for Individuals, the most common of which is called the Dasha system where the individual is apportioned 120 years to their life, and they then divide the 120 years up into different time periods, each based on a different planet.

So while your birth chart tells you what would happen in your life, you also have to factor in the Transits of the planets over your birth chart (which tell you When things will happen); you still have to recognize and accept that the birth chart and the Transits are consummated within the Time lords, which work both on a Micro (individual cycles) and on a Macro level (Humanity cycles). On the Micro level, you are for large periods of time under the Rulership of a specific Time lord planet for that cycle, which determines how your life would be for specific periods. And if a person has, let us say, the Sun in his chart exalted in Aries in the 5th house, and one of these micro time lord periods ruled by the Sun arrives in his life, then he will have an even more exalted sun, very powerful, and it will lift him up, it will take his good luck up, maybe either he or one of his children will become very successful or make a fortune, or maybe it will be his first child. Because it will be a period of time when he will be super exalted, and the influence of the time lord will really be good for him. In Western astrology there are things which are very similar. The Greeks and Romans also used time lords. The Persians also had a time lord system called the Faderia. And it was very prevalent in its time, and it has

made a comeback in the world of Western astrology over the last ten years or so. But these are all micro time lord cycles.
In this series of talks, we are going to look at the Time periods from the Jewish Kabalistic astrology perspective, which in this case deals with the macro time periods of history. So this series will be about a system called the 18 Time periods. In brief, the 18 Time periods in Judaism are based on the Torah teachings that the history of the human world is 7000 years long (made up of a 6000 years period followed by another 1000 year period). The 7000 years are then broken up into 18 periods. And in each of these 18 time periods God is going to direct the world in a particular way. Of course God rules the world all the time, He runs it and directs what happens, but in each of the time periods there is a specific influence. So the history of the world is basically divided into 18 periods that are the broadest categories of how Time is divided and how the energy comes down from above in a fixed way in these 18 periods.

But before we start on these 18 Time periods, I would like to mention that there is another system in Kabbalistic astrology called the Fixed Planetary Time system. Some of this Fixed Planetary Time system has found its way into Western astrology and is called the "Planetary Hours", where it takes the 7 days of the week and assigns a ruling planet to each day, like Sunday ruled by the Sun and Monday ruled by the Moon etc., and then to break the days down into hours, with each hour being ruled by a different planet. So the ruling planet of the day and the ruling planet of the night will depend on which planet rules the 1st hour of the Day (6 am) and which rules the 1st hour of the Night (6 pm). And with this information they can then get a limited idea of what is going to happen to the individual concerned in his lifetime, on the micro level. But this is a limited system and only takes into consideration the days of the week, and the hours. The source of the 'Planetary Hours' system of Western astrology is found in the Talmud, which was written about 1500 years ago, at the end of Tractate Shabbat, where the Fixed Planetary Time system is explained and also in the Bible (Book of Genesis).
{I have a 12 part series for anybody interested in that, of Jewish astrology based on the writings of Rabbi Avraham Bar Chiya, where he goes into depth regarding that system}.
There is much more to the Fixed Kabbalistic Planetary Time system than what is found in the Planetary hours system of Western astrology. In other words the Kabbalists did not only use the days of the week and the hours, but also longer periods, like weeks, the months, and the 7 year cycles (called the Shmita cycles) and also the 50 year cycles (know as the Jubilee cycles, which

consisted of 7 x 7 year cycles plus 1 year = 50 years, which has its own special laws), and also the 1000 year cycles. They used these both as a micro and macro time system. This whole Fixed Planetary Time system in fact comes from the 7 days of creation in the Bible. In other words, God created the world in 7 days, with each day and hour being ruled by a different planet. And it is says in Psalms 90:4; "A 1000 years are as 1 day in the eyes of God". Which means that each day of creation refers also to a 1000 year period of the world's human existence: The 1st day refers to the first 1000 years that the human world existed; the 2nd day refers to the second 1000 years in the world's human history, and so on until you have the 7 days, which refer to the seventh 1000 years, totaling 7000 year. So the 7 days of the week are a variation to the 7000 year cycle and this adaptation is what the Western astrologers use. And to really understand this system one has to go to the root of this system which is found in the beginning of the Bible, where the 7 days of creation are discussed. This is the source of the primary wisdom, which was originally given to the first man Adam, and he then transmitted it onwards, passing on a lot of the astrological knowledge, of how the star system and planetary system work, to his descendents. And that knowledge came down eventually to Avraham, the first Jew, who came from Babylon, where the wisdom of astrology was concentrated at that time, the time of the dispersion after the Tower of Babel, when God mixed up all the nations and their languages, and everybody then left Babylon. So that knowledge spread all over the world, and everyone took some pieces of that knowledge from there, and that is how latter generations in the world got the idea of the 7 day week. Babylon was a transit point. And if you don't learn like that, then how can you explain the global 7 day week idea? How did everyone in the world come to this system of a 7 day week? There are books which talk about this, like Josephus, in his History of the World, where he talks about this ancient knowledge that was passed on from Adam's children. And in the famous Jewish philosophy book, Sefer HaKuzari, which talks about this too. But in any case, the Kabbalists built this whole system, dividing the world's history into 6000 years, plus a final 1000 years (during which the world will be somehow different to the preceding 6000 years) making up the 7000 year cycle. So according to this Fixed Kabalistic Time Planetary system/cycle, we have the first 1000 years being ruled by the Sun. So those people had good health and lived long lives, as mentioned in the Bible. Some lived for 900 years, and some were almost 1000 years old when they died. The 2nd thousand years' period was ruled by the Moon. And there was the great flood during that period etc....But today is not the time to get into that system and I am only trying to show you the roots of this system and to introduce the idea that in Jewish astrology, just like the life of Individual is divided up into time periods, so is Human history.

This idea of having Astrological Human History, is not something dealt with in Indian astrology, or Arab or Greek/Roman astrology. There could be a philosophical reason for that. Many of the early nations held that the world and universe was an ongoing eternal cycle with no beginning or end. In other words they didn't believe that the world had been Created, and believed that it always existed. And if it always existed, then it would always keep existing, and there is no way to divide history or find any meaning in History except for the utility of its study. So maybe that is one reason why they didn't talk about time periods. But in Judaism, the world had a Beginning. History has a starting point and an ending point as well. The human time world is divided into seven 1000 year periods, and there is a definite beginning and a definite meaning and purpose to History, and God is directing that history. God uses the planets as one of his agents to send down influences to the world. And while we are not able to understand God, we can at least try, by studying astrology, to understand how God runs the world. And this is the whole idea of Kabbala, to understand the way God runs the world and see His intention in creating the world, and try, through this, to get a glimpse of Him, since we can't understand His essence. So soon I hope to do a comprehensive series on the Torah Fixed Planetary Time system, showing how to expand the Western Planetary hour system. But let's get back to the main topic of this series, the 18 Time period of Human history.

So just like a person's life is broken into time periods, so is Human History. In Kabala we have the famous saying, that "as below, so above", that whatever is found below is found above. This world and the upper worlds are all broken into time periods. There is also a relationship between the Micro and the Macro, between a person and the whole of humanity. This series is based on the writings of the early Kabbala, from a little bit earlier then the Ari Zal (Rabbi Luria). It is going to be based on the writings of Rabbi Moshe Kordovero, and a book called Chesed LeAvraham, written by Rabbi Avraham Azulai. Both R. Kordovero and R. Azulai were major Kabbalists who lived in Zfat in the 1500s, which was the time of the end of the early kabbala, and the beginning of the Lurianic kabbala. This material is dealt with in the latter kab bala studies of the Ari Zal, but I want to use the earlier Kabala because it brings this subject down in a more precise format.

So let us start now. I am going to translate a little bit from his book and then comment and move forward in that pattern. Let us start in the Chesed

LeAvraham where R. Azulai says, **"It is known to everybody that it should not go up in their mind, and they should not believe, that any action in the world, weather little or big, might happen by chance. Nothing in the world happens by chance, but rather, they are all directed from a higher source. And it has not been directed, not by the power of man, and not from the power of anything that was created"**. In other words, direction is coming from the Source before Creation, and not from anything that didn't exist before creation, like Angels or Sefirot (Kabalistic Spheres), or the Planets or different things like that. **"But rather, anything that is coming from the secret of the world is being directed from what is called the Ein Sof, the ineffable light, the limitless light, the high unending light, who knows good and who knows bad. And He does good with His will, in order to punish people and in order to reward people, everything according to His own calculations. And He doesn't add to it, and nothing is subtracted from it, not even a little dot, God forbid, even a hand's breadth"**.

So in his first paragraph, R. Azulai wants to show you that first of all, everything is being run from a higher source. And you shouldn't think that the planetary system runs the world, which had always been the mistake of the idol worshipers. They thought the world is run by the planets and constellations, with nothing above that. But we have already learned that there are many worlds above the universe we are living in. And above that, there is the higher power called the Ein Sof, and even He was only an emanation of a higher level above that, which we shouldn't even talk about. And everything is being run from this Higher source, and eventually by God himself. And the introduction given here is that the world is being run from a higher source.

"Even so, you have to know that this light, the Ein Sof, which the world is being run by, directing the world and everything that happens in it, and there is nothing that happens by chance. Even so you have to know that the way the world is being directed from above does change from different Time period to different time periods, and these Time periods are these". Rabbi Azulai will now list them in brief and latter do them in detail.

"The 1st Time period was right after the first man was created, and Man had complete contentment, he was completely contented. It was a period when he was completely contented with contentment". Man had everything he needed, he was content and everything was good. That was the first period. The common opinion of the scientists today is that all humanity in the world started from one man, and that is very consistent with ancient Jewish theology, that the world started with one man. And I guess the anthropologists even call him Adam, and his wife Eve. And you have to assume that they were indeed the first couple, for otherwise, without the idea of a primary couple, you can't have the idea of common archetypes. The whole archetype system is built on the idea that all people in the world are subservient to these archetypes. And had there been more than one couple as the source of humanity, there would be more than one set of archetypes: the descendents of each would have a different archetype to be based on. So from this point of view too, you have to hold that the whole world came from one man. So the first time period was when the first man was created. And he lived in contentment.

"The 2nd time period started after the first man sinned and was expelled from the Garden of Eden, until after the Flood". If you look in the Bible, you see that during the first thousand years, people had very long life spans. It was only after the flood that the life span shortened to around 300 years. And later it became 120 years, which continues until our very day. So during the second period, people still had very long lives, despite the sins and things like that. People were still in contentment, like our rabbis explained.

"The 3rd time period is that of the Avot, the Forefathers of the Nation of Israel; Abraham, Isaac and Jacob". Abraham had a big impact on the world; For example the Indian astrology came from Avraham. It is says in the Bible that when Avraham had a concubine and children from her, he sent them to the east with 'gifts'. And over there, the major Talmudic commentators say that these were Spiritual gifts, and he sent a lot of Holy names to the people in the east, so they could use them. Avraham was a master astrologist, so a lot of his knowledge got to the east. The word Brahmin, in Indian society, is very similar to the name of Abraham, which is like A-Braham. So there is a connection along these lines. Avraham was born in 1948, according to the Jewish calendar, according to which today date is 5771. So that means that Abraham lived around the 1700s and the 1800s B.C. He wrote the Sefer HaYetzira, which is the oldest known astrology book, from around 1800 B.C. That was the time of the fathers. And the divine presence dwelled with them, and they had great success.

But you see that their lives were, already, much shorter, and none of the Fathers got to be 200 years old.

The 4th time period is the going down of Yaakov, with his children, to Egypt. And they were still having success. Even though they had to go down to Egypt, and leave Israel, they still had success.

The 5th time period is the exile of the children, and the suffering they had in Egypt. In other words, after Jacob died, and Joseph too, the children of

Israel slowly became enslaved in Egypt, and they experienced a lot of suffering.

The 6th time period is their redemption from Egypt, the success they had in the desert, and all the different miracles they witnessed. If you go to the Bible, in the Book of Numbers, its talks about how the Israelites, due to sins they did after leaving Egypt, had to spend forty years in the desert. And during those years, great things happened to them. So they had to wonder in the desert, but great miracles happened to them there. For example, since they didn't have food in the desert, every day food was dropped for them from heaven. And the clothing that they wore never withered. And there were all sorts of other miracles in the deserts, which we don't see today. That was a different period in the world, where the directions of things were different. And so it is possible to see all the different ways in which God directs the world. And you have to see, again, that everything is actually inside everything. It is not only one period, which completely ends, with nothing remaining out of it. Things in each period go the main way, but actually, all other periods somehow exist within each period. The main direction of the world is what sticks out each period, but directions from other periods still exist. Like you see today that there are still miracles, though not as great and revealed as during the Israelite time in the desert.

The 7th time period is when the Israelites entered the Land of Israel and had success when the conquered the land from the seven nations who were there. And that whole generation was under this particular energy when the Jews came back to their land. And that happened again today where recently, some 60 years ago, Jews started to come back to their land again.

The 8th time period is when the Israelites were subservient to the nations, during the time of the Judges. This was a more difficult period.

The 9th time period was the success of the Israelites during the days of the kings. Like when King Shlomo (Solomon) ruled the world, and after that there were other kings, and the Israelites were very successful. But they were most successful when Solomon ruled the world, which was one of the highest points, if not the highest point, in Jewish history, when they had the First Temple.

The 10th time period is the destruction of the First Temple, and the exile of the Jewish people, slowly and by stages. I guess this is still going on today, because many Jews are still in exile, though many Jews came back to Israel. And slowly we might get to a point where the majority of Jews will find themselves in Israel.

The 11th time period is the exile of the Jews to Babylon, and the little bit of success they had there, in Babylon.
The 12th time period was the redemption of the Jews, when they came back to Israel from Babylon, and built the Second Temple.
The 13th period was the sufferings of the Jews during the Second Temple period, and also the successes that they had during that time.
The 14th period is the exile of the Jews. This was of time when sometimes it was in sorrow and sometimes in prosperity and blessing. During this period the Jews have been sent throughout the world, they were tremendously persecuted in some countries, but in others they had some success, and became extremely wealthy. And again it also depends on periods. During some periods in one country, Jews were successful, while during other periods, they were persecuted. And it is not just Jewish history which I am talking about; this is really connected to the whole world. The whole world is also influenced by the 18 Time periods which the Jews underwent. And we will also explain that as we go on.
The 15th time period is the success Jews will have at the end of days, during the time of redemption, and the future sufferings that will be in that time period. Now we are talking about present day events. While the fourteenth time period is the exile, the fifteenth time period is already the coming out of exile, which you see has already began, with the Jews coming back to the land of Israel and forming their own nationality. Also he mentions the successes and the suffering that will be at the time of redemption, with all the nations in the world slowly developing antipathy towards the State of Israel, with Anti Zionism replacing Anti Semitism. Rabbi Avraham Azulai and Rabbi Moshe Kordovero talk about that and we will deal with this in the series.
The 16th time period is when the dead come back to life. We will talk about that later because it is a hard concept.
The 17th time period is the destruction of the world. These are things that you should still be looking forward to!
The 18th time period is the renewal of the world.

R. Azulai continues: **"All these time periods have everything that happens in the world included in them. In other words, all the things that already happened in the past, and everything that is going to happen in the future (are included these 18 Time periods). And it is important for people to know all these changes, and all the different ways that God directs the world in each and every time, according to the time period".** And indeed, you can't be a great astrologer if you don't really know history.

You have to know what is going on in the world. And if you hold that the world just always existed and is always going to exist, and that there is no guiding principle in history or anything, and no end of days, then what is it all about? How do you know what is going on in the world? As an astrologer, if you don't know what time period the world is in, how can you predict for a person? Individuals are subservient to higher forces and higher energies. If you see the whole history of the world, with people who had such crazy ideas, and who did such stupid things, like they worshiped idols, they took their kids and passed them in fire, sacrificed children, and that went on for the last five thousand, or even six thousand years. And at each time period, people thought that that was the real way to live. One could say that people live today in the Western world in a way which back a few hundred years ago, people would pass out if they heard of what is going on today. What would people say about all the crazy stuff which goes on today, some two hundred years from now?

So Rabbi Avraham Azulai is emphasizing here that you really have to understand that there are different Macro Time periods in the world. And the way God is running the world is always changing, but there is always an overlapping theme to the history of the world, and to the responsibility of the Individual to the world and the way he has to behave.

R. Azulai then talks about Micro Time periods of the Individual: **"Just like there are different Time periods for the world, there are time periods for the individuals, and they have their own directions in life"**. So there are also Time periods in the life cycle of the Individual, on each and every person. We know that there are 4 types of scenarios where good happens to righteous people, and bad happens to bad people. And there are times when bad happens to good people and good happens to bad people. And you see that in this world, unfortunately, we don't exactly get rewarded according to our behavior. If we were instantaneously rewarded or punished according to our behavior then everyone would know what to do, and there would be no free choice, because of the immediate repercussions. Unfortunately, the world doesn't work that way. If you don't start to see how the world functions, and the context in which things are happening (that good people have bad lives and bad people have good lives), then that is enough to take you away from your belief in God, until you come to believe in the idea that the world is run by its nature, or, as some people hold, by the judgments and decrees of the planets, or by other energies or things. Take the Holocaust for example. So the fundamental idea is to understand that nothing happens by chance, and it is all directed by a higher force.

R. Azulai continues: **"Before I explain all these matters, I am going to talk about all the different ways God directs the world, according to how they happen".**
So before getting into all the different time periods in detail we are going to discuss and hopefully understand a bit more, all the different ways that God runs the world.

Chapter 1
So besides the fact that there are Time periods in individual human beings, there are also Time periods in the history of the Humanity as a whole, in the history of the human species. This will give you a new way to look at human evolution, human history, how the world progresses, and how your chart fits into the broader Macro climate of what is happening in the world. This is because each time period in history and even in every generation, is really very different from the previous one. Each generation has a whole different energy, and a completely different world. The illnesses people contract have changed through the generations, and so have life expectancies and also sorts of other things. For example we knew from the Zohar that Mankind, after the year 1840, would experience a tremendous breakthrough in scientific knowledge, and so, while before that Mankind would live 50 years, and a 60 or 70 years lifespan was considered a long life, today a life span of 100 years is no longer rare. So if, for example, you are going to predict the life expectancy of an individual, its best to know the macro Time period he lives in and the country he lives in ect... before you look at the chart.
Now let us start with the 1st Time period, which began from when Adam Harishon was born until the time that he sinned. That was the first period, which we hope will come back and be similar in the future days, when we get to the end of the days, where we hope that the world will be directed the same way it was directed when Adam Harishon was first created, before he sinned. Because in the future everything is going to be like what we experience on the Sabbath today, where the energy of peace and tranquility will come down to us and there is going to be a contentment down below, in the body and in the soul, **"and the world will be fixed from all its curses, and all the garments of impurity will be removed, and there will not be death anymore in the world. And all this is going to be because of the light of Wisdom, which will come down into the light of Understanding, and the light of Understanding will come down into the 6 directions, the 6 Sefirot/Spheres, from Chesed to Yesod, and they will come down into Malchut/Kingship** (Malchut is the lower world we are in). **And this will never**

happen in any other Time period, except for the first and the last ones (of the 18 Time periods). **Even during the time of the First Temple, in the times of King Solomon, who was wiser then all the wise men of the east, and yet the world wasn't fixed as it was during the time of Adam Harishon, because there was still death and all other curses in the world".**

So here we have the idea that the ideal time from when Adam Harishon was created until the time he sinned, will be repeated in the stage of the end of days, when the world is going to be revived, and evil will be neutralized, with no death in the world and were there will be the contentment of the soul and the body. And these are really the times of the ideal state of things, which occurred in the 1st Time period and which will reoccur in the future, in the time of 'the world to come', just like it was in the time of the first man. Then the light of Wisdom will light up into the light of Understanding. **"And Man will receive the Wisdom of heaven through his mind, and cling to it, to the Garden of Eden in the secret of the tree of life, and he will grow up and connect himself with the high angels, up until the Throne".** This world of the Throne is the highest part of the world of Creation. This is the world which is underneath the world of Atzilut/Emanation, the world of Beriah/Creation. And in fact the contentment is going to be on an even higher level, because at the time of Adam Harishon, even before his sin, there was an evil force and impurities in the world which eventually caused Man to sin. But in the future, all these evil forces and impurities are going to be completely nullified. So the End of days, in the 18th Time period, it is going to be an even better than during the time of Adam, before the sin. **"Because at the time of Adam there were imperfections such as 'the diminishing of the moon', which would wax and wane, starting from the 4th day of creation. And also we have another difference in that the world (during the time when Adam was created) was missing the Shabbat (which only occurred after the sin)".** So you see that other things were lacking during this 1st Time period which will not be lacking in Time period 18. The symbolic example is the moon, which waxed and waned, and the lack of Shabbat in the world. In the future there is not going to be any of this fluctuating moon. It will be more constant and every day is going to be like the Sabbath. So the whole story of the sin of Adam Harishon is a big kabalistic discussion, and is not our aim here to go into details on this matter. But what R Azulai is saying is that had Adam been able to avoid messing up until the Sabbath came, and refrained with Eve from getting involved with the snake and the apple, then the world would have been corrected then and there, and instead of all these 18 Time periods of history, we would have had just 1 Time period throughout.

The 2nd Time period starts after the sin of Adam Harishon, and lasts until after the flood. **"And the sin of the first man is comparable to the destruction of the First Temple. And the 2 letters Hey (of Hashem's name)" got exiled due to that, because of his sins and the sins of the generation of the First Temple.** In other words God has two of the Hebrew letter H in His holy name, and since they were exiled, His name is not complete, and that caused the destruction of his presence in the world.

"And all those doors above in Heaven became blocked up, and haven't been opened again, since the sin of Adam Harishon". In other words, the higher energies from the upper worlds, which bring down the best sustenance, got blocked up at the time of Adam's sin, and haven't been opened again since.

"And that is the secret of the 'opening up of the ground/path to the Wisdom'. And the sin of Adam Harishon caused the Ketet/Crown, which is of the highest Sefira/Sphere, to block up". This means that it could not give its Wisdom properly to the 2 Sefirot/Spheres of Chochmah/Wisdom and Binah/Understanding, and enable them to receive from this high Crown/Keter, which has all the other things included in it, including Wisdom and Understanding, which it (Keter) is supposed to give to the Sefirot of Wisdom and Understanding. Unfortunately, due to the sin of Adam, it couldn't be given properly. **"And that caused all of the worlds to fall inside the Impurities"**, what are called in Kabala, 'klipot'. **"This cannot be fixed again until the Time of the 'the World to Come', when the world will go out from its evil. This happened once before, to the Jewish people, during one short period when the Jews stood on the Mountain of Sinai and received the Torah from Hashem. At that moment, the evil and the impurity stopped existing in the people's bodies. But after that, what happened is that the Jews went and sinned, and everything got destroyed as it was originally. And the main 'fixing' which could have taken place is now only going to happen in the future, in the Time of 'the world to come"**. So there was a short respite on Mount Sinai, when God reveled himself to the Jews and gave them the Torah. And all of the higher energies briefly functioned, and all the evil left the world for a certain period of time. But, unfortunately, due to the sin of the golden calf, all these impurities and evil came back into the world, and death returned to the world. And we are waiting for the end of days, when all the higher energies will come back to the world again.

Don't think it is only about what happened almost six thousand years ago, at the time of Adam Harishon, and that it has already happened and is not going to happen again. And don't think that it is something which is not going to affect our lives. You have to know that all these different time periods are, in a way, also within us now. If we are in one time period, it doesn't mean that we don't have the influences of other time periods. It just means that the time period we are in has the strongest emphasis. The time period we are in, is the one that sticks out and rules our lives. But the other ones also exist and influence us in a weaker way. In the kabala there is the principle of everything being inside everything else. Today we refer to this as being Holistic; which in the Western sense means everything being interconnected somehow with everything else. But in kabala, it goes in a deeper way because everything, in any Time period, is interconnected with everything else in that and other Time periods, going back and forwards in history. All Time and History is interconnected, and becomes one story. Like the principle that every person is a descendant of Adam Harishon. All individuals have a remnant of all their ancestors who are connected to them. Whether it is my parents, my grandparents or my great grandparents, I have something of them in me too. And I also have all my children within me, and their children and all the other descendants in the future too. All that is interconnected and everything is impacting on everything else. In other words, you are influenced by all your ancestors, who are in you coming from the past. And also you are influenced by all the people who are in you and will come from you in the future, which are your descendants. For example, in the Torah we have many cases of people who should have died according to the Divine decree but, because they were destined to have a very important child being born to them, God let them live, so they can give birth to that child. So everything is interconnected with everything else, including the past and the future. So we all have all the 18 Time periods within us, although we live in a specific Time period energy now at the beginning of the 21st Century.

"And all the generations continued, after the sin of Adam Harishon, and they were in a limited way fixed, and on the other hand they were also destroyed in a limited way. But because they were so close to the original light, they still had these lengths of days and years, which is from the side of the Arikh Anpin". Arikh Anpin means 'the long suffering one' and is connected to Keter/Crown, which is the highest Sefira/sphere. So in Biblical history during the first 1000 years, people lived for very long periods: Adam lived 930 years, and his descendants at that time lived for as many years too. And this went on up to the time of Noah. After the flood, people's lives became shorter. When we will discuss the 'Planetary system' in future lessons, we will also see that in that system the first 1000 years are connected to the Sun. Just like the first day of the week, which is called Sun-day, which is a hint that the Sun rules that day. So the first 1000 years had the power of the sun, when everything was very strong, with a lot of energy and long life. But from the time of Adam's sin up to the generation of Noah, people consistently sinned and caused damage and destruction, and made things worse. They destroyed and did not fix anything, and strengthened the power of evil, which had the effect of closing up more and more doors in the upper worlds, so that less and less energy could get down to us. And though there were some righteous people in those generations, who were going on the proper way and fixing things, they didn't have enough power in their actions to turn the tide. These righteous individuals were able to give just enough support to the Divine presence to enable it to remain in this world and maintain a little mercy down here. But as time progressed, before the arrival of Abraham, the evil people increased their evil so much, that the righteous people didn't have the ability in their hands to fix the things which so many people messed up.

Then came the 3rd Time period, the Time period of the Avot/Forefathers of the nation of Israel (Abraham, Isaac and Jacob), which starts in the period of the great Dispersion, when all the people in the world were still one people and spoke one language, with one tradition which was passed down from Adam Harishon. And they gathered in Babylon, to build the Tower of Babel. And the Bible tells us how God got their languages all mixed up, and dispersed them to different parts of the world. Abraham witnessed this great dispersion, and after that, through him the Jewish people were born. **"After the great dispersion, the evil people were no longer able to cause deficiencies in the upper world, because from that time onwards, God only looked to Avraham, who was like God's inheritance. And all the people who came after him, from his seed, were God's inheritance too; so all that came down from the upper worlds, God filtered it onto Avraham and his descendants. And the other nations, when they did all the evil that they did, they were doomed to be destroyed. And this is what happened to Sodom and Gomorrah and other places like that. But from that time onwards, the nations who do evil are no longer able to cause damage to the world of the Sefirot/Spheres, the world of Atzilut, but rather they destroy and cause the deficiency to themselves down here, for they no longer have any connection to the upper worlds. So their influence is in the lower worlds. The person just sins to his own body, like it says in the Zohar, 'I will darken also myself, because of the sin that I do'. The Zohar**

further explains how the Forefathers; Abraham, Isaac and Jacob came along and started fixing the sins of Adam Harishon". (The Zohar is a mystical explanation of the 24 books of the Jewish bible. The Bible is made up of the five books of Moses, the Prophets and the Holy Writings, 24 in total.) And the author of the Zohar was Rabbi Shimon Bar Yochai, and he mentioned there in the Zohar, that **"Adam Harishon was reincarnated in each of the three Fathers in order to correct the 3 kinds of sins that Adam succumbed too: Sexual sins, Murder and Idol worshiping. These are the only 3 sins that a Jew is told that he should rather give up his life for, rather than transgress them. And these 3 categories of sins were fixed by the 3 Fathers, who had to pass through all these various tests and purification processes in order to do this rectification. And the Divine presence was revealed to the Fathers in a limited way, and this was the beginning of the 'fixing' of Man. The Sefirot/Spheres was still plugged up and blocked, and the foundations in the upper worlds were not opened, but only the world of Yetzirah, the world of Formation";** Which means that up until then only the world of Asiyah, the world of Action, the lowest of the 4 worlds, was opened. But from the time of the Fathers, they could see in the 2nd of the upper worlds too, the world of Yetzirah/Formation; like it says in the Zohar, **"because of this 'there was a famine in the land' in the days of Abraham and Isaac and Jacob, because of the closing up of the wells".** There has always been a problem with the closing up of the wells. And this is a hint that these 'wells' are infact the Sefirot/Spheres in the upper worlds, especially in the world of Atzilut. **"And the Fathers taught their children, and gave instructions to their souls. And due to that, they started to do good, and traveled without being in complete exile (from the upper worlds); but they weren't redeemed, but rather they were somewhere in the middle, in order that they could purify the souls that were damaged in each of the generations that fell before the days of Noah. At that time, there was a chance for things to be fixed a little bit through Abraham, and after that through Isaac, and even more through Yaakov. They were able to begin that process of fixing the Sefirot/Spheres. And the direction of the world at that time was through the angels; The Ophanim (angels of the world of Assiyah) and the angels of the Metratron (angels of the world of Yetzirah)".** So these are still the lower 2 worlds (excludes the upper worlds of Beriah and Atzilut). **"And because of the good that the Fathers were doing in the upper worlds the Divine presence was always with them, and directed them. And the Fathers began the fixing of the different Sefirot/Spheres in**

the upper worlds, that is to say, they were Chariots for these things". In other words: Avraham was the aspect of mercy, of doing good deeds, which is the right side of the tree of life, the Sefira/Sphere of Chesed/Mercy. So he was the embodiment of that in this world, and he fixed the Sefira through his actions. Isaac fixed the left side of the tree of life, which was the side of Gevurah/Strength. He fixed the world through his strength and resilience and his ability to overcome things. And Jacob was in the middle, a combination of both, and he fixed the Sefira which is called Tiferet/Truth/Compassion. And because of the fixing that they did, the world was strengthened and became better established. Until then the world was not on 'solid ground'. **"Until Avraham came and fixed the right side of mercy, which strengthened the world, and then Isaac came and fixed the left pillar of justice/strength, and finally Yaakov came and established the world as it should be, then the world would never be destroyed again due to actions of evil people. And this caused the world to be directed by God in a middle way, sometimes somehow successful, and sometimes in need for prayers, because of the destruction. And they were continually walking and supporting and uniting with the divine presence."**

So that is the period when things in the upper worlds started to be fixed only through Avraham and his descendants. In other words, what a descendant of Avraham, Isaac and Jacob can fix, even the president of the United States, can't fix, because he doesn't have this ability anymore; the nations of the world were not given the ability to fix those higher worlds, from the time of the great dispersion onwards. All the fixings of the upper worlds was done by Abraham, Isaac and Jacob and their descendents. So from the time of the sin of Adam, up to before Avraham, the sins of Mankind got worse, until the world almost couldn't be fixed. But when Avraham came along and found God, and God decided to put all the tools of fixing into Avraham's hands and the hands of his descendants, they are the ones who are able to fix the worlds and what the others do will not have a significant effect on the upper worlds. Evil could no longer make things worse, at least not in the upper worlds. So that was the third time period.

<u>Chapter 2</u>

The 4th Time period started, **"when Jacob and his children went down into Egypt. Initially, after they went to Egypt, they had a lot of success. Joseph went down first into Egypt and by the time the rest of his family came, he was second only to Pharaoh, and he was basically running the country, and made sure that his Father, Brothers and Sisters were taken**

care of. Yaakov's going down into Egypt could be called 'Exile' since they were leaving the land of Israel and were going down into Egypt. And eventually the Jews became slaves in Egypt. It started slowly with no fixed beginning but somehow led to enslavement. But since Yaakov and his children were all holy and righteous people, and united together with the Divine presence, the Exile did not rule over them at that time. Yaakov and his descendants had the ability to work with the external forces to do their bidding. And the Divine presence that dwelled with the Jews was able to light itself up, even though it was outside the land of Israel. The external forces had no rulership over them. This is similar to the idea that when the righteous people pass through hell, its fires do not harm them at all. When the Jews entered Egypt, "the fire of hell cooled down and became weaker", and so did the power of exile weaken and that reduced the power of the forces that tried to hurt all the Jews in Egypt. And in fact the opposite occurred because the Jews ruled over Egypt until their enslavement. When the Divine presence comes down and encloses itself in the forces of evil, the forces of evil have no power over it, God forbid. The Divine presence rules over those forces of evil. So when Yaakov and his righteous descendants went down to Egypt, they were attached to the Divine presence, and were on such a high level that they ruled above the evil forces".

So Joseph and his generation made the evil forces submissive, because of the merit of their purity and cleanliness, and the way they distanced themselves from the impurity of the exile, and managed to keep themselves very close to levels of holiness. And because they did this, even though they were in exile, they managed to stay attached to the forces of holiness, which are above the forces of evil, **"So Egypt did not rule over them at all, until that whole generation of the righteous people passed away. While they lived, they were on such a level that they were clinging to the highest world of Atzilut. But they gave birth to children whose souls were reincarnated, souls that were coming back to the world, souls that were not on such high levels as their parents and grandparents (at lower levels of development). And then the exile began in earnest, and the forces of evil started to have power over the Jewish people. The Divine presence only went down with the first generation from Israel to Egypt due to the fact that they were learning the Torah, and did not 'throw off the yoke of Torah and Mitzvot'. So they could live then in peace and with blessings. And they were even sending sustenance to the external forces, through the blessing they got, and they had the best of the land.**

And the Sefirot/Spheres were fixed through the learning of the Torah that they did, and through the 600 000 Torah students that Yaakov established in Egypt. And Yaakov didn't leave the world and wasn't taken away from it, until he completed the task of having 600 000 students learning the Torah". So there is the principal that there is the 'burden of Torah' and the 'burden of the world'. And if a person takes upon himself to do the will of heaven and the Torah, then all his troubles in this world, to a certain extent, are made easier so that he can fulfill the burden of heaven that is placed on him, to be a righteous person. But if he moves away from the Torah, and starts worrying too much about how he is going to make a better income, and gets attracted to and caught up in this world's pleasures, then he is going to end up suffering from the problems of this world, and he will have to deal with the problems of this world. So originally, when the Jews went down into Egypt, they were at a very high level, learning the Torah all the time, and they did not throw off the yoke of Mitzvot (the commandments), and so all the other worldly things were done for them. But once they started to lose this attachment to the Torah and Mitzvot, then the burdens of this world were placed on them. But Yaakov was able to increase the practice of Torah, with up to 600 000 Jews studying in Egypt, **"as is written in the Torah, that God said to Yaakov, 'don't worry, for a great nation I will place for you there', meaning in Egypt. And it is written, 'your servants will be the Shepherds of the Sheep'. And in the Zohar it is explained, that the Hebrew word 'Roeh' (which means a Shepherd) comes also from the Hebrew word 'Hitroea' (shake, shook), which indicates that the world would shake, because they were subduing the 'Tale', the sheep, which is the Mazal of Egypt, Aries, the ram".** So by their holy studies and practices, they ruled over the sign of Aries, the ram which was the emissary of Egypt in the upper worlds. **"The Jews increased their light there, and extinguished the external forces. And Joseph was the one who was supplying the wheat for the whole country, he was like the Sefira/Sphere of Yesod/Foundation, which is the one who feeds and gives sustenance to everything. Because the Yesod of Zeir Anpin gives to the Malchut/Kingdom, and the Malchut sustains all the lower worlds. So through Joseph all the energies were coming down. And it was supporting the Egyptians too, even during that time of subjugation. And therefore they succeeded in the exile in the beginning".** And if we could conduct ourselves today as they did, and increased our holiness in the place of the external forces, we would also subdue them and diminish their power by breaking them into little pieces, and we would rule over them and give them sustenance to do good. But the evil inclination/yetzer hara inside us, does not let us achieve this. And therefore we had a big success at the beginning, and the divine presence did not hold back any of its beneficent energy, and the Souls got fixed and they were blessed.

That is the 4th Time period. You have to remember that each of the 18 Time periods have some pieces of all the other 17 Time periods within it. It is not that these periods are in the past and are not relevant in subsequent Time periods. We learn that all periods are working and operating even today, but they are below the specific ruling energy assigned to this current Time period. So we only see these subordinate energies occasionally and to a lesser degree, but they are operating.

So let us now start the 5th Time period, which is the 5th way God runs the world. **"The 5th Time period was the actual enslavement of the Jews in Egypt. And there is no doubt that the divine presence went down to Egypt with the people of Israel in the exile, like it is said in the Zohar; 'the man in his house came to Egypt'. But it did not last. And the secret of this exile in Egypt is that it was even more severe then the exile we are still undergoing today. Because they forgot the Torah of God, and because they took the burden of learning the Torah and of doing the mitzvot off themselves. And they put upon themselves the burden of having to take care of having to survive in this world. That is to say, the forces of evil burdened them, and placed on them heavy responsibilities, and gave them heavy punishments and injuries. Because the main reason for that exile was to purify the impure souls from the bad deeds they did in the past. And all souls of the bad generations of before, like the generation of Sodom and Gomorrah, and that of the time of the Tower of Babylon, were reincarnated into the Jewish people at that time in Egypt. And had they engaged in purifying themselves with the moral teachings of the Torah and done repentance/Teshuva, then there would not have been any need for those reincarnations. Because the reincarnation is only to complete what a person is lacking in repentance, so had the Jews clung to their righteousness, they would not have needed to be purified, and they would not have had their first sons thrown into the Nile, (which was one of the decrees of Pharaoh). And they would not have had those difficult labors that they had, to build for the Egyptians with bricks and straw. And the people had to die 'a thousand times' and come back until they got purified. Because of their behavior they put themselves into this difficult period which was placed upon them".** In other words, the period of being enslaved in Egypt was due to the souls having to undergo purification. So they had to come back and be tremendously oppressed in Egypt. If you read the books of the Ari Z"L, you will see that he spends a lot of time talking about all of these things. But if they had been righteous, and had fixed themselves through learning the Torah and doing good deeds and repenting, they wouldn't have been oppressed, because repentance is more powerful than reincarnations after death. But since they threw off the burden of the Torah, and attached themselves to the pleasures of Egypt, they didn't have the merit of fixing themselves at all, except through the fate of reincarnations.

"If the Jews had done like their fathers did, and had they made the Egyptian people submissive to them by stopping the forces of evil with their good deeds, it would have been better for them. But they didn't want to, and they fell under the power of the forces of evil; the idols, energies, rituals and cultures. At that time all the forces of evil, which latter manifested in the world, all of them were inside the crucible of Egypt, to punish the reincarnated souls. In the beginning of the exile, the Jews ruled in Egypt and had power over them, due to the righteousness of the tribes of Jacob. But then gradually the nation of Israel was enveloped in the evil (the klipot/shells) of the Forces of evil. The only way for them cut out this cancer was for them to 'take the sword', which in the case of Israel is the Torah, and cut out the cancer. And from these actions with 'the sword', freedom would be regained. But this did not happen and so the forces of evil swallowed them up and disgraced them, and threw them down from one disgraceful level to the next. And slowly they went into the depths of servitude to Egypt and into the most deprived state possible. And they did not have the power and ability to bring down the holiness at all. And the only food they had was what they got from Pharaoh". So we see that originally when the Jews went down into Egypt, not only were the Jews getting energies from above, but they even were able to pass on this sustenance to the Egyptian people. But the next generations got it wrong and became deprived, and eventually all that they had left was the little food that Pharaoh would give them. The Jews were forced to build the cities for Pharaoh in poverty and misfortune, they had to build the cities of Pitom and Ramses, which in Hebrew have a root meaning of: 'The depths of the mouth' (Pitom), which swallowed them up, and the 'evil that chews up' (Ramses), so they got chewed up by the evil. So the Jews got into 49 levels of impurity in Egypt until God, in His mercy, redeemed them. **"And God broke the evil into little pieces including all the images that were before the Jews and all the layers of impurity that they were in, as**

it says, 'from the first born of Pharaoh... to the first born of the slave, who sits behind the grindstone'". After the first born of the Egyptians died through God's decree, the Jews were finally redeemed. Had God not done so, the Jews would have disappeared from History.

Although this 5th Time period of the exile was more than 3000 years ago, I think you can see how it has a lot in common with the current exile of the Jews in America and what remains of the Jews in the Western world. Jews originally went to these countries with good intentions, and gradually they threw off the yolk of Torah, and they then became more and more deprived. You see today in the news how prominent Jews are involved in all sorts of degenerate behaviors, which was not the norm for Jewish people. What is happening to people in the Western world is awful, it's unbelievable! When I was a kid, we thought things were bad, but we didn't realize how bad, and how much more things would degenerate. It is really shocking. Hopefully the Jews today in the Western world will realize the basic principle at work here, not to move away from Torah, and will get themselves out of this slippery slope. But if not, then God will have to come and rescue them like he did in Egypt. So I think you can learn a lot from this 5th Time period in human history. So now let us start the 6th Time period:

The 6th Time period starts from the Redemption of the Jews from Egypt and the success they had in the desert and all the miracles they witnessed there. **"During all of the days of Moshe Rabenu (Moses), may his memory be blessed; Israel had a tremendous and complete success, with all sorts of miracles taking place. And this was because they were being directed by God and by the Ein Sof (the Endlessness), which is the Sefirah of Crown/Keter and the Wisdom/Hochma, in the secret of miracles and wonders, as it says 'which I took them out from the hidden place'. They were being directed by the world of Atzilut/Emanation, which was working through the world of Beriah/Creation, even on the weekdays. Because Moshe Rabenu did not want them to have to receive the divine direction via the lower world of Yetzirah/Formation, and that is what Moses meant when he said, 'your face is not coming down and reaching here'. And it is says, 'Go now God in our midst'. And he chose that Atzilut would enclose itself inside Beriah, because it is not possible to direct things through Atzilut without the 'garment' of Beriah. And even on the holy day of the Sabbath, Atzilut still has to enclose itself in Beriah. And when the Jews sinned with the golden calf as was done in the sin of Adam Harishon, some of the evil that left them during the Redemption came back and re-attached itself to them. But this impurity did not**

completely attach itself to them, because finally the purity that the Jews managed to achieve mostly remained, but again death still ruled over them. And the strength of Moshe Rabenu was very great because it was because of him only that Atzilut could work through Beriah, and not through the lower world of Yetzirah. The Divine presence enclosed itself in the world of Beriah/Creation (Kisey Hakavod/Throne of Glory). And because of that they would be directed according to their deeds".

Chapter 3

The 6th Time period started with the Redemption from Egypt and the success the Jews had in the desert with all the different miracles and wondrous events that took place there. This was a unique period in the world's history. **"During all the days of Moshe (Moses) our father, may his memory be blessed, Israel had great success, wondrous success, through visible complete miracles. This is because at that time they were being directed from the 'Nothingness' (Ayin) and also from the 'There is' (Yesh). The Ayin is the highest sefira of Keter/Crown, and the Yesh is the sefira of Hochma/Wisdom. These two highest sefirot/spheres were running the world. And that is the secret of 'with wonders and great deeds', and the main place of direction is from the place of the hidden. So the direction of the world was through the world of Atzilut/Emanation, by way of the world of Beriah/Creation, even on the weekdays".**

We today are not able to reach such high levels of consciousness. But back then they were on a very high level, working directly with the high level of the world of Atzilut, through the world of Beriah. They did not have to go through the lower worlds of Asiya or Yetzira, as we do today to reach Beriah. They were able to get direct contact. **"Because Moshe Rabenu our Father did not want the direction of the divine flow to this world to be enclosed (and received) from the world of Yetzira/Formation, but rather from Beriah. And that is the meaning of the verse; 'if your face is not going to lead us (through the world of Beriah), do not take us out from there'. And it also says, 'go my Master, in our midst', in other words, through Beriah. And when the Jews sinned with the golden calf, which was very similar to the sin of the first man Adam, the impurities which were removed at Sinai came back. But although these impurities came back, they didn't come back completely, because the purification process that the Jews underwent at the beginning of the Redemption stood in its place".** So the Jews did not go back to the low level they were back in Egypt, which was the 49th level of impurity. And they held on to most of the purity. The only significant thing that happened was that death ruled over them again due to the sin of the golden calf. **"Even though the Jews had these deficiencies, through the spiritual power and strength of Moshe, the divine flow and energy did not go down through the lower world of Yetzira/Formation, and instead came down through the Divine presence that enclosed itself in the Throne of Glory, the top 3 sefirot/spheres of the world of Beriah"**. All the energy and all the sustenance which is sent from above, when it comes down from the highest places in the kabbalistic universe, it usually passes through every level of these worlds. Sometimes when it passes through, the energy is changed by the levels it passes through, while other times it is not changed by the levels it passes through. It is like a subway which has both express trains and local trains going through. So when it is an express train it doesn't stop at every stop, while the local train does. And that is what happens when the energy comes down. It passes a level without being changed by that level, and it is not accounted for in that level and does not enclose itself in that level. So Moshe Rabenu, who ruled over the people of Israel at that time, didn't want the energies to be enclosed and affected by the lower worlds. He just wanted them to pass through. So the energies came down and first got enclosed in the Atzilut, and then in the top three sefirot/spheres of Beriah, and then they just passed right through the rest of the worlds (Yetzirah and Assiya) all the way to us without being affected by that. And for this reason, the direction of the Jews at that time was according to their actions. **"Despite the merit and strong leadership of Moses, the Jews didn't completely fix things in the upper worlds and did not fully raise themselves up and connect with the upper worlds in that high place at that time. This eventually happened in the Time of King Shlomo, when the Nation of Israel was at its peak. But at this Time in the desert, they had not been able to rebuild everything. As it is said, 'by the house that you have build, you have build it little by little'"**. In other words, although the Jews were in a very high level with Moses as their leader, they were only at the beginning of the process that, many hundred years latter, lead to the great days of King Solomon. **"And due to this deficiency the Jews were complaining all the time and were bothersome in the desert. Sometimes they were complaining about the water, sometimes about not having bread, sometimes about not having meat, and all this because the Divine Presence, the Shechina, was not firmly fixed and attached to them yet. And they did not have a Temple yet while in the desert, but what they had was the Mishkan, the Tabernacle, which is the secret of the 'youth' of the Angel Mem Tet (Metraton), which is the level of the Tabernacle,**

which is talked about in the Zohar. And yet this is a difficult idea, because earlier as we said, the Mem Tet angel was pushed off by Moses, like it is said, 'come now God, and dwell in our midst', which means to dwell and work through Beriah. So how could they have a Tabernacle with this angel who was pushed off? So it appears to me, that the building of the Tabernacle was all below, and these angels were in the Throne of the Tabernacle (Beriah). And they would enclose themselves into the Tabernacle, and reveal themselves there, through the name of Adnut. So the Jews did not constantly have the light of the Divine Presence, but they had the light of the name of Adnut, from which they connected with Beriah." So the Divine flow that came down to them was coming through Atzilut and enclosed itself in Beriah, and not in the lower worlds. And even though they got the divine flow through the Tabernacle here on earth, the angel that was ruling it was up in the world of Beriah, the Throne of Glory. And due to all these energies coming from those very high levels, God performed many great miracles for them at that time.

The 7th, 8th and 9th Time periods all have something in common but are still considered separate time periods. The 7th Time period started when the Israelites entered the Land of Israel and conquered the Land from the seven nations who were there, which was the time of Joshua. It also includes the times of the Judges, when things started to decline and the 8th Time period started when the Israelites were oppressed in the Land of Israel and were subservient to the nations up to the time of the Prophet Shmuel. And the 9th Time period was the success and failures of the Israelites during the days of the Kings. **"After the death of Moses, and after they entered the Land of Israel, on the one hand the Jews were worthy, and on the other, it was a great responsibility for them. They were worthy in the sense that when they came into the Land of Israel, the external forces of evil were subservient and at a low point there, and the Jews were breathing the holy air of the Land of Israel, and experiencing the holiness and purity of the land. That made them worthy. At that time there were no forces of externality that captured the land. But that was only for that one period, when the Jews originally came into Israel. And this pure state did not even exist in the past during the time of the Fathers; Avraham, Yitzchak and Yaakov, when they lived in the Land of Israel. But the disadvantage and responsibility was that God was now directing the world though the Mem Tet (Metatron) of Yetzira (below Beriah). This was the Mem Tet angel of Yetzira that Moses was able to push off**

resulting in God running the world through Beriah, as it is said in the book of Yehoshua, 'I am the army minister of the Lord, and now I came'. And they, the Sages, explain that 'now I came' means in the time of Yehoshua, but not in the time of Moshe Rabenu, may his memory be blessed. So that means that once Moshe left, the Jews didn't have the power to push off the world from being directed through the world of Yetzirah, which was a lower direction. And the Divine Presence was not fixed, because the light of the sefira/sphere of Yesod/Foundation was not yet opened at all. Yesod is in the world of Yetzirah/Formation. The aspect of Yesod was hidden and concealed, as it says in the Zohar. And due to that, they had difficult things happening to them at that time, even at the time of Kind David, like the famine of his time. And this time period, from the coming of the Jews to Israel up to King David, lasted a long time. And even at the time of King David, the Divine Presence was still being fixed. And it wasn't completely fixed enough in order to open itself up to its main place, which didn't happen, until the days of King Solomon, may his memory be blessed. However, in the days of King David and all the other generations that came before going back to Joshua, all of the direction and divine flow was by way of the Divine Presence while it enclosed itself in the angel Mem Tet of the world of Yetzira/Formation". So the 7th, 8th and 9th Time periods were from the time the Jews came into the Land of Israel until the time of King Solomon. **"And it lit up the essence of its light, but not from the upper sefirot/spheres, because the energy that came from the higher sefirot could not be brought down because the Yesod was still closed off and hidden. And the Yesod did not light up the Divine Presence. And therefore, Hochma/Wisdom went into Bina/Understanding, and Bina went into the six sefirot (Hesed to Yesod), which is associated with the world of Yetzira. And these six sefirot were hidden and concealed, from the day the world was created until now. And even though the Torah was given, and this opened up access to Higher sources, this was in relation to the giving of the Torah, but in relation to how the world was being directed, it was still hidden and concealed, because they were not yet worthy of this level at all, until the time of King Solomon, may his memory be blessed. And when they were holy, they succeeded, and when they did evil they fell.** This whole period, from the time they went into Israel, the world was being directed from the world of Yetzira, and its angel, Mem Tet. And when the Jews did good, good happened to them, and when they did bad, bad happened to them. Which is also a high level. Today if you do good, you sometimes don't get the reward right away, and it may be delayed for a long time. Or if you do bad, you often don't get punished for a long time. And you may eventually think you didn't really do bad, and maybe you may come to think you really did good. But in those 7th, 8th and 9th Time periods, if you did good you were rewarded soon, and if you did bad you were punished quickly. **"It was a difficult time for the Jews because even though they were in the Holy land with all the advantages, they were not able to properly connect with Heaven, because the spiritual sustenance was still closed up above, and couldn't be drawn down. But on the other hand, they were also very successful during this time period because the forces of evil were at rest. And due to their righteousness and good deeds, they brought about their success in this period, where the world was directed according to their actions, according to their righteousness and according to the deeds of each generation. This was in the 8th and 9th Time periods, at the time of the Judges and later. And it also depended on how much the judges acted righteously in their judgments, and if the generations were engaged in idol worship or other sins. Idol worship gave the power to the forces of evil and allowed the evil to grow. And 'what the Jews planted, they couldn't eat', because the external forces were taking the energy. So everything depended on how the Jews were behaving. And this would determine if the forces of evil had power over the Jewish nation, or if those forces were submissive to them because of their righteous deeds".** Everything depended on whether the Jews did good or evil. And there was no time laps in the repercussion. It started in the times of the Joshua and the Judges, then went on to the times of Shmuel the Prophet, and then to King Shaul and even during the days of King David and King Solomon. Everything was run by the same way from above except for the fact that the 7th Time period was directed in the way of the Judges, and the 8th Time period in the way of the Prophets, and the 9th Time period in the way of the Kings.

The next group of Time lords in human history is the 10th, 11th, 12th, 13th and 14th Time periods. The 10th Time period was the time the First Temple was built and the gradual spiritual decline that followed in the Land. The 11th Time period started when the First Temple was destroyed and the Jews were exiled to Babylon and what happened there. The 12th Time period started about 70 years later with the building of the Second Temple. The 13th Time period was the spiritual decline that followed and the sufferings and successes of that time up to the destruction of the Second Temple by the Romans. The 14th Time period was the long Exile of the Jews throughout the world.

"Our rabbis explain that in the days of King Solomon, the moon stood in its fullness". At that point in history, this was the fifteenth generations from after the time the Jews went out of Egypt, and just as the moon becomes full on the fifteenth day of the month, so did the Jews reach their peak at that time of King Solomon and the first Temple. **"Then, at the time of the first Temple, the Divine Presence was completely fixed and operating with its full force, working with the wisdom of King Solomon. The lights from the high Hochma/Wisdom, working through Bina/Understanding, which then lit up to the six sefirot/spheres (Hesed to Yesod), and the six sefirot were able to take all that energy from Bina and Hochma and send it all into Malchut/Kingship, the Kingship of the people at that period. And through that, it completed the lower Wisdom (Malchut). The lower Wisdom is Malchut/Kingship and the first Temple is the light of Bina/Understanding through which the higher Wisdom works. But things were not perfected, and the sin of Adam Harishon was still strong, it still stood in its place and didn't stop, and death was still present in the world. The world did not nullify its punishment for the sin of Adam Harishon"**. But again, this was a very high spiritual level which was close to being the final rectification, the final Tikun/Fixing. They were only one step away from that. And there was lighting up from Keter/Crown and Hochma/Wisdom all the way down to Malchut/Kingship.

"And then Israel eventually accumulated sins, during the time of King Yerovam (who rebelled against King Solomon, and later against King Solomon's son, King Rechovam), when he as King of the 10 tribes made 2 golden calves for idol worship. And this was similar to the sin of the golden calve in the Desert and all these three calves are from one subject matter. And so the Divine Presence slowly started to become darkened, and the moon started to diminish itself. And all that light that was originally coming down direct to Malchut during the time of King Solomon started to darken; more and more until the destruction of the 1st Temple. The light which flowed down during the whole period of the first Temple was the light of Bina/Understanding. And Binah has both aspects of Judgment and Mercy, and through their actions the direction would switch to one or the other. So the Jews would have mixed results, sometimes going up and sometime going down. They were either very successful in winning battles, or they were defeated. And eventually first the 10 tribes were exiled, and then the remainder of the Jews, the tribes of Judah and Benjamin, were exiled to Babylon for 70 years. There are 7 sefirot/spheres from Binah to Malchut, and each sefirah has 10 in

it, so 7 X 10 = 70, so in the 70 years of exile their spiritual consciousness went all the way down from the upper world of Binah/Understanding to the world of Assiya/Action. And during the time of that exile often things were being run through the strict judgment of Malchut and by way of the lowest world of Assiya, as opposed to how it was in the past through the world of Beriah and Yetzirah. And because of this they had mixed results. But sometimes they did have prophecies and a bit of success. Fortunately the righteous ones of Israel, who were also in exile in the Kingdom of Babylon, had some success right up until the 2nd Temple was rebuilt. And had the Jews at that time not made themselves impure by their attachment to the pagan women of the land and mixed their seed with them, they could have been redeemed back to Israel, to build the 2nd Temple, through miracles that were even greater than the ones of the exodus from Egypt. As it says in the Zohar, those miracles weren't performed. During the time of the building of the 2nd Temple, all the accusing angels and other forces of evil were working hard against the Jews. And due to that they were not prepared for the redemption. And because of this the era of the 2nd Temple sometimes looked as if it was 'broken', as if it was ruled in exile, underneath the hand of their enemies, and some other times it 'stood' right and everything was pleasant. Everything was according to the direction of the light of the Divine Presence, which was now working more through the world of Assiya, sometimes with judgment and sometimes with mercy. There was always trouble surrounding the Jews at the time of the second Temple. And eventually the light of the Divine Presence got darkened completely, and was fully enclosed in the lowest world of Assiya/Action. And the 2nd Temple was destroyed and the Jews went into complete exile, which was the exile of Edom, the Romans, which we are still in. And the Divine Presence began to come down through the 3 lower Palaces of the world of Assiya. And the time it fell down was the length of the exile. And during all that time, everything was being directed through the world of Assiya. And the world was being nourished by way of the prayers of the Jews. And sometimes in the exile things would go from bad to good, especially when the Jews were good and God responded by decreeing it so".

So we see that the 10th, 11th, 12th, 13th and 14th Time periods are lumped together; from the building of the 1st Temple, followed by its destruction and the Jews being exiled for 70 years in Babylon, and then coming back to rebuild the 2nd Temple, and then loose it again and go into the exile of Edom. But again, these were much higher levels of spiritual connection and consciousness than we have today.

Chapter 4

Let us now do a very interesting set of Time periods; the 15th,16th ,17th and 18th Time periods, which are very significant for us. We are already living in these Time periods. It is very important for people to understand what the Prophets and Sages held regarding the Time period we live in, and the predictions they made about what it was going to be like. Every generation has different problems, and there are different degrees of severity for these problems. So the Time periods are like the backdrop for the drama of Humanity in a way, and this Time period energy runs throughout each generation. In every Time period in history you see the world is being run in a different way. And in order to focus on what is happening, you have to have an understanding of that background noise, and see what is actually going on in history. Human history has a common thread to it, and the world is run differently in each Time period. And you have to be able to focus in on that, and factor that into your astrology and chart reading.

I would like to remind everybody that these ideas in this series of 5 talks, are taken mostly from the early Kabbalists. I have also seen these ideas in the Ari Z"l . The Ari Z"l has structures which are very similar to this, but he uses a different language, maybe more complicated. I wouldn't say it isn't clear, because the Ari Za"l is very clear in what he is talking about, but it is not as accessible to the average reader as in the way it is brought down in the early kabbala, by Rabbi Moshe Kordovero and Rabbi Avraham Azulay. So I am reading it from there. Also remember that in Jewish history there are basically 6000 years of Human history as we know (followed by a unique 1000 year period and onwards). And now we are almost in 5772, which means it is 228 years from the maximum Time period set for the 'end of the Exile'. But our tradition is that the 'end of the Exile' could come earlier, it does not have to run its full time period and go to the exact end. And also remember that there will be transitional periods.

"In the end of our exile, just before the Redemption, there will be a tremendous increase in the suffering of Israel. And it will come to a point that they will say to the mountains, 'crush me!' And they will say to the hills, 'you should fall on me!' This will be because of all the great suffering that is going to befall Israel, from all sides, in every corner".
And if you look back at the Holocaust, which was in this time period, a few

decades ago, I think many people said that back then. The suffering was unbearable. But that was physical suffering. In our generation its more mental and psychological suffering, because I think we don't have the strength of the last generation anymore, we would collapse if we had to undergo their physical suffering. So I think the suffering of our times is the tremendous amount of mental and emotional suffering that we experience, and it is growing. Someone told me that his kid went to summer camp, and in the camp, many kids were lining up in the morning to take their medicines, their mental pills for stress and other problems. It is a terrible and stressful period we are living in.

"And there will be an increase in suffering, up to a point where fathers will not have time for their children. And fathers will not be able to help their children. And anyone who will find any life support will be considered a strong person and a winner. And why is it going to be so bad in this period? Because the Divine Presence is going to judge the house, and there is going to be tremendous judgment in the world, in order to purify everybody before the Redemption. To prepare them for all the good that will come to them, as promised by God and the Prophets, the good that is going to be of such proportion that today the mind can't even comprehend this good. The good is going to be so great and abundant, that the Sages said, regarding the Redemption, that people will no longer be talking about the great Redemption from Egypt. While today, through all the prayers and other Mitzvot we do every day, time after time, we remember and mention how 'God took us out of the Land of Egypt, with miracles and great deeds'. But in the future, we are not going to remember that first, for we are going to remember how it is in the 'end of the days', and the great miracles and wonders that God will perform for us during the time of the Redemption. This is how odd it will be, as it is says, 'they will not say anymore, on the life of God, who took us out of the Land of Egypt, but, on the life of God, who took and brought Israel back here, from all the different countries'". This book was written some 500 years ago, and yet we see how today that the Jews are being redeemed from all the different countries. Jews were already in Israel, but the bulk of Jews came to Israel after the Second World War from Europe and the Arab countries. And later it was a miracle that the Jews from the former Soviet Union returned as they did to Israel in massive numbers. And the Jews are continuing to come back to Israel from all over the world. **"And in this time there are going to be miracles, and the revelation of the Divine Presence to Israel in wonderment. And all people who are worthy of this**

will say, 'here is our God that we have waited for, and He redeemed us', and you will be able 'to point with your finger' and say 'look, here He is, God that we have been waiting for'". So there has been a tremendous amount of suffering in this 15th Time period, but all this suffering is to make the final accounting, so that people are going to purify themselves now, to prepare for what is going to be in the final days, and be ready for all the good that is going to come. If people didn't suffer now and weren't purified, they wouldn't be able to handle all the good that is going to come. They did a study on people who won millions of dollars in the lottery, and discovered that years after wining the money, most of these people regretted it. Because they were not equipped to handle that amount of money, and eventually they lost it or got into all sorts of trouble because of it. So people have to prepare themselves to handle something big that is coming their way, and we also have to be ready to handle all the good that is going to come down. So time is running out, and people have to become purified, and due to the purification that is taking place today, you see so much suffering in the world.

"And if there is somebody who is worthy of living in those days, he is going to see a tremendous amount of suffering, and all this is in order to refine and purify Israel, according to the judgment by which they have been judged. And everybody has to suffer according to their obligations. And anybody who resists this punishment, and doesn't repent, will be wiped out". So a lot of the suffering comes to urge people to repent and change their ways. **"And anyone who puts their neck in the alter of repentance, and accept all these sufferings upon themselves, with some kind of joy and acceptance, being prepared to suffer in order to refine themselves, in order to be able to receive the great good which will come in the future, with the nullification of the evil, will survive and be rewarded.**

And all this time, while a portion of the Jews still do evil, there will still be evil in the world that is still attached to them. And if so, how is it possible to nullify the external forces of evil? God, who is the God of judgment, righteousness and truth, can't accept this. And therefore He refines them, with refinement after refinement, until the Jews will become like pure silver. And this direction of the world will be with tremendous judgment. Because the forces of evil are going to resist it as much as they can, because they know that their existence is in danger, since they are about to be nullified".

This is another prediction we see in our generation, that a large amount of people are turning to religion. This is happening in the Jewish world. It is also happening in Christianity. For example in America, there is a big Evangelical Christian movement, and people are becoming more attached to their religion. And in the Muslim world there is a return to Islam. So if you look around you see that a lot of these things are happening throughout the world and among all its nations. So there are parallels between what happens today to Jews and to what happens to other nations. My main audience is Jewish, but many are not, and this is also relevant to them. And there are professional astrologers who listen to my lectures, many of whom are not Jewish, and I think they can also learn a lot from this material from the Kabbalists. I think it is very important.

This passage above also has a hint with respect to gold and silver. In the Torah, gold and silver, but especially gold, is a hint to, and is associated with, the Jewish people. Just like you see the price trend for gold and silver consistently going up in our recent history, so it will be for the Jews. The highest world in the Kabalistic Universe is the world of Atzilut/Emanation. There is a principle in Kabbala that whatever comes from this highest world down to this world here is only found in minimal quantities, and whatever comes from the lower worlds above to here, is found here (in this world) in large amounts. So as to the question of why Jews make up such a small proportion of the worlds population, the answer in Kabbala is that they are spiritually from the world of Atzilut, which is the highest world. So only a certain number can come down and work down here. That is why today there are maybe about 6-7 billion people in the world, and only about 15 million Jews. But despite these very low numbers, the impact of the Jews in the world is probably more than that of any other civilization. This is because our source is in the world of Atzilut. And the same thing goes with gold and silver, especially gold, which is in such a minimal amount. All the gold in the world, including all the gold that has been mined throughout history, can only fill 3 Olympic size swimming pools. So this is a hint. Just as silver and gold are associated with the world of Atzilut, and are scarce here on earth, so are the Jewish people. And I suggest that just as gold and silver will become more important, so Israel is going to become more important in the world.

"In these days, at this time, there is going to be a big war, one nation against another, a man against his neighbors". And we see this in this period with many people rising up against their leaders and revolutions, as well as the increase of wars between countries. **"Israel is going to be between them in big suffering because all of these nations will want to 'shorn the sheep' of Israel"**. For centuries now, while in exile, the Jews used to live among all other nations, but each nation made sure that the Jews were concentrated in one place, like the ghettos. But there was always a way to escape. And today, the nations of the world want the Jews of Israel, who are gathered in this tiny ancestral land, to be limited in their ability to defend themselves and 'escape' from all the violence directed at us. The world is like one entity today, a global village, with Israel as its ghetto. And slowly every nation is turning against Israel. **"So they all want to trap the 'sheep', the Jewish people and 'eat their flesh'. But God is going to have mercy on the Jews, through the merit of the three Fathers, and He is going to refine and purify Israel. And He is going to destroy Amalek, the eternal enemy of the people of Israel, and wipe out its name from underneath the Heaven. And afterward, the judgment will focus on the descendants of Esau, the evil one, until there will not be a chance for Esau 'to rise up anymore'. And then the Jews will start to slowly rise up and redeem themselves from their sufferings. And God is going to pass judgments on the nations of the world, but the Jews will still be suffering, as it is said in the Book of Ezekiel, that God wants to clean up Jerusalem and the rest of Israel, just as a man cleans his garment, by taking it out to the sunlight and shaking it with his hand, and getting rid of all the dust and impurities. So is God going to do to the Land of Israel, and especially to Jerusalem. And He is going to clean out all those people who worship idols, and He is going to wipe out idolatry itself from Jerusalem. And all other unclean things that are here are going to be wiped clean in Jerusalem. And at that time, the People will gather and go to the desert, to be closer to God. And there will be hunger for 45 days. And they will be refined and further purified, and Prophet Elijah will appear to them, and the Messiah is going to appear to them, amid the great poverty".** And we start to see the increase of poverty in the world. People are going to start lacking money. All my life I cannot remember us worrying too much about money or food, on the contrary, we had too much of everything. And now you finally see that the wheel is turning, and it is hard for people, especially for the young who haven't had a chance, to make a good living. There is going to be a lot of financial poverty. **"And Moses is also going to reveal himself at that time. And the Divine Presence is also going to reveal herself, and is going to be fixed. And the holy temple is going to come down to earth. And when it will be rebuilt, the Jews are going to come to Jerusalem, with the Divine Presence, just like when the Jews left Egypt. And there is going to be a tremendous increase in miracles, and such great revelations the mouth can't speak about and the mind can't imagine. The amount of wonders and miracles that are going to be**

performed for Israel, will be enormous. And the fountains of wisdom are going to be opened. And that is how the world is going to be run at the end of days".

So these were the 15th and the start of the16th Time periods. And about these periods of the final redemption, the Sages of old prayed that it should happen as fast as possible, but they also prayed that they did not want to be reincarnated in those Times, because they knew how bad things were going to be. Nobody wanted to live through the Holocaust. And today people are preparing another holocaust for us in Israel, but hopefully it will not happen. We will now cover the rest of the 16th Time period and the 17th and 18th Time periods:

"At the time of the final redemption of Israel, God is going to run the world with Chochma/Wisdom, and it will light up to Bina/Understanding, and Chochma is going to get its light from Keter/Crown. And we never saw this before, that it gets its light from such a high level. And due to that, there is going to be tremendous amount of miracles, overpowering the laws of nature. And Israel is going to succeed in an unimaginable way, even more than the success they had during the days of King Solomon. Because in the days of Solomon, only Bina/Understanding got light from Chochma/Wisdom, but there was no involvement from Keter/Crown. But in the final days, the Chochma is going to get its light from the Keter, because by that time the world will get closer to fixing all the imbalances caused by the forces of evil. But at this stage we will still not have the final fixing, and there is going to be a certain amount of delay, until all external forces of evil will be nullified. And during this transitional period, from the period of suffering to the period of good, people will no longer be able to repent and reap the rewards of fixing ones wrongs, because repentance is from Bina, and at that time the world is not going to be run by Bina anymore, but by Chochma instead".

Because repentance comes from the situation where there is good and evil, and people are confused as to what is right or wrong, and make wrong choices which sometimes they can repent for and fix the damage. But at that stage, there are going to be so many miracles and revelations, that it will be obvious which side is right and what is wrong, and therefore to do wrong will make no sense and repentance no longer justified. **"And the evil ones will no longer be accepted anymore, and will be destroyed. But through the secret of Reincarnation, some will be reborn, for up to forty years later, at which point even reincarnations will stop. And then the stage of the Resurrection of the dead will take place, when the dead will come back to**

life, and people who died in the past are going to be resurrected, refined and purified. And the people are going to become tremendously wise, to a great extent, and they will uncover many of the deep secrets of the Torah".

Here we see that there are many parallels between what is going to be in the religious world and the secular world. Where the Wisdoms of the spiritual world and the material world are going to expand and work together, synergistically, to reach the ultimate goal. There is a famous Zohar that states that from the year 1840, 'the gates of Wisdom are going to be opened up'. That date is considered to be the beginning of the Time periods we have been talking about tonight: the end of the exile, this final stage of exile, when the suffering is going to grow and yet there will be an increase in Wisdom. But still what has taken place up to now, are only the beginning of the massive advancements that are coming our way, after the Redemption. But some of this surge in Wisdom destined for the 16th ,17th and 18th Time periods has already started, and overlaps the 15th period identified as the period of suffering. We see that the mid 1800's was the beginning of the industrial revolution. And up until then, the main technique for healing used by the doctors was bloodletting, which was done if nothing else worked. And so you see how medicine has progressed since that time. And this is so in every field of science. When I came to Israel, nobody had telephones, we had to go to the central post office to make a phone call to America, and stand in line for an hour. Today everyone walks around with their own telephones in their pockets, and that happened within 30 years. So you see the tremendous upsurge in technological wisdom in the secular world in the last 100 years or so. And although the upsurge of Wisdom in the religious/spiritual world took a devastating blow during the Holocaust, it has slowly recovered and a momentum has started to take root in Israel and there will be tremendous revelations of the secrets of the Torah that will be re-discovered. Today there are many people learning and practicing the Torah. Someone told me that 65 years after the Holocaust, after six million Jews were killed, there are more Jews learning the Torah today than in any other period in the world's history. And eventually this is also going to lead to big revelations of the deep secrets of the Torah. **"And people are going to become refined, and are going to do great acts of charity, and they will get to high levels of prophecy. And because they had already purified themselves, even the secrets of the Torah they will grasp. Insights and experiences which we could not even imagine or understand in our generation, they will have. And they are going to increase the light more and more as time goes on. And all of this Time**

period is going to continue, until the end of the 6000th year". Today we are about 220 years away from the 6000th year in the Jewish calendar, and at the time of the Holocaust we were 290 years away, so you see we are close. He is talking about our time, and it is very important to know this. **"And after the 6000 years, the world is going to be directed by Keter/Crown, which means that the world will be on an unimaginable higher level of consciousness. After the 7000th year, the world will be reborn. And then there is going to be such light that you can't even conceive in you mind, how high it can be. And people will get to levels that are impossible to conceive let alone achieve today. And then the whole world is going to be drawn after the will of God, who knows the Truth. All this is due to the purification we are going to undergo".** There is not going to be anything that can stop us from receiving this great light which is going to lift us up and allow us to have tremendous breakthroughs in spiritual understanding and our spiritual practice. And this is similar to what you see in all the breakthroughs we are having today in the physical world of science. Something like genetics didn't even exist a hundred years ago. What did we know about Astronomy 100 years ago compared to what we know today? So in all areas of life we are witnessing what Rabbi Moshe Kordovero and Rabbi Avraham Azulay talked about in a book that was written about 500 years ago. And it should give astrologers some humility, for astrologers only predict one year forward at most, while the kabbalists predicted what was going to happen hundreds of years later. We see that what was written in these books has come true, as if the vision was in front of the eyes of the Kabbalists who brought these detailed predictions down. They didn't just hint about it, but they said it clearly. And I think they knew more than what they wrote, because there are some things that you are not allowed to say. Like a great Sage used to say, 'not everything you think you should say and not everything you say should be written down'. And astrologers too should realize the tremendous difficulty that people are undergoing today, and we should have more respect for people who are trying to cope with their problems. I have a friend who is a doctor. And he told me that 30 years ago he enjoyed practicing medicine. People used to come to him and he used to help them, and he would get great satisfaction out of it. But he says that today people come with such difficult problems that he does not even know where to begin to help them. So these are difficult times, and people need to realize that. Today I think many astrologers in the world have the goal of helping people maximize their pleasures in the world, like money, love etc. But I don't know if this helps people in the end, because I don't think the world is about that, certainly not in this time period. The world is basically going through the Time period of purification, and it is a period where God is helping people purify themselves through suffering, in an attempt to hasten the redemption. So helping people improve their pleasures is advising them in the wrong direction. We should take into account what kind of 'background noise' is permeating our lives in this time. Unfortunately the pursuit of pleasure is the mindset of America today. And we are witnessing the dissolution of America. America and the 'American dream' are undergoing a tremendous crisis now. Because people thought that it was 'the land of milk and honey', and it was a dream. And now people see the dream fading, and that the dream was just an illusion. People should be worried about the future in America. And if it is not good for America, maybe it will not be good the rest of the world either.

So in this series I have tried to emphasize that there are different time periods in history, and you have to factor that in. And if you are going to try to help people, then you have to understand what kind of Time period we are living in. I don't think that people today come to astrologers to get advice on how to attain pleasure anymore, because in a certain sense, pleasure had been destroyed. People have difficulty experiencing real pleasure today. I think people today want 'peace of mind' more than anything else, to get a kind of blueprint for the future, that can give insight into why 'what is happening to me is happening to me'. People today want to find some meaning in their lives at this time, to find what their life purpose is at this time, and where they are heading in the world at this time. That broader perspective and background, is what you find in the Kabalistic 18 Time periods of history.

NOTES
ON THE PLANATERY HOUR SYSTEM

NOTES ON THE PLANATERY HOUR SYSTEM

The planetary hour system is a division of the week into days and hours. Each day has the influence of a specific planet over it, and each hour has the rulership of a specific planet.

The beginning of this system and its history is clouded in mystery. It is fair to say that nothing is known of its origins or why the planetary influences were arranged the way they were. In the western literature it says that the arrangement of the planetary hours was according to the Chaldean order (Saturn, Jupiter, Mars, Sun, Venus, Mercury, and Moon), and because of this it must have had a Chaldean beginning. The Chaldean order is a fancy name meaning that the planets are more or less counted from the farthest out from the earth to the closest planet. There are numerous explanations for this order. I prefer that of Harvard trained astronomer Rabbi Nissim Vidal that the ancients looked at the sky from a spiritual perspective not from a scientific measurement oriented perspective and this is the order from top down in a spiritual sense with the earth the most gross of all the planets stationed below them.

To bring clarity to the subject, I must first ask a few questions. If we are working from top down, then the first hour of the first day should be Saturn, and the second hour of the first day should be Jupiter and so on. More than that, the order of the days should also be from top to bottom. The first hour of the first day should be Saturn, the first hour of the second day should be Jupiter, the first hour of the third day Mars, and so on. Neither the order of the hours nor the order of the days goes from top down starting with Saturn, nor is the order of the hours the same as the order of the days. The order of the hours is Sun, Venus, Mercury, Moon, Saturn Jupiter, and Mars. The order of the days is Sun, Moon, Mars, Mercury, Jupiter, Venus and Saturn. As far as I know, there is no astronomical or any other explanation for the arrangement of the days.

Why was a top down order used for the planetary hours, why not bottom up or some other arrangement? To say it is the Chaldean order is not an explanation

See the appendix for a chart of the planetary hours.

We already have an astrology system based on where the planets are in the sky at any moment. Why do we need another system? Also the system seems incomplete using only hours and days. Why is there no mention of bigger time periods like weeks and months and years or smaller periods like minutes or seconds?

The chart of planetary hours is mathematically correct only for the times when the hours of day and night are equal. Thus the chart is only accurate 2 days a year. Almost all the time either the amount of daylight is greater than the amount of darkness or the reverse, thus making the 12 hours of daylight longer or shorter than 60 minutes. Should we use equal hours all the time or unequal hours?

To answer all these questions and shed light on the planetary hour system we must turn to a system of astrology that has been disregarded and to a book my teacher Zoltan Mason once said "all of astrology is in it, if you know how to find it", the five books of Moses, the Bible

On the first night of creation it says, "and there was evening and morning one day", so we see in the Jewish calendar the night comes first, for example, Sunday would be what we call Saturday night and Sunday day.

Concerning the fourth day of creation it is written "and God made the two great luminaries, the greater luminary to rule the day and the lesser luminary to rule the night; and the stars. And God set them in the firmament of heaven to give life upon the earth, to rule by day and by night, and to separate between the light and the darkness. And God saw that it was good. And there was evening and morning, a fourth day."

If you look now at the chart of the planetary hours, you will see that on the fourth night the first hour is ruled by Saturn, and then the second hour Jupiter and so on from top down. Now we have answered the question why the first hour of the first day is not Saturn and it is because the creation of the planets was not until the fourth night and we start counting from there.

Why do we count from top down? The answer is already given. Since the creation was from top down according to the ancients with the last being the earth the lowest and most gross of all the spheres , and on the fourth night the creation of this world began it is natural to start with the planet farthest out and the first to be created.

Now we also understand the order of the rulers of the days. On the fourth night the first 7 hours are from Saturn to the moon. Then five hours Saturn Jupiter Mars Sun and Venus and the first hour of the fourth day becomes Mercury. The fourth day has 24 hours. After counting 3 sets of 7 starting from mercury you have a remainder of 3, mercury moon and Saturn and Jupiter becomes the ruler of the fifth day and so on.

Now to the question of why this system is incomplete and only talks about days and hours, no measurement greater nor lesser. To answer this we must turn to another ancient book the "Talmud" which is the repository of the oral teachings of the Torah, was redacted between the years 200 to 500 of the Common Era, although the teachings date from much earlier time periods.

In the Talmud there is a discussion of when it is permissible and when not to bloodlet.The law is based on planetary hours. On days of the week where Mars falls in an even hour bloodletting is forbidden, on days where it does not bloodletting is permissible.

See appendix for the discussion.

Since in the case of bloodletting the only relevant factors in the discussion are hours and days there was no need to consider other time periods, however, in truth the planetary hour system expands out to months and years and seven year cycles and fifty year cycles and one thousand year cycles as is known from the Kabalistic literature . It appears to me that the western astrologers whom had translations of the Talmud thought that only hours and days were useable because they did not have access to the kabalistic teachings of which there were no translations.

In truth it is a very ancient time system which has its roots in the Bible. The seven days of creation are each one thousand years of history and each one thousand years are ruled by a different planet. (See my translation of the book 'Light of the eyes' for a development of this idea)

The planetary hour system has its roots in the creation of time. According to a famous Rabbi of the 18th century, Moshe Sofer, when God created time he placed planetary influences within all the different time periods themselves. Thus hours, days, months, years, 7 years 50 years and 1000 year cycles have different astrological forces embedded within them. In this 7 thousand year cycle we see history unfolding.

In western astrology the hour system is used as an event oriented system. What time to start an event, Marriage in a Venus hour. To begin learning or meditation a Jupiter hour. Saturn to build, etc. This they also learned from bloodletting. The event of bloodletting when is a good time to start and when is not a good time to start.

Finally the question of equal versus unequal hours, the 20th century western mind so scientifically measure oriented with computer printouts of the hours of every place on the globe sees a no-brainer that we use unequal hours. Vedic astrology with a different mindset is divided on which to use. Some even saying the astrologer should use his intuition in deciding on each occasion.

If the Jewish nation took the laws of bloodletting seriously and extended it out to other areas like when to start building houses, planting, marriage, journeys and more than we are talking about 3 million Jews at the time of the second temple, then it is hard to imagine all of them sitting down and working out the calculations for uneven hrs every time they needed to do so. I imagine even the most gung ho astrologer of today without a computer program would not work them out by hand, yet he expected 3 million people neither astrologers nor mathematicians to do so? It seems to me that they used standard hours and the rationale behind it was the metaphysical idea that the sustenance coming from the upper worlds must be able to be received by the living beings down here, too little sustenance and the organism cannot function properly and too much can cause it to burst. Here to since the nation could not receive according to unequal hours, the energy was sent in standard hour form. A proof for this can also be found in the case of bloodletting, we see that on Fridays the Jews blood let even though Mars feel in an even hour because they knew that they would have a good Sabbath meal that night which would enable them to regain their strength which was not the case the rest of the week, and why were they not hurt? The Talmud answers because "God watches over fools". Here also since they were fools In the sense that they did not have the capabilities to work out unequal hours, he made the flow according to standard *hours and watched over them*

SATURDAY Evening	Friday Evening	Thursday Evening	Wednesday Evening	Tuesday Evening	Monday Evening	Sunday Evening (SAT Night)	Time of the hr	ORDER of the hours
MARS	Moon	SUN	SATURN	Venus	Jupiter	Mercury	6-7	1
Sun	Saturn	Venus	Jupiter	Mercury	MARS	MOON	7-8	2
Venus	Jupiter	Mercury	MARS	Moon	SUN	SATURN	8-9	3
Mercury	Mars	Moon	SUN	SATURN	Venus	Jupiter	9-10	4
Moon	Sun	SATURN	Venus	Jupiter	Mercury	Mars	10-11	5
SATURN	Venus	Jupiter	Mercury	MARS	MOON	SUN	11-12	6
Jupiter	Mercury	MARS	MOON	SUN	SATURN	Venus	12-1	7
MARS	MOON	SUN	SATURN	Venus	Jupiter	Mercury	1-2	8
SUN	SATURN	Venus	Jupiter	Mercury	MARS	MOON	2-3	9
Venus	Jupiter	Mercury	MARS	Moon	SUN	SATURN	3-4	10
Mercury	MARS	Moon	SUN	SATURN	Venus	Jupiter	4-5	11
Moon	SUN	SATURN	Venus	Jupiter	Mercury	MARS	5-6	12
SATURN	Venus	Jupiter	Mercury	MARS	MOON	SUN	6-7	1
Jupiter	Mercury	MARS	Moon	Sun	SATURN	Venus	7-8	2
MARS	Moon	SUN	SATURN	Venus	Jupiter	Mercury	8-9	3
Sun	SATURN	Venus	Jupiter	Mercury	Mars	Moon	9-10	4
Venus	Jupiter	Mercury	Mars	Moon	Sun	SATURN	10-11	5
Mercury	MARS	Moon	Sun	Saturn	Venus	Jupiter	11-12	6
Moon	SUN	SATURN	Venus	Jupiter	Mercury	MARS	12-1	7
SATURN	Venus	Jupiter	Mercury	MARS	Moon	SUN	1-2	8
Jupiter	Mercury	MARS	Moon	SUN	SATURN	Venus	2-3	9
MARS	Moon	SUN	SATURN	Venus	Jupiter	Mercury	3-4	10
SUN	SATURN	Venus	Jupiter	Mercury	MARS	Moon	4-5	1
Venus	Jupiter	Mercury	MARS	Moon	SUN	SATURN	5-6	12

Samuel said: The correct interval for blood-letting is every thirty days; in middle age3 one should decrease [the frequency];4 at a [more] advanced age5 he should again decrease [the frequency]. Samuel also said: The correct time for bloodletting is on a Sunday Wednesday and Friday, but not on Monday or Thursday, because a Master said: He who possesses ancestral merit may let blood on Monday and Thursday, because the Heavenly Court and the human court are alike then.6 Why not on Tuesday? Because the planet Mars rules at even-numbered hours of the day.7 But on Friday too it rules at even-numbered hours? Since the multitude are accustomed to it,8 'the Lord preserveth the simple.'9

commentary: any day of the week where mars falls in an even hour bloodletting is forbidden (dont look at night hrs bec they did not blood let at night) monday and thurs mars also falls in even hrs but did not mention it bec the other reason they give is more important. Wednesday even though the last hr of the day mars falls in an even hr we say either it is so close to the night that it is as if night or it was so late in the day people would not blood let at that hr. mars is a malefic and even hrs demons have power, a double negative. the whole day is forbidden bec the Rabbis thought the bloodletter would mix up the hrs or because that one hr influenced negatively the whole day.

THE LETTER OF RABBI ABRAHAM BAR HIYA

This is the letter of the brilliant scholar, the prince Rabbi Hiya the Sefardi, may his memory be blessed. He was also called Isahab El Shorta. Concerning events that happened to him. The letter was sent to Rabbi Yehuda the son of Rabbi Barzili El Bartsaloni, may his memory be blessed.
It is written (Psalms 34 verse 15) "Turn away from evil and do good", in your business dealings and in the works of your hand. "Seek peace and run after it" in your interpersonal relationships.
Another explanation: Turn away from evil and do good" if your desires turn to that which wisdom and understanding consider undesirable, turn away from the evil desire and accept the advice of good wisdom. “Seek peace and run after it" if you see your friend receive improper advice, seek peace and run after it and warn him as if you were seeking and running after the peace of your own soul. The explanation of the matter: If you are preparing to go on a journey and a wise man, one of your friends, says don't start the journey at that hour because it is dangerous, whether because it is an even hour or the hour of Saturn, or the hour of Mars, or he will say to you don't start out on this day because the planets are unfavorable for a journey, be concerned with what he says and don't start out on the journey. Similarly, if there will be before you food that you desire to eat and the doctor will say to you don't eat it because it is bad for people of your age group, heed his words and don't eat. This is the meaning of "turn away from evil and do good". Stop the evil and take the good advice. "Seek peace and run after it": If your see your friend starting a journey or beginning a task on an even hour which is dangerous or on a day on which the planetary forces are unfavorable for that task, warn him against starting out on the journey or from beginning the task and you will have fulfilled seek the peace of your friend and run after his good. For men of understanding it is proper to guard themselves from all danger and to be cautious and not begin work at an improper hour or on a day that is astrologically unfavorable, and just like it is proper for them to be cautious and guard themselves, so is it proper for them to caution and warn their friends.

We learn this is proper behavior from our rabbis, may they be blessed, who warned us about this matter in one place and taught us to do and act like this in all places. They said (Sabbat 129 B): "Blood should be let on Sunday, Wednesday or Friday but not on Monday or Thursday since the master taught only those whose ancestors had great merit should blood let on Monday or Thursday because on those days the celestial court and the Earthly court are as one. On Tuesday why not blood let? It is because Mars is in an even hour. But on Friday is it in an even hour? Since people disregarded it we say "God watches over simpletons" (Psalms 116 verse 6).

The explanation is that Mars rules an even hour on that day and it was known to the masters of Astrology that it is not proper to begin in general a new venture on an even hour, and all the more so if a destructive planet rules that hour. They worried about bloodletting in a Martian hour because Mars rules over blood, and they warned not to let blood on a day that Mars rules over an even hour like Monday and Thursday where Mars rules an even hour. These two days are dangerous in respect of the planetary rulership of the hours and they are also dangerous because the celestial court and the earthly court are as one, and we see that Tuesday is dangerous because Mars rules over the first and eighth hour. We see that those days or those even hours that Mars rules over are dangerous, according to our rabbis, for bloodletting. From here we learn that anyone who wants to build a house, or plant a vineyard or dig a well or any action which Saturn rules over should start on Sunday or Wednesday and should be careful from beginning on Monday, Tuesday and Friday because on those days Saturn rules over even hours. We can make other rules when to start a specific job depending on which planet rules and we can rely on what the rabbis taught us. No man can protest what I said because it is revealed before their eyes.

However, it once happened to me concerning this matter and I need to explain what happened and make known all the complaints, doubts and questions which arose and to answer them (one by one) until the truth becomes clear. I had a talented student whom I loved and cared about greatly. He was to be married on Friday and he suggested to me to be married in the third hour of the day at the time the congregation leaves the synagogue. His suggestion appealed to me very much because it was an odd hour and the moon was ruling and according to everyone it is proper to begin a good thing in the moon's hour. Further more, the planetary positions were good at that time. However he was forced to delay the wedding because of a "met mitzvah" which chanced upon the city. The wedding contingent saw that the heads of the congregation and the important men of the community were going to the funeral and the entrance of the bride was delayed until the congregation returned from burying the dead at the end of the fifth hour, the beginning of the sixth hour of the day which is ruled over by Mars and it also didn't seem right from the planetary positions and the rising sign. When I saw this I said to him since you waited until the sixth hour, delay a little longer and do the wedding in the seventh hour which is odd and the sun rules. It is always proper to start at this time and further more the planetary positions are better. He listened and was convinced by my reasoning and he and his friends decided to wait. However, there was someone who disagreed and said " this waiting is similar to ' asking a Chaldean' and our rabbis, may they be blessed, said " we don't ask Chaldeans'", and whoever does this deed transgress the words of our rabbis and concerning what Samuel said that we let blood on Mondays etc. is only concerning bloodletting because of the weakness it cause the body but we can't learn other things from that ruling. He went on again and again until the bridegroom was forced to begin his marriage in the sixth hour. Since all this happened because of me, I felt as if all those who heard the story considered me a transgressor and sinner, therefore I have to give the reasoning behind what I said and to acquit myself before G-d and his people, as it says (in the desert 32 verse 22) " you are clean before G-d and Israel". I stick to my words and say that my accuser was being strict when there was no reason for strictness, and ruled something forbidden that there was no reason to forbid because whoever says that hour so and so of day so and so is good for something or says it is proper to start something in the hour of Jupiter or in the hour that Aries or Taurus rises or descends it is as if he said the water of this grass is good for the eyes or this food is good for the teeth or the stomach or this medicine causes diarrhea or this medicine causes constipation. Just like this drug and this food and this grass each work in their own way, similarly each hour affects a person in a different way. Also as there is no reason to forbid medicine so there is no reason to forbid acting according to the hours.

Similarly one who says about a child born when Jupiter is ruling that he will be honest or modest or about a girl born when Venus is strong that she will be attractive and pleasant is not " asking a Chaldean" and is not behaving like a Chaldean and is not turning away from the way of the Torah even by a hair's breath because all Israel acknowledges and believes that the power that was delegated to the stars was delegated on condition and it is not in their hands to benefit or to hurt according to their will and understanding rather they do what they are told and commanded. This is the way of all G-d fearing men who delve into the wisdom of Astrology and one who is suspicious of them is suspicious of kosher people and his thoughts are not kosher thoughts. It appears to us through logical reasoning after careful consideration that one who is careful not to start his work in even hours or in hours which are unsuitable because of the planetary positions has not sinned, he can rely on the words of Samuel and has transgressed neither a Rabbinical nor biblical injunction. What he did is not "asking a Chaldean" like it went up in the heart of the strict one (who opposed us). However we must investigate what the Rabbis meant when they said "we don't ask the Chaldeans".

Now we must examine and investigate what our Rabbis meant when they said "we do not ask Chaldeans". Do we not listen to them because we shouldn't worry about what they say and we shouldn't take their advice or maybe we are only warned concerning the asking? Let us arrange our investigation in this way and say that one who asks a Chaldean and listens to his advice and is concerned over what he hears he transgresses the words of our sages and is guilty of death because our sages said not to ask and he asked and he went even further and was concerned by what they said. And from his actions is he guilty for both of them or only once? However, if Shimon asked a Chaldean and didn't worry over what they said and Levi listened to their advice but didn't ask them. Is it for us to say that both of them are guilty of one transgression or do we say that the transgression of Shimon is greater than that of Levi or do we say that only Shimon is guilty but not Levi? We cannot acquit Shimon from his transgression and since we are delving into the matter it goes out that Levi, who worried about what they said and listened to their advice but did not ask them, is absolved of all guilt because of what our Rabbis said " Rabbi Akiva had a daughter and a Chaldean said to him on the day that your daughter is to be married a snake will bite her and she will die, and Rabbi Akiva was very concerned". We can't say that Rabbi Akiva asked the Chaldeans because our Rabbis didn't say so and heaven forbid that rabbi Akiva would transgress the words of the sages. Rather the Chaldeans told him and he didn't ask and since he was greatly concerned we see that you can be concerned with what they say. Similarly we say that you can take their advice from the story of the mother of Nachmon the son of Yitzhak. A Chaldean said to her, your son is going to be a thief , don't let him go with his head uncovered. She told him to cover his head. She listened to their advice and commanded her son to cover his head and the sages were not angered. By this we see that you can take the advice of Chaldeans and it is clear that our Rabbis only warned us from asking Chaldeans however we can be concerned with what they say and take their advice and there is nothing wrong with it.

Now let us investigate further concerning the warning from asking Chaldeans. Is it from the side that their science that they engage in has an element of idol worship or blasphemy and we were warned from asking them because their science is forbidden, or perhaps they didn't warn about asking except concerning the asking itself because in their astrological investigation they seek out that which is forbidden and it is as if we participate in their transgression. To answer this question we need to investigate what are the words of the Chaldeans and what is their wisdom until we find if there is a forbidden side to it. We find in the Rabbinic Literature the words the Chaldeans used to teach the mother of Rav Nachman " your child will be a thief" and this is similar to those who delve into the ways of the stars who say " if one is born under such and such a constellation, or if this planet rules over a person he will be a thief or a rich person or a wise person. We find it taught in the Rabbinical Literature not in the name of the Chaldeans, but for extra emphasis, as found written in the journal of Rabbi Joshua Ben Levi. One born under the sun will be like this, one born under Venus like this until one born under Mars will be a blood spiller. Rav Ashi said" or a thief or a blood letter or an animal slaughterer or mohel". Rava said "I am born under Mars", Abaya* said to him "you also punish and kill". These words are similar to the words of the Chaldeans and were said by Rabbi Joshua Ben Levi and Rava and Abaya* (each one gave s strong reason), how can we say there is a forbidden side to it? Rather we see from here that our Rabbis engaged in the study of the planets and constellations (astrology), and they delved into it and they did not hold their hand back from it. We can say that in this respect because what the Chaldeans said does not differ from what the Rabbis said there can be no forbidden side to it, rather because they investigate it in a forbidden way our Rabbis warned us from asking them. Now we will explain this matter in another way and say that those investigators of the of the stars and their influences are similar to our father Abraham that our Rabbis said about him " Abraham said before G-d , Master of the universe, I looked at my horoscope and I am not suitable to have a child". G-d replied- get out from your astrology the Jews are not under the influence of the constellations. What's your reasoning? That Jupiter is in the west? I will return it and place it in the east, like it says in Isaiah 42-2 "who lit up the east with righteousness" (Jupiter). We see from this story that the movement of the planets which speak about the fate of man and what will happen to him depending upon the placement of the planets and signs at the time of birth is alright because it is similar to what Abraham practiced. Or perhaps you can say what the Chaldeans practiced is something else, because when Abraham our father said "I looked and saw that I couldn't have children" he said it according to the traditional way that astrologers analyze horoscopes. And furthermore because nobody can say about our father Avraham (who recognized the existence of the creator at the age of three and G-d said about him, "since Abraham listened to my voice and guarded my commandments, laws and teaching") that he would engage in anything that was stigmatized or sinful. Rather we have to say that anything that one engages in, which is similar to what our father Abraham did; there can be nothing wrong with it. Here we can say concerning astrology that there is no stigma to it and we can say about the words of the Chaldeans if they are similar to the words of the wise astrologers then there is no stigma attached because they are similar.

This is the first thing we can say from the story. It also appears that astrology is a true knowledge and it is proper to encourage and study it, because G-d said to our father Abraham "Leave astrology because the Jews are not under planetary influences" and he didn't say leave astrology because it is not a science and it is not a true and proper study. All of this he could have said if astrology wasn't a science that should be encouraged and learned. From this we can say that astrology is called a science and its principals are true and you should search after it and study it. The third thing you can learn is that the Jews are not under the planetary influence, that is to say that the righteous ones of Israel can nullify evil decrees by their righteous behavior and prayer, which isn't the case of the rest of the nations like we learnt " Rabbi Johanan said how do we know the Jews are not under the planetary influences because it is said (Jeremiah 10,2) "thus G-d said don't learn from the ways of the non Jew, and from the signs of heaven don't be afraid because the non Jew is afraid", the non Jew will be afraid the Jew will not be afraid. Further more, it was said that the Jews are not under the planetary influences because the whole world was created only for the Jews, if the Jews didn't accept the Torah the whole world (the planets and constellations) would have returned to nothingness. And if the planets and constellations only exist because of the Jews how can they rule over the Jews? rather the strength of the Jews and their merit which allowed the world to exist is greater than the power of the stars, and because of this we say the Jews are not under the planetary influences, because there isn't enough strength in the constellations to fulfill their [evil decrees] on Israel, since the righteous ones of Israel are able through their merit to nullify the power of the constellations. Like it says "charity saves from death".

Even though we said that there is no mazal to Israel, we do say that the constellations testify for Israel. Like it says "Rabbi Hanina said mazal makes you wealthy, mazel makes you wise and there is mazal to Israel". Rabbi Hanina's words were not against rabbi Yohanan, and Rav and Rabbi Yehuda, and Shemuel and Rabbi Akiva who all said " there is no mazal to Israel, rather the reasoning of Rabbi Hanina why there is mazal to Israel which brings wealth and wisdom or poverty or stupidity is that the merit of Israel can nullify the testimony of the planets. It comes out there is mazal to Israel and there isn't mazal to Israel. since the mazal doesn't testify for them the testimony isn't established rather it is dependant on the deeds of Israel and their merit. If G-d wants to nullify the decrees of the planets from Israel he doesn't nullify the power of the planet that testifies to that decree rather the decree is automatically revoked, because the planets and signs have no rulership over Israel. However if G-d wants to nullify the planetary decrees on the nations of the world, first he removes the power of the planet which has rulership over that decree, and nullifies its rulership and afterwards he does what he wants with that nation.

We found this since it was right in G-d's eyes to increase the life span of King Hezkeyah and to add on to the testimony of the birth planets which concerning it the prophet Ishayahu prophesized " you will die and not live ". We do not see that he removed the planetary power and nullified the sign rulership rather he said "I am adding on to your life fifteen years" and similarly with daughter of Rabbi Akiva who G-d saved from death. Rabbi Akiva didn't say that G-d nullified the rulership of the constellations rather he expounded "charity saves from death" and the Jews are not under the planetary influences. And it is not so with the nations of the world, rather the decree that came on the generation of the flood.

He said remove one star from the constellation of Tauras and bring on the flood because the flood would not have come to the world if the influence of the constellations hadn't been nullified and the star cima which is in Taurus hadn't been removed. He didn't remove a star from any other constellation because the flood was in the month of Eyar where cima rises in the east or Mar Heshvan where cima sets in the west. Because the rabbis argued , in which of these two months the flood took place. In these two months cima rises and sets and rules over the rains and thunder and testifies concerning all the increases and decreases in every year according to all those versed in astrology. Because the flood was in the days of the rulership of cima from there it was said remove a star from cima and bring the flood. If the flood was in Eyar remove the star from cima which is rising, and if it is in Mar Heshvan remove it when it is setting. All this is to make known that God only nullifies the planetary power which rules at that specific time. Which in the future He will reinstate or nullify on the nations, but on Israel God does not have to nullify the planetary powers because the planets do not rule over them.

G-d in the story of Abraham our father informed us of these two matters. He informed us of the power of Israel, that they have no mazal, and He informed us of the power of the stars over the nations of the world. Jupiter is in the West, then I will move it to the East. He brought these two matters because from Avraham came forth many nations who the stars rule over and concerning them he said Jupiter is in the West then I will move it to the East. He also nullified the power of the stars (because there is no mazal to Israel) and this is what He said to Avraham "Ishmael will live before you", who for him I nullified the power of the constellations. He said "So it will be" and further "my covenant I will establish with Yitzhak whose power is greater than the hosts of heaven". About Yitzhak he said "He will be called offspring" and his offspring will be established and the stars will have no influence over them.

Already we have seen from the story of Abraham that there is nothing wrong with astrology because Abraham our father practiced it or something similar. We see it is a true science because G-d did not nullify testimony of the stars on Abraham until he changed their placement and put Jupiter in the East. We see that the constellations rule over the nations of the world and the testimony of the stars rule and are established over them and if G-d wants to nullify it he must remove the power of the planets and nullify their advice. Raba said "Jupiter is in the West, I will move it to the East", and we also see the stars have no power over Israel. Furthermore we see a fifth thing that with the knowledge of the stars one thing can be derived from another thing like it says "the son of my house inherits me". He didn't see this, rather he saw that he wouldn't have a son and he learnt from it that his servant would inherit him. This is similar to the wise man who said to a man your children will be from illicit relationships. He answered him where do you know this from and where did this wisdom come from? He answered back, I saw that every woman that you will marry with a marriage covenant will be barren and I also saw you will have children and I derived from this that your children will be from an illicit relationship. This is how you derive knowledge from astrology.

From everything we said up to now we see that it is proper to study astrology and to hold to it. However since it could go up in the heart of man that the knowledge of the Chaldeans that our rabbis warned us about consulting, is the wisdom we have been talking about until now; we need to investigate the difference between the two. We must say that astrology gives us the insight to what will be in the future in a general way but it cannot inform us in detail or tell us the specifics of the subject. If it informs us that this man will own fields and vineyards, it can't tell us which man's field he will buy or the vineyards what will be their specific location. The astrologer doesn't have the power to add on to this and cannot explain it another way because he only sees the power of the mazel and its testimony when it is in the sky and doesn't see its particulars down on the earth. Rather he sees the categories and the general. This is a matter which is very clear and agreed on by all who practice this science.

The Chaldeans' words are not like this, rather they predict about a specific thing like it teaches in the Talmud Shabbat concerning " Yosef who honors Shabbat". There was a non-Jew in his neighborhood and he had a lot of possessions. The Chaldean said to him" Yosef who honors Shabbat will eat all your possessions." They informed him the name of the man who will eat his possessions and this isn't the way of astrologers because even if they knew that someone would eat his possessions they wouldn't be able to name a specific person like the Chaldean said " Yosef who honors Shabbat will eat them". Similarly it was said "a Chaldean said to the mother of Rav Nachman" Your son will be a thief don't let him go with his head uncovered". This isn't the way of astrologers because they are able to see if he is a thief but they don't know if covering his head will help him and this isn't learning one thing from another that we explained above because covering the head has nothing to do with thievery in any way. This is similar to that which the Chaldean said to Rabbi Akiva about his daughter that when she enters the wedding room a snake will bite her. It is not in the power of the astrologers to predict where she will die, if they see she will die in a field they can't say in Mr. X's field or Mr. Y's garden. From there we learned that the power of the astrologers and the power of the Chaldeans are unequal. Furthermore, it was taught that Shmuel and Avlat were sitting and they saw a man going to the lake. Avlat said to Shmuel "he is going but he will not return ". Now this is something that any astrologer can predict, on the road at this hour something will happen to him. Because of this the Talmud called him Avlat by his name because he was an astrologer and didn't call him a Chaldean like it said in the stories about Rabbi Akiva and the mother of Rav Nachman.

It appears to us that astrology and the "work of the Chaldeans" is not the same thing. Rather the Chaldeans investigate more deeply and because of this we say that the "work of the Chaldeans" where they investigate what will be in the future is not carried out in the same way as the astrologers carry out their investigations. If we clarify all the different sciences and works which comprise astrology, what they are and on what side man studies the science of astrology and engages in the work of the heavenly bodies we can see from there what the Chaldeans do, if it is one of these sciences or not.

We will say that the first of the sciences that comprise astrology is the study of the shape of the earth and the heaven and their pictures and to give proofs and signs for them that they are circular like the picture of a ball and the earth is planted and stands in the middle of the firmament, which surrounds it and travels around it from the east to the West and to investigate the shapes of the planets and where they dwell in the firmament and how the planets are one underneath the other. To know the shape of their orbits from the East to the west (and where their Northernmost point and southern most point are) and how the constellations move and how sometimes they are closer or farther from the earth and to calculate all their movements in order to know where each planet is standing in terms of the constellations and if it appears in the north or south of the kav ofen ha mazalot[the belt of the constellations] and if they're closer or further from the earth and if their orbit is direct or retrograde and many other investigations which I don't have time to expand on. This science is the most exalted of all the sciences that comprise astrology. The wise men of Israel and those of the nations were studying and explaining it and they praised its study and the wise men of Israel only disagree with the wise men of the nations on a few points.

The second science which comprises astrology and is dependant on the first is to know the rulership and the power which were given to the planets and the constellations in their orbits around the earth and if this power that was given to each planet stands when it is in every constellation and how this power changes as the planet moves through the firmaments when it is in the North and in the South, when it draws closer to the earth and when it distances itself from the earth, when it is travelling direct or retrograde and the power of them on the earth and everything on the earth and each person on his birthday and new events when they arise, this knowledge was handed over and expounded on by the wise men of this science. Whether it was handed over to them by way of the tradition or it came to them through divine revelation or they learned it through experience in their lifetime.

And the wise men of Israel investigated this science and we find a hint to this that they say who is born under Saturn will be like this, and under Jupiter will be like this and their works are expanded on more than here in the "braitot of Shemuel" in their name and here also on the rulership of the planets there is no significant difference between the Jewish sages and the wise ones of the nations except on their power to force an event, the wicked ones of the nations who have no fear of heaven say that the power of the stars is a complete and full power and are able to start and damage according to their will and understanding and their decrees are unconditionally fulfilled. But the believers whose strength is in the fear of God, and make themselves holy by learning his book and who received this wisdom from the holy spirit: the mouth of the prophets say that the power of the planets is not a complete power and they don't have the power to start and damage according to their understanding and will. Rather everything is in God's command and any time God wants he can remove their rulership and change their decree. This is the difference between the Jewish sages and the wise ones of the nations.

Our rabbis blessed these two sciences and studied and practiced them. And on both they obligated "everyone who can calculate the seasons and the constellations to calculate them" to fulfill what is written "it is your wisdom and understanding in the eyes of the nations. You are not able to say what they meant by 'to calculate the seasons and constellations'" is talking about the four seasons (handed over with the intercalculation of the year)because this is something easy and it is not a difficult calculation and not dependant on a special knowledge and all the nations can calculate them. If you say the calculation of the seasons and constellations is about all seven planets where they are in the constellations. The seasons are the calculation of the sun and the constellations is said about calculating the planets. With the calculation of the seasons the Jewish sages knew when the festivals would fall in the year, with the calculation of the planets what knowledge would be added? However, just like the sun orbits in the sky, so all the planets orbit in the sky and like the sun has four seasons in the sky that switch during its travels around the earth and in truth there are four seasons of the year for all the planets since they all have four points in the sky where they switch their direction. They all have these four points in the days of their orbits and it was enough for them to say "to calculate the four seasons", and because they said "the seasons and the constellations" we know that "the seasons" is the calculation of the orbits of the planets and "the constellations" is the calculation of their decrees as they appear on the earth. For we call the testimony and decrees of the planets mazalot. When the planets signify good we say " mazal tov" and for the opposite which isn't good, "mazal raa" and for this I bring a proof from the passage. " It is your wisdom and understanding in the eyes of the nations" because the calculation of the planetary motions is not a singularly Jewish wisdom compared to the nations rather the majority of the nations are greater in this than the Jews. Rather the wisdom of the Jews and there understanding in the eyes of the nation: it is that their righteousness nullifies for them the decrees of the heavens but the decrees of the nations is established and not nullified except if G-d removes the power of the planet and weakens it and the power of the planet is not weakened for Israel because it has no power over them.

If two nativities that are similar in their mazel, one of a non-Jew and the second of a Jew will be brought to a wise man of one of the nations he will find that all the difficult decrees in the birth chart of the Jew, he was saved from them and the unrighteous non-Jew was tripped up by all of them. This will be a great wonder for the wise men of the nations and they are startled when they see the greatness of Israel. There is another difference between Israel and the nations. If there is a decree that is suitable to come on Israel and the nations and G-d wants to nullify it from the nations he removes the power of the planet and nullifies it and when he removes the power of the planet and nullifies the decree for the Jew and non-Jew alike because there doesn't remain to the planet damage or help. And if G-d wants to nullify from Israel he doesn't weaken the power of the planet because the planet has no rulership over Israel and because its power is not weak and its decree is established over the non-Jew and on this the passage says "for what great nation is there that has G-d so close to them the Lord our G-d whenever we call to him." He says your wisdom will be for the eyes of the nations who will see that the decrees of the planets are nullified from you in your calling out to G-d and it is not nullified from them. With this you will see the wisdom of Israel because all the astrologers saw that Hezekiah king of Judah was destined to rule no more than 14 years and because of his righteousness and prayers he ruled for twice that number of years decreed by the stars and the astrologers recognized this honor.

Similarly Ahaziyahu the son of Ahaz, king of Judah they(astrologers) decreed about him, that he would recover from his illness and similarly the priests of Baal Zvuv, the god of Akron to whom he sent to ask of the idol(said he would live). However the prophet came and decreed upon him "the bed you are lying on, you will not rise from it, for surely you will die. You can't say that this decree was decreed before he went to ask Baal Zvuv, because if so what was the necessity of the prophet saying to us." He will surely die. Rather his asking Baal Zvuv caused his death. And similarly he said to him "since you sent messengers to ask Baal Zvuv, the god of Akron therefore the bed you are on, there you will die, and if he didn't send them it wouldn't have been decreed on him.

And also with Rabbi Akiva who the Chaldeans frightened [with their prediction] when the decree was nullified, he didn't say the Chaldeans lied rather he said "charity saves from death", similarly Shmuel when the words of Avnet the Heshoni were not fulfilled he didn't say "he is a liar" rather he said "charity saves from death."

Because of this it is an obligation that everyone who knows the calculation of the seasons and the constellations to calculate them and if he sees testimony that good things will happen don't trust this rather guard yourself and be careful lest the sin will cause [you lose the good things] and if you see testimony that isn't good, repent, fall down and supplicate before God maybe it will be proper in his eyes to nullify the decree.

We find that this art, it is an obligation on all who know it, to practice it, so that his belief will be strengthened as well as his fear [of heaven] and he will increase his prayers and his righteousness at all times. Concerning this our rabbis said "the one who knows how to calculate the seasons and the constellations" is about the calculation of the movement of the planets and an explanation of the damages of their decrees. He had to mention the seasons and the constellations because there is no value to the planets, and their testimony is not known except through their movement, and of these two sciences that are attached to the fear of heaven it is the wisdom of the stars that Israel is obligated to study and engage in. There are other sciences that are dependent on the planets which most of the nations engaged in and the Jewish people were not permitted to engage in them because they are connected to idolatry and they degrade one's fear of heaven. Because all the nations that believe that the planets benefit or destroy with their own knowledge, will eventually add to their wickedness and brazenness until it appears to them that their serving and making offerings to the planets helps them before the planets. And it went up in the hearts of many after an impure spirit came to them from the planets to command them, warn them and to teach them the way they must be served. These evil ones caused their generation to sin, they made for them idols and statues to be served and worshipped and they taught them how they should be worshipped and they enacted evil ceremonies to be performed before them. These false prophets, prophets of idols they are called in Arabic Etziel Vathi which means "the founders of the ceremonies". And their students who performed the crooked religious ceremonies were called El Atba, meaning "the ones who were drawn after the evil". Each of the idolatrous nations, worshippers of statues to whom they dedicated themselves and enacted forms of evil worship and who many followed after them were called a sect – and after them another sect called in Arabic Mustonol Beel Kavi meaning "those that draw down the powers". These sinners to their own souls, trapped and apportioned the different times when they wanted to draw down celestial powers from his dwelling place above. In one of the nice portions they claimed that it was given to a certain planet in the sky and they would burn incense to that planet or offer to it certain things that it was suitable to offer it at that specific time according to their knowledge. With this they would draw down the power of the planet to the earth to do their will and answer their questions and these two evil sects were certainly idolatrous and bowing down to strange gods, may they be cursed, and all those that do like them. We also find a third sect "Abael Talezmat" meaning "the masters of the pictures". They would ponder the movements of the planets and investigate the order of their movements through different pictures in the sky and when they passed through the place where the image they wanted appeared to them, at the time they saw the planet pass through that image in the constellations when it is in the north side or the south side, they would make an image like that image from different types of metals that were suitable for this. If the planet is one of the favorable planets he increases the strength of that image, and if a destructive planet he nullifies its power. They know when to stop and when to increase the power of different things in this world, and there remain even to our times all sorts of images from the work of these wicked ones.

After them is the fourth group which knows the movement of the planet on which day and at what hour it is beneficial to collect different herbs from all the herbs and to gather different seeds from all the seeds to gather honey, beat the olives, to pick grapes and other fruits, to chop wood and collect it. They would know what was gathered on each day and what its nature was and for what it was beneficial. Everything was stored with them and when they were needed they would combine the different herbs that were stored with them that were beneficial to use at that time, to do their work, to increase the power of one thing or to reduce the power of something else. While they were doing this, when they were gathering from the field, or combining herbal formulas they would whisper incantations and unclean names and the names of demons. This sect was called in Arabic Atzchav el Hel meaning "masters of the capture", and this sect was also called in Arabic Atzchav el Ashar.

All these four sect's wisdom and understanding depended on the movement of the planets in different ways then those of the God fearers. It appears to me that all four sects are mentioned in the Book of Daniel in the dream of the wicked Nebuchadnezzar like it is written (Daniel 2,2)" Nebuchadnezzar dreamt dreams, his spirit was agitated and his sleep was interrupted, the king said to call the Hartumen, Ashpen,Chasdim and Mecashfin to tell the king his dream." These four names we explained them by their skills "Hartuman" they are the capturers, the "Ashapen" are the "senders of the power", the Mecashfin" are the "masters of pictures" and the Chasdim are the "drawers". We find these four are also mentioned in the Book of Daniel in Aramaic Hartumia, Ashpin, Cusdi, Gezri (Daniel 4:4) and it is also written(Daniel 8,11)"Hartumia Ashpin

Cusdi and Gezri and your father the king made him (Daniel) chief of them". It is clear that the Hartumen, Ashapen, and Chasdim that are mentioned first in Hebrew are the hartumia, Ashpin and Cusdi that are mentioned a second time in Aramaic but the mecashfin that are mentioned in Hebrew, is it possible that they are Gezri in Aramaic because it is not their way to talk about the future and the four that are mentioned in Aramaic their way is to talk about the future or is it possible that Gezri are those that study the constellations deeply and they are called gezri (laws) because their opinion is that the testimony of the planets is fixed and cannot be changed but that they have permission to decree and establish. This opinion is right in my eyes because it says in Nebuchadnezzar's first dream the Chaldeans responded before the king and said (Daniel 2,10) "There is no man on earth who can relate the king's matter that is why no king, leader or ruler has ever requested such a thing of any necromancer or astrologer or Chaldean." Of the four Nebuchadnezzar only mentions three and he leaves out mechasfin (magicians) because it is not their way to make known things like this. Rather their job is to explain the different forces that are on the earth and when they increase or decrease. In a similar vein Daniel didn't mention them when he said to Nebuchadnezzar (Daniel 2,27)"the secret the king requests no wise men, Ashpen,Hartumen Gezrim are able to tell the king." He didn't mention the magicians because it is not their way to reveal secrets or the future but he mentioned the Gezri who ponder the movement of the planets through the constellations because it is their way to speak about the future which is hidden from the rest of mankind. He didn't mention the Chasdim before Nebuchadnezzar rather he mentioned the Hartumen, Ashpen because the chasdim were not mentioned before the king at that time. Similarly Daniel didn't mention them among the wise men, Ashpen, Hartumen, Gezren because they were students of the Ashpen and were drawn after them and they sullied themselves in idol worship more than the Ashpen and because of this he saw no reason to mention them. In another place the Hartumen were left out like it says (Daniel 5,7) "just then fingers of a human hand came forth and wrote in the plaster of the wall of the king's palace facing the candelabrum and the king saw the palm of the hand that was writing. The king's appearance thereupon changed and his thoughts bewildered him, the belt on his waist opened and his knees knocked one against the other. The king cried aloud to bring in the ashpen, the Chasdim and the gezri. The king exclaimed to the sages of Babylonia that a person who would read this writing and tell its interpretation would wear royal purple with a chain of gold on his neck and rule a third of the kingdom." He didn't mention among them the Hartumen because it is not proper to ask them about something which requires deep wisdom and understanding like the writing that was written on the plasters of the wall of the king's palace. We find one place where all three were left out where they were not needed and only the mecashfim (magicians) by themselves were mentioned. Like it says (Exodus 4,11) "And pharaoh called out to the wise men and the magicians." He called to the wise men who were magicians at the time he saw the staff turn into a snake. Right away he called the magicians who know the times when the powers of all that are found in the world would be strengthened, to see if at that time, if there was power in the form of the snake or if there was power in the wood or in the staff to do this according to the movement of the stars. They took advice together and agreed that the snake has only the powers to bite and doesn't have any other power. The wisdom of the magicians is not dependent on the movement of the stars, and it has no power over it.

However, the Hartomen whose work is hidden with them from times past, they hurried to do and because the magicians didn't protest, it as if they were considered partners. Like it says(Exodus 4,11) "And the Hartoman of Egypt they also did with their staffs." It could have said "The Hartomen of Egypt did." However, since it said "they also did" we see that the magicians were considered one with them because they didn't protest.

We also see here that every plague God brought on the Egyptians in Egypt, none of them were able to be caused by the movements of the planets. In order to make known to the nations of the world their lack of wisdom before God's might, and similarly you can say that all the decrees that God decrees on the evil nations of the world, he doesn't decree them except to a time when the planets do not testify to the decree, and if the prophecy could be learned from the planetary movements, then what is the prophet coming to reveal to us? However it is right that the prophecy will not be in accordance with the movement of the constellations and planets. So that all the wise men of the nations will consult and be confused and shocked in the face of God's might; at the time they see their testimony and thoughts go against them. And similarly the prophet Isaiah(19,12) said: "Where are they? Where are your wise men? Let them tell you now, let them try to know what God, master of the legions, has prepared for Egypt." To tell you that the decree which He advised to bring on Egypt, the experts in the

wisdom of astrology they saw it but their wisdom was nullified. Like it says(ibid 11) "Pharaoh's wisest advisors offer boorish counsel." And the text is not coming to teach that the wise men of Egypt were liars but rather to teach you God's strength, that He nullified the powers of the planets and took away their power until the wise men appeared fools in their eyes, like it says(ibid 44,25) "I am god.... Who abrogates the omens of the stargazers, and makes fools of the astrologers; who makes wise men retreat and makes their knowledge foolish." No one except for the master astrologers can see the awesome strength of God at the time when they see the decrees of the planets nullified before the righteous ones and evil ones and it increases fear and belief.
From here you can see that this wisdom (astrology) increases fear of heaven and knowledge of God and it reveals the awesomeness of His name and His might. But the other four types of wisdom of the stars we mentioned they do not increase fear of heaven and they are forbidden to engage in because they lead the person to idol worship and cheapen the fear of heaven. There are other crafts like them and if they are not suitable to be called wisdom they are called crafts or cunning and the text called them, or most of them, divination. Like it says(Ezekiel 21,26) "For the King of Babylonia stood at the crossroads, at the head of the two roads, to practice divination- and he shot arrows, inquired of terephim and looked into the liver ".These three crafts that are done with arrows, teraphin and liver are called divination and it is one category which includes all. The arrows mentioned here were possibly sharp arrows "BeholdI will say to the lad go and find the arrows(hetz)". These are the arrows shot from the bow. The King of Babylonia divined with them. It is also possible that the arrows are gravel like it says(Lamentations 3,16) "He ground my teeth in gravel(hetzetz)" also "the bread of falsehood is sweet to man, but afterwards, his mouth will be filled with gravel(hetzetz}". It is possible the divanation was with gravel. And also we find the Arabs that lived in the Land of Keder their expertise was to polish stones on the earth, and they would know by this which way to travel, and they would know what to do and it is possible that this is the meaning of hetz

.

The terephem were shapes and pictures like visions in glass, many images which they were gazing at, whenever they would try to decide to do something they would look to see if it was good and would benefit them, and what they would see in that vision they would rely on. Now we find in these lands something similar to teraphim, like those who gaze in glass bottles filled with water which are placed on something red and they don't lift up their eyes from it until the image of that which they asked about appears to them in the water in the glass. Similarly they would look at the fingernail or the shoulder or an egg that was painted by something polished and bright like pitch or olive oil. All these are similar to asking Teraphim. Teraphim comes from the word toref which is the essential part or the root of the thing and it is translated in Aramaic zalmania. Rabbi Saddiya Gaon translates it as images and pictures.

It is good for a man to forbid himself from doing all those works which the king of Babylonia asked through them because they are called divinations and the Torah forbids us from divining, like it says(Deuteronomy 18,10-11) "They shall not be found among you one who causes his sons and daughters to pass through the fire, one who practices divinations, one who knows the times(mevnan), one who reads omens, a sorcerer, or an animal charmer, one who inquires of Ov or Yidoni or one who consults the dead". And you will say all the works are called divination and when he says "one who practices divination" it is a general rule and the details will be :one who knows the times, one who reads omens, a sorcerer, or an animal charmer, one who inquires of Ov or Yidoni or one who consults the dead. Here we have a general rule and a detail and a general rule you can judge only on the detail and you can say that only these specific things which have been mentioned in the text have been forbidden as divination and nothing else. These will come to make light, and the first one will be to make heavy. A proof that for you 'divination' is a general rule and not a specific work by itself, from what it says here on who inquires of Ov or Yidoni and he calls what one does with the Ov "inquiring" and later on it says(Shmuel A 28,5) "But the women said to him 'surely you know what Saul has done – that he has eliminated the necromancer and diviner from the land" Here he said diviner and not inquirer to teach you that all of these arts that are forbidden are called divination.

Another proof is that you find a mevnan, one who reads omens and all the others that are mentioned in the text are clearly mentioned by our rabbis, may they be blessed, each one what he does and what his work is, and they don't mention among these diviners because it is a general name which includes all of them. And rabbis said "you shall not find among you one who passes his son or daughter through the fire;" here we learn son or daughter,

where do we learn son of the son, or son of the daughter? It says somewhere else in the text "God spoke to Moses saying: say to the Children of Israel, my man from the children of Israel, and from the proselyte who lives with Israel, who shall give of his seed to Molech shall be put to death".
They said about Mevnan , Rabbi Akiva said "this is one who fixes periods and hours. Today is a nice day to go out, tomorrow will be a fine day to engage in business, buy nothing to profit from. Before the seventh year the wheat is good quality, uproot (not harvest) the beans so they don't go bad, and will not spoil". These people who fix periods and hours they rely on their experience which they experienced during their lifetime and what they learned from it. They didn't learn this from the wisdom of the movement of the constellations, and not from the wisdom of the movement of the planets because they don't give importance to one day of the week over another. If Monday this week is good for something it doesn't mean next Monday will also be good, it's possible that next Monday could be dangerous. Similarly the seventh year is not always good for the wheat crop. Not every year is the same according to the astrologers. The Mevnan according to Rabbi Akiva treats the days and years as the same always and because of this it was said that the mevnan's artistry does not always go along with the wisdom of the constellations and not according to the wisdom of the world and not according to Rabbi Akiva who said he considers the times and the hours, and not according to the scholars that "they hold peoples' eyes" and not according to Rabbi Yishmael who says" they pass seven types of semen over the eye".

They said who is a reader of omens, He says "bread fell from his mouth, his staff fell from his hand, the deer stopped in the path, a snake is on his right and a fox is on his left . And our rabbis said "Don't read omens, for example, those that read omens in huldot and birds, and those who speak about what will happen in the World according to what they see "in signs" from the planets and animals and birds. This art is found in the world today mainly among sailors and farmers. Like those who say if the moon on the first or second day of the month has a black ring surrounding it, this is a sign of much rain during that month, and similar to a black ring surrounding the moon, if the sun shines bright and the air that surrounds it is red, there will be heavy winds from the direction where the red air appears. Similar to this is one saying things like this concerning any of the seven planets or the bright comets and also one saying the voice of the raven at night and the voice of chickens at the beginning of the night testify to rain, and the Hulda who lifts up its voice and dances testifies to cold weather and other signs like these are the ways of the readers of omens from birds and the planets.

Sorcerers are ones who do a deed and don't just "hold onto the eyes" and what the sorcerers do we already mentioned above, they know when different powers are found in the world and also those who gather herbs and trees at specific times, these are also deeds and not just holding the eyes.

Baal Ov is someone who speaks from his joints or under his armpits. Baal Yidoni is someone who puts a special bone in his mouth and speaks from it. The rabbis said "one who asks the dead" this is someone who starves himself so that an unclean spirit rests on him.

All the different forms of divination our rabbis explained us what they are about and how their work is performed. They said all of them are forbidden to do like they said "don't learn to do, but you can study them in order to learn and teach", from it itself they derived it was forbidden to ask of them because it is written(Deuteronomy 18,12-13) "It is an abomination all who do those, be simple with the lord your G-d" From there they saw that you don't ask them like it says "from where do we learn that you don't ask the Chaldeans from be simple with the Lord your G-d, and it is learned from the section of the Talmud where the rabbis expound all the different kinds of work that are forbidden to engage in . From here they also warned us from searching them out and asking them. And the word Chaldean here means all those who engage in forbidden works- hartumem ashphem,cashdim, mekashfim and all those that divine things. They are called Chaldeans because the people of Babylonia and the Land of Shinar were engaged in all these arts. It is known that all the people of these lands are Aramaic like it says "And the Cashdim spoke to the king in Aramaic. They spoke in the language of the nation they were from(genesis 10,23) " and the children of Aram; otz, chol, neter, mash" and among them are not mentioned , not the Cashdim and not the Chaldean. The people who lived in the Land of Shenar were called Chaldean and they were also called Cashdim and Soranime and other names and the name that includes all these is "false prophets" and afterward the "Chaldeans", and on this name in the language of the Rabbi's they were called Chaldean. The Cashdim they were from the governmental families in the days of Nebuchadnezzar the evil one

and they filled their hands with idol worship and they were priests in their house of worship and from this they were called Cashdim those who draw down the forces of the planets, because they were priests, in their house of idolatry and Chaldeans are the rest of the population who engage in divination and the other forbiddin works. The Cashdims are one of the families and all of the Cashdim are called Chaldean but not all of the Chaldean are called Cashdim.
Since our rabbis said "we don't ask the Chaldeans" they included among them the Cashdim, who drew down forces from above, and all those who engaged in wisdoms like these concerning knowing the future. The Rabbi's words were as if they said, we don't ask sorcerers, Chaldeans, readers of the times and all the other wisdoms that are similar to them because the Chaldeans engaged in all those arts. Now we have come to distinguish clearly what it means "we don't ask the Chaldeans" and it has been revealed to us what are the wisdoms that are suitable to learn and practice and what are those that are permitted to learn but not practice. It appears from this that one who practices what is permitted and his intention is for the sake of heaven then he can be called a truly righteous one even though the whole world calls him misguided but if he forbids what is permitted and permits what is forbidden like we see today those who permit the asking of trophem; and looking at stones and they forbid those who investigate the wisdom of the stars (astrology) we don't call this person misguided. Because he has left the true path we call him guilty and a sinner.
It is enough for us now with all the reasons we have given to have shown that the one who was strict concerning the bridegroom, who caused us to write all this, was in fact so strict that he forbid what was permitted and even though it was known and clear to all that what he did was for the sake of heaven and he was G-d fearing..
Everything we have taught until now from his mouth(his teachers) we have learnt from, his water it has been drawn and all the wisdom that is known to all the people on earth is lit up in him like the streets of Nehardia. If it is suitable before him, if it is straight in his eyes and it is good before him, and if he sees that these words of mine are good and proper then he will reveal his heart before us and honor us with an announcement from his lips and not leave us standing in doubt and walking in darkness because pointing out the truth and the proper way is the characteristic of the wise man and the way of acting of the right and complete man. It is proper for us and all those who hear his words to thank him and praise him because of his great righteousness and goodness, his

humbleness and modesty and if he will see that my words are riddled with errors and craziness, words of nonsense and insanity, words not proper to speak, words which only confuse, then let his mercy and righteousness grow and open his hand and show us in which ways my words are broken and why they should not be relied upon. On the day I will hear his complaints I will confess my sin and say I recant my words and I will say about myself(Job 6,13) "is not mine own help with me". If you don't answer me satisfactorily and you don't pay attention to my words to answer one of the two questions that I asked,and you will say to me "your words don't make sense to me but I don't have the power to destroy your reasoning" I will say to him "far be it from me - until I perish – to say you are right! I will not renounce my innocence from myself." But if I am mistaken in what I write and in my arguments, I implore my rabbis don't hold me guilty for all the words I have spoken for the lord of justice knows and all hidden things are revealed before him, that I didn't come to teach and expound, nor to adorn myself, nor to build myself up, G-d forbid, and to incite, rather my whole intention was to clear my name. Maybe I will be acquitted, for from my youth until this day I was taught the wisdom of astrology and practiced it. I delved into and explored its depth and I considered myself one who has acquired wisdom and discernment, one who is guilt-free and innocent.

Now when I have seen wise men straight in judgment and modesty that have studied the sciences and are knowledgeableand they disagree with me. They have ruined my work. In my childhood and youth I was judged leniently because of the honor I required before ministries and kings and now in my old age I will have this before me as an accuser. It is good that I search for judgment and speak out for my innocence perhaps until I awaken the anger of those that hate me, who spoke evil about me and they will tell me my obligations, they will criticize me and maybe there will be power in their words, to prove to me to follow their way.

And now you, my rabbis, men of strength and torah, defenders and mighty ones who have the power to rule over the wisdom, don't put a stumbling block before the blind, tell me which way to go, put me on the path of the king, because all of Israel are responsible for each other and the fat one is obligated to pour out his oil to the skinny one. To light up the eyes, to lead the blind, the one satiated with water will pour water for the thirsty until the day comes when everyone will be happy in his portion and find his true desire. It should be your will, Lord of Heaven, to honor us at that time and to fulfill what is written in Jeremiah "no longer will a man teach his friend or his brother to know G-d because all of them will know me from the smallest to the greatest - the word of G-d – when I will forgive their iniquity and no longer recall their sin.

Printed in the USA
CPSIA information can be obtained
at www.ICGtesting.com
LVHW082306111023
760515LV00072B/636